Footprint

Egypt

The travel guide

Handbook

Anne McLachlan & Keith McLachlan

A corner which no stranger can explore
Where no one bores you, and you no one bore.

Ibn-i Yamin (Translated by Edward Browne)

Egypt Handbook
Third edition
© Footprint Handbooks Ltd 2000

Published by Footprint Handbooks
6 Riverside Court
Lower Bristol Road
Bath BA2 3DZ. England
T +44 (0)1225 469141
F +44 (0)1225 469461
Email discover@footprintbooks.com
Web www.footprintbooks.com

ISBN 1 900949 68 7
CIP DATA: A catalogue record for this
book is available from the British Library

In USA, published by
NTC/Contemporary Publishing Group
4255 West Touhy Avenue, Lincolnwood
(Chicago), Illinois 60712-1975, USA
T 847 679 5500 F 847 679 2494
Email NTCPUB2@AOL.COM

ISBN 0-658-01084-0
Library of Congress Catalog Card
Number 00-132902

Credits

Series editors
Patrick Dawson and Rachel Fielding

Editorial
Editor: Claire Boobbyer
Maps: Sarah Sorensen
Additional editorial assistance: Katrina
O'Brien and Alasdair Dawson

Production
Typesetting: Emma Bryers and
Leona Bailey
Maps: Claire Benison and Robert Lunn
Colour maps: Kevin Feeney

Cover: Camilla Ford

Design
Mytton Williams

Photography
Front cover: Impact Photo Library
Back cover: Impact Photo Library
Inside colour section: Art Directors and
Trip, Chris Barton, Impact Photo Library,
Jamie Marshall, Robert Harding Picture
Library, Travel Ink, Lawson Wood

Print
Manufactured in Italy by LEGOPRINT

Every effort has been made to ensure
that the facts in this Handbook are
accurate. However, travellers should still
obtain advice from consulates, airlines
etc about current travel and visa
requirements before travelling. The
authors and publishers cannot accept
responsibility for any loss, injury or
inconvenience however caused.

Egypt

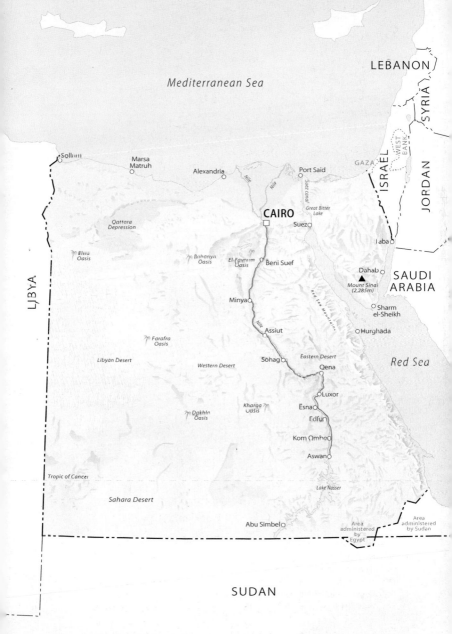

Mediterranean Sea

LEBANON

SYRIA

ISRAEL

JORDAN

GAZA

WEST BANK

Sollum

Marsa Matruh

Alexandria

Port Said

Suez canal

Great Bitter Lake

CAIRO

Suez

Taba

Nile

Qattara Depression

Siwa Oasis

Bahariya Oasis

El-Fayum Oasis

Beni Suef

Dahab

Mount Sinai (2,285m)

SAUDI ARABIA

Sharm el-Sheikh

Minya

Nile

Red Sea Mountains

Hurghada

Farafra Oasis

Assiut

Libyan Desert

Western Desert

Sohag

Eastern Desert

Qena

Red Sea

Dakhla Oasis

Kharga Oasis

Luxor

Esna

Edfu

Kom Ombo

Aswan

Tropic of Cancer

Lake Nasser

Sahara Desert

Abu Simbel

Area administered by Egypt

Area administered by Sudan

SUDAN

LIBYA

N

0 km 100

0 miles 100

Contents

Left: Anyone for tea? Catching up on daily life at the El Fishawi café, Cairo

4

Right: *the gold, quartz, turquoise and lapis lazuli striped death mask of the boy-king Tutankhamen, exhibited in the Egyptian Museum, Cairo*

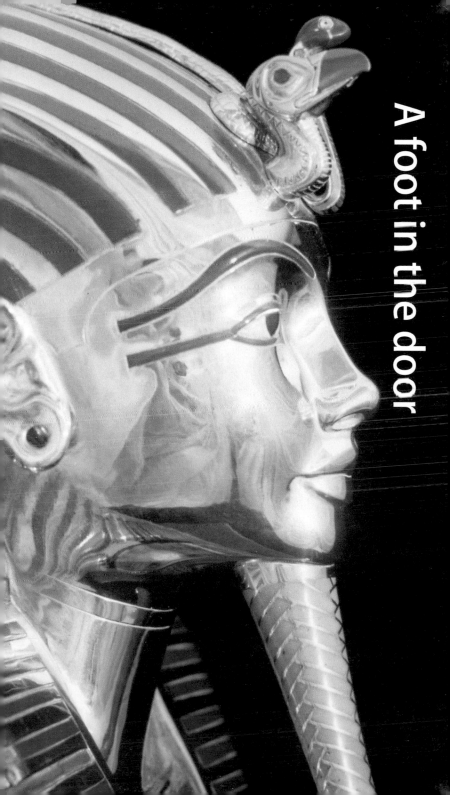

A foot in the door

Right: A sphinx stands guard at the Temple of
Luxor. *Below*: The Eye of Horus, a sought after
charm to ward off evil, here displayed as an
appliqué work.

Above: Camels stride by one of the Seven
Wonders of the Ancient World: The Pyramids
at Giza. *Right*: Carry on up the Nile: the life
blood of the country flanked by luscious
palms. *Next page*: Taking a snooze in the
Khan Al Khali Bazaar before starting to barter
in earnest.

Highlights

The sheer scale of Egypt is awe-inspiring. Its river, deserts, monuments and modern cities are all truly impressive in size and without serious rival in the Middle East and Africa. The historic record represented in major buildings like the pyramids, the written word in hieroglyphic forms and intricate religious philosophies of the ancient past are worldwide nowhere so well developed as in Egypt. Egypt's chronology is of vast span, encompassing more than 5,000 years of civil government in the downstream lands of the Nile in addition to a notable contribution to the earlier development of crops, domesticated animals and tools. Islam, Judaism and Christianity touched Egypt and gave new architectures, cities and ways of life to enrich the pharaonic past.

Egypt - The magnificent

And there is a modern Egypt buzzing with vibrant life as 60 million people set about modernisation and economic growth in the 21st century. Mega state funded economic projects and a mass of small scale private ventures can be seen propelling Egypt into a new industrial age - all side by side with unchanging rhythms of rural life in the fields of the Delta and Nile Valley. Contrasts were never so brilliantly etched on an ancient landscape.

Egypt is a desert except only for the cultivated triangle of the Delta and narrow strip of the Nile Valley. The Nile waters thus dominate the country as a single giant river in what is otherwise an arid landscape. On average 75 cubic kilometres of water every year soundlessly traverse Egypt's barren land bringing a controlled flow of water for irrigation, drinking and industry. The river has a million moods depending on the time of year, the time of day and place from which it is seen - each reflected in a gorgeous range of colours and lights. A lush manicured garden of cultivated land clings to the banks of the Nile, worked by each succeeding generation of farmers into a fine patterned patchwork of greens, yellows and reds overlain by a tall umbrella of palms, and brightly tinted fruit blossoms. From a Nile steamer or a felucca the sight of the eternal river and the farmed land adjacent is a panorama of traditional ecological harmony. The structures along the river reflect all the ages of hydraulic engineering and irrigation from pharaonic "nilometers" that measured the fluctuating height of Nile waters to the great 19th century storage dams and their service canals and the massive 20th century man-made reservoir that is Lake Nasser. And all around the Nile are sited many of the world's most spectacular monuments - the grand temple complex of Karnak and the incomparable tomb-temples of Luxor's West Bank. This panoply of sound, light and movement can be enjoyed from the river itself, through the soles of one's feet on land or by balloon from the air.

The River Nile

Few countries have contributed so much to the civilized world as Egypt. Literature and the papyruses of the ancient kingdoms of Egypt are synonymous. Pharaonic hieroglyphics gave us a first footing into writing, formulating knowledge on a permanent basis and a means of managing day to day government. The ancient Egyptians bound learning to religion to capture it for long-term benefit of society in a way that had never before been achieved. All the crafts of ink and paper-making, the storage of documents and taxation, organizing the calendar, together with the administrative systems that perpetuated the kingdoms from 31 BC to the end of Cleopatra's reign in 30 BC arose within the Egyptian arena. How far they went - to America, the far Orient or the Pacific Ocean possibly - the papyrus boats of Egypt carried traded goods and ideas that were absorbed by other peoples both close to, in the Eastern Mediterranean, and far from in Mesopotamia and Persia. It was the ancient Egyptians that handed on medical knowledge, the art of embalming and an understanding of human anatomy long before most of the world were aware of other than rudimentary science.

The Great Civilization

The amazing achievement of pyramid building suggests just what considerable skills in geometry and construction engineering were accumulated in the Nile Valley at a very early period. A continuity of empire through five thousand years indicates too how the pharoanic administration was in its day, by invention and adaption, at the forefront of the arts of warfare and diplomacy.

Islamic Heritage Egypt contains within it many of the finest of the world's Islamic buildings - mainly in central Cairo, in which a wealth of interesting and intricate mosques, tombs and Islamic schools are concentrated. All Islamic artifacts that are the product of the creative activities of man over fourteen centuries and which contribute so much to the civilization of human life in the broadest sense are present here in abundance. From architecture to technology and from cuisine to silver work, all matters that are part of the Islamic culture of the Middle East and North Africa can be found in Egypt in brilliant physical forms, whether contemporary or relict.

Visitors may use Egypt as an unsurpassed source of examples of Islamic material culture to understand the basis of Islamic science and technology and as a means of bridging the cultural divide between themselves and their Islamic neighbours in the Middle East, North Africa and elsewhere. In particular, appreciation of the way in which Islamic culture has matured over the centuries since the death of the Prophet Mohammed enables an enjoyment of all those valuable skills and technologies from manufacture of astrolabes to precious jewellery that are Egypt's latter day gifts to mankind.

Christian Continuity Egypt has one of the longest continuing traditions of the Christian faith encapsulated in diverse forms - "Old Cairo's" congested townscape, the working monastic communities of the Western Desert and the unique oddity of St.Catherine's old monastery in Sinai.

St.Mark the Evangelist travelled in Egypt during the rule in Rome of the Emperor Nero in the first century AD. From this tradition developed a distinctive form of Christianity - in which monasticism and martyrdom were important features - and from which developed quite separate art, architecture and liturgy. The Coptic language is a direct line successor to the pharaonic past and is currently enjoying a revival of use and interest. There is also an engaging vocal music and an art which successfully merges classical with ancient Egyptian traditions in painting and sculpture. Religious art, well exhibited in a range of monasteries and specialist museums, has a charming character all of its own and perhaps is closer to the rich original Christian format than its Western counterparts. It can only be seen in its great variety in Egypt.

The Desert Lands Some 98 per cent of Egypt is desert, most of it absolutely arid sand and rock waste. This adds up to one million square kilometres of desert terrain as varied as a brown and yellow kaleidoscope image. The bulk of southern Egypt is uninhabited sand seas and deserts interspersed with gravel and stone plains, called *hamadas*.

In Sinai the desert is broken hill lands with rugged passes and narrow valleys in contrast to the sand seas, open plains and wide depressions of the Western Desert. For peace and solitude the great voids of the desert cannot be equalled and the challenge of travel in extreme conditions is incomparable as a sport, a world of temptation for the true individualist.

The Lost Oases Oases, green and welcoming, abound in the better watered niches of the great deserts. Many such as Siwa, near the frontier with Libya, stand as isolated societies of considerable eccentricity. They perpetuate ways of life and economy of an ageless kind with their date palm cultures, clever use of limited water supplies and close local and tribal lineages. Several of the oases of the New Valleys area such as Bahariya have

Left: Praying at the monastery of St Simeon, Aswan. *Below*: Weird and wonderful: the white desert near Farafra Oasis.

Above: Painted house in Gorma Village. *Left*: Muslim women outside the Temple of Karnak. *Next page*: Silhouetted minarets standing tall as the sun sets on the biggest city in Africa.

Right: Diving the depths. Red Sea riches are some of the best in the world. **Below**: A possible 17 million inhabitants would get to see this Omar Sharif movie billboard in downtown Cairo.

Above: The Mohammed Ali Mosque, in the Citadel, Cairo. **Right**: Not the rush hour in Midan Talaat Harb, Central Cairo.
Next page: The monumental statues of megalomaniac Ramses the Great stare out across the Nile at Abu Simbel.

not only a contemporary element but are also adjacent to desert centres of ancient civilisations that have but recently come to light. Exploration in this context takes on two dimensions - desert travel and sights of settlements that are formulating a new historic perspective on the evolution of civilized man.

Within the desert areas are a number of extensive dry wadis which enable transport access and give modest availability of underground water. Shallow topographic basins at Qattara, el-Fayoum and the New Valley system from Bahariya to Kharga also have sub-surface water available at shallow depths. There are dry salt lakes throughout the deserts, the greatest number being in the Western and Southern Deserts.

The oases have never been heavily populated. They acted as stop-over points for trans-Saharan caravans. Siwa was a set of scattered palm grove villages in a large low plain in which water seepages occurred. Recent changes in the New Valley and Toshka regions have resulted in considerable building activity both for new agricultural estates on the perimeter of the settlements and administrative, military and other buildings.

In effect, Egypt is now in many areas spreading activity and settlements out into the desert in an exciting but by no means certain gamble against the most extreme of physical elements.

An underwater World

Egypt has experienced an explosion of development of diving and snorkelling activities and their support facilities in the very recent past. The hubs for diving take advantage of Egypt's year-round good weather - mainly a hot desert climate tempered by sea breezes - and the almost limitless access to the waters and reefs of the Red Sea, the Gulf of Aqaba and the Mediterranean Sea. The coral reefs are extensive, including 500 coral species, and still lightly dived over much of their length. Aquatic life is prolific and in great variety—the fish most of all of which there are some 1,000 species identified so far. There are submarine wrecks to explore such as the famous Thistlegorm in the Straits of Gubal. Diving in the Red Sea began with Jacques Cousteau and Dr Hans Hass in the 1950s and has brought to light new, lightly used dive sites in an amazing underwater world, just three/four hours from Western European population centres. The discovery of ancient cities under the sea at Alexandria enlarge this under water world.

Africa's Greatest City

Cairo is among the world's largest cities. It is bursting with activity as a teeming population centre of 10 million people in its metropolitan area and many more clinging to its outskirts. This is the city made famous by Nobel Prize for Literature winner Naguib Mahfouz in his novels such as *Midaq Alley*, a warm hive of few rich and many poor people in an environment that is still wonderfully antique except for the noisy swell of motorised traffic.

This hubbub of a city is totally welcoming to visitors. The biggest urban centre in Africa boasts one of the world's best museums with the very best exhibit - the Tutankhamen treasure - to be found anywhere on earth. There are representative mosques, large and small, of almost every style. Cairo has close connections with Saladin, Napoleon, Mohammed Ali, General Gordon, Gamal Abdel Nasser and has never been other than the leading light of the Arab Middle East for two centuries. It is thus a place heavily touched by recent and contemporary political events, a circumstance that reflects itself in buildings, monuments, shrines and social scars in a very intense way. There is nowhere quite so wealthy in the relicts of history and current lifestyles as Cairo.

Essentials

2

Essentials

Planning your trip

Where to go

Underwater enthusiasts and those looking for a relaxed break can choose between the dedicated holiday resorts of which the best are, El-Gouna for wind surfing, Hurghada for diving and Sharm El-Sheikh for all-round entertainment. At these sites, warm sea water and all year warm to hot weather offer ideal conditions. Those who wish to taste the bustling life of contemporary Egypt will do this best in Cairo, including Giza. Here the wide range of accommodation allied to the facilities of a 10 million population city, magnificent monuments, wonderful Egyptian Museum and the nearby pyramids offer scope for a busy week. A third choice under this head is a break in either Luxor or Aswan, the former for those looking for the opportunity for a dabble among the great monuments of Thebes as well as a relaxing stay in a friendly town and the latter for people really wanting to get away from it all with a briefcase of good books and some easy touring of magnificent antiquities.

Seeing the country as a whole is possible thanks to that great artery of Egypt - the Nile – which runs the length of populated and cultivated land like a perfect axis from the north in the delta to the south as far as Abu Simbel. Exploit this singular feature by travelling top to bottom on the river itself, in the train, by road or by a mixture of transport. The ideal would be to train the Cairo Luxor section of the route, transfer to a Nile cruiser between Luxor and Aswan and sail on the *Eugenie* up Lake Nasser from Aswan to Abu Simbel. Fly back to Luxor or Cairo to connect with return flight home. For the whole River Nile transect travelling would take up ten days and would need days off to see Cairo – say two weeks for the voyage of a lifetime. A multiple visit strategy: For those with time for an extended period in Egypt or with the means for multiple visits there is great pleasure to be had in developing knowledge of both Egyptian modern and ancient cultures together with an understanding of its diverse regions. In best circumstances a programme of this kind would begin in Cairo to take in both Coptic (Old Cairo) and Muslim (al-Ghawri) centres, the Egyptian Museum and Giza. Luxor/Thebes is the next prime target to see Karnak and the West Bank sites at leisure and in detail which includes a good selection of decorated tombs of the nobles, workmen and the pharaohs as well as the usual monuments such as the Ramesseum, Nefertari tomb and Hapshetsut temple. Aswan and a Nile cruise to the town from Luxor is a high scoring experience. Aswan redefines the word "relaxed" aided by a luxurious cruise on Lake Nasser to Abu Simbel.

In the Egyptian cycle of entertainment outside the Nile Valley for the active and inquisitive traveller are Sinai and St.Catherine's monastery; the west Mediterranean Coast, Alexandria to El-Alamein, with Siwa Oasis; and the Western Desert and the Great Desert Circuit through Farafra and Bahariya. Each of these requires at least five to seven days but are preferably treated as separate trips. Public transport, albeit at times in the form of shared taxis, is available for all these areas, though the Western Desert and Central Sinai are really to be seen as four-wheel drive vehicle expeditions under canvas. Egypt is well served by internal air transport links so that rapid transfers are possible between distant sites – but there is still nothing so satisfying and memorable as bussing and training even the longest journeys in company with the locals.

Short trips

Longer trips

Essentials

Essentials

👉 *Main UK tour operators featuring Egypt*

Abercrombie and Kent*#
Sloane Sq House, Holbein Road, London,
SW1W 8NG, T020-77309600, F0845-
0700607, www.abercrombiekent.co.uk

African Safari Tours
113-119 High St, Hampton Hill, Middlesex,
NW12 1PS, T020-89417400, F020-
89417502, www.lawsoninternational.com

Amoun Travel#
56 Kendal St, London, W2 2BP,
T020-74023100, F020-74023424,
sales@amountravel.co.uk

Ancient World Tours
PO Box 12950, London, W6 8GY,
T07071-222950, F01483-237398,
www.ancient.co.uk

Bales Worldwide
Bales House, Junction Rd, Dorking, Surrey,
RH4 3HL, T01306-885991, F01306-740048,
www.balesworldwide.com

British Museum Traveller
46 Bloomsbury St, London, WC1B 3QQ,
T020-73238895, F020-75808677,
www.britishmuseumtraveller.co.uk

Destination Red Sea*#
T020-84409900, F020-84409905.

Diving World#
Bank Chambers, 6 Borough High St,
London, SE1 9QQ, T020-74070017,
F020-73781108, www.diving-world.com

Egyptian*#
Longcroft House, Arnewood Bridge Rd,
Sway, Hampshire, SO41 6DA,
T01590-677665, F01590-683364.

El-Sawy Travel Ltd*#
80 Park Rd , London NW1 4SH,
T020-72581901, F020-77248003.

Exodus Travels
9 Weir Rd, London, SW12 OLT, T020-8772
3822, F020-86730779, www.exodus.co.uk

Explore Worldwide
1 Frederick St, Aldershot, Surrey, GU11 1LQ,
T01252-319448, F01252-760001,
www.explore.co.uk

Explorers Tours#
223 Copermill Rd, Wraysbury, TW19 5NW,
T01753-681999, F01753-682660,
www.explorers.co.uk

Goodwood Travel
St Andrews House, Station Rd East,
Canterbury, CT1 2WD, T01227-763336,
F01227-762417, www.concord.co.uk

Hayes and Jarvis*#
152 King St, London, W6 OQU,
T020-82227800, F020-87410299,
www.hayes_jarvis.com

The Imaginative Traveller#
14 Barley Mow Passage, Chiswick, London,
W4 4PH, T020-87428612, F020-87423045,
www.imaginative-traveller.com

Jasmin Tours*#
53-55 Balham Hill, London, SW12 9DR,
T020-86758886, F020-86731204,
www.Jasmin-tours.co.uk

Kuoni Travel*#
Kuoni House, Dorking, Surrey, RH5 4A2,
T01306-743000, F01306-744222,
www.kuoni.co.uk

When to go

Best time to visit The sun shines the whole year round and rainy days are the exception. The temperature increases as one travels south with Luxor being about 10°C warmer than Cairo. The high summer temperatures in the desert will be of greatest concern for visitors.

Each section has at least one climatic table with the best season(s) shaded for easy reference. The best time for travelling everywhere except possibly the Alexandria region is the period October-April but best of all is November-February. Travellers in Egypt in April-May should be prepared for the *khamseen* wind – the wind of 50 days – which blows sand and heat to the discomfort of those caught in the open. Relative humidity can be high (over 70%) on the coast and the Delta. Inland, humidity is not a problem with Aswan, for example having averages of less than 50% for the whole year and a mere 30% in the summer months. At the height of the summer, humidity falls in many places to less than 20%.

Longwood Holidays#
3 Bourne Court, Southend Rd, Woodford
Green, IT8 8HD, T020-85514494, F020-
85500086, www.longfordholidays.co.uk
MISR Travel*#
Rm 201, 2nd floor, Longham House,
308 Regent St, London, W1R 5AL,
T020-72551087, F020-76372973.
Oonas divers*#
20 St Leonards Rd, Eastbourne, E Sussex,
BN21 3UH, T01323-648924,
F01323-738356, www.oonasdivers.com
Peltours Ltd#
Sovereign House, 11-19 Ballards Lane,
Finchley, N31 4UX, T020-83430590,
F020-83430579, www.peltours.com
Prospect Music & Art Tours
36 Mancester St, London, W1U 7LH,
T020-74865704, F020 74065808,
enquiries@prospecttours.com
Regal Holidays*#
22 High St, Sutton, Ely, CB6 2RB,
T01353-778096, F01353-777897,
www.regal-diving.co.uk
Seafarer Cruising and Sailing
30 Hartston Rd, Poole, BH15 2PG,
T020-72340500, F020-72340700,
sales@seafarercruises.co.uk
Soliman Travel#
113 Earls Court Rd, London, SW5 9RL,
T020-72446855, F020-78351394,
www.Solimantravel.co.uk
Somak Holidays
Somak Hse, Harrovian Village,

Bessborough Rd, Harrow on the hill,
Middlesex, HA1 3EX, T020-84233000,
F020-84237700, www.Somak.co.uk
Swan Hellenic
77 New Oxford St, London, WC1A 1PP,
T020-78002200, F020-78311280,
www.swanhellenic.com
Tailor Made Holidays*#
5 Station Approach, Hinchley Wood,
Surrey, KT10 05P, T020-83984464, F020-
83986007, www.tailormadeholidays.co.uk
Thomas Cook
PO Box 36, Thorpe Wood, Peterborough,
PE3 6SB, T01733-563200.
Thomson Holidays#
T0870-502555.
Top Deck Travel
131-135 Earls Court Rd, London, SW5 9RH,
T020-73704555, F020-73736201,
www.topdecktravel.co.uk
Travelbag Adventures#
15 Turk St, Alton, Hants, GU34 1AG,
T01420 541007, F01420-541022,
www.travelbag-adventures.com
Travelscope Worldwide#
T01483-569453, F01483-569466.
Wind, Sand & Stars
2 Arkwright Rd, Hampstead, London,
NW3 6AD, T020-74333684,
www.windandstars.co.uk

* = provision for disabled   # = diving
holidays

Crusader Travel, 57 Church Street, Twickenham, Middlesex, TW1 3NR, T020-87440474,   **Tours & tour**
F020-87440574, www.crusadertravel.com The division known as Red Sea Travel Centre   **operators**
is particularly interested in watersports – scuba diving, wind surfing, sailing and
snorkelling – they own the Aquasport dive and Watersports centres (at Sharm el Sheikh
and Hurghada), offer two-centre and tailor-made visits as well as Nile cruises.
Egyptian Dream, 244 Earl's Court Gardens, London, SW5 0TA, T0207-3736055.
Explore Worldwide Ltd, 1 Frederick St, Aldershot, Hants, GU11 1LQ, T01252-319448,
F01252-343170. For hotels/camping in oases of Siwa and Western Desert, also Nile
cruises, Abu Simbel, Felucca sail-trek, Red Sea and Sinai. **Guerba Safaris and Expeditions**,
Wessex House, 40 Station Road, Westbury, Wiltshire, BA13 3JN, T01373-826611,
F01373-858351, www.guerba.co.uk **The Imaginative Traveller**, see table for details.
Camping, walking, cycling also first class quality tours. **Oonasdivers**, see table for details.
Quality liveboard accommodation for divers, also a fascinating Red Sea Diving Safari,
camping and diving off the remote southern Red Sea Coast of Egypt. **Soliman Travel**, see
table for details. Made to measure service, specialist tours to famous battle fields of
Western Desert, follow route of Holy Family in Egypt. **Sunbird**, PO Box 76 Sandy,

Bedfordshire, SG19 1DF, T01767-682969, F01767-692481, www.sunbird.demon.co.uk A variety of locations in Egypt with emphasis on bird life and history. *Tailor Made Holidays*, 5 Station Approach, Hinchley Wood, Surrey KT10 0SP, T0208-3987424, F0181-3986007. Offer Hooked on the Nile – Fishing on Lake Nasser, they have six boats fed by a supply boat on Lake Nasser, a civilized safari in a steel hulled boat, with ample opportunities to fish. *The British Museum Traveller*, 34 Bloomsbury Street, London, WC1B 3QQ. Offer a variety of accompanied tours such as Christmas on the Nile, Monasteries in the desert, Egypt at Easter in the footsteps of Howard Carter; Egypt and the Nubian Temples; New Year in Thebes. *Travel Bag Adventures*, 15 Turk St, Alton, Hampshire, GU34 1AG, T01420-541007, F01420-541022. Cheaper end of the market, felucca travel, explore the Western desert by jeep and camel. *Travelscope Worldwide (Gaz Tours)*, PO Box 158 Guildford, Surrey GU2 6PU, UK, T/F01483-569453. An excellent independent travel company, which has been in business since 1972, and which arranges individual and group tours not only to classic sites in Cairo, Luxor and Aswan but also to the oases. Special tours for Christian groups can follow the Holy Family's flight from Egypt, while tours to Sinai cover all the major sites to the Israeli border. The service is excellent because the company specializes in providing a personalized service. Dr Sadek has direct access to the *EgyptAir* computers and can therefore make and confirm flight reservations. *Wind, Sand & Stars*, 2 Arkwright Road, London, NW3 6AD, T0207-4333684, F0207-4313247. For special tours in Southern Sinai and the Western Desert. Also see table above.

Egyptian embassies and consulates

Embassies

Australia, 1 Darwin Ave, Yarralumla, ACT 2600 Canberra, T62-2734437.

Austria, 1190 Wien, Kreindll Gasse 22, Vienna 1190, T1 4788800.

Belgium, Av de l'Uruguay, 19 1000 Bruxelles, T26635800, Egypt.embassy@skynet.be

Canada, 454 Laurier Ave East, Ottawa, Ontario, K1N 6R3, T613-2344958.

Denmark, Kristianiagade 19, DK - 2100, Copenhagen, Denmark, T35437070.

France, 56 Ave d'Iena, 75116 Paris, T1-47209770.

Germany, Kronprinzen Str, Bonn 2, T228-364000.

Greece, 3 Vassilissis Safies Street, Athens, T1-3618612/3.

Ireland, 12 Clyde Rd, Dublin 4, T1-606566.

Israel, 54 Rehov Rosel, Tel Aviv, T5465131.

Italy, 00199, Roma-Villa Savoia, Via Salaria, 267, Roma, CP 7133, T06-8440191.

Morocco, 31 El-Gazaer St, Sawmaat Hassan, Rabat, T7-731834.

Netherlands, Boweg 1-2597, The Hague, T70-3542000.

Norway, Drammensveien 90A, 0244 Oslo 2, T222-00010.

Portugal, Av D Vasco Da Gama No 8, 1400 Lisbon, T1-3018342.

Spain, Velazquez 69, Madrid 28006, T1-5776308.

Sudan, Sharia Al-Jama'a Al-Mojram, Khartoum, T72836.

Sweden, Strandvagen 35, Stockholm, T8-6603145.

Switzerland, 61 Elfenauweg, 3006 Berne, T31-3528012.

UK, 26 South St, London W1Y 6DD, T020-74993304, F020-74911547, www.egypt-embassy.org.uk

USA Embassy and Consulate, 3521 International Court, NW Washington DC 20008, T202-8955400.

Consulates

Canada, 3754 Côtes-des-Neiges, Montreal, Quebec, H3H 7V6, T514-937781.

Libya, 5th floor, Omar El-Khayam Hotel, Ben Ghazi, T61-92488.

UK, 2 Lowndes St, London SW1X, T020-72355684, F020-72359777, www.MFA.gov.eg, open 1000-1200 Monday-Friday for visas.

USA, 1110 Second Ave, New York, NY10022, T212-7597120; 3001 Pacific Ave, San Francisco, CA 94115, T415-3469700, F415-3469480, www.cgy2000.com

Finding out more

Austria, Ellsabeth Strasse, 4/Steige 5/1, Opernringhof, 1010 Vienna, T5876633, aegyptnet@netway.at **Belgium**, 179 Av Louise 1050, Brussels, T26473858, TOUREGYPT2@SKYnet. BE **Canada**, 1253 Mc Gill College Avenue, Suite 250, Quebec, Montreal, T514-8614420. **France**, 90 Ave Champs Elysees, Paris, T1-45629442, Egypt.Ot@Wanadoo.Fr **Germany**, 64A Kaiser Strasse, Frankfurt/Main, T69252319. **Greece**, 5 Soloms St, Kolonaki, Athens, T3606906. **Italy**, 19 Via Bissolati, 00187 Rome, T6-4827985. **Japan**, Hoshina Building, 3F, 4-2, 2-chome, Minato-ku, Tokyo, T3-35890653, Tourism@ egypt.or.Jp **Spain**, Torre de Madrid, planta 5, Oficina 3, Plaza de Espana, 28008 Madrid, T91-5592121. **Sweden**, Dorottningatan 99, Atan 65, 11136 Stockholm, T468-102584, egypt.Ti.Swed@alfa.telenordia.se **Switzerland**, 9 rue des Alpes, Geneva, T022-329132. **UK**, 170 Piccadilly, London W1V 9DD, T0900-1600299/020-74935283. **USA**, 630 5th Ave, Suite 1706, New York 10111, T212-3322570, egyptourst@ad.com

Egyptian State tourist offices

The official language is Arabic, however many Egyptians are proficient in foreign languages, in particular English and French. See Language for Travel, page 553 for a simple vocabulary.

Language

Essentials

Essentials

Before you travel

Visas & immigration
Passports are required by all and should be valid for at least six months beyond the period of intended stay in Egypt.

There are few closed areas in this region but certain sensitive border zones can be mined or be restricted to military personnel. Do not stray into clearly marked boundary or no-go areas. Details of any known sensitive areas are given in appropriate sections of this *Handbook*.

Visas are required by all except nationals of Ghana, Guinea and Malta and most Arab countries. Tourist visas cost around US$20 equivalent. In UK this is £15 for a single entry and £18 for up to three entries. Business visas cost £53 and £91 accompanied by a letter of authorization. Payment must be by cash or postal order, cheques are not accepted. Visas are valid for three months from date of issue and one month from date of arrival and cannot be post dated.

A renewable 30 day tourist visa can easily be obtained at all international airports and ports, and even on the boat; £10, but not when entering from Israel or Palestine. Entrance without a visa is permitted for visits of up to a week to South Sinai and St Catherine when entering through Sinai entry points of Taba, St Catherine and Sharm el-Sheikh airports, Nuweiba and Sharm el-Sheikh seaports. Do not permit officials to stamp your passport at these entry points.

As part of the easing of controls on travellers in this area, most countries will issue entry visas at principal border posts.

Visa extensions can be obtained (with difficulty) at the Mogamma, Midan Tahrir, Cairo; Sharia Khaled Ibn el Walid in Luxor; 28 Sharia Talaat Harb in Alexandria and at the port in Sharm el Sheikh. You will need your passport, two new photographs, cash to pay for renewal, and receipts proving you have exchanged US$180 for each extra month you wish to extend. Overstaying by one or two days does not matter, but after a couple of extra weeks be prepared for a fine.

Entry into Israel, Palestine, Libya and Sudan With the appropriate visas entry is comparatively straight forward although bilateral relations with Sudan are currently very strained.

Identity & membership cards
If you are in full-time education you will be entitled to an International Student Identity Card (ISIC), which is distributed by student travel offices and travel agencies in 77 countries. The ISIC gives you special prices on all forms of transport (air, sea, rail etc) and access to a variety of other concessions and services. Contact ISIC, Box 9048, 1000 Copenhagen, Denmark, T(+45) 33939303.

Insurance
Comprehensive travel insurance is essential. Consider one which offers immediate repatriation for illness or accident. Claims for lost or stolen items must be backed by evidence of reporting the matter to the police. Obtaining this matter will not be easy. There is a problem of language, getting it written in English and hardest, getting someone high enough in authority to accept the responsibility.

Vaccinations
Vaccinations are not required unless travelling from a country where yellow fever or cholera frequently occurs. You are advised to be up to date with polio, tetanus and hepatitis protection. Evidence of an HIV test is required for visits over 30 days – although this requirement is not always enforced (see Health for further information, page 55).

Travellers tend to take more than they need though requirements vary with the **What to take**
destination and the type of travel that is to be undertaken. Laundry services are
generally cheap and speedy. A travelpack, a hybrid backpack/suitcase, rather than a
rigid suitcase, covers most eventualities and survives bus boot, roof rack and
plane/ship hold travel with ease. Serious trekkers will need a framed backpack.

Clothing of light cotton or cotton/polyester with a a woollen sweater for evenings,
more northern regions, higher altitudes and the clear desert nights. Comfortable
shoes with socks as feet may swell in hot weather. Modest dress for women including
a sunhat and headscarf.

Checklist: Sun hat; sun protection cream; sunglasses; money belt; air cushions for hard
seating; bumbag; earplugs; eye mask; insect repellent and/or mosquito net, electric
mosquito mats, coils; neck pillow; International Driving Licence; photocopies of
essential documents; spare passport photographs; Swiss Army knife; tissues/toilet
paper; torch; umbrella (excellent protection from sun and unfriendly dogs); wipes
(*Damp Ones, Baby Wipes*); zip lock bags.

Those intending to stay in budget accommodation might also include: Cotton
sheet sleeping bag; padlock (for hotel room and pack); soap; student card; toilet paper;
Universal bath plug.

Health kit: Antiacid tablets; anti-diarrhoea tablets; anti-malaria tablets; anti-infective
ointment; condoms; contraceptives; dusting powder for feet; First aid kit and
disposable needles; flea powder; sachets of rehydration salts; tampons; travel sickness
pills; water sterilizing tablets.

If you would like to take presents for Egyptians you meet, men would appreciate
American cigarettes and alcohol. It is not appropriate to give presents to women.

Declarations On arrival you may be asked to declare video cameras and computers **Customs**
on the D form. This is now rarely the case. In case of theft report to police or they will
assume you have sold them and charge duty.

Goods may be imported into Egypt as follows: 200 cigarettes or 50 cigars or 250 gm of **Duty-free**
tobacco, one litre of spirit, one litre of perfume or toilet water, gifts up to the value of
E£500. Duty-free export of purchases can be arranged through the larger shops and
tourist agencies.

Money

E£1 =100 Piastres. Notes are in denominations of E£1, F£5, E£10, E£20, E£50, E£100 and **Currency**
5, 10, 25 and 50 Piastres. Coins (which are not worth carrying) are 5 and 10 Piastres.

Visitors can enter and leave Egypt with a maximum of E£10,000. There are no **Regulations**
restrictions on the import of foreign currency provided it is declared on an official **& money**
customs form. Export of foreign currency may not exceed the amount imported. All **changing**
cash, Travellers' cheques, credit cards and gold over E£500 must be declared on arrival.

Access/Mastercard, American Express, Diners Club and Visa are accepted in all major **Credit cards**
hotels, larger restaurants and shops but, in the main, Egypt is still a cash economy.

Travellers' cheques can be honoured in most banks and *bureaux de change*. US$ are the **Travellers'**
easiest to exchange particularly if they are well-known like Visa, Thomas Cook or **cheques**
American Express. There is always a transaction charge so it is a balance between using

Essentials

Discount flight agents in the UK & Ireland

Usit Campus, 52 Grosvener Gardens, London SW1W 0AG, T08702-401010, www.usitworld.com; 53 Forest Rd, Edinburgh EH1 2QP, T0131-225 6111; Fountain Centre, College St, Belfast BT1 6ET, T01232-324073; 19 Aston Quay, Dublin 2, T01-6021777. Student/youth travel specialists with branches also in Birmingham, Brighton, Bristol, Cambridge, Glasgow and Manchester.
Council Travel, 28a Poland St, London W1V 3DB, T020-74377767, www.destinations-group.com
The London Flight Centre, 131 Earl's Court Rd, London SW5 9RH, T020-72446411; 47 Notting Hill Gate, London W11 3JS, T020-77274290.
STA Travel, 86 Old Brompton Rd, London SW7 3LH, T020-74376262, www.statravel.co.uk Also have other branches in London, as well as in Brighton, Bristol, Cambridge, Leeds, Manchester, Newcastle and Oxford and on many University campuses. Specialists in cheap student/youth flights and tours, and also good for student Ids and insurance.
Trailfinders, 194 Kensington High St, London W8 7RG, T020-79833939.

high value cheques and paying one charge and carrying extra cash or using lower value cheques and paying more charges. A small amount of cash, again in US$, is useful in an emergency. Egypt has a fixed exchange rate – wherever the transaction is carried out.

Banks There are five national banks and more than 78 branches of foreign banks. Banking hours are 0830-1400 Sunday-Thursday.

Cost of living Egypt is very cheap. Depending on the standards of comfort and cleanliness one is prepared to accept for accommodation, food and travel, it is possible to survive on as little as E£25-30 pp per day. Petrol (super) 100 piastres per litre, coffee or tea E£1 (depending where you purchase), soft drink E£0.75-E£1, medium beer E£1.50.

Getting there

Air

It is possible to fly direct to Egypt from Europe, the Middle East, North Africa, most adjacent African countries and also from the USA and Canada.
Carriers include: British Airways, www.britishairways.com, Air France, www.airfrance.com, KLM, www.klm.uk.com
   There are regular flights from most European and African capitals, New York and Tokyo. Check with your travel agent.
   Air Sinai operates return services: Cairo-Tel Aviv; Cairo-El-Arish, Cairo-St Catherine-Eilat; Cairo-Ras el-Nakab-Luxor-Sharm el-Sheikh. Details from *Nile Hilton Hotels*, T760948/776893.
   The national airline is EgyptAir, www.egyptair.com **UK** Sales: 29/31 Picadilly, London, T020-77342343. **USA** 720 Fifth Avenue, New York 10019, T212-5862678, **Australia** Suite 1601, 130 Pitt St, Sydney, T6122326677. **Canada** 151 Bloor St, Suite 300, Toronto, Ontario, T9602441. **France** 1 Bls Reu Auber, 75009, Paris, T44948500. **Netherlands** Singel 450, 1017 AZ Amsterdam, T6256661.
   Flight times to Cairo: from London about four hours 40 minutes; from Paris 4½ hours; from Athens two hours; from Tunis 1¾ hours. Package tours which frequently offer cheaper flights generally operate smaller planes which take longer.
   An increasing number of tourists fly direct to airports such as Sharm el-Sheikh and Hurghada.

Discount flight agents in North America

Air Brokers International, 323 Geary St, Suite 411, San Francisco, CA94102, T01-800-8833273, www.airbrokers.com Consolidator and specialist on RTW and Circle Pacific tickets.
Council Travel, 205 E 42nd St, New York, NY 10017, T1-888-COUNCIL, www.counciltravel.com Student/budget agency with branches in many other US cities.
Discount Airfares Worldwide On-Line, www.etn.nl/discount.htm A hub of consolidator and discount agent links.

International Travel Network/ Airlines of the Web, www.itn.net/airlines Online air travel information and reservations.
STA Travel, 5900 Wilshire Blvd, Suite 2110, Los Angeles, CA 90036, T1-800-7770112, www.sta-travel.com Also branches in New York, San Francisco, Boston, Miami, Chicago, Seattle and Washington DC.
Travel CUTS, 187 College St, Toronto, ON, M5T 1P7, T1-800-6672887, www.travelcuts.com Specialist in student discount fares, Ids and other travel services. Branches in other Canadian cities.

The cheapest time of year to travel is May to September when it is extremely hot in Egypt.

It is possible to obtain significantly cheaper tickets by avoiding school vacation times, by flying at night, by shopping around and by booking early to obtain one of the quota of discounted fares. Group discounts apply in many instances. — **Discounts**

General airline restrictions apply with regard to luggage weight allowances before surcharge; normally 30 kg for first class and 20 kg for business and economy class. An understanding of the term 'limited' with regard to amount of hand luggage varies greatly. Some airlines can be strict and will decline to permit large or in some cases more than one item of hand luggage on board with the passenger. — **Airline restrictions**

International airlines vary in their arrangements and requirements for security over electrical items such as radios, tape recorders and lap-top computers (as does the interest of the customs officials on arrival and departure). Check in advance if you can, carry the items in your hand luggage for convenience and have them wrapped for safety but available for inspection. — **Airline security**

Train and steamer

There is no international rail link either east to Israel or west to Libya and the ferry connection across Lake Nasser between Aswan and Wadi Halfa in Sudan has been suspended due to political tensions.

Road

For coaches to Israel (Tel Aviv and Jerusalem) contact *Travco Travel Agency*, 112 Sharia 26 July, Zamalek, Cairo, T3420488; the *East Delta Bus Company* (Sinai International Station) runs a/c buses daily except Saturday to Tel-Aviv. Contact Sinai International Station, T824753 or East Delta Buses, 14, Sharia Mustafa Abu Hef, Cairo, T743027. — **Bus & service taxi**

Service taxis run between Marsa Matruh and Sollum on the Libyan border. Reach Marsa Matruh by bus (a/c or service) from Midan Sa'ad Zaghloul, Alexandria. *Arab Union* superjet buses leave from Midan Almaza, Cairo at 0200 for Amman, Jeddah, Damascus, Kuwait, Bahrain and Qatar.

Essentials

Discount flight agents in Australia and New Zealand

Flight Centres, 82 Elizabeth St, Sydney, T13-1600; 205 Queen St, Auckland, T09-3096171. Also branches in other towns and cities.
Quantas, Shifly Square, Sydney, T02-99570111.
STA Travel, T1300-360960, www.statravelaus.com.au; 702 Harris St,

Ultimo, Sydney, and 256 Flinders St, Melbourne. In NZ: 10 High St, Auckland, T09-3666673. Also in major towns and university campuses.
Thomas Cook, 321 Kent St, Sydney, T02-92486100.
Travel.com.au, 80 Clarence, St, Sydney, T02-92901500, www.travel.com.au

Motoring Vehicles drive on the right in Egypt. Road signs are international with Arabic script. The main international road west goes to Libya and to the east under the Suez Canal and via El-Arish to Palestine and Israel. Other international routes are along the Nile Valley or along the northern Sinai and the Red Sea coasts. Entry for private cars requirements – a Carnet de Passage en Douane and an International Driving Licence. Contact Egyptian Automobile Club, 1 Sharia Kasr el-Nil, Cairo, T743355. Vehicles must be petrol, not diesel, and four-wheel drive vehicles require permission from the Ministry of Defence. Extra vehicle insurance may be required at the border.

Boat

Ferries The region is served by a number of ferry services, particularly across the Red Sea/Gulf of Aqaba, most catering for both vehicles and foot passengers. Most ferries are reliable and moderately comfortable.

The main coastal ports are Alexandria, Port Said and Suez. Ferries operating in this area can be contacted in UK at: **Viamare Travel**, Graphic House, 2 Sumatra Road, London NW6 1PU, T020-74314560.

For connections to Southern Europe contact Adriatica's representive at Mena Tours Agency, 14 Sharia Talaat Harb, Cairo, T740955/740864; 28 Sharia al-Ghorfa al-Tigariya, Alexandria, T809676.

For connections with Jordan, from Nuweiba to Aqaba contact **Egyptian Shipping Co**, Cairo, T758278, daily from Aqaba at 1300 and 1800 – except Saturday, only one sailing so check carefully.

Cruise ships calling in at ports in Egypt: **Airtours Cruises**, Wavell House, Holcombe Road, Helmshore, Rossendale, Lancs, BB4 4NB, T0870-2412567, F01706-236154, call in at Alexandria. P&O Cruises, 77 New Oxford Street, London, WC1A 1PP, T020-78002345, F020-78311280, call in at Alexandria and Port Said. Titan Travel/Costa Cruises, HiTours House, Crossoak Lane, Selfords, Surrey, RH1 5EX, T01737-760033, F01293-440034, www.titantravel.co.uk, call in at Alexandria and Port Said.

Ferries ply between Suez and Jeddah in Saudi Arabia via Aqaba, contact **Mena Tours Agency**, 14 Sharia Talaat Harb, Cairo, T740955 or **Misr Travel**, 1 Sharia Talaat Harb, Cairo, T3930010.

Touching down

Airport information

Egypt's international airports are Cairo International (CAI) 22 km northeast of the city (travel time 30 minutes); Alexandria Airport (ALY) 5 km southeast of the city; Luxor Airport (LXR) 5½ km from the town.

Cairo Airport (CAI) is far out to the east of the town – about 22 km, travelling time about 30 minutes. Terminal One is mainly EgyptAir and domestic travel. The newer terminal Two is about 3 km away and takes all other flights. Terminal One T2448977, Terminal Two T

Departure There is no departure tax. Confirm airline flights at least 48 hours in advance. Have all currency exchange receipts easily available. Before passing into the departure lounge/area it is necessary to fill in an embarkation card. Only a limited amount of currency can be reconverted before you leave. This is a tedious process and is not possible at Luxor airport. Sometimes suitable foreign currency is not available. It is better to budget with care, have no excess cash and save all the trouble. A maximum of E£1,000 may be carried into or out of Egypt.

Airport tax

Tourist information

All visitors to Egypt must register with the police within seven days of arrival. This is generally done by the hotel. Independent travellers are responsible for their own registration which can be done at a main police station or the Mogamma building off Cairo's Medan Tahrir. If you do not register be prepared for a fine.

Registration

Over such a large country the provision of tourist information is vary variable. Offices that were helpful become outdated and new offices are built. In every case, other than for accommodation, the best place to ask is one of the good quality hotels.

Tourist offices

There is very little provision for the disabled. Some of the newer museums have ramps and some of the buildings have lifts. Access to the main sites – Pyramids, Temples and Tombs is very limited.

For those with access to the internet, a Globa Access – Disabled Travel Network Site is www.geocities.com/Paris/1502 It is dedicated to providing travel information for disabled adventurers and includes a number of reviews and tips from members of the public.

Disabled travellers

Being openly gay could be difficult, as homosexuality is forbidden in the Koran, and it is not the country in which it is advised to look for a partner. HIV is a serious consideration.

Gay & lesbian travellers

Student identification cards are best obtained through the backpacker hostels. They cost E£40 (more if it is obtained for you), require a passport photograph and an official letter from a university or college. As these cards give cheap access to all places worth visiting and cheaper travel – they are a must. The International Student Identity Card (ISIC) can also be contacted at The ISIC Association, Box 9048, 1000 Copenhagen, Denmark, T+45-33939303.

Student travellers

Women face greater difficulties than men or couples. Young Muslim women rarely travel without the protection of a male or older female, hence a single Western woman is regarded as strange and is supposed to be of easy virtue – a view

Women travellers

Essentials

Touching down

Business hours *Government offices From 0900-1400 every day except Friday and national holidays.* **Banks** *Open 0830-1400 Saturday-Thursday.* **Shops** *are open 0900-1230 and 1600-2000 in summer and 0900-1900 in winter. Hours on Friday and Sunday will vary.* **Directory enquiries** **Emergency services Cairo** *Police: 122,*

Ambulance: 123, Fire: 125, Tourist Police: 126. **IDD** *140* **Museums** *etc close for Friday prayers, 1130-1330.* **Official time** *GMT + 2 hours.* **Voltage** *220 volts AC. Sockets take standard continental two round pin plugs. Continental adaptors are useful.* **Weights and measures** *Egyptians use metric measurements.*

perpetuated by Hollywood. To minimize the pestering that will certainly occur, dress modestly, the less bare flesh the better (see page 31), steadfastly ignore rude and suggestive comments directed at you but aimed at boosting the caller's ego, avoid any behaviour which would aggravate the situation, and keep a sense of humour. Single men often attract greater attention from customs officials and are more liable to receive unwelcome propositions.

Working in the country Opportunities for casual work in Egypt are very limited. Those with journalistic skills and/or English teaching skills might find informal employment with the private sector. Other than that, foreigners working abroad are recruited outside Egypt for specific projects.

Business travellers will be well looked after. Egyptians are excellent hosts. Transport, accommodation and business facilities of the highest quality are available at the better hotels in the larger cities.

Rules, customs and etiquette

Travelling in Islamic countries Egypt is a deeply Islamic country in which religion is a total way of life. Some Egyptians are used to the ways of the Arab countries and a handful are more widely travelled: most, however, are conservative and parochial in attitude. While Islam is similar to Judaism and Christianity in its philosophical content and the three revealed religions are accepted together as the religions of the book (Ahl Al-Kitab), it is wise for travellers to recognize that Islamic practices in this traditional society are a sensitive area. Public observance of religious ritual and taboo are important, just as is the protection of privacy for women and the family. Islamicism of an extremist kind is on the wane in Egypt but bare-faced arrogance by visitors will engender a very negative response even among normally welcoming Egyptians who have no tendencies towards fundamentalist views.

Travel, tourism and foreign workers are common throughout the region so that the sight of outsiders is not unusual. Tourists attract particular hostility, however. They are seen as voyeuristic, short-term and unblushingly alien. Tourists have become associated with the evils of modern life – loose morals, provocative dress, mindless materialism and degenerate/Western cultural standards. In many cases these perceptions are entirely justified and bring a sense of infringed Islamic values among many local people, most of whom are conservative in bent. Feelings are made worse by apparent differences in wealth between local peoples whose annual per head income is approximately US$1,500 and foreign tourists living on an average of US$32,000 per head in the industrialized states. Tourists, whose way of life for a few weeks a year is dedicated to conspicuous consumption, attract dislike and envy. Muslims might wonder why a way of life in Islam, seen as superior to all other forms of faith, gives poor material rewards vis-à-vis the hordes of apparent "infidels" who come as tourists. The areas where sensitivity can best be shown are in dress and courtesy:

Daily dress for most Egyptians is governed by considerations of climate and weather. **The dress code** Other than labourers in the open, the universal reaction is to cover up against heat or cold. For males other than the lowest of manual workers, full dress is normal. Men breaching this code will either be young and regarded as of low social status or very rich and Westernized. When visiting mosques (where this is allowed), medressa or other shrines/ tombs/religious libraries, men wear full and normally magnificently washed and ironed traditional formal wear. In the office, men will be traditionally dressed or in Western suits/shirt sleeves. The higher the grade of office, the more likely the Western suit. At home people relax in loose jallabah. Arab males will be less constrained on the beach where Bermuda shorts and swimming trunks are the norm.

For women the dress code is more important than for men. Quite apart from dress being tell-tale of social status among the ladies of Cairo or Alexandria or of tribal/regional origin, decorum and religious sentiment dictates full covering of body, arms and legs. The veil is increasingly common for women moving in public as a reflection of growing Islamic revivalist views. There are many women who do not conform, including those with modern attitudes towards female emancipation, professional women trained abroad and, remarkably, many Berber women or women with genuinely nomadic or semi nomadic lives. The religious minorities – Copts and Jews for example do not wear the veil. Jewellery (see Jewellery in Background) is another major symbol in women's dress especially heavy gold necklaces.

The role of dress within Islamic and social codes is clearly a crucial matter. While some latitude in dress is given to foreigners, good guests are expected to conform to the broad lines of the practice of the house. Thus, except on the beach or 'at home' in the hotel (assuming it is a tourist rather than local establishment), modesty in dress pays off. This means jeans or slacks for men rather than shorts together with a shirt or T-shirt. In Islamic places such as mosques or medressa, hire jallabah at the door. For women, modesty is slightly more demanding. In public wear comfortable clothes that at least cover the greater part of the legs and arms. If the opportunity arises to visit a mosque or medersa open to tourists, jallabah and slippers are available for hire at the doors. Elsewhere full covering of arms and legs and a head scarf is necessary. Offend against the dress code – and most Western tourists in this area do to a greater or lesser extent – you risk antagonism and alienation from the local people who are increasingly fundamentalist in their Islamic beliefs and observances.

Do not enter mosques during a service. In other places dedicated to religious **Forbidden** purposes behave with decorum – refrain from shouting, unseemly laughter and take **places** photographs only when permitted. Outsiders have spent much time and ingenuity in penetrating Islam's holiest shrines. This is not worth the effort here since the most interesting sites are open to visitors in any case. People who are clearly non-Muslim will be turned away by door keepers from places where they are not wanted. Those who try to slip past the guardians should be sure they can talk their way out of trouble!

Islam has its codes of other practices and taboos but few will affect the visitor unless he **Good manners** or she gains entry to local families or organizations at a social level. A few rules are worth observing in any case by all non-Muslims when in company with Muslim friends. (i) Do not use your left hand for eating since it is ritually unclean. If knives and forks are provided, then both hands can be used. (ii) Do not accept or ask for alcohol unless your host clearly intends to imbibe. (iii) If eating in traditional style from a common dish, use your right hand only and keep your feet tucked under your body away from the food. (iv) Never offer pork or its derivatives to a Muslim visitor. Buy hallal meat killed in accordance with Muslim ritual and/or provide a non-meat dish. Do not provide alcoholic drink.

Essentials

Essentials

 ## The inner sanctum – realities of the harem

Hollywood and the popular image have vested the 'harem' with a fanciful aura that fails entirely to approximate to reality. Perhaps the fact that women in urban great houses and the courts of rulers in North Africa and the Middle East were contained within a protected zone, forbidden to all males but the patron and his eunuch managers, gave the harem a certain mystique to inquisitive Europeans. Architecturally, too, the marvellous apartments with their geometrically decorated mashrabiyya, spacious rooms and wonderful plaster arches have an alluring atmosphere of quiet and peace. In the same way the gardens set out for the ladies of the harem to take exercise remain fine monuments to the use of sheltered space.

The romantic side of the harem and those – generally young men of good but undisclosed royal antecedents – who sought to find their loved ones locked within its fortresses is possibly a legacy of the tales of A Thousand and One Nights, which early found their way into western literature in romanticized and bowdlerized forms.

In the 19th century a number of European artists such as Delacroix, Roberts and Gleyre were attracted to North Africa by the exotic images of a different and colourful culture. Paul Lenoir, who travelled with Gérôme in the 1860s, indicated that the harem took prime attention: "... during the 19th century, the harem, the bath and the guard to the seraglio remained amongst the most popular manifestations of Orientalism in painting and literature".

Inevitably it was images of the Ottoman seraglio and the Islamic harem that were widely painted by Europeans in North Africa. Paintings of women in the bath house such as the Harem in the Kiosk and the Moorish Bath by Gérome did much to give graphic pictures of the subject. In Great Britain, there was also a flurry of orientalist painting, poetry and other literature, with J F Lewis (1805-75) particularly concentrating on the subject of the harem. He travelled in Morocco and Spain and later lived in Egypt for many years. His watercolours have a particular attraction and were widely acclaimed in their day. In addition to The Hareem of 1854, pictures like The Intercepted Correspondence with its portrayal of richly elaborated backgrounds in the oriental house and images of Islamic domestic action in the harem, set the tone of interest in the West. The works of the European orientalist artists and their romantic preoccupation with women of the seraglio has been roundly attacked by feminists but, for better or worse, remains the dominant influence on mental pictures of the harem.

The harem in Islamic society was and is an urban rich man's way of interpreting the words of the Koran "good women are obedient, guarding the unseen because God has guarded them". In the harem women are kept totally unseen and unable to defile themselves. In all Muslim houses, rich and poor, the women's part of the establishment is forbidden to outsiders, although in many cases in the houses of the ordinary people the harem is no more than a section of the house separated only by an imaginary line or hoddud across the floor space. Women themselves, who might circulate throughout the house, withdraw to their quarters when a stranger is about. Even in contemporary Egypt and North Africa

Bargaining Bargaining is expected in the bazaars. Start lower than you would expect to pay, be polite and good humoured, enjoy the experience and if the final price doesn't suit – walk away. There are plenty more shops. Once you have gained confidence, try it on the taxi drivers and when negotiating a room.

there are women's movements that propagate the notion that the greater the seclusion and veiling of women, the more their purity and religious/social standing. Segregation of men and women in public places is a growing feature of Islamic society: the harem is merely a reflection of that same feature in the rich and conservative. In the geography of the family the male has sole access to the world beyond the door of the house and women must stay within according to the teachings of recent Islamic theologians such as al-Mawdudi.

Of course, the containment of women in a harem also had an important function in a community where purity of ancestry permeated traditional tribal and extended family groups. The worst slur on a man's origins could be eliminated where all the women of the family were kept permanently separated from male company of any kind but that authorized by the senior male. The limitations on female mixing outside her own house were once defined as "a woman should leave her house only on three occasions – when she is taken to the house of her husband, when her parents die and when she is carried to her own grave".

The harem was populated by the ladies of the house, usually the wives of an extended family. Given that families were large and that any one man could marry four wives, the harem in a noble house would be very large. Additionally, unlimited numbers of concubines could be brought into the harem without benefit of matrimony. The religious sanction for concubinage has always been disputed but it was practised widely regardless of this. The number of women in a harem of a major ruler could be as high as 300. In effect, a large house and its harem even in rural areas had a great variety of people within it and women could socialize freely within that group. Similarly, visiting groups of women would be met and entertained by the women of the house.

A vicarious pleasure in the larger houses and palaces was watching events through a mashrabiyya or wooden grill protecting the women's quarters. By a paradox, it was often the wives of the richest men of traditional social inclination who saw least of the world and who literally saw few visitors, went visiting little themselves and whose only outings were to the hammam.

The harem on the model of the Ottoman seraglio is no more. But segregation of the sexes in the home is common unless families are thoroughly westernized. A significant number of women are cloistered in their homes and veiled outside it. Women's rights in law are gradually increasing but in traditional households change is very slow, impeded as much by a rising tide of Islamism as by neglect by the authorities.

Meanwhile, the architecture of the traditional family house continues to reflect the need for exclusive areas for women. Naguib Mahfouz in his book (in English translation) Midaq Alley shows how 20th century realities in a tightly packed urban community play tricks with the seclusion and the frustration of the women trapped within the home. For an insight into the magnificent provision for the women of the harem in the past visit the **Palace of Amir Bashtak** or the **Beit al-Sihaymi** both in Cairo, where the vestiges of harems can be seen.

Clothing Cotton clothes in summer, warmer garments for winter and desert evenings. Egyptian cotton garments are good value. Trousers and long sleeved shirts provide protection from the sun and insects. A wide brimmed hat or sun glasses will offer protection from the glare of the sun. Comfortable shoes are necessary for sightseeing. Open sandals let the sand and dust in. Egypt is a Muslim country and scanty clothing can cause offence. Efficient laundry services are provided by most hotels. See section on clothing (see page 31).

● ●

☞ *Female circumcision*

It is small comfort to know that despite pressure from Islamic extremists the Egyptian authorities say they will ignore a court recommendation to lift the ban on female circumcision in state hospitals. The Mufti has issued a fatwa decreeing that it should be allowed.

● ●

Courtesy Politeness is always appreciated. You will notice a great deal of hand shaking, kissing, clapping on backs on arrival and departure from a group. There is no need to follow this to the extreme but handshakes, smiles and thank yous go a long way. Be patient and friendly but firm when bargaining for items and avoid displays of anger. Be very careful never to criticize as officials, waiters and taxi drivers can understand more than you think. **However** when it comes to getting onto public transport, forget it all – the description 'like a Cairo bus' will need no explanation.

Mosque etiquette Visitors to mosques (where permitted) and other religious buildings will normally be expected to remove their shoes and cover-all garments will be available for hire to enable the required standard of dress to be met.

Photography Egypt's fine weather, clear skies and varying scenery gives opportunities for spectacular pictures. However, photographs of police, soldiers, docks, bridges, military areas, airports, radio stations and other public utilities are prohibited. Photography is also prohibited in tombs where much damage can be done with a flash bulb. Photography is unrestricted in all open, outdoor historic areas but some sites make an extra charge for cameras. Flashes are not permitted in the Egyptian Museum in Cairo nor for delicate relics such as the icons in St Catherine's Monastery. Taking photographs of any person without permission is unwise, of women is taboo and tourist attractions like water sellers, camels/camel drivers etc will require payment. Even the goat herder will expect a tip for providing the goats.

Video Cameras: Always check that use of a video camera is permitted at tourist sites and be prepared to pay a heavy fee (E£100+) for permission.

Police Report any incident which involves you or your possessions. An insurance claim of any size will require the backing of a police report. If involvement with the police is more serious, for instance a driving accident, remain calm, read the section on how to deal with the bureaucracy (see page 37) and contact the nearest consular office without delay.

Prices Understand what prices are being asked for taxis, meals and hotels. Do not accept 'favours', like 'free lunches' they do not exist. Shop owners will attempt to give you gifts. At best these are used as a lever to get you to buy other items expensively or can lead to disputes over alleged non-payment for goods. It is also a matter of discretion how you handle friendly relations with locals who invite you home for a meal/visit.

Tipping Tipping is a way of life – everyone except high officials expects a reward for services rendered or supposed. Many people connected with tourism get no or very low wages and rely on tips to survive. Advice here is to be a frequent but small tipper on the principal of 'often and little'. Usually 10% is added to hotel and restaurant bills but an extra tip of about 5% is normal. Taxi drivers expect between 5-10%. In hotels and at monuments tips will be expected for the most minimal service. Rather than make a fuss have some very small coins handy. Tips may be the person's only income.

Tourist numbers recover

The number of tourists visiting Egypt fell dramatically after the massacre at Luxor in November 1997. After a very hard time for the industry in Egypt with the flow of visitors down to less than one million annually in 1998, the tourists are now flooding back.

The Islamic fundamentalists have been in political retreat in the face of enhanced security and some concessions to Islamic sentiment by the government. Egypt now offers immensely good value both in terms of costs and facilities, factors which have bolstered the attraction of the country and brought visitor numbers back to more than three million per year (3.5 million in 1999). It is planned to lift the number of hotel rooms available from 105,000 to 186,000 by 2005 when it is hoped that total tourist numbers will rise to 6.6 million. The increase in the number of hotel rooms will also cater for the development of travel within Egypt by the country's own nationals, some of whom had the chance to use foreign tourist facilities at a discount during the 1997-99 recession, and now prefer Egypt to travel abroad – which is a new benefit from domestic tourism since Egyptian tourists' spending abroad costs the exchequer US$1.4 bn per year.

Essentials

Prohibitions

The main areas of difficulty affect relations with the bureaucrats, police and other officials To avoid trouble bear in mind:

Documents Do not lose your passport and ensure that all travel documents are in order. Passports are lost but they are also traded for cash/drugs and officials can be very unsympathetic. Long and often expensive delays can occur while documents are replaced. Keep all forms such as landing cards and currency documents together with bank receipts for foreign exchange transactions.

Drugs Ignore all offers of drugs. It is more than likely that the 'pusher', if successful, will report you to the police. Drug enforcement policies are strict in Egypt. The **death penalty** may be imposed for those convicted of smuggling or selling narcotics. Possession of even small quantities may lead to prosecution.

Firearms Firearms including hunting guns may not be imported without prior permission. Permits can be obtained for hunting guns through the hotel/tour organizer. It is forbidden to take into UK – ivory, crocodile, snake or lizard skin. It is forbidden to take from Egypt genuine Egyptian artifacts.

Politics Keep clear of all political activities. Nothing is so sensitive as opposition to the régimes. By all means keep an interest in local politics but do not become embroiled as a partisan. The mokharbarat (secret services) are singularly unforgiving and unbridled in taking action against political dissent.

Black market Make use of black market currency only when it is private and safe. Most countries have tight laws against currency smuggling and illegal dealing.

Driving Keep to driving regulations and have an appropriate international licence. Bear in mind that the incidence of traffic accidents is high and that personal rescue in the event of an accident can be protracted and not necessarily expert.

Antiquities Trading in antiquities is illegal everywhere. Most items for sale are fakes. Real artifacts are expensive and trading in them can lead to confiscation and/or imprisonment.

Essentials

 With friends like the tourist police

Those travelling in Egypt outside the confines of the tour bus, Nile cruise boat and the main tourist sites will often find themselves in the bear hug of the police authorities – mainly the tourist police. This is especially the case in Western Sinai and Northern Sinai, the Canal Zone and the New Valleys areas, where individual or small-group foreigners will find their transport under rather closer official gurad than is comfortable albeit at nil cost to themselves.

If you find yourself in the grip of a police escort, there is little that can be done to gain liberty. The Egyptian government is determined in the wake of the 1997 massacre at Luxor that no further tourist lives will be lost by terrorist attack. Police chiefs know that any publicized tourist deaths by Islamists in their district will mean instant transfer to an isolated Nubian village in the deep south! The best way to handle the problem is to create as profound a cordon sanitaire around your vehicle as possible; keep well out of sight line of the weapons of your watchdogs and keep as great a distance between your own car and that of your escort so as to avoid a collision. Egyptian driver psychology when in official convoy is to tailgate the vehicle in front – far more of a hazard than any terrorist might be! As always approach the game with a sense of humour.

Keep cool Remain patient and calm whatever the provocation. Redress against officials is next to impossible. Keep the matter from becoming serious by giving no grounds for offence to officials. Be genial and low key. Aggression and raised voices do little to help. Where you feel you are right, be smilingly persistent but not to the point of a break down in relations.

Safety

The level of petty crime in Egypt is no greater than elsewhere. It is unlikely that you will be robbed but take sensible precautions. Leave your valuables in a hotel deposit box and never leave valuables or money around. Avoid carrying excess money or wearing obviously valuable jewellery when sightseeing. There will be pickpockets in crowded places. It is wise not to walk around at night away from the main thoroughfares. External pockets on bags and clothing should never be used for carrying valuables. Bag snatching and pick pocketing is more common in crowded tourist areas. **NB** It is wise to keep a record of your passport number, Travellers' cheques number and air ticket number somewhere separate from the actual items.

Egypt is a Muslim country and Friday is the day of rest when offices and many shops are closed. The Christians celebrate Sunday as their sabbath when many of their shops are closed. As the Islamic year is shorter than the Western year the dates of their religious holidays change. The Christian Coptic calendar gives a third set of variable dates. It has 12 months of 30 days with the extra five days added every fourth year.

Beggars Beggars are a fact of life in Muslim countries where alms-giving is a personal duty. It is unlikely that they will be too persistent. Have a few very small coins ready. You will be unable to help many and your donation will most probably be passed on to the syndicate organizer!

Confidence The most common 'threat' to tourists is found where people are on the move, at ports
tricksters and railway and bus stations, selling 'antiques', 'gems', offering extremely favourable currency exchange rates and spinning 'hard luck' stories. Confidence tricksters are, by definition, extremely convincing and persuasive. Be warned – if the offer seems too good to be true that is probably what it is.

Getting help can often be cheap or free. Start off with agencies used to foreigners, namely travel agents, airline offices and hotels. They will have met your problem before and might offer an instant or at least painless solution on the basis of past experience. They will know the local system and how it works. They act as free translators. Friends who are either locals or who live locally can act as translators and helpers. They will often have networks of family and acquaintances to break through the bureaucratic logjams. Last, and only last, turn to your embassy or consulate. Embassies are there principally to serve the needs of the home country and the host government, not the demands of travellers, though they have ultimate responsibility for official travel documents and, at their own discretion, for repatriation in cases of distress. Treat embassy and consular officials calmly and fairly. They have different priorities and do not necessarily feel themselves to be servants for travellers in trouble.

Getting help

Essentials

Security

The large and complex organizations of state and society in Egypt make generalizations difficult. It is currently clear that the government faces political problems. The opposition, principally a long established Islamic revivalist group known as Ikhwan Al-Musalmin (**Muslim Brotherhood**), is large and well organized. In addition to the assassination of President Sadat in 1981, it is claimed that Islamic fundamentalists have murdered a number of leading individuals within the régime and there have been attacks on tourists. The government has held elections of sorts and has a political mandate on that basis, but the régime is unpopular at a variety of levels. The economy is performing only moderately well. There is no sense among Egyptians that the economic struggle against rising population numbers is being won, while external threats to reduced flows of Nile water adds to tensions. The close association of the régime with the USA and the history of links with Israel since the Camp David accords, distances the government from mass opinion. Yet the régime has its supporters through the co-option of the military and many senior Egyptian families. A deeply conservative streak runs through the population and a feeling that Egypt should look, as the régime does, first to Egyptian interests rather than 'Islamic' or 'Arab' ideals.

The support for the régime from the USA has a strong positive side. Aid and food supply are guaranteed within limits so that the population can be fed and the state kept on an economic even keel. Care for foreign visitors by the régime is vital to keep the tourist industry alive and the opposition has in the past deliberately targeted tourist facilities to make a political point. Egypt is a large country and 'troubles' tend on most occasions to be regional rather than national. A day's rioting in Giza will leave the Upper Nile and Sinai untouched. Similarly, some towns are far more fundamentalist inclined than others with Assiut and Qena being noted for their Islamic revivalist sentiment.

Although Egypt has a troubled history of foreign relations in the 1950s-1970s, it is now comparatively stable. Travellers should check with their national authorities before departure for Egypt.

It is wise in circumstances of political uncertainty for a foreigner to be very discreet:
1 Stay in your hostel or hotel.
2 If the telephones are working, get in touch with your embassy or consulate so that your location is known.
3 Conserve any rations you might have.
4 Do not join in any action by locals. Your motives could be misunderstood.
5 Make contact in your hostel or hotel with other foreigners so that you can form a mutual-assistance group.
6 Listen carefully to the advice given by local hostel or hotel officials.

What to do if unrest occurs

The disturbances caused by religious extremists have ceased but the national and local security services are still very much in evidence to offer protection at all major tourist areas. While the region containing Assiut, Minya and Qena ought to be avoided, travellers should encounter no problems elsewhere.

Risks are not necessarily higher in this region than in other parts of the 'developing world' but they do exist. Any traveller who intends to be travelling for a protracted period should check with his/her national authorities on the advisability of visiting the area. In the UK, the relevant Foreign and Commonwealth Office T020-72333000 desk will give you the latest assessment from their embassies overseas. If you are deeply concerned, where possible phone your national embassy direct and ask for the press/information officer.

Restricted areas   Permission must be obtained to visit areas near Egypt's frontiers and off-road areas in Sinai. Contact Ministry of Interior travel permit department corner of Sahria Sheikh Rihan/Nubar in central Cairo.

Survival in the desert

For those travellers staying in well regulated accommodation in good hotels, the realities of the desert can be disguised for as long as electricity and pure water supplies are sustained. Much of the information in the following section can thus be ignored, though not with total impunity. Trips into the desert even by the most careful of tour operators carry some of the hazards and a knowledge of good practice might be as helpful on the beach or tourist bus as for the full-blooded desert voyager.

There is a contemporary belief that the problems of living and travelling in deserts have been solved. Much improved technology in transport together with apparent ease of access to desert areas has encouraged these comfortable ideas. The very simplicity of the problems of deserts, lack of water and high temperatures, make them easy to underestimate. In reality, deserts have not changed and problems still arise when travelling in them, albeit with less regularity than twenty or so years ago. One aspect of the desert remains unchanged – mistakes and misfortune can too easily be fatal.

Desert topography   Desert topography is varied. Excellent books such as Allan JA & Warren A (1993) *Deserts: a conservation atlas*, Mitchell Beazley, show the origins and constant development of desert scenery. In the region covered by this *Handbook*, desert and semi-desert is the largest single surface area and so has an importance for travellers rarely met with elsewhere. Its principal features and their effects on transport are best understood before they are met on the ground. The great ergs or sandseas comprise mobile dunes and shifting surface sands over vast areas. Small mobile barkhans, which are crescent shaped, can often be driven round on firm terrain but the larger transverse and longitudinal dunes can form large surfaces with thick ridges of soft sand. They constantly change their shape as the wind works across them. While not impassible, they can be crossed only slowly and with difficulty. The major sand seas such as those at Calanscio, Murzuq, and Brak should be treated as no-go areas for all but fully equipped and locally supported expeditions. The wadi beds which penetrate much of the Sahara, serirs and gravel plains provide good access for all-terrain vehicles.

Aridity   The main characteristic of the desert is its aridity. Aridity is calculable and those navigating deserts are advised to understand the term so that the element of risk can be appraised and managed with safety. CW Thornthwaite's aridity index shows water deficiency relative to water need for a given area. There is a gradient from north to south throughout the region, of rising temperatures, diminishing rainfall and worsening aridity. Aridity of the desert is thus very variable, ranging from the Mediterranean sub-tropical fringe to a semi-arid belt to the south and a fully arid

Sand on the move

Egypt has some 97% of its surface area under deserts and is therefore rich in sand dunes. The main areas of dunes occur in the west of the country with the most accessible large sand seas in the Western Desert.

Dunes form under various wind conditions. Barchan or crescent dunes tend to be found where a steady wind blows from one direction and where the volume of loose quartz sand is limited. The sand in the horns of the crescent is blown ahead of the main mass of the dune as it migrates across the usually flat landscape. Ridge dunes occur at right angles to the direction of the wind, though other theories for their form are proposed by the experts and are known as linear or in Arabic saif dunes. They are well developed in the Egyptian desert lands and can be several kilometres in length and rise to 170 m high. Typical of some of the greatest sand masses in the Sahara and the sand seas such as the Western Desert, particularly south of Siwa oasis, adjacent to the Libyan border, where sand sheets and dune formations are both found covering large surface areas. In Egypt there are star dunes, in which wind prevails from different directions or is erratic in direction, giving what appear to be multiple crescent shaped dunes in the configuration of a star when seen from above. The star dunes can become centres of massive sand accumulation as with altitudes of 300 m and a length of 1 km.

The mobility of dunes varies. The largest move perhaps no more than a metre each year. Barchans can, especially if of low altitude, travel more quickly, at up to 50 m per year. Mobile dunes create a hazard for transport since roads can be covered quickly in high wind conditions, as is frequently the case on roads linking settlements in the New Valley. Elsewhere, cultivated lands can slowly be inundated with sand.

Stabilizing sand dunes is a difficult matter. The large dune systems are unstoppable and man's attempts to halt their advance have rarely succeeded for long. Smaller dunes can be stabilized by planting them with a close graticule of drought resistant grass or other plants, which once established can be inter-planted with desert bushes and shrubs. This process is slow and expensive though generally very effective even in very dry conditions. More cheap and dramatic is to build sand fences to catch moving sand, tar-spraying dunes or layering dunes with a plastic net. The results are less aesthetically pleasing than using the traditional vegetation cover system and are less long-lasting unless combined with planting, though in the driest areas of the Sahara these are the only possible methods of fixing mobile dunes.

desert interior. In basic terms, the further south you are the more dangerous the environment. Do not assume that conditions on the coast properly prepare you for the deep south. The Sahara is also very varied in its topography, climate and natural difficulties posed for the traveller. Rapid transition from rough stone terrain to sand sea to salt flat has to be expected and catered for.

For practical purposes, aridity here means lack of moisture and very high temperatures. The world's highest temperatures are experienced in the Sahara, over 55°C. Averages in the southern desert run in summer at more than 50°C in the shade at midday. In full sun very much higher figures are reached. High temperatures are not the only difficulty. Each day has a large range of temperature, often of more than 20°C, with nights being intensely cold, sometimes below freezing. In winter, air temperatures can be very low despite the heat of the sun and temperatures drop very rapidly either when the sun goes down or when there is movement from sunlight to shade, say in a deep gorge or a cave.

Increasing aridity means greater difficulty in water availability. Scientists define the problem in terms of water deficits. The region as a whole and the deep Sahara in particular are very serious water deficit areas. Surface waters are lacking almost everywhere except in the case of the River Nile in Egypt. Underground water is scarce and often available only at great depths. Occasional natural seepages of water give rise to oases and/or palmeries. They are, however, rare. Since water is the key to sustaining life in deserts, travellers have always to assume that they must be self-sufficient or navigate from one known water source to another.

Isolation Isolation is another feature of the Sahara. Travellers' tales tend to make light of the matter, hinting that bedouin Arabs will emerge from the dunes even in the most obscure corner of the desert. This is probably true of the semi-desert and some inland wadi basins but not a correct assumption on which to build a journey in the greater part of the Sahara. Population numbers in the desert are very low and most of these are concentrated in small oasis centres. Tarmacked road systems are gradually being extended into and through the Sahara but they represent a few straggling lines across areas for the most part without fixed and maintained highways. The very fact that oil exploration has been so intense in the Sahara has meant that the surface of the desert is criss-crossed with innumerable tracks, making identification of all routes other than tarmacked roads extremely difficult. Once off the main roads, travellers can part from their escorts and find no fixed topography to get them back on course. **Vanishing individuals and vehicles in the Sahara are too frequent to be a joke.** To offset this problem read on.

The most acute difficulty with off-road emergencies is finding the means of raising assistance because of isolation. Normal preventative action is to ensure that your travel programme is known in advance by some individual or an institution to whom regular check-in is made from points on the route. Failure to contact should automatically raise the alarm. Two vehicles are essential and often obviate the worst problems of break-down and the matter of isolation. Radio communication from your vehicle is an expensive but useful aid if things go wrong.

Bear in mind the enormous distances involved in bringing help even where the location of an incident in the desert is known. Heavy rescue equipment and/or paramedical assistance will probably be 500 km or more distant. Specialist transport for the rescuers is often not instantly available, assuming that local tele-communications systems work and local administrators see fit to help.

Living with the climate Living with desert environments is not difficult but it does take discipline and adherence to sensible routines at all times. It is an observed fact that health problems in hot and isolated locations take on a greater seriousness for those involved than they would in temperate climates. It is still common practice with Western oil companies and other commercial organizations regularly engaged at desert sites to fly ill or injured persons home as a first measure in the knowledge that most will recover more rapidly without the psychological and environmental pressures of a desert site. Most health risks in the desert are avoidable. The rules, evolved over many years, are simple and easy to follow:

1 Allow time to acclimatize to full desert conditions. Conserve your energy at first rather than acting as if you were still in a temperate climatic régime. Most people take a week or more to adjust to heat conditions in the deep Sahara.
2 Stay out of direct sunlight whenever possible, especially once the sun is high. Whenever you can, do what the locals do, move from shade to shade.
3 Wear clothes to protect your skin from the sun, particularly your head and neck. Use a high Sun Protection Factor (SPF) cream, preferably as high as SPF15 (94%) to minimize the effects of Ultraviolet-B. Footwear is a matter of choice though many of those from the temperate parts of the world will find strong, light but well ventilated boots ideal for keeping sand, sun, venomous livestock and thorns off the feet. Slip on boots are best of all since they are convenient if visiting Arab encampments/ housing/religious sites, where shoes are not worn

4 Drink good quality water regularly and fully. It is estimated that 15 litres per day are needed by a healthy person to avoid water deficiency in desert conditions, even if there is no actual feeling of thirst. The majority of ailments arising in the desert relate to water deficiency and so it is worth the small effort of regular drinking of water. Too much alcoholic drink has the opposite effect in most cases and is not, unfortunately, a substitute for water!

5 Be prepared for cold nights by having some warm clothes to hand.

6 Stay in your quarters or vehicle if there is a sand storm.

7 Refrain from eating dubious foods. Deserts and stomach upsets have a habit of going hand in hand. Choose hot cooked meals in preference to cold meats and tired salads. Peel all fruit and uncooked fresh vegetables. Do not eat 'native' milk-based items or drink untreated water unless you are absolutely sure of its good quality.

8 Sleep off the ground if you can. There are very few natural dangers in the desert but scorpions, spiders and snakes are found (but are rarely fatal) and are best avoided.

Safe travel

The key to safe travel in desert regions is reliable and well equipped transport. Most travellers will simply use local bus and taxi services. For the motorist, motorcyclist or pedal cyclist there are ground rules which, if followed, will help to reduce risks. In normal circumstances travellers will remain on tarmacked roads and for this need only a well prepared two wheel drive vehicle. Choose a machine which is known for its reliability and for which spares can be easily obtained. Across much of the region only Peugeot and Mercedes are found with adequate spares and servicing facilities. If you have a different type of car/truck, make sure that you take spares with you or have the means of getting spares sent out. Bear in mind that transport of spares to and from rural Egypt might take a tediously long time. Petrol/benzene/gas is available everywhere, though diesel is equally well distributed except in the smallest of southern settlements. Four-wheel drive transport is useful even for the traveller who normally remains on the tarmacked highway. Emergencies, diversions and unscheduled visits to off the road sites become less of a problem with all-terrain vehicles. Off the road, four-wheel drive is essential, normally with two vehicles travelling together. A great variety of four-wheel drive vehicles are in use in the region, with Toyota and Land Rover probably found most widely.

All vehicles going into the southern areas of North Africa should have basic equipment as follows:

1 Full tool kit, vehicle maintenance handbook and supplementary tools such as clamps, files, wire, spare parts kit supplied by car manufacturer, jump leads.

2 Spare tyre/s, battery driven tyre pump, tyre levers, tyre repair kit, hydraulic jack, jack handle extension, base plate for jack.

3 Spare fuel can/s, spare water container/s, cool bags.

For those going off the tarmacked roads other items to include are:

4 Foot tyre pump, heavy duty hydraulic or air jack, power winch, sand channels, safety rockets, comprehensive first aid kit, radio-telephone where permitted.

5 Emergency rations kit/s, matches, Benghazi burner (a double-skinned metal water boiler).

6 Maps, compasses, latest road information, long term weather forecast, guides to navigation by sun and stars.

Driving in the desert is an acquired skill. Basic rules are simple but crucial:

1 If you can get a local guide who perhaps wants a lift to your precise destination, use him.

2 Set out early in the morning after first light, rest during the heat of the day and use the cool of the evening for further travel.

3 Never attempt to travel at night or when there is a sandstorm brewing or in progress.

4 Always travel with at least two vehicles which should remain in close visual contact.

Other general hints include not speeding across open flat desert in case the going changes without warning and your vehicle beds deeply into soft sand or a gully. Well maintained corrugated road surfaces can be taken at modest pace but rocky surfaces should be treated with great care to prevent undue wear on tyres. Sand seas are a challenge for drivers but need a cautious approach – ensure that your navigation lines are clear so that weaving between dunes does not disorientate the navigator. Especially in windy conditions, sight lines can vanish, leaving crews with little knowledge of where they are. Cresting dunes from dip slope to scarp needs care that the vehicle does not either bog down or overturn. Keep off salt flats after rain and floods especially in the winter and spring when water tables can rise and make the going hazardous in soft mud. Even when on marked and maintained tracks beware of approaching traffic.

In the desert border areas of Egypt, **unexploded mines** are a hidden danger. Maps of mined areas are unreliable, some were never marked. Always obey the precautionary signs. Floods can move mines considerable distances from the original site. Be warned, people do die.

Emergencies The desert tends to expose the slightest flaw in personnel and vehicles. Emergency situations are therefore to be expected and planned for. There is no better security than making the schedule of your journey known in advance to friends or embassy/consulate officials who will actively check on your arrival at stated points. Breakdowns and multiple punctures are the most frequent problem. On the highway the likelihood is always that a passing motorist will give assistance, or a lift to the nearest control post or village. In these situations it is best simply remain with your vehicle until help arrives making sure that your are clear of the road and that you are protected from other traffic by a warning triangle and/or rocks on the road to rear and front.

Off the road, breakdowns, punctures and bogging down in soft sand are the main difficulties. If you have left your travel programme at your last stop you will already have a fall back position in case of severe problems. If you cannot make a repair or extricate yourself, remain with your vehicle in all circumstances. Unless you can clearly see a settlement (not a mirage) stay where you are with water, food and shelter. The second vehicle can be used to search for help but only after defining the precise location of the incident. In the case of getting lost, halt, conserve fuel while you attempt to get a bearing on either the topography or the planets/stars and work out a traverse to bring you back to a known line such as a highway, mountain ridge or coastline. If that fails, take up as prominent a position as possible for being spotted from the air. Build a fire to use if and when you hear air activity in your vicinity. Attempt to find a local source of water by digging in the nearest wadi bed, collecting dew from the air at night. If you have fuel to spare it can be used with great care both as a means of attracting attention and a way of boiling untreated water. A Benghazi burner, two crude metal cones welded together to give a water jacket and space for a fire in the centre can achieve this latter purpose. As ever in this region, be patient and conserve your energy.

Hotel classifications

AL US$150+   Luxury hotel. All facilities for business and leisure travellers are of the highest international standard.
A US$100-150+   Central heated, a/c rooms with WC, bath/shower, TV, phone, mini-bar, daily clean linen. Choice of restaurants, coffee shop, shops, bank, travel agent, swimming pool, parking, sport and business facilities.
B US$75-100   As **A** but without the luxury, reduced number of restaurants, smaller rooms, limited range of shops and sport.
C US$50-75   Best rooms have a/c, own bath/shower and WC. Usually comfortable, bank, shop, pool.
D US$25-50   Best rooms may have own WC and bath/shower. Depending on management will have room service and choice of cuisine in restaurant.
E US$10-25   Simple provision. Perhaps fan cooler. May not have restaurant. Shared WC and showers with hot water (when available).
F under US$10   Very basic, shared toilet facilities, variable in cleanliness, noise, often in dubious locations.

Where to stay

As tourism is one of Egypt's major industries, accommodation is available at the main sites and in all the major cities. This varies from deluxe international hotels to floor or roof space for a sleeping bag – at prices to suit all pockets, currently there are 77,000 hotel rooms available. Most top quality hotel chains are represented offering top class facilities in their rooms and business centres. There are also cheap hotels which though often clean are very basic and spartan. There is a pronounced seasonality to demand for accommodation and in the spring, autumn and winter months the main tourist areas can be very busy and the hotels fully booked. Reservations in advance are recommended, especially for luxury hotels. Finding cheap accommodation is easy throughout the area, except in high season. Tax and a service charge will be added to the bill. Always ask to see the room first. **Hotels**

It should be noted, however, that, while price is a reasonable reflection of the type of hotel and service you can expect, some hotels are expensive but very ordinary while there are some wonderful hotels which are real bargains. International hotels have an uncomfortable habit of changing owner and name. Be prepared for this and if confused ask for what it was called before. If you are unsure about whether a cheap hotel is any good, only book in for one night, leave your baggage there and then go and explore the other choices.

Prices for the top class hotels are on a par with prices in Europe while medium range hotels are generally cheaper in comparison. In almost every case, the advertised room price, that charged to the individual traveller, is higher than that paid by the package tourist and it may be worth bargaining. The categories used in this *Handbook* are graded as accurately as possible by cost converted to American dollars. Our hotel price range is based on a double room with bath/shower in high season and includes any relevant taxes and service charges but no meals.

Normally the facilities indicated will be available and are therefore not repeated in the descriptions.

Abbrevations in the listings: a/c = air conditioning, T= telephone, F = Fax. Bath denotes bath and/or shower.

Information from Egyptian Youth Hostels, 7 Sharia Dr Abdel Hamid Said, Marouf, Cairo, T43799. There are 16 hostels (all but one are of simple grade) located in Egypt's main historic and tourist towns which are open all year round, closed 1000-1400 and 1300-0700. Minimum age six years. Overnight fees range from E£5-25 including **Youth hostels**

Essentials

breakfast. Visitors may stay more than three consecutive nights if places are available. Although cheap meals are available (breakfast is included, lunch E£2, dinner served from 2000-2100, E£5), all the big hostels have a member's kitchen where guests can prepare meals for themselves (use of the kitchen is free). Holders of membership cards can obtain significant reductions on train journeys. Those who do not already have cards can obtain them from any of the hostels in Egypt. The rules include no alcohol or gambling, single sex dormitories, lights out between 2300-0600. Groups must make advance bookings at least two weeks before their arrival. Booking is recommended at all hostels.

Camping There are only a few official camp sites with good facilities and guards. Sites of varying quality exist in Aswan, Luxor, Cairo, Giza, Sharm el-Sheikh and Marsa Matruh. Hotels are very cheap and are probably a more comfortable option. Assess the security of any site you choose and where possible ask permission to avoid any unpleasantness.

Getting around

Air

Domestic airlines link the main towns. The services are reliable and can be recommended where long distances of otherwise hot and dusty land travel are involved such as between Cairo and Abu Simbel.

There are daily flights between Cairo, Alexandria, Luxor, Aswan, Abu Simbel, New Valley and Hurghada and much less frequently to Marsa Matruh. Contact Egyptair T922444, www.EgyptAir.com.eg There are regular flights from Cairo to St Catherine, El-Arish (perhaps) and Sharm el-Sheikh. Contact Air Sinai at *Nile Hilton* T760948.

Alexandria	Aswan	Assuit	Beni Suef	Cairo	Damanhur	Dumyat	El Arish	El-Fayoum	El-Tur	Giza	Hurghada	Ismailia	Luxor	Marsa Matruh	Minya	Port Said	Qena	Sohag	Suez	Tanta	Zagazig
1128																					
604	524																				
347	781	257																			
224	904	380	123																		
64	1064	540	283	160																	
229	1095	571	314	191	165																
506	1277	753	496	373	455	370															
329	826	302	45	105	265	296	478														
605	1286	762	505	376	542	516	476	487													
232	896	372	115	8	168	199	381	97	390												
759	513	467	562	529	695	629	718	634	637	521											
272	1043	519	262	140	208	185	232	244	331	147	486										
895	223	303	557	676	831	866	1017	594	936	660	299	785									
288	1416	892	635	512	352	517	794	617	893	504	1047	560	1185								
472	656	132	125	248	408	439	621	170	630	240	608	387	433	760							
357	1128	604	347	224	215	60	320	329	466	232	569	85	895	645	472						
864	282	242	499	622	382	813	952	544	1004	614	234	720	65	1134	374	846					
703	425	99	357	479	639	670	852	401	851	471	368	618	205	991	231	703	134				
364	1044	520	363	134	300	276	323	245	242	147	395	91	810	652	388	174	762	619			
130	998	474	217	94	66	120	376	199	473	102	612	142	768	418	342	175	716	573	231		
191	989	465	208	85	127	122	315	190	390	93	565	81	759	479	333	172	707	564	170	61	

Distances between main towns in Egypt in kilometres

Flight times: Cairo to Luxor one hour, Cairo to Aswan two hours, Aswan to Abu Simbel 40 minutes, Cairo to Hurgarda one hour and Cairo to St Catherine's Monastery 50 minutes.

Bus

Conditions vary from excellent dual carriageways to rural roads and unnerving one vehicle wide and far flung roads which are a rough, unsurfaced *piste*. Problems include fierce flash floods and encroaching sand.

Buses, the main mode and cheapest means of transport, link nearly all the towns. Air-conditioned coaches which are more expensive connect the biggest cities and keep more strictly to the timetable. Smaller private vehicles require greater patience and often work on the 'leave when full' principle. Book in advance wherever possible. Orderly queues become a jostling mass when the bus arrives. Inner city buses are usually dirty and crowded and getting off can be more difficult than getting on. They keep to the timetable within reasonable (Egyptian) limits. Sorting out the routes and the fares makes taking a taxi a better option.

Car hire

Car hire quality varies greatly. Car hire is not cheap and the condition of vehicles can be problematic. Make sure that you are well insured as the road accident rate is exceedingly high. Some companies place restrictions on areas that can be visited. The problems of driving your own or a hired car are two fold – other drivers and pedestrians. Give serious consideration to hiring a car and a driver.

The main car hire firms are Avis, Hertz and Budget. See entry for each town. An International Driving permit is required but own country driving licence is often accepted. Remember driving on the right is the rule in Egypt. Petrol (super) E£1 per litre.

Approximate journey times from Cairo by road:

Alexandria	3 hours
Sharm el-Sheikh	6 hours
Aswan	16 hours
Luxor	10 hours
Port Said	3 hours

Boat

The traditional Nile sailing boats *feluccas*, can be hired by the hour but are not recommended for travelling between towns. The Sudanese railway operate a steamer service from Aswan to Wadi Halfa but this is currently suspended. Regular Nile cruises operate between Luxor and Aswan and sometimes between Cairo and Aswan for five days (standard tour), seven days (extended tour) and 15 days (full Nile cruise). The leading Nile cruise companies are Seti, Sheraton, Hilton, Presidential, Sphinx, Pyramid and Eastmar.

Cruises now operates between the Aswan Dam and Abu Simbel – go for the experience and scenery, not for speed.

Ferry routes

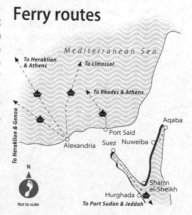

Essentials

Essentials

Train

Rail networks are limited, slow and generally more expensive than the alternative – the bus. First class is always more comfortable; offering air-conditioning and sometimes sleeping accommodation. There are strict restrictions on the trains which can be used be foreigners. Check carefully. Cheaper carriages can be crowded and none too clean. Train travel offers the advantage of views available only from the track.

The rail network extends west to Sollum on the Libyan border, south along the Nile from Alexandria and Cairo to Luxor, Aswan and Abu Simbel. There are links to Port Said and Suez. There are several luxury a/c trains with restaurants to Luxor and Aswan with sleeping accommodation. Contact International Sleeping Cars, T761319. Inclusive tickets with reduced hotel charges in Luxor and Assan can be negotiated. Reductions on train tickets are available for students (see Tourist Office in nearest town) and members of the YHA (see Youth hostels below). Cheaper student and group tickets are available. Contact T753555.

Approximate journey times from Cairo by train:

Alexandria	2¾ hours
Aswan	15 hours
Luxor	12 hours
Port Said	2½ hours

Other land transport

Bicycles & motorcycles Bicycle hire is becoming widely available although the mechanical fitness of the machines is often dubious. Traffic conditions can make cycling a very dangerous sport. Motorcycles can also be hired. Comments above regarding cycles apply also to motorcycles – but more so.

Hitchhiking This is really only a consideration in outlying places not served by the very cheap public transport. Rides are often available on lorries and in small open trucks but payment is always expected. Hitchhiking has a measure of risk attached to it and is not normally recommended, but in out of the way places is often the only way to travel.

Taxi The larger, long distance taxis with metres are good value, sometimes following routes not covered by service buses and almost always more frequent. They run on the 'leave when full' principle and for more space or a quicker departure the unoccupied seats can be purchased. In general these taxis are 25% more expensive than the bus but it is always possible to negotiate. In 'sensitive areas' foreigners are not permitted to use shared taxis. Inner city taxis are smaller, may have a working meter, and can also be shared.

Satellite TV

Egyptian satellite TV began broadcasting on 31 May 1998, beaming programmes across the Middle East and Mediterranean. There is scope for 84 channels, however, private broadcasters have been denied the opportunity to use this facility and it is feared that the output will be no more enlightened than previously. Government control of newspapers and magazines also extends to television. The highly conservative influence of Saudi Arabia currently dominates all Arab language broadcasts, Islamic rules being strictly applied. The new satellite transmission will reach every corner of the country but the material will be strictly controlled.

Keeping in touch

Communications

Internet facilities are found in most large cities and in all large hotels. In Cairo cybercafes can be found in Garden City, Heliopolis, Maadi, Mohnadessin, Nasr City and Zamalek. Cost is generally between E£20-40 an hour. In Alexandria there are cybercafes in several places including Semouha Shopping Mall and costs are lower than Cairo. Service providers are available on http://ce.eng.usf.edu/pharos/access.html **Internet**

Local services: all post offices are open daily except Friday and the Central Post Office in Cairo is open 24 hours. Airmail letters cost E£0.80 and local letters E£0.10. Postage stamps can be purchased from cigarette kiosks and from hotels where mail can be posted too. Mail services are unreliable so away from the capital do not expect a quick service. **Post**

International telegram services are available at the main post offices in Cairo, Alexandria, Luxor and Aswan. **Parcels** for abroad may only be sent from a main post office. Do not seal it until it has been examined. Shops will arrange to send items you purchase. Receiving a parcel may involve import duty.

Country code: 20. **Internal area codes for Governorates** are: Cairo: 02, Alexandria: 03, Aswan: 097, Luxor: 095, Sharm el-Sheikh: 062, Hurghada: 065, Sadat City 015. 10th of Ramadan: 010, Ismailia: 064, 6th October: 011. **Telephone**

Cheapest time to telephone is between 2000-0800. Local calls can be made from coin operated machines in shops (tip the shop keeper), cigarette kiosks and hotels (which normally add a premium in any case). Long distance and international calls can be made from telephone offices and the better hotels. For International calls dial 00 before country code and subscriber's number. The telephone office has an orange circular dial sign rather than a handset. Most large towns have a 24-hour service. Outside of Cairo the system is overburdened and requires immense patience. International phone calls from Egypt can be paid for with a E£15 phone card which lasts three minutes. The Egyptian minute is shorter than most but the use of the card saves time. The phone card can be used in all official phone centres. These cards – available from telephone exchanges, airports and post offices are generally in short supply – get your full holiday stock when you can.

Media

The *Egyptian Gazette* is a daily paper in English. The most influential Egyptian daily is *Al-Ahram*. It publishes an English language *Al Ahram Weekly* on Thursday, 50 piastres. Newspaper-weekly *Middle East Times* for coverage of Egypt and the region E£2 per

Essentials

Hollywood on the Nile

The Egyptian State Broadcasting Company are all set to build another Hollywood – on the Nile. They have signed a £190 mn contract to build 'Media Production City', a huge studio complex on the outskirts of the capital. The Egyptian film industry is 100-years-old – the oldest in the Middle East – and Egyptian-made productions dominate the viewing. The demand for more material cannot currently be satisfied – hence the planned investment.

copy, http://metimes.com *Egypt Today*, a monthly publication in English gives up-to-date information.

Short wave radio guide The BBC World Service (London) broadcasts throughout the region. Reception quality varies greatly: as a general rule lower frequencies give better results in the morning and late at night and the higher ones in the middle of the day.

Food and drink

Bearing in mind the suggestions in the Health section on food best avoided in uncertain conditions, a wide choice still remains. Forget the stories of sheep's eyes and enjoy the selection of filling, spicy and slightly unusual meals. For the less adventurous, Western style food (other than pork) can be found in most hotels.

Food Egyptian food is basically a mixture of Mediterranean cusines, containing elements of Lebanese, Turkish, and Greek cooking, with few authentic local dishes.

Breakfast is usually *fuul*, fava beans simmered slowly overnight, the national dish and a cheap meal at most cafés. These are served in a thick spicy sauce, either with an egg on top or in a sandwich. Equally cheap and popular is *taamaya*, deep fried balls of ground fava beans spiced with coriander and garlic, again often served in a sandwich garnished with *tahina* (sesame seed dip) and *torshi* (brightly coloured pickled vegetables such as turnips, carrots, and limes). These constitute Egyptian fastfood with the addition of *shawarma*, sliced lamb kebab sandwiches, and *fitir*. The latter sold in special *fatatri* cafés, where the thin dough pancake is made to order with either sweet or savoury fillings.

Bread is the staple of the Egyptian diet, its Arabic name *aish* meaning life. The local *aish baladi*, a brown flat loaf similar to pitta, tastes good fresh but should be eaten on the day of purchase. The white flour *aish shami* is less common.

Lunch is the main meal of the day, eaten anytime between 1400 and 1700. Carbohydrates, usually rice and bread, form the bulk of the meal accompanied by fresh seasonal vegetables and either meat or fish. *Mezzas*, a selection of small salads, are served at the beginning of the meal and include *tahina*, *babaghanoug* (*tahina* with mashed aubergines), olives, local white fetta-style cheese, *warra einab* or stuffed vine leaves, and *kobeiba*, deep fried bulgar wheat stuffed with meat and nuts. Like most Middle Eastern countries, *kebab*, lamb pieces grilled over charcoal on a skewer, and *kofta*, minced lamb, are common main dishes. Chicken and pigeon are also widely available, the latter considered a local delicacy when stuffed with rice and nuts. All meat should be eaten well-done to avoid stomach upsets. Fish is less commonly eaten but nevertheless good. From either the Red Sea or the Mediterranean, try the Sea Bass or the Red Snapper but watch the bones in the latter. Lobster and shrimp are relatively cheap.

Particular Egyptian main dishes include *molokia*, finely chopped mallow leaves, prepared with garlic, spices and either rabbit or chicken, and a good deal more tasty than its glutinous texture suggests; *fatta*, layers of bread, rice, chunks of lamb or beef,

Wines, beers and spirits in Egypt

Egypt is Mediterranean by climate but certainly not affected by the Latin love of the vine and its products despite the colonial activities of the French. A mere 10,000 ha of vines are cultivated and annual output is something over a quarter of a million tons of grapes.

Vines grow well enough in the favourable climate of the northern coast lands, producing modest amounts of table grapes and a minor volume of feedstock for wine making. Some 3.5 million litres of wine are produced annually in the Alexandria area.

A fairly reliable red is the Omar Khayyam for those with a good sense of humour about their wines. The white and rosé wines such as Cru des Ptolemees are very ordinary and should only be taken well cooled.

Egyptian beers, Stella for example, are cheap and light. Imported beers are very expensive in the major hotels and bars.

Local spirits such as brandy, gin and whisky are quite palatable and reasonably cheap. Try zibeeb, the Egyptian version of Ouzo (see also page 50).

Rather than risk uncertain brews, why not have an alcohol-free vacation instead?

yogurt, raisins and nuts, drenched in a vinegar garlic broth; *koshari*, a mix of macaroni, rice and brown lentils covered with fried onions and a spicy tomato sauce; and *mahshi*, vegetables, typically black or white aubergines, tomatoes, green peppers, and courgettes, stuffed with rice and mincemeat.

Fruits, like vegetables, are seasonal although there is a wide variety available all year round. Winter offers dates of various colours ranging from yellow to black, citrus fruits, small sweet bananas, pears, apples, and even strawberries. Summer brings plums, peaches, figs, pomegranates, guava, mangoes, grapes, melons and a brief season, for a few weeks in May, of apricots.

Traditional Egyptian desserts are sweet, sticky, fattening, and delicious. The best of all is *Om Ali*, or Mother of Ali, a warm pudding of bread or pastry covered with milk, coconut, raisins, and nuts. But try the oriental pastries including *atayef*, deep fried nut-stuffed pancakes; *baklava*, honey-drenched filo pastry layered with nuts; *basbousa*, a syrupy semolina cake often filled with cream and garnished with pistachio nuts and *konafa*, shredded batter cooked with butter and stuffed with nuts.

Vegetarianism is not a concept with which Egyptians are familiar. While vegetable dishes are plentiful, and the majority of Egyptians eat any quantity of meat only once a week, it is difficult to avoid tiny pieces of meat or meat stock in vegetable courses. Even the wonderful lentil soup, like most Egyptian soups a meal on its own, often has the addition of a chicken stock cube.

Drink Tea is the essential Egyptian drink, taken strong without milk but with spoonfuls of sugar. A pleasant alternative is tea prepared with mint, *chai bil na'ana*, which is good for the digestion. Instant coffee just called Nescafe, is available but avoid the local Misr Café which tastes like sawdust. The thick Turkish coffee, which can be laced with cardamom or cinnamon, should be ordered either *saada*, with no sugar; *arriha*, with a little sugar; *mazbut*, medium; or *ziyada*, with extra sugar. The *mazbut* is the most popular – and one is expected to leave the thick mud of coffee grains in the bottom half of the cup. Coffee grinds, like tea leaves elsewhere, are believed to indicate the future. Other hot drinks include a cinnamon tea, *irfa*, reportedly good for colds; and the less common *sahleb*, a milk drink with powdered arrowroot, coconut, and chopped nuts. Cold drinks include the usual soft drink options of Coca-Cola, Pepsi Cola, 7-Up, and Fanta. Of more interest are the traditional *ersoos*, licorice juice; *karkade*, made from the dried petals of the red hibiscus; and *tamarhindi*, from the tamarind. Freshly squeezed juice stands are located throughout the cities, but these may not be very hygenic. Bottled water, either Baraka or Siwa, is sold widely but check that the seal is intact and that the bottle has not been refilled.

Although Egypt is a Muslim country, alcohol is available in bars and good restaurants. While five-star hotels are beginning to import beer in barrels, the local 'Stella' beer is the most popular sold, with the better-quality 'Stella Export', in half litre bottles. Nonetheless, quality for both brands remains variable. The local spirits are bottled to resemble international brands, and include an ouzo called *zibib*, a rum 'Zattos', and a 'Big Ben' gin.

Water Be prepared for shortage or restriction of water, never regard tap water safe to drink. Bottled water is cheap and easily available.

Where to eat & drink The better hotel restaurants serve international cuisine of a high standard and often have speciality Egyptian restaurants. From there the price but not necessarily the standard falls down to the street stalls which perhaps are best avoided for hygiene reasons. See entries under separate town sections.

Shopping

Places to shop Normal opening hours are summer 0900-1230 and 1600-2000, winter 0900-1900, often closed Sunday but shops in tourist areas seem to stay open much longer. The most interesting shopping is in the bazaars. This takes time but bargains can be found. The main bazaar in Cairo, *Khan el-Khalili*, has a wide selection of ethnic items. By contrast the smaller *Aswan bazaar*, parallel to and one block behind the Corniche, has less hassle and more time to ponder on the purchases.

Best buys Jewellery (sold by weight) and precious stones – particularly lapis lazuli, perfumes, spices, carpets, copper and brass ware, inlaid wooden boxes with intricate designs and cotton garments.

Photography Most types of film are available. Check the sell by date and purchase from shops that appear to have a rapid turnover of films. Bring specialist films with you and take back home all exposed film for processing. High speed film (ISO400) is recommended for night time photography such as Sound and Light shows, and interiors of buildings where a flash is not permitted. Lower speed film is more suitable for the brighter outdoor conditions. The best time to take photographs is early morning or late afternoon as the amount of reflective light in the middle of the day requires a filter. Protect your camera from the fine invasive desert sand with a sturdy polythene bag.

Voltage 220 volts AC. Sockets take standard continental two round pin plugs. Continental adaptors are useful.

Holidays and festivals

Holidays & festivals The Islamic year (Hejra/Hijra/Hegira) is based on 12 lunar months which are 29 or 30 days long depending on the sighting of the new moon. The lengths of the months vary therefore from year to year and from country to country depending on its position and the time at sunset. Each year is also 10 or 11 days shorter than the Gregorian calendar. The Islamic holidays are based on this Hejarian calendar and determining their position is possible only to within a few days.

Ramadan is a month of fasting (see below). The important festivals which are public holidays (with many variations in spelling) are Ras el Am, the Islamic New Year; Eïd al-Fitr (also called Aïd es Seghir), the celebration at the end of Ramadan; Eïd al-Adha (also called Aïd el Kebir), the celebration of Abraham's willingness to sacrifice his son and coinciding with the culmination of the Haj in Mecca; Mouloud, the birthday of the Prophet Mohammed.

Caveat Emptor – the art of bargaining

Haggling is a normal business practice in Egypt and surrounding countries. Modern economists might feel that bargaining is a way of covering up high-price salesmanship within a commercial system that is designed to exploit the lack of legal protection for the consumer. Even so, haggling over prices is the norm and is run as an art form, with great skills involved. Bargaining can be great fun to watch between a clever buyer and an experienced seller but it is less entertaining when a less than artful buyer such as a foreign traveller considers what he/she has paid later! There is great potential for the tourist to be heavily ripped off. Most dealers recognize the wealth and gullibility of travellers and start their offers at an exorbitant price. The dealer then appears to drop his price by a fair margin but remains at a final level well above the real local price of the goods.

To protect yourself in this situation be relaxed in your approach. Talk at length to the dealer and take as much time as you can afford inspecting the goods and feeling out the last price the seller will accept. Do not belittle or mock the dealer – take the matter very seriously but do not show commitment to any particular item you are bargaining for by being prepared to walk away empty handed. Never feel that you are getting the better of the dealer or feel sorry for him. He will not sell without making a very good profit! Also it is better to try several shops if you are buying an expensive item such as a carpet or jewellery. This will give a sense of the price range. Walking away – regretfully of course – from the dealer normally brings the price down rapidly but not always. Do not change money in the same shop where you make your purchases, since this will be expensive.

The day of rest for Muslims is Friday. Observance of Friday as a religious day is general in the public sector though privately owned shops may open for limited hours. The main exception is tourism where all systems remain operative. Holy days and feast days are taken seriously throughout the country.

Ramadan, the 9th month of the Muslim calendar, is a month of fasting for Muslims. The faithful abstain from eating between dawn and sunset for the period until an official end is declared to the fast and the start of the festival of the Eïd al-Fitr. During the fast, especially if the weather is difficult or there are political problems affecting the Arab world, people can be depressed or irritable. The pace of activity in official offices slows down markedly. Travellers have to manage in these conditions by leaving even more time to achieve their aims and being even more patient than usual. If you have a choice, stay out of the area during Ramadan and particularly the Eïd al-Fitr. Travel, services and the atmosphere are all better at other times of year. Travel facilities immediately before and immediately after Ramadan are often very congested since families like to be together especially for the Eïd al-Fitr.

1 January	New Year's Day
15 March	El Fayoum National Day
Sham al-Nessim	(Sniffing of the Breeze, or the first day of Spring) is celebrated second Monday after the Coptic Easter Day with family picnics.
25 April	Liberation of Sinai
1 May	Labour Day
18 June	Evacuation Day – the day the British left Egypt
23 July	Anniversary of 1952 Revolution
26 July	Alexandria National Day
6 October	Armed Forces' Day – parades and military displays
13 October	Suez Day
23 December	Victory Day

Approximate dates of Islamic festivals 2001/2002:

2001		2002
17 November	Beginning of Ramadan	6 November
15 December	End of Ramadan	5 December
5 March	Feast of Sacrifice	22 February
26 March	Islamic New Year 1422	15 March
4 June	Prophet's Birthday	24 May

Approximate dates of Coptic celebrations in 2001/2002:

2001		2002
7 January	Christmas	7 January
19 January	Epiphany	19 January
7 April	Annunciation	7 April
15 April	Easter	5 May
3 June	Pentecost	23 May
19 August	Transfiguration	19 August

Sport and special interest travel

Sport opportunites range from riding horses or camels in the desert to under-water swimming over coral reefs, from floating in balloon over the temples to a leisurely sail in a *felucca* on the River Nile in addition to the more usual golf, tennis, swimming etc.

Diving Climatic and geographic features make the Red Sea **the** place to scuba dive and snorkel. An experience not to be missed. Training and equipment are available. See entries under individual towns.

Balloon flights This is a splendid way to see Egypt – away from the push of people and noise and crush of traffic. Contact *Balloons over Egypt* in Luxor, T370638, F376515, who also have representatives in Luxor at *Hilton International*, *Sheraton* and *Movenpick Jolie Ville*.

Normally collection is from the hotel, the flight lasts between 45 and 90 minutes and takes place on the West Bank over the Valley of the Kings and Valley of the Queens. A post-trip breakfast is often served. These trips are subject to weather conditions over which there is no control. Agility is required to climb into the basket and children under 4'6" are not accepted.

Fishing This is becoming a very popular sport, especially on Lake Nasser where there are over 32 species of fish. Specialist operators organize camping/fishing safaris (see page 22). A permit is required both to fish and to visit the lake – costs US$65. All tackle can be hired in Aswan.

Ornithology For bird watching information contact Sherif and Minay Baha el Din, 4 Sharia Ismail el Mazni, Apl 8, Heliopolis, Cairo.

Watersports Windsurfing, water skiing and other watersports are dealt with in chapters concerning the Red Sea.

Annual sporting events **January**: Egypt International Marathon – Luxor; National Tennis Championships. **February**: International Fishing Festival – Hurghada; International Tennis Championships; International Bridge Tournament.

Golf in Egypt

Egypt has come late in its provision of golf courses for its visitors but the number is increasing and the quality is high.

Alexandria
The course at Alexandria was constructed in 1898 and lies partly within a racetrack. The 18 holes are considered quite challenging because wind can be an important factor. T025433627, F025433678.

Cairo
Gezira Sporting Club. The course here, which is located on the island of Zamelek, was built 110 years ago. There are 9 holes with 15 greens, par 70. T023410434, F02346000.

The Mena House course is overshadowed by the great pyramid of Cheops. It is 5,265 yds long, par 68. T023833/222/444.

Cairo outskirts
Dreamland is located very close to the Pyramids Road and is one of the nicest things about 2 October City. A long course offers three sets of tees and a moderate degree of difficulty but some holes are a bit repetitious. The fairways and greens are in great condition – a haven for all golfers whatever the handicap. From some holes there are views of the pyramids. T011400577/8.

Katamey Heights is the most mature of the new courses and probably the most difficult because as the name implies once you are on the fairway you are rarely level with your ball. There are 27 holes of world class standard and three sets of tees to choose from. Villas overlook the fairway. An easy drive from Maadi or Heliopolis. T027580512-7.

The Mirage City course is located right off the Cairo-Suez road where it intersects with the ring road. It is well designed. Many of the holes can be played in a number of ways, depending on the capabilities of the player, The holes offer a great variety and are not replicas of one another. The Club House is unusual having been inspired by a Roman Spa. Convenient access from Maadi and Heliopolis. T024085200/5300/5400.

Pyramids Park (Suleymaneya) is 200 km northwest of the tollgate on the Cairo-Alexandria Desert Road. Luxuriant landscaping greets the visitor. The course is dotted by a great number of ponds providing a feeling of Equatorial lushness. It is a long and difficult course and while some holes are superbly designed others are on the verge of absurd. Another four courses and a floodlit executive course is planned along with residential units.

El Gouna
El Gouna just 20 km north of Hurghada boasts a course designed by Gene Bates (USA). There are 18 holes, T065580009, F023661041/2. Open daily, 0800-1700. Fees E£75 for 9 holes.

Hurghada
The Cascades championship course is 40 km south of Hurghada adjacent to the new Sheraton and Robinson complex. It was designed by Gary Player and this challenging 9 hole course provides spectacular views of the Red Sea (where a lot of balls end up!!). Wind can be a factor in nearly every shot – a Red Sea version of a links course. T065544901/023407510.

Luxor
The new Royal Valley course is just outside Luxor. Take the road to Qena and the sign is just after the police check point. It was 'sculpted out of the desert'. Black tees 6,730 yds, blue tees, 6,250 yds. The BMW International Golf Cup washeld here for the inauguration in October 1999. T0122129204, F024146538.

Sharm el Sheikh
The new Movenpick hotel in Sharm el Sheikh is a huge complex of accommodation and restaurants with a high quality health centre. But its pride and joy is a beautifully designed championship course among gentle hills with 18 lakes and the inevitable palm trees. This 18 hole course, 6,021 m long, par 72, is seeded with special Bermuda grass. There are weekly golf tournaments and golf schools arranged for guests. T2062603.

18 hole championship course with 18 lakes 6,700 yd, par 72 5 km east of Na'ama Bay, T062600625.

Essentials

March: International Marathon – Cairo-Alexandria.
May: National Fishing Competition – Sharm el-Sheikh; Sharkia Arab Horse Breeding Festival – Sharkia.
July: National Fishing Festival – Hurghada.
September: Red Sea International Wind Surfing Competition – Hurghada.
October: International Competition for Long Distance Swimming – Giza; Port Said National Fishing Competition – Port Said; Pharaoh Rally – Nationwide.
November: Duck Shooting; International Yacht Regatta – Alexandria; Zahra'a Arab Horse Breeding Festival – Ain Shams, Cairo; International Fishing Championship – Sharm el-Sheikh. **December**: Nile International Rowing Regatta – Cairo and Luxor.

Cultural events

January: Cairo International Book Fair – Nasr City, Cairo.
February 22: Ramses II Coronation – Abu Simbel.
March: Cairo International Fair; Annual Spring Flower Show – Andalucìa Gardens, Cairo.
July: International Festival of Documentary Films – Ismailia.
August: International Song Festival – Cairo; International Folklore Dance festival – Ismailia; (Wafa el Nil) Nile Festival Day – Giza.
September: World Alexandria Festival (every two years); International Festival for Vanguard Theatre – Cairo; International Movie festival – Alexandria; World Tourism Day; (Wafa el Nil) Nile Festival Day – Cairo.
October: International Folk festival – Ismailia; Oct 22 Ramses II Coronation – Abu Simbel; Oct 24 Commemoration of Battle of El-Alamein – El-Alamein.
November: Luxor National Day; International Children's Book Fair – Nasr City, Cairo.
December: International Film Festival – Cairo; Festival for Arab Theatre – Cairo; Festival for Impressionist Art (every two years) – Cairo.

Health

Before you go

What to take Take out medical insurance. You should have a dental check up, obtain a spare glasses prescription and, if you suffer from a longstanding condition such as diabetes, high blood pressure, heart/lung disease or a nervous disorder, arrange for a check up with your doctor who can at the same time provide you with a letter explaining details of your disability (in English and French). Check the current practice for malaria prophylaxis (prevention) for the countries you intend to visit. For a simple list of 'Health Kit' to take with you, see Before you travel.

Medical facilites The traveller to this region is inevitably exposed to health risks not encountered in North America or Western Europe. Despite the countries being part of Africa where one expects to see much tropical disease this is not actually the case, although malaria remains a problem in some areas. Because much of the area is economically under-developed, infectious diseases still predominate in the same way as they did in the West some decades ago. There are obvious health differences in risks between the business traveller who tends to stay in international class hotels in large cities and the backpacker trekking through the rural areas. There are no hard and fast rules to follow; you will often have to make your own judgements on the healthiness or otherwise of your surroundings.

There are many well qualified doctors in the area, a large proportion of whom speak English or French but the quality and range of medical care is extremely variable and diminishes very rapidly away from big cities. In some places, there are systems and traditions of medicine rather different from the Western model and you may be confronted with unusual modes of treatment based on local beliefs. At least you can be reasonably sure that local practitioners have a lot of experience with the particular diseases of their region. If you are in a city it may be worthwhile calling on your Embassy to obtain a list of recommended doctors.

If you are a long way from medical help, a certain amount of self medication may be necessary and you will find that many of the drugs that are available have familiar names. However, always check the date stamping and buy from reputable pharmacists because the shelf life of some items, especially vaccines and antibiotics is markedly reduced in hot conditions. Unfortunately many locally produced drugs are not subjected to quality control procedures and can be unreliable. There have, in addition, been cases of substitution of inert materials for active drugs.

With the following precautions and advice you should keep as healthy as usual. Make local enquiries about health risks if you are apprehensive and take the general advice of European and North American families who have lived or are living in the area.

Smallpox vaccination is no longer required. Neither is cholera vaccination. Cholera vaccine is not effective which is the main reason for not recommending it but occasionally travellers from South America, where cholera is presently raging, or from parts of South Asia where the disease is endemic may be asked to provide evidence of vaccination. The following vaccinations are recommended: **Vaccinations**

Typhoid (monovalent): one dose followed by a booster in a month's time. Immunity from this course lasts 2-3 years. Other injectable types are now becoming available as are oral preparations marketed in some countries.

Poliomyelitis this is a live vaccine, generally given orally and the full course consists of three doses with a booster in tropical regions every 3-5 years.

Tetanus: one dose should be given with a booster at six weeks and another at six months and 10 yearly boosters thereafter are recommended.

Children should, in addition, be properly protected against diphtheria, whooping cough, mumps and measles. Teenage girls, if they have not yet had the disease, should be given rubella (German measles) vaccination. Consult your doctor for advice on BCG inoculation against tuberculosis. The disease is still common in the region. North Africa lies mainly outside the meningitis belt and the disease is probably no more common than at home so vaccination is not indicated except during an epidemic.

On the road

Staying healthy Mosquitoes and flies can be a problem in certain areas. Buy a fly spray, take good repellent creams and antihistamine cream if you are prone to bites. Raw food is best avoided unless you can wash it or peel it. The sun is hot all year round so take adequate precautions. **Health/ disease risks**

Water Bottled water is easily available, cheap and safer to drink, but cleaning your teeth with tap water will not be harmful.

This is common. It seems to be frequently caught by travellers probably because, coming from countries with higher standards of hygiene, they have not contracted the disease in childhood and are therefore not immune like the majority of adults in developing countries. The main symptoms are stomach pains, lack of appetite, nausea, lassitude and yellowness of the eyes and skin. Medically speaking there are two types: the less serious, but more common, is hepatitis A for which the best protection is **Infectious Hepatitis (Jaundice)** careful preparation of food, the avoidance of contaminated drinking water and scrupulous attention to toilet hygiene. Human normal immunoglobulin (gammaglobulin) confers considerable protection against the disease and is particularly useful in epidemics. It should be obtained from a reputable source and is certainly recommended for travellers who intend to live rough. The injection should be given as close as possible to your departure and, as the dose depends on the likely time you are to spend in potentially infected areas, the manufacturer's instructions should be followed. A new vaccination against hepatitis A is now generally available and probably provides much better immunity for 10 years but is more expensive, being three separate injections.

The other more serious version is hepatitis B which is acquired as a sexually transmitted disease, from a blood transfusion or injection with an unclean needle or possibly by insect bites. The symptoms are the same as hepatitis A but the incubation period is much longer.

You may have had jaundice before or you may have had hepatitis of either type before without becoming jaundiced, in which case it is possible that you could be immune to either hepatitis A or B. This immunity can be tested for before you travel. If you are not immune to hepatitis B already, a vaccine is available (three shots over 6 months) and if you are not immune to hepatitis A already then you should consider vaccination (or gamma globulin if you are not going to be exposed for long).

AIDS HIV is probably less common than in most of Europe and North America but is presumably increasing in its incidence, though not as rapidly as in Sub-Saharan Africa, South America or South East Asia. Having said that, the spread of the disease has not been well documented in the North African/Red Sea region so the real picture is unclear. The disease is possibly still mainly confined to the well known high risk sections of the population ie homosexual men, intravenous drug abusers, prostitutes and children of infected mothers. Whether heterosexual transmission outside these groups is common or not, the main risk to travellers is from casual sex, heterosexual or homosexual. The same precautions should be taken as when encountering any sexually transmitted disease. In some of these countries there is widespread female prostitution and a higher proportion of this population is likely to be HIV antibody positive. In other parts, especially high class holiday resorts, intravenous drug abuse is prevalent and in certain cities, homosexual, transsexual and transvestite prostitution is common and again this part of the population is quite likely to harbour the HIV virus in large measure. HIV can be passed via unsterile needles which have been previously used to inject an HIV positive patient but the risk of this is very small indeed. It would, however, be sensible to check that needles have been properly sterilized or disposable needles used. The chance of picking up hepatitis B in this way is much more of a danger. Be wary of carrying disposable needles yourself. Custom officials may find them suspicious. The risk of receiving a blood transfusion with blood infected with HIV is greater than from dirty needles because of the amount of fluid exchanged. Supplies of blood for transfusion are now largely screened for HIV in all reputable hospitals so the risk must be very small indeed. Catching HIV does not necessarily produce an illness in itself; the only way to be sure if you feel you have been put at risk is to have a blood test for HIV antibodies on your return to a place where there are reliable laboratory facilities. The results may not be ready for many weeks.

Altitude Mountain sickness is hardly likely to occur. A not-too-rapid ascent is the sure way to prevent it. Other problems experienced at moderate altitude are: sunburn, excessively dry air causing skin cracking, sore eyes (it may be wise to leave your contact lenses out, especially in windy and dusty areas) and stuffy noses. Many travellers, as long as they are physically fit, enjoy travelling in the mountains where it is generally cooler and less humid and there are fewer insects.

Full acclimatization to high temperatures takes about two weeks and during this **Heat & cold** period it is normal to feel a degree of apathy, especially if the relative humidity is high. Drink plenty of water (up to 15 litres a day are required when working physically hard in hot, dry conditions), use salt on your food and avoid extreme exertion. Tepid showers are more cooling than hot or cold ones. Large hats do not cool you down but prevent sunburn. Remember that, especially in the mountains, there can be a large and sudden drop in temperature between sun and shade and between night and day so dress accordingly. Clear desert nights can prove astoundingly cold with a rapid drop in temperature as the sun goes down. Loose fitting cotton clothes are still the best for hot weather; warm jackets and woollens are essential after dark in some desert areas, and especially at high altitude.

These can be a great nuisance. Some, of course, are carriers of serious diseases such as **Insects** malaria and yellow fever. The best way of keeping insects away at night is to sleep off the ground with a mosquito net and to burn mosquito coils containing Pyrethrum. Aerosol sprays or a 'flit' gun may be effective as are insecticidal tablets which are heated on a mat which is plugged into the wall socket (if taking your, own check the voltage of the area you are visiting so that you can take an appliance that will work. Similarly check that your electrical adaptor is suitable for the repellent plug).

You can use personal insect repellent, the best of which contain a high concentration of Diethyltoluamide. Liquid is best for arms and face (take care around eyes and make sure you do not dissolve the plastic of your spectacles). Aerosol spray on clothes and ankles deters mites and ticks. Liquid DET suspended in water can be used to impregnate cotton clothes and mosquito nets. Wide mesh mosquito nets are now available impregnated with an insecticide called Permethrin and are generally more effective, lighter to carry and more comfortable to sleep in. If you are bitten, itching may be relieved by cool baths and anti-histamine tablets (care with alcohol or driving) corticosteroid creams (great care – never use if any hint of sepsis) or by judicious scratching. Calamine lotion and cream have limited effectiveness and anti-histamine creams have a tendency to cause skin allergies and are therefore not generally recommended. Bites which become infected (commonly in dirty and dusty places) should be treated with a local antiseptic or antibiotic cream such as Cetrimide as should infected scratches. Skin infestations with body lice, crabs and scabies are unfortunately easy to pick up. Use Gamma benzene hexachloride for lice and Benzyl benzoate for scabies. Crotamiton cream (Eurax) alleviates itching and also kills a number of skin parasites. Malathion lotion 5% is good for lice but avoid the highly toxic full strength Malathion used as an agricultural insecticide.

Practically nobody escapes this one so be prepared for it. Some of these countries lead **Intestinal** the world in their prevalence of diarrhoea. Most of the time intestinal upsets are due to **upsets** the insanitary preparation of food. Do not eat uncooked fish or vegetables or meat (especially pork), fruit with the skin on (always peel your fruit yourself) or food that is exposed to flies. Tap water is generally held to be unsafe or at least unreliable throughout North Africa with the exception of large cities in Morocco. Tap water in Israel is also usually safe. Filtered or bottled water is generally available. If your hotel has a central hot water supply this is safe to drink after cooling. Ice for drinks should be made from boiled water but rarely is, so stand your glass on the ice cubes, instead of putting them in the drink. Dirty water should first be strained through a filter bag (available from camping shops) and then boiled or treated. Bringing the water to a rolling boil at sea level is sufficient but at high altitude you have to boil the water for longer to ensure that all the microbes are killed. Various sterilizing methods can be used and there are proprietary preparations containing chlorine or iodine compounds. Pasteurized or heat treated milk is now widely available as is ice cream and yoghurt produced by the same methods. Unpasteurized milk products including cheese and yoghurt are sources of

Essentials

tuberculosis, brucellosis, listeria and food poisoning germs. You can render fresh milk safe by heating it to 62°C for 30 mins followed by rapid cooling or by boiling it. Matured or processed cheeses are safer than fresh varieties.

Diarrhoea is usually the result of food poisoning, occasionally from contaminated water (including seawater when swimming near sewage outfalls). There are various causes – viruses, bacteria, protozoa (like amoeba) salmonella and cholera organisms. It may take one of several forms coming on suddenly, or rather slowly. It may be accompanied by vomiting or by severe abdominal pain and the passage of blood or mucus when it is called dysentery. How do you know which type you have and how do you treat it?

All kinds of diarrhoea, whether or not accompanied by vomiting, respond favourably to the replacement of water and salts taken as frequent small sips of some kind of rehydration solution. There are proprietary preparations consisting of sachets of powder which you dissolve in water or you can make your own by adding half a teaspoonful of salt (3.5 grams) and four tablespoonfuls of sugar (40 grams) to a litre of boiled water. If you can time the onset of diarrhoea to the minute, then it is probably viral or bacterial and/or the onset of dysentery. The treatment, in addition to rehydration, is Ciprofloxacin 500 mgs every 12 hours. The drug is now widely available as are various similar ones.

If the diarrhoea has come on slowly or intermittently, then it is more likely to be protozoal ie caused by amoeba or giardia and antibiotics will have no effect. These cases are best treated by a doctor, as is any outbreak of diarrhoea continuing for more than three days. If there are severe stomach cramps, the following drugs may help: Loperamide (Imodium, Arret) and Diphenoxylate with Atropine (Lomotil).

The lynchpins of treatment for diarrhoea are rest, fluid and salt replacement, antibiotics such as Ciprofloxacin for the bacterial types and special diagnostic tests and medical treatment for amoeba and giardia infections. Salmonella infections and cholera can be devastating diseases and it would be wise to get to a hospital as soon as possible if these were suspected. Fasting, peculiar diets and the consumption of large quantities of yoghurt have not been found useful in calming travellers' diarrhoea or in rehabilitating inflamed bowels. Oral rehydration has on the other hand, especially in children, been a lifesaving technique. As there is some evidence that alcohol and milk might prolong diarrhoea, they should probably be avoided during and immediately after an attack. There are ways of preventing travellers' diarrhoea for short periods of time when visiting these countries by taking antibiotics but these are ineffective against viruses and, to some extent, against protozoa, so this technique should not be used other than in exceptional circumstances. Some preventives such as Enterovioform can have serious side effects if taken for long periods.

Malaria This disease occurs in all the regions covered by this book but is, however, only common in the area bordering the Nile Valley in Egypt. Despite being nowhere near so common as in Sub-Saharan Africa, malaria remains a serious disease and you are advised to protect yourself against mosquito bites as described above and to take prophylactic (preventive) drugs where and when there is a risk. Start taking the tablets a few days before exposure and continue to take them six weeks after leaving the malarial zone. Remember to give the drugs to babies and children and pregnant women also.

The subject of malaria prevention is becoming more complex as the malaria parasite becomes immune to some of the older drugs. This phenomenon, at the time of writing, has not occurred in this region so the more traditional drugs can be taken with some confidence. Protection with Proguanil (Paludrine) two tablets per day, or Chloroquine two tablets per week will suffice and at this dose will not cause any side effects. You will have to find out locally the likelihood of malaria and perhaps be prepared to receive conflicting advice on how to prevent yourself from catching it. You can catch malaria even when taking prophylactic drugs, although it is unlikely. If you do develop symptoms (high fever, shivering, severe headache, sometimes diarrhoea) seek medical advice immediately. The risk of the disease is obviously greater the further you move from the cities into rural areas with limited facilities and standing water.

First time exposure to countries where sections of the population live in extreme poverty or squalor and may even be starving can cause odd psychological reactions in visitors. So can the incessant pestering, especially of women which is unfortunately common in some of these countries. Simply be prepared for this and try not to over react.

Psychological disorders

If you are unlucky enough to be bitten by a venomous snake, spider, scorpion, lizard, centipede or sea creature try (within limits) to catch the animal for identification. The reactions to be expected are fright, swelling, pain and bruising around the bite, soreness of the regional lymph glands, nausea, vomiting and fever. If in addition any of the following symptoms supervene, get the victim to a doctor without delay: numbness, tingling of the face, muscular spasms, convulsions, shortness of breath or haemorrhage. Commercial snake bite or scorpion sting kits may be available but are only useful for the specific type of snake or scorpion for which they are designed. The serum has to be given intravenously, so is not much good unless you have had some practice in making injections into veins. If the bite is on a limb, immobilize it and apply a tight bandage between the bite and body, releasing it for 90 secs every 15 mins. Reassurance of the bitten person is very important because death by snake bite is in fact very rare. Do not slash the bite area and try and suck out the poison because this kind of heroism does more harm than good. Hospitals usually hold stocks of snake bite serum. Best precaution: do not walk in snake territory with bare feet, sandals or shorts.

Snake & other bites & stings

If swimming in an area where there are poisonous fish such as stone or scorpion fish (also called by a variety of local names) or sea urchins on rocky coasts, tread carefully or wear plimsolls. The sting of such fish is intensely painful and this can be helped by immersing the stung part in water as hot as you can bear for as long as it remains painful. This is not always very practical and you must take care not to scald yourself but it does work. Avoid spiders and scorpions by keeping your bed away from the wall and look under lavatory seats and inside your shoes in the morning. In the rare event of being bitten, consult a doctor.

The burning power of the sun is phenomenal, especially at high altitude. Always wear a wide-brimmed hat and use some form of sun cream or lotion on untanned skin. Normal temperate zone suntan lotions (protection factor up to 7) are not much good. You need to use the types designed specifically for the tropics or for mountaineers or skiers with a protection factor (against UVA) between 7 and 15. Certain creams also protect against UVB and you should use these if you have a skin prone to burning. Glare from the sun can cause conjunctivitis so wear sunglasses, especially on the beach.

Sunburn & heat stroke

There are several varieties of heat stroke. The most common cause is severe dehydration. Avoid this by drinking lots of non-alcoholic fluid and adding some salt if you wish.

Athletes foot and other fungal infections are best treated by exposure to sunshine and a proprietary preparation such as Tolnaftate.

Other afflictions

Dengue fever is not common in North Africa but there have been cases of this virus transmitted by mosquito bites producing severe headache and body pains. There is no treatment: you must just avoid mosquito bites.

Hydatid disease is quite common in Egypt but can be avoided by keeping well clear of dogs, which is good advice in any case.

Intestinal worms do occur in insanitary areas and the more serious ones, such as hook-worm, can be contracted by walking bare foot on infested earth or beaches.

Leishmaniasis is a parasitic disease transmitted by sandflies, that tend to bite at dawn and dusk. The cutaneous form causes a crusty sore or ulcer that persists for several months. The rare but more serious visceral form causes a persistent fever. Protect against sandfly bites by wearing impregnated long trousers and long sleeved shirt, and DET on exposed skin. Sleep under an impregnated bed net. Seek advice for any persistent skin lesion or nasal symptom.

Prickly heat is a common itchy rash avoided by frequent washing and by wearing loose clothing. It can be helped by the regular use of talcum powder to allow the skin to dry thoroughly after washing.

Schistosomiasis (bilharzia) occurs particularly in Egypt and can easily be avoided because it is transmitted by snails which live in fresh water lakes so do not swim in such places or in canals.

Rabies is endemic throughout North Africa and the Middle East. If you are bitten by a domestic animal try to have it captured for observation and see a doctor at once. Treatment with human diploid vaccine is now extremely effective and worth seeking out if the likelihood of having contracted rabies is high. A course of anti-rabies vaccine might be a good idea before you go.

When you get home
Remember to take your anti-malarial tablets for six weeks. If you have had attacks of diarrhoea, it is worth having a stool specimen tested in case you have picked up amoebic dysentery. If you have been living rough, a blood test may be worthwhile to detect worms and other parasites.

Further health information
The following organizations give information regarding well-trained English speaking physicians throughout the world: International Association for Medical Assistance to Travellers, 745 Fifth Ave, New York, 10022; Intermedic, 777 3rd Ave, New York, 10017.

Information regarding country by country malaria risk can be obtained from the World Health Organisation (WHO) or the Ross Institute, The London School of Hygiene and Tropical Medicine, Keppel St, London WCIE 7HT, which publishes a strongly recommended book entitled *The Preservation of Personal Health in Warm Climates*. The organization MASTA, (Medical Advisory Service to Travellers Abroad), also based at The London School of Hygiene and Tropical Medicine, T020-76314408, F020-74365389, will provide country by country information on up-to-date health risks.

Further information on medical problems overseas can be obtained from Dawood, Richard (ed), *Travellers Health, How to Stay Healthy Abroad*, Oxford University Press, 1992, costing £7.99. We strongly recommend this revised and updated edition, especially to the intrepid traveller heading for the more out of the way places.

General advice is also available in Health *Advice for Travellers* published jointly by the Department of Health and the Central Office of Information (UK) and available free from your Travel Agent.

The following information has been prepared by Dr David Snashall, Senior Lecturer in Occupational Health, United Medical Schools of Guy's and St Thomas' Hospitals and Chief Medical Officer, Foreign and Commonwealth Office, London.

Further reading

Antoniou, J, *Historical Cairo, a walk through the Islamic City*, American University in Cairo Press, 1998.

Buckles, G, *The Dive Sites of The Red Sea, New Holland, 1997.*

Durrell, L, *Alexandria Quartet*, Faber & Faber: London.

Edwards, A, *A Thousand Miles up the Nile*, Parkway Publishing, 1997 (first published 1877).

Edwards, IES, *The Pyramids of Egypt*, Pelican Books, 1947/1961.

Emery, WB, *Archaic Egypt*, Pelican Books, 1961.

Fakhry, A, *Siwa Oasis*, American University of Cairo Press, 1991.

Faulkner, RO, *The Ancient Egyptian Book of the Dead*, British Museum Press.

Ghisotti, A, & Carletti, A, *The Red Sea Diving Guide, includes* 100 illustrations of fish and three dimensional diagrams of coral reef dives, E£95.

Goodman, SM, & Meininger, PM, *Birds of Egypt*, Oxford Univ Press, 1989.

Haag M, *Alexandria*, AUC Press 1993, a full colour guide to Alexandria past and present.

Heikal, M, 1975; *Autumn Fury and The Road to Ramadan*, London.

Hewson, Neil, *The Fayoum*, American University of Cairo.

Hirst, D, & Beeson, I, *Sadat*, London, 1981.

Hobson, C, *Exploring the World of the Pharaohs – a complete guide to Ancient Egypt*, Thames and Hudson Inc, 500 Fifth Avenue, New York, 1987.

Murnane, William J, *A Penguin Guide to Ancient Egypt*, Penguin Books, 1983.

Pick, Christopher, *Egypt: A Travellers Anthology*, John Murray Publishers Ltd.

Seton, MV, *A Short History of Egypt*, Rubicon Press.

Spence, L, *Egypt – Myths and Legends*, Studio Editions, Eastcastle Street, London, 1994.

Steindorff, G, & Seele, KC, *When Egypt Ruled the East*, University of Chicago Press.

Stephens, R, *Nasser – a Political Biography*, London, 1971.

Vatikiotis, PJ, *The History of Modern Egypt: From Mohammed Ali to Mubarak*, Weidenfeld & Nicolson: London.

Waterbury, J, T*he Egypt of Nasser & Sadat*, Princeton, 1983.

Watterson, B, *The House of Horus at Edfu, Ritual in an Ancient Egyptian Temple*, Tempus Publishing Ltd, Stroud, GL5 2QC. Also by the same author: *Introducing Egyptian Hieroglyphics*, *The Gods of Ancient Egypt* and *Women in Ancient Egypt*.

The *Shire Egyptology* series: Shire Publications Ltd, Princes Risborough, Bucks, UK, have a fascinating series £4.99 each including *Egyptian Coffins, Mummies, Pyramids and Household Animals, Temples, Tools & Weapons. Common Birds of Egypt*: American University in Cairo Press, helps to sort out some of the less usual birds. Brown and Rachid, *Egyptian Carpets*, American University in Cairo Press, E£10.

Egypt Focus, a monthly newsletter published by Menas Associates Ltd, PO Box 444, Berkhamsted, Hertfordshire, HP4 3DL, T01442-872800, F01442-876800, www.menas.co.uk

Books

Michelin map No 154 covers Egypt. The Oxford Map of Egypt by Oxford University Press is very good. Sinai printed in Switzerland by Kümmerly and Frey gives most of the sites. Look out for three maps produced by SPARE – Society for the Preservation of Architectural Resources of Egypt – with detailed information of The Citadel, Islamic Cairo and Khan al Khalili. Several maps of the whole of Egypt and of the major towns are available from the the the Egyptian Tourist Board.

Maps & town plans

Egypt on the web

www.touregypt.net/ This is described as the official internet site of the Ministry of Tourism – very detailed – examples include internet cafes, dive sites off Hurghada with illustrations of wrecks, and on-line shopping from the Khan el-Khalili bazaar.

www.ce.eng.usf.edu/pharos/ This is Egypt's world wide web index with 18 main categories including Egyptology, cuisine, education and travel, breaking down into hundreds of fascinating sites.

www.presidency.gov.eg This is the presidential web site and offers photographs of the palaces and biographies of former rulers. Fascinating.

www.egy.com Deals with historical issues on Cairo – where to put the blue plaques etc. Interesting.

www.telefax.com.eg This is a useful Business Directory aiming to cover the whole of Egypt.

www.bibalex.gov.eg Very detailed information and up-to-date news on the new Alexandria Library. Not to be missed.

www.egyptyellowpages.com.eg Everything you need to know on hand.

Cairo

64

Cairo

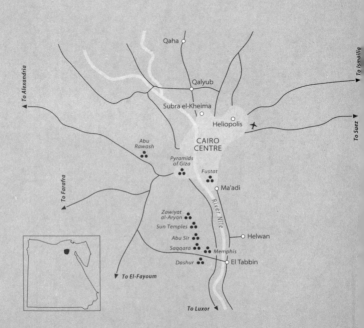

Cairo today is the result of many different cities which have been built on top of one another over the centuries and a cosmopolitan population with connections far beyond the Arab world. It is a teeming mega-city with an estimated 13 million people living in a fabric designed for two million. Standing at the crossroads of Africa and the Middle East it has dominated the region for centuries.

Cairo

Ins and outs

Getting there

Phone code: 02
Colour map 2, grid B2
Population: 17,000,000
Altitude: 75 m

For further transport information see page 136

As one of the world's most crowded and noisy cities, arriving in Cairo can initially seem a very daunting experience. Independent travellers, without the advantage of being met at the airport, have to cope with the problems of finding the way to their hotel and must fend off the unsolicited offers of cheap hotels and taxi rides. The best thing to do is to refuse all offers of help, except from official sources, having worked out in advance where you are going and how you are going to get there.

The airport is 22 km east (30 mins) of Cairo. Terminal 1(T2448977) caters for EgyptAir and domestic travel. The newer Terminal 2 (T2914255) is 3 km away and takes all other flights. Visas are on sale just before passport control and the desk clearly marked.

Taxis are available immediately on exit from customs for E£50. There is an airport service bus that will drop passengers at any central Cairo hotel for E£20 a head. The cheaper and easier way, (less than E£1) is to take the bus No 410 to Midan Ataba or the no 400 every 30 mins or no 27 minibus to the bus terminal at Midan Thrir in the city centre.

There are hotels within the airport complex such as *Movenpick Heliopolis* and *Novotel* which have shuttle buses. Walking is not a safe or serious option.

Getting around

There is a local bus service, metro system and taxis. Taxis are the best way of getting around. There are tourist offices in the main air terminals (T667475; T2914277), Ramses Train Station (T764214) or by the Pyramids at Giza (T3850259). The best information can be obtained at the desks in quality hotels. The main tourist office is at 5 Sharia Adly, near Midan Opera. Advertized hours are 0800-2000, reduced at Ramadan, T3913454. It is not easy to find and limited help is available. The Tourist Police are next door.

Best time to visit

The best time to visit is between March and May and between September and October.

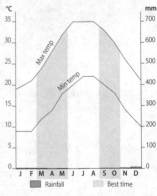

Climate: Cairo

A foot in the door - Cairo

A day in the Egyptian Museum is an essential component with time to admire the treasures of King Tutankhamen's tomb and the immense collection of amazing antiquities.

Climb the Cairo Tower and, on a clear day, get a breathtaking view of the city.

Enjoy a private trip down the River Nile to

get a glimpse of the pyramids or take a companiable evening dinner cruise with Egyptian music to entertain.

Walk in the quiet of the morning in the Coptic heart of Old Cairo, push through the throngs in Khan el-Khalili bazaar and with walks through Islamic Cairo still to plan, take time off for a leisurely lunch at Helnan Shepheards.

History

Since the Arab conquest in AD 641 most Egyptians have called both the city and the whole country **Misr** (pronounced Masr), which was the ancient Semitic name for Egypt and was also mentioned in the Koran. Having rejected Alexandria as the capital of their Egyptian province, because it was considered a Christian stronghold, the Arabs chose **Fustat** (encampment) in the middle of modern-day Cairo as their administrative and military capital. Consequently Cairo rapidly grew in size and importance and it is thought that the name Misr was used in order to distinguish the new city from the many other towns called Fustat in the Arab world. **Al-Qahira** (the Conqueror), which is the city's official but less commonly used name, is derived from Al-Qahir (Mars) because the planet was in ascendance when the Fatimids started the construction of their new city in AD 971. **Cairo** was the Latin version of the name which was given to the city in mediaeval times.

Although the city of Cairo is younger than Alexandria the surrounding region has a very ancient and impressive past. **Memphis**, which lies 15 km south of Cairo across the River Nile, was established as the capital in 3100 BC because of its geographical and symbolic position in controlling both Upper and Lower Egypt. It was during this period that the huge necropolis was developed across the river on the west bank first at **Saqqara** and then at the site of modern-day Giza where the largest pyramids were built.

Memphis was temporarily eclipsed by the new capital of **Thebes** (Luxor) during the New Kingdom. Then another cult centre known as On, or **Heliopolis** to the Greeks, and later Aïn Shams (Spring of the Sun) by the Arabs, was developed further north when a canal was cut between the River Nile and the Red Sea. Although the gradual westward movement of the Nile left it stranded and miles from the river, a small east bank fortress which became known as **Babylon in Egypt**, was expanded during the Persian occupation (525-404 BC). At the time of the Roman occupation in 30 BC the fortress had been deserted and Memphis was still the country's second city after Alexandria. Recognizing the strategic importance of the site, the emperor Trajan (AD 98-117) rebuilt and reinforced Babylon and a thriving town soon sprung up around its walls. During the subsequent Christian era Memphis was completely abandoned and never rose again, while Babylon became the seat of the bishopric and the west bank village of **Giza** grew into a large town.

When the **Arabs** conquered Egypt in AD 641, they were given specific instructions by Khalifa Omar in Damascus to establish their administrative capital in Babylon rather than at the larger Alexandria. His general Amr Ibn

Al-As built his encampment (or Fustat) in the middle of a deserted triangular plain on the east bank which was bounded by Babylon in the south, Aïn Shams (ancient Heliopolis) to the northeast and Al-Maks (the Customs Point), which was the Arab name for Heliopolis' former port of Tendunyas and is now the site of Ramses Station, to the northwest. The Amr mosque was the first of a number of new and permanent buildings which were erected as the plain was developed and the foundations of modern Cairo were laid.

Under successive Muslim dynasties additions were made to the area as new mini-cities, each to the northeast of the previous one, were built. By the time the Fatimid heretical Shi'a invaders arrived from North Africa in AD 969, under the military command of Gohar, only the south of the plain had been developed. He therefore chose to build a new walled city (which included the Al-Azhar mosque, palaces, pavilions and gardens for the sole use of the Khalifa, his family and retainers), about 1½ km north of the Fustat complex and called it Al-Qahira. Two centuries later in AD 1168 calamity struck the Fustat area when, fearing occupation by the invading Crusaders, the Egyptian wazir Shawar set fire to the city. Over 54 days the

Greater Cairo

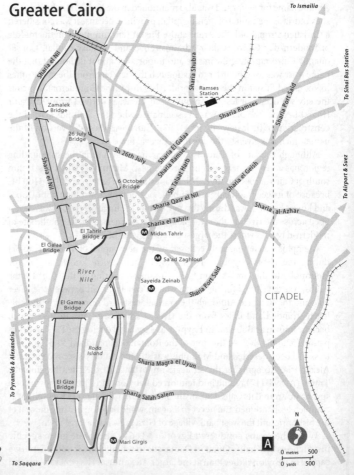

Related map
Central Cairo, page 70

24 hours in the city

First stop the Citadel. Here visit the Mosque of Mohammed Ali Pasha, its architecture showing strong Ottoman influence. From the terrace are excellent views over the city.

On leaving pass the Mosque of Ibn Tulun, Cairo's oldest mosque with an amazing spiral minaret. Near here are the Al-Rifai Mosque Cairo's most modern mosque completed in 1912 and the more ancient (1462) Sultan Hassan Mosque. Both are well worth a visit but you may only have time for one.

Spend the rest of morning in the Egyptian Antiquities Museum going first to see the treasures of Tutankhamen before the crowds arrive.

Book at Shepheards for lunch, an interesting walk south along the Corniche. Service can be slow, keep pressing, as time is short.

After lunch visit Coptic Cairo. In the heat of the afternoon the cool interiors of the museum and the churches are very welcome. Visit the Coptic Museum and

either the Hanging Church or the Church of St Sergius, which is equally decorative. The beautifully restored Ben Ezra Synagogue (Egypt's oldest synagogue) is an optional extra. The Nilometer is accessible from here, but only if you have not seen one elsewhere to the south.

In the early evening make your way to Khan el Khalili (closed on Sundays) the main souq in Cairo since 1382. Stop for tea at Al Fishawi café just west of Midan Hussein. Enjoy the atmosphere of the bustling markets.

Purchases complete, cross the footbridge over Sharia ul-Azhar and walk south through the magnificent complex of Sultan al-Ashruf Qansah II al-Ghawri at least as far as Bab el-Zoueila for another splendid view. Take evening drinks at Mena House Oberoi before the amazing spectacle of sound and light staged at the Pyramids. Shows in English are early, allowing time to eat a relaxing dinner on a floating restaurant.

fire almost totally destroyed Fustat whose inhabitants fled to Al-Qahira and constructed temporary housing. Three years later the last Fatimid khalifa died and his wazir, the Kurdish-born **Salah al-Din**, assumed control of the country and founded the Sunni Muslim orthodox Ayyubid Dynasty (AD 1171-1249). He expelled the royal family from Al-Qahira which he then opened to the public and it soon became the commercial and cultural centre of the metropolis.

Salah al-Din actually only spent one third of his 24-year reign actually in Cairo. Much of his time was spent fighting abroad where he recaptured Syria and eventually Jerusalem from the Crusaders in 1187 and finally died in Damascus in 1193.

He expanded the walls surrounding the Fatimid city and in the southeast built a huge **Citadel**, which became the city's nucleus, on an outcrop of the Muqattam Hills. Under Mamluke rule (AD 1250-1517) the city grew rapidly to become the largest city in the Arab world. As the east bank of the River Nile continued to silt up, the newly elevated areas provided additional space which were developed to house the expanding population.

Under the **Ottomans** (AD 1517-1798) both Cairo and Alexandria were relegated to the position of mere provincial cities with little in the way of public building undertaken in the whole of the 17th and 18th centuries. This changed, however, with the combination of the arrival of the French in 1798 and the coming to power in 1805 of the Albanian-born Ottoman officer Mohammed Ali. As part of his ambitious plan to drag Egypt into the modern world by introducing the best that Europe had to offer, he embarked on a project which included a huge public building programme in Cairo and turned it into a large modern capital city.

Central Cairo

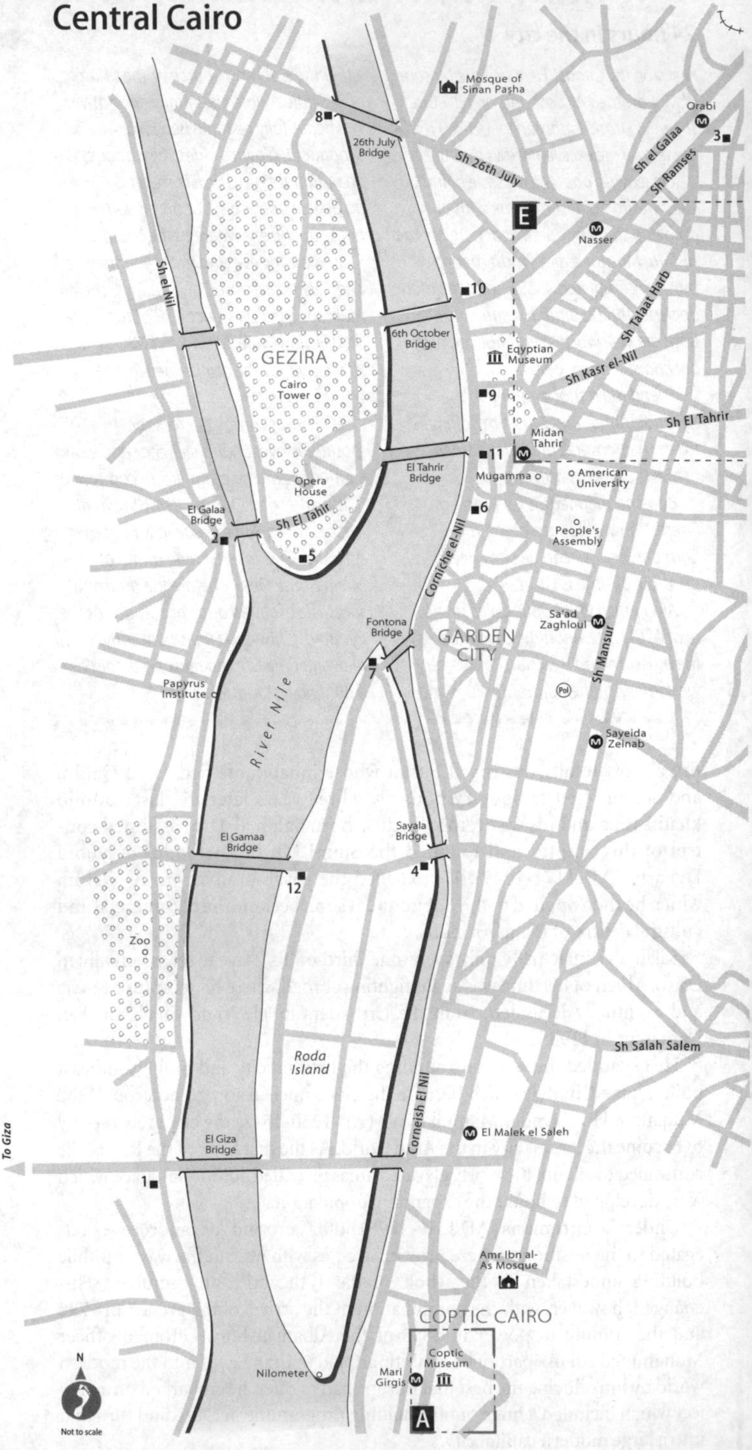

Cairo

8■

Mosque of
Sinan Pasha

26th July
Bridge

Sh 26th July

Orabi

3■

Sh el Galaa

Sh Ramses

E

Nasser

Sh Talaat Harb

10■

Sh el Nil

6th October
Bridge

Egyptian
Museum

Sh Kasr el-Nil

GEZIRA

Cairo
Tower

9■

Sh El Tahrir

Opera
House

El Tahrir
Bridge

Midan
Tahrir

11■

Mugamma

American
University

El Galaa
Bridge

Sh El Tahrir

2■

6■

Corniche el-Nil

People's
Assembly

5■

Sa'ad
Zaghloul

Fontona
Bridge

GARDEN
CITY

Sh Mansur

Papyrus
Institute

7■

Pol

Sayeida
Zelnab

River Nile

Sayala
Bridge

El Gamaa
Bridge

12■

4■

Zoo

Sh Salah Salem

Roda
Island

Corniche El Nil

El Giza
Bridge

El Malek el Saleh

1■

To Giza

Amr Ibn al-
As Mosque

COPTIC CAIRO

Coptic
Museum

N

Nilometer

Mari
Girgis

A

Not to scale

The combination of very rapid population growth and extensive rural-urban migration to the city, particularly since World War Two, has totally overwhelmed Cairo. It has totally outgrown its infrastructure and today a city, intended to house only two million people, is home to over 13 million. The result is that the transport, power, water and sewage systems are completely inadequate and hundreds of thousands live on the streets or wherever they can find shelter including the infamous 'Cities of the Dead' cemeteries. What is amazing is that, despite all its problems, this ancient city actually functions as well as it does and that in adversity the Cairenes are so good natured and friendly.

Sights

It certainly makes sense, if time permits, to visit the major sights of this area in chronological order. Therefore, rather than rushing to the large and exhausting Egyptian Museum, start outside the city at the pyramids and trace their development from the earliest in Saqqara to the splendours of Giza (see separate section **The Pyramids**, page 144). In Cairo city there are few remains from the pre-Christian era other than in the Egyptian Museum, so the logical sequence of visits would be – **Coptic Cairo** in the ancient fortress of Babylon-in-Egypt; the mosques, cemeteries and *souqs* of **Islamic Cairo**; and the modern sites and museums of **Contemporary Cairo**.

Cairo

■ **Sleeping**

1 Abu el-Hoal Palace
2 Cairo Sheraton
3 Capsis Palace
4 Club Med (Manial Palace)
5 El-Gezira Sheraton
6 Helnan Shepheard
7 Le Méridien Le Caire
8 Marriott
9 Nile Hilton
10 Ramses Hilton
11 Semiramis
12 Youth Hostel

Related maps
A Coptic Museum,
page 72
B Islamic Cairo, page 82
C The Citadel, page 106
D Southern Cemetery,
page 116
E Cairo downtown,
page125

Coptic Cairo

This settlement was constructed by the Persians in about 500 BC to guard the junction of the River Nile and the canal linking it to the Red Sea. During the Christian period the fortified settlement of Babylon in Egypt grew into a large town. It was perhaps named by the fort's homesick building workers from modern-day Iraq or from the name for Gate of Heliopolis (Bab-il-On). Later the Arabs called it Qasr al-Sham'ah (Fortress of the Beacon). Whatever its origins it is now known, not entirely accurately, as Coptic Cairo.

Copts – the native Christians of Egypt

The Copts take their name from a corruption of the Greek word *aigupioi* for Egyptian. The Copts were concentrated in the region from Girga to Assiut and had a community in old Cairo until recently. Now many have moved to the metropolitan area of Cairo and its suburbs. The number of Christians of all kinds in contemporary Egypt is put officially at 3.5 million but is thought to be much larger (6 million) of which the majority (4.4 million) are of the Coptic Church. There are also some 90,000 members of the Alexandrian rite, affiliated to Rome and quite separate from the Coptic Church proper.

The Coptic language is no longer spoken. It originated from the language spoken in Egypt in the early Christian era, at that time written in Greek characters. Although there were regional variations in the Coptic language, by the fifth century AD they had merged into a universal form throughout Egypt. The language has been in disuse since the sixth century as a working language though it survived in use in religious rituals. Arabic is the language of the Coptic church services. The Coptic Church is very old – for it is believed that St Mark, who wrote the gospel, preached in Egypt during the time of Emperor Nero and founded a church in Alexandria. He is considered the first patriarch. The Coptic Church is close in belief and form to the Armenian, Ethiopian and Syrian Orthodox rites and differs from Rome which believes in the dual nature of Christ and God while the Copts believe in the unity of the two. The Arab invasion of Egypt in the seventh century put the Coptic Church under siege and made it a minority religion in the country. It survived, however, despite some persecution.

The Coptic Church is led by the patriarch of Alexandria and all Egypt from Cairo with 12 bishops. The Church runs a series of Coptic Churches and monasteries throughout the country and has a foundation in Jerusalem. The Copts are heirs to a rich Christian literature going back to the 3rd century AD. Egyptian governments have normally recognized the historical and religious importance of the Coptic community by giving cabinet posts to at least one of its members. The appointment of Boutros Boutros Ghali as Secretary General of the United Nations in January 1992 did much to highlight the strength of the Coptic role in Egypt.

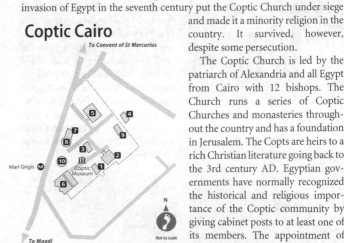

Coptic Cairo

To Convent of St Mercurius

Mari Girgis Ⓜ

Coptic Museum

To Maadi

N

Not to scale

1 Ben Ezra Synagogue
2 Church of St Barbara
3 Church of St Sergius
4 Church of the Virgin
5 Convent of St George
6 Hanging church
7 Monastery of St George
8 New church of St George
9 Old church of St George
10 Tower of Roman Fortress

Related map Central Cairo, page 70

Months in the Coptic Calendar

*All the months have 30 days except
Ayam el Nasite which has 5 or 6.*

Kiyahk	Abib
Tuba	Misra
Amshir	Ayam el Nasite
Baramhat	Tut
Baramoda	Baba
Beshens	Hatur
Bauna	

Coptic Cairo is located on the east bank of the River Nile about 5 km south of Midan Tahrir opposite the southern tip of Roda Island to which it was connected by a pontoon bridge. From Midan Tahrir there are taxis and buses (Nos 134 and 814) and the metro (a better option) to **Mari Girgis** (St George), four stops in the Helwan direction. The churches are open 0900-1800, 1200-1800 on Sunday. Some charge may be made to visitors.

Coptic Cairo has been inhabited since 313 AD

Leaving the station, you are confronted by two circular Roman towers some 33 m in diameter which comprised the west gate of the fortress built on what was at that time the east bank of the Nile, now 400 m further west and on foundations now smothered beneath 10 m of Nile silt and rubble. Much of the original fortress was demolished as part of extensive alterations and today only its towers which supported a drawbridge and gates have survived. The new **Church of St George**, built in 1904 and the only circular church in Egypt, is actually built on top of the north tower and is part of the **Monastery of St George**, which is the seat of the Greek Orthodox Patriarchate of Alexandria, with the **Convent of St George**, the **Church of the Virgin** and the remains of the original fire-damaged **Church of St George** to the northeast.

Church of Al-Mu'allaqah (The Hanging Church)

Old Wing of Coptic Museum

0 metres 10
0 yards 10

1 Entrance from Sharia Mari Girgis
2 Passage
3 Covered courtyard
4 Narthex
5 Nave (wagon-vaulted)
6 Aisle
7 Marble pulpit
8 Altar screen
9 Sanctuary of St George
10 Sanctuary of Virgin Mary
11 Sanctuary of St John the Baptist
12 Shrine of Takla Hamanout
13 Baptistry with basin

To the south of the Roman towers is the Church of the Virgin (Coptic masses held on Friday 0800-1100 and Sunday 0700-1000), better known as the **Hanging Church** (Al-Mu'allaqah or 'The Suspended One') because it stands on top of the three stone piers of the semi-flooded Roman **Water Gate** from where the Melkite bishop Cyrus, the last Byzantine viceroy, fled by boat as the Muslim army arrived. The gate below the church is reached via a stairway behind the piers, by buying a ticket at the Coptic Museum.

The original church built in the 4th century was demolished in AD 840 by Ali Ibn Yahya who was the Armenian Governor. It was rebuilt in AD 977 and modified several times, most recently in 1775. The church is approached though a wonderful narrow courtyard from which steps lead, via a 19th century vestibule, to the church's entrance. In the vestibule is a more modern approach – the sale of videotapes and religious artefacts. It is divided into a wide nave and two narrow side aisles by two rows of 8 columns, 15 of white marble and one of

Cairo

black basalt, all columns with Corinthian capitals. Look out for the odd black basalt capital. The vaulted roof is of timber. There are three supporting columns in the centre of the nave and an 11th century marble pulpit supported by 15 delicate columns arranged as seven pairs and a leader. Examination of the marble steps up to the pulpit will reveal a shell and cross design. On examination each pair of columns is identical but no two pairs are the same. A very fine piece of work. The 13th century *iconostasis* (wooden screen supporting icons), which separates the congregation from the three *haikals* (altar areas) behind the marble pulpit is an incredible feat of fine woodwork and appears virtually transparent. The central icon depicts Christ on the throne, with the Virgin Mary, Archangel Gabriel and St Peter to the right and John the Baptist, Archangel Michael and St Paul to the left. To the right of the altar is a room which is built over the eastern tower of the southern gateway of the old fortress. Here in the baptistry the basin is of red granite. It contains the shrine of Takla Hamanout, an Ethiopian saint, and a small room with a font. The screen dividing this room from the main church is a very delicate woodwork – the mother of pearl inlay is enhanced by holding a candle or torch behind. To its left and right, two secret passageways lead down to the foundations. These recent discoveries are thought to be escape routes used by the Christians during times of persecution.

Immediately to the east of the main Roman towers, down a narrow cobbled lane, is the fifth century **Church of St Sergius**, the oldest church in Cairo. It is dedicated to two soldiers, St Sergius and St Bacchus, who were martyred in Syria in 303. The earliest pieces of the building date from the 5th century. It lies some 3 m below street level. It was rebuilt in the Fatimid period after having been virtually destroyed by fire in the 8th century. The architecture of the church, which contains many antiques recovered from ancient monuments, follows the style of a traditional basilica with the nave divided from the side aisles by marble pillars – two rows of six pillars. Eleven of these monolithic columns are marble and one is of red granite. The remains of illustrations on these pillars represented the apostles or saints. The arched nave roof is of timber. The altar is edged with a raised moulding in which there is a break. It closely resembles an offering table. This is separated from the main part of the church by a 13th century wooden sanctuary screen which has fine encrustations and beautiful ornamentation. The marble pulpit is supported by ten columns. Pieces of an earlier pulpit, rosewood with inlays of ivory and ebony, is on show in the nearby museum. The crosses in the upper section are ivory. Some of the icons here are 17th century and show various scenes of the life of Christ, Virgin Mary and some of the saints.

The partially flooded crypt, to the left of the sanctuary, the only remaining vestige of the original church, is intriguing because it is claimed that the Holy Family sought refuge here during their flight to Egypt and the places where they sat are still visible.

Church of St Sergius

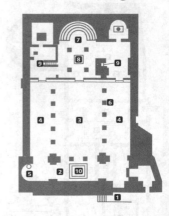

N

0 metres 10
0 yards 10

1 Entrance
2 Narthex
3 Nave

4 Aisle
5 Baptistry
6 Columns with Corinthian capitals
7 Apse
8 Altar
9 Steps to Sanctuary of Holy Family
10 Plunge bath

A fair deal for horses

Some of the owners of horses do not have perhaps as much consideration for their animals as European visitors might expect. Some animals are 'a sorry sight.' Something can be done to improve their lot. See first the Box Brooke Hospital for Animals, page 225. As a guest it is not permissible to intrude but gentle persuasion can be used.

Before accepting a ride in a horse-drawn carriage cast your eye over the horse. You don't need to be a vet to recognize an underfed animal, a limp or an untreated open sore. Refuse to use the carriage and quietly explain your reason to your guide or the driver. Free treatment is available. Does the driver know? As tourism pays the driver's wages the opinion of a tourist may have some sway. If tourists only rode in carriages pulled by healthy horses, the message would be loud and clear.

If you want to take this further the driver's licence number is displayed at the back of the carriage. This can be given to the Brooke Hospital and they can try to get treatment for the animal.

The crypt measures 6 m by 5 m and is 2.5 m high. There are niches on the north, south and east walls. It has always been a popular place of pilgrimage. A special mass is held annually on the 24th day of the Coptic month of Bechens (June 1) to commemorate the Flight into Egypt of the Holy Family. There are two smaller chapels, one on either side of the altar.

Just behind the church of St Sergius is the very similar 11th century **Church of St Barbara** standing on the site of an older church dedicated to St Cyrus and St John in AD 684 which was destroyed during an Arab assault. It is told that when some Christians from Damanhur, including Cyrus and John confessed to their faith they were shot with arrows, burned in a furnace, tied to a horse's tail and dragged through the streets and survived – to be beheaded. The remains of these two martyrs are in the side chapel approached from the left of the altar. The 3rd century's St Barbara's relics were brought to the church and are now contained in a lovely little chapel to the left of the altar. The 13th century iconostasis (screen) is another fine example of encrustation work with some very fine inlaid carved ivory. The original screen is in the nearby museum and the wooden panel linking the columns is an equally characteristic example of delicate Coptic architecture. The domed apse behind the main altar has seven steps which are decorated with bands of marble – red, black and white. The baptistry in the chapel dedicated to Cyrus and John has a polygonal font. The plunge bath was a tank filled with water and used for the Maundy Thursday service – the washing of the feet and on the feast days of St Peter and St Paul. Today a smaller receptacle is used. This church is now dedicated to St Barbara, an attractive young woman from Nicomedia in Asia Minor. In one version of her history she tried to convert her father to Christianity and he killed her. In the second version she was denounced by her family

Church of St Barbara

0 metres 5
0 yards 5

1 Entrance
2 Narthex
3 Nave
4 Ambon
5 Altar screen
6 Altar
7 Chapels of St Cyrus & St John
8 Aisle
9 Shrine to St Barbara
10 Domed apse
11 Baptistry

when she decided to become a nun – then tortured and finally put to death by the Romans along with her faithful attendant St Juliana.

Just to the south of the Church of St Barbara is the **Ben Ezra Synagogue** in the former sixth century Church of St Michael the Archangel, which itself had been built on the site of a synagogue destroyed by the Romans. Hence, this is the oldest surviving synagogue in Egypt. In the 12th century it was sold back to the Jews by the Copts in order to raise funds to pay taxes being raised to finance the Ibn Tulun mosque. The synagogue is built in the basilica style with three naves and an altar hidden by doors, which are wonderfully worked and encrusted with ivory. When the synagogue was extensively repaired in the 19th century, medieval Hebrew manuscripts, known collectively as the **Geniza documents** and providing details of the history of the 11th-16th centuries, were discovered.

Women sit outside the **Church of the Virgin** selling bunches of the herb basil as this church is also known as 'the container of basil'.

The Convent of St George. St George was a Roman soldier and one of the many Christians who fell foul of Diocletian. His body was brought to Egypt in the 12th century. One remarkable feature of the central room is the wooden doors which lead to the shrine. They are 6 m high. The convent is closed to visitors except for the chaplet which has some interesting icons. The custodians here are very keen to display a chain which, it is claimed, was used to secure early martyrs.

The **Convent dedicated to St Mercurius** is situated just north of this central Coptic area. After a vision in which he was presented with a luminous sword (hence his Arabic name Abu Seifein – Mr Two Swords), with which he was to fight for the cause of Christianity, he was persecuted and killed for his faith. Relics are said to be here in the convent and also in the adjacent church. The convent has its origins in the sixth century but has gone through many stages of rebuilding especially in the 10th century. The **Church of St Mercurius**, the largest church here is actually a church and four large chapels, that on the ground floor dedicated to St Jacob (containing the font used for adult baptism) and those upstairs dedicated to St George, John the Baptist and the Children killed by Herod.

The church contains a plunge bath in the narthex, many recycled marble columns in the nave, some/all of which once decorated with religious illustrations and a very attractive dome-shaped wooden canopy dating back to the 10th century over the altar. One side chapel is dedicated to Angel Raphael and contains a baptistry with a shallow font, the other is dedicated to the Virgin Mary. A flight of stairs near the north aisle leads up to a small unlit crypt, the abode of St Barsum (known as Barsum the Naked) for 20 years of his life.

In the **Church of St Shenuda**, adjacent to and slightly south of the church of St Mercurius, a central nave is divided from the side aisles by two rows of marble columns, 5 in each row connected by a wooden architrave. The screen dividing the altar from the main body of the church is a lovely red cedarwood. There are seven icons in the screen, the central one shows the Virgin Mary and the others each have pictures of two apostles. This church is noted for its 18th century icons. Shenuda is associated with the Red and White monasteries (see page 186).

Beside the Hanging Church is the **Coptic Museum**, the other main tourist attraction in Coptic Cairo. ■ *Closed on Sun, Sat-Thu 0900-1700, Fri 0900-1100 and 1300-1600, but the old wing when it can be visited closes 30 mins earlier. Entry for all the Coptic sites here is E£16 (students E£8), cameras E£10.* The museum is regarded as among Egypt's principal display of antiquities and houses a fine collection of mainly Coptic treasures. It was founded by a rich and influential Copt, Morcos Simaika, with the support

Coptic Museum

New wing - ground floor

1 Architectural sculptures
2 Burial ground reliefs
3 Frescoes
4 Carved masonry
5 Stone reliefs & capitals
6 Monastery objects
   from Saqqara
   (Graeco-Coptic)

7 Graeco-Egyptian
   sculptures & friezes
8 Reliefs & figures of
   Biblical scenes
9 Christian & traditional
   Egyptian murals
18A Funerary stelae

New wing - upper floor

10 Mummy case & Graeco-
   Byzantine tapestries.
   Manuscripts &
   documents
11 Textiles
12 Religious textiles
13 Female ornaments &
   toiletries. Icons

14 Metalwork, silver &
   glass. Crucifixes
15 Eagle statue. Roman
   metalwork
16 Keys, door furniture &
   surgical instruments
17 Church wallpaintings

Old wing - upper floor

22-23 Church frescoes &
   furniture
24 Frescoes
25 Woodwork friezes
   & lintels

26 Woodwork - toys
27 Woodwork panels
28 Woodwork - doors
29-30 Ceramics &
   terracotta

of the royal court. The collection began in 1908 as a means of preserving Coptic artefacts and Egypt's Christian heritage against the acquisitive activities of local and foreign collectors. From 1931 the museum has been managed by the Egyptian Government. There was an expansion programme in 1947 which enabled the collection to include a number of small but very valuable private holdings of objects and items from Coptic churches throughout Egypt and much of the Coptic collection of the Cairo Museum was transferred here too. The enclosed garden is neatly laid out with benches for a well earned rest. Here many large pieces of old stonework have been incorporated into the garden design. There is also a small café.

The Coptic Museum gives an excellent insight into the evolution of Christian and to some extent secular art and architecture in Egypt in the period AD 300-1800 and shows some of the interchange of ideas and forms with the larger Islamic community. The displays are arranged thematically, with the Old Wing of the museum holding glass, ceramics and masonry and the New Wing showing manuscripts, metalwork and textiles. Begin in the ground floor of the New Wing. Leave the museum from the ground floor of the New Wing through the garden via the steps that lead down to the Water Gate.

The most convenient way of getting the best from the displays is to circulate round each main room in a clockwise direction. Key items to look out for on the ground floor of the New Wing are: **Room 18A** to the right of the entrance is a pagan gravestone with intricate relief carvings: **Room 1** pediment fragment showing Orpheus and Eurydice, another showing Pan, both from 4th century; **Room 2** some early Christian reliefs which give strength to the suggestion that the Christian cross developed from the Pharaoic *ankh*; **Room 3** the main semi-dome of the sixth century Bawit Monastery south of Dairut which shows a wonderful painting of

Christ enthroned with four mythological creatures of the Apocalypse; **Room 4** the classical depiction of the sacred eagle with wings spread out and the figure of a saint above and two cuddly children, naked, with lovely curly hair carrying a cross encircled with a garland; **Room 5** complicated capital made of limestone with traces of original green colouring; **Room 6** in which all the artefacts come from the fifth century monastery of St Jeremiah in Saqqara. Huge columns march the length of the hall with lotus leaves, vines, palm fronds and acanthus leaves as decoration. A sixth century stone pulpit (the earliest recorded), and a perfectly preserved and fresh painted niche of Christ floating above a sitting Virgin Mary holding an infant; **Room 7** friezes of fruit and flowers with musicians and labourers; **Room 8** dominated by biblical themes in which all the figures face forwards and have somewhat enlarged heads; **Room 9** the 11th century Fayoumi painting of Adam and Eve in the Garden of Eden is well executed and a good Coptic example of biblical stories told in pictures.

Upstairs in **Room 10** is a cabinet displaying what is claimed to be the oldest surviving book in the world – 1,600 years old. It is a small wooden covered book containing 500 handwritten pages of the Psalms of David and here also there is a fine mummy case, painted in full colour of a robed inmate, who was not necessarily a Christian. Upstairs in **Room 11** there are some exquisite Coptic funeral robes carrying traditional symbols such as the sign of the fish; **Room 12** look for the copes and other priests' garments, mainly 18th century, with clever silk embroidery; **Room 13** displays a feast of delicate toiletry objects, including illustrations of women dressed for high days; **Room 14** has ecclesiastic paraphernalia, some, like the marvellous set of crucifixes, not to be missed; **Room 15** contains a figure of a Roman eagle from the Babylon site; **Room 16** some heavy bolts and keys off monastery doors, musical instruments and at one side a fascinating collection of surgical instruments specifically for childbirth; also a fine collection of early Christian wall paintings from Nubia – the faces being rounder and the eyes larger than in the Egyptian illustrations.

In the Old Building, there are rewarding sights. The ceiling carvings throughout this section are from Coptic houses in Old Cairo and have been incorporated into the building along with panels and tiles. They make a magnificent background to the exhibits. Also look for the very varied and ornate woodwork, heavy work being executed in acacia and palm and finer work in imported cedar, pine and walnut. Ebony too was very popular. **Room 22** has the original Fatimid pine altar dome from the Church of St Sergius (see page 74) It is the oldest wooden altar found in Egypt. **Room 24** contains a 6th-century fresco of the head of Christ within a garland of flowers. A frieze in **Room 25** depicts a large crocodile, with flowers, suggested as a Nilotic scene while a long wooden lintel of sycamore has a Greek inscription and numerous small figures.

The wooden toys in **Room 26** which retain some of their colouring are presumed to come from children's graves. **Room 28** has a delightful wooden litter made of ivory, bone and mother of pearl. It is almost 2 m in length and was designed to be carried by two camels. This room also displays a door from the Church of St Barbara. The wood used is sycamore and pine and the carvings are of religious scenes. The pottery in **Room 29** is arranged according to decoration and size. There are two handled red clay jugs, small pots for make-up, a lamp with a frog decoration – all fascinating. **Room 30** has more pottery, some from the Monastery of St Jeremiah at Saqqara (see page 149). The library contains priceless manuscripts. Here is the only biblical text found in an Egyptian tomb.

There are more than 100 Coptic Orthodox churches in Cairo but the special pride is the new (1965) **Coptic Orthodox Cathedral** dedicated to St Mark. This is just off Sharia Ramses. This can seat 5,000 worshippers, houses the patriachal library and accommodates the patriarch Pope Shenuda III.

No peace for the holy either

In the grim, barren desolation of the Moqattam hills to the south of Cairo were a number of abandoned windmills. These had been used by the British army during the First World War to produce flour supplies and were no longer required.

In 1936 a monk called Mina obtained one to use as a place of retreat and prayer. With the door replaced and the roof made safe he constructed a small living area downstairs and an even smaller chapel above. His intention to devote himself to peaceful contemplation proved impossible. The monk in the windmill was good news to those needing a release from their mental and physical problems. The number of visitors increased and set times were allocated for services each day.

The area was declared unsafe during the Second World War and Mina moved, with some reluctance, to the neighbouring churches of Archangel Michael and St Mary in Old Cairo, just 3 km distance.

After the hostilities Mina purchased the land adjacent to the former windmill site and built a church dedicated to St Mina the martyr. To this was added a large monastic complex complete with accommodation where he stayed until he was elected patriach in 1971 and became Pope Shenuda III.

Whereas the monasteries in Egypt had suffered from serious decline the influence of a Pope who had spent so many years in retreat caused a revival of interest in monasticism among the Coptic community. Buildings have been restored, visitors welcomed and the number of monks has increased.

Islamic Cairo

As already noted in the history of Cairo (see page 68), the city was initially developed as a series of extensions and new walled mini-cities which radiated in a northeast direction from the original encampment of Fustat outside the walls of the Babylon in Egypt fortress. There are literally hundreds of mosques in this Islamic city and it is difficult to know where to begin. All the mosques in Cairo are open to the public outside prayer times except those of Sayyidah Hussein and Sayyidah Nafisah. Broadly speaking, however, the most important places to visit in Islamic Cairo are away from modern Cairo and the River Nile in a broad belt to the east of the main Sharia Port Said. The exceptions to this are the **Amr Ibn al-As Mosque**, the oldest mosque in the country which is just near Babylon in Egypt (visit this while seeing Coptic Cairo) and the **Mosque of Sinan Pasha** nearer the River Nile and further north. The rest of Islamic Cairo can be visited by following a series of routes most beginning from the **Al-Azhar Mosque**.

Islamic Cairo has been occupied since 641 AD

Mosque of Sinan Pasha at Bulaq

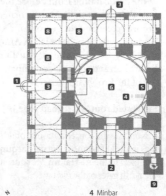

Not to scale

1 Main entrance
2 Entrances
3 Passage
4 Minbar
5 Marble Mihrab
6 Central domed chamber
7 Stairs to gallery
8 Shallow domes over arcade
9 Minaret

Cairo

The **Mosque of Sinan Pasha** (1571) is located in Bulaq.

The Albanian-born Sinan Pasha was recruited for service as a boy at the Sublime Porte in Istanbul and rose to become Sulayman the Magnificent's chief cupbearer. He was governor of Cairo between 1571-72 and is best remembered for his building activities rather than political events. He erected buildings in Alexandria and re-excavated the canal between the River Nile and Alexandria but the major buildings he initiated in Egypt were at Bulaq and included the mosque, essential as the focal point of the community, a *sabil*, a *maktab*, commercial buildings, a *hammam*, residential houses, shops, a mill and a bakery.

The small, square Ottoman mosque stands in a garden. There are entrances into three sides of the mosque into the large central domed chamber which is surrounded on three sides by a colonnade with shallow brick domes. The decorative S-shaped curved windows – 16 in the dome and eight in the outer area – provide, together with the distinctive marble *mihrab*, the only colour. The *dikka* is above the northwest entrance, a gallery running round the brick interior of the dome is reached from the entrance passage while the minaret and ablution area are to the south.

While most of the Sinan Pasha complex has long since disappeared the adjacent public bath, (men only), is still in operation.

The original **Mosque of Amr Ibn al-As (Gama Amr)**, 500 m north of Mari Girgis metro station, was built in AD 642 by Amr Ibn el-As, commander of the Arab army which captured Egypt in that year. Built near both Babylon in Egypt and the Arabs' encampment (Fustat) it is the oldest mosque in Egypt and one of the oldest in the entire Islamic world. Because of the continual enlargements, which began in AD 673 only 10 years after Amr's death aged 93, and included major restoration work in the 15th and 18th centuries and the most recent work in the 1970s, nothing of the original mud-brick 30 m by 17 m thatched-roof mosque exists. Recently repainted and cleaned, its aspect today is virtually modern. As is often the case in the older mosques the interior includes many pillars taken from the ancient Egyptian monuments. As a result the whole mosque is a hybrid with parts of the fabric dating from before the conquest of Egypt until the 19th century alterations. In the north corner under the dome and surrounded by a bronze screen, on the site of Amr's house in Fustat, is the tomb of his son Abdullah who was born when Amr was only 13, became a Muslim before him and was a close companion of the Prophet.

Suggested routes (see map page).

1. North via the concentration of buildings in the **Qalaoun/Al-Nasir/Barquq** complex, to the **Al-Hakim Mosque** at the north gates of the old city.

2a. South to the **Al-Muayyad Mosque** which stands at the **Bab el-Zoueila** gate at the south edge of the old city and the buildings on Sharia Darb al-Ahmar to the **Sultan Hassan Mosque** and the modern **Al-Rifai Mosque**.

Mosque of Amr Ibn al-As

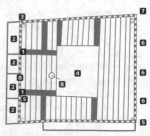

Not to scale

1 Entrances
2 Portal (recent)
3 Tomb of Abdullah
(son of Amr Ibn al-As)
4 Sahn
5 Position
of minaret
6 Mihrab
7 Tomb
8 Fountain

2b. Continuing to the mosques and museums in the imposing **Citadel** and the huge ancient **Ahmed Ibn Tulun Mosque**.

3. To the mosques and tombs in the **City of the Dead** which lies in the 'Northern Cemetery' to the east of Islamic Cairo.

The ancient **Al-Azhar Mosque (1)** and the nearby *souqs* in the **Khan el-Khalili (2)** district are at the centre of modern-day Islamic Cairo. They are located south east of Midan Ataba (reached by taxi or No 66 bus from Midan Tahrir). You can either walk east from Midan Ataba beneath the flyover along Sharia al-Azhar or, better still, along the congested but fascinating Sharia Muski which, once across the tramlines of busy Sharia Port Said, becomes more attractive as you approach Khan el-Khalili.

Although it also refers to a specific street, the **Khan el-Khalili** ■ *daily except Sun,* is the general name given to this district of Cairo which has a large number of individual *souqs*. The Arab/Islamic system of urban planning has traditionally divided the *souqs* by professions or guilds. While the system is less rigid than formerly there is still a concentration of one particular trade in a particular area. The Khan el-Khalili includes streets which almost exclusively sell gold, silver, copper, perfume, spices, cloth or any one of a number of particular products. Many of the products are manufactured within the *souq*, often in small workshops behind or on top of the shops.

The **Khan el-Khalili** has been the main *souq* in Cairo since 1382 when it was first created around a caravanserai by Amir Jarkas al-Khalil who was the Master of Horse to the first of the Burji Mamluke Sultans, Al-Zahir Barquq (1382-89). The caravanserai attracted many foreign and local traders and expanded rapidly, to become a base for the city's subversive groups and was consequently frequently raided. Much of the area was rebuilt by Sultan Al-Ashraf Qansuh al-Ghawri (1501-17) but it still maintained its role as Cairo's main area for traders and craftsmen. Today the main area of the *souq* is occupied by tourist shops but a few of the streets to the west are more authentic and much more interesting. Here you will find souvenirs including gold, silver, copperware, leather goods, perfume oils, alabaster, boxes, herbs and spices. Many of the shops are closed on both Friday and Sunday. **NB** It is essential to bargain because the traders will always start at about double the price they actually expect. It is traditional to respond by offering them about

Mosque of Al-Azhar

Not to scale

1 Entrance
2 Gawhar Medersa
3 Aqbugha Medersa
4 Taybars Medersa
5 Sahn
6 Bab Qaitbai (Barber's Gate)
7 Bab al-Muzayyinin
8 Bab al-Abbas
9 Bab al-Maghariba
10 Bab al-Shawam
11 Bab al-Saayidal
12 Bab al-Haramayn
13 Bab al-Shurbah
14 Bab and minaret of Qaitbai
15 Tomb of Sitt Nafisa
16 Tomb of Abdel al-Rahman Karkhuda
17 Toilets
18 Minaret of Qahnsuh al-Ghawri
19 Riwaq of Abbas II
20 Riwaq Al-Hanafiyyah
21 Qibla
22 Mihrab

Islamic Cairo

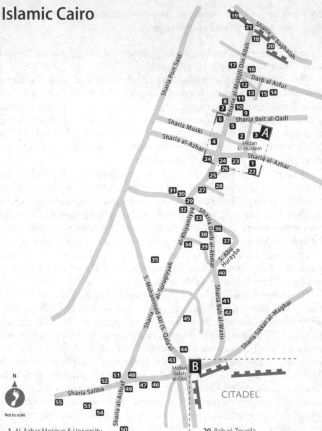

1 Al-Azhar Mosque & University
2 Khan el-Khalili
3 Sayyidah Hussein Mosque
4 Medersa of Sultan al-Ashraf Barsbay
5 Medersa & Mausoleum of Sultan al-Salih Ayyub
6 Medersa of Sultan al-Mansur Qalaoun al-Alfi
7 Medersa of Sultan Al-Nasir Mohamed
8 Medersa & Tomb of Sultan Barquq
9 House of Uthman Kathuda
10 Palace of Amir Bashtak
11 Sabil-Kuttab of Abd al-Rahman Kutkhunda
12 Mosque of al-Aqmar
13 Medersa & Tomb of Tartar al-Higaziya
14 Musafirkhana Palace
15 Mosque of Mohammed Muharram
16 Beit al-Sihaymi
17 Mosque & Sabil-Kuttab of Suleyman Agha al-Silahdar
18 Mosque of al-Hakim
19 North Wall
20 Bab al-Nasr
21 Bab al-Futrah
22 Wikala & Sabil-Kuttab of Sultan Qaitbai
23 Wikala of Sultan al-Ashraf Qansuh II al-Ghawri
24 Ghuriyya
25 Fakahani Mosque
26 House of Gamal al-Din al-Dhahabi
27 Sabil-Kuttab of Tusan Pasha
28 Hammam as-Sukariyah
29 Bab el-Zoueila
30 Mosque of Sultan al-Muayyad Sheikh
31 Hammam of Al-Muayyad
32 Zawiya & Sabil of Sultan al-Nasir Farag
33 Mosque of Vizir al-Salih Tala'i
34 Mosque Gani-bak al-Ashrafi
35 Mosque of Malika Safiya
36 Mosque Qajamas al-Ishaq I
37 Mosque & Tomb of Amir Aslam al-Silahdar
38 Mosque & Tomb of Ahmed al-Mihmandar
39 Mosque of Altunbugha al-Maridani
40 Medersa of Sultan al-Ashraf Sha'ban II
41 Mosque of Amir Aqsunqur
42 Medersa & Tomb of Amir Khayrbak
43 Mosque of Sultan Hassan
44 Al-Rifai Mosque
45 Medersa of Amir Sayf al-Din Ilgay al-Yusfi
46 Sabil-Kuttab of Sultan Qaitbai
47 Mosque of Qanibai al-Muhammadi
48 Mosque of Amir Shaykhu
49 Khanqah of Amir Shaykhu
50 Mosque of Sayyidah Nafisah
51 Sabil-Kuttab of Um Abbas
52 Mosque of Amir Taghri Bardi
53 Mosque of Ahmed Ibn Tulun
54 Beit al-Kridliyah (Gayer-Anderson Museum)
55 Medersa & Tombs of Salar & Sangar al-Gawli

one third of what they originally quoted. This is not so for precious metals which are sold by weight, prices for gold and silver being given daily in the paper. On a bracelet for example a small percentage is added for workmanship, and this is the only thing that is negotiable. Antique jewellery is of course more expensive.

Both Khan el-Khalili's Sharia Muski which is virtually a pedestrian precinct and the more congested Sharia al-Azhar lead east into Midan El-Hussein.

On the southwest of the Midan El-Hussein, an underpass below the busy Sharia al-Azhar leads to the famous and very influential **Al-Azhar Mosque & University (1)** whose leader, known as the Sheikh al-Azhar, is appointed for life and is Egypt's supreme theological authority. ■ *Sat-Thu 0900-1500, Fri 0900-1100 and 1300-1500, E£12 entry fee plus tip for any guides, no bare legs allowed, shawls provided for women. At present this mosque is undergoing renovation and entry is restricted.*

The mosque was built in AD 970 and established as a university in AD 988 which, despite a counter-claim by Fes' Qarawiyin Mosque in Morocco, may make it the world's oldest university. With the exception of the main east *liwan*, however, little remains of the original building because additions and modifications were made by successive rulers, including modern buildings to the north, designed to house the university's administration block.

Initially during the Shi'a Fatimid era (969-1171), the university was used as a means to propagate the Shi'a faith in a predominantly Sunni city, but it fell into disrepair under Salah al-Din and his successor Ayyubids (1171-1250), Sunni Muslim rulers, before being reopened by the Bahri Mamlukes (1250-1382) and eventually became a bastion of Sunni orthodoxy. Later during the rise in Arab nationalism in the late 19th and early 20th centuries, Al-Azhar became a stronghold for independent thinkers. It is no coincidence that in 1956 President Nasser made his speech against the Suez invasion in the university.

The entrance to the mosque is through the Barber's Gate (where students traditionally had their hair shaved), which was built in the second half of the fifteenth century by Qaitbai (1468-96). This opens out on to the 10th century Fatimid *sahn* (courtyard) which is 48 m by 38 m and is overlooked by three minarets. With the exception of the Mamluke *medressa* (theological schools) surrounding the *sahn*, most of the buildings date back to the Fatimid period. The carpeted east *liwan* is particularly impressive with a great number of ancient alabaster columns. The *mihrab* is strangely placed in the middle of the *liwan*, with no *qibla* wall behind it. An extension of the *liwan* by Sultan Abd el-Rahman in 1751 left the *mihrab* in this unusual position. Take the opportunity to climb one of the five minarets for an excellent view over the surrounding area.

Immediately to the south of Al-Azhar is an area known as **Butneya,** once notorious as the base for Cairo's underworld where drugs were openly traded by powerful and locally popular gangsters. After a major crack-down in 1988 most of them left but the area is still home to minor local gangs who tend to prey on shops, restaurants and middle-class Egyptians rather than on tourists who should be perfectly safe.

The area with the greatest concentration of historic buildings in Islamic Cairo lies north from the Al-Azhar complex and the Khan el-Khalili to the north gates of the old city. On the north side of Midan El-Hussein is the **Sayyidah Hussein Mosque (3)**, Cairo's official mosque where some 10,000 people pray daily and President Mubarak and other dignitaries worship on important occasions. This is closed to non-Muslims. This mosque is named after and contains the head of the Prophet Mohammed's grandson Hussein. The rest of his body is perhaps in

Route 1: North from Al-Azhar

Cairo

Iraq. He was killed at Karbala in AD 680 at the climax of the struggle which led to the early and continuing schism in the Muslim world between the orthodox Sunni (followers of the way) and the Shi'a (party) followers of Ali. Hussein, son of Mohammed's daughter Fatima, was the father of the Prophet's only direct descendants, who revere Hussein as a martyr and a popular saint like his sister Zeinab. His mosque is the focus of his annual *moulid*, one of the city's most important festivals which is held over a fortnight in September, and attracts

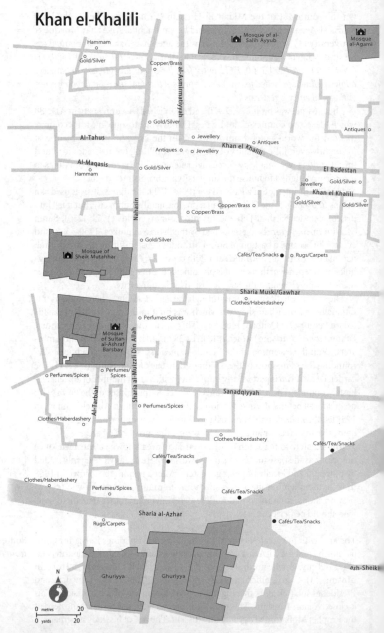

Khan el-Khalili

thousands who camp in the streets. Walk back 200 m northwest along Sharia Muski to Sharia al-Muizzli Din Allah. **NB** On the southwest corner of the crossroads is the **Medersa of Sultan al-Ashraf Barsbay (4)** (1422-37), ■ *E£6*. This liberal and enlightened Mamluke Sultan, originally from the Caucasus, financed his capture of Cyprus in 1426 by turning the spice trade, which in Cairo is based just to the south of the *medersa*, into a state monopoly. The *medersa* is cruciform in plan with the *sabil-kuttab* near the entrance which is marked by a splendid onion-shaped dome. An offset corridor leads into the courtyard in the centre of which are two marble tombs, those of the wife and the son of the sultan who is himself buried in the Northern cemetery. At the northwest corner is the **Mosque and Sabil-Kuttab of Sheikh Mutahhar** erected in 1744. Turn right at the crossroads and head north along Sharia al-Muizzli Din Allah passing some of the many goldsmiths and coppersmith shops. These are concentrated in the alleys to the right including the actual Sharia Khan el-Khalili. Although its façade is largely hidden by shops, at the right hand side of the street, on the site of the former slave market, is the **Medersa & Mausoleum of Sultan al-Salih Ayyub (5)** (1240-49) who was the last of the Ayyubid Sultans and who was the first to introduce the foreign Mamluke slave-soldiers. The *medersa* was special because it was the first built to include all four of Egypt's schools of law while the tomb is the first example where it is placed next to the *medersa* of its founder. Most significant now is the minaret standing tall above Sharia al-Muizzli.

Opposite, with a wonderful unbroken 185 m long façade, stands an amazing complex of three *medressa* founded by three of the most influential mediaeval sultans, Qalaoun, Al-Nasir and Barquq. This section of the street is known as Bayn al-Qasrayn (between two palaces) because of the Fatimid period's magnificent Great Western Palace and Eastern Palace which stood on either side.

The earliest and most impressive *medersa* is the **Qalaoun (6)** complex built by Sultan Al-Mansur Qalaoun al-Alfi (1280-90), ■ *E£6*. Like so

Map labels:
Mashad el Khalili
Sayyidah Hussein Mosque
El Radaatun
Rugs/Carpets
Cafés/Tea/Snacks
Khan el Khalili
Ahmed Pasha
Cafés/Tea/Snacks
Fishawi's
Midan El-Hussein
Cafés/Tea/Snacks
Cafés/Tea/Snacks
Hussein
Radwan
Al-Bustan
Cafés/Tea/Snacks
Cafés/Tea/Snacks
Taxis
Midan al-Azhar
Mosque of Muhammed Abul Dahab
Al-Azhar Mosque
Mohammed Abdul
Fruit & Vegetable Market

Cairo

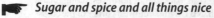

Cairo

☞ Sugar and spice and all things nice

A visit to the spice market (Souq al-Attarin) is highly recommended both for the visual impact and the tremendous aromas. Anything that could possibly be wanted in the way of herbs, spices, henna, dried and crushed flowers and incense are on display, piled high on the ancient pavements in massive burlap bags or secreted away in tin boxes in various drawers inside. Ask if what you want does not appear to be in stock but do not be fobbed off with old merchandise, fresh spices are always available. Prices are extremely low by western standards and shopkeepers are prepared to sell small amounts, weighing out the purchase into a little paper cornet. Saffron is the best buy, far cheaper than at home, but sometimes only the local rather than higher quality Iranian saffron is available. The main street of the spice market runs parallel to Sharia al-Muizzli Din Allah beginning at the Ghuriyya. Here, many of the shops have been in the same family for over 200 years. Some of the owners are also herbalists etara, practising traditional medicine and offering cures for everything from bad breath to rheumatism. Cairo's most famous herbalist, however, is Abdul Latif Mahmoud Harraz, 39 Sh Ahmed Maher, T923754, near Bab el-Khalq. Founded in 1885, the shop attracts a devoted following throughout the Middle East.

The Arabic names for the more common herbs and spices are:

Allspice	kebab es-seeny
Arabic gum	mystica
Bay leaf	warra randa
Basil	rihan
Cardamon	habbahan
Cayenne	shatta
Celery salt	boudra caraffs
Chervil leaves	kozbarra
Chilli	filfil ahmar
Cinnamon	erfa
Cloves	orumfil
Coriander	kosbara
Cumin	kamoon
Dill	shabat
Fennel	shamar
Ginger	ginzabeel
Horseradish	figl baladi
Mace	bisbassa
Marjoram	bardakosh
Mint	naanaa
Oregano	zaatar
Paprika	filfil ahmar roumi
Peppercorns	filfil eswed
Rosemary	hassa liban
Saffron	zaa'faran
Sage	maryameya
Savory	stoorya
Sesame	semsem
Tarragon	tarkhoun
Tumeric	korkom

many other Mamlukes ('possessed') slave-soldiers he was a Kipchak Turk who used the name Al-Alfi because he was originally bought for the high price of 1,000 (or alf) dinars. He subsequently diluted the influence of his own Kipchaks amongst the Mamlukes by importing Circassians whom he billeted in the Citadel. These Burgis Mamlukes (*burg* = tower) were rivals to the Bahri Mamlukes (1250-1382) stationed on Roda Island and eventually created their own dynasty (1382-1517). Qalaoun was constantly fighting the Crusaders and eventually died of a fever in 1290 aged 79, on an expedition to recapture Acre.

The complex was built in just over a year in 1284/85 on the site of the Fatimid's Western Palace and includes a *medersa* and mausoleum to the left and right, respectively, of the entrance with a *maristan* down a now closed 10 m high corridor to the rear of the two linked buildings.

The 20.5 m by 17 m *sahn* of the *medersa* has only two *liwans* while the north-east wall has three storeys of tunnel-vaulted alcoves which were used as student rooms. Of particular interest is the *qibla liwan* and the *mihrab* arranged into three aisles with a glass mosaic around the *mihrab*.

On the north side of the corridor is the beautiful mausoleum ■ *0900-1700* which is a 21 m by 23 m rectangular room with four pillars and four piers arranged in an octagon below an 11.5 m diameter, 30 m high dome built in 1903 to replace the original wooden dome which was demolished in the 18th century. The rose granite pillars have Corinthian capitals and the ceilings are finely carved. The walls are decorated with beautiful marble and mosaics topped by a frieze. The 7 m high horse-shoe shaped *mihrab* is particularly outstanding with columns on either side and covered with rich mosaics and marble. The tomb of Qalaoun and his son Al-Nasir Mohammed is in the middle of the room surrounded by a beautifully sculpted wooden rail.

The *maristan* is now reached via an alley along the southwest wall of the *medersa*, but little remains of the original hospital except for one of the *liwans* and the remnants of a marble fountain. Since 1910 it has been the site of a modern eye clinic.

To the north is the **Sultan Al-Nasir Mohammed (7)** complex which was started by Sultan Kitbugha in 1295 and finished by Al-Nasir during his second reign in 1304 which is commemorated by over 30 mosques and other public buildings throughout the city. Qalaoun's eldest son Khalil (1290-94), was assassinated in 1294 and his 9-year-old brother Mohammed (1294-95) was elected Sultan. He was deposed the following year by the Mongol regent Kitbugha (1295-97) who in turn was soon forced into exile. Kitbugha was replaced by Lajin (1297-99) but he was assassinated after a short reign while playing chess. Following this chapter of 'accidents', Mohammed was restored to the throne, but was kept in terrible conditions by his regent until he escaped to Jordan 10 years' later. He eventually returned with a large army the following year, executed his enemies, and ruled happily for another 30 years until his death in 1341.

The complex ■ *0900-1600* consists of a mosque, *medersa* and tomb. Although restoration work is still in progress it is worth trying to get in to see the *qibla* wall which still has its original decoration and Kufic inscriptions. The *mihrab*, although incomplete, is also interesting because it is one of the last stucco *mihrabs*. Little remains of the mausoleum and parts of the walls have been removed to the *Museum of Islamic Art*. It was originally built for Al-Nasir, but he was buried next door in his father's mausoleum, and the two tombs here belong to his mother Bint Suqbay and Anuq, his favourite eldest son who died the year before his own death. The three-storey minaret is very beautiful with a richly ornamented Andalusian style first storey and the other two storeys surmounted with delicate stalactite cornices. The main door is Gothic and was brought back from the Church of St George in Acre during a campaign against the Crusaders.

Medersa & Tomb of Sultan Barquq complex

Not to scale

Sh al-Muizzli Din Allah

1 Entrance
2 Sahn
3 Qibla Liwan
4 Ancient column
5 Stairs to Sufi monks' cells
6 Tomb of Sultan's daughter
7 Water for ablutions
8 Base of minaret
9 Minbar
10 Mihrab

This is followed to the north by the *medersa* and tomb which make up the **Sultan Barquq (8)**, complex which was built in 1384-86, ■ E£6. The marble entrance and the silver-encrusted

Cairo

☞ Islamic Monuments – A chronological list

641-2	Mosque of Amr Ibn al-As
814	Nilometer
876-9	Mosque of Ahmed Ibn Tulun

Fatimid Monuments

970-2	Mosque of Al-Azhar
990१-10l3	Mosque of Al-Hakim
1087	Bab al-Nasr
1087	Bab al-Futrah
1090	Bab el-Zoueila
1125	Mosque of al-Aqmar
1154	Mosque of Sayyidah Hussein
1160	Mosque of Visir al-Salih Tala'i

Ayyubid Monuments

1176 etc	Citadel
1211	Mausoleum of the Imam al-Shafi'i
1240-49	Medersa and Mausoleum of Sultan al-Salih Ayyub

Mamluk Monuments

1295-96	Medersa and Mausoleum of Sultan al-Nasr Mohammed
1298	Medersa and Mausoleum of Zayn al-Din Yusef
1303	Medersa and Tombs of Sakar and Sangar al-Gawli
1318-35	Mosque of Sultan al-Nasr Mohammed (Citadel)
1324	Mosque and Tomb of Ahmed al-Mihmander
1334-39	Palace of Amir Bashtak
1339-40	Mosque of Altunbugha al-Maridani
1344-45	Mosque and Tomb of Amir Aslam al-Silahdar
1346-47	Mosque of Amir Aqsunqur
1349	Mosque of Amir Shaykhu
1350	House of Uthman Kathuda
1355	Khanqah of Amir Shaykhu
1356-63	Mosque of Sultan Hassan
1360	Mausoleum of Tatar al-Higaziya
1368-69	Mosque of Sultan al-Ashraf Sha'ban II
1373	Medersa and Mosque of Amir Sayf al-Din Ilgay al-Yusufi
1384-86	Medersa of Sultan al-Zahir al-Barquq

bronze-plated door are very impressive and lead through an offset corridor to the *sahn* which has four *liwans* arranged in a cruciform shape. The *qibla liwan*, to the east, is divided into three aisles by four ancient pharaonic columns which support beautifully carved and painted ceilings. Upstairs there are cells for the Sufi monks who once inhabited the building. To the north of the *medersa* a door leads to the mausoleum where Sultan Barquq was originally buried before being transferred to the mausoleum specially built by his son Al-Nasir Farag (1399-1405 and 1405-12) in the city's northern cemetery (see below).

Sultan Al-Zahir Barquq, whose name means plum, (1382-89 and 1390-99) reigned twice and was the founder of the dynasty of Circassian slave-soldiers who became the Burgis Mamlukes rulers of Egypt. He was reportedly an enlightened Sultan, who admired piety and intelligence and surrounded himself with learned scholars, before dying of pneumonia aged 60 in 1399.

1384-89	*Medersa and Tomb of Sultan al-Zahir Barquq*
1409	*Zawiya and Sabil of Sultan al-Nasir Farag*
1413	*Mosque of Qanibai al-Muhammadi*
1415-21	*Mosque of Sultan al-Muayyad Sheikh*
1420	*Hammam al-Muayyad*
1423-37	*Medersa of Sultan al-Ashraf Rarsbay*
1426	*Mosque of Amir Gani-bak al-Ashrafi*
1432	*Mausoleum of Sultan al-Ashraf Barsbay*
1440	*Mosque of Amir Taghri Bardi*
1444-53	*Mosque of Yehia Zein al- Din*
1456	*Mausoleum of Barsbay*
1472-77	*Medersa, Mausoleum and Sabil-Kuttab of Sultan al-Qaibai*
1480-81	*Mosque of Qajamas al-Ishaqi*
1502	*Medersa and Mausoleum of Amir Khayrbak*
1503-04	*Wikala and Mosque of Sultan al-Ashraf Qansuh II al-Ghawri*
1501-16	*Gates of Khan Khalili*
1501 17	*Ghuriyya Complex of Sultan al-Ashraf Qansuh II al-Ghawri*

Ottoman Monuments

1528	*Mosque of Suleyman Pasha*
1567	*Mosque of Sinan Pasha*
1610	*Mosque of Malika Safiya*
1631	*Beit al-Kridliyah*
1637	*House of Gamal al-Din al-Dhahabi*
1648	*Beit al Sihaymi*
1697	*Mosque of Ahmed Katkhuda al-Azab*
1735	*Fakahami Mosque*
1744	*Sabil-Kuttab of Abd al-Rahman Katkhunda*
1792	*Mosque of Mohammed Muharram*
1820	*Sabil-Kuttab of Tusan Pasha*
1824	*Qasr al-Gawharah*
1824-57	*Mosque of Mohammed Ali Pasha*
1837-39	*Mosque and Sabil-Kuttab of Suleyman Agha al-Silahdar*
1867	*Sabil-Kuttab of Umm Abbas*
1869-1911	*Mosque of Al-Rifa'i*
1893-9	*7 Mosque of Sayyidah Nafisuh*

Besides the Qalaoun/Al-Nasir/Barquq complex which is on the west side of Sharia al-Muizzli Din Allah there are a number of other interesting, if less important buildings on and near the east side of the street on the route north to the Al-Hakim mosque. This area, which is heart of Islamic Cairo, is definitely worth exploring for a full day.

Directly opposite the Qalaoun complex is Sharia Beit al-Qadi and 40 m down on the left hand side is the modern looking house No 19 which is marked with a green plaque where visitors should knock to be shown around in return for a little *baksheesh*. This is the remains of a palace built in 1350 but better known as the **House of Uthman Kathuda (9)** who restored it during the 18th century.

Further north opposite Barquq's complex are the beautiful if neglected remains of the **Palace of Amir Bashtak (10)** (Al-Nasir's son-in-law) built in 1334-39 a fine example of the domestic architecture of the time. The original five storey structure has been reduced to two and the windows in the rather plain façade are covered with *mashrabiyya*. Access is via an offset courtyard ■ E£6 and the warden who is usually to be found at the nearby **Sabil-Kuttab of Abd al-Rahman Kutkhunda (11)** has keys to both properties. There used to be many of the these Ottoman-influenced *sabil-kuttab*, which combine a water supply for the public at street level and a Koranic school in the building above, throughout Cairo. This elegant example, built in 1744 by a powerful amir seeking absolution for his former sins, stands on a triangular piece of land where two roads meet. The building is tall and slim. A beautifully carved timber screen on the upper storey protects the *kuttab* on its three open sides and the balcony permits a good view. Below, the double arches are supported by delicate columns. The *sabil* is faced with Syrian tiles.

About 75 m further north on the right up the main road is the **Mosque of al-Aqmar (12)** which was built in 1121-25 by the Fatimid visir of Khalifa al-Amir (1101-31).

It was originally at the northeast corner of the great eastern Fatimid palace. It is particularly important because: it was the first Cairo mosque with a façade following the alignment of the street, rather than the *qibla* wall, so that its ground plan was adjusted to fit into an existing urban environment; it was the first to have a decorated stone façade, the colour giving it its name which means moonlight; it introduced the shell motif and the stalactite into architectural styles which subsequently became favourites in Cairo.

The mosque has been restored over the centuries. Amir Yalbugha al-Salami restored the *minbar, mihrab* and ablution area in 1393 and added the minaret in 1397. The minaret was apparently removed in 1412 because it had started leaning, but the current structure includes the original first storey which is made of brick covered with very uncommon carved stucco decorated with chevron patterns. Because the street level has risen since the mosque was built there are steps down to the entrance which is offset from the main part of the mosque. Despite its importance and unique features the original interior of the mosque is unspectacular. Around the base of the almost square *sahn* the arches bear Koranic verses in the early angular and unpointed Kufic script on an arabesque background.

The **Medersa-Mausoleum of Tartar al-Higaziya (13)** is located in a small street which connects Sharia al-Gamaylia with Midan Bayt al-Qadi. It was built in two phases with the mausoleum, which was connected to the princess's palace, being built in 1347 for her recently murdered husband and the palace itself being converted into a *medersa* in 1360 which explains its irregular shape.

Tartar was the daughter of Sultan al-Nasr Mohammed, the sister of Sultan Hassan and the wife of the Amir Baktimur al-Higazi. The mosque was built on the site of the residence of Amir Qawsun who had married one of Tartar's sisters in 1347. Little else is

Medersa-Mausoleum of Tartar al-Higaziya

Not to scale

1 Entrance	**7** Porch
2 Domed mausoleum	**8** Ablutions liwan
3 Sahn	**9** Qibla liwan
4 Sarcophagus of Tatar	**10** Princess's liwan
5 Mihrab	**11** External courtyard
6 Octagonal minaret	

known about Tartar except that she died of the plague in 1360. Her tomb is still visited by women seeking her blessing.

Entrance to the building is via a corridor which leads via a porch with a lovely ceiling into the *sahn* which has a *qibla liwan* to the southeast, the ablution *liwan* to the northwest and the princess's much larger liwan to the southwest which contains a large and most attractive *mihrab* with marble pillars. The *liwans* are united by a beautiful inscription, bands of Koranic script on a blue background which surround them. The triple arcade is supported by reused Byzantine columns. A series of stucco niches are set in the upper section of the *sahn* and the semi-domes of the two *mihrabs*. The high quality craftsmanship is matched by three carved and painted wooden ceilings. The octagonal minaret to the southwest of the *sahn* has been missing its top for over a century. Access to the minaret, the ablution area and storage areas are all via doors off the *liwans*. The ribbed stone dome, one of the earliest in Cairo, over the mausoleum is in the north end of the complex on the corner of two streets and passers-by can solicit a blessing or invoke a prayer via the open windows.

The restoration work carried out in the 1980s was done with care and consideration. Further east stands the Ottoman **Musafirkhana Palace (14)** (House of Guests), a rather fine rambling building constructed between 1779 and 1788 by the merchant Mohammed Muharram, who also built the adjacent mosque **(15)**, named after him, and had the misfortune to die of sunstroke after returning from a pilgrimage to Mecca. Mohammed Ali bought the building which is noted as the birth place of Khedive Ismail in 1830. It is possible to enter and examine the products of the resident artists and sculptors and see the intricate *mashrabiyya* in the harem on the second storey. Note the two wind catchers which provide cool air. Return to the main thoroughfare.

Take the next right hand turn for a brief detour to No 19 Darb al-Asfur which is 50 m along the left hand side of the street. This is the **Beit al-Sihaymi (16)** ■ *0900-1600*, actually two houses, built in 1648 and 1796 and inhabited until 1961, and probably one of the finest examples of a luxurious Mamluke mansion in the whole of the city. It has a lovely courtyard and a *haramlik (harem)* for the women including a domed bathroom.

Returning to the main street and continuing north, one reaches the **Mosque and Sabil-Kuttab of Suleyman Agha al-Silahdar (17)**, built in 1837-39 by one of Mohammed Ali's ministers who also built many other *sabils* throughout the city. The style of the building is very much influenced by the contemporary style in Istanbul including the minaret with an Ottoman-style cylindrical shaft and conical top.

Mosque of Al-Hakim

Sh al-Muizzli Din Allah

Sh al-Baghalah

North wall of Cairo

Not to scale

1 North minaret
2 West minaret
3 East dome
4 South dome
5 Mihrab dome
6 Great stone porch
7 Sahn
8 Northwest arcade
9 Southwest arcade
10 Northeast arcade
11 Qibla arcade
12 Qibla

Continuing to the north end of the street is the giant **Mosque of Al-Hakim**, named after the third Fatimid caliph, **(18)** ■ *0900-1600, E£6 plus a tip for both your guide and minder in the mosque*, which abuts the **North Wall (19)** of the old city of Fustat/Cairo between the **Bab al-Nasr (20)** and **Bab al-Futrah (21)** gates and commemorates its most notorious ruler (see box, page 92).

Cairo

➤ *Al-Hakim – The Vanishing Despot*

In AD 996 at the age of 11 Al-Hakim succeeded his father as the second Egyptian Fatimid Khalifa and began a despotic reign. At the age of 15 he had his tutor assassinated and started his extremely cruel and relentless persecution of Christians, Jews, Sunni Muslims, women and dogs. He prohibited any Christian celebrations and had the Church of the Holy Sepulchre in Jerusalem demolished. He also prohibited Sunni ceremonies and tried to established Shi'a Islam as the only form of Islam. Women were forbidden to leave their homes and, in order to enforce this, cobblers were not permitted to make or sell women's shoes. At one time all of Cairo's dogs were exterminated because their barking annoyed him. Merchants who were found to have cheated their customers were summarily sodomized by his favourite Nubian slave while Al-Hakim stood on their head. Wine, singing, dancing and chess were also prohibited and the punishments for disobeying these laws were very severe and usually resulted in a gruesome death.

His erratic rule, with laws often changing overnight, led to tensions within Fustat/Cairo, particularly between the various religious communities. In 1020, the news that Al-Hakim was about to proclaim that he was a manifestation of Allah provoked serious riots to which he

responded by sending in his Sudanese troops to burn down the city where they clashed not only with the civilians, but also the Turkish and Berber soldiers. An alternative story is that one particular quarter of Fustat was torched because he thought that was where his favourite sister Sitt al-Mulk (Lady of Power) took her lovers, but when she was proved to be a virgin by the midwives he examined the ruins and asked "who ordered this?" Whatever the truth, he then sent his chief theologian Al-Darazi to Syria for safety where he is believed to have originated the theology of the Druze who consider Al-Hakim to be divine.

Despite his ruthless public acts Al-Hakim's personal life was very abstemious and he was a very generous alms-giver. He took to riding around the city and surrounding countryside on a donkey with only a couple of servants but disappeared in February 1021. Following the discovery of his knife-slashed robe, it is believed he was murdered, possibly on the instructions of Sitt al-Mulk with whom he apparently argued because of her refusal to begin an incestuous marriage with him. The fact that his body was never discovered led the Druze to believe that he had retreated from the world to return at a later date, while the Copts believe that he had a vision of Jesus, repented and became a monk.

■ *Entrance fee E£6 gives access to both gates.* It was begun in 990 by the Shi'a Muslim Fatimid Khalifa Al-Aziz (975-996) and was eventually finished some 23 years later by his son who took the name **Al-Hakim bi-Amr Allah** (Ruler by God's Command) and ruled between 996-1021.

Possibly having a Christian wife was the reason why his reportedly tolerant and humane father Al-Aziz had been more forbearant towards Christians and Jews than towards the indigenous Sunni Muslim population. In contrast his son was very intolerant to everyone. With such a colourful history, the large 122 m by 115 m mosque itself is actually rather plain. It is organized around a large central *sahn* and built of bricks with a large porch in the traditional Fatimid style. It has been restored many times throughout the centuries, notably after the major earthquake in 1302 and by Sultan al-Hassan in 1359. Originally the two minarets stood separate from the walls, the huge salients, added in 1010 to strengthen them, are in fact hollow shells. After the 14th century it was converted to house Crusader prisoners-of-war, then as a stable by Salah al-Din, during the French occupation as a fortified warehouse, as a school, and in the mid-19th century to store items destined for the **Museum of Islamic**

Mosque of Ahmed Ibn Tulun

Art which opened in 1896. Since 1980 the mosque has been restored, practically rebuilt, in white marble by the Indian-based Bohra sect of Ismaili Muslims who claim direct spiritual descent from the Fatimid imams whom they worship. Its twin minarets have been reinforced by stone carvings and from these and from the roof there is a wonderful view over Cairo.

The route south from Al-Azhar mosque has a number of very interesting buildings including the **Mosque of Sultan Al-Muayyad Sheikh** at the medieval **Bab el-Zoueila**. Further to the south of Fustat is the **Sultan Hassan Mosque** and the much more modern **Al-Rifai Mosque** which stand side-by-side below the mighty **Citadel** (see page 102) and its various mosques. One can then head west to the huge and very old **Mosque of Ahmed Ibn Tulun** and the nearby *Gayer Anderson Museum* before returning to the river. Allow a minimum of half a day to take in all of the sites on this tour of the south part of Islamic Cairo.

Immediately to the south of the Al-Azhar complex are a few of the 20 remaining *wikalas*, hostels for merchants which were usually above a bonded warehouse for their goods, which numbered over 200 in the 1830s. Directly opposite the mosque is the **Wikala and Sabil-Kuttab of Sultan Qaitbai (22)** the first of two hostels founded by this sultan. The wonderfully preserved **Wikala of Sultan al-Ashraf Qansuh II al-Ghawri (23)**, which was originally built in 1504, is just off the southwest corner of Al-Azhar: it now houses a permanent exhibition of desert life and is also used as workshops for artisans. Traditional handicrafts for sale. ■ *Daily (except Fri) 0900-1700 or 0900-1100 and 1400-1600 during Ramadan, E£6.*

50 m to the northwest back on Sharia al-Azhar just near the footbridge, is the **Ghuriyya (24)**, the magnificent complex of **Sultan al-Ashraf Qansuh II al-Ghawri** (1501-17), which is bisected by a continuation of Sharia al-Muizzli Din Allah. The complex, made up of his domed mausoleum to the east of the street and his mosque and *medersa* to the west, was built in 1504-05 and was the last great Mamluke public building before the Ottoman conquest. He died of a stroke in 1516, aged about 76, during a battle near Aleppo against the Turks, who then immediately invaded and captured Egypt, and began their long

Route 2a: South from Al-Azhar

Mosque of Ahmed Ibn Tulun

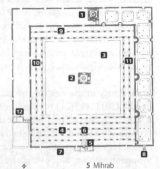

Not to scale

1 Minaret
2 13th century fountain
3 Sahn
4 Sanctuary arcade
5 Mihrab
6 Minbar
7 Qibla
8 To Gayer Anderson Museum
9 Northwest arcade
10 Southwest arcade
11 Northeast arcade
12 Sabil of Sultan Qaitbai

rule which lasted from 1517 to 1805. Because Al-Ghawri's body was never found, he was not buried in this magnificent and hugely expensive tomb. The north side is open and on Wednesday and Saturday evenings at 2000 holds a short exhibition of Dervish dancing, good entertainment, no charge.

Sharia al-Muizzli Din Allah between the two buildings, originally roofed, was the site of the exotic silk market. Today mainly household goods are sold in the shops. Each section of this main thoroughfare, Islamic Cairo's main street, was named after the merchandise sold in that particular stretch. For example the fruit-sellers had their own mosque, the **Fakahani Mosque (25)** (built in 1735), about 200 m down the street on the left hand side. Make a detour by walking left from its northwest corner and then left again where, 70 m to the east at No 6, is the **House of Gamal al-Din al-Dhahabi (26)**, Cairo's richest gold merchant in 1637 when this beautiful house was built. It is used as a documentation centre and is open to visitors. ■ *Daily 0900-1400 except Fri.* Back to the south of the mosque, is the ornate **Sabil-Kuttab of Tusan Pasha (27)**, built in his name by his father Mohammed Ali Pasha in 1820. From here the south gates of the ancient city are just ahead. Before going through the gates turn left or east at the *sabil-kuttab.* About 75 m along the side street is an old 18th century men's bath-house known as **Hammam as-Sukariyah (28)** which was originally owned by a rich woman who also owned the nearby *wikala* and *sabil* of Nafisah Bayda. Although like the other remaining bath-houses in the city it is no longer a den of vice, it is still an interesting place to visit and relax. Today it helps the local community by allowing its fire for heating the water to be used to cook *ful mudammas* (beans) for the locals' breakfast.

Bab el-Zoueila (29), built by Badr al-Gamali in 1092 when Fatimid fortifications were being reinforced, was one of the three main gates in the city walls. It is named after mercenaries from the Al-Zoueila tribe of Berbers who were stationed in the nearby barracks. The gate was soon inside the city following the successive expansions and Salah al-Din's construction of larger walls further out from the centre. Cairo was in effect divided into two with the inner walls still in existence and both sets of gates locked at night.

Bab el-Zoueila also has a more popular history linked to the caravans departing both to Mecca and the south. It was not only the location of street performers including snake-charmers, story tellers and dancers, but after the fifteenth century it also became the site of public executions. Common criminals were beheaded, garrotted or impaled, while cheating merchants were hanged from hooks or rope. Defeated Mamluke Sultans, including the last one in 1517, were hanged and sometimes nailed to the doors. Even today the 20 m high Bab el-Zoueila, which comprises a 4.8 m wide multi-storey arch between two solid stone towers, is still an impressive sight particularly from the south.

Immediately to the west of the gate is the **Mosque of Sultan al-Muayyad Sheikh (30)** (1412-21) built on the site of the old Kazanat al-Shamaii prison. ■ *E£6.* Al-Muayyad had been incarcerated here on a number of occasions because of his love of alcohol when he was a Mamluke slave-soldier. On being released after one particularly long and unpleasant stretch, he vowed to replace the prison with a mosque which he began in 1415 after becoming Sultan.

The mosque, which is sometimes known as the Red Mosque because of the colour of its external walls, was one of the last to be built in the ancient large enclosure style before the Turkish style was adopted as the norm. The superb bronze-plated wooden entrance doors leading to the mosque were originally intended for the Sultan Hassan Mosque but were purchased by Al-Muayyad for his own mosque. The entrance leads into a vestibule with an ornate stalactite ceiling. From the vestibule, the door on the left leads to the Al-Muayyad's mausoleum and marble tomb with Kufic inscription, while nearby is the tomb of his son, Ibrahim, who died in 1420.

From the mausoleum a door leads to the east *liwan* which was restored at the beginning of this century and gives an impression of the mosque's past splendour. Many of the columns were taken from ancient monuments but the most exceptional sight is the *mihrab* and the surrounding wall because of the perfect harmonization of the coloured marble stucco. The *minbar* is an example of fine woodwork, but has also been restored. The courtyard is now planted with shrubs and palm trees. From the top of one of the two minarets (expect to pay extra for this climb ■ *E£10*, there is an excellent view over the surrounding area and the adjacent Bab el-Zoueila.

From here a 20 minutes' walk or five minutes' ride on bus No 75 to the west of Bab el-Zoueila along Sharia Ahmed Maher brings you to the *Museum of Islamic Art* (see page 118).

En route immediately next to the mosque is a large and elegant building which looks like a small palace but is in fact the **Hammam al-Muayyad (31)** bath-house, built in 1420. This has fallen into disrepair and is now often flooded. The area between the two is known as the Bab el-Khalq after a mediaeval gate which has long since vanished.

From the south of Bab el-Zoueila there are two routes you can take to reach the **Sultan Hassan** and **Al-Rifai mosques** which stand north of the *Citadel*. One is to continue southwest along what is officially known as Sharia al-Muizzli Din Allah but which, like so many other long roads, changes its name in different sections and at this point is also known as Sharia al-Khiyamiyya (Tentmakers) because of its bazaar. After about 1 km you reach a major crossroads where you should turn left or southeast along Sharia al Qala'a which leads to the rear of the two mosques. A much more interesting route includes a few nearby sites on Sharia al-Khiyamiyya before heading east along Sharia Darb al-Ahmar, after which the whole area is named, towards the Citadel.

Immediately south of the gates are two buildings which are bisected by Sharia al-Khiyamiyya. To the west is the *zawiya* (Sufi monastery) and *sabil* (public fountain) of **Sultan al-Nasir Farag (32)** (1405-12) who was Barquq's son and successor. To the east is the much more magnificent **Mosque of Visir al-Salih Tala'i (33)** which was both the last Fatimid mosque and, when it was built in 1160, was the country's first suspended mosque resting on top of a series of small vaulted shops which, with the rise in the street level, are now in the basement. Tala'i reportedly died

Mosque of Visir al-Salih Tala'i

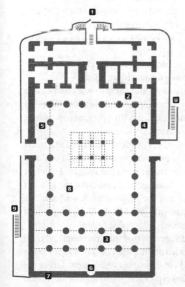

Not to scale

1 Entrance (uniquely above shops)
2 Northwest liwan
3 Southeast liwan
4 Northeast liwan
5 Southwest liwan
6 Mihrab
7 Qibla wall
8 Sahn
9 Steps to street level

Cairo

The Hammam

A visit to the hammam or Turkish bath is still part of the way of life for many Egyptians. Many Egyptian families have no bathing facilities at home and rely on the public hammam. A ritual purification of the body is essential before Muslims can perform prayers, and even for the well-off classes in the days before bathrooms, the 'major ablutions' were generally done at the hammam. Segregation of the sexes is of course the rule at the hammam: some establishments are open only for women, others only for men, while others have a shift system (mornings and evenings for the men, all afternoon for women). In the old days, the hammam, along with the local zaouia or saint's shrine, was an important place for women to gather and socialize, and even pick out a potential wife for a son.

In the older parts of the cities, the hammam is easily recognizable by the characteristic colours of its door. A passage leads into a large changing room cum post-bath rest area, equipped with masonry benches for lounging on and (sometimes) small wooden lockers. Here one undresses under a towel. Hammam

gear today is football or beach shorts for men and knickers for women. A token must be purchased at the cash desk for a massage/scrub down, where shampoo can also be bought.

This is the procedure. First into the hot room. 5-10 minutes with your feet in a bucket of hot water will see you sweating nicely, and you can then move back to the raised area where the masseurs are at work. After the expert removal of large quantities of dead skin, you go into one of the small cabins or mathara to finish washing. (Before doing this, catch the person bringing in dry towels, so that they can bring yours to you when you're in the mathara). For women, in addition to a scrub and a wash, there may be the pleasures of an epilation with sokar, an interesting mix of caramelized sugar and lemon. Men can undergo a taksira, which although it involves much pulling and stretching of the limbs, ultimately leaves you feeling pretty good. And remember, allow plenty of time to cool down, reclining in the changing area before you dress and leave the hammam.

regretting the construction of the mosque because, being located directly outside the walls of the city, it could be used as a fortress by an enemy.

In 1160 the enfeebled Fatimid Dynasty was about to fall as one child khalifa succeeded another, ruling in name only, while a powerful visir really wielded royal authority. When the Armenian-born Tala'i ibn Ruzzik came to power he called himself al-Salih hence the mosque's name.

The mosque, about 60 m by 20 m in size, was originally intended as a mausoleum for the remains of the martyr Hussein which were brought to Cairo from Ashkalon when the latter was under threat from the Franks. The great earthquake of 1303 severely damaged the mosque and destroyed the minaret which was restored together with the rest of the mosque by Amir Baktimur al-Gukandar (Polo-Master) and subsequently in 1440, 1477 and lastly and very badly in the 1920s after the minaret had collapsed yet again.

It was only in about 1920 that it was discovered that the street level had risen so much and that the mosque was suspended on shops below. The shops – seven at the front, 12 on either side but none below the *qibla* wall – were part of the *waqf* and whose rents supported the upkeep of the mosque. The northwest entrance porch, with its large portico and an arcade of keel-arches raised on ancient columns with Corinthian capitals, is unique in Cairo. The decoration around the entrance is, however, similar in style to the earlier al-Aqmar mosque. The porch's *mashrabiyya* dates from the first restoration and the bronze facings on the exterior door are also from 1303 while the carvings on the inside of the door are a copy of the original which is now in the Islamic Museum.

From the entrance a tunnel-vaulted passage leads into the *sahn* surrounded on four sides by *liwan* but the northwest *liwan* is not original. In the northeast *qibla liwan* the tie-beams, which are inscribed with Koranic inscriptions in what is known as floriated Kufic script, are original but the ceiling is modern.

The highlight of the interior is the exquisite *minbar*, the fourth oldest in Egypt and a very fine example of Mamluk wood carving, which was donated to the mosque in 1300 by Amir Baktimur al-Gukandar. Above is the first appearance in a Cairo mosque of a *malqaf* (wind vent) which was an ingenious early Islamic form of air conditioning.

Medersa & Mosque of Amir Gani-Bak al-Ashrafi

Not to scale

1 Entrance
2 Cruciform medersa
3 Mihrab
4 Minbar
5 Domed tomb

Mosque of Malika Safiya

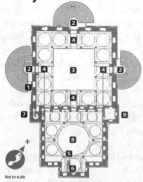

Not to scale

1 Main entrance
2 Entrances
3 Sahn
4 Domed arcade
5 Minbar
6 Mihrab
7 Minaret
8 Central dome
9 Women's room
   behind screen

Further south down the street is what is probably the city's best preserved example of a **roofed market** which, because of the multitude of coloured printed fabrics sold here, is known as the **tentmakers' bazaar**. Situated slightly further along the street is the **Medersa-Mosque of Amir Gani-Bak al-Ashrafi (34)** which was built in 1426 and is named after a favourite of Sultan al-Ashraf Barsbay (1422-37). Although the mosque has similarities with a number of other Mamluk mosques of the same period and despite the loss of both a coloured marble lintel over the portal door and the windows, its decoration even now is more ornate than other examples.

You enter the mosque from the south and pass through a serpentine corridor arriving in the central domed cruciform area with the usual *qibla* wall, *mihrab* and *minbar*. There is a 2-storey minaret, to the right of the entrance, which is very plain and utilitarian.

The Amir Gani-Bak al-Ashrafi had been brought up by Sultan al-Ashraf Barsbay and his meteoric rise to amir in 1422 naturally created many enemies. He was poisoned and died aged 25. He was such a favourite that the Sultan had his body transferred to a tomb in the Sultan's own Eastern Cemetery complex.

Nearby is what little remains of the **Souq al-Surugiyyah** (saddle-makers market).

The **Mosque of Malika Safiya (35)**, built in 1610, lies to the west in a small street off Sharia Mohammed Ali (see map, page). It is one of the few mosques in Cairo which bears a woman's name although Queen Safiya acquired it deviously rather than constructed it herself.

Safiya, who was from the noble Venetian family of Baffo, was captured by pirates along with a large party of other women in 1575 on their way to Corfu where her father was governor. Because of her beauty she was presented to the Sublime Porte where she became chief consort of Sultan Murad III. He made her his *Sultana Khasski* (favourite) which gave her considerable power and influence which was increased further when she produced Murad's first-born son who succeeded his father in 1595. At her son's death Safiya was exiled to a harem where she lived in obscurity until she died in 1618.

This Turkish style mosque, which was originally set in gardens, is entered on the southwest side via some very high steps which lead to a square courtyard. The cloister which runs all round the forecourt has three arches above columns on each side, and is vaulted by a series of small supported Byzantine style domes of a type unknown in Egypt before the Turkish conquest. The roof in the centre of each side is oblong in plan.

One small Mamluk-style dome, entirely distinct from the others, covers a small room in the northeast corner of the sanctuary. This room was probably intended for women because a *mashrabiyya* separated it from the sanctuary.

A fine stalactite doorway leads into the sanctuary over which lies the great brick dome, resting on six pointed arches, and surrounded by smaller arches. The *mihrab*, which except for the blue Iznik tiles is in the earlier Mamluk style of coloured marble panels, stands at the back of a square domed annex. The beautiful *minbar* is characteristically Turkish, being entirely carved in white marble with a pointed conical top.

Returning to Bab el-Zoueila and turning right (east) into Sharia Darb al-Ahmar (Red Road) there is an interesting 1¼ km walk to the Citadel. The street gets its name from the incident in May 1805 when the Mamlukes were tricked into going to discuss their grievances with Mohammed Ali Pasha (1805-48). He had them slaughtered as they travelled 'Between the Two Palaces' and their heads sent to Istanbul as a demonstration of his power and independence. In March 1811 he did a similar thing again on the same street when 470 Mamlukes and their retainers were persuaded into going to a banquet at the Citadel to celebrate his son's imminent departure to fight the Wahabis in modern day Saudi Arabia. They were slaughtered on their return near Bab el-Zoueila.

About 150 m after the Mosque of Wazir al-Salih Tala'i the road bends towards the south and on the corner of the fork in the road is the beautiful late-Mamluke era **Mosque of Qajamas al-Ishaq I (36)** who was Sultan Qaitbai's Viceroy of Damascus where he died and was buried in 1487. Although the mosque was built in 1480-81, it is now known locally as the **Mosque of Abu Hurayba** after the 19th century sheikh who occupies the tomb.

At this point you can could make a detour off the main road east up Sharia Abu Hurayba where the left hand fork leads 250 m to the **Mosque & Tomb of Amir Aslam al-Silahdar (37)** built in 1344-45 and then follow the road around southwest and back to the main Sharia Darb al-Ahmar.

Alternatively you can forget about the detour and just continue south from the Mosque of Qajamas al-Ishaqi along Sharia Darb al-Ahmar. About 50 m on the right is the **Mosque & Tomb of Ahmed al-Mihmandar (38)**, built in 1324 but restored in 1732, but much more interesting is the beautiful, relaxing and very peaceful **Mosque of Altunbugha al-Maridani (39)** (1339-40) which is 100 m further along the street. This is among the most impressive 14th century buildings in Cairo. Altunbugha (Golden Bull), who was originally from the Turkish

Adhan – The Call to Prayer

This is known as the adhan and is performed by the muezzin who calls the faithful to prayer, originally by the strength of his own voice from near the top of the minaret but today, taking advantage of technological advances, it is probably a recording timed to operate at a particular hour. Listening to the first call to prayer just before the sun begins to rise is an unforgettable memory of Egypt.

There is no fixed tune, perhaps tune is too definite a description, but in Egypt there is one particular rhythm used all over the country for the adhan. The traditional Sunni adhan consists of seven phrases, with two additional ones for the morning prayer. There are some variations which the well-tuned ear will pick up.

1. Allahu Akbar (Allah is most great) is intoned four times. This phrase is called al takbir.

2. Ashhadu anna la ilah ill'-Allah (I testify that there is no god besides Allah) is intoned twice.

3. Ashhadu anna Muhammadan rasul Allah (I testify that Mohammed is the apostle of Allah) is intoned twice. This and the preceeding phrase are called the shihada, a confession of faith.

4. Hayya 'ala 'l-salah (come to prayer) is intoned twice.

5. Hayya 'ala'l-falah (come to salvation) is intoned twice. This and the preceeding phrase are called tathwib.

6. Allahu Akbar is intoned twice.

7. La ilah ill'Allah (there is no god besides Allah) is intoned once.

The two additions to the morning prayer are: Al-salatu khayr min al-nawm (Prayer is better than sleep) which intoned twice between the fifth and sixth phrases, and Al-salatu wa'l-salam 'alayka ya rasul Allah (Benediction and peace upon you, Oh Apostle of Allah) intoned after the seventh phrase.

town of Mardin, rose through the ranks to become amir and then married one of Sultan al-Nasir Mohammed's daughters and became his cupbearer (*saqi*). After the sultan died in 1340 his successors imprisoned Altunbugha until 1342 when he was made governor of Aleppo in modern-day Syria. He died there the following year at the age of 25.

Altunbugha's courtyard mosque, which was extensively restored in 1895-1903, is one of the oldest remaining buildings in this area. The minaret, to the right of the entrance, was the first in Cairo with an entirely octagonal shaft. It was built by Mu'allim al-Suyufi, who was the royal chief architect, who also built the minaret of Aqbugha at al-Azhar. The shafts of both are decorated by two-coloured inlaid stone work. Fortunately the restoration work followed the original plans so that the bulb crowned canopy supported on stone pillars, the earliest existing example, was retained.

The main entrance in the northeast wall is composed of a high-pointed vaulted recess which is decorated by a stalactite frieze and inlaid black and white marble. Inside the mosque the large *sahn* with a later Ottoman octagonal wooden fountain canopy, is surrounded by four *riwaq* but the *qibla riwaq* is separated from the rest of the mosque by a beautifully carved part-original, part-restored *mashrabiyya*. There is a three-bay by three-bay domed area, supported by eight red granite pharaonic columns, in front of the marble mosaic and mother-of-pearl *mihrab* and the wooden carved and inlaid *minbar*. There is a stone *dikka* on raised pillars where the Koran is recited. The painted and gilded ceiling above has been partially restored which reveals the glorious original colour but also shows the need for further renovation.

Another 200 m further south past a small Turkish mosque, by which time the road is now called Sharia Bab al-Wazir in memory of the Gate of the Wazir which once stood there, is the large **Medersa of Sultan al-Ashraf Sha'ban II**

(40) (1363-78). It was built in 1368 when he was only 10, for his mother, who was one of al-Nasir Mohammed's (1310-40) concubines, which is why it is known locally as *Umm Sultan Sha'ban* ('mother of Sultan Sha'ban') but he died before her and is buried there.

On the road south is the **Mosque of Amir Aqsunqur (41)** who was the son-in-law of al-Nasir Mohammed and later became Viceroy of Egypt. It is sometimes known as the **Mosque of Ibrahim Agha** by locals and the **Blue Mosque** by Europeans because of both the exterior's blue-grey marble and the beautiful indigo and turquoise tiling of the *qibla* wall. In the 1650s Ibrahim Agha usurped the mosque started in 1346 and decorated it with imported tiles.

The **Medersa-Mausoleum of Amir Khayrbak (42)** was built in stages with the earliest, the mausoleum, which was attached to his palace, being erected in 1502. Because it was squeezed between existing buildings the shape of the complex is very irregular. The complex is best viewed from the Citadel end to the south from where one can see that the minaret, undated, which has the upper storey missing and the intricately carved dome of the tomb raised above arched windows.

Unlike most Mamluk *medressa* it was initially not a Friday mosque although this was subsequently introduced in 1531 when the *minbar* was added. Documents show that the *medersa* staff included one imam, six *muezzins*, two *qari* (Koran readers) at the *medersa*, nine *qari* to recite the Koran at the windows, a sufi shaykh, 10 *qari* to perform daily in two shifts, and two *qari* at the mausoleum.

The entrance is through a corridor to the left of which is the *sabil-kuttab* and to the right of which is the portal entrance to the mosque which one enters by stepping over a piece of pharaonic stone. Three cross vaults cover the mosque's interior but it is noticeable that the arches strangely obscure the windows on the *qibla* wall suggesting a change in plan during construction. The stonework is red and yellow and the *qibla* wall of coloured marble. To the left of the *mihrab* with its pointed arch is a door which leads down stairs direct to the adjacent Alin Aq palace which Khayrbak had requisitioned. Past the wooden *minbar* is the entrance to the rather plain but extraordinarily tall tomb containing the sarcophagus of Ganbalat, Khayrbak's brother. From the windows of the tomb one has a good view of the ruined Alin Aq palace and Salah al-Din's city walls.

For the record, as you admire this building, Khayrbak who was the Mamluk governor of Aleppo, betrayed his master Sultan al-Ghuri at the Battle of Marj Dabiq in 1516 when the Turks routed the Mamluks which led to the Ottoman occupation of Egypt. He was

Medersa-Mausoleum of Amir Khayrbak

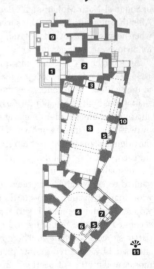

Not to scale

1 Entrance
2 Courtyard
3 Portal
4 Domed tomb chamber
5 Mihrab
6 Sarcophagus of Ganbalat
7 Steps to Alin Aq's palace
8 Sahn
9 Sabil
10 Qibla wall
11 Viewpoint

rewarded for his treachery by being appointed as the first Ottoman governor of Egypt where he was reportedly known for his cruelty and greed.

From here the road slopes up to the left to meet the approach road to the Citadel but we continue right to the two imposing mosques.

Directly below the Citadel are two adjacent mosques. The **Sultan Hassan Mosque (43)** ■ *E£12* was started in 1356 and finished six years later during the second reign of Sultan Hassan (1354-61). The building is a masterpiece of Islamic art and is of incomparable simplicity and beauty. The main entrance is through a large, impressive doorway decorated with stalactites and finely sculpted ornaments. This leads into an antechamber connected to the main courtyard. The magnificent cruciform courtyard has an ablutions fountain at the centre covered by a large dome which was originally painted blue. Each of the vaulted *liwans* served as a place for the teachings of one of the four doctrines of Sunni Islam. The *liwan* containing the *mihrab* has richly decorated marble lined walls and a Koranic frieze in Kufic writing carved in the plaster work. The marble *minbar* here is one of the finest in Cairo. Its height is accentuated by hanging lamp-chains. The original glass lamps from these chains can be found in the *Museum of Islamic Art* in Cairo and in the Victoria and Albert Museum in London.

Mosque of Sultan Hassan

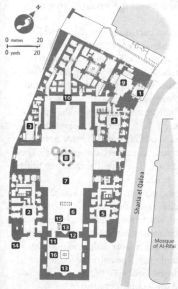

0 metres 20
0 yards 20

Sharia el Qalaa

Mosque of Al-Rifai

1 Entrance
2 Hanifi medersa
3 Hanabali medersa
4 Malaki medersa
5 Shafi'i medersa
6 Sanctuary/liwan
7 Sahn
8 Water for ablutions
9 Antechamber (domed)
10 Corridor
11 Bronze-faced door with gold and silver inlay
12 Qibla
13 Mihrab
14 Base of minaret
15 Minbar
16 Tomb chamber/ mausoleum

From here an ornate bronze door with gold and silver motifs leads to the square mausoleum of Sultan Hassan, again a room of grand proportions. The room is dominated by a large 21 m diameter dome which was actually built later during the Turkish period.

The three-section 86 m minaret by the mausoleum is the highest in Cairo, with each new section richly decorated at its base with numerous stalactites. Another much smaller 55 m minaret on the east side of the mosque was built in 1659 to replace the existing one which was decaying. The building also contains four *medressa* with one for each of the four – Malaki, Hanafi, Hanabali and Shafi'i – Islamic schools of law. Each *medersa* forms a virtually autonomous part of the building. The ground floor is used as a place for teaching, meditation and praying and the first floor as lodgings for the students. Sultan Hassan was murdered and his body never recovered to place in here but two of his sons are buried here.

This huge building, one of the largest mosques in the world, was at times used as a fortress, being conveniently placed for hurling roof-top missiles at enemies in the Citadel.

Cairo

Despite its appearance, the **Al-Rifai Mosque (44)** ■ *E£12*, directly to the east of Sultan Hassan Mosque, was only started in the late 19th century and was actually finished in 1912. However the mosque, which is named after Sheikh Ali al-Rifai who was the founder of the Sufi Muslim *tariqa* bearing his name and who was originally buried there, blends remarkably well into the surroundings. It was built over and expanded by the Dowager Princess Khushyar, the mother of Khedive Ismail who died in 1885 before it was finished, and was intended to contain the tombs of her descendants. Besides Al-Rifai and herself it contains the tombs of Khedive Ismail (1863-79), his sons Sultan Hussein Kamil (1914-17) and King Ahmed Fouad I (1917-36) but not King Farouk who died in exile and is buried in the Southern cemetery. It is also the last resting place of the last Shah of Iran (Mohammed Reza Pahlavi), who died in exile in 1980 and, on President Sadat's instructions, was buried with great ceremony in a tomb made of green marble imported from Pakistan.

The **Medersa of Amir Sayf al-Din Ilgay al-Yusfi (45)** built in 1373, is located on Sharia Souq al-Salih to the north of Bab Mangak al-Silahdar (1346-47).

Sayf al-Din Ilgay rose through the ranks to become an Amir of the Sword and eventually commander-in-chief of the army. He married Khwand Baraka, who was the mother of Sultan Shaban (1363-77), and he found himself one of the powers behind the throne. After his wife died, however, he quarrelled with the Sultan over her property and lost his influence. He had to flee the court and was drowned in uncertain circumstances while trying to cross the River Nile on horseback. His body was recovered and he was buried in the *medersa* that he had built a few years earlier in 1373. His tomb lies beneath the dome at the western corner of the mosque.

It is a late Mamluk complex with an unusual curved and fluted dome which is quite unique. The ribs twist across the dome at an angle of 45° to the right and then swing back to the left before fusing together at the apex. The minaret has an octagonal base and the usual further two storeys above, the galleries of the first of which are supported by attractive corbels of stalactite form. The upper storey of the minaret is a later reconstruction with a pillared pavilion.

The main façade is made up of an ornate formal entrance on the extreme north corner with the remaining façade being divided into two recesses headed with stalactite cornices and crennellated hoods separated by two narrower full-height ornamental arches headed with decorated fluted stone. The recesses and arches carry 36 windows in three courses; the second and third courses are elegant windows with tracery masonry lights.

The entrance to the traditional Mamluk cruciform mosque is via the northwest steps near the street corner which lead via a winding corridor into the central *sahn* which is surrounded by four *liwan* each of which have a frontal arch and above which is gilded decoration, now somewhat deteriorated in quality. The *qibla liwan* has been depleted of its former marble dado and the *minbar* has lost its top but still has fine carving and inlay. The entrance to the Ilgay's tomb is between the northwest and southwest *liwans*. To the right of the *minbar* on the southwest wall is an exit to the small outside courtyard.

Route 2b:
The Citadel
See Citadel map page 106

The magnificent **Citadel** reached direct from Midan Tahrir by taking a No 82 bus, is also known as Al-Qala'a al-Gabal (Citadel of the Mountain) or Al-Burg. ■ *Daily 0800-1700 in winter, 0800-1800 in summer (except 1130-1300 on Fri), E£20 for the mosque of Mohammed Ali Pasha and E£20 for the second section of the complex containing the mosque of Suleyman Pasha, the Carriage museum and the Seized museum. 50% student discount. Camera tickets E£10 and E£100 for video cameras. Tips should be reserved for guides in the museums but not the*

Police or Military museums. Entrance into the museums ends at 1530. Enter via *Bab al-Gabal*.

The Citadel was built by Salah al-Din (1171-1193) as part of a very ambitious general fortification plan which included enclosing the whole city with a new wall which could be controlled from the Citadel. The original fortress and remaining fortifications were strongly influenced by the architecture of castles built in Palestine and Syria by the Crusaders. It was built on a steep hill which stands 75 m high on the eastern side of the city. The work on the Citadel began in 1176 when pieces of demolished Fatimid mosques and tombs and blocks from the pyramids of Giza were incorporated in the defensive system. It was built in two walled enclosures, linked by their shortest walls, with the military area to the northeast and the residential quarters in the southwest. Every 100 m or so along the walls there is a tower connected to its neighbours by upper ramparts and by internal corridors that run the full circuit of the walls. The whole complex is still under military control and there are large areas which are closed to the public.

Later the Citadel was abandoned until the Mamlukes' arrival, when it became the Sultan's residence and the *Burji Mamlukes* (1382-1517) took their name from their base in the Citadel. In the 14th century Sultan al-Nasir Mohammed (1310-40) added a number of buildings including a mosque and later, because of the development of warfare and the use of canons, the Turks undertook major reinforcements. The most recent modification to the Citadel was by Mohammed Ali Pasha (1805-40) who built an impressive mosque on the site of the original palaces. Today the most interesting features of the Citadel are the **Mosque of Mohammed Ali Pasha**, which provides an amazing view west over Cairo and the restored **Sultan al-Nasir Mohammed Mosque**.

Walls, Towers and Gates The Ayyubid walls and towers (1176-83) around part of the Northern enclosure are from the time of Salah al-Din. The dressed stone walls are 10 m high and 3 m thick and 2,100 m in circumference interspersed with half-round towers. Some of the larger/later towers (1207) such as Burg at-Turfa which enclose parts of the wall were built by al-Kamir (nephew of Salah al-Din and the first Ayyubid sultan to live in the Citadel). **Bab al-Azab** enclosed by a pair of round headed towers stands on the west side of the Citadel. It was the original entrance to the Southern enclosure and is no longer open to the public. The brass bound wooden doors date from 1754.

Bab al-Qullah (16th century) connects the two separate parts of the Citadel. The original Mamluk gate was replaced after the Ottoman conquest and was widened in 1826 to allow Mohammed Ali's carriage to pass through. **Bab al-Gadid** (New Gate) was built in 1828 and is in reality a large tunnel with a vaulted ceiling. There are guard rooms on either side.

Burg as-Siba (Lion's Tower) was built in 1207 by the Mamluk Sultan Baybars. The frieze of stone lions, the sultans' heraldic symbol, gives it its name. **Burg al-Muqattam** (16th century) is the largest tower in the citadel, being over 25 m high and 24 m in diameter. The 7 m thick walls were built to withstand artillery attack.

Mosque of Mohammed Ali Pasha, Citadel

Not to scale

1 Main entrance
2 Entrance from courtyard
3 Domed turret
4 Octagonal minaret
5 Northeast arcade
6 Southwest arcade
7 Mihrab
8 Sahn
9 Ablutions fountain
10 Clock tower
11 Tomb of Mohammed Ali
12 Subsidiary mihrab
13 Minbar (1848)
14 Minbar (1939)
15 Cistern

The **Mosque of Mohammed Ali Pasha,** ■ *E£10, E£5 students,* was started in 1824 but only finished eight years after his death in 1857. The architecture was strongly influenced by the Ottoman mosques of Istanbul with the characteristic high, slender, octagonal minarets and an imposing dome which had to be rebuilt in the 1930s. The marble floored courtyard is very finely proportioned, with a beautiful central ablutions fountain. To the northwest is a small square tower for a clock which was a gift from King Louis-Philippe of France in 1846 in exchange for the obelisk now sited in Paris' Place de la Concorde, but the clock has never worked. The mosque is covered by a large dome with four half domes on each side. Once inside, it takes some time to become accustomed to the dim lighting. The white marbled tomb of Mohammed Ali is to the right after the entrance, behind a bronze grille. This mosque is unusual, having two *minbars.* The large wooden construction, carved, painted and gilded was installed by Mohammed Ali. It was too large to erect in the conventional space by the *mihrab* and was placed under the central dome making the weekly sermon inaudible to most of the congregation. In 1939 King Faruq installed a smaller alabaster minbar carved with a geometric pattern – to the right of the *mihrab.*

The **Sultan al-Nasir Mohammed Mosque** was built between 1318 and 1335. It is certainly the best preserved Mamluk building in the Citadel and is claimed to be one of the finest arcade-style mosques in Cairo, the arches being supported by pharaonic and classical columns plundered from elsewhere. The two distinctive minarets, one above each entrance, are covered in the upper part with green, blue and white ceramic tiles attributed to craftsmen from Persia as are the onion-shaped bulbs on the tops of the minarets. The magnificent marble which covered the floors and lined the walls to a height of 5 m was unfortunately removed on instructions of the Ottoman ruler Selim I. The *mihrab* is still in good condition.

The **Mosque of Suleyman Pasha** (1528), in the northern enclosure of the Citadel, was the first domed mosque to be built in Cairo during the Ottoman period and is believed to be dedicated to the janissary corp of soldiers of which Suleyman Pasha was earlier governor. It may have been designed by one of the architects sent to Cairo to repair the damage caused to the Citadel and the city walls by the Ahmed Pasha revolt.

The main entrance to the mosque is to the right of the minaret. Its stalactite portal leads not directly into the paved courtyard like most Ottoman mosques but into the prayer hall on its southwest side. This is due to its cramped position by the Citadel's walls. The minaret is typical of the style common in Istanbul, a tall slender cylinder with a conical top, but like the Mamluk minarets it has two galleries. Like the domes of the surrounding mosque and prayer hall the minaret's pointed cap is covered with green tiles which are similar to a number of Cairo's mosques of the period.

The mosque interior comprises a richly painted domed central area flanked on three sides by three supported semi-domes. The *sahn* is surrounded by a shallow-dome roofed arcade and in the northwest corner is the slightly larger dome of the mausoleum containing tombs of a number of janissaries.

Mosque of Suleyman Pasha, Citadel

Not to scale

1 Entrance
2 Domed central area
3 Sahn
4 Roofed arcade
5 Marble minbar
6 Mihrab
7 Mausoleum of
   Suleyman
8 Maq'Ad
9 Minaret

The Marabout

The landscape in western Egypt is dotted with white painted monuments scattered about the hillsides, hilltops and cemeteries. These are the burial places of the holy men or marabouts (marabit in Arabic) though the practice of adopting seers and ascetics is thought to have preceded the coming of Islam. The marabout was a religious teacher who gained credibility by gathering disciples around him and getting acknowledgement as a man of piety and good works. Marabouts were in many cases migrant preachers travelling to and from Mecca or were organizers of sufi schools. Place names of marabout sites are mainly after the names of the holy man interred there usually prefixed by the word `sidi'. Some sites are very modest, comprising a small raised tomb surrounded by a low wall, all whitewashed. Other marabouts have a higher tomb several metres square topped by a dome (koubba). In some instances, the tombs of saints, especially in Egypt, are large house-like structures acting as mausoleums and shrines. Most tombs in rural areas can carry stakes bearing flags in green cloth as symbols of the piety of their donors and as a token of the continuing protection provided by the marabout.

Annual processions or pilgrimages are made to the marabout shrines for good luck, fertility and protection against the evil spirits. This is particularly the case where the area around is occupied by a tribe claiming descent from the holy man in question.

Cairo

The frescoes on the walls were restored in the 19th century and it is uncertain how faithful they are to the original Ottoman decoration. The *mihrab* is situated under one of the half-domes. There was insufficient space here adjacent to the *mihrab* for the *minbar* which had to be placed under the central dome. The conical top of the marble *minbar*, is decorated with a Mamluk inspired geometric pattern based on the stars and polygon forms, similar to the Ottoman minarets.

The **Mosque of Ahmed Katkhuda al-Azab** was built in 1697, in Ottoman style on the site of an earlier mosque. The slender minaret stands tall above the ruins of the main building.

The **Carriage Museum** is in the dining hall used by British officers who were stationed in the Citadel and on display are eight carriages once used by the Egyptian royal family and some painted wooden horses. The **Military Museum** is situated in the **Harim Palace** built in 1827 as the private residence of Mohammed Ali. There are three extensive wings with many halls and side rooms all decorated in lavish style. King Farouk ordered its conversion into a museum which traces the history of the Egyptian army from pharaonic times to the present day. There are military uniforms, rifles and cannons on display. Tanks captured in the October 1973 conflict are in the courtyard. ■ *Daily 0900-1400 except Mon.* The **National Police Museum** has some strange and interesting exhibits of policing problems ranging from assassination attempts to protection of Egyptian antiquities. It is constructed on top of Burg as-Siba and the view from the terrace takes in the Pyramids on the left to the minaret of the Mosque al-Fath in Midan Ramses to the right. Absolutely breathtaking –

Citadel Museums
See Citadel map page 106

on a clear day. **Seized Museum**, ■ *E£40*, provides a very interesting hour. In two small rooms the exhibits, confiscated from dealers in the antiquities black-market, span the history of Egypt. The first room is set aside for Pharonic items including a painted wooden sarcophagus and funerary beads in excellent condition. The second room is cramped with an assortment of treasures, including a collection of Byzantine, Islamic and European gold coins, a small group of beautiful books in the Arabic script, seven stunning Coptic icons and a set of official seals from the reign of the Mohammed Ali.

Qasr al-Gawhara (Palace of Jewels) stands on the site of the palace of the Circassian Mamluk sultans. It was built in 1814 as the first of two palaces with French-style salons that Mohammed Ali built in the Citadel. It contains an impressive audience hall and guest rooms. Having been the residence of Egypt's rulers since the 12th century he predicted that his descendants would rule Egypt as long as they lived in the Citadel: sure enough, Ismail's move to the Abdin Palace foreshadowed the decline in their fortunes.

Today it is a museum with displays of portraits, costumes, furniture and ornaments which belonged to King Farouk. Much of this has neither beauty nor historical interest. The **Archaeological Garden Museum** in the Northern Enclosure contains an interesting collection of bits and pieces – monuments and statues – as well as welcome benches.

Joseph's Well named after Salah al-Din built in 1183 is also known as the well of the snail as there is an enclosed spiral staircase which leads down some 87 m through solid rock to the water level of the River Nile. There are two platforms where pumps operated by oxen raised the water which was then carried to the surface by donkeys. It is possible to go down, but take great care. It was built by Crusader prisoners and provided a secure supply of drinking water for

The Citadel

▲ **Gates & Towers**		
1 Bab al-Azab	11 Burg al-Imam (Imam's Tower)	19 Burg at-Turfa
2 Bab al-Gabal	12 Burg al-Matar (Flight Tower)	(Masterpiece Tower)
3 Bab al-Gadid	13 Burg al-Muballat	20 Burg Kirkilyan
4 Bab al-Mudarrag	(Paved Tower)	(Tower of the 40 Serpents)
5 Bab al-Qarafah	14 Burg al-Muqattam	21 Lion's Tower
6 Bab al-Qullah	15 Burg al-Muqusar	22 Tower of Muh 'Ali
7 Bab al-Wustani	(Concave Tower)	
8 Burg al-Wustani (Middle Tower)	16 Burg ar-Ramia (Sand Tower)	**🏛 Museums**
9 Burg al-Ahmar (Red Tower)	17 Burg as-Sahra (Desert Tower)	1 Qasr al-Gawhara
10 Burg al-Haddad	18 Burg as-Suffa	2 Carriage Museum
(Blacksmith's Tower)	(Alignment Tower)	3 Harim Palace Military Museum

4 National Police Museum	**🕌 Mosques**
5 Seized Museum	1 Ahmed Katkhuda al-Azab
6 Archaeological	2 Sultan al-Nasir
Garden Museum	Mohammed
	3 Mohammed Ali Pasha
	4 Suleyman Pasha

Related maps
Central Cairo, page 71

all of the Citadel. It is covered by a tower and stands just south of the Mosque of Sultan al-Nasir Mohammed.

Qasr al-Ablaq (Striped Palace) was built in 1315 by al-Nasr Mohammed for official receptions. Mohammed Ali Pasha had the building torn down but a remaining portion of outer wall shows it was constructed in alternating bands of black and yellow marble, hence the name.

From Midan Salah al-Din to the west of the Citadel and in front of the Sultan Hassan Mosque make your way west along Sharia Saliba. On the left is the second decorated **Sabil-Kuttab of Sultan Qaitbai** (1477) (**46**). This is another *sabil* and *medersa* but has, unusually, no connection to a larger religious foundation. Continue west past the small **Mosque of Qanibai al-Muhammadi** (**47**) to the imposing architectural buildings with matching minarets which face each other across the Sharia Saliba. On the right, north, is the **Mosque of Amir Shaykhu** (1349) (**48**) and on the left, south, the **Khanqah of Amir Shaykhu** (1355) (**49**). Amir Shaykhu was the Commander in Chief of the Mamluk army during the reign of Sultan Hassan. The *khanqah* had small cells for up to 70 sufis around the inner courtyard and in the northeast corner of the arcaded prayer hall is Amir Shaykhu's tomb. There is an option to turn left here and travel south down Sharia al Ashraf. After 500 m one reaches Midan Sayyidah Nafisah on the corner of which is the Gate of Ali Pasha Hakim. Turn left through here to the modern **Mosque of Sayyidah Nafisah** (**50**), one of the very few mosques closed to non-muslims. Sayyidah Nafisah was a direct descendant of the Prophet Mohammed. She was born in Mecca and came to Egypt with Imam Shafi where she settled in Cairo and lived on the site where this mosque now stands. She was known for her piety, her complete knowledge of the Quran and the more dubious fact that she dug her own grave. Large crowds gathered to receive her blessing and perhaps healing. She died in 824 and the first shrine over the tomb was constructed soon afterwards. The shrine has been rebuilt and enlarged many times, the present construction, the last of a series of tombs, which dates from 1893-7 was erected following a destructive fire.

Continue beyond the mosque entrance, turn right at the end of the covered passage and right again into the courtyard into the cemetery. Among the many tombs the one of note is the domed mausoleum in the centre, the mid-13th century square tomb of the Abbasid Caliphs.

The next turning left going south down Sharia al Ashraf is Sharia al Sayyidah Nafisah which leads to the Southern Cemetery (see page 115). Return to the main route turning west (right) at the cross roads, with the **Sabil-Kuttab of Um Abbas** (**51**) on the corner, passing the small but impressive **Mosque of Amir Taghri Bardi** (1440) (**52**) with a carved stone dome. While the external structure of this building follows the east-west line of Sharia Saliba the interior is aligned southeast to Mecca.

The largest mosque in Cairo and the oldest one which retains its original features is the **Mosque of Ahmed Ibn Tulun (53)** ■ *Daily 0900-1600, entrance fee E£6*, which is located about 15 minutes' walk west of the Citadel along Sharia Saliba on the way towards the river. Alternatively it can be reached from Midan Tahrir by bus No 72 or minibus No 54 which go to the Citadel via the Saiyida Zeinab area and then past the mosque. Although the Saiyida Zeinab metro station is only two stops from Midan Tahrir it is probably a 30 minutes' walk from there to the mosque.

West from the Citadel

See Islamic Cairo map page 82

Cairo

It was built between 876-879 by Ahmed Ibn Tulun, the son of a Turkish slave who became governor of Egypt but who then declared independence from the Baghdad-based Abbasid Khalifas. He thereby became the first of the Tulunids (AD 868-905), at the new town of Al-Qata'i (the Concessions or the Wards) northeast of Al-Askar which, in turn was northeast of Fustat, and near the foothills of the Muqattam Hills. When the Abbasids regained power in Egypt in AD 905 they destroyed much of the town except for the mosque which fell into decay until it was restored in 1296 by Sultan Langin who had hidden there after he was implicated in an assassination attempt against his predecessor.

The mosque was originally designed in 876 by a Syrian Jacobite Christian architect which probably explains the presence of many designs and motifs inspired by Coptic art. Legend says that the sycamore beams were brought from Mt Ararat and were part of Noah's ark. Despite the extensive restoration work by Sultan Lagin, apart from the addition of a minaret with an unusual outside spiral staircase which appears to be a copy of the one at Samarra in Iraq, no major changes were made. External measurements are 140 m by 122 m making it the largest place of worship in Cairo. The central courtyard is 92 m square yet despite its huge size, the overall impression is of harmony, simplicity and sobriety. The walls have been plastered but the ornamentation is sculpted and not moulded. **NB** The long Kufic script inscriptions, almost 2 km long, of about 20% of the Koran circle the mosque several times below the roof. The marble plated *mihrab* is surrounded by an elegant glass mosaic frieze. Directly above is a small wooden dome. The *minbar*, presented by Sultan Lagin in 1296, is a fine work of art. The view from the top over the surrounding area is excellent and worth the climb.

The **Gayer-Anderson Museum**, which is also called108 **Beit al-Kridliyah (54)** (House of the Cretan Woman), abuts the southeast corner of Ahmed Ibn Tulun's mosque and has its own entrance into the mosque precinct. ■ *0800-1700, Fri 0900-1100 and 1330-1530, E£16, E£8 for students, E£10 for cameras using the same ticket as for the Islamic museum, T3647827.* It is contained in two houses, the one on the west dating back to 1540 and the one to the east to 1631, on either side of a small alley called Atfat al-Gami which originally belonged to the Al-Kiridhi family. Originally one house was for men's accommodation *salamlik* and the other for women *haramlik*. The roof area was solely for the women who crossed from one building to the other by a small bridge on the second floor. A screened balcony *mashrabiyyah* which overlooks the large two-storey sitting room *qa'ah* with its marble floor and ornately tiled fountain permitted the women to see the male visitors and the entertainments without being seen themselves.

The houses were sold to the government which in 1934 gave them to Major Robert Gayer-Anderson (1881-1945), a retired doctor and member of the Egyptian Civil Service, when he expressed a desire in restoring them and refurnishing them with Ottoman furniture and fittings. A tour of the houses give a good insight into the decoration and organization of a house during the Ottoman rule. Each of the main rooms has a different theme, Damascus room, Persian room, Turkish room and Byzantine room. Other rooms include a library, a writing room and a display room for the Major's collection of pharaonic antiquities.

The Medersa and Tombs of Amirs Salar and Sangar al-Gawli (55). This was once a much larger set of buildings, even so the remaining tombs and the *medersa* indicate the original grandeur. The domes over the tombs are of different sizes, that to the east being the largest. The slender minaret immediately to the right of the entrance stands about 45 m high. The first storey is square, the second is octagonal and the third is cylindrical, culminating in a cornice of stalactites capped with a ribbed dome. The entrance is up the steps through a stalactite arch into a porch. Further steps lead to the vaulted corridor and to the tombs. The Tomb of Amir Salar, 7 m sq, is encircled by a wooden frieze and has a fine marble mihrab. Note the design of the windows in the dome. The adjacent Tomb of Amir Sangar is smaller at 6.5 m sq and is less ornate than its neighbour. Still further west is a third tomb called the Tomb of the Unknown Amir. Even smaller, at only 4.5 m sq, the unnamed occupant died in 1348. Turning east from the stairs leads to the mosque. The larger courtyard had small rooms for students (the grills over the doors need some explanation) and a smaller courtyard off which is the *mihrab*.

The area to the west of the giant mosque is known as **Sayyidah Zeinab** after the Prophet Mohammed's granddaughter Zeinab (AD 628-680) who settled in Fustat/Cairo in 679 with her five children and the son of her brother Hussein who was murdered at Karbala in the Sunni-Shi'a conflict. Because of her position as closest kinswoman to the martyred Ali and Hussein the area has become a site of pilgrimage for foreign Shi'a Muslims. This is focused on the mosque built and continuously rebuilt over her tomb which is located off Sharia Bur Said but is closed to non-Muslims. Her moulid (saint's day) between 13-27 Ragab (December 1994) attracts up to half a million revellers who come to watch the wild Sufi parades and evening festivities.

The **Cities of the Dead** is the name given by Europeans to Cairo's two main cemeteries which spread from the Citadel. The **Southern Cemetery** is older and spreads to the southeast but there are few monuments to see. The **Northern Cemetery**, which is known locally as Qarafat al-Sharqiyyah (the Eastern Cemetery) because it was east of the old city, is much more interesting and has been the burial place of the sultans since the 14th century. It contains a number of interesting mausoleums including those of Barquq and Qaitbai.

Route 3: The Cities of the Dead

Medersa & Tomb of Amirs Salar & Sangar al-Gawli

Not to scale

1 Entrance	7 Corridor to tombs
2 Domed tomb of Salar	8 Mihrab
3 Domed tomb of Sangar	9 Liwan
4 Tomb of unknown amir	10 Rooms for students
5 Porch	11 Small cemetery
6 Stairs up to roof	

Getting there

The easiest way to the Southern Cemetery from the Sultan Hassan and Ibn Tulun mosques, is to head south along Sharia el-Khalifa for about 1 km. The easiest way to the Northern cemetery is either by taking a taxi direct to Qarafat al-Sharqiyyah or by walking east along Sharia al-Azhar from the Al-Azhar mosque for about 15 mins until you reach the roundabout junction with the north-south dual carriageway of Sharia Salah Salem and then north for 250 m. Then cut into the cemetery and head for the dome and minaret which are clearly visible.

Warning This area is densely populated by Cairenes who live in or near the tombs. In Egypt there has long been a tradition of living close to the dead but the very large numbers are a relatively recent trend caused by an acute scarcity of housing. Consequently the people who live in the cemeteries tend to be comparatively poor and, although certainly not dangerous, it is obviously advisable not to flaunt your wealth, dress modestly and remember that this is where people live.

In the Northern Cemetery the **Mausoleum of Sultan al-Zahir Barquq** (1382-89 and 1390-99) was built over a 12 year period in 1398-1411 by his son Al-Nasir Farag (1399-1405 and 1405-12). It was the first royal tomb to be built in this modern necropolis after Barquq had expressed a wish to be buried alongside a number of pious Sufi sheikhs who were already buried there. Therefore his body was moved from the *medersa* on Sharia al-Muizzli Din Allah once the 75 sq m complex had been completed. It is square with two minarets symmetrically placed on the façade. The entrance in the southwest corner leads along a corridor to the *sahn* which has an octagonal fountain in the centre and is surrounded by four *liwans*. The north and south *liwans* have one aisle whereas the west has two, and the east, three. The east *liwan* has three very simple *mihrabs* and an extraordinarily finely sculpted stone *minbar*. Doors lead from either side of the *liwan* into mausoleums. The north mausoleum contains Barquq's own marble cenotaph which is richly decorated with Koranic inscriptions, together with the tombs of an unknown person and another intended for Farag whose body was left in Damascus after he had been assassinated on a military campaign in Syria. The mausoleum to the south holds the tombs of Barquq's wife and two granddaughters.

A little to the south is the **Medersa & Mausoleum of Sultan al-Qaitbai Mosque** (1468-96), built in 1472-74, which is a magnificent example of 15th century Arab art and possibly one of Egypt's most remarkable monuments from the Arab era. From the outside the building has very harmonious proportions with the dome finely decorated with polygonal motifs. The minaret is also remarkable because it has a square base, octagonal middle section and a cylindrical top tier. The mosque is reached by climbing 17 steps to the entrance which leads into the southeast *liwan*. The cruciform *medersa* has side *liwans*, and a relatively small covered *sahn* with an octagonal roof lantern. The superbly decorated coloured

Northern Cemetery

marble floors are somewhat damaged but still attractive. The *liwans* are very narrow but the east *liwan*, which has a modern ceiling, still has a very well preserved and finely encrusted *minbar*. A door in the south corner of the *qibla liwan* leads to the mausoleum which is decorated with the same sort of marbles as the *medersa*. Its high dome is simply decorated, in contrast with the highly ornate walls. Sultan Qaitbai's tomb is enclosed behind an elaborate wooden *mashrabiyya* while the other tomb is that of one of his sisters.

Contemporary Cairo

Contemporary Cairo has developed further west on both sides of the river into a modern and increasingly Europeanized capital. Although residential suburbs spread outwards in all directions any visit to Cairo should include the **Egyptian Museum**, the **Museum of Islamic Art**, the **Manial Palace** on Roda Island and, provided it is a clear day without too much pollution haze, the **Cairo Tower** on Gezira Island.

The Egyptian museum

The Egyptian Museum (called in Arabic **el-Mathaf el Misri** and sometimes, albeit mistakenly, referred to as The Cairo Museum) rates as one of the wonders of the country. Its most famous exhibits are the world-renowned and spectacular Tutankhamen displays. It has an enormous wealth of materials covering early history, ancient Egypt and the Islamic period which is unrivalled even in the grand museums of Berlin, London, New York and Paris. For tourists and scholars alike, the museum is a must if only for a few hours.

The museum is situated in the centre of Cairo taking up the north side of Midan el-Tahrir. Entry is from the sculpture garden fronting the building. The museum is worth visiting either early in the day or during the late afternoon since at other times it is taken over by coach parties. The Tutankhamen exhibit is particularly in demand and it might be necessary to queue for entry. ■ *Daily 0900-1645, Fri 0900-1115, 1330-1600, (Ramadan closes at 1500). From time to time rooms are closed for repair, decoration and for setting up new exhibitions. Similarly there are changes in the lay-out of exhibits. Tickets cost E£20, E£10 for students. Cameras E£10, E£100 amateur videos, no flash photography. There is an additional fee of E£40 (students E£20), for the Royal Mummy Room, reopened in March 1991. Not recommended except for specialists. It is worth buying a detailed guide to the rooms (E£5), where the layout of displays can change from time to time (but also see plan of Egyptian Museum in this Handbook). There is a souvenir shop outside of the Museum on the right of the entrance and an official sales area on the left inside the main building. Café and restaurant facilities are available on the first floor. T5754319.*

The new museum was set up and opened in 1902, the brainchild of Francois Auguste Ferdinand Mariette (1821-81), a Frenchman who was a distant relation of Champollion, the decipherer of Egyptian hieroglyphic writing. He was a great scholar of Egyptology who excavated widely in Egypt throughout the second half of the 19th century. He won the confidence of the crown prince Sa'id Pasha proposing greater preservation of monuments and artefacts and more controls on the export of antiquities. Mariette was appointed to oversee all excavations in Egypt through the Egyptian Antiquities Service and also took responsibility for the setting up of the museum of antiquities. His reign was not without its upsets since he quarrelled violently both with Egyptian officialdom and with rival archaeologists but he was successful in creating the present museum which was specially designed to house the Egyptian national collection. It remains well planned for its age and a great treasure house of objects. There are hopes of a new purpose-built museum to be established, possibly at Giza to overcome the complaint that the present rooms are inadequate to handle exhibits in a satisfactory way and that too many major objects are never seen by the public.

A visit to the museum begins in the sculpture garden, where there is a statue and tomb of Auguste Mariette, a number of sphinx-headed statues and a sarcophagus. The main museum building has two floors, both with 51 principal exhibition rooms. Circulate from the entrance in a clockwise direction. The exhibits are distributed in a generally chronological order beginning in the hallway (Room 48-GF). **NB** GF = Ground Floor; UF = Upper Floor rooms. Rooms and galleries are both included as 'Rooms'.

The museum is fairly large and for a full initial viewing of both floors and all rooms needs some four hours. A shortened tour is recommended for those with only two hours to spend in the museum, with a circuit of the ground floor followed by a visit to the Tutankhamen Gallery in rooms on the upper floor. If there is scope for a 1-hr visit then the entrance hall (Room 43-GF) and the Tutankhamen galleries, though bear in mind that there can be queues/congestion in this area, especially in Room 3-UF where the principal treasures are stored.

Egyptian Museum - ground floor

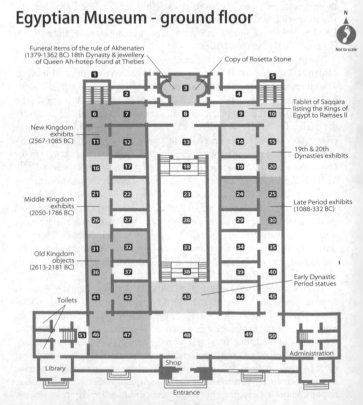

N
Not to scale

Funeral items of the rule of Akhenaten (1379-1362 BC) 18th Dynasty & jewellery of Queen Ah-hotep found at Thebes

Copy of Rosetta Stone

Tablet of Saqqara listing the Kings of Egypt to Ramses II

New Kingdom exhibits (2567-1085 BC)

19th & 20th Dynasties exhibits

Middle Kingdom exhibits (2050-1786 BC)

Late Period exhibits (1088-332 BC)

Old Kingdom objects (2613-2181 BC)

Early Dynastic Period statues

Toilets

Library

Shop

Administration

Entrance

The museum also has many other individual objects of great distinction on display. The guide that follows is no more than a check list of items than those in the collections above in this museum's rich holding of objects. In the entrance room (48-GF, display unnumbered) is a cast of the Rosetta Stone, from which Frenchman Jean-Francois Champollion decoded the hieroglyphic writing of ancient Egypt. The original is in the British Museum. In the same room are recent additions to the museum's collection out of chronological sequence. Room 43-GF holds a number of Early Dynastic period statues. Old Kingdom (2613-2181 BC) objects take up GF Rooms 47, 46, 41, 42, 36, 31 and 32. In Room 42-GF there is a notable standing wooden statue of the priest Ka-aper and a statue of King Chephren, one of the builders of the Giza pyramids. There is also a painted stone statue of a Fifth Dynasty scribe, cross legged on a plinth. In Room 32-GF, display 39, is a painted effigy of Seneb the dwarf and his family. He was a keeper of the royal wardrobe in the fifth Dynasty. A well sculptured painted statue of Ti, a noble of the same period and other figures such as Prince Ra-hoptep and his wife Nofert are also to be found in Rooms 32 and 31-GF (display 27).

The Middle Kingdom period (BC 2050-1786) is represented in Rooms 26, 21, 22 and 16-GF. The painted statue of King Menutuhotep is in Room 26-GF (display 67). It was found at Bahr el Bahari and is 11th Dynasty. Room 26-GF also houses a series of sarcophagi of painted limestone from this period. In particular see the Sarcophagus of Dagi (display 71), a tomb beautifully illustrating objects in everyday use such as sandals and linen items together with hieroglyphs of magic spells and offerings. King Senusert

Touring the museum

Cairo

Egyptian Museum - upper floor

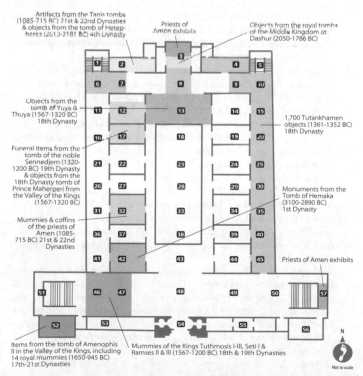

Artifacts from the Tanis tombs (1085-715 BC) 21st & 22nd Dynasties & objects from the tomb of Hetepheres (2613-2181 BC) 4th Dynasty

Priests of Amen exhibits

Objects from the royal tombs of the Middle Kingdom at Dashur (2050-1786 BC)

Objects from the tomb of Yuya & Thuya (1567-1320 BC) 18th Dynasty

1,700 Tutankhamen objects (1361-1352 BC) 18th Dynasty

Funeral items from the tomb of the noble Sennedjem (1320-1200 BC) 19th Dynasty & objects from the 18th Dynasty tomb of Prince Maherperi from the Valley of the Kings (1567-1320 BC)

Monuments from the Tomb of Hemaka (3100-2890 BC) 1st Dynasty

Mummies & coffins of the priests of Amen (1085-715 BC) 21st & 22nd Dynasties

Priests of Amen exhibits

Items from the tomb of Amenophis II in the Valley of the Kings, including 14 royal mummies (1650-945 BC) 17th-21st Dynasties

Mummies of the Kings Tuthmosis I-III, Seti I & Ramses II & III (1567-1200 BC) 18th & 19th Dynasties

N

Not to scale

I (Sesostris) is depicted in 10 limestone statues in Room 22-GF though these are outshone for visual impact by the 56 cm wooden statuette of Senusert I (display 88) carrying sceptres in both hands to denote his royal authority. A granite statue of Amenemhat III is occasionally on show in the same room (display 105) and there are a double statue of that king as the Nile god (display 104) and several sphinxes of the same provenance in Room 16-GF (display 102). The four sphinxes are in grey granite and come from the find by Auguste Mariette at Tanis.

The New Kingdom ran from BC 2567-1085. The exhibits in the set of galleries 11, 12, 6 and 7 are mainly from the 18th Dynasty, with more complex garments and headgear than in previous eras. Room 12-GF is well endowed with notable objects, mainly statues in granite. Most important are the statues of Senenmut, steward of Queen Hatshepsut and tutor to her daughter. He was responsible for designing the temple of Hatshepsut at Deir el-Bahari. The examples here in Room 12-GF include his block statue (display 132) with his pupil, Princess Neferure, peering below his chin. The plaque carries inscriptions of his titles and merits. Queen Hatshepsut is seen in a variety of statues (Room 12-GF, display 952) and in the remnants of her red sandstone sarcophagus (Room 28-GF, display 131), while there is a variety of statues of Tuthmosis III and Isis, his mother. Hatshepsut is represented in a large restored statue in Room 7-GF.

Room 3-GF is given over to objects from the reign of Akhenaten (Amenhotep IV), who set up his capital at Tell el-Amarna (North of Assiut) and altered the mode of public art and architecture in Egypt to one of realism. There are sandstone statues of Amenhotep IV, of which the presentation of an offering tablet (display 160) is perhaps the most interesting, and a gilded coffin lid of Amenhotep's brother, Smenkhkara. Several heads of women are on display in Room 3-GF, with the unfinished head of Nefertiti (display 161) being the most famous, and the head of a princess (display 163) most exquisitely portrayed. Representations of the 'royal family' in the form of what seems to be a shrine (display 167) are also on show.

The central hall of the museum (Rooms 13, 18, 23, 28, 33 and 38-GF) is used to exhibit giant statues of a mixture of periods. As an example, it is worth while to look at the 7 m statue of Amenhotep III and his wife Tyi (display 610).

Objects of the 19th and 20th Dynasties are displayed in Rooms 9, 10, 15, 14 and 20-GF. Room 9-GF contains the Tablet of Saqqara (display 660), which lists the kings of Egypt to Ramses II. The crystalline limestone head of General Nakhtmin (display 195) is in Room 15-GF and shows fine workmanship. The painted bust of Meritamoun, daughter of Ramses II and queen in succession to Nefertari, when available, is also in Room 15-GF.

Best of the Late Period (BC 1085-332) is concentrated in Rooms 25, 24 and 30-GF. Key items include the Psametik group of statues in greenstone of which those of the Psametik, a head jeweller, with Hathor (display 857) and of Isis, wife of Osiris (display 856), are particularly well executed. A statue of Princess Amenartais in alabaster (display 930 in Room 30-GF) is a beautiful example of 25th Dynasty sculpture.

The pride of the museum is contained in the Tutankhamen collection of the 18th Dynasty (years 1361-52) in rooms 3, 4, 6, 7, 8, 9, 10, 15, 20, 25, 30, 35, 40 and 45-UF with 1,700 objects on exhibition. This remarkable treasure was found intact by the Englishman Howard Carter in 1922 in the Valley of the Kings. Tutankhamen ruled for only nine years between the ages of 9-18. His tomb was saved from heavy destruction grave robbers by its position low in the valley and by the construction of workmens' huts across its entrance. Unlike most other archaeological finds before 1922, the

Muslim cemeteries

One of the lasting monuments in Islam is the qarafah or graveyard. All are different, ranging from undefined rocky areas near villages, where unnamed head and foot stones are barely distinguishable from the deserts surrounding them, to the elaborate necropoli of Cairo, where veritable cities of the dead are established. In all cemeteries bodies are interred with head towards the qibla – Mecca.

In Egypt, graveyards often contain a series of simple whitewashed mud brick tombs of holy men or marabouts (see box page 105), around which his disciples and their descendants are laid. More grandly in Cairo at the City of the Dead is the Eastern Cemetery, known as the Tombs of the Mamlukes (see page 109), a set of Muslim grave yards, developed particularly from the 15th century. It contains large numbers of notable tombs, most important of which is the Tomb of Sultan al-Zahir Barquq. A second and even more elaborate cemetery is Cairo's Southern Cemetery, situated close to the Citadel. This ancient graveyard includes a number of the earliest examples of Muslim funerary architecture in Egypt and is home to the Tomb of the Imam Shafa'i, the most significant mausoleum in Cairo. The Imam Shafu'i was born in Palestine in 767 and was the originator of the Shafi'ite School of Islamic jurisprudence, one of the four great Sunni Schools of Law. The Imam ash-Shafa'i spent his last years (until his death in 820) in Fustat in Cairo. Salah al-Din set up the Shafa'i Mosque in 1180, which included the Imam's new tomb. Although subject to numerous subsequent reconstructions, of which the last was under the Khedive Tawfiq in 1891, the tomb is in an adequate state of repair to justify a visit. The large Shafa'i complex takes in a mosque, a ceremonial gateway and the mausoleum itself. The tomb is simple but decorated at various times with silver and paintings. The mausoleum has some fine beams and a wooden cupola together with much of the original inscriptions and ornamentation undertaken by Salah al-Din's builders. Shafa'i's tomb lies to the north of the building. Its religious focus is a delicate 20th century sandalwood screen or maqsurah and a marble stela. These are kissed by visiting Muslims as a sign of faith. Also entombed at the site are Mohammed abd al-Hakim and Princess Adiliyyah, the mother of Sultan al-Kamel, while the Sultan Kamel Ayyub himself (interred elsewhere) is commemorated by an uninscribed tomb in the south of the chamber. A walk along Sharia Sidi Uqbah and Sharia Imam Shafa'i will take the visitor past a wide variety of funerary constructions, many in a sad state of decay. Also visit the al-Basha Housh ('house') which backs on to the Shafa'i tomb on a parallel road (Shariyah Imam al-Lais) to the west. This is the family mausoleum of the family of Mohammed Ali Pasha in a set of pavilions of 19th century origin.

Muslim graveyards have no flowers unless they grow wild and by chance. Instead of buying flowers to decorate family graves on their routine weekly visit, relatives will often give a simple dish to the poor to provide a meal for their children.

Death and funerals are times for noisy outbreaks of wailing and crying. In traditional families, the approach of a person's death is signified by wailing, increased on actual death by the addition of the mourning neighbours and relatives. Occasionally in villages the body is laid in a large room where funeral dances are performed by wailing women, singing the praises of the deceased. Corpses are washed and wrapped in a simple shroud for interment. Mourners follow the cortege to the cemetery often in large crowds since every person who walks 40 paces in the procession has one sin remitted. At the grave side a shedda or declaration of Islamic faith is recited. Urban funerals are more ornate than those in the country districts and the passing of public figures is often accompanied by some pomp.

Cairo

Tutankhamen treasure was retained in Egypt and its full glory can be seen in the Egyptian Museum. All the exhibits have their own value both decorative and academic. Visitors are recommended to look at the entire set of Tutankhamen displays. If time is very short at least look at the following items: (1) **Colossal statue of Tutankhamen** (Room 9-UF, display 173). This is executed in painted quartzite which shows Tutankhamen as a youth and complete with ceremonial beard and hieroglyphs of Horemheb who stole the statue for his own tomb; (2) **The gold mask of Tutankhamen** (Room 4-UF, display 174). The mask is made of gold garnished with carnelian, coloured glass, lapis lazuli, obsidian, quartz, and turquoise. The 54 cm high figure came from the head of the mummy. The blue stripes are in lapis lazuli, there is a ceremonial beard and a head-dress knotted at the back of the neck. There is a gold ureaus and vulture head above the brow; (3) **The gold coffin of Tutankhamen** (Room 4-UF, display 175). This is rendered in gold and semi-precious stones with coloured glass. It is the inner of three coffins, the outer two made in wood. Some 187.5 cm long and weighing 110.4 kg, the coffin is in the form of a mummy in the shape of Osiris with the crossed arms carrying divine emblems. The body is covered by carved feathers and the representations of Upper and Lower Egypt – the vulture and cobra; (4) **Lid of canopic jar** (Room 8/9-UF, display 92), **The goddess Selket** with **The golden shrine** (Room 8/9-UF, display 177). This group of objects includes a wooden shrine gilded with gold and with silver which was in the antechamber of the king's tomb. It is ornately decorated with family and hunting scenes. The jar lid, containing the remains of the king's entrails, is of alabaster, carrying the king's image and lightly painted. There were four Canopic jars as miniature sarcophagi in the tomb. The golden shrine was protected by four goddesses, of which Seket, the water goddess, is displayed in gilded and painted wood about 90 cm high; (5) **Wooden funerary bed** (Room 9/10-UF, display 183). Made of stuccoed wood, these three funerary beds gilded and painted. The most remarkable is the couch in the image of the primordial cow with cow's heads and lyre-like horns set about sun disks; (6) **The Throne of Tutankhamen** (Room 25-UF, display 179). The throne is 102 cm high and 54 cm wide, made of gilded wood and ornamented with semi-precious stones. In addition to the winged serpent arms of the throne, the seat back carries a gilded and painted scene in which Tutankhamen's wife anoints him with oil; (7) **Ceremonial chair** (Room 25-UF, display 181). The finely inlaid ebony and ivory chair of Tutankhamen is regarded as among the best examples of Egyptian cabinet-making ever found. It is decorated with uraeus snakes and divinities; (8) **Funerary statues 'shawabti'** (Room 35-UF, display 182). The tomb of Tutankhamen contained 413 small, approximately 50 cm high, figures of the king as workers, foremen and overseers, giving one workman per day of the

Southern Cemetery

Midan Salah al-Din
Sh Tariq Salah Salem
Turban al-Sultaniyyah
Mohammed Ali Fort
Tomb of Tankizbugha
Tomb of Zain al-Din Yussef
Sh imam ash-Shafa'i
Sh Sa'd
Sh al-Farisi
Sh Muwasalah
Sh al-Kurdi
Sh imam al-Lais
Housh al-Basha
Tomb of Imam ash-Shafa'i
Sh Kamel
Sh imam al-Lais
Sh Sidi Uqbah
Tomb of Imam al-Lais
N
Tomb & Mosque of Sidi Uqbah

Related map Central Cairo, page 71

Not to scale

Egyptian antiquities in Paris

Every serious student of Egyptology undertakes a course of study, before travel, from libraries or at museums. Most visitors from Europe have the benefit of proximity to a wide range of high calibre artefacts in their homeland. The most recent collection to come to the eyes of the public is in the Louvre which until now has had insufficient room to display its very numerous high quality possessions. Egyptian antiquities are the centre piece of the newly opened extension there where an amazing 30 rooms and galleries on

three floors display over 6,000 objects ranging from minute scarabs to monumental sphinxes. This is just over 10% of the full collection. When, if ever, will the rest be displayed? The curators have done a fine job of balancing the needs of the casual viewer with that of the serious specialist with both thematic galleries and dynastic chronological displays, as best suit the materials and hopefully the visitor. If the opportunity arises for a visit here or to the British Museum in London or the Egyptian Museum in Turin – take it.

year. They are made of wood, which is painted and gilded; (9) **Tutankhamen with a harpoon** (Room 35-UF, display 182). Among the seven royal statuettes found in the tomb of Tutankhamen, the two gilded wooden statues of Tutankhamen hunting in gallery 35 are most pleasing. One shows the king on a papyrus board hunting in the marshes, harpoon in hand. A second is of the king wearing the crown of Upper Egypt riding the back of a panther. (10) **Painted chest** (Room 40-UF, display 186). This is a 44 cm tall/61 cm wide wooden chest, stuccoed with paintwork above. It is in a good state of preservation and carries pictures of battle against Asians and Africans and a set of hunting scenes; (11) **Anubis chest** (Room 45-UF, display 185). A carrying chest made in stuccoed wood and ornamented with black resin, gold, silver and varnish. The chest itself contained jewellery, cups and amulets. Anubis as a jackal sits on the chest ready to act as a guide for Tutankhamen in the after-world; (12) **Ka statue of Tutankhamen** (Room 45-UF, display 180). This large (192 cm tall) statue is one of two guardians of the tomb. It is made in wood and painted in bitumen. The king holds a mace in his right hand and a staff in his left. He is wearing a **khat** head-dress and has a gilded kilt.

On leaving the Tutankhamen galleries there is much still to see in the museum, including jewellery and monuments. Important objects include the wonderful 25-piece collection of **Meketra's models**, in fact models found in the tomb of Meketra, a noble of the Middle Kingdom (2000 BC), at a site south of Deir el-Bahari.

The miniatures show the form, dress, crops, vessels and crafts of the period. The best known is the offerings bearer (display 74), 123 cm high and made of painted wood. It shows a servant, carrying a basket of vases on her head and a duck in her right hand. There are also models of fishermen, cattle, weavers and carpenters in displays 75, 76, 77 and 78, respectively. In Room 32 (display 117) is a **Ka statue of King Auib-re Hor** in wood now bereft of its stucco coating. The head-dress of up-raised arms symbolizes **ka**, the vital force of the king.

Worth looking out for if you have time are the **Fayoum portraits** in Room 141-UF for the most part encaustic (wax) painted in wooden bases and painted by Greek artists in the second century AD to leave a likeness of the deceased for his family. (See page 168.)

The Museum of Islamic Art

It contains the rarest and most extensive collection of Islamic works of art in the world. ■ *Daily Sat-Thu 0900-1600, Fri 0900-1100 and 1330-1600, E£16, students E£8, ticket is also valid for Gayer-Anderson House – see above. Guides available. T3901520.* It is ideally located on the junction of Sharia Port Said and Sharia Qalaa about equidistant between Midan Ataba and the Bab el-Zoueila.

It was originally established in the courtyard of the Al-Hakim Mosque (see above) in 1880 but it was moved to the present building, containing over 75,000 exhibits from various Islamic periods, in 1903. The dates indicated in the museum's exhibits are AH (After the Hegira), which is the starting point of the Islamic Calendar in AD 622 when Mohammed is thought to have fled from Mecca. The rooms follow a chronological order through from the Umayyads to the Abbasids, Fatimids, Ayyubids, Mamlukes and Ottomans. Of particular interest are **Room 1** which contains recent discoveries like the very long papyrus over in the right hand corner; **Room 2** is the beginning of the Umayyad collection, considered the first true Islamic period with the first pieces of Islamic coinage in bronze and gold; **The Fatimid panels** in **Room 4** which depict animals and birds because, unlike the Sunni Muslims, the Fatimid Shi'a have no objection to portraying living things; the doors to **Room 6** which were originally from the Al-Azhar Mosque; the reconstruction of an 18th century Ottoman patio in **Room 10**; the Mamluke astrolabe used by Muslim navigators in **Room 11**; just before leaving **Room 13** on the right the 10th century 'Fayoumi' plate in Chinese style; **Room 20** Persian carpets; the glassware in **Room 21** and the Persian art in **Room 22**. The oil lamps from the mosque of Sultan Hathor, considered one of the most beautiful exhibits in the museum, are in a central case in **Room 21**. Take

Museum of Islamic Art

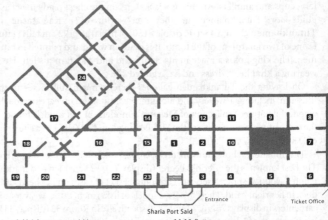

Sharia Port Said

Entrance

Ticket Office

1 Mainly recent acquisitions
2 Ommayyad (7-8th century) - mainly from Fustat
3 Abbasid (8-10th century) - stucco pannels
4 Fatimid (10-12th century) - panels depicting living things
5 Mamluk (13-16th century) - woodwork & ceramics
6-10 Woodworking in chronological order
11 Chandeliers & other metalwork
12 Armour & weapons
13 A mixture - a room not to miss

14-16 Pottery
17 Upstairs from garden - textiles & carpets
18 Outdoors - Turkish headstones/tombs/sundial
19 Books & manuscripts - a changing exhibition
20 Turkish art - wall hangings, china & jewellery
21 Glass - lamps from mosques arranged in chronological order
22 Persian exhibition - mainly pottery
23 Temporary exhibitions
24 Library

refreshment in the shaded garden by a fountain moved from Roda Island and marble panels with Fatimid reliefs. Sometimes the exhibits are not illuminated, ask the custodian to turn on the light for you but do not tip him.

No smoke without fire

Long renowned for its exotic cigarettes, Egypt does not actually grow its own tobacco. In fact growing tobacco is illegal.

Other museums

■ *Note that most museums are closed at midday prayer time on Fri, 1130-1330.*

Abdin Presidential Palace Museum This imposing building completed in 1872 became the official royal residence until 1952. For the previous 700 years the Citadel had housed the rulers. It is situated just east of Midan el Gumhurriya with the entrance in Sharia Mustafa Abd el Raziq. ■ *Daily 0900-1500 except Fri, E£10, students E£2. No cameras permitted.*

The rooms of the actual palace are not for viewing but 21 halls contain exhibits.

The first section, President Mubarak's Hall, contains a selection of the gifts he received – a varied collection of medals, portraits, clocks and plaques. The second section is of silverware, porcelain and crystal owned by the descendants of Mohammed Ali Pasha, indicating a very luxurious lifestyle. Who lifted the 125 kg silver tray when it was laden?

The Military Museum takes up 13 of the halls in the same building displaying weapons, suits of armour, as well as unusual items such as Rommel's dagger and two guns belonging to Napoleon Bonaparte. In the courtyard is a shrine to Sidi Badran.

Agricultural Museum It is adjacent to the Ministry of Agriculture in Dokki at end of 6th October Bridge. Oldest agricultural museum in world, stuffed animals, Egyptian farming practices. Here the artifacts are placed in context, the flax plant beside the linen, the papyrus plant beside the rope and paper. The many animals that were worshipped, hunted or eaten – cats, ostrich, Apis bulls and falcons are there as mummies or skeletons. Unfortunately the labels, in a variety of languages, give little information and often there are no labels at all. ■ *Daily 0900-1330, closed Mon, 10 piastres, T3614999, F3607881.*

Cotton Museum Next to Agricultural Museum, survey of cotton growing in Egypt. ■ *0900-1400, closed Mon and Fri afternoon, free.*

Entomological Museum It houses an old (it was founded by King Fuad) but interesting collection of Egyptian birds and insects and is very useful if you could not name what you saw, what ate your crops or what bit you. ■ *Daily 0900-1300 except Fri and 1800-2100 Mon, Wed and Sat. 14 Sharia Ramses near the railway station.*

Ethnological Museum This stands at 109 Sharia Qasr el Aini, just south of Midan Tahrir. Here in this small, neat museum are displays of village crafts, costumes and everyday utensils as well as details of farming and water control. ■ *Daily 0930-1400 except Fri. T3545450.*

Mahmoud Khalil Museum Giza has his collection of impressionist paintings and some fine sculptures. ■ *Daily 1000-1730, closed Mon, E£25, T3362378. 1 Sharia Kafour.*

Cairo

Cairo

 Never smile at a crocodile

Here in the Ancient Egyptian Agricultural Museum the 5 m long crocodile complete with wicked grin is fortunately very dead as are the many other animals here on display. A dog lies on its side, prostrate, seemingly sleeping in the sun and a baboon sits back resting on its haunches, huge hands hanging over its knees. Collected here are the animals worshipped, pampered, hunted and husbanded by the Ancient Egyptians: fat cats, even fatter Apis bulls, domesticated sheep and horses; birds ranging is size from the falcon and duck to the ostrich and fleet of foot gazelles and the venerated ibis. The animals depicted in hunting scenes on countless reliefs and tomb paintings have not, fortunately, come to life, but their skeletal and mummified remains are on display.

The **Manial Palace** on Roda Island in the middle of the Nile is an oasis of tranquillity in noisy Cairo and is well worth visiting. ■ *Daily 0900-1600, E£5 for foreigners, E£2.50 for students. Fee for normal cameras E£10, video cameras, E£100.*

The palace, which was built in 1903 and is now a museum, was the home of King Farouk's uncle Prince Mohammed Ali and comprises a number of buildings in various styles including Moorish, Ottoman, Persian, Rococo and Syrian. The first is the Reception Palace at the gate which is beautifully decorated with polychrome tiles and stained glass. Upstairs are a number of luxurious rooms, of which the Syrian Room is the finest, and a mother-of-pearl scale model of Sultan Qaitbai's mausoleum. To the right is a mosque with a tall mock Moroccan minaret and then a revolting Trophies Museum with tatty and poorly stuffed animals including a hermaphrodite goat and a table made of elephant's ears. Much more interesting is the royal residence in the middle of the garden which is a mixture of Turkish, Moroccan, Egyptian and Syrian architectures and contains a number of rooms, nearly all of which are decorated with blue earthenware tiles. The Throne Hall behind the residence is of little interest but the Private Museum, which includes a very varied collection of Korans, manuscripts, carpets, plates and glassware, is fascinating.

Mustafa Kamel Museum Midan Salah el-Din, has the tomb and personal belongings of this nationalist and leader. ■ *Daily 0900-1500. T5109943.*

National Museum of Egyptian Modern Art Gezirah Exhibition grounds, Zamalek: Works date back to early 20th century and exhibitions are changed regularly. ■ *Daily 1000-1300 and 1700-2100. Closed Mon.*

New Egyptian Museum. The foundation stone was laid in Jan 2000 on a site of 600,000 sq m on the outskirts of the city. Costing an estimated US$400 mn it will be the world's largest historical gallery – to display the hundreds of priceless monuments that now lie gathering dust in the store rooms of the existing museum in Cairo– due to lack of space.

Post Office Museum, Midan El-Ataba, second floor in main post office building. Here there are displays of memorial stamps and illustrations of the ways in which the post was transported. ■ *Daily 0900-1300 except Fri, free.*

Railway Museum, next to Ramses station, automated display, coaches for Khediv Ismail's private train. ■ *Daily 0830-1300, closed Mon, E£1.50, Fri E£3.*

See also *Coptic Museum* page 76, *Gayer-Anderson Museum* page 108, *Carriage Museum* page 105.

Having been satiated with mosques, mausoleums and museums it is probably worth visiting the top of **Cairo Tower** to get a bird's eye view of the city before treating yourself to a relaxing mini-cruise along the Nile and away from the noisy traffic. The 87 m tower ■ *daily 0900-2400, E£14*, is located on Gezira Island and its lotus-shaped top is one of the city's most visible landmarks. It was built with Soviet help in 1957-62. Although the restaurant and cafeteria are OK it is the viewing platform that is most important. Providing the pollution is not too bad, which it often is, you can look east across the modern city centre to the minarets and mosques of Islamic Cairo and the Muqattam Hills beyond; west beyond the residential areas to the Pyramids and the edge of the desert; north towards Zamalek and beyond; or south upstream to Roda Island and the original pre-Coptic settlement of Babylon in Egypt where this teeming mega-city first began almost 2,000 years ago.

Dr Ragab's Papyrus Institute is in a boat moored alongside Cornich el-Nil opposite *Cairo Sheraton*. The museum displays the processes involved in the making of papyrus. It is possible to purchase copies of illustrations and writing on papyrus found in tombs. ■ *Daily 0900-2100, E£4.*

Other places to visit

Dr Ragab's Pharaonic Village is more fun than culture, a great place, especially for those with children. It is located on Jacob Island 3 km south of the city centre. Numerous actors perform the daily activities of the ancient Egyptians. It gives background to the main sites and as the pace is set by the boat tour through the village on the bullrush-fringed Nile allow at least two hours. Avoid February when the boat does not run as the river is too low and the journey then is on foot. ■ *Daily 0900-1700 in winter and until 2100 in summer, E£40.*

Nilometer on southern tip of Roda island, originally built in 9th century BC, stands in a small kiosk. There has probably been a nilometer here since ancient times but this was constructed in AD 861. The original measuring guage remains today.

October War Display This illustrates the October 1973 War with the crossing of the Suez Canal and the attack on the Bar-Lev line, the air battle led by the Egyptian Air Force and an almost life-size painted scene of the battle to take Qantara. The commentary is in Arabic. ■ *Daily except Tue. Shows at 0930, 1000, 1230, 1800 and 1930, E£10. Junction of Sharia Oruba and Ismail el-Fangari, Heliopolis.*

Rare Books and Special Collections Library Definitely for the specialist. ■ *0800-1700. Closed Fri and Sat and all Aug. 22 Sharia Sheikh Rihan.*

Gardens

There are several spacious gardens for the visitor to find some tranquillity away from the city bustle. These include the **Zoological Gardens** in Giza, The **Fish Gardens** in Zamalek with several large aquaria, ■ *Daily 0900-1530.* The **Japanese Gardens** in Helwan, the **Meryland Gardens** in Heliopolis, the **International Garden** in Nasr City and the **Kanater al-Khaireya Gardens** (the Good Barrage) about 25 km from the capital. Unfortunately at present there are a number of open spaces which need more attention and others which have been closed down (**Andalusian Garden** closed since 1987) as they are being worn away by too much public use! Perhaps a charge will have to be made for entry to pay towards upkeep. The **River Nile Promenade**, constructed at huge expense and opened in 1996, has also been closed to protect it from the wear and tear.

Manial Palace Garden. After years of neglect the rare botanical garden annexed to Mohammed Ali Palace on Roda Island is to be renovated. The garden is 5,500 sq m and contains a rare collection of trees brought back to Egypt by Mohammed Ali. Once returned to its original splendour it will be opened to the public who will have to pay to enter.

Giza Zoo has many claims to fame. In particular it is the biggest exhibitor in Africa, having on display the largest number of endangered species. Its situation near the west bank of the River Nile at Giza makes it easily accessible over El Gamea Bridge. The zoo is organized into five huge grottos, one holding statues of rare Egyptian mammals. There are over 6,000 animals and birds on display from around 40 species. Features include the Reptile House and the Lion House. The zoo is proud of its record in breeding and returning to the wild Barbary Sheep, Nubian Ibex, Dorcas Gazelle and Sacred Ibis. Visitors used to western zoos may find a visit here very distressing and hence not a recommended stop.
■ *Daily 0800-1800 in summer, 0900-1700 in winter, 10 piasters.*

Essentials

Sleeping As the largest city in Africa and the Middle East, and one of the world's great tourist destinations it is not surprising that Cairo has hundreds of hotels ranging from deluxe accommodation, often run if not owned by the major international chains, to some really unpleasant places. The listing below, which has sought to avoid the worst, provides a wide range to suit every budget. The expensive and medium price hotels have been grouped by region for convenience.

City Centre: **AL** *Cairo Marriott Hotel and Casino*, 16 Sharia Saray el-Gezira, Zamalek, T3408888, F3406667. 1,250 rooms, built around a lavish 19th century Gezira Palace built to commemorate the opening of the Suez Canal and still retains some of its real splendour. 12 restaurants, bars, night club and Egypt's largest casino Omar El Khayyam (ext 8503), located in the heart of the city, has own sporting facilities – tennis court, health club, etc, beautiful gardens, simply palatial, a good place to unwind from the bustle of Cairo, non floating restaurant and Nile cruiser. **AL** *Cairo Ramses Hilton*, 1114 Corniche el-Nil, Maspero, T5754999, F5757152. 836 rooms, in heart of Cairo, overlooking the River Nile near Midan Tahrir, within walking distance Egyptian museum. Tower block of 28 floors, do your birdwatching from the balcony, pool, healthclub, plus a variety of restaurants, bars, lounges and boutiques, first class business centre. **AL** *Cairo Sheraton*, Midan Galaa', Dokki, Giza, T3369700, F3364601. 660 rooms, located just south of the Gala bridge, views of River Nile, Sheraton high quality service, visible as twin towers on west bank of River Nile, views of the pyramids from the restaurant, circular pool. **AL** *El-Gezira Sheraton*, Gezira Island, PO Box 264, Orman, Giza, T3411555, F3413640. Opposite the *Cairo Sheraton*, circular tower, 27 floors, on the south tip of Gezira Island is one of Cairo's most distinctive landmarks, business provision is excellent, *El-Samar*, riverfront restaurant/nightclub and *Regine's* discotheque. **AL** *Helnan Shepheard*, Corniche el-Nil, Garden City, T3553900, F3557284. 270 rooms, all with good views, south end of Gezira Island, varied cuisine, pool, business centre. A modern structure named after the original hotel which burnt down in 1952, good Nile view, Casino d'Egypte glory is fading. **AL** *Le Méridien Le Caire*, Corniche el-Nil, Garden City,

● ●

Take a deep breath – if you dare

According to UN figures lead pollution in the atmosphere in Cairo is equivalent to 1 tonne per car per year and Cairo now has over 1.5 million cars.

It has been suggested that by Egypt's Environmental Affairs Agency that lead pollution and other suspended particles in the air over Cairo, which last October reduced visibility down to a few metres and breathing to a desperate struggle, is responsible for between 15,000 and 20,000 additional deaths annually.

To combat this pollution the government plans that by 2001 all petrol consumption will be lead-free. Over 65% of the cars in Cairo are more than 10 years old and the implementation of this law would entail the impossible task of scrapping these old vehicles.

If the government could enforce this Cairo would be a delightful place to visit.

● ●

13621717, F3621927. 275 rooms, very well-managed French hotel, located by the River Nile on north tip of Roda Island, with excellent service for businessmen and tourists, and popular French restaurant. **AL** *Nile Hilton Hotel*, Corniche el-Nil, Midan Tahrir, T5780444, F5780475. 434 large rooms, located on the River Nile, adjacent to Egyptian Museum, recently modernized but showing its age as it was opened in 1959 by President Nasser. Like many international Hiltons, it is the place for the jet set of the capital. The Ibis Club is the meeting place for coffee, Jacky's one of the best nightclubs in the city swinging until the early hrs, for the more active the pool is recommended. Business centre for those who must keep in touch. **AL** *Semiramis Inter-Continental*, Corniche el-Nil, Garden City, T3557171, F5653020. 743 rooms, an ugly building and very expensive, is possibly the best hotel in Egypt with French cuisine, excellent service and a good view of River Nile overlooking the southeast end of Gezira Island, outdoor pool.

A *Golden Tulip Flamenco Hotel*, 2 Sharia el-Gezira el-Wasta, Abu el-Feda, Zamalek, T3400815, F3400819. 132 rooms, new hotel, located on quieter but less scenic northwest corner of Gezira Island, high standard and spotlessly clean, Spanish restaurant, 24-hr café, cocktail bar, conference room for 30-40 people, ballroom, takeaway shop, tea room, shops, bank, business centre.

B *Alnubila Cairo Hotel*, 4 Sharia Gamiat ad Duwal al-Arabia, Mohandiseen, T3461131, F3475661. 170 rooms. **B** *Belair Cairo Hotel*, Mokattam Hill, PO Box 996, T916177, F922816. 276 rooms, good view of the Citadel, badly located for downtown Cairo. **B** *Manial Palace (Club Mediterranee)*, Kasr Mohammed Ali, El-Manial, T846014, F3631737. 190 rooms and bungalows, huge pool, an oasis of peace and tranquillity in exquisite gardens of Manial Palace on the north end of Roda Island, half board only, discotheque open from 2300-dawn.

C *Cairo Uncle Sam*, 54 Sharia Abul Mahasen El-Shazli, Agouza, Cairo, T3465377, Tx20147. 150 rooms, family-run, on west bank, just behind the *Atlas Zamalek*. **C** *Concorde Hotel*, 146 Sharia el-Tahrir, Dokki, T708751, F717033. 72 rooms, on main street running west from the Gala' bridge. **C** *Marwa Palace*, 11 Sharia el-Khatib, Dokki, T3433380, very noisy but clean. **C** *Pharaohs*, 12 Sharia Lutfi Hassuna, Dokki, T712314, friendly, very clean, family-run hotel with good service but a poor breakfast, located in a street parallel to the River Nile and north northwest between the Gala' and 6th Oct bridges. **C** *President Hotel*, 22 Sharia Dr Taha Hussein, Zamalek, T3400718, F3413195. 119 comfortable clean rooms, very good well-run hotel, provides good value for money, quiet and convenient location in the middle of the north end of Zamalek, restaurant with good food and excellent service, try downstairs for snacks and atmosphere, business facilities, slow and inadequate lift.

Airport: **AL** *Baron Hotel Heliopolis*, 8 Sharia Ma'ahad el-Sahara, off Sharia el-Uraba (also known as Airport Rd), PO Box 2531, El-Horriya, Heliopolis, T2902844, F2907007. 126 rooms located in Heliopolis overlooking palace, a good business-man's hotel. Clean and comfortable, if unspectacular, decent food and good service, 2 restaurants, 24-hr coffee shop, bar, ballrooms and discotheque. **AL** *Le Méridien Heliopolis*, 51 Sharia el-Uraba, PO Box 2928 El-Horriya, Heliopolis, T2905055, F2908533. Pool, good hotel located only 10 mins from airport, French restaurant very popular, well equipped health club. Business centre recommended. **AL** *Movenpick Heliopolis* (also known as *Movenpick Concorde*), Cairo International Airport Rd, El-Horriya, Heliopolis, T2470077, F4180761. 415 soundproofed rooms, one of best hotels in Cairo, located next to the airport, used by transit and business passengers, good food and really excellent service. **AL** *Sheraton Heliopolis*, Sharia el-Uraba, PO Box 11361, Heliopolis, T2677730, F2677600. 90 rooms, located near airport, currently only the front building is in use.

A *Novotel Cairo Airport*, PO Box 8, Cairo Airport, Heliopolis, T2918520, F2914794. 209 rooms, an unspectacular airport version of the Novotel 4-star chain, almost all the guests are transit and business passengers as it is so convenient for airport.

C *Beirut Hotel*, 56 Sharia Beirut, Heliopolis, T662347, 91 rooms. **C** *Egyptel*, 93 Sharia el-Merghani, Heliopolis, T2907444, 78 rooms, near the *Baron Hotel*. **C** *Horriya Hotel*, 14 Sharia el-Horriya, Heliopolis, T2903472, Tx94332. 57 rooms, budget hotel near *Baron Hotel*.

Pyramids: **AL** *Cairo Jolie Ville Movenpick*, Alexandria Desert Rd, PO Box 1, Giza, T3852555, F3835006. 240 rooms, located near the Pyramids, lovely gardens and excellent food. **AL** *Intercontinental*, Desert Rd, T3838666, F3839000. 481 rooms, good service, located 2.5 km outside Cairo near the Pyramids, 4 restaurants, nightclub with oriental floorshow, pool, health club, gym, sauna, tennis, and nearby golf course and horse-riding clubs. **AL** *Le Meridien Pyramids*, Alexandria Desert Rd, T3830383, F3831730. 523 rooms, a/c, some with balcony, recently renovated, rooms with view of pyramids cost more, many facilities. Small charge made for shuttle bus to town centre which takes minimum of 35 mins. A really grand hotel, able to cope with busi-nessmen and honeymooners. **AL** *Mena House Oberoi*, 6 Sharia Pyramids, El-Ahram, T3833222, F3837777. 487 rooms, very attractive old style hotel built in 1869, excellent view of Pyramids, set in 16 ha of gardens, superb nightclubs and restaurants, disco-theque, casino, largest outdoor pool in Cairo, tennis, a nearby 18 hole golf course, horse and camel riding with experienced instructors, take a room in the renovated older part for preference.

A *Siag Pyramids Penta Hotel*, 59 Mariuteya, Saqqara Rd, PO Box 107, Ahram, T3856022, F3857413. 352 rooms, large hotel located near, and with a good view of the Saqqara pyramids, good room service reportedly better than eating in the restaurant.

B *Kaoud Delta Pyramids*, end of King Faisal Rd, El-Ahram, T3833000, F3830957. 140 rooms, pool, a room with view of Pyramids, also suffers from traffic noise. **B** *Oasis Hotel*, Cairo/Alex Desert Rd, PO Box 44, Pyramids, T3831777, F3830916. 260 rooms, good motel style hotel near Pyramids, large clean pool and a 24-hr restaurant.

C *Chateau des Pyramides Hotel*, 10 Sharia Sadat, PO Box 167, Cairo-Alexandria Desert Rd, T3871342, F3838545. 75 rooms, very good. **C** *Pyramids Hotel*, 198 Sharia el-Ahram, El-Ahram, T3875100, F3874974. 84 rooms, located on the main road to the Pyramids, caters for budget groups. **C** *Saqqara Country Club & Hotel*, Saqqara Rd, Abu el-Nomros, T3852282. 20 rooms, located outside the city near the Saqqara pyra-mids, very highly recommended, well run with good food and excellent horse-riding facilities, temporary club membership available.

Maadi: **AL** *Sofitel Maadi Towers*, 29 Corniche el-Nil, PO Box 217, Ma'adi, Cairo, T5260601, F5261133. 176 excellent rooms, good view of the Nile, excellent service, located at south end of Corniche and a long way from downtown Cairo.

A *Ma'adi Hotel*, 55 Sharia Misr Helwan, PO Box 196, Ma'adi, T3505050, F3518710. 145 rooms, 219 beds, a long way from downtown Cairo in the south suburb of Ma'adi.

B *Residence*, 11th Rd 18, PO Box 418, Ma'adi, T3507189. 28 rooms.

C *Atlas*, Sharia Mohammed Rushdi, Midan Opera, T3918311, 110 rooms, a decent downtown hotel but is noisy because it is next to a large mosque.

D *Abu el-Hoal Palace*, 161 Sharia el-Ahram, El-Ahram, T3856043. 20 rooms, located on way to the Pyramids. **D** *Arabia*, 31 Sharia Abdel Aziz al-Saud, El-Manial, T841444. 16 rooms, family run hotel on Manial Island which specializes in budget groups. **D** *Cairo Crillon*, 19 Sharia el-Montaser, Agouza, T/F3477570. 38 rooms, very good hotel in the west bank area of Agouza. **D** *Caesar's Palace Hotel*, 45 Sharia Abdel Aziz Fahmi, Heliopolis, Cairo, T2457241, F2457240. 60 rooms, family-run hotel near the main Heliopolis Hospital. **D** *Carlton*, 21 Sharia July 26th, Azbakia, T755323, 60 rooms, family-run, located on a noisy downtown street. **D** *Cosmopolitan*, 1 Sharia Ibn Tahlab, Kasr el-Nil, T3923845, F3933531. 84 a/c rooms incl 6 suites, recently refurbished, located in centre of downtown Cairo in a relatively quiet side-street in an elegant building, restaurant which serves reasonable food, bars, café, nightclub, excellent laundry service. **D** *El-Manar*, 19 Sharia Abdel Hamid, off Sharia Luth, Mohandiseen, T709299, 85 rooms, caters for budget groups. **D** *Fontana*, Midan Ramses, T5922145. 93 rooms, cheap hotel with pool, located near the very noisy and crowded Ramses station. **D** *Horus House Hotel*, 21 Sharia Ismail Mohammed, Zamalek, T3403977, F3403182. 35 rooms, friendly, clean, cheaper tariff for extended

Cairo downtown

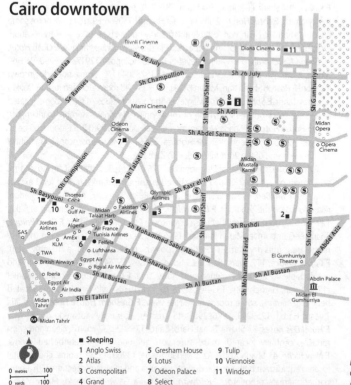

■ **Sleeping**

1 Anglo Swiss	5 Gresham House	9 Tulip
2 Atlas	6 Lotus	10 Viennoise
3 Cosmopolitan	7 Odeon Palace	11 Windsor
4 Grand	8 Select	

0 metres 100
0 yards 100

*Related map
Central Cairo,
page 70*

visits. **D** *Kemet Hotel*, Midan Abbasiya, PO Box 46, Abbasiya, T824018, 96 rooms, poor location halfway between Heliopolis and downtown Cairo but good hotel. **D** *King Hotel*, 20 Sharia Abdel Rahim Sabri, Dokki, T3350939, 90 rooms, family-run hotel. **D** *Longchamps*, 21 Sharia Ismail Mohammed, Zamalek, T3409644. 30 rooms, decent well located hotel run by a very helpful and friendly family. **D** *Odeon Palace Hotel*, 6 Sharia Abdel Hamid Said, Kasr el-Nil, T776637, 30 rooms, modern hotel with a roof garden in a noisy but central location. **D** *Salma Hotel*, 12 Sharia Mohammed Kamel Morsi, Mohandiseen, T700901, F701482. 54 rooms, good view of Cairo from the rooftop bar and on a clear day you can see pyramids, good and friendly service, an English pub, bar, restaurant with good food and cheap drinks. **D** *Saqqara Palm Club*, Saqqara Rd, Badrashin, T200791, 21 rooms, clean, excellent pool, set in beautiful gardens, excellent hotel but located right outside Cairo. **D** *Sheherazade*, 182 Sharia el-Nil, Agouza, T3461326, F3460634. 160 rooms, budget hotel with a good view of the Nile overlooking the Gezira Island. **D** *Vendome*, 287 Sharia el-Ahram, El-Ahram, T5818904, F5854138. 60 rooms, clean and comfortable family-run hotel on the way to the Pyramids. **D** *Victoria*, 66 Sharia el-Gumhorriya, Midan Ramses, T918766. 105 rooms, located in noisy, crowded area near Ramses station, has large a/c rooms, restaurant, bar. **D** *Windsor*, 19 Sharia Alfi Bey, T915277, F921621, recommended as best 3-star hotel in downtown Cairo, clean, well-run, one of the nicest bars in the city. Michael Palin stayed here while going around the world in 80 days. Not very reliable plumbing!

E *Amun*, Midan Sphinx, Agouza, T3461434. 40 rooms, noisy hotel a the busy west end of the 26th July bridge. **E** *Grand Hotel*, 17 Sharia July 26th, Azbakia, T757700, F757593. 99 rooms, 180 beds, located in a crowded downtown area, has much of its original Art Deco fixtures and furniture. **E** *Green Valley*, 33 Sharia Abdel Khalek Sarwat, Kasr el-Nil, T3936317. 28 rooms, a decent budget hotel near the noisy Opera Square. **E** *Kinow*, 382 Sharia el-Ahram, El-Ahram, T859260. 36 rooms, located on way towards the Pyramids. **E** *Lotus Hotel*, 12 Sharia Talaat Harb, T5750966, F921621. 50 rooms some have bath and a/c, clean, comfortable and friendly budget hotel in very central location, reception is on the 7th floor and is reached via the *Malev Airlines* arcade. **E** *Oasis Hotel*, 15 Sharia Abdel-Wahab el-Kadi, Kolleyet el-Banat, Heliopolis, T2917312, F2907912. 60 rooms. **E** *Omayad Hotel*, 22 Sharia July 26th, T5755044. 72 rooms, noisy downtown location. **E** *Rose*, 6 Sharia Iran, Midan Dokki, T707059. 40 rooms, located just off Dokki's Sharia el-Tahrir. **E** *Sphinx*, 8 Sharia Magles el-Sha'b, Abdin, T3557439. 80 rooms, located in a tower block on the south side of the Peoples' National Assembly (parliament). **E** *Tiab House Hotel*, 24 Sharia Mohammed Khalaf, Dokki, T709812. 33 rooms, 60 beds. **E** *Zayed*, 42 Abul Mahasen el-Shazli, Agouza, T3463318. 40 rooms, near Midan Sphinx and the west end of the 26th July bridge to Zamalek.

F *Anglo-Swiss*, 14 Sharia Champollion, T751479. 1930s style, decaying charm, downtown *pensión* with fairly clean shared bathrooms, drinks, but no food except breakfast. **F** *Big Ben*, 33 Sharia Emad el-Din, T908881. 37 rooms, near Ramses Station, reception is on the 8th floor. **F** *Blue Nile*, 4 Sharia el-Hokama, off Manshiet el-Bakri, T291078. 27 rooms, located between downtown Cairo and Heliopolis. **F** *Cairo Palace*, Sharia el-Gumhorriya, Midan Ramses, T906327. 24 clean rooms, located in the very noisy area outside Ramses Station, rooftop restaurant and a friendly staff. **F** *Capsis Palace*, 117 Sharia Ramses, Midan Ramses, T5754219. 72 rooms, clean and comfortable, located in crowded and noisy area. **F** *Garden City*, 23 Sharia Kamel el-Din Salah, Garden City, T3544969. 38 rooms, 1930s style *pensión* hotel located behind *Semiramis*, some rooms have Nile view. **F** *Gresham House Hotel*, 20 Sharia Talaat Harb, T759043, F762298. 45 rooms, centrally located downtown. **F** *Hotel Des Roses*, 33 Sharia Talaat Harb, Cairo, T758022. 32 rooms, clean and comfortable, centrally located, make sure you get one of the refurbished rooms. **F** *New Riche*, 47 Sharia Abdel-Aziz, Midan Ataba, T3900145. 37 rooms, cheap hotel located equidistant between the downtown area and the Islamic section with a sympathetic female proprietor. **F** *Radwan*, 83 Sharia Gawhar el-Kaaid, Midan Azhar,

T901311. 45 rooms, noisy, not advisable for single women. **F** *Safa Inn Hotel*, Sharia Abbas el-Aqqad, Medinet Nasr, Cairo, T4037409, F2619022. 50 rooms, located far from centre. **F** *Select*, 8th Floor, Sharia Adli. Highly recommended. Downtown budget hotel located on 8th floor, breakfast included. **F** *Tulip*, 3 Midan Talaat Harb, T766884. 22 rooms, good location on 3rd floor and above an office block in the heart of downtown Cairo, clean and comfortable. **F** *Viennoise*, 11 Sharia Mahmoud Bassyouni, Kasr el-Nil, T5751949. 26 rooms, atmospheric downtown hotel which retains its turn of the century character.

Camping Because there are so many hotels there is little demand for camping. One of the very few is called *Salma Camping*, T3849152, E£7 per person per night, which can be reached by turning off from Harraniya village on the road between the Pyramids and Saqqara. It offers both cabins, a camping ground, hot showers, a buffet and a bar.

Youth hostel 2 km south of city centre, 135 Sharia Abdel-Aziz al-Saud, El Manial, near University Bridge, T3640729. 167 beds, kitchen, meals available, family rooms, laundry, overnight fee E£20, station 3 km. Book 1 month in advance. Places for disabled, credit cards accepted. *Egyptian Youth Hostel Association (EYHA)*, 7 Sharia Dr Abdel Hamid Said, Marouf, Cairo, T2758099.

The numerous high quality hotels can be relied upon to serve good, anxiety-free **Eating** meals and usually have a range of expensive and average meals. Cheap meals are available in the many *fuul* restaurants (see Food and drink in Essentials). Opening times and menus may change during Ramadan.

Expensive: *Arabesque*, 6 Kasr el-Nil, Downtown, T5747898. The surroundings are ele- **City Centre &** gant, service is excellent and the food, whatever the dish chosen, first class. Open **Garden City** 1230-1530 and 1930-0030. *Asia House*, in Helnan Shepheard Hotel, T3553800 – serves Chinese and Indian meals in the magnificent dining room, high ceilings and *mashrabiyya* style walls. Central fountain adds to the ambience. Food is delicious but service leaves much to be desired. Open 1230-1600 and 1900-1330. *Bird Cage*, in *Semiramis Inter-Continental*, T3557171, tasty Thai cuisine complete with live (caged) birds. Very expensive. Open 1200-1500 and 1800-2400. *Le Champollion*, in *Le Meridien Hotel*, T3621717, Nile view and expensive French cuisine. Absolutely delightful. Leave space for a delicious dessert. Open 1930-2330 *Sapporo*, Cairo Sheraton, T3369700, Japanese chef produces authentic meals at table. Take the seven-dish fixed menu to leave space for a fresh fruit dessert. Open 1230-1500 and 1900-1230. *Sea Market*, in Conrad International, T5808000, freshly caught fish, open 1200-1700 and 1900-0100.

Mid-range: *Alfi Bey*, 3 Sharia El-Alfi, Downtown, T5771888 in pedestrian precinct, authentic Egyptian food, especially kebabs, kofts, lamb chops and shank, grilled and stuffed pigeon with pastas and rice. Smart waiters provide an efficient and friendly service, no alcohol served. Open 1300-0200. *Felfela*, 15 Sharia Talaat Harb, T3922833. One of downtown's most famous and popular tourist restaurants, serves good food and beer. *Le Rendezvous*, in shopping arcade of Hotel Ramses, open 1000-2000. *Peking* behind *Diana Cinema*, T5912381, friendly atmosphere under paper lanterns, extensive menu, staff rely on customers' patience. Open 1200-2400.

Expensive: *Al-Adin*, in *Cairo Sheraton*, Lebanese and Middle Eastern specialities. A **Giza & Dokki** very sophisticated setting. Live entertainment of exceptional quality, open 1300-1600 and 2000-2400; *Amici*, 20 Sharia El-Haram, T3830088. Spanish/Italian food spiced with a view of the Pyramids. Best choice is the seafood, choose your own fish. Limited takeaway menu. Price reflects the location so stay and eat, open 1000-0100; *La Mamma* in *Cairo Sheraton* cheerful atmosphere, serves Italian food with live

Cairo

Chicken for Ramadan

2 medium chickens (about 1 kg each)	Clean the chickens and season inside
salt and pepper to season	and out.
melted butter for basting	Heat butter in pan, fry onion until soft, add
Filling	chopped hearts and livers and cook until
Butter for frying.	the meats go lighter in colour. Over a low
Heart and liver from both chickens clean	heat add the stock, rice, herbs and
and chopped	seasoning and cook for 5 mins.
1 large onion chopped finely	Divide filling and place half in each
200 ml of chicken stock	chicken. Truss to secure.
150 gm of cooked rice.	Bake in a moderate oven (180 C) for
Chopped mint and chopped parsley	75-90 mins, basting with melted butter.
to taste	Turn the birds every 10-15 mins to ensure
Salt and pepper to season	even cooking.

entertainment which makes conversation difficult, open 1000-0100; *Le Chalet*, *Swissair* restaurant, El Nasr Building, Sharia el-Nil, T3485321, Swiss and French specialities, good service, open 1200-2400.

Mid-range: *Cortigiano*, 44 Sharia Michel Bakhum, Dokki. Pizzas and Italian specialities continue to delight customers. Good choice of desserts. No alcohol. Open 1300-0100; *Fish Market*, 26 Sharia El Nil, Giza, T5709693 – the ultimate choice in seafood; *L'Entrecote Café de Paris*, 24 Sharia Ibn el-Walid, Dokki, T3606262. Chicken breast or beef steak cooked to order and served with salad and french fries. Choice of desserts. Good service. Open 1100-1400; *Pizza Express*, 52 Sharia Michel Bakhum, Dokki T3881838. These are excellent pizzas, made to order as you wait. Wide choice of starters and desserts. Excellent service. Open 1230-0100; *Silver Fish*, 39 Mohy El Din, Sharia Abu El Ezz, Dokki, T3492272, good seafood in a relaxed setting.

Cheap: *Kenny Rogers Roasters*, roast chicken, 21 Sharia Nadi el-Seid, Dokki, T3366344.

Heliopolis & Nasr City **Expensive:** *Al-Sarraya*, Movenpick Heliopolis, T2470077, French cuisine, seafood specialities, and gourmet menu, live piano. Open 1800-2400; *Chinois,* Sheraton Heliopolis, T2677730. Oriental cuisine, stir fried at the table with tasty side dishes. Leave room for fried toffee bananas. Good service. Open 1300-0100; *Starlight*, in *Baron Hotel*, 8 Sharia Maahad El-Sahari, international food, panoramic views, open 1930-0030.

Mid-range: *Ataturk*, 80A Sharia Al Thawra, Heleopolis, T4170955/53, newly opened, Turkish specialities such as chicken stuffed with perfumed rice and vegetables, or cubed meat and vegetables served in tomato sauce, all well cooked and well presented, open 7 days a week 1000-0200. *Chilli's*, 18 Sharia el-Thawra, T4188048, Spicy food in colourful surroundings, mouth-watering desserts, no alcohol, sharp service. Open 1100-0100. *Cortigino*, behind Almaza Central, T4142202, excellent Italian cuisine, pizzas to write home about. Open 1300-0100. *Full Moon*, 100 Sharia El-Mirghani, T4184860, recommended are the seafood spaghetti and the waffles with icecream. No alcohol served. Open 0800-0200.

Cheap: *El-Shabrawi*, 7 Sharia Ibrahim, T4178191, for *ful* and *tameya*. *Pizza Express*, 16 Sharia El-Mirghani, T4505871. Excellent pizzas made to order. *Smiley's Grill*, 75 Sharia Abu Bakr el-Sedik, Midan Safir, Heliopolis, T2406258, open 1000-0200, except Sun;

Turkish Sandwich Bar, (home-made bread) and restaurant with Turkish delicacies, 80A Sharia El-Thawra, Heliopolis, T4170953.

Mid-range: *Bua Khao*, 9 Road 151, Thai food, open 1200-2300. *Peking*, 29 Sharia **Maadi** El-Nasr, T5164218. Lively with families, extensive menu, allow plenty of time for your meal. Open 1200-0030.

Cheap: *Lan Yuan*, 84 Road 9, T3782702, for Chinese food with Chinese music, open 1200-1500 and 1700-2300. *Pizza Express*, Sharias El-Nasr/Laselky – usual high standard of food and service. Open 1200-2400.

Mid-range: *Ataturk*, Sharia Riyadh, T3475135, an unusual find – Turkish food, served **Mohandiseen** fresh with tasty breads and rice dishes. No alcohol. Open 1000-0200; *Mr Muxim*, Sharia El Shaheed Abdel Moneim Riyadh, T3606121, restaurant, lunch and dinner, French, Lebanese, Moroccan and Greek food, sea food speciality, open 1200-0200; *Tia Maria*, 32 Sharia Jeddah, T713273, a quiet Italian restaurant, all meals made with fresh meats and vegetables. Live entertainment some nights. Open 1200-0100.

Cheap: *El Omda* behind *Atlas Hotel*, T3452387, famous for Egyptian food, especially *ful* and *koshari*, served very speedily. No alcohol. Open 1200-0200; *Marqush*, Lebanese cuisine, 64 Midan Lebanon, T3450972, no alcohol served, open 0900-0200.

Expensive: *Moghul Room*, *Mena House Oberoi*, T3833222, authentic Indian food, **Pyramids** soothing atmosphere, live Indian entertainment every evening, open 1200-1445 and 1930-2345.

Mid-range: *Christo's*, 10 Sharia El-Haram, another restaurant with a view of the Pyramids. Here the speciality is fish – choose your own as you enter. Sometimes busy at lunch times with tour groups. Open 1100-0300; *Felfela*, 27 Cairo-Alexandria Rd, T3830234, excellent Egyptian food served indoors and outdoors. Thirteen varieties of *ful* served with freshly baked bread. Slick service. Open 0830-0130.

Cheap: *Andreya*, 59 Mariuteya Canal, T3831133, specialities are chicken/pigeon, eat out of doors; *La Rose*, 58 Sharia Mariuteya Canal, T855712, clean surroundings, tasty food.

Expensive: *Chin Chin*, at The Four Corners, 4 Sharia Hassan Sabri, Zamalek, **Zamalek** T3412961, high quality Chinese food, beautifully presented, home delivery also available but why miss the ambience? Open 1930-2400; *Ciao Italia*, *Gezira Sheraton*, T3411333, excellent cuisine, well presented food, slick service. Finish with a high calorie ice cream. Very expensive, open 1200-1500 and 1900-2400; *Justine's*, 4 Sharia Hassan Sabri, Zamalek, at The Four Corners, T3412961, excellent service, noted for high quality French food, the place for a special meal. Open 1230-1500 and 2000-2300; *La Piazza*, Four Corners, 4 Sharia Hassan Sabri, Zamalek, T3412961, very welcoming and friendly service. Desserts are a weight-watcher's nightmare, open 1230-0030; *Tokyo*, 4 Sharia el-Maahad el-Swissry, Zamalek, T816610, excellent service, interesting Japanese food, if this is what you came to Egypt for!

Mid-range: *Ali Hassan el-Hati*, 8 Sharia 26th July, T918829, fish and kebab both recommended, open 1100-2200; *Roy's*, in *Marriott Hotel*, serves Mexican food from 1200-2400; *The Marina* opposite *Cairo Marriott Hotel*, fish specialities, open 1800-2400.

Cheap: *Al-Dente* for pasta, 26 Sharia Bahgat Ali, Zamalek T3409117. *Zamalek Restaurant*, 118 Sharia 26th July, for *ful* and *tameya*.

For international fast food ask a taxi driver for *Pizza Hut*, *McDonalds* or *KF Chicken* –
they are all in the same street.

Floating restaurants *Nile President*, good efficient service, clean, well maintained,
excellent and varied food; *The Nile Maxim*, T3408888, 2 nightly cruises at 2000 and
2300 and weekend lunch at 1430, wide choice of menu, fish specialities, live entertainment and show, moored opposite entrance to *Cairo Marriott Hotel*; *Le Steak* on *Le
Pacha 1901*, Sharia Saray el-Gezirah, T3406730, an elegant Nile River boat, steaks plain
or with all the trimmings. Book to get a river view seat, open 1200-0200.

Nile Crystal – *Onyx*, *Topaz* and *Hamis* – either a la carte or open buffet – pick up at
Corniche el Nil at beginning of Maadi Road. T3639021, F3639074; Pharaonic Luxury
cruising restaurants – *Nile Pharaoh* and *Golden Pharaoh* with very distinctive gold
painted hulls 138 Sharia El Nil, Giza T5701000. Meals at 1430-1630, 2015-2215,
2245-0045; *Aqarius*, Sharia Abdel Azzia al Seoud, 1500-1700, 2000-2200, 2230-0030,
T5253690; *Scarabee*, Corniche el Nil, alongside *Helnan Shepheard*. T3554481, meals at
1430-1630, 2000-2200, 2230-0030.
     Look out also for evening meals on *The King, Sofitel*, and *Nile Trocadero*.

If you want something that stays open a bit later try the following; *Cairo Cellar* under
President Hotel, cosy, often bordering on crowded; *Deals*, cheap, cheerful and very
noisy at 2 Sharia el-Maahad el-Swissri; *Harry's Pub* in *Cairo Marriott Hotel*;
Johnny's Pub on *Le Pacha 1901* (see above) rather pricey; *Piano-Piano*, in World
Trade Centre, open until 0300 serving Chinese and French cuisine.

Cafés: *Abu Ali Café*, *Nile Hilton*; *Badaweia*, 33 Nasr Ahmed Zaki, Nasr City; *Coffee
Roastery*; Sahria Shooting Club, Mohandiseen; *Garden Promenade Café*, *Marriott
Hotel*, Zamalek; *Maroush*, 64 Midan lebanon, Mohandiseen; *Orangerie*, *Movenpick
Hotels*; *Picasso Café*, 17 Sharia Kambis, Dokki; *Simonds*, Sharia 26th July, Zamalek;
Tornado, 3 Midan Aswan, Mohandiseen; *Zezenia*, 15 Ahmed Orabi, Mohandiseen.

Bars &   **Casinos**: found in the following hotels: *Cairo Heliopolis Movenpick*, *Cairo Marriot*, *Cairo*
nightclubs *Sheraton*, *El Giza Sheraton*, *Mena House Oberoi*, *Nile Hilton*, *Ramses Hotel*, *Semiramis
Intercontinental*, *Helnan Shepheard Hotel*, *Sheratan Heliopolis*.

Nightclubs all have live entertainment and most with belly dancers: *Abu Nawas*, in
Mena House Oberoi Hotel, open 2000-0300, closed Wed, T3833444; *Aladin*, open air,
and *Alhambra*, in *Cairo Sheraton Hotel*, summer only, closed Mon, T336970; *Belve-
dere*, in *Nile Hilton*, open 2000-0230, closed Tue, T767444; *Candella*, in World Trade
Centre, open 2200-0400, T5785347/8; *City Club*, Nile Tower 21, 23 Sharia Giza, open
1000-0400, T5701279; *El-Samar*, in *El-Gezira Sheraton Hotel*, T3411555; *El-Torero*, in
Hotel Sofitel, T3506092; *Empress*, in *Cairo Marriott*, T3408888, is very popular; *Haroun
el-Rachid*, in *Semiramis Intercontinental Hotel*, closed Mon, T3557171; *La Belle Epoque*
in *Le Méridien Cairo Hotel*, T3621717; *Shishow*, in *Sheraton Heliopolis Hotel*, 1000-0400
closed Mon, T2677730; *Ya Salam*, in *El-Salam Hotel*, closed Mon, T2974000, ext 7003.

Most popular discos with young and affluent Egyptians and expatriates: *Atlantis* at
Helnan Shepheard Hotel, open 2300-0400, entrance E£50; *Barracuda* in *Le Meridien*,
Heliopolis, T2905055, open 2200-0300, not Mon; *Borsalino's*, 15 Sharia Rustum
Basha, Garden City, open 2300-0300, entrance E£20, for a more basic club playing
African influenced pop and reggae; *Castle* in *Helnan Shepheard*, T3553800, open
2200-0300; *Churchill* in *Baron Hotel*, Heliopolis, T2902844, open 2200-0300, closed
Wed; *Galaxy* in *Pyramisa*, T3367000, open 2200-0400, closed Mon; *Papillion*, in
Movenpick Heliopolis, T2470077, open 2200-0400; *Saddle* at the *Mena House Oberoi*,

Mummy Come Home

An elegant new tomb has been constructed, its pillars supporting a deep blue ceiling studded with gold stars. This is an attempt by the Egyptian Museum in Cairo to recreate the ambience of Thebes in around 1300 BC and provide a final resting place for some of its most famous pharoahs.

The mummies have suffered many indignities. Take Meneptah, grandson of Seti I. Having survived a spectacular first burial with all the pomp and splendour due to Egyptian royalty, tomb robbers flung his mummy aside and 21st Dynasty priests rewrapped him and placed him with eight other displaced persons in a side chamber in the Tomb of Amenhotep II. Rediscovery in 1898 was followed by transport to Cairo where he was put on view. Queen Nedjemet, another resident was slashed by the knives of those who unwrapped her. The great Ramses II unwrapped in public in 1886 in an unseemly 15 minutes strip, has also found a decent home here. In 1946 public display of mummies was banned as improper. But in March 1994 the special tomb tastefully displays these bodies neatly wrapped once again, complete with dimmed lighting and dehumidifiers to protect the desiccated remains. Among the 11 who have found, hopefully, a final resting place here beside Queen Nedjemet, Meneptah and Ramses II are Merytamum his queen and his father Seti I.

open 2200-0400, closed Sun, entrance, E£40, T3834010; *Tamango* in *Atlas Zamalek Hotel*, T3466567, open 2200-0300, entrance E£40.

Cinemas: Current information on cinema performances is given in the Egyptian Gazette and Egyptian Mail as well as the monthly Egypt Today publication. Commercial cinemas change their programmes every Mon so check the programme. Arabic films rarely have subtitles. The World Trade Centre offers two venues, *Upstairs* and *Katcho's*.

Entertainment

Cinema in English: *Al Tahrir*, 122 Sharia al Tahrir, Dokki, T3354726, daily at 1000, 1300, 1500, 1800, 2100. *Cairo Sheraton*, Sharia Giza, 17606081. *Cosmos 1 and Cosmos 2*, 12 Sharia Emad el Dine, T5742177, shows at 1030, 1300, 1530, 1830 and 2130. *Diana*, 17 Sharia el Alfi, T5924727. *Drive In*, entrance to Shourouk City, Cairo-Ismailia Desert Road, T2190831. *El Haram*, 147 Sharia El Haram, T5742177, shows at 1230, 1530, 1830, and 2130, midnight shows Thu, Fri and Sat. *El Salam*, 65 Sharia Abdel-Hamid Badawi, Heliopolis, T2931072, daily at 1530, 1830, 2130 and midnight. *French Cultural Center* start at 1900, English subtitles, 1 Sharia Maddraset El-Huquq El-Faransiya, Mounira, T3457679. Films at *Goethe Institute* start at 1830 with English subtitles, 5 Sharia El-Bustan, Downtown, T5759877. *Italian Cultural Centre* – 3 Sharia Sheikh El-Marsafi, Zamalek T3408877791. *Karim I/Karim II*, 15 Sharia Emad el Dine, T5924830, shows at 1000, 1300, 1500, 1800 and 2100; *Metro* in *Swissotel el-Salam*, T393/566; *MGM*, 4th Floor Maadi Grand Mall, T5195388. Shows at 1230, 1530, 1830 and 2130 with midnight shows Thu and Fri; *New Odeon*, *Cairo Sheraton*, Sharia El-Galaa, Giza, T3606081 (50% discount for students), daily 1000, 1300, 1500, 1800, 2100 and 0000; *Tiba 1 & Tiba 2*, 75 Sharia el Nasr, Nasr City, T2621089. *Ramses Hilton Cinema*, 7th floor of the hotel's shopping annex.

Galleries: *Arabesque*, 6 Sharia Kasr el Nil, Downtown, open all week. *Cairo Opera House Arts Gallery*, Gezira, daily except Fri. *Ewart Gallery*, Main Campus, American University in Cairo, Sharia El-Sheikh Rihan, open daily except Fri and Sat 0900-2100; *Faculty of Fine Arts*, 4 Sharia Mohammed Thaab, Zamalek, daily except Fri. *French Cultural Centre*, 27 Sharia Sabri Abu Alam, Midan Ismailia, open daily except Fri and Sat 1000-1400 and 1700-2000; *Khan el-Maghraby Gallery*, 18 Sharia

☛ Egyptian handmade carpets

The variety and high quality of Egyptian handmade carpets is still not fully known outside the country. Yet they are every bit as valuable and decorative as most Persian and Turkish products. Nothing can be better as a memento of Egypt than a locally made carpet or rug and a better choice will be made with a little knowledge and by taking your time in making your selection. If you do buy, make sure that you pick a rug that you like and can live with. Acquiring carpets as an investment is only for the experts.

In Egypt there are two main types of handmade carpet, the flat woven kilims and knotted carpets usually of wool on a cotton base.

Kilims are flat woven rugs and include tapestries with woven scenes. They have the great virtue of being cheap, light in weight and easily packed. Very decorative are the thin Bedouin rugs in bright reds and golds, while there are also coarse rag rugs made from scraps of material common in Egypt. Most valuable are the kilims made entirely of wool and dyed in natural colours or mixed fibres, some in very bright hues.

Handknotted carpets and rugs are more expensive than kilims. The number of knots per square centimetre determines the quality of a handknotted carpet, as does the materials of which it is constructed. The backing (the warp) may be of cotton, wool or silk and the knots of wool or silk. Coarse woollen material is used when knot densities are low, on average about 25 per centimetre, while the fine wools and silks require higher densities of up to 69 knots per centimetre, take longer to make and therefore cost more.

Designs for the handknotted carpets are very varied, though the best usually take their patterns from tile designs from the walls of the famous mosques. Often however designs are adapted from traditional patterns made popular elsewhere in the Middle East – Persian, Turkish and Caucasian being most widespread. Pleasing designs on small rugs follow the classical patterns of the tree of life, formal hunting scenes, the Persian garden, bird carpets and central medallions. Most small rugs were, and to an extent, are still produced as prayer mats and incorporate a triangular top portion to act as the indicator of the direction to Mecca copied from the mihrab in the wall of the mosque.

The Egyptian carpet industry is relatively recent in origin, though there is evidence in ancient Egyptian monuments such as the Tomb of Kheti at Beni Hassan, that mat weaving existed from at least 2000 BC. In Egypt today carpets are woven by the Bedouin, household weavers and by workers in small workshops. Most weaving is done on a horizontal loom with the weaver sitting on the ground. More recently the vertical loom has been used for manufacturing high quality and ornate Egyptian hand-knotted carpets and tapestries. Handlooms are all different and little credit is given in the traditional weaving areas to mathematical accuracy. Expect, therefore, that even best quality carpets and rugs will be slightly misshapen.

Most wool for carpet making is imported though some Bedouin still use wool from their own or neighbours' flocks. Camel hair and cotton are also important parts of rug-making, camel hair giving a natural colour for traditional rugs and cotton providing the long warps through which the wool is woven.

Designs vary greatly from the simple provincial mosque wall derived patterns of Assiut to the ornate medallions of the Senna and Persian types. Colours are most subtly used in the complicated designs of the hand-knotted carpets of the small workshops but the brightly-coloured narrow strips of the Bedouin weavers have their own charm.

Machine-made carpets, normally to be avoided, can be distinguished by the fringe which will often have been sewn on later, or by the sides which are much neater and flatter than handmade rugs, and by the back which does not show the pattern very clearly and is quite smooth. Fold back the carpet for a close examination of the knots and pattern on the rear of the carpet to check the mathematical precision of weaving which gives away the fact that it is factory made.

Purchase Each carpet will need to be bargained for with patience and humour. The following points might help during this process. (1) Before entering the bargaining process make sure that you know what you are looking for – rug, tapestry or carpet – and what size of carpet your rooms can accommodate (and you can comfortably carry with you out of Egypt). (2) If possible take an independent Egyptian friend with you to the shop who understands carpets and rugs. He will help to overcome language and bargaining hurdles. (3) Take your time by shopping around and culling more than once at a shop before purchase. There is no need to be rushed whatever the inducement. (4) Remember that you must pay for your purchase in Egyptian pounds – exchanging currency through a shop keeper can be very expensive – and that posting a carpet home from Egypt is technically difficult and best avoided.

The most famous carpet shops in Egypt are to be found in Cairo, first in the Khan el-Khalili where the best and most expensive wares are on sale. The Cairo city centre and main streets of Zamalek also have their specialist carpet dealing shops, while Alexandria and its adjacent villages such as Hammam have both a carpet school and commercial carpet shops.

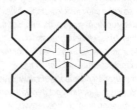

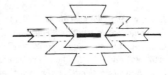

El-Mansour Mohammed, Zamalek, daily except Sun, 1030-2100; *Mashrabiya Gallery*, 8 Sharia Champollion, Downtown, daily except Fri 1100-2100; *Salama Gallery*, 36a Sharia Ahmed Orabi, Mohandiseen, 1000-1400 and 1700-2100, closed Fri.

Sound & light shows: 3 performances daily at the Sphinx and Pyramids, Giza: at 1830, 1930 and 2030 in Winter, 2030, 2130, 2230 in Summer. Entrance: E£33. Information: T3852080. Bring a sweater as it gets quite chilly in the evening and use insect repellent as the mosquitoes become active at dusk. **Mon**: English/French/German, **Tue**: English/French/Italian, **Wed**: English/French, **Thu**: Arabic/English/Japanese, **Fri**: English/French, **Sat**: English/Spanish, **Sun**: French/German/Japanese.

Theatres: current information for theatre performances is given in the *Egyptian Gazette* and *Egyptian Mail* as well as the monthly *Egypt Today* publication.

The 7-storey *Opera House*, T3420601, in the Gezira Exhibition Grounds at the end of Ksar el-Nil bridge has a main hall with 1,200 seats for opera, ballet and classical music performances, a second hall with 500 seats for films and conferences and an open air theatre. Advance booking is recommended. Men must wear jacket and tie. *Al-Gumhorriya*, 12 Sharia Gumhorriya, T3907707; *Balloon*, Sharia el-Nil near al-Zamalek Bridge, T3471718; *Mohammed Farid*, in Sharia Mohammed Farid, T741204; *Puppet Theatre*, Azbakiah, T910954; *The National*, in Midan Ataba, T5917783. Apart from the *Opera House*, all performances are likely to be in Arabic; Whirling dervishes – Egyptian members of the Sufi sect – perform at the *Ghuriyya Cultural Centre* housed in the Mausoleum of al-Ghawri, Sharia al-Azhar on Wed and Sat evenings, starting about 2000, T909146.

Cairo

☞ *The souq way to secure a bargain*

An enduring characteristic of all souqs is their use of pricing through bargaining for every transaction, however large or small. This bargaining, so unfamiliar to the European, has brought rather differing responses. On the one hand bargaining is seen as a sign of the efficiency of the souq. Each separate business transaction is done with the finest of margins so that prices are very sensitive and really reflect the value. Contrary opinions strongly maintain that, far from being efficient, bazaar transactions only maximize profits for the seller for each article sold rather than getting the best potential profit flow. Souqs or bazaars thus actually act as a brake on the expansion of commerce as a whole.

They also rely on the ability of the seller to exploit the absence of quality controls, trade mark conventions and other types of consumer protection. In these situations, the seller treats each transaction as an opportunity to cheat the customer. Souqs are, in this view, places where the buyer must be doubly wary since short measure, adulteration of goods and falsification of origin of goods for the benefit of the seller is normal. By definition this system can operate only in countries like Egypt with minimal regulatory régimes and where consumer information is un-organized.

When shopping in Egypt the best advice is to be fully aware that the system is designed to work to the seller's advantage.

Festivals/ cultural events **Jan** *International Book Fair*, Jan 7, Coptic Church *Christmas*, Jan 19, Coptic Church *Epiphany*. **Mar** *International Fair: Annual Spring Flower Show*. **Apr** Apr 7, Coptic Church *Annunciation*, Apr 15 Coptic and Roman Catholic *Easter*. **Jun** Jun 3 2001/Jun 23 2002/Jun15 2003, Coptic Church *Pentecost* **Jul** *International Festival of Documentary Films*. **Aug** *International Song Festival; Nile Festival Day* at Giza. Aug 19, Coptic Church *Transfiguration*. **Sep** *Nile Festival Day* in Cairo; *International Festival of Vanguard Theatre*. **Nov** *International Children's Book Fair* at Nasr City. **Dec** International Film Festival; *Festival for Arab Theatre; Festival for Impressionist Art* (alternate years).

Shopping Egypt's low labour costs mean that a number of western clothing chains manufacture high quality cotton goods in-country including Benetton, Naf Naf, Mexx. Prices are considerably lower than in the West. Visit Cairo's trendiest shopping mall, *The World Trade Centre*, 1191 Corniche el-Nil, Maspero, for the full selection. Moiré silk handmade shoes available from *Atlas* near *Nagib Mahfouz Café* in Khan El Khalili, T5906139, or in *Semiramis Intercontinental Hotel*. Among the most attractive areas to shop is the *Khan el-Khalili Bazaar* and *Sagh* comprising an array of shops dating from the 14th century. Renowned for craftsmanship in silver and gold, embroidered cloth, copper ware, leather and ivory inlaid goods. (Remember that the import of ivory is for-bidden into most Western countries.) The Kerdassa village, east of Giza, is noted for its embroidered cotton and silk dresses, *galbeyas*, and other handmade goods while Haraneya, west of Giza, is the main centre for quality carpets.

Bookshops: those selling books and periodicals in European languages. *Academic Bookshop*, 121 Sharia el-Tahrir, Dokki, open 1000-1500 and 1700-2000, closed Thu evening and all Fri; *Al-Ahram*, 165 Sharia Mohammed Farid, downtown in *Nile Hilton*, open 0830-2200; *Al-Arab Bookshop*, 28 Sharia Faggala, T908025, open 0900-1400, 1700-2000, closed Sun; *American University in Cairo Bookstore*, on main campus, open 0830-1630, closed Fri, Sat evening and all Aug, also has a store in Sharia Mohammed in Thakeb, Zamalek open 1000-1830, closed Sun; *Anglo-Egyptian Bookshop*, 165 Sharia Mohammed Farid, Downtown, open 0900-1330 and 1630-2000, closed Sun; *Baron Books*, *Méridien Heliopolis Hotel* 0830-2330; *Dar el Bustan*, 29 Sharia Faggala, Downtown. Open 1000-1900, closed Sun; *Everyman's Bookshop*, 12 Sharia Baghdad, Heliopolis, open 0930-1430 and 1700-2130 except Sun;

The tax man plays the tune

Nothing escapes the tax man.

*Egypt's 12 highest earning belly dancers
pay a total in annual taxes equivalent to
US$250 mn.*

*This makes them the country's fifth largest
source of income.*

*Only the receipts from traffic on the Suez
Canal, tourism, oil exports and cotton
exports are more important.*

Cairo

Lehnert & Landrock, 44 Sharia Sherif, books in German and English, open 0930-1330 and 1530-1930, closed Sat afternoon and Sun; *Livres de France*, 36 Sharia Kasr el-Nil, T3935512. Open 1000-1900, morning only on Sat and closed Sun; *L'Orientaliste*, 15 Sharia Kasr el-Nil, near Midan Tahrir, T5753418, for oriental and rare books – old maps, lithographs and post cards, open daily 1000-1930 except Sun, has been in the hands of the same French family for generations. *Reader's Corner*, 33 Sharia Abd el-Khalek Tharwat, open 1000-2200, closes from 1500 on Sat and all day Sun. *Zamalek Bookstore*, Sharia Shagaret el-Dorr, open 0830-2000, closed Sun.

Billiards: *Ramses Hilton Mall*, T572752 and *Al Buston Centre*, T3950100   **Sports**

Bowling: *Cairo Land*, 1 Sharia Salem Salem, open 1000-0100; *Maadi Family Land*, Corniche el Nil, open 1000-0200; *MISR Bowling Centre*, 9th floor, Al Bustan Centre, Bab Ellouk, T392229; *Sport Mall*, 80 Sharia Shehab, Mohandiseen.T3026432

Cycling: T3526310 for meeting each Fri at 0700 by Cairo American College.

Diving: Meeting 1900 first Mon each month at *Helnan Shepheard Hotel*, T3553900. *Sub Aqua Club* at British embassy each Tue. Monthly dive trips and training schedule, T3654567, *Cairo Divers' Club*, T3400889.

Golf: there is a public golf course at the foot of the pyramids. Also at *Mina House Oberoi* and *Pyramid Park Sofite*. *Katameya Heights Golf Course* is located just 23 km south east of Cairo. Here the annual membership is E£5,000 with a restriction of 600 players. Currently it has 18 holes with another 9 being constructed.

Gym: at *Nile Hilton*. *Ramses Hilton* and *Marriot* welcome visitors. *Gold's gym and fitness centre*, 121 Sharia el-Nil, Giza, T7480003, F7480004 offers serious fitness for everyone – if not fully satisfied your old body will be returned to you!

Horse riding: Gezira, T3405690. But much more pleasant to ride in the desert by the pyramids, particularly for sunrise or sunset. Avoid the haggard looking horses lined up for tourists by the pyramid's gate and head for the stables in Kafr el-Gabal (straight on past the entrance to the Sound and Light). *AA Stables* (T3850531) and *MG Stables* (T3583832) are the most highly recommended, have regular Western clients, and offer a variety of excursions from the standard hour-long ride around the pyramids (E£15), riding lessons (E£20 per hour) to a trip to Saqqara (E£60). More elaborate excursions and night rides need to be booked in advance.

Rugby: Club meets for training at 1830 each Mon and Wed at the Victory College fields, T3750840 for details.

Running: Cairo Hash House Harriers, meet each Fri approximately 2 hrs before sunset. For differing venues contact T3476663.

Shooting: *Shooting Club*, Dokki, T3498479.

Swimming: use the pools at the hotels. Those in the 5-star establishments cost more. Heliopolis, Giza and Gezira sporting clubs have pools; daily and weekly membership available. Public pools are to be avoided.

Tennis: tennis courts can be booked at the *Marriott Hotel*. *Katameya Tennis Resort*, 23 km south east of Cairo, has 10 clay courts and 2 of grass.

Yachting: *Yacht Club*, Maadi, T3505169.

Spectator sport **Football**: at the stadium in Heliopolis, weekends at 1500. The season extends from Sep-May.

Horse racing: weekends in winter at the Gezira race-course at 1300 and weekends mid Oct-end of May at Heliopolis race-course at 1330.

Rowing: races each Fri on the River Nile.

Tour operators *Abercrombie and Kent*, 5 Sharia Bustan, Tahrir, T3936255; *Academy Tours*, 95 Sharia el-Herghani, Heliopolis, T345050; *American Express*, 21 Sharia Giza, Nile Tower Building, T3703411; *Astra Travel*, 15 Sharia Demashk, Mohandiseen, T3446445; *Egyptian Express*, 8 Sharia Kasr el-Nil, T750620; *Etam Tours*, Egyptian Tourism and Medical Services, 3 Sharia Kasr el-Nil, T754721, F5741491, ask for Dr Bishara, a long established firm offering specialized handling of handicapped visitors; *Gaz Tours*, 7 Sharia Bustan, T752782; *Hermes Travel*, 1 Montaser Bldg, Sharia Sudan, Sahafeyeen, T3451474; *Isis Travel*, 48 Sharia Giza, Orman Bldg, T3494326; *Karnak Travel and Touristic Services*, 12 Sharia Kasr el-Nil, T750600; *Mena Tours*, El-Nasr Bldg, Sharia el-Nil, Giza, T3482217 and 14 Sharia Talaat Harb, T740955; *Misr Travel*, 1 Sharia Talaat Harb, T3930010, ask for Mr Mohammed Halawa; *Seti First Travel Co*, 16 Sharia Ismail Mohammed, Zamalek, T3419820, F3400855; *Thomas Cook Overseas*, 12 Midan El-Sheikh Youssef, Garden City, T3564650.

Transport **Local Bus**: buses in Cairo are only for the strong and the brave. They are very crowded. They tend to slow down rather than stop which requires some agility. One enters at the rear and leaves by the front which means pushing the length of the bus. The main bus station is in Sari al Gala behind the Egyptian Museum. Bus No 997 goes to the pyramids and Nos 356 and 400 (hourly) to the airport. **Calèche**: for a tourist ride. This is expensive but an experience. **Car hire**: *Avis*, 16 Sharia Ma'amal el-Soukkar, Garden City, T3547400, also at *Hotel Méridien*, *Nile Hilton Hotel*, *Hotel Jolie Ville* and *Sheraton Hotel*; *Bita*, 15 Sharia Mahmoud Bassyouni, T746169; *Budget*, 1 Sharia Mohammed Ebeid, Heliopolis, T666027, also at *Marriott Hotel*; *Hertz*, 27 Sharia Libnan, Mohandiseen and also at the airport, T3474712. *Hertz*, 195 Sharia July 26, Mohandiseen, T3034241, F3474172, also at *Ramses Hotel*, *Sonesta Hotel*, *Maadi Hotel* and *Semiramis Intercontinental*. **Metro**: in addition to the Heliopolis Metro connecting Midan Ramses to Heliopolis, Nasr City and Mattareya, there is the Metro from Helwan to El Marg and Shubra al-Kheima to Giza with a third line under construction, stopping at 14 stations including Old Cairo and Maadi. Operates daily every 6 mins from

0530-2400 (summer 0530-0100). (See page 137 for map.) Tickets E£0.50. Don't lose your ticket as you will need it at the exit and don't smoke. There are separate 'women-only' carriages on all trains, generally the first one. Many stations are only named in Arabic. **Taxis**: ramshackle but the best way of getting around. Check current prices with locals or at your hotel. Best not to ask the price first or to bargain but just pay the current price at the destination and don't ask for change.

Long distance Air Cairo International Airport, 15 km northeast of Midan Tahrir (Tahrir Sq) in downtown Cairo, has two terminals which are about 3 km apart. The new Terminal 2 is used by most of the Western airlines while Terminal 1, which is the old airport, is used by Egyptair and all of the other airlines who cannot or will not pay the higher landing charges. Taxis are available immediately on exit from customs for E£50 (check current official fare from airline or airport official). A fixed price limousine service taxi at E£20 per head for a max of four people (check before you get in) leaves from Misr Travel's stand at Terminal 1. The airport service bus drops a minimum of five passengers at any central Cairo hotel at E£20 per head and E£25 for Giza which makes a taxi a cheaper option. The cheaper and easier way, costing less than E£1, is bus No 410 to Midan Ataba or the No 400 bus every 30 minutes or No 27 minibus every hour from Terminal 1 to the bus terminal at Midan Tahrir which is right in the centre of the city. From here one can get transport to everywhere else in Cairo. Cairo Airport: T2472548/2914255.

For both **Train** and **Bus** transport restrictions apply for foreigners moving south or east and only certain services may be used. **Bus**: long-distance buses arrive at Sinai Bus Station, also known as Abbassiya Station, about 5 km northeast of Midan Tahrir

Cairo Metro

—○— Under construction

Cairo

☛ Room for one more inside…

An average of seven million commuters use Cairo's public transport on a daily basis, with two million using the metro and three million the microbus and taxis. Looks like the other two million were all on the bus that just went by.

which can be reached by the cheap No 32 minibus or taxi from outside the terminal (expect to pay E£5 to get downtown). Buses from Luxor and Hurghada arrive at the Ahmed Helmi Terminal behind Ramses Station. The city's other two arrival points are the Koulali Terminal, in front of the Ramses Station, for buses from the Suez Canal Zone and the Delta while the Al-Azhar Terminal for those from the Western Desert, is about 450 m east of Midan Ataba which is only one stop from both Midan Tahrir and Ramses Station. For destinations outside Cairo: **East Delta Bus Co**, from Midan Abbassiya, T824753; **Tel Aviv** on Sun, Tue, and Thu at 0500, reservations Hepton Tours at Cairo Sheraton, price US$50; Daily departures to **Rafah** 0800 and 1300; **El Arish** 1600 and 2400; To **Suez**, Ismailia and **Port Said** every hour from 0600-2000. *Middle Delta Bus Co*, T946286; *West Delta Bus Co*, T759701. The Cairo-Fayoum City bus leaves every 30 mins from Midan Ahmad Helmi just behind Ramses Railway Station.

Train All trains arrive at Ramses Station, T5764214, with different sections for Nile Valley and Delta tracks. It is at the north end of downtown Cairo about 2 km from Midan Tahrir which can most easily be reached by Metro (2 stops) although bus (No 95) or taxi can also be taken. **Sleeping cars**: T753555/3484633. To **Alexandria**: 17 daily; **Aswan**: 0730, 1545, 1900, 1915, 1930, 2000, 2030, 2100; to **Beni Suef and Assiut**: 0700, 1000, 1240, 1410, 1600; to **Luxor**: 0100, 1200, 1400; to **Port Said and Ismailia**: 0620, 0845, 1240, 1425, 1830.

Directory **Airline offices** *Air France*, 2 Sharia Talaat Harb, T5743300, at airport T661028; *Air India*, 1 Sharia Talaat Harb, T3927467; *Air Libya*, 37 Sharia Kasr el-Nil, T3924595; *Air Sinia*, 12 Sharia Kasr el-Nil, T5760948; *Alitalia*, Nile Hilton Commercial Complex, T5743488 (Airport T665143); *British Airways*, 1 Sharia Abdel Salam Aref, T759977, airport T3934873; *EgyptAir*, 9 Sharia Talaat Harb, T3932836, or Nile Hilton (Airport 697022); *Iberia*, 15 Midan Tahrir, T3910828, (Airport T4177297); *KLM*, 11 Sharia Kasr el-Nil, Cairo, T5740999 (Airport T662226); *Lufthansa*, 6 El-Sheikh el-Marsafi, Zamalek, Cairo, T3420471, airport T666975; *Orascom* (charter to El-Gouna), 66 Sharia Abuel Mahassen el Shazli, T3052401; *Quantas*, 1 Sharia Kasr el-Nil, T749900; *Royal Air Maroc*, 16 Bustan, T3934574; *Swissair* 22 Sharia Kasr el-Nil, T3921522; *Tunis Air*, 14 Sharia Talaat Harb, Cairo, T5753420, (Airport 2680188).

Banks *American Express*, 4 Sharia Syria, Mohandiseen, T3605256; *Bank of Alexandria*, T3913822-3, and *Egyptian Central Bank*, in Sharia Ksar el-Nil, T3926211; *Barclays International Bank*, 1 Sharia Latin America, Garden City, T3540431, 3542195; *British-Egyptian Bank*, 3 Sharia Abu El Feda, Zamalek, T3409186; *Chemical Bank*, 3 Sharia Ahmed Nessim, Giza, T3610393; *Citibank*, 4 Sharia Ahmed Pasha, Garden City; *National Bank of Egypt*, 24 Sharia Sherif, T3924022, F3924177. Western Union Money Transfers are now available from branches of *International Business Associates* throughout the city, T3571300.

Couriers *DHL*, T3029801; *Express Mail Service*, T3905874; *TNT* (International Express), T3608921; *Western Union* (Money Transfers), T3495199.

Communications Internet: *Arabia Internet Café*, Osman Towers, Corniche El Maadi, open 1000-2400, E£10 per hour, T5249000; *Café Internet*, Sharia Gameat El Dowal, Mohandiseen, open 1000-2400, E£12 per hour, T3050493; *Connections*, 15 Sharia El Meraashly, Zamalek, open 24 hrs, E£10 per hour, T3408650; *Cyber Café Internet*, Nile Hilton Shopping Mall, Midan Tahrir, open 1000-2400. E£12 per hour, T578 0325; *Future Access*, 13 Osman Towers Corniche el-Nil, Maadi, open 1000-2330, E£7 per hour, T5261081; *Internet Egypt*, 2 Sharia Simon Bolivar, Garden City, open 0900-2200, E£12 per hour, T2599793; *Internet Egypt*, 1 Sharia Shafik Ghorba, Heliopolis, open 1000-2400, E£12 per hour, T2599793; *Nile Net*, 5 Sharia Nadi Tersana, Mohandiseen, open 0100-1000, E£10 per hour, T3024270; *Road 9 Café*, Road 9 Amaadi, open 1000-2400, E£10 per hour, T3784514; *The Way Out*, 18 Sharia Abdel Hadi, Heliopolis, open 24 hrs, E£13 per hour, T4180995.

The Fourth Pyramid

The taxi driver has put his favourite cassette on. Who does that forceful voice, rising above the slithering quarter tones of the violins, belong to? It could well be that of Umm Kalthoum, the best known Egyptian of this century after Gamal Abd al Nasser and still the most popular Arab singer. There was nothing in her background to suggest that Umm Kalthoum was to become the greatest diva produced by the Arab world.

Born in 1904 in a small village in the Nile Delta region, Umm Kalthoum became interested in music through listening to her father teach her brother Khalid to sing religious chants for village weddings. One day, when Khalid was ill, Umm Kalthoum accompanied her father and performed instead of her brother. The guests were astonished at her voice. After this, she accompanied her father to sing at all the weddings. In 1920, the family headed for Cairo. Once in the capital, Umm Kalthoum's star rose fast. She met the poet Ahmad Ramzi and made her first commercial recordings. In 1935, she sang in her first film. She subsequently starred in numerous Hollywood on-the-Nile productions.

In 1946, personal and health problems made Umm Kalthoum abandon her career, temporarily as it turned out. Due to her illness, she met her future husband, the doctor Hassan el Hafnawi, whom she married in 1954. She then resumed her career. Songs such as Al awal fil gharam wal hubb ('The first thing in desire and love'), Al hubbi kullu ('Love is all') and Alf layla wa layla ('A Thousand and One Nights') made her name across the Arab lands. In the 1960s, her Thursday evening concert on the Cairo-based Radio Sawt al Arab ('Voice of the Arabs') became an Arab-wide institution. During the Yemeni civil war, the Monarchist troops knew that Thursday evening was the best time to attack the Egyptian troops supporting the Republicans as they would all be clustered round their radio sets listening to their national diva. So massive was her fame that she was dubbed 'the Fourth Pyramid'.

Umm Kalthoum's deep, vibrant voice was exceptional, of that there is no doubt. Nevertheless, the music may be difficult for western ears. Though the lyrics are often insufferably syrupy, the diva's songs continue to enjoy wide popularity and her films, subtitled in English or French are often shown on Egyptian satellite channel Nile TV. In Ramadhan 1999, a TV series on her life drew huge audiences. If there is one piece of modern Arab music you should try to discover, it has to be the Umm Kalthoum classic love song, Al Atlal, ('The remains of the camp fire'). The theme, a lament sung over the ashes of the camp fire for the departed lover, goes way back to the origins of Arab poetry.

Umm Kalthoum died in 1975, and her funeral cortege filled the streets of Cairo with hundreds of thousands of mourners. Her voice lives on, played in cafés and cars, workshops and homes all over the Arab world.

Post Office: Cairo's main post office is on Midan Ataba. Major hotels can possibly provide the same services without the crowds. **Telecommunications:** there are International telephone, telex and fax services at all major hotels.

Cultural Centres *American*, US Embassy, 5 Sharia Latin America T3549601, closed Fri and Sat; *Austrian*, Austrian Embassy, Sharia El-Nil T5702975; *British* in British Council, 192 Sharia El-Nil, Agouza. T3031514, closed Sun; *Canadian*, Canadian Embassy, 5 Sharia Sarayal Kubra, Garden City, T3543110, only Tue and Wed; *Dutch*, 1 Sharia Dr Mahmoud Azmi, Zamalek, T3400076; Egypt Crafts Centre, 27 Sharia Yehia Ibrahim (off Sharia 26th July open Sun-Thu 0900-1600, Wed from 0900-0730; *Egyptian*, 11 Sharia Shagaret El-Dor, Zamalek, T3415419. *French*, 1 Sharia Madraset El Hoquq El Faransia, Mounira, T3553725; *German*, Goethe Institute, 5 Sharia Abd El-Salam Arif, T5759877; *Israeli*, Israeli Embassy, 92 Sharia El-Nil, Dokki, T3488995; *Italian*, 3 Sharia Sheikh el-Masrafi, behind *Marriott Hotel*, Zamalek T3408791, closed Fri and Sat; *Japan,* Japanese Cultural Centre, 106 Sharia Kasr El Hoq El Faransia, Mounira, T3553725; *Swiss*, Swiss Embassy, 10 Sharia Abdel-Khalek Tharwat, T5758284, closed Fri and Sat.

Cairo

Embassies & consulates Most Consulates take a two day weekend, between Thu and Sun. *Australia*, 12th floor, World Trade Centre, Sharia Corniche el Nil, T5750444; *Canada*, 5 Sharia Sarayal Kubra, Garden City, T3543110/9; *France*, 29 Sharia Morad, T5703919; *Germany*, 8B Sharia Hassan Sabri, Zamalek, T3406017; *Libya*, 7 Sharia el-Saleh, Zamalek, T3401864; *Netherlands*, 36 Sharia Mohammed Mazhar, T3401936; *Spain*, 41 Sharia Ismail Mohammed, T3406397; *Switzerland*, 10 Sharia Abdel Khalek Sarwat, T5758284; *Sudan*, 3 Sharia El Ibrahimi, Garden City, T3545043, letter of recommendation required; *UK*, 7 Sharia Ahmed Raghab, Garden City, T7940852; *USA*, 5 Sharia America al Latiniya, Garden City, T7957373.

Language schools Arabic classes available at the *Egyptian Cultural Centre*, 11 Sharia Shagaret El-Dor, Zamalek, T3415419; *Afro Arab Language Institute*, T685858584; *Amoun School*, T7947077; *British Council*, 192 Sharia El Nil, T3031514; *Berlitz Worldwide*, 2 Sharia El Meleihi, T3381350; *International Language Institute*, T3463087.

Medical services Chemists: 24-hr service: *Ali and Ali*, 9 Outlets, T3604277; *Ataba Pharmacy*, Midan Ataba, T920831; *Helwan Pharmacy*, 17 Sharia Ahmed Anas, T38018; *Isa'f Pharmacy*, Sharia Ramses, T5743369; *Magsoud*, 29 Sharia Mahmoud Shahk, Heliopolis, T2453918; *New Cairo airport*, T2446032; *Old Cairo airport*, T2903964; *Zamalek Pharmacy*, 3 Shagaret El Dor, Zamalek, T3402406. Dentists: *American Dental Centre*, Heliopolis, T2468670; *Maadi Dental Centre*, Digla, T5198736; *Smile Clinic*, Heliopolis, T4175068. Hospitals: *Anglo-American Hospital*, behind Cairo Tower, T3406162; *Coptic Hospital*, Sharia Ramses, T904435; *Damascus Hospital*, 1 Sharia Damascus, Mohandiseen, T3470194; *El-Salam International*, Maadi, T3507592; *Shaalan Surgical Centre*, 10 Abdel Hamid Loth, Mohandiseen, T3605180.

Places of worship Anglican/Episcopalian, *All Saints Cathedral*, 5 Sharia Michel Lutfalla, behind Marriott Hotel, Zamalek, T3418391, international English speaking congregation, Sun services, Holy Communion 0800 and 1030 on 1st/3rd/5th, Matins at 1030 on 2nd and 4th; Evensong 1915 on 2nd and 4th Sun, for weekday services please enquire; *St John the Baptist*, Sharia Port Said, Maadi, services Sat at 1730; *St Michael's*, interdemoninational and international, T4142409; 10 Sharia Seti, off Sharia Baghdad, Heliopolis, Eucharist Sat at 1830, Sun at 1030 and 1930 in Arabic and 1800 in English; *Armenian Church*, 28 Sharia Sabri Abu Alam. Sun 0815-0915, 1930, T9441163. Christian Science Society, 3 Midan Mustafa Kamel, T3929032, Sun at 1900 and Wed at 1930, reading room available; Coptic/Orthodox, *Church of St Anthony and Girgis*, Heliopolis, T821274, mass in English 3rd Sun in month at 0800; *First Baptist Church*, 28 Sharia Khalafawi, Shubra; Sun at 1000 and 1930, T9941163. German Evangelical/Lutheran Church, 6 Sharia Gaber Ben Hayyan, Dokki, T3614398, 1st and 3rd Sun at 1730; Quaker, alternate Sun at 1900, T3576969; Roman Catholic, *Holy Family Church*, Maadi, T3502004, daily Mass Mon-Thu at 0615, Fri at 0900, service in English Sat 1730 and Sun 1800, French at 0630, Spanish Sat at 1700; *St Joseph's Church*, T3408902, 2 Sharia Bank Misr, Downtown, Mass in French daily at 0730 and 1830, also Sun in Fresnch 1100, and 1900, in Arabic at 1000, and English at 1900; *St Joseph's Church*, 4 Sharia Ahmed Sabri, Zamalek, Mass (English) Sun 1800. *St Theresa Catholic Church*, Coptic Rite Mass and Latin Rite Mass at 0630/1730 confessions in Arabic, French, Italian, Spanish, English and Maltese.

Useful addresses and telephone numbers Major police offices: at Railway Station, Cairo Airport, Midan Tahrir, Sharia 26th July/Mansour Mohammed. **Accident:** T123; **Fire:** T125; **International collect call:** T146; **Meteorological information:**, (weather forecast), T2447988; **Police:** T122; **Pyramids Office:** T850259; **Tourist Police:** T126 or T926028; **Tourist Police Head Office:** T3906027.

Cairo Environs: The Pyramids & El-Fayoum

4

The Pyramids & El-Fayoum

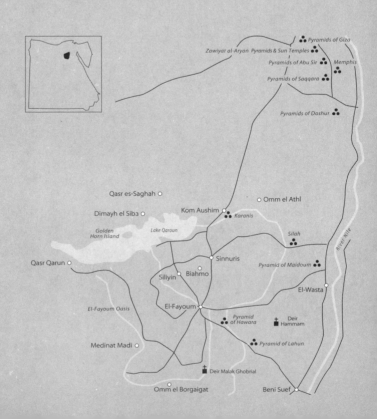

Pyramids of Giza

Zawiyat al-Aryan Pyramids & Sun Temples

Pyramids of Abu Sir

Memphis

Pyramids of Saqqara

Pyramids of Dashur

Qasr es-Saghah

Omm el Athl

Dimayh el Siba

Kom Aushim Karanis

Golden Horn Island

Lake Qaroun

Silah

Qasr Qarun

Sinnuris

Pyramid of Maidoum

River Nile

Siliyin Biahmo

El-Wasta

El-Fayoum Oasis

El-Fayoum

Pyramid of Hawara

Deir Hammam

Medinat Madi

Pyramid of Lahun

Deir Malak Ghobrial

Omm el Borgaigat

Beni Suef

*Ever since the Greek and Roman era, if not earlier, the Pyramids at Giza just to the west of Cairo have been one of the world's great tourist attractions. Although there are other pyramids in Egypt, the ones at Giza are almost certainly the largest, most imposing and best preserved ancient monuments in the world. In order to see the development from the simple underground tomb to the audacious concept and awesome majestic splendour of the Pyramid of Cheops it is undoubtedly worth visiting Saqqara before going on to Giza but tourists rarely do. Whether sooner or later, when you come to Egypt, this is the site to visit. And, after the heat, the crowds, the pushing and waiting and the pollution of Cairo, slip away to El-Fayoum. The **El-Fayoum** oasis, which includes **Lake Qaroun**, is literally a breath of fresh air. It offers both Egyptian and foreign visitors a relaxing break from city life, a day at the beach and a chance to see oasis life without having to venture too far. It has few ancient monuments. A relaxing day or two in El-Fayoum is strongly recommended for those in Cairo who are beginning to feel claustrophobic.*

Memphis

The oldest known imperial city on earth, was founded in the First Dynasty (3100-2890 BC) at the start of the Early Dynastic Period (3100-2686 BC), and lies 15 km south of Cairo. It was established sometime around 3100 BC by Menes who may have actually been several successive kings rather than a single person. It was the Pharaohs' capital city throughout the Old Kingdom (2686-2181 BC) and was inhabited for four millennia, until it was eventually abandoned by the Moors, and returned to the Nile silt from which it was originally constructed. Sadly all that remains today is a limestone Colossus of Ramses II (1304-1237 BC) and a giant alabaster sphinx weighing 80 tonnes, both of which may have stood outside the huge Temple of Ptah, and the remains of the Embalming House, where there are several alabaster tables, weighing up to 50 tonnes, which were used to embalm the sacred Apis bulls before burial at Saqqara. Beyond these its former glories can only be imagined.
■ *E£14, students E£7, camera E£10, video camera E£100.*

Saqqara

Getting there To reach Saqqara by public transport take the No 121 bus from Giza Pyramids to Badrashin (E£0.35) and then Badrashin to Saqqara village (E£0.40), after which it is a 3 km walk. Giza to Saqqara by camel costs E£150 per person and takes 4-5 hours or E£100 and 2 hours by horse. People who really want to ride a camel around the pyramids could get a 10 minutes ride for E£15. Horses can be hired to ride from Giza to Saqqara. Avoid the Sphinx stable where the horses are reported to be tired and in poor condition. There are better stables such as AA or MG at the right of the main entrance. Because of the hassle of public transport and the fascinating information an informed tour guide can provide about the area it is probably best to spend E£50-E£60 to go with a

Cairo environs

reputable tour group. All guides will expect *baksheesh* of a few E£ at the end of the tour but only give it if you genuinely feel that they have been good. On the journey between Saqqara and Giza most tour coaches will stop at some of the numerous carpet schools. Avoid Fridays, Saturdays and public holidays when Egyptians turn out for picnics, games of football and general merriment in such numbers that it is hard to get through the crowds. You would do well to avoid the expensive cafeteria too and take some sandwiches.

Saqqara, which faces Memphis across the River Nile from the west bank, was the enormous necropolis for the first pharaohs. It extends for over 7 sq km. With many tombs believed to be still undiscovered it is currently Egypt's largest archaeological site. From its inception it expanded west into the desert until the fourth Dynasty (2613-2494 BC) when the Giza plateau superseded it. At the end of the fifth Dynasty (2494-2345 BC) a more systematic construction of pyramids and *mastabas* began which resulted in many splendid monuments around Saqqara. In 1883 a Middle Kingdom (2050-1786 BC) necropolis was found to the east but it was not until the New Kingdom (1567-1085 BC) that Saqqara is thought to have regained its importance as a burial ground. ■ *Daily 0900-1600, E£20, E£10 for students with cards, camera fee E£10, E£100 for video cameras.*

Zoser's Funerary Complex

This complex, the largest in Saqqara, is an example of some of the world's most ancient architecture. The whole complex, including but not confined to the **Step Pyramid**, was designed and built by **Zoser** (2667-48 BC), the second king in the third Dynasty, under the control of his chief architect Imhotep who some regard as the world's first architect. At its heart is the Step Pyramid, the first of its kind, which can be seen as a prototype for the Giza Pyramids. This marked the evolution of burial tombs from *mastabas* with deep shafts for the sarcophagus to imposing elevated mausoleums. It was constructed in steps building up from the traditional square *mastaba* (1) of Tura faced local stone measuring 71.5 m each side and 8 m high. The sides faced the cardinal points. This original tomb (1) was then faced with a further casing (2) on all sides and an extension to the east (3) before being expanded to a four-step (4) and then later to a six-step (5) pyramid. Although the external fine white limestone casing, brought from quarries across

The Step Pyramid at Saqqara

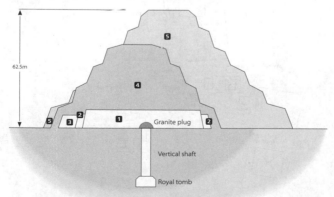

The Pyramids & El-Fayoum

the Nile at Memphis, has disappeared over time this step structure is still clearly visible. The pyramid eventually reached a height of 62.5 m on a base 109 m by 121 m, which, although small by comparison with those at Giza, is still an amazing feat because of the primitive building techniques. The advances represented by Zoser's Pyramid were not in the building techniques or materials, which were already established, but the concept, design and calculations involved which made such a monument possible.

The entrance is in the north face. In accordance with the traditional *mastaba* technique, the Royal Tomb lies 28 m underground at the bottom of a vertical shaft. The shaft was then sealed with a three tonne granite block but this still did not prevent the tomb from being looted. Another 11 shafts were found, 32 m deep, under the east side of the Pyramid, which lead to the tombs of the queens and royal children. Unfortunately these are no longer open to the public.

The whole funerary complex was completely surrounded by buttressed walls which were over 544 m long, 277 m wide and 10.4 m (20 cubits) high. Although 14 fake doors were built, only the one in the southeast corner, which leads into the colonnade **Hypostyle Hall** actually gives access to the site. It is thought that the area was walled in order to deter intruders and thieves, and to provide space for the Pharaoh's *Ka* (spirit) to live in the after-life. Before entering the Colonnade, observe the fake door complete with hinges and sockets in the Vestibule on the right. The Colonnade leads through to the **Great Court** or **Southern Court**, on the south side of which there is a frieze of cobras. This represents the fire-spitting goddess of destruction Edjo who was adopted as the Uraeus, the emblem of royalty and of protection, which was worn on the pharaonic head-dress (see box Cobras).

Further along this south wall is a deep shaft at the bottom of which lies **Zoser's Southern Tomb** which some believe held the King's entrails. More importantly there is a relief, depicting the King running the Heb-Sed race,

North Saqqara

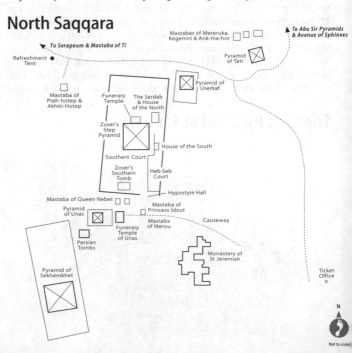

The Sacred Scarab

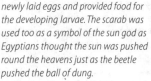

Scarabaeus sacer, a dung beetle, is the celebrated beetle held sacred by the ancient Egyptians. They were fascinated by the beetles' strange habit of fashioning perfectly round balls from animal-droppings. These balls, larger than the insect itself, were moved backwards using the rear legs, the head being thrust against the ground to give purchase. The balls were buried with

newly laid eggs and provided food for the developing larvae. The scarab was used too as a symbol of the sun god as Egyptians thought the sun was pushed round the heavens just as the beetle pushed the ball of dung.

The dung beetle is called Kheper in the Egyptian language and is associated with the verb kheper *which means to come into being. As new beetles emerge from the ground as explained above the two words and the two actions are easily associated. Models of the beetle made in clay were supposed to have healing powers while live beetles, secured by a small chain through the wing-case, were actually worn as decoration.*

The scarab seal was used to stamp letters into the clay seal on letters, bottles, wine jars etc with the owner's mark.

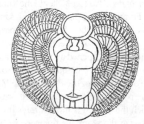

which illustrates the purpose of the surrounding buildings and monuments. The buildings in the funerary complex, some of which are mere façades like a Hollywood film-set, simply represented a pastiche for the after-life of this crucial ceremony. Their intended purpose was to eternalize the symbol of the unification of a greater Egypt and the power of the pharaoh even in death.

This symbolism is echoed in the lotus and papyrus capitals on top of the columns fronting the **House of the South** and the **House of the North** which represent the heraldic emblems of Upper and Lower Egypt, respectively. The **House of the South** is interesting because its columns, which are precursors of the Greek Doric style, and its New Kingdom graffiti offer a fascinating reminder of the continuity of human civilization.

On the north side of the Step Pyramid there is a stone casket, known as the **Serdab** (cellar), containing a copy of a life-size statue of Zoser. The original is in the Egyptian Museum in Cairo. The Serdab has two cylindrical holes to enable the statue to communicate with the outside world and to preserve the Pharaoh's *Ka*. To the west of the Serdab the **Funerary Temple** is in ruins but some of the walls and the entrance can still be seen. A tunnel originally linked it with the royal tomb.

Dash for the Altar – The Heb-sed Race

The Heb-Sed race took place during the festival held to mark the 30th anniversary of Zoser's reign. He would sprint between two altars, which represented Upper and Lower Egypt, *thereby not only re-enacting his coronation in both parts of the country and symbolizing the unification of the two lands but also demonstrating his continuing vigour.*

South of Zoser's Funerary Complex

The Pyramid of Unas, which was built for the last pharaoh of the Fifth Dynasty (2494-2345 BC), appears from the outside to be a heap of limestone rubble but the inside is still very well preserved and contains some beautiful hieroglyphs. Originally when clad in its granite casing it stood 44 m high but is now reduced to 19 m. As always, the entrance is from the north side down a passageway leading to the Burial Chamber. This was originally closed off with three granite portcullises. This is largely undecorated except for the star-covered ceiling and the sarcophagus which is made from a single block of black basalt and bears no inscriptions. The most interesting inscriptions are in the passageway, painted in green and organized in vertical lines. The hieroglyphs are magic formulae and prayers, known as the Pyramid Texts, for the Pharaoh to help his passage into the after-life. They were the first to be found inside a tomb and formed the basis for the *Book of the Dead* (see Valley of the Kings, page 243). To the east, a few remnants of the **Funerary Temple** can be seen, some granite columns with palm capitals and pieces of granite floor. Beyond this the remains of a causeway linking the Funerary Temple to the Valley Temple 700 m away has been discovered. The pyramid was excavated and opened as a tourist attraction in 1881 by the director of antiquities Gaston Maspero with financial sponsorship from Thomas Cook & Son.

To the north of the Pyramid the **Mastaba of Queen Nebet**, who was Unas' wife, is also fascinating and well preserved. It is divided into three rooms of which the second is most interesting because it contains some rare scenes of Nebet in the women's quarters, or harem, in the palace. From here, a door leads to a gallery with beautifully decorated walls.

Opposite, to the northeast, is the **Mastaba of Princess Idout**. The tomb is divided into 10 rooms but only five are decorated. The wall paintings give us a glimpse of life in Idout's day with the many tableaux of rural and domestic scenes. Two rooms are dedicated to the offerings to the Princess and are designed to provide for her in the after-life.

Slightly to the east is the **Mastaba of Merou** containing some exceptionally well preserved paintings. In the **Grand Offerings Room** the paint scarcely seems to have faded thereby giving a good idea of the original splendour of these tombs.

South of the Pyramid of Unas a stone hut covers the access to three small **Persian Tombs** 25 m underground and composed of two shafts. In order to lower the heavy sarcophagus, an ingenious system was devised involving the use of an additional smaller shaft. The main shaft was dug out, then filled with sand. The sarcophagus was then placed on top of the sand which was gradually removed from below via the smaller shaft. The tombs dating from the 27th Dynasty (525-404 BC) are interesting because they have very similar inscriptions to those found in Unas' Pyramid constructed over 2,000 years earlier.

To the southwest are the remains of the **Pyramid of Sekhemkhet** which was at the centre of an unfinished and unused funerary complex, very similar to that of his predecessor Zoser, which was only discovered in 1950 and to which there is no public access.

The Pyramids & El-Fayoum

To the east of the Pyramid of Sekhemkhet can be seen the remains of the **Monastery of St Jeremiah** which was founded in the fifth century but destroyed by the Arabs five centuries later. Following its discovery in 1907 many of the paintings and other items of interest were removed and are now on display in the Coptic Museum in Cairo.

Northeast of the Funerary Complex

The **Pyramid of Teti**, the founder of the Sixth Dynasty (2345-2181 BC), was discovered by Mariette in 1853 but is now little more than a pile of rubble in constant danger of being submerged by sand. It is entered via a steep pathway leading to the funerary chamber in which the ceiling is decorated with stars.

Mastaba of Mereruka. To the north are a number of well preserved *mastabas*. The most outstanding is that of **Mereruka**, who was Teti's visir, chief judge and inspector, an important person in Sixth Dynasty society. This is one of the largest Old Kingdom *mastabas* to have been found. Its 32 rooms are divided into three parts for Mereruka (21 rooms), his wife (six rooms) and his son (five rooms). In the main entrance passage Mercruka is depicted painting the three seasons which leads to the next room containing some interesting hunting scenes. Particularly worth noting is the indication of the types of animal that they hunted and the techniques being used. Scenes of everyday life are beautifully depicted throughout the tomb giving a valuable insight into contemporary life. The largest room, with six pillars, has a statue of Mereruka to the north and some unusual mourning scenes on the east wall. On the left are scenes of Mereruka carried by his son and surrounded by dwarfs and dogs. To enter Mereruka's wife's rooms go back to the main entrance and take the door on the left.

To the east, the **Mastaba of Kagemni** who was also a visir and judge of the 6th Dynasty has some excellent reliefs and paintings of a much a higher standard, but unfortunately less well preserved, than those in Mereruka's tomb. Further east is the **Mastaba of Ankh-ma-hor**, the visir and overseer of the Great House in the Sixth Dynasty, which is also known as the Doctor's Tomb because of the paintings depicting circumcision and an operation on a broken toe! The other rooms are interesting and show the usual scenes of the preparation and transportation of the offerings and various representations of hunting and daily life. Look on the south wall for the mourners fainting at the burial ceremony.

Northwest of the funerary complex

Situated about 200 m south of the road to the refreshment tent is one of the finest of all the *mastabas*. The **Double Mastaba of Ptah-Hotep and Akhiti-Hotep** contains some of the finest Old Kingdom art and some fascinating unfinished work which demonstrates the techniques used in painting reliefs. Ptah-Hotep was a priest of Maat in the reign of Djedkare, who was Unas' predecessor. His son Akhiti-Hotep was visir, judge, and the overseer of the treasury and the granaries.

The entrance leads into a long corridor decorated with unfinished agricultural scenes. The red paint indicates the preliminary drawing before the wall was carved and painted. The outstanding masterpiece, however, is in the **Sanctuary** dedicated to Ptah-Hotep. On the walls behind the entrance Ptah-Hotep is seated watching a concert while his servants wash and manicure him. Other walls bear scenes of Ptah-Hotep receiving offerings. On the left wall, which is the most interesting and impressive, the figure in the first boat is being given water by a boy. The inscription describes him as the Chief Artist,

Music

Music played an important part in the lives of the ancient Egyptians. This bas relief discovered in a nobleman's tomb at Saqqara is a good illustration of entertainments of that era. Here three musicians entertained the owner of this fifth Dynasty tomb while he feasted from a huge basket of fruit.

Sometimes musicians played to placate an angry goddess such as Hathor. Music was produced on harps as shown here which were very common, though some had fewer string, single and double flutes, drums and by hand clapping. A number of wall reliefs show blind singers and instrumentalists.

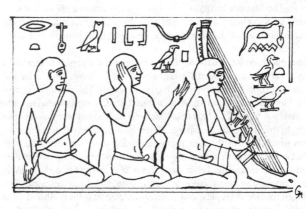

who is thought to have been Ankhen-Ptah, and this scene may well represent the first known example of an artist's signature.

The Serapeum. This was a burial place for the sacred Apis Bulls which were believed to be manifestations of Ptah's blessed soul and were identified with Osiris after his death. They were given full honours in a ceremony worthy of any Pharaoh or important noble and were then embalmed and the mummified body placed in a sarcophagus and buried in the Serapeum. The sarcophagus was then sealed off from the main gallery by means of a richly decorated wall. The high priests would then start searching for the new Apis Bull within the sacred herd. It had to be the only calf of its mother, be black in colour except for a white diamond-shaped marking on the forehead and have a scarab symbol on its tongue.

The cult was a significant one and the Serapeum represents an important funerary complex which, besides the tombs themselves, included the priests' quarters, schools and inns catering for passing pilgrims. The cult of the Apis Bulls lasted well into the Ptolemaic period.

The Serapeum is situated 300 m to the northwest of the refreshment tent and is one of the most impressive sites in Saqqara. It is reached via a long, sloping path, at the bottom of which a door leads to the three galleries. Only two are accessible, and the 24 surviving sarcophagi are set in small galleries on either side of the main one. Each sarcophagus was made from a single piece of rock and weighed around 60 tonnes. Only three of the enormous basalt or granite sarcophagi bear inscriptions, and these are marked with the cartouches of different pharaohs, Amasis, Cambyses and Khababash. The Serapeum was discovered in 1851 but, with the exception of one tomb, most had already been looted. The artifacts discovered are now displayed in the Musée du Louvre, Paris.

The **Mastaba of Ti** is one of the wonders of the Old Kingdom, and its beautiful reliefs provide some interesting insights into life during that period. Ti was a Fifth Dynasty royal hairdresser who married well and became steward of the sun temples of Neferikare and Nyuserre and whose children later bore the title of 'royal descendant'.

The *mastaba* stands 400 m north of the refreshment tent, very close to the Serapeum, and is centred around a square pillared courtyard. The entrance is through a vestibule with portraits of Ti on the two entrance pillars. The reliefs in the courtyard have been damaged but their representations of daily life – breeding birds (north wall left), Ti on his litter with dogs and dwarfs (east wall, centre), and Ti with his wife (west wall centre) – are still worth seeing. In the centre of the courtyard an undecorated shaft leads to the tomb. A corridor leads from the southwest corner through to the main shrine. On the left of the corridor, just after the door, servants are depicted bringing offerings while on the right are musicians and dancers. Further on, to the right, is a false door bearing a representation of Ti's wife.

Further down the corridor on the right is a storage room and then the main hall of offerings and shrine which has a number of scenes depicting the offerings ceremony, the brewing of beer and the baking of bread. The main shrine is remarkable for its abundance of scenes depicting daily life including one illustrating boat construction. Note the extreme simplicity of the tools used.

The south wall holds the **Serdab**, where a copy of Ti's statue, the original being in the Cairo Museum, can be seen through the slit. Around the two slits there are scenes of daily market life, carpenters, tanners, and various other artisans. Around the second slit, Ti is entertained by musicians while servants burn incense. These paintings should be taken on one level as literal depictions of Egyptian life but it is also important to realize the importance of symbolism and allegory. The north walls show Ti in a boat observing a hippopotamus hunt in the Delta region. The hippopotamus was symbolic of evil so there is probably more to the picture than meets the eye.

The **Pyramids of Abu Sir** are situated 2½ km further northeast of the Mastaba of Ti. The site originally contained 14 Fifth Dynasty pyramids but only four are still standing. The temples are solidly constructed with black basalt floors and red Aswan granite pillars and are well worth visiting. When arriving from the main Saqqara complex the **Pyramid of Neferefre** is the first to be encountered. It was never finished and is now in very poor condition. The next also unfinished pyramid to the north was built for **Neferikare** and towering over the others is, at 68 m, the tallest of the group. To the northeast, the **Pyramid of Nouserre** is worth noting for its **Funerary Temple** which, although originally built for the Neferikare, was used by Nouserre because of Neferikare's premature death. About 100 m to the northeast lies the tomb of **Ptah-Cepses**. The *mastaba* is not in good condition and has been closed for safety but from outside the columns with lotus capitals which are the oldest so far discovered can still be seen.

The remaining one, **Sahure's Pyramid**, is directly north and its **Funerary Temple** is not too severely damaged. Excavation work around it has led to the discovery of the remains of a 240 m ramp which connected it to the **Valley Temple**. Sahure was brother to Userkaf whose pyramid is at Saqqara. The ceilings of this Funerary Temple were yellow stars on a blue background and the reliefs carved on the limestone walls showed the king's defeat of his neighbours in the desert and those from Asia. Some have been removed and placed in museums, but a few remain and are quite well preserved.

The **Sun-Temples of Abu Ghurab**, built in the Fifth Dynasty when the solar cult had been declared the State religion, are about 1 km northeast of Sahure's Pyramid. Unlike earlier temples their purpose was solely devotional and the pharaohs who built them were not buried in them. There were twin temples but only the **Sun-Temple of Nyuserre** remains with the **Sun-Temple of Userkaf** being little more than rubble. Fortunately because they were identical little is lost.

The Pyramids & El-Fayoum

At the western end of an enclosed courtyard a massive 70 m obelisk once stood. The obelisk was the symbol of the primordial mound, the sun's resting place at the end of the day. An alabaster altar stands in the centre of the courtyard which would have been at the eastern side of the obelisk's base. Animals were sacrificed at the northeast corner of the courtyard from which channels cut in the paving carried the blood to 10 alabaster basins, nine of which survive.

South Saqqara

This completely separate necropolis, founded by the pharaohs of the Sixth Dynasty (2345-2181 BC), is situated about 1 km south of the Pyramid of Sekhemkhet which is the most southerly of all the pyramids in North Saqqara. It has a few interesting tombs, based on the Pyramid of Unas as an architectural model, but sadly has been plundered by unscrupulous stone-masons or their suppliers. The pyramids of **Pepi I** and **Merenre** are in ruins.

To the east of the latter lies the **Pyramid of Djedkare**, known in Arabic as the Pyramid of the Sentinel, which is 25 m tall and is open to visitors. The entrance is on the north side through a tunnel leading into the funerary chamber but there is comparatively little to see.

The most important and interesting tombs are further south. The **Pyramid of Pepi II** is surrounded by an entire funerary complex. The inside chamber is decorated with stars and funerary inscriptions. Within the complex are a number of other smaller pyramids belonging to his queens. They are all based on the same design as Pepi's pyramid and contain a miniature funerary complex. The **Pyramid of Queen Neith** is interesting and has some wonderful inscriptions and decorations.

To the east is the **Mastaba Faraoun**, the tomb of **Shepseskaf**, the last Pharaoh of the Fourth Dynasty (2613-2494 BC). The inside is interesting but undecorated and the walls are made from large blocks of granite. From the outside the tomb looks like a gigantic sarcophagus and the exterior was originally covered in a thin layer of limestone. About 1 km further south are two more pyramids. The first is the brick **Pyramid of Khendjer** which has a funerary chamber made out of quartzite. The second is larger, but unfinished, and bears no inscriptions or signs of use. It has impressive underground white stone chambers and a quartzite funerary chamber.

The Pyramids at Dhashur – The Red Pyramid and The Bent Pyramid lie about 2 km south of the Mastaba Faraoun. They were constructed by Snefru (BC 2575-51) first ruler of the 4th Dynasty, at the time of the great pyramid construction. He built the two pyramids in Dhashur and was perhaps responsible for the pyramid at Maidoun. His constructive tendencies were continued in his son Cheops.

The **Red Pyramid** to the north, named after the reddish local limestone used in the core, is considered to be older. It is thought to be the first true pyramid to be constructed to have sloping sides rather than steps. Each side measures 220 m, the slopes measures 43°40' and the total height is 101 m. Some of the original Tura limestone facing stones still remain on the eastern side. Limestone fragments of the monolithic pyramidion exist. The entrance 28 m above the ground on the north side leads down to two corbelled antechambers from the second of which the burial chamber can be reached. The **Bent Pyramid** (also known as the Southern Shining Pyramid) which lies further to the south was constructed of local limestone with a casing of polished Turah limestone, the casing blocks slope inwards making them more stable and also difficult to remove. The side at the base measures 188.6 m and the height is 97 m (originally 105 m). If construction had continued at the original angle it would have been 128.5 m high.

The pyramid is unique on two counts. First the angles change. The lower angle is 52° enclosing some 70% of the bulk of the pyramid. It then reduces to 43.5° up to the peak. There is a number of theories for the unusual shape. It is suggested that the builders got tired and changed the angle to reduce the volume and so complete sooner. It is suggested that the change in slope indicated a double pyramid – two pyramids superimposed. It is also suggested that the architect lost his nerve for this was being built when the pyramid at Maidoun collapsed. That too had an angle of 52° so a quick rethink was necessary.

A pyramid with two entrances is also unique. The first entrance in the middle of the north face is about 12 m above the ground and leads to the upper chamber. The second in the west face is only just above ground and leads to the lower chamber. Both chambers are corbelled and the floors of both were built to a depth of 4 m with small stone blocks. ■ *There is unrestricted access for E£20, E£10 for students, camera E£5.*

There are three other pyramids here (from north to south) belonging to the 12th Dynasty Kings, Amenemhat II, Senusert III and Amenemhat III.

The Bent Pyramid at Dhashur

(After IES Edwards)

Section looking east

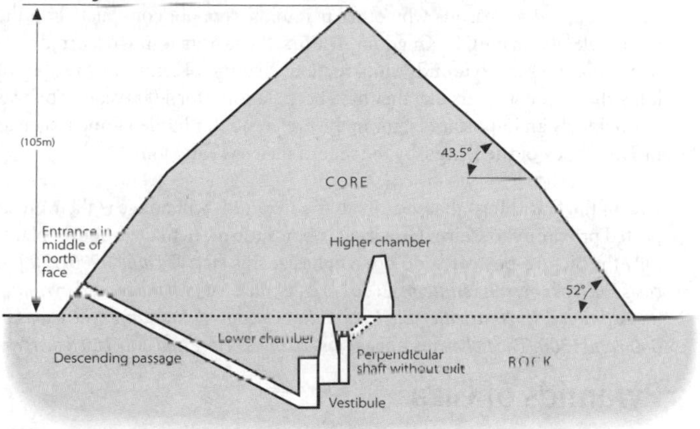

Section looking south

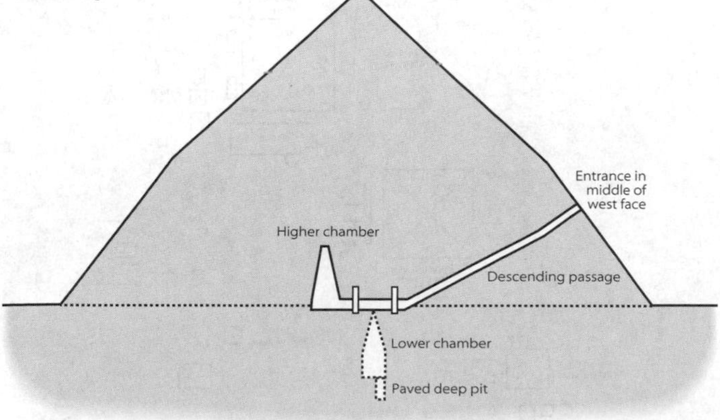

The Pyramids of Giza

Of the Seven Wonders of the ancient world only the **Pyramids** remain. Those at **Giza** outside Cairo are by no means the only ones in Egypt but they are the largest, most imposing and best preserved. When **Herodotus**, chronicler of the Ancient Greeks, visited them in 450 BC they were already more ancient to him than the time of Christ is to us today! That the huge blocks were quarried, transported and put into place demonstrates how highly developed and ordered the Old Kingdom was at its peak. Herodotus claimed that it would have taken 100,000 slaves 30 years to have constructed the great **Pyramid of Cheops**, but it is more likely that the pyramid was built by peasants, paid in food, who were unable to work the land while the Nile flooded between July and November. Happily, the high waters also made it possible to transport the casing stone from Aswan and Tura, virtually to the base of the pyramids. The enormous Pyramid of Cheops, built between 2589-66 BC out of over 2,300,000 blocks of stone with an average weight of 2.5 tonnes and a total weight of 6,000,000 tonnes to a height of almost 140 m, is the oldest and largest of the pyramids at Giza. The **Pyramid of Chephren** and **Pyramid of Menkaure** date from 2570 BC to 2530 BC.

A breakdown in the structure of society, and the reduction of wealth, have been proposed as reasons why other pyramids were not constructed on the same scale later in the Old Kingdom. The first thefts from tombs occurred relatively soon after the Pyramids' construction. A couple of centuries, or so, is not long when one considers that they have been standing for 4,000 years! This was undoubtedly an important factor in the preference for hidden tombs, such as in **The Valley of the Kings**, by the time of the New Kingdom.

One of the first things that visitors to the Pyramids will notice is their unexpected proximity to Cairo. Giza itself is now little more than a suburb. Naturally the picture-postcards do not emphasize this fact! ■ *Daily 0900-1700. It costs E£20 per person (students E£10) to enter the area and the second pyramid, an additional E£20 to enter the Pyramid of Cheops. Admittance to Cheops at 0800 and 1300. The ticket office opens just 20 mins before and only 150 tickets are*

Pyramids of Giza

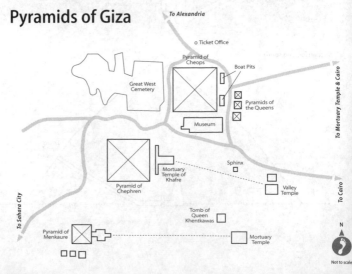

Flinders Petrie – The beginnings of systematic archaeology

Flinders Petrie applied the first systematic excavation techniques to archaeological sites in Egypt. He was born in 1853 in Scotland and arrived in Egypt in 1880 in search of measurements of pyramids. He stayed and excavated many sites, recording in detail each item and layer of his work with consistency and accuracy, which was in sharp contrast to the acquisitive and unscientific digging of this and earlier periods. It was he who set the chronological framework within which most archaeologists and their colleagues later

worked. Petrie had the reputation even as a young man for wanting his own way and there were constant skirmishes between himself and his financing committee in London. In 1886 Petrie left his employment with the Egypt Exploration Fund but remained in Egypt for a further 37 years, actively excavating and recording his finds. He eventually left Egypt in 1923 when the law on the division of archaeological finds was changed after the discovery of the tomb of Tutankhamen by Howard Carter. He died in 1942.

issued each time. It costs E£10 to visit the pyramid of Menkaure, plus E£10 for cameras inside the pyramid but no flash photography is allowed. For sound and light performances see page 133. All the official guides demand a tip but most have already been tipped by the tour operator so don't give much. It is difficult but possible to avoid amateur guides who then demand money. The café has a minimum charge and should be avoided so make sure that you take water with you. The hassling camel owners will demand much more but don't pay more than E£10 for a short ride and make sure you agree the price first and don't pay until you are back on the ground. The whole complex can be fairly busy at peak times and very dusty. Claustrophobics should avoid the inside of the pyramids.

Pyramid of Cheops (Khufu)

Very little is known of Cheops. His tomb, which could have provided some answers, was looted long before the archaeologists arrived. He is believed to have been the absolute ruler of a highly stratified society and his reign must have been one of great wealth in order to afford so stupendous a burial site. Although he was buried alone his wives and relations may have merited smaller *mastabas* nearby.

Originally the 230 m x 230 m pyramid would have stood at 140 m high but 3 m has been lost in all dimensions since the encasing marble was eroded or removed. The entrance, which was at the centre of the north face, has been changed in modern times and access is now 15 m lower via an opening created by the plundering Khalifa Ma'mun in AD 820. From this entrance a tunnel descends steeply for about 25 m until it reaches a point where it is met by an ascending corridor which climbs at the same angle.

If one were to continue down the very long, narrow and steep descending shaft, which is closed to ordinary visitors and is definitely not for those who are either unfit or claustrophobic, one would eventually reach a lower unfinished chamber which lies 20 m beneath the bedrock of the pyramid's foundations! Even though the chamber is empty, except for a deep pit where the sarcophagus would have been lowered, the sensation of standing alone under six million tonnes of stone blocks is overpowering. Despite the speculation that the chamber was unfinished because of a change of plan by either Cheops or his architect the later pyramid of Chephren follows an identical pattern.

Going up the 36 m long ascending corridor, which is 1.6 m high and has a steep 1:2 gradient, one arrives at the start of the larger 47 m long **Great Gallery** which continues upward at the same incline to the **King's Chamber** 95 m beneath the pyramid's apex. The gallery, whose magnificent stonework is so well cut that it is impossible to insert a blade into the joints, narrows at the top end to a corbelled roof which is 8.5 m high.

At the beginning of the gallery there is a second horizontal passage, 35 m long and 1.75 m high, which leads to a room misleadingly known as the **Queen's Chamber**. In fact no queen was buried there and the small room, measuring 5.2 m by 5.7 m with a 6.13 m pointed roof, is more likely to be the Serdab which contained the icon of the Pharaoh. In 1872 two triangular holes were made by a British engineer in the chamber's north and south walls in order to discover the location of the air or ventilation shafts.

The walls of **The King's Chamber** are lined with polished red granite. The room measures 5.2 m by 10.8 m by 5.8 m high and contains the huge lidless Aswan red granite sarcophagus, which was all that remained of the treasures when archaeologists first explored the site. It was saved because it was too large to move along the entrance passage and, therefore, must have been placed in the chamber during the pyramid's construction. Above this upper chamber there is a series of five relieving chambers which are structurally essential to support the massed weight of the stones above and distribute the weight away from the burial chamber. A visit to the collapsed pyramid at Maidoum (see Fayoum, page 167) will illustrate why this was necessary! As in the Queen's Chamber the north and south walls bear air shafts but in this case they are the original ones.

One of the great mysteries of the massive Pyramid of Cheops is the four tiny meticulously crafted 20 cm square shafts, which travel, two from the King's Chamber and another two from the Queen's Chamber, at precisely maintained angles through the body of the pyramid to the outer walls. Obviously serving a significant function, they were originally thought to be ventilation shafts. However, Egyptologists now are more inclined to believe that they are of religious significance and relate to the Ancient Egyptian's belief that the stars are a heavenly counterpart to their land, inhabited by gods and souls of the departed.

Pyramid of Cheops (section)

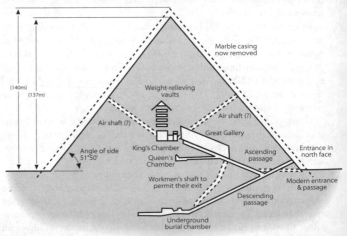

(140m)
(137m)

Marble casing now removed

Weight-relieving vaults

Air shaft (?)

Air shaft (?)

Great Gallery

Angle of side 51°50'

King's Chamber

Queen's Chamber

Ascending passage

Entrance in north face

Workmen's shaft to permit their exit

Modern entrance & passage

Descending passage

Underground burial chamber

The main feature of the ancient night sky was the Milky Way, the bright band of stars which was believed to be the celestial River Nile. The most conspicuous of bright stars which appeared in the night sky were those of Orion's Belt, which because their reappearance after 70 days coincided with the yearly miracle of the Nile flood, were associated with Osiris, the protector god. The brightest star in the sky, Syrius, was his consort the goddess Isis because it was bright, beautiful, and followed Osiris across the sky. Linked into the creation myth, the texts on the great pyramid's walls repeatedly tell of the dead pharoah, seen as the latest incarnation of Horus, the son of Isis and Osiris, travelling in a boat between various star constellations. At an angle of exactly 45°, the southern shaft of the King's Chamber points directly at where Orion's Belt would have been in the sky in ancient times. Meanwhile, the southern shaft of the Queen's Chamber points to Syrius, his consort Isis. The northern shaft of the King's Chamber is directed at the circumpolar stars, important to the Ancient Egyptians as the celestial pole because these stars never disappear or die in the sky. The 'star shafts' thus appear to be directed so that the spirit of the dead pharoah could use the shafts to reach the important stars with pinpoint accuracy.

Around the Cheops Pyramid

In accordance with the Pharaonic custom, Cheops married his sister Merites whose smaller ruined pyramid stands to the east of his together with the pyramids of two other queens, both of which are attached to a similarly ruined smaller sanctuary. Little remains of **Cheops' Mortuary Temple** which stood to the east of the pyramid. It was connected by a causeway, which collapsed only in the last 150 years, to the Valley Temple which stands near the modern village of **Nazlat al-Samman**. The temples and causeway were built and decorated before Cheops' Pyramid was completed.

West of the Cheops Pyramid is an extensive Royal Cemetery in which 15 *mastabas* have recently been opened to the public after having been closed for over 100 years. A 4,600-year-old female mummy, with a totally unique internal plaster encasement unlike that seen anywhere else, was discovered at the site.

The **Boat Pits and Museum** ■ *daily 0900-1600, E£20, students E£10* is located at the base of the south face of the Cheops Pyramid where five boat pits were discovered in 1982. The boat, which is encased in the stones, is amazingly intact and was held together with rope with no nails being used at all. The exact purpose of these buried boats is unclear but they may have been regarded as a means of travelling to the after-life, as can be seen in the 17th to 19th Dynasty tombs at Thebes, or possibly as a means of accompanying the Sun-God on his diurnal journey. One boat has been located at the site and can be seen in the museum. It is best to avoid visiting the sun ship at prayer time because you cannot get in.

Pyramid of Chephren (Khafre). Built for the son of Cheops and Hensuten, the Pyramid of Chephren, or Khafre as he is sometimes known, stands to the southwest of the Great Pyramid of Cheops. Although, at 136.5 m high, and an estimated weight of 4,880,000 tonnes, it is actually a few metres smaller than the Cheops Pyramid. The fact that it was built on a raised limestone plateau was a deliberate attempt to make it appear larger than that of his father. The top of the pyramid still retains some of the casing of polished limestone from Tura that once covered the entire surface, thus providing an idea of the original finish. The entrance to the tomb was lost for centuries until 1818 when Belzoni located and blasted open the sealed portal on the north side.

Although he believed that it would still be intact, he found that it had been looted many centuries earlier. As with the Pyramid of Cheops there is an unfinished and presumed unused chamber below the bedrock. The passageway now used to enter the burial chamber heads downwards before levelling out to the granite lined passageway that leads to the chamber. To the west of the chamber is the red granite sarcophagus, built into the floor, with the lid lying nearby. This pyramid has just reopened after months of restoration. Better ventilation and new interior lighting has been provided by the number of daily visitors is to be strictly limited.

The **Mortuary Temple of Khafre** lies to the east of the pyramid and is more elaborate and better preserved than that of his father. Although the statues and riches have been stolen, the limestone walls were cased with granite which is still present in places. There are still the remains a large pillared hall, a small sanctuary, outhouses and a courtyard.

A 500 m causeway linked the Mortuary Temple to the **Valley Temple**, ■ *daily 0900-1600*, which is better preserved than any other because it lay hidden in the sands until Mariette rediscovered it in 1852. It is lined with red granite at roof height which protects the limestone. Two entrances to the Temple face east and lead to a T-shaped hall supported by enormous pillars. In front of these stood 23 diorite statues of Khafre. The only one which has remained intact can be found in the Egyptian Museum. Side chambers lie off to the south of the hall. A passage which joined the causeway is now closed off.

The Sphinx is next to Khafre's Valley Temple to the northeast. We are extremely lucky that it still exists because it was built of soft sandstone and would have disappeared centuries ago had the sand not covered it for so much of its history. Yet it is equally surprising that it was ever carved because its sculptor must have known that such soft stone would quickly decay. The Arabs call it *Abu'l-Hawl*, the awesome, or terrible one. Nobody can be certain who it personifies but it is possibly Khafre himself and would then be the oldest known large-scale royal portrait. Some say that it was hewn from the remaining stone after the completion of the pyramid and that, almost as an afterthought, Khafre set it, as a sort of monumental scarecrow, to guard his tomb. Others claim that the face is that of his guardian deity rather than Khafre's own.

Pyramid of Chephren (section)

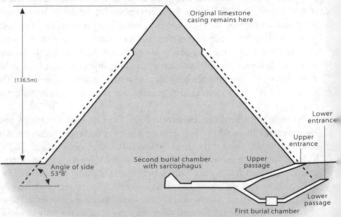

Original limestone casing remains here

(136.5m)

Angle of side 53°8'

Second burial chamber with sarcophagus

Upper passage

Lower entrance

Upper entrance

First burial chamber

Lower passage

Save our Sphinx

The carefully planned, six-year-long, restoration of the Sphinx programme is in its third and final stage. In the 1980s over 2,000 new limestone blocks were added to the ailing body of the sphinx and it was subjected to injections of chemicals. Unfortunately this 'treatment' flaked away taking with it parts of the original rock surface. The next attempt at restoration was certainly unkind and unscientific. Various mortars and numerous workers, untrained in restoration, carried out a six-month repair. The result was further damage and in 1988 the crumbling of the left shoulder and falling of blocks.

The present attempts to restore the Sphinx are under the control of archaeologists from the Supreme Council of Antiquities. Work has been concentrated so far on draining away the subsoil seepage which is damaging the rock and on repairing the damaged shoulder with smaller blocks more in keeping with the original size. After all, said the Minister of Culture, "It is an objet d'art". We admire his sentiments and wish them every success.

The Sphinx was first uncovered by Tuthmosis IV (1425-17 BC) thereby fulfilling a prophecy that by uncovering the great man-lion he would gain the throne. Recent efforts to conserve the Sphinx are now complete but the rising water table threatens to accelerate its decay. Earlier attempts to restore it caused more harm than good when the sandstone was filled, totally inappropriately, with concrete. The Sphinx is incomplete. The 'beard' is exhibited in the British Museum.

The name 'sphinx' which means 'strangler' was given first by the Greeks to a *fabulous creature* which had the head and bust of a woman, the body of a lion and the wings of a bird. The sphinx appears to have originated in Egypt in the form of a sun god with whom the pharaoh was associated. The Egyptian sphinx is usually a lion with the head of a king wearing the characteristic wig-cover. There are however ram-headed sphinxes associated with the god Amun.

The Pyramid of Menkaure (Mycerinus) is the smallest of the three Giza Pyramids and marks the beginning of a steep decline in the standards of workmanship and attention to detail in the art of pyramid-building. At the time of the death of Menkaure, who was Chephren's successor and was later known by the Greek name of Mycerinus, it was unfinished and the granite encasement intended to cover the poor quality local limestone was never put in place by his son Shepseskaf who completed the rest of the pyramid. The base is 102 m by 104 m (the original measurements much reduced by removal of stones) and rises at 51° to 66.5 m high, considerably lower than the earlier pyramids. It also differs from those of Khufu and Khafre in that the lower chamber was used as the burial tomb. The walls are lined with granite hewn into the rock below the level of the Pyramid's foundations. The fine basalt sarcophagus was discovered in the recessed floor but unfortunately lost at sea en route to Britain.

There is a theory that the odd plan of the three Pyramids of Giza, progressively smaller and with the third slightly offset to the left, correlates to the layout of the three stars of Orion's Belt. But this is highly controversial as it suggests that the Ancient Egyptians chose to reproduce, on land and over a great distance, a kind of map of the stars.

East of the Pyramid of Menkaure lies the **Mortuary Temple** which is relatively well preserved. The walls were not encased with granite or marble but with red mud bricks and then lined with a thin layer of smoother limestone. It is connected to the Valley Temple via a 660 m mud-brick causeway which now lies beneath the sand.

Subsidiary Pyramids

South of the Pyramid of Menkaure are three smaller incomplete ones. The largest, to the east, was most likely intended for Menkaure's principal wife. The granite sarcophagus of the central tomb was recovered and was found to contain the bones of a young woman.

The Tomb of Queen Khentkawes, who was an obscure but intriguing and important figure, is situated to the south of the main Giza pyramids. Although she appears to have been married to Shepseskaf, who was the last Fourth Dynasty pharaoh, she subsequently married a high priest of the sun-god Re at a time when the male dynastic line was particularly weak. By going on to bear a number of later kings who are buried in Saqqara and Abu Sir, she acted as the link between the 4th and 5th Dynasties. Her tomb is an enormous sarcophagus and is linked to a Mortuary Temple cut out of the limestone.

The Zawiyat al-Aryan Pyramids are roughly halfway between Giza and North Saqqara and one has to ride through the desert to see them. A visit would probably only be rewarding to the devoted Egyptologist. There are two pyramids of which the southernmost one is probably a 3rd Dynasty (2686-13 BC) step pyramid. The granite suggests that it is Fourth Dynasty (2613-2494 BC) but it would appear to have been abandoned after the foundations had been laid. The **Pyramids of Abu Sir** and **The Sun Temples of Abu Ghurab** are about 3 km further south (see Saqqara, page 151).

For those interested in the Coptic Monasteries look out for the **Monastery of St Mercurius** (Abu Seifein) in Tamouh just 12 km south of Giza, now used as a training centre.

Pyramid of Menkaure (section)

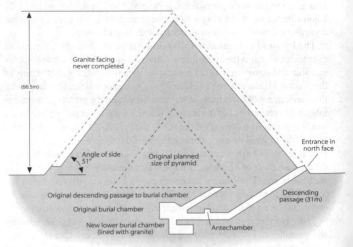

Granite facing never completed

(66.5m)

Angle of side 51°

Original planned size of pyramid

Entrance in north face

Descending passage (31m)

Original descending passage to burial chamber

Original burial chamber

New lower burial chamber (lined with granite)

Antechamber

El-Fayoum and Lake Qaroun

Although usually described as an oasis **El-Fayoum** is not fed by underground water, like the Western Desert oases further southwest, but by water from the Nile which is transported to this natural triangular depression by a series of canals. The water comes from the River Nile leaving the Ibrahimeya canal at Assiut as the Bahr Yusef which itself divides into a number of smaller canals west of Fayoum City. Having irrigated the oasis the water runs into Lake Qaroun which, despite having dramatically shrunk over the past few thousand years, is at about 215 sq km still Egypt's largest natural salt-water lake ranging in depth from 5 m in the east to 12 m in the west. The oasis which covers 4,585 sq km has five main centres and 157 villages. It is 8% water, 39% cultivated area and 63% housing and desert.

Phone code: 084
Colour map 2, grid C2

About 70,000 years ago the Nile flood first broke through the low mountains which surround the large Fayoum depression and formed Lake Qaroun and the surrounding marshes. This is believed to be one, if not the first, site of agriculture in the world as plants which grew around the lake were collected, land was fenced in, and dry and guarded storage areas were built. Even today Fayoum is still famous for fruit and vegetables and its chickens. To describe food as *fayoum* means delicious.

The 12th Dynasty pharaoh Amenemhat I (1991-62 BC) first drained part of the marshes to develop the area for agriculture and also dug a large canal from the River Nile controlled by a regulator at El-Lahun to the northwest of Beni Suef. The result of this and further developments by Amenemhat III (1842-1797 BC), who showed great interest in the area and built a pyramid at Hawara (see page 167), was Lake Moeris (Great Lake), twice the present size and teeming with fish, and an agricultural area to the south renowned for its rich and varied crops.

The Romans, who called the area **Crocodilopolis** (because of the ever present crocodiles) changed Fayoum's previous system of crop rotation and forced the area to supply grain exclusively to the Roman market. Muslims believe that the prophet Joseph developed the area during his captivity in Egypt through the canalization of the Bahr Yusef River and by building the world's first dam. Although Fayoum's national strategic importance diminished with the canalization of the Nile Delta it remains one of the most productive agricultural areas in the country.

The water level in Lake Qaroun had been falling for about 2,000 years as it received less and less water until the construction of the Aswan High Dam led to far greater stability in the level of the River Nile. By mediaeval times the lake had become far too salty to sustain freshwater fish and new species were introduced. The shrunken lake now lies 45 m below sea level and 40 m lower than its original level of 70,000 years ago and 1/6 of its original size. It now appears that the water table is rising again as houses and fields at the lakeside have been flooded in recent years. Evidence of this is clear in notices excusing the rising damp in the walls of the Auberge du Lac and raised sills over which one must step to gain access to hotels along the lake shore.

Despite its stagnant and polluted water the beach resorts around Lake Qaroun still attract the more affluent visitors to the region. The oasis is declared free from bilharzia, a recommendation in itself. The number of visitors is increasing and while half are Egyptian about a third are European. The season runs all year round, but from January-April it is considered too cold to swim. As part of its efforts to persuade tourists to visit areas outside the Nile valley the Egyptian Tourist Association is trying to encourage tours from

The Pyramids & El-Fayoum

Cairo, via Fayoum and the Middle Egypt sites, to both the Red Sea coast and Upper Egypt which would undoubtedly be a wonderful and fascinating tour.

Fayoum City is the main town in the oasis and the province's capital, 103 km southwest of central Cairo and 85 km from Giza and the Pyramids, an estimated one hour journey along the four-lane carriageway. The majority of the oasis' population of 1.8 million people are not Nile Valley Egyptians but settled and semi-nomadic Berber people who are related to the Libyan Arabs. Although few reminders of its ancient past have survived it is still a relatively attractive town though visitors are not advised to stay in the city for long but rather to enjoy the peace and tranquillity of the oasis' gardens and the lake.

In addition, the climate is splendid. The summers are not as hot as Luxor/Aswan and the winters are not as wet as Cairo or the delta. The atmosphere is clear – so beware of the sun.

In the quieter areas there is a rewarding amount of wildlife to observe. While the fox is common in the town, the wolf is found only in the desert periphery. Sightings of the wild cat are very rare. Thousands of egrets roost in the oasis, herons are common and many migrating birds take a rest here in spring and autumn.

Getting there The Cairo-Fayoum City bus leaves every 30 min from Midan Ahmad Helmi behind Ramses Railway Station. Tickets cost E£3 and can be purchased in advance from the building behind the grey church in the middle of the square. The Bahr Yusef canal bisects Fayoum, the many bridges being numbered for convenience, and buses and taxis from Cairo all terminate close to the canal in the centre of town. Negotiate the price then take one of the *hantours* (horse-drawn carriages) to your destination. Local buses and service taxis serving the oasis can be obtained from the Al-Hawatim terminal to the south of the Bahr Yusef canal. Private taxis hired through the tourist information kiosk, *Hotel Auberge du Lac* and the Kom Aushim museum, cost about E£10 per hour.

Tourist offices There is a particularly active and helpful local tourist administration, main office (T342313) in the centre of town on Sharia Gumhorriya. The office by the waterwheels is T325211.

The El-Fayoum Oasis

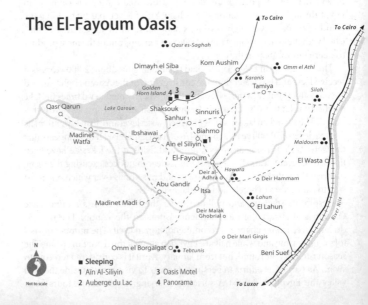

N
Not to scale

■ Sleeping
1 Aïn Al-Siliyin
2 Auberge du Lac
3 Oasis Motel
4 Panorama

Spring clean

In January each year every canal in the country undergoes cleaning and repair. The sluices are shut, the canals are dry, silt is dredged, walls are strengthened and the water wheels, now white with dead algae, are lifted and overhauled. Although the wheels are considered to be ancient in fact no part is more than about 10 years old. It is said the state of the canals is a mirror of the condition of the whole country.

There is comparatively little to see in Fayoum City itself although the covered *souq* and the adjacent street of goldsmiths, **es-Sagha**, found across the fourth bridge to the west of the central tourist office, are worth a visit. A little further west along the south side of the Bahr Yusef is the attractive **Mosque of Khawand Asal-Bay** believed to have been built in 1490, or earlier, making it the oldest in the oasis. It was built by the Mamluke Sultan **Qaitbai** (1468-98) who was noted as a warrior, a builder and a torturer, for Asal-Bay who was not only his favourite concubine but also the mother of his assassinated successor Mohammed IV (1496-98), sister of Qansuh I (1498-1500) and wife of Janbalat (1500-01) who were both deposed and murdered. When, however, Tumanbay I (1501-01) married Qaitbai's official wife Fatima he insulted and disgraced Asal-Bay but he was soon deposed and exiled. Remains of its former impressive structure, most of which fell into the Bahr Yusef in 1892, include the dome supported by ancient pillars, some with Corinthian capitals, the rather plain *mihrab* and the gilded teak *minbar* elaborately carved and inlaid with ivory from Somalia. A small plaque on the wall by the *mihrab* gives information about the construction of the building.

Other mosques are worth visiting in town, particularly during the *moulids*. The **Mosque and Mausoleum** in honour of **Ali er-Rubi** has a large plain white dome and a minaret. The entrance leads into a covered courtyard at the far right hand corner of which is the door to the mausoleum. The birthday feast of Ali er-Rubi is a very important *moulid* in this area. The so called **Hanging Mosque** or **El Moalak Mosque** was constructed in limestone in 1375 by Prince Soliman Ibn Mouhamed. It is built above five arches, each of which housed a workshop, and with a double flight of steps leading to the main door. It is north of the Bahr Yusef up a small street.

The 13 m red granite **Obelisk of Senusert I** (12th Dynasty) to the northeast of town, estimated weight over 100 tonnes, serves as a useful point of reference. Originally it was situated in the settlement of Abgig to south but now it stands in the middle of a traffic roundabout.

The locals are particularly proud of their water-wheels, a magnificent sight. They were first introduced by the Ptolemies and are used now as the official symbol of El-Fayoum province (See box 'The Groaning Water-wheels of El-Fayoum', page 166). There are over 200 to see in the region about 4 m to 5 m in diameter and black with layers of protective tar. Besides the four large ones behind the tourist office on the main Sharia Gumhorriya the most famous is the series of **Seven Water-wheels** about 3 km north along the Bahr Sinnuris. It takes about half an hour. Walk north out of town following the Bahr Sinnuris first on the west bank then on the east. A solitary wheel at a farm is followed by a spectacular group of four and then the final two wheels by a bridge. They are powered by the water in the stream and run all the time. The slope of the land from south to north encourages fast flowing streams, thus enabling this type of water lifting to be constructed. When the water is not required for irrigation it runs back into the main stream. Maintenance takes place each spring but should an urgent repair be required it takes a team of strong men to stop the wheel rotating.

The Pyramids & El-Fayoum

There are four churches in the town, that of the Holy Virgin (Coptic Orthodox) being the oldest and having historical interest. The date of construction is given as 1836. Ignore the less tasteful items and look out for the large altar screen decorated with light and dark wood inlay work and the Bible stand and Bishop's throne both inlaid with ivory.

The church contains a shrine to Anba Abram who died in 1914, one time Bishop of Fayoum and Giza.

Sleeping **B/C** *Auberge du Lac*, located on Lake Qaroun, T700002, F700730. 88 a/c rooms with telephone, TV and bath, laundry, 24-hr room service, 4 restaurants open 0600-2300 (only in season), disco open 2200-0300 (only in season). Tennis, squash, 2 pools, watersports, boats for hire, duck shooting, poorly equipped gym and health club, parking, facilities for handicapped, major cards taken. Comfortable, but not luxurious. The view from the more expensive rooms is ruined by the cheaper chalets built in the gardens beside the lake. King Ibn Saud and Winston Churchill met here in 1945, ask to have a look at the suite used by King Farouk, now all very faded and lacking in care, someone has decorated the stairs – all over the dark red carpet. Don't stay here – go to the *Oasis.* **C** *Panorama Shakshuk*, on Lake Qaroun, T701314, F701757. 30 a/c rooms with balcony and lake view, TV room, pool, watersports, fishing, wind surfing, water, skiing, duck shooting, garden, restaurants inside and out, seafood speciality.

D *Oasis Motel*, on Lake Qaroun shore, T701565. 28 rooms, 2 restaurants, 1 over the lake, pool over lake, cheerful staff, caravan and camping facilities.

E *Aïn al-Siliyin*, T500062. 32 chalets, restaurant with good range of basic foods, gardens. **E** *Palace Hotel*, on Sharia Horriya, very central. 35 clean a/c rooms, cars, motorbikes and bicycles for hire. Mixed reports.

F *El Montazah*, Minsht Lutfallah, Fayoum City, T324633. Located next to the Bahr Sinnuris canal to the north of the town centre, run by Copts. **F** *Geziret el-Bat*, Manshat el-Sadat, Lake Qaroun, T749288. 22 rooms. lakeside location, very cheap. **F** *Honey Day Hotel*, Sharia Gamal Abdel Nasser, Fayoum Entrance, T341205. 25 rooms, restaurant, coffee shop, spacious and clean with friendly staff, 25% discount

Fayoum City

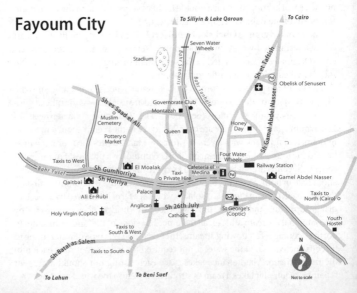

for groups. **F** *Queen*, Sharia Manshat Luftallah, Fayoum City, T326819. 32 beds, reasonable and newish hotel.

Camping *Aïn al-Siliyin Hotel, Oasis Hotel, Kom Abu Muslim* camp site and *Kom Oshim* near Karanis.

Youth hostels *Fayoum Hostel*, in Fayoum City, T323682. *Fayoum Stadium Hostel*, *Fayoum City*, T327368. *Shakshuk Hostel*, in Shakshuk, near Lake Qaroun, T323164. *Siliyin Hostel and Scout Camp*, T500062. *International Hostel* at Flat No 7, Housing Block No 7, Hadaka, 24 beds, T350005, self catering facilities. Station 3 km.

Expensive: *Aïn el Shayr*, near springs at Aïn Siliyin. *Café Gabal el Zinah*, on Qaroun   **Eating** Lake, play areas for children, boatlanding, fish is main item on menu. *El Medinah*, overlooking the 4 water wheels in Fayoum City. *Karanis Tourist Restaurant*, Kom Oshim, eat in shaded garden, T600783. The *Auberge du Lac-Fayoum* provides average quality food in interesting surrounding.

Mid-range: *Al Jowhara (Gem) Restaurant*, at Aïn Siliyin, in disappointing garden. *Café al-Louloua*, at Qaroun Lake, at major junction serving Western food. *Lake Plage Café*, overlooking Qaroun Lake and 1.5 km of beach, play areas for children, adequate but unimaginative. *Zahret el Shateu Restaurant*, at Aïn Siliyin.

Cheap: *Mokhimar*, 100 m west of central tourist office.

Fayoum chickens, fresh fruit and straw baskets.   **Shopping**

Bus: to Cairo's Ahmed Helmi and Giza stations buses leave every 30 mins between   **Transport** 0630-1830 from the main bus station in the centre of town on Sharia el-Hadqa by bridge No 3. There are also regular buses south to Beni Suef with connections south up the Nile Valley. **Service taxis**: are quicker but more hair-raising than buses and leave the depot next to the bus station for Cairo's Midan Giza, and thence on to central Cairo, and for Beni Suef.

Train These are so slow and inefficient that they are not worth taking, except to El-Wasta and Beni Suef.

Banks *Bank of Alexandria, Banque du Caire, Banque Misr* and *National Bank of Egypt*, in town   **Directory** centre. You may have to try all for exchange facilities. **Communications** **Post Office**: central post office is on the south side of the Bahr Yusef canal opposite the central tourist office. **Medical services** Hospital: T322249. **Places of worship** There are four churches in El-Fayoum where services are held in Arabic or Coptic/Arabic. **Useful telephone numbers** Ambulance: T123; Fire: T180; Police: T122; **Tourist Police:** T324048.

Excursions from El-Fayoum

Outside town at **Aïn al-Siliyin**, 9 km north of the city towards Lake Qaroun, is a popular park which has natural springs and a stream. This is a very tatty area, the springs, Aïn Siliyin and Aïn Alshayr, rarely flow yet it is very crowded on Friday and holidays. ■ *25 piastres*. Further north is **Lake Qaroun** which, despite the stagnant and salt encrusted water, is a favourite beach resort. Although it is calm much of the time, in winter it is reported to be quite rough and teeming with ducks and geese which bring the hunters to the lakeside hotels. Qaroun means 'Lake of the Horn'. It is possible to negotiate a row boat from the *Auberge du Lac* to the barren **Golden Horn Island** or to the north shore.

The Groaning Water-wheels of El-Fayoum

Because the land in the El-Fayoum oasis varies from +26 m to -42 m in three main steps, self-powered water-wheels were essential and the construction of one particular type, which is exclusive to Fayoum, began in pharaonic times. There are often whole series of these 'sawaqih al-Hadir' (or 'roaring water-wheels'), *which produce a perpetual groaning noise and can last 10 years if they are properly maintained, and there are over 200 in the oasis which has adopted the water-wheel as its official symbol.*

To the east of the lake and 25 km from the city on the main road towards Cairo, **Kom Aushim** is adjacent to the site of the ancient city of **Karanis**. Karanis, founded in the third century BC and inhabited by mercenaries of Ptolemy II, was once the centre of a large agricultural area exporting cereals to Rome via Alexandria. Walking to the remains of two Roman temples, the Temple of Pnepheros and Petesouchos (yet more crocodile gods) is the larger, one crunches across ground covered with broken pottery. Expect to be shown the oil/wine presses, tank for crocodiles, Roman baths with evidence of heating pipes, a row of headless sphinxes and the former residence of British High Commissioner Sir Miles Lampson. The site is very large, has a café, play area and offers camping sites with 50 tents available. ■ *Daily 0900-1600 in winter and to 1700 in summer, E£10.* The results of excavations carried out in the 1920s by the University of Michigan are displayed, together with exhibits from other sites around the Fayoum, in a small circular **museum**. The most interesting exhibits are the carefully restored pottery and glassware, the central mummy, the necklaces and the minute statues. ■ *Tue-Sun 0900-1600 in winter and 1700 in summer, E£5.* Trips to **Qasr es-Saghah** and the ruins of the Ptolemaic settlement of Soknopaiou Nesos, which used to be on the lakeside but is now 11 km away and 65 m above the current lake, can be arranged at the museum and it is strongly recommended to take a guide.

Madinet Madi about 30 km southwest of Fayoum City contains the ruins of a 12th Dynasty temple, built by Amenemhat III and Amenemhat IV dedicated to Sobek the crocodile god and Renenutet the serpent goddess. This site retains an attractive avenue of lions and winged sphinxes. The walls are constructed of limestone, a soft medium for the many reliefs including one of Sobek on the outside wall at the back. The cartouches of both Amenemhats are in the sanctuary with the elegant feet and ankles (all that remains) of several statues. Access by normal vehicle. **Dimayh el Siba** would have been situated on the north coast of the lake which is now almost 3 km away. This old Ptolemaic city with ruins of small temple dedicated to Soknopaios (crocodile) was once the starting point of a camel trade route to the oases of the Western desert. The goods first crossed the lake by boat, still a good way to reach this site. **Omm el Athl**, east of Karanis is the ruins of Bachias city, 700 mud brick houses and a small mud brick temple dedicated to a crocodile god. Pedestals of **Biahmo** – two large stone pedestals each about 6 m high in Biahmo village some 7 km north of Fayoum – each once supported a seated colossus of Amenemhat III. Records suggest that each statue of red quartzite was 13 m above the top of its pedestal and each colossus and pedestal was surrounded by a huge solid wall. **Omm el Borgaigat** with the ruins of **Tebtunis** are 30 km south of Fayoum. This temple was dedicated to Sobek and was constructed of locally quarried coarse limestone but little remains of the walls. Some of the paving remains. A cache of mummified crocodiles was found here at the beginning of the last century. **Qsar Qarun**, to the west end of the lake, has the remains of the Graeco-Roman city of Dionysias, and a well preserved limestone Ptolemaic temple dedicated to a crocodile god and decorated with a symbol of a winged sun. The date is not certain as there are no inscriptions. It is a small structure but inside there are many small rooms, corridors, cellars and tunnels. It is fun to explore – with a torch. Watch out for scorpions. There are two spiral staircases up to the roof which provides a superb view.

There are four separate pyramid sites in the vicinity. **Hawara** pyramid, about 10 km southeast from Fayoum is a mud brick pyramid of Amenemhat III of 12th Dynasty, 58 m high and side of base measures 100 m. All the decorative casing has long since been removed. Contrary to normal practice the entrance was situated on the south side in an unsuccessful attempt to confuse looters. Adjacent to this pyramid is the legendary Labyrinth, a mortuary temple built by Amenemhat III, covering an area of 105,000 sq m. It was half carved into the interior of the rock and was composed of over 3,000 rooms but today few traces remain of this spectacular construction. Nearby is the tomb of his daughter Princess Sobek-Nefru Btah which was discovered intact in 1956.

The ruined **Pyramid of Senusert II** (1897-78 BC) near **Lahun** was built by Amenemhat III's grandfather. It was built on a rocky outcrop on which limestone pillars were constructed and then covered over with mud-brick and finally encased in stone. A 'sponge' made of sand and flint was placed around the base in order to prevent any flooding. Once again the unusual south facing entrance did not deter the tomb robbers who looted Senusert's sarcophagus but left some wonderful jewellery which is now in the Egyptian Museum and New York's Metropolitan Museum. The walled pyramid complex also include the ruins of a subsidiary pyramid for the queen, the mortuary temple and the mastaba tombs of other members of the royal family.

The collapsed **Maidoum Pyramid**, located to the northwest of El-Wasta on the River Nile, is most easily reached from there by a one hour early morning train journey followed by a 15 minute taxi ride to the village of Maidoum and a short walk. Originally it was 144 m sq and 42 m high but over the centuries the imposing pyramid, which is built on the edge of an escarpment above the cultivated area, has collapsed leaving only a central three stepped core of stone

The pyramids of El-Fayoum

The Pyramids & El-Fayoum

Maidoum Pyramid (section)

(After IES Edwards)

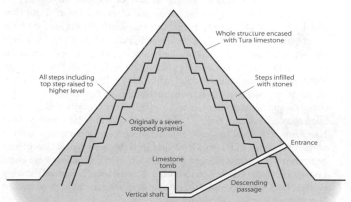

Whole structure encased with Tura limestone

All steps including top step raised to higher level

Steps infilled with stones

Originally a seven-stepped pyramid

Entrance

Limestone tomb

Descending passage

Vertical shaft

 *Fayoum portraits*

While excavating in a cemetery in the vicinity of the Hawara pyramid Sir Flinders Petrie found 146 quite remarkable hand painted portraits varying in quality of style and preservation. These funeral masks or portraits were executed in tempra or encaustic – a mixture of paint and wax – on slices of cedar or other wood. They were of children and of men and women of all ages.

They are dated from Graeco-Roman times, 30 BC to 395 AD, and are among the earliest portraits known. It is assumed that they were commissioned during the person's lifetime and used as decoration in the home until required. When the diseased was emblamed the portrait would be attached to the coffin or mummy case. Examples can be seen in the museum in Cairo.

standing 65 m high which looks rather like a mediaeval fort. The difficult entry is up a 30 m stairway on the north side from which visitors descend into a long 57 m sloping passage which levels out to reach a short vertical shaft leading to the limestone-lined and corbel roofed burial chamber which is on the same level as the pyramid's foundations.

While it is generally agreed that the Maidoum Pyramid housed the first Fourth Dynasty (2613-2494 BC) pharaoh Snefru, because he also had two other pyramids at Dashur, it is now believed that it was started by his father Huni and completed by Snefru. The theory as to why it collapsed is that, unlike the pyramids at Giza which distributed the stresses inwards, the incorrectly calculated outward stresses in this progression from the early step-pyramid to the later standard pyramid caused its collapse. Slightly further north are the rubble remains of the **Seila/Silah** step pyramid of limestone from Second Dynasty and adjacent rock tombs, thought to be Christian. This excursion requires four-wheel drive, a guide and a short walk.

The monasteries of El-Fayoum Saint Anthony (AD 251-356) acted as an inspiration for hermits and there were soon numerous monasteries throughout the country including the Fayoum depression. A number still stand today. The 12th century **Deir al-Adhra (Monastery of the Virgin)** just off the road to Beni Suef about 6 km outside Fayoum City is the most accessible. It was inhabited until the 18th century then fell into disuse. Bishop Anba Abram was buried here in 1914. The *moulid* of the Virgin is celebrated here each August and the number of pilgrims, already large, is increasing each year. Further south is the beautiful seventh century Coptic **Deir Malak Ghobrial (Monastery of the Angel Gabriel)** which is located on the desert escarpment at Naqlun above the cultivated lowlands. There is a large number of cells in the area – cut into the hillside – and these were accommodation for the monks. The last rebuilding/refurbishment took place this century, so today pilgrims to the annual celebration find more comfortable places to stay in the monastery buildings which surround the church. The church is of a simple classic design. Elements of older buildings have been incorporated giving an impression of greater antiquity. There are icons from the 19th century. **Deir Hammam**, which was originally built in the sixth or eighth century, is 6 km northeast of Luhun and Coptic **Deir Mari Girgis (Monastery of St George)** can be reached by boat from Sidmant al-Gabal which is 15 km southwest of Luhan. Even more isolated is **Deir Anba Samwail (Monastery of St Samuel)** which is about 30 km south of the rim of the Fayoum depression and can only be reached by pack animal or four-wheel drive vehicle.

Middle Egypt – Cairo to Luxor

5

Middle Egypt – Cairo to Luxor

Although most tourists tend to concentrate on Cairo and the splendours of Luxor and Aswan in Upper Egypt, the area stretching along the River Nile between Cairo and Luxor, termed Middle Egypt, should not be missed, security conditions permitting. There are many interesting sites and the slower provincial pace of life is most acceptable after the noise and hassle of Cairo.

Warning Middle Egypt in general and the towns such as Beni Suef, Assiut, Minya, Mallawi and Qena in particular are Islamic fundamentalist strongholds and as such could pose a threat to non-muslims. The threat should not, however, be exaggerated or be allowed to deter tourists from visiting Middle Egypt for all visitors will find themselves under the protection of the Tourist Police. In order to minimize the risks it is probably best for independent travellers to avoid staying in Beni Suef, Mallawi, Assiut and Qena which, besides any potential threat, are unpleasant towns with little or nothing to see. Instead most sites can be seen on trips from the attractive provincial capital of Minya or even further afield. The wonderful temples at Abydos and Dendera can be visited on long but worthwhile day trips from Luxor or Sohag rather than staying nearby in less pleasant circumstances. If planning to visit Middle Egypt it is **very** important to obtain the very latest security/risk information from an unbiased source such as your embassy.

Beni Suef

Phone code: 082
Colour map 2, grid C2
130 km south of Cairo, with a population of 86,000, Beni Suef is the northernmost provincial capital in Middle Egypt but is best avoided (see above) if possible and the few nearby sites can be seen on day trips from Cairo or the Fayoum Oasis.

Sights Besides the **Maidoum Pyramid**, which is best seen on a trip from the Fayoum Oasis or even Cairo, there is little to see in Beni Suef except a small museum and the ancient and very poorly preserved cities of **Heracleopolis** and **Oxyrhynchus**. They are located 15 km west of Beni Suef and 9 km west of Beni Mazar on the route to Minya.

Excursions can be made from here to the monasteries of St Anthony and St Paul (see pages 447 and 447).

Sleeping
& eating
D *Semiramis*, Sharia Safir Zaghloul, Midan El-Mahat, T322092, F316017. 30 rooms, a poor quality hotel in an unpleasant city. For safety and comfort, but not gastronomic delight, eat here. **F** *Bakri Hotel*, to east of station or **F** *Rest House*, west of canal on Sharia Port Said. May be useful if held up in Beni Suef.

Transport **Train** It is easy to make a quick getaway from Beni Suef because almost all express and slower trains travelling up and down the Nile Valley stop at the station in the centre of the city. **Bus**: can be caught from the bus station, to the south of the railway station across the canal, every 30 mins to Cairo or Fayoum. Less frequent direct services go to Alexandria and some of the Delta towns. **Service taxis**: north to Cairo, west to Fayoum, south to Minya and east to Zafarana on the Red Sea coast can be caught from the depot by the bus station.

Directory **Banks** Bank of Alexandria in Midan Gumhorriya. **Communications** Post Office: located opposite the *Semiramis Hotel* in Midan El-Mahat. Telephones at railway station.

Minya

Phone code: 086
Colour map 3, grid B1
Minya, 110 km south of Beni Suef and 245 km from Cairo on the West Bank of the River Nile, was until recently one of the nicest, friendliest and most relaxed towns in the whole country. At present it is to be avoided.

The centre of Minya is bounded on the east by the River Nile which here runs southeast-northwest, and the parallel railway line and Ibrahimiya Canal to the west. Beyond to the west is agricultural land.

Hermopolis – The City of Thoth

Hermopolis was the city of Thoth, the gods' scribe and visir, the reckoner of time, the inventor of writing and, following his association with Khonsu, a moon-god with mastery of science and knowledge. Thoth is depicted either with a man's body and the head of a sacred ibis or as a white and very well endowed baboon. Although his cult originated further north in the Nile Delta, its greatest following was in Middle Egypt.

In the city's complex creation myth, known as the Hermopolitan cosmogony, the chaos before the world's creation was thought to have had four characteristics – water, infinity, darkness and invisibility – each represented by a male and a female god who collectively are known as the Hermopolitan Ogdoad (company of eight). A primordial mound and the cosmic egg arose from the chaos and hatched the sun god who then began to organize the world from the chaos. While most people believed the Ogdoad itself produced the cosmic egg, Thoth's devotees alone credited him with having laid it and therefore having been connected with the creation of the world. A modern interpretation of the link between his representation as a baboon and his role in the Creation is associated with the habit of baboons shrieking at sunrise thus being the first to welcome the sun. The baboon is also connected to the moon and there are often statues of baboons with moons on their head. This is probably because of the ancient Egyptians' love of puns and word-play because the word for 'to orbit' was apparently similar to that for 'baboon'. Although by the New Kingdom this Hermopolitan version of creation myth had been supplanted by the Heliopolitan cosmogony, Thoth's cult continued until the later Ptolemaic era.

Head of Thoth

Getting there

Train: At the train station exit, across a colonial looking square, is the town's main street called Sharia Gumhorriya which runs northeast to the Corniche and the river front about 1 km away. **Road** The main service taxi depot and the bus terminal are both five minutes' walk to the right (south) of the railway station exit along the parallel Sharia Sa'ad Zaghloul. The service taxi depot for Abu Qirkus, the jumping off point for Beni Hassan only, is 250 m further south just across the railway and the canal bridge. Two buses a day from Alexandria to Assiut stop at Minya. Picking the bus up for return is difficult.

Sights

First go south taking the track along the river bank to visit the Temple of Hatshepsut in the area popularly called Istabl'Antar. It is about 3 km. The temple/shrine is dedicated to a lioness goddess called Pakhet. The outer court has/had eight columns, the four at the front being wider in girth. It is thought that the capitals represent Hathor's head. The back wall has remains of scenes of Hatshepsut with gods. The inner hall, access in the centre of this back wall, contains a high level niche with a rough stone statue of Pakhet.

Beni Hassan (Beni Hassan al-Shurruq), which is named after an ancient tribe, is about half way between Minya and Mallawi. It is the site of a neat row of almost forty 11th and 12th Dynasty (2050-1786 BC) tombs which were dug into the rock face of hills overlooking the River Nile. The tombs are important because they are the first to show illustrations of sports and games as well as the daily life of the people of the Middle Kingdom.

■ *To reach Beni Hassan by service taxi to the small town of Abu Qirkus on the main Minya to Mallawi road, cross over the canal and walk about 1 km straight down its main street until the road forks from where you can take a E£0.25 pick-up to the banks of the River Nile. The efficient little ferry across the river costs E£4.50 return but this also includes the short minibus ride to the tombs. Entry is permitted to four tombs. Daily 0800-1600, E£8, E£4 for students, E£10 to take photographs.*

The tombs are interesting because they mark a stage in the evolution of tomb design from the lateral Old Kingdom (2686-2181 BC) style *mastabas* to the deep New Kingdom (1567-1085 BC) royal tombs of the Valley of the Kings (see page 230). At Beni Hassan some of the earlier tombs have no vestibules and consist only of a simple chamber carved in the rock while the later ones contain a vestibule and a more intricate arrangement of the chamber. Another interesting feature is that they were not royal tombs but were built for regional rulers and military leaders. Their illustrations tend to be more personal and to depict feudal or military life rather than those of offerings and magic formulae for reaching the after-life which are more commonly associated with the royal tombs. Of the 39 tombs only 12 were decorated and only four can currently be visited.

Tomb of Amenemhat (No 2) He was the regional governor and commander-in-chief at the time of Senusert I (1971-28 BC) and his tomb has a columned portico facade and a lintel bearing a list of his titles. The texts inside the door relate to his numerous military campaigns south to Kush and praise his administrative skills. Particular reference is made to a year when there was heavy flooding of the River Nile but taxes were not increased. The main chamber has a vaulted roof which is supported by four columns and decorated in a

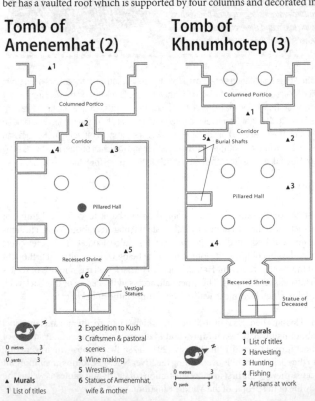

Tomb of Amenemhat (2)

Tomb of Khnumhotep (3)

▲1
Columned Portico
▲2
Corridor
▲4   ▲3
Pillared Hall
▲5
Recessed Shrine
▲6
Vestigial Statues

0 metres   3
0 yards   3

▲ **Murals**
1 List of titles

2 Expedition to Kush
3 Craftsmen & pastoral scenes
4 Wine making
5 Wrestling
6 Statues of Amenemhat, wife & mother

Columned Portico
▲1
Corridor
5▲ Burial Shafts   ▲2
▲3
Pillared Hall
▲4
Recessed Shrine
Statue of Deceased

0 metres   3
0 yards   3

▲ **Murals**
1 List of titles
2 Harvesting
3 Hunting
4 Fishing
5 Artisans at work

chequered pattern. To the back of the chamber the niche once contained a statue of Amenemhat. The chamber walls are finely decorated with a cooking scene on the right of the south wall. In the middle Amenemhat is seated during an offering ceremony while the north wall has scenes of hunting and military preparations. On the east wall there are pictures of wrestling, an attack on a fortress and boats sailing towards Abydos.

Tomb of Khnumhotep (No 3) This tomb is very similar and is that of Amenemhat's successor Khnumhotep who was also governor of the Eastern Desert. The façade has a proto-Doric columned portico leading into a central chamber with a niche for his statue at the far end. Inscriptions of great historical importance about feudal life in the 12th Dynasty were discovered in the tomb. Clockwise around the tomb there are scenes of ploughing, the harvest and his voyage to Abydos. Below the next scene of desert hunting on the north wall is the lower register showing the arrival of an Asian caravan which offers gifts to the governor. All is shown in minute detail. This is followed by Khnumhotep and his wife who are shown fishing and fowling in the marshes on the left and harpooning fish from a punt on the right of the niche for the statue. On the south wall he inspects boat-building and then sails to Abydos while other registers show dyers, weavers, carpenters and other artisans.

Tomb of Baqet III (No 15), who was governor of the Oryx Nome, is much simpler than the others and dates back to the 11th Dynasty (2050-1991 BC). In the chamber are two columns with lotus capitals. On the north wall are scenes of a desert hunt with four mythological animals in the midst of the normal animals including copulating gazelles. On the east wall there are illustrations of 200 wrestling positions while the south wall illustrates scenes from Baqet's turbulent life including an attack on a fortress.

Tomb of Kheti (No 17), who was Baqet's son and heir, is quite similar to that of his father. The same wrestling scenes are to be found on the east wall and there are very similar representations of craftsmen and desert hunts. On the south wall Kheti is shown watching agricultural scenes and receiving offerings from under a sunshade attended by his servants and a dwarf.

Middle Egypt

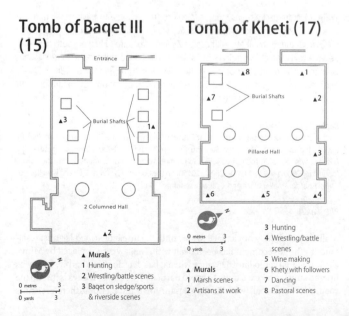

Tomb of Baqet III (15)

Entrance

▲3   Burial Shafts
1▲

2 Columned Hall

▲2

▲ **Murals**
1 Hunting
2 Wrestling/battle scenes
3 Baqet on sledge/sports & riverside scenes

0 metres   3
0 yards   3

Tomb of Kheti (17)

▲8   ▲1
▲7   Burial Shafts   ▲2

Pillared Hall   ▲3

▲6   ▲5   ▲4

0 metres   3
0 yards   3

▲ **Murals**
1 Marsh scenes
2 Artisans at work

3 Hunting
4 Wrestling/battle scenes
5 Wine making
6 Khety with followers
7 Dancing
8 Pastoral scenes

Essentials

Sleeping **C** *Etap Nefertiti*, Corniche el-Nil, T326282, F326467. River-side location about 2 km north of the town centre on both sides of the beautiful tree-lined corniche, recently expanded, 96 rooms (30 decent rooms in main building, 24 satisfactory garden chalets without a river view, and 42 chalets adjacent to the River Nile), 3 restaurants (*La Palma*, *Banana Island* and *Darna*), a bar, tea and coffee shops, pool, tennis, sauna, small gym, efficient and very friendly staff, reduction in tourist trade has resulted in some of the facilities being closed.

E *Beach Hotel el-Shata* T322307, 32 rooms and 2 suites, a/c with bath, good location by the river.

F *El-Shatek*, 31 Sharia el-Gumhorriya, T322307. 32 rooms. **F** *Ibn Khassib*, 5 Sharia Rageb T324535 is near to the station, 20 rooms of very varying quality, restaurant. **F** *Lotus*, 1 Sharia Port Said, T364541, F364576. 42 extremely clean rooms with rather noisy a/c and bath, 92 beds, River Nile 1 km, station 1 km, pleasant hotel.

Youth hostels The youth hostel has dormitory beds and a pool, 1.5 km out of town near the stadium.

Eating Besides restaurants in the *Nefertiti* and *Lotus* hotels, which offer different standard but reasonably priced good quality food and good views, the *El-Fayrouz* restaurant on the Corniche about 150 m north of Sharia Gumhorriya provides excellent meat dishes and juices. The *Ibn Khassib* restaurant is cheap with limited menu. The *Ali Baba* cafeteria is not recommended. Good cheap food can be bought at many of the other local cafés such as *Cafeteria Ali* on the corniche north of Sharia Port Said.

Shopping While the more up-market shops are on Sharia Gumhorriya the best and main shopping streets bisect it about half way between the station and the river. There has been a Mon market since Ottoman times.

Transport **Train** Most inter-city trains stop at Minya so it is possible to travel easily north to Cairo (4 hrs) via Beni Suef or south to Luxor via Assiut and Qena. **Bus**: almost hourly buses from the terminal on Sharia Sa'ad Zaghloul to Cairo (5 hrs) or south to Assiut. **Service taxis**: which are quicker but still cheap can be caught to the same destinations from the nearby depot under the railway arch. Those for Abu Qirkus (30-45 mins), the jumping off point for Beni Hassan, can only be caught 250 m further south just across the railway and the canal bridge.

Directory **Banks** There are two banks, open Sun-Thu 0830-1400 and 1700-2200, next to the tourist office on the Corniche. **Communications** Post Office: in the main square called Midan Sa'a, directly outside the railway station, open Sun-Thu 0830-1400 and 1700-2200. **Tour operators** The Minya provincial government is very keen to promote tourism and the tourist information office (open daily 0800-1400 and 1700-2200, T320150) on the Corniche is very helpful and is well worth a visit. Another smaller office at the railway station.

Mallawi

Colour map 3, grid B1 Mallawi is definitely not a place to stay until the threat of armed Islamist resistance to the government has been dealt with. Mallawi was replaced by Minya as the regional capital in 1824 since when it has deteriorated sharply. Today its littered streets make it a town to avoid particularly because Minya is just up the road. Although Mallawi is an unpleasant town the fact that there are some

Ibis – the sacred bird

This bird has been held in great esteem by man for over 5,000 years. Mummies of ibis were found in Saqqara though now this bird is rare in Africa north of the Sahara.

The ibis is sacred as a representation of Thoth (see page 217). It is depicted in coronation scenes listing the years of the king's rule. The birds' 'ability' to write is traced to the movements of the beak in the water and the resemblance of that beak to a held writing implement.

The main cult centre of the ibis-god Thoth was Hermopolis Magna (see page 177) but mummies of the sacred ibis have been found all over the country. They were

found in tombs of kings and queens and in cemeteries set aside just for ibis mummies. A simple explanation equates the annual flooding of the Nile with the arrival of this bird and its disappearance as the water receded. Ceremonies to greet the rising water incorporated the large flocks of these migrating birds.

SM

important archaeological sites has persuaded the regional tourist authority to plan two new three or four star hotels. Located beside the River Nile, mercifully outside the town. They will have berthing facilities for nine tourist boats while the chalets will be able to accommodate 404 tourists. This unfortunately still remains at the planning stage.

Today little remains of the ruined 7th Dynasty (2181-73 BC) city of **Hermopolis Magna** and its necropolis at nearby **Tuna el-Gabel** which are located to the northwest of **Mallawi**, about 50 km south of Minya.

Antinopolis

It is necessary to travel north from Mallawi to take the ferry east across the River Nile to visit Sheik Abada, the ruined Roman town of Antinopolis. Construction started here in AD 130 in memory of Antonius, a favourite who was accompanying Emperor Hadrian on an official visit to the area. It is said that he drowned himself in the River Nile to prevent a danger, which had been prophesied for the Emperor. (It had been prophesied that someone of importance would drown in the Nile on this visit.) Early travellers described the splendid columns and archways, now dismantled and dispersed, but the plan of the town can still be traced.

Hermopolis Magna as it was known in Ptolemaic times, was the ancient city of Khmunu the capital of the Hare Nome, and had a dual function as a secular and religious centre and was ruled by the High Priest. It was once quite large, extending to both sides of the River Nile's banks, with a temple surrounded by a 15 m thick wall at its centre. The town regained importance under the Ptolemies who associated the ibis-god Thoth with their god Hermes and gave the town its name.

At the same time a vast necropolis, now known as **Tuna el-Gabel**, was established west of the town. Today, however, little remains of the city except a large mound of rubble and mud-bricks and 24 rose granite columns. The Tuna el-Gabel Necropolis ■ *daily 0900-1700, E£7* is 6 km west across a very hot and empty desert road from the small town of that name and 10 km southwest of Hermopolis. There is comparatively little to see above ground because most of the tombs lie below the sand dunes which would soon cover the whole site if it were not for the workers' constant efforts to keep them at bay.

Tuna el-Gabel is best known for the **Sacred Animal Necropolis** which is to the right of the entrance. It is set in catacombs which are thought to stretch as far as Hermopolis, but only a small area is now open to the public. Many mummified remains of ibis and baboons were found here. These were sacred

Middle Egypt

Revolutionary Art: Akhenaten and Nefertiti's New Designs

The new settlement of Akhetaten was not only revolutionary in its religion but also in the arts. A number of excellent craftsmen and artists were recruited to work on the decoration of the new city. Rather than focusing almost exclusively on the theme of resurrection and the after-life they also depicted daily life and nature in greater detail than before. There were two main art styles with the first depicting Akhenaten with an elongated face, protruding stomach, and female-style thighs, as demonstrated by the famous colossi from his temple at Karnak which are now in the museum in Cairo, while the later style is much less distorted. It has been suggested, although not proven, that the earlier distortions were partly due to the difficulties that the artists had in radically altering their style. Alternatively it may have been that the decoration was undertaken too hastily using inferior limestone and varying quality carvings.

It has been suggested that Akhenaten intended that the depictions of himself and his family, which appear in the shrines of private houses in Tell el-Amarna, should be worshipped and that only he could directly mediate with the god. The Aten disc is only shown when he or the Royal family are present. While the pharaoh was always, at least nominally, accepted as a god or the gods it appears that Akhenaten may have been particularly literal about this convention.

Very unusually, in scenes of royal dinners both the pharaoh and his wife were depicted and the presence of both their cartouches almost as co-rulers demonstrated the difference in Amenhotep IV's approach. Wives had never previously been portrayed as equal to the pharaoh and their names had never appeared side by side.

animals because they were the two living images of Thoth. The ibises were bred here. A large number of mummified animals were found but the best have been removed to museums and the remaining ones are poorly preserved.

A few hundred metres to the south is the main part of the **City of the Dead** which was modelled on a real city with streets and some tombs which resemble houses. Egyptians traditionally went to visit their dead relatives and took a meal or spent the night in the mausoleum. Some of the tombs therefore have more than one chamber and a few have an additional floor or even a kitchen. The City of the Dead's most interesting building is the splendid tomb-chapel of **Petosiris** who was the High Priest of Thoth at Hermopolis and whose inlaid wooden coffin is on display in the Museum in Cairo. It was built in 300 BC and the wall decorations are a blend of Pharaonic and Greek art work as illustrated by the Greek clothes. The mausoleum was a family tomb. The vestibule has illustrations of traditional activities; farming, wine and brick making, wood working and jewellery construction. The inner shrine is dedicated to the father and brother of the tomb owner. On either side of the door to the shrine are offering and sacrifice scenes. In the shrine are colourful illustrations from traditional Egyptian funerary texts with the east wall depicting a funerary procession. The actual burial chambers, where three generations of high priests were buried, is 8 m below the shrine. Much of the important material found at these two sites is in the museum in Cairo but the Mallawi museum open mornings only has a number of items from here.

Another interesting two storey tomb-chapel is that of **Isadora** which dates from 120BC and still contains the well-preserved mummy of the young girl. Because she drowned in the sacred River Nile this led to the brief establishment of a cult for her. Also worth a visit is the tomb known as the **House of Graffiti** which has been restored and contains a kitchen, various rooms and a chamber where the deceased was exposed before being buried in the funerary shaft.

Tell el-Amarna

12 km south of Mallawi, Tell el-Amarna is the East Bank city which was founded by Pharaoh Amenhotep IV (1379-62 BC), who is better known as **Akhenaten**, after he had left Thebes (Luxor) to establish the totally new and heretical monotheistic religion. Although little remains today because most of the temples and palaces were destroyed by subsequent pharaohs who reverted back to the previous polytheistic religion, the site still has plenty of atmosphere. There is another school of archaeologists who believe that, far from introducing a radical new monotheism, Akhenaten chose to ignore a religion which through a multiplicity of myths and images was able to present a surprisingly complex view of the world.

In order to reach Tell el-Amarna, drivers should head south from Mallawi to the village of Deir el-Mawas and then east to the ferry crossing, E£2 return. The river can easily be reached by catching any southbound bus or pick-up from the depot just south of the Mallawi train station at the bridge between the canal and the railway tracks or taking a private taxi. Pick ups cost 50p. The River Nile can be crossed by car ferry, motorboat or felucca to the East Bank village of El-Till, where you will be greeted by adults and children hawking basketwork and other handicrafts. The ticket kiosk is just to the left of the landing stage and there is a little café to the east of the village. On arrival independent travellers will be expected to pay a 'local tax' of a few E£ to keep El-Till functioning. Alternatively there is also a small car ferry from nearby Beni Amar to the nicer village of Hagg Qandil, to the south of El-Till, but the only tickets and transport are at El-Till. **NB** Neither ferry can be relied on to carry cars after 1600. The tractor ride to the Northern Tombs costs E£10, expensive but the only realistic option. ■ *Daily 0700-1700, E£6, students E£3. Make sure the guide includes Tomb 6 in the itinerary. The Northern Palace costs a further E£5 to visit.*

Getting there

Middle Egypt

Tell el-Amarna

To Mallawi ▶

Northern Palace
Northern Tombs
El-Till
Great Temple of Aten
King's House (Enclosure with Record Office, Harem & Coronation Hall)
Great Palace & Bridge
To Royal Tomb
Deir el-Mawas
Hagg Qandil
Central City
El Amarea
Roman Camp
Maru-Aten
Southern Tombs
El Hawata

To Assiut

River Nile

Royal Road

N

0 km   1
0 miles   1

Sights

The huge site is made up of a number of different areas – the **city ruins** to the south of El-Till; the **Northern Tombs,** 5 km to the east and up an 80 m escarpment for which a donkey or tractor-driven trailer is almost essential; the **Royal Tomb,** 5 km further away up a hidden valley, and closed to the public; the rarely visited **Southern Tombs** southeast of El-Till; and the **Northern Palace** near the riverbank to the north of the village. At least half a day is required for the site and a full day if the Southern Tombs are to be included.

Amenhotep IV was the son of Amenhotep III (1417-1379 BC) and his dark-skinned and possibly Nubian 'chief wife' Queen Tiy who may have ruled jointly for 12 years with her son after he ascended the throne in 1379 BC. The cult of Aten, which was one aspect of the sun-god, had been mentioned in earlier texts

👉 The Nile ran red

As the story goes – Re, the sun-god, creator of all men and all things, began to grow old and the men he had so carefully created began to mock him. They criticized his appearance and even complained about his neglect of them. Re was very angry at their lack of reverence due to his position, after all he was their creator. He called a secret council of gods and goddesses (Geb, Shu, Tefnut, Nut and Hathor), where it was agreed to destroy all mankind and thus remove the unnecessary aggravation.

The task of destruction was handed to Hathor, the daughter of Re. She seems to have been happy in her work, 'wading in blood' as the story goes. The gods realized, almost too late, that without the men the tasks on earth in the temples would not be performed. It was essential therefore to protect those who remained from slaughter. The drug mandrake was mixed with freshly brewed beer and the blood of the already slain making 7,000 vessels in all. This liquid was poured out across the land (symbolic of the Nile floods) and Hathor, waking, mistook this liquid for blood, drank it all and was too stupefied to complete her gruesome task.

and shown as a human being but may have been a private and personal royal belief during his father's reign. Amenhotep IV, however, espoused it very strongly at the expense of Amun and the other gods very early in his reign which naturally upset the high priests of Amun in Thebes (Luxor).

Therefore, in the 5th year of his reign in 1374 BC, he and his wife Nefertiti moved the capital to Akhetaten ('horizon of Aten') half way between Thebes and Memphis at Tell el-Amarna in order to make a clean break with previous traditions. For those of a romantic disposition the large gully or river *wadi* cutting through the eastern cliffs have been likened to the Egyptian symbol for the horizon. It has been suggested that it was because the sun rose from behind these cliffs that Akhenaten chose this as the site for his new city of Akhetaten.

On arriving in Akhetaten he changed his name to Akhenaten or 'servant of Aten' while Nefertiti became Nefernefruaten or 'beautiful are the beauties of the Aten'. In the 12th year of his reign he adopted a more confrontational approach to the old cults and his decision to close down all the old temples probably led to unrest because of the detrimental economic effect caused by the temple being closed. There is some evidence that Akhenaten was criticized for not defending Egypt's borders and for jeopardizing the territories previously won by his expansionist father.

How Akhenaten's reign ended is still a mystery. One theory is that Akhenaten rejected his wife Nefertiti and made his son-in-law Smenkhkare the co-regent. Some have interpreted the fact that the two men lived together, and some of their poses in the murals, as proof of a homosexual relationship. Smenkhkare, who was both the husband of Akhenaten's eldest daughter and his half-brother, is thought to have continued ruling for a year after Akhenaten's death in 1362 BC but soon died himself. The other, more contentious, interpretation of events is that, far from splitting up with Nefertiti, the pharaoh actually made her co-regent and his equal. She may then have adopted Smenkhkare as her official name and been illustrated in a different way. However only the cartouches can be used to identify the figures which makes the theory a suitably interesting alternative. The reality is that no-one knows the truth which may be very dull compared with these stories.

Worship of Aten did not long outlive its creator. In 1361 BC Smenkhkare was succeeded by Tutankhamen (1361-52 BC), another of Amenhotep III's sons and therefore Akhenaten's half-brother, who returned to the

Thebes-based cult of Amun. He and his successors attempted to eradicate all traces of Akhenaten and the city of Akhetaten was subsequently destroyed and completely pillaged by Seti I (1318-04 BC) so that nothing was known of the city or its cult until the second half of this century.

Apart from the romantic story of Akhenaten, the importance of the city lies in its short history. Although about 5 km long, the city was built and occupied for no more than 25 years. When abandoned a record of life in the late 18th Dynasty was left which ranged from peasants in small houses to the official buildings and palaces. Most urban sites in Egypt have either been lost under modern towns and villages or have been badly damaged so that Tell el-Amarna offers a unique record.

Leaving El-Till you pass the remains of the massive **Great Temple of Aten** on the right which is now partly covered by the modern cemetery. There are then the vague ruins in the sand of a mixture of administrative and residential buildings until one reaches the **Small Temple of Aten** which is currently being preserved and re-excavated by the Egyptian Exploration Society. Although it is not yet open to tourists a good view of the temple can be had from a local tractor-trailor.

Just before the temple there is a large mud-brick structure on either side of the road. This is the remains of the **bridge** which crossed the road and connected the **King's House** to the east with the so-called **Great Palace** to the west which runs along and partly under the cultivated area. This area including the palace, temple and ancillary buildings is the **Central City** which was the administrative and religious centre of the ancient city.

The Northern Tombs, which are the most interesting site at Tell el-Amarna, was the necropolis for the nobles many of whom were not originally from Thebes but were elevated to their position by Akhenaten once he arrived at Akhetaten. Most of the tombs also devote more space and decoration to Akhenaten himself than to the occupant. It is **advisable to carry a torch** but there is now electric lighting in the Northern Tombs.

Tomb of Huya (1)   # Tomb of Mery-Re II (2)

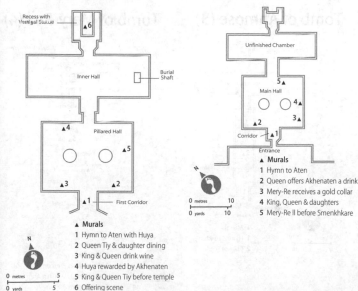

Tomb of Huya (1)

Recess with Vertical Statue ▲6

Inner Hall

Burial Shaft

Pillared Hall

▲4

▲5

▲3   ▲2

▲1 — First Corridor

▲ Murals
1 Hymn to Aten with Huya
2 Queen Tiy & daughter dining
3 King & Queen drink wine
4 Huya rewarded by Akhenaten
5 King & Queen Tiy before temple
6 Offering scene

0 metres 5
0 yards 5

Tomb of Mery-Re II (2)

Unfinished Chamber

Main Hall

5▲

4▲

▲2   3▲

Corridor

Entrance

▲ Murals
1 Hymn to Aten
2 Queen offers Akhenaten a drink
3 Mery-Re receives a gold collar
4 King, Queen & daughters
5 Mery-Re II before Smenkhkare

0 metres 10
0 yards 10

Tomb of Huya (No 1). Huya was the Superintendent of the Royal Harem and Steward of Akhenaten's mother Queen Tiy and may have died during her visit to Akhetaten in 1367 BC. At the entrance he is pictured praying next to a hymn to Aten and on either side of the door are highly unusual scenes of Queen Tiy drinking wine with Akhenaten, Nefertiti and princesses. On the left wall is a scene showing Akhenaten in a procession being carried on his litter towards the Hall of Tribute where ambassadors from Kush and Syria await his arrival. To the left and right of the entrance to the shrine are somewhat damaged scenes of Huya being decorated by Akhenaten from the Window of Appearances with the sculptor's studio below. On the right hand wall Akhenaten leads Queen Tiy to see the temple he has built for his parents while the staff who worked on the temple are displayed below. The shrine is undecorated but the niche has some scenes of funerary offerings, mourning, and a curious representation of the funerary furniture.

Tomb of Mery-Re II (No 2). This tomb of the Royal Scribe, Overseer of the Two Treasuries and Overseer of the Harem of the Great Royal Wife Nefertiti was started during Akhenaten's reign but finished by Smenkhkare and follows a similar plan to Huya's tomb. After the now destroyed Hymn to the Aten at the entrance, Mery-Re is shown worshipping the Aten and then to the left Nefertiti offers Akhenaten a drink next to three young princesses. Further along the upper register depicts Mery-Re receiving a golden collar from Akhenaten while foreigners look on and then being acclaimed by his household. Further along the right wall Akhenaten, Nefertiti and their daughters are at the centre of a scene divided into three subjects. The first shows black slaves, with their faces painted red, carrying gold bars and coins. The tables are heaped with piles of gold and a number of slaves are shown carrying their children. In the second scene, Asian people pay homage to Akhenaten and bring him treasures and a number of female slaves. The last scene shows a double procession with the empty royal litter and the royal guard while treasures are offered to the Pharaoh. The rest of the tomb was never finished except for a defaced scene on the back wall of Mary-Re being rewarded by Smenkhkare and his wife.

Tomb of Ahmose (3) Tomb of Mery-Re I (4)

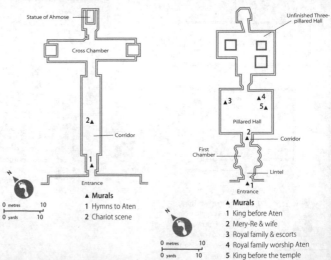

Tomb of Ahmose (3)

Statue of Ahmose

Cross Chamber

2▲

Corridor

1▲

Entrance

N

0 metres 10
0 yards 10

▲ **Murals**

1 Hymns to Aten
2 Chariot scene

Tomb of Mery-Re I (4)

Unfinished Three-pillared Hall

▲3   ▲4
      5▲

Pillared Hall

2▲

Corridor

First Chamber

Lintel

▲1

Entrance

N

0 metres 10
0 yards 10

▲ **Murals**

1 King before Aten
2 Mery-Re & wife
3 Royal family & escorts
4 Royal family worship Aten
5 King before the temple

Tomb of Ahmose (No 3) Who was Akhenaten's fan bearer and therefore had the right to a noble's tomb, is with another group of four tombs just beyond the next valley. The tomb was unfinished and some of the scenes are damaged. Most of them depict aspects of the palace including the throne room, the royal apartments and some of Akhenaten's army preparing for battle.

Tomb of Mery-Re I (No 4) The High Priest of the Aten and the father of Mery-Re II, has three chambers and is probably the best of all. On the entrance wall he is shown in adoration before the Aten while in the columned and flower decorated vestibule Mery-Re and his wife Tenro are shown in prayer. On the left hand wall of the main chamber, which now only has two of the original four columns, Mery-Re is invested with the High Priest's gold collar by Akhenaten. The royal family and escorts are then portrayed in an important scene, because it shows the height of the buildings, leaving the palace for the Great Temple in chariots. There are hymns to the Aten and offering scenes above the entrance to the unfinished inner chambers. On the right of the main chamber Akhenaten, accompanied by Nefertiti and two of their daughters, is in the Great Temple making sacrifices to the Aten. Other scenes show Akhenaten after the sacrifice with his daughters playing musical instruments while beggars await alms in the corner. Below is a scene which has given archaeologists a rare insight into the original appearance of the city. Mery-Re is seen showing the Pharaoh the stocks in the temple with views towards the port, a stable and the royal boats on the River Nile.

Tomb of Panehsi (6) Tomb of Pentu (5)

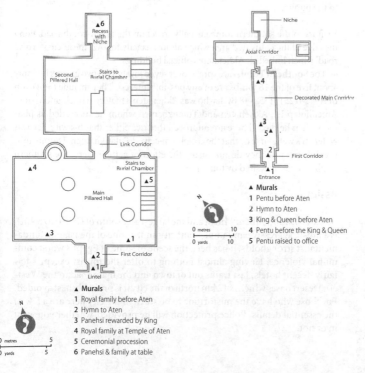

▲ **Murals**

Tomb of Panehsi (6)
1 Royal family before Aten
2 Hymn to Aten
3 Panehsi rewarded by King
4 Royal family at Temple of Aten
5 Ceremonial procession
6 Panehsi & family at table

Tomb of Pentu (5)
1 Pentu before Aten
2 Hymn to Aten
3 King & Queen before Aten
4 Pentu before the King & Queen
5 Pentu raised to office

Middle Egypt

The nearby **Tomb of Pentu (No 5).** The royal scribe and chief physician, is badly disfigured and it is better to see the **Tomb of Panehsi (No 6):** which is 500 m to the south. This High Priest's tomb, which has four columns in each of the two chambers, was later transformed by the Copts into a chapel but many of the original decorations are still in place. In the first chamber are scenes of Akhenaten decorating Panehsi. On the left hand wall, the royal family worship the Aten in front of their household. There are further scenes of Akhenaten including one on the far wall on the left behind a Coptic baptistery and one by the stairs leading down to the funerary chamber, showing him with Nefertiti and their daughters in their chariots surrounded by troops. The rest of the tomb is either unfinished or has been damaged.

The **Royal Tomb,** which is located in a secret valley 5.5 km east of the main plain, has been closed since 1934 and cannot normally be visited. Although if really keen it is possible to arrange a visit beforehand with the antiquities department at Minya. Although there are electric lights, because there is no source of power, it is necessary to take your own generator. It is a very rough ride, best undertaken by tractor, because it will damage all but the strongest of four-wheel drive vehicles.

People with their own transport can see the **Northern Palace** about 1.5 km north of El-Till which was recleared several years ago by the Egyptian Antiquities Service. Although it is only really for enthusiasts it is possible to walk around and enter this large mud-brick ruin where a section of mosaic can still be seen. There is a temple to the south called Kom el-Nana which is being excavated by a British mission but it is not accessible or currently open to the public.

Visitors to the southern tombs usually travel on the north-south road along the edge of the cultivated area which almost exactly follows the ancient 'royal road' which linked all Akhetaten's official buildings.

The **Southern Tombs** are spread over seven low hills in two groups but only about five of the 18 tombs are of any possible interest. They include the **Tomb of Ay** (No 25) (1352-48 BC), who was Akhenaten's maternal uncle and visir to Amenhotep III, Akhenaten and Tutankhamen whom he succeeded as pharaoh when he died. There are unproven theories either that his wife Tey was Nefertiti's wet-nurse or that the couple conceived Tutankhamen. Despite this, possibly because they do not justify the effort of getting there, the southern tombs are rarely visited by tourists.

Assiut

Phone code: 088
Colour map 3, grid B2

Assiut, 109 km south of Minya and the largest city south of Cairo (375 km), is a noisy, aggressive and unpleasant city and, as one of the Islamic fundamentalist strongholds, it has been the scene of some of Egypt's worst communal violence. Having almost nothing to offer the tourist except a few fairly decent hotels, fast trains out of town and the main road to the Western Desert oases which is 12 km north of the city it is probably best avoided. For those who have the misfortune to be stuck in the city here are a few of the essential details. Police protection will be provided-whether you want it, or not.

Diagnosis just 3,000 years too late ...

The German Institute of Archaeology in Cairo has successfully used DNA tests on mummy tissue to diagnose a 3,000-year-old disease. The mummy from a noble's tomb suffered in life from tuberculosis of the left lung. Due to problems of contamination of ancient tissue this is the first time such a diagnosis has been possible. With this breakthrough a carefully controlled analysis of ancient Egyptian mummies may provide insights into infectious diseases of ancient individuals and population. One hopes diagnosis today is completed with greater speed!

The train, bus and service taxi stations are all located on Sharia el-Geish and most of the best hotels are situated on or near the same street. Roads in front of the stations run to the River Nile while those behind the railway station lead to the *souqs*. The airport 10 km northwest of the city has no bus connection. **Getting there & around**

There is comparatively little to see in Assiut itself although the **Nasser Museum** in the village of Beni Marr just to the south of the city and the very large **Monastery of the Virgin** (Deir el-Adhra) ,originally built by Empress Helena in AD 328, where Copts believe the Holy Family sought refuge from Herod in the caves at Dirunka 12 km west of Assiut, are worth a visit. Every year in August in the presence of up to 50,000 pilgrims the icons are paraded around its cave-church during the **Moulid of the Virgin**. Further afield, 5 km out of El-Qusiya which is 42 km north of Assiut, is the **Burnt Monastery** (Deir el-Muharraq) – dating back to the 4th century AD which gets its name from its location on the edge of the burning, roasting desert, but which, given the attacks on Coptic churches by the area's Islamic fundamentalists, is a particularly apt name. The Burnt Monastery is the largest and wealthiest in Middle Egypt. It is considered a place of healing and the Feast of Consecration, the annual moulid with up to 50,000 pilgrims, takes place before Easter. It is claimed that the **Church of the Blessed Virgin Mary** was the first church built in Egypt, although the current church was constructed in 1964 and badly damaged by Islamic extremists in 1988. It is better to visit Tell el-Amarna from Minya and Abydos from Sohag rather than from Assiut. **Sights**

Middle Egypt

Essentials

If you have to stay in Assiut the decent hotels are near the train station, but there are also some really unpleasant places. The long promised luxury hotel is not yet completed. **Sleeping**

C *Badr Touristic*, Sharia el-Thallaga, T329811/2 F322820. 44 rooms, some with TV, comfortable hotel, restaurant and bar. **D** *Assiutel Hotel*, 146 Sharia Nile, T312121 F312122, 31 fairly comfortable rooms, Nile views, restaurant. **D** *Casa Blanca*, Sharia Mohammed Tawfik Khashaba, T337662, F336662, 48 rooms, cheaper than above.

E *Akhenaten Touristic*, Sharia Mohammed Tawfik Khashaba, T327723, F321600. 35 rooms. **E** *Reem Touristic*, Sharia el-Nahda, T326235, F329102. 40 rooms, very cheap.

F *El-Salam*, Sharia Thabet, T332256. 40 rooms. **F** *YMCA*, Sharia Gumhorriya, T323218. Located about 10 mins walk from the train station, clean, cheap a/c rooms, pool.

Camping It is possible, but unadvisable to camp near the Assiut barrage (built by the British in 1898-1903 and carries a wide road), at the Officers Club (T323134) and the Sporting Club (T233139) or on Banana Island where there are no facilities.

Youth hostels Building 503, Sharia El-Walidia, Assiut, T324846, 40 beds, 2 km from station, E£5.

Eating All the better hotels have restaurants which offer decent food as do the various clubs which usually admit better-dressed tourists. The best is *Badr Touristic* but there is little competition. There are a number of good cheap and cheerful restaurants between the back of the station and the *souq* in the main commercial district. The cheap ones including: *Express Restaurant* and *Mattam al-Azhar*, as well as others along Sharia Talaat Harb and Sharia 26 July. Ahmed Wagdy's coffee shop is recommended.

Entertainment Renaissance Cinema has four screens.

Transport **Air** Internal flights to Cairo (2 a week) and Kharga from the airport, 10 km northwest of the town.

Train Runs 12 times a day to Cairo (7 hrs) via Mallawi (2 hrs) and Minya (3 hrs), but less frequently to Luxor (6-7 hrs) via Sohag (2 hrs) and Qena (4-5 hrs).

Road Bus: 7 daily buses Cairo (7 hrs), 5 to Kharga Oasis (5 hrs) which go on to Dakhla (8-9 hrs), and 4 to Qena (4 hrs), as well as buses every 30 mins between 0600-1800 north to Minya (2 hrs) and south to Sohag. **Service taxis**: which are quicker than buses, run to every town between Minya and Sohag, as well as to Kharga (5 hrs), and are easy to catch from the depot in the mornings but are less frequent later in the day.

Directory **Banks** There are a number of banks, including the *Alexandria Bank* (open Sat-Thu 0830-1400 and 1800-2100, Fri 0900-1230 and 1800-2100) in the commercial district around Talaat Harb. **Communications** There is a telephone beside the railway station. **Post Office**: near the railway station and open Sun-Thu 0830-1400 and 1700-2200. **Tour operators** There is an office on Sharia Thawra but it is best to ask for information at the better hotels. **Useful numbers**: Emergency police 322225, Hospital 323329.

Sohag

Phone code: 093
Colour map 3, grid C2

A small agricultural and university West Bank town, 97 km south of Assiut along the River Nile, Sohag has a large Coptic community among its 90,000 population. Although it has few minor sites it is not really geared to tourists (who receive no encouragement to stay) but it does have the advantage of being relatively close to the beautiful temple at Abydos and within half a day's journey from Dendera.

Sights The small **White Monastery** (Deir al-Abyad) and **Red Monastery** (Deir al-Ahmar), at 10 km and 14 km south of Sohag are of interest. The **White Monastery**, with light coloured walls of limestone, was founded in the 5th century by St Pjol and dedicated to St Shenuda, one of the most prominent figures in the history of the Coptic church. There is a moulid each July. Once it had a population of over 2,000 monks. The church which dominates the monastery is divided with decorated columns into a central nave and two aisles. The three altars are dedicated to St Shenuda (centrally placed), also St George and The Holy Virgin. St Shenuda worked in the White and Red Monasteries for over 80 years. (He is believed to have lived for well over 100 years.) He introduced both spiritual and social support for the local community including medical help. Just 3 km to the north of here is the smaller **Red Monastery** founded by St Bishoi who was a disciple of Shenuda. It is built of burnt brick, hence the name. It is said to have been

Americans in the Nile Valley

Although the history of enquiry into Egyptology in the 18th and 19th centuries was largely determined by the Europeans, the Americans put in a late but important appearance. There is a consensus that the work of recording the reliefs and paintings of the Nile Valley sites is among the most pressing of tasks before theft, looting and other damage take too great a toll. This task, the accurate recording of inscriptions or epigraphy, was begun with British encouragement by the Archaeological Survey in the 1890s. Among its most scholarly members was Norman de Garis Davies and his wife Nina, working first for the (British) Exploration Fund and later for the Metropolitan Museum of Art, New York. His work inspired US interest in the matter and the foundation of Chicago House at Luxor in 1924.

The arrival of US academic concern was the achievement of James Henry Breasted. He was born in Rockford, USA, in 1865 and rose to become the USA's first professional Egyptologist at the University of Chicago in 1894. He began a process of recording all known Egyptian hieroglyphs and continued his work in a series of scientific expeditions to Egypt and Nubia in the period 1905-07. He was particularly concerned to record all inscriptions that were at risk of damage or decay. His enthusiasm was rewarded by JD Rockefeller Jnr, who funded the establishment of an Oriental Institute at Chicago. The Institute's field centre in Egypt was sited in Luxor and a comprehensive study of a number of sites was accomplished, most famous were those of Medinet Habu and the Temple of Seti I at Abydos. Breasted died in 1935 after major archaeological successes for the Institute both in Egypt and Iran.

An American businessman, Theodore Davis, became a major backer of archaeological work in Egypt, eager to find new tombs and artifacts. He was a generous sponsor of excavations but impatient of the academic requirements of good archaeology. He fell out with all the inspectors of antiquities appointed by the Antiquities Service – Carter, Quibell and Ayrton – and was responsible for more haste than discipline in the excavation of some sites, notably that of the tomb of Smenkhare, brother, it is thought, of Tutankhamen. Davis did, however, use his money to finance the publication of many books on the archaeology of the sites he paid to have excavated. Davis died in 1915 sure that the Valley of the Kings was exhausted of new archaeological finds.

the centre of a monastery of 3,000 monks. The church of St Bishai has some interesting wall paintings and a sanctuary screen with icons of St Bishai, St Shenuda and St Pjol.

Akhmin is not to be ignored, **Deir al Shuhuda** (Monastery of the Martyrs) is an important place for pilgrims. It is here that papyrus scrolls containing the Book of Proverbs was found. In the town too is **Deir al-Adra** (Convent of the Holy Virgin) with a *moulid* on 22 August

On the way south the beautiful **Temple of Seti I** at **Abydos** is an absolute must and better visited from here than from Qena.

Abydos on the west bank of the River Nile is 12 km southwest of El-Balyana and halfway between Sohag and Qena and can be reached by service taxi from Sohag to El-Balyana (E£2) and then on to Abydos (E£0.5). It was the holiest town of all for the ancient Egyptians and pilgrims were making the journey to Abydos from the 7th Dynasty (2181-73 BC) until well into the Ptolemaic era (323-30 BC). ■ *Site daily 0700-1800, E£12.*

It was the cult-centre for **Osiris**, the god of the dead who was known as 'Lord of Abydos', because according to legend either his head or his whole body was buried at the site (see Temple of Isis, Aswan, page 300). Abydos was considered the door to the after-life which looked out over the Western Desert where the gates were thought to be. Initially, in order to achieve resurrection it was necessary to be buried at Abydos but the requirement was later changed to a simple pilgrimage and the gift of a commemorative stela.

There are cemeteries and tombs scattered over a very wide area in Abydos but there are only a few buildings left standing. They do, however, include the **Temple of Seti I**, the **Osireon** (Cenotaph) and the **Temple of Ramses II** which are open daily ■ *0700-1800, E£6, E£3 for students.*

Next to the ticket booth is an excellent little café with green tables which is cheap and clean and serves very welcoming cold drinks.

The Temple of Seti I, was constructed in fine white marble by Seti I (1318-04 BC) as an offering in the same way that lesser individuals would come on a pilgrimage and make a gift of a stela. Most of the work on the temple and its convex bas-reliefs, which are among the most beautiful of all New Kingdom buildings, was carried out by Seti I, but when he died, his son Ramses II (1304-1237 BC) completed the courtyard and façade. This can be seen from the quality of workmanship which changes from Seti I's beautiful bas-reliefs to Ramses II's much cruder, quicker and therefore cheaper sunken reliefs. It is a very unusual temple because it is L-shaped rather than the usual rectangular and because it has seven separate chapels rather than a single one behind the hypostyle halls. This may have been because of the water table or the presence of the older Osirieon behind the temple.

Temple of Seti I, Abydos

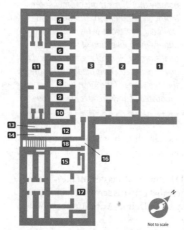

Not to scale

1 First & second court (destroyed)
2 First hypostyle hall
3 Second hypostyle hall
4 Chapel/Sanctuary of Horus
5 Chapel/Sanctuary of Isis
6 Chapel/Sanctuary of Osiris
7 Chapel/Sanctuary of Amun-Re
8 Chapel/Sanctuary of Re-Harakhiti
9 Chapel/Sanctuary of Ptah
10 Chapel/Sanctuary of Seti I
11 Suite of Osiris
12 Suite of Sokar & Nefertum
13 Chapel of Sokar
14 Chapel of Nefertum
15 Hall of the Books
16 Gallery of the Lists
17 Hall of Sacrifice
18 Corridor of the Bulls

The temple was originally approached via a pylon and two fore-courts, built by Ramses II below the main temple so that the concept of the temple sloping upwards from the entrance to the inner sanctuary was maintained, but they have now been largely destroyed. The temple's front is now the square-columned façade behind 12 rectangular pillars decorated with Ramses welcoming Osiris, Isis and Horus. Originally there were seven doors through the façade which led on to the seven chapels but Ramses altered the construction and only the central one is now unblocked.

The theme of the seven separate chapels is evident in the **First Hypostyle Hall**, built and decorated by Ramses II's second-rate craftsmen, where the columns with papyrus capitals depict Ramses with the god represented in the corresponding sanctuary. In the much more impressive **Second Hypostyle Hall**, built by Seti, the first two rows of columns also have papyrus capitals but the last row have no capitals at all. On the right-hand wall Seti is pictured before Osiris and Horus who are pouring holy water from vases and making offerings in front of Osiris' shrine as five

Brick making in Egypt

Sun dried bricks were made from the dried Nile mud. This mud shrinks a great deal when it dries and has to be protected from the sun and the wind to prevent the brick collapsing even before it is used. To reduce the breakage rate the mud was mixed with chopped straw or reeds.

The Bible tells of the Israelites being forced to make bricks while in captivity in Egypt as the tomb painting shows. Each brick-maker had a daily target to reach, only whole bricks being counted. Forcing them to make bricks without straw meant more journeys to collect mud as it was then the only ingredient and the bricks were fragile and more frequently broken.

Painting from the Tomb of Rekhmire (see page 250).

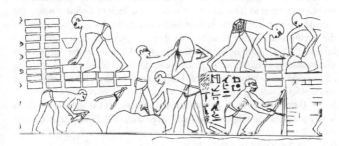

Middle Egypt

goddesses look on. The quality of the work in this hall contrasts sharply with the rougher decoration in the outer hall which was probably because Ramses had ordered all the most skilled craftsmen to concentrate on his own temple!

Behind the inner hypostyle hall there are seven separate **Sanctuaries** or chapels which are dedicated to the deified Seti I, the Osiris triad of Osiris, Isis and Horus, and the Amun triad of Amun, Mut and Khonsu. Many of the wonderful bas-reliefs are still coloured, which gives a good idea of the temple's original decoration, but some of the finest are unpainted and show the precision and great artistry used in the moulding. The sanctuary to the left is dedicated to Seti and contains a beautiful scene of the Pharaoh being crowned by the goddess of Upper and Lower Egypt.

Cenotaph (Osireion)

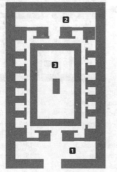

N

Not to scale

1 First transverse chamber
2 Second transverse chamber
3 Sarcophagus chamber

Each of these sanctuaries would have contained the god's barque as well as his stela placed in front of a false door. The sanctuary was locked and only High Priests had access because the Ancient Egyptians believed that the gods lived in their sanctuaries. The daily rituals which were carried out included a sacrifice as well as the dressing and purification of the stelae. Unlike the others, the **Sanctuary of Osiris** does not have a false door at the back of the chapel but connects with the pillared **Suite of Osiris**. It is decorated with scenes from the Osiris myth and has three shrines on the west wall dedicated, with magnificent and incredibly vivid paintings, to Seti, Isis and Horus. The Mysteries of Osiris miracle play would have been performed in the hall and in the unfinished and partially destroyed **Sanctuary of Osiris** which is reached through a narrow entrance on the opposite wall.

Back in the Second Hypostyle Hall the temple changes direction on the left-hand or southeast side with two entrances leading to a number of other halls. The nearest is the 3-columned **Hall of Sokar & Nefertum**, northern deities subsequently integrated into the Osirian cult, with the separate **Chapel of Sokar** and **Chapel of Nefertum** at the back. Through the other entrance is the narrow star decorated **Hall/Gallery of Ancestors/Lists** which, very usefully for archaeologists, lists in rows the names of the gods and 76 of Seti's predecessors although, for political reasons, some such as Hatshepsut, Akhenaten and his heirs are omitted. The gallery leads on to the **Hall of Barques** where the sacred boats were stored, the **Hall of Sacrifices** used as the slaughterhouse for the sacrifices, and other store-rooms: they are currently closed to visitors. Instead it is best to follow the side **Corridor of the Bulls**, where Ramses II is shown lassoing a bull before the jackal-headed 'opener of the ways' Wepwawet on one side and driving four dappled calves towards Khonsu and Seti I on the other, before climbing the steps to the temple's rear door and the Osirieon.

The **Osirieon**, built earlier than the main temple and at water level which has led to severe flooding, is sometimes called the Cenotaph of Seti I because it contains a sarcophagus. Although it was never used by Seti I, who is actually buried in the Valley of the Kings in Luxor (see page 242), it was built as a symbol of his closeness to Osiris. Many other pharaohs built similar 'fake' tombs, which were modelled on the tombs at Luxor, in Abydos but were eventually buried elsewhere. The Osirieon is the only remaining visible tomb but is unfortunately inaccessible because of the inundation of sand and the flooding caused by the rise in the water table.

The small **Temple of Ramses II**, near the village 300 m northwest from the Temple of Seti I across soft sand, is naturally an anticlimax after the scale and sheer beauty of the Temple of Seti I. It was originally a very finely built shrine which was erected in 1298 BC for Ramses' *Ka* or spirit in order to give him a close association with Osiris. The workmanship is better than in most of Ramses II's monuments because it was probably decorated by craftsmen trained in his father's era. Although the temple was reportedly almost intact when first seen by Napoleon's archaeologists, it has since fallen into ruin except for the lower parts of the limestone walls which are still brightly coloured.

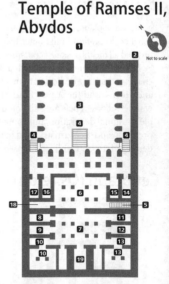

Temple of Ramses II, Abydos

Not to scale

1 First pylon & first courtyard (in ruins)
2 Second pylon
3 Second courtyard with square pillars
4 Steps to raised courtyard
5 Stairs to roof (no roof now)
6 First octosyle hall
7 Second octosyle hall
8 Chapel to Osiris
9 Chapel to Min
10 Chapel to Onuris
11 Room for linen
12 Room for ornaments
13 Room for offerings
14 Temple to Seti
15 Temple to Royal Ancestor
16 Temple to Ennead
17 Temple to Ramses II
18 Temple to Onuris
19 Main sanctuary

Nag Hammadi At Hiw to the south of Nag Hammadi in the curve of a meander of the River Nile stands a complex known as the Monastery of St Palomen. This is a rich agricultural area and the bell tower can be seen from quite a distance. There are three churches, St Palomen, St Mercurius and St Damyanah. St Palomen died of excessive fasting. To the north of here in 1947 the famous Gnostic codices were discovered (see page 76, Coptic Museum).

It is not recommended to stay in Sohag. If necessary the grade **C** *Merit Amoun Hotel* is best, T601985 F603222, 30 rooms, across the River Nile by the Governovale building. **D** *Cazalovy Hotel* beyond the *Merit Amoun* T601185. There are four hotels directly outside the railway station of which the best are **F** *Al-Salam* and **F** *Andolous*, both clean but noisy budget hotels which mainly cater for Egyptian train travelers, there are fans but only inadequate shared shower and toilet facilities.   **Sleeping**

Youth hostels 5 Sharia Port Said, T324395. 28 beds, parking, station 1.5 km. Another on road from Assiut to Sohag in front of Elmanzalawy factory, T/F311430, 72 beds, family rooms, disabled facilities, parking, kitchen, laundry.

There are a number of small cheap restaurants and cafés in the streets around the railway station including *El-Eman* to the north of *Andolous*.   **Eating**

Train To all regional destinations, but those to Cairo and Luxor (4 hrs) are much slower than buses or service taxis and are not worth taking.   **Transport**

Road Bus: 5 daily buses north to Minya and Cairo and south to Luxor, as well as much more frequent ones to Assiut (2 hrs), El-Balyana (for Abydos) and Qena (3 hrs), which can be caught from the bus depot, 5 mins to the left of railway station. **Service taxis**: run north as far as Assiut and south to Qena via El-Balyana and Nag Hammadi.

Useful numbers: Emergency/Police 24239, Passport office 323746.   **Directory**

Qena

Although not as bad as Mallawi, Beni Suef or Assiut, the town of Qena, 147 km south of Sohag and 58 km north of Luxor, is another place which is best avoided. It is an unfriendly, fairly dirty town with difficult transport connections and still some problems of Islamic fundamentalism. You will certainly get a police escort.The only reason for stopping in the town is to see the magnificent temple at Dendera about 8 km from the centre of town. At least note the lovely mosque on the main road named Abdur Rahim as you pass through.   *Phone code: 096*
Colour map 4, grid A2

From the train station and the southbound service taxi depot, which are on either side of the main canal, yet another Sharia el-Gumhorriya leads southeast to a major roundabout and the town's main street, to the west end of which is the bus station and the northbound service taxi depot. Tourists on excursions from Luxor may travel north to Dendera either by cruise ship or in convoy by coach. Expect delays from the additional security procedures associated with visiting this area. Coaches and taxis are driven in convoy from Luxor and the intervention of the tourist police can result in a lengthy wait (½ hour or more) at both ends of the journey.   **Getting around**

Middle Egypt

Sights

Visitors should immediately head for Dendera. Because Qena's transport terminals are so far apart the easiest way of getting there is to forget about the cost, which in Western terms is still very modest, and take a taxi direct from Qena to the temple and thereby avoid a long hot walk or misdirections and total confusion. Alternatively service taxis between Qena and Sohag which can be caught next to the bus station will drop you at Dendera village which is only a 1 km walk to the temple.

Dendera was the cult-centre of Hathor since pre-dynastic times and there are signs of earlier buildings on the site dating back to Cheops in the 4th Dynasty (2613-2494 BC). Hathor, who is represented as a cow or cow-headed woman, was the goddess associated with love, joy, music, protection of the dead and, above all, of nurturing. Her great popularity was demonstrated by

Site of Temple of Hathor at Dendera

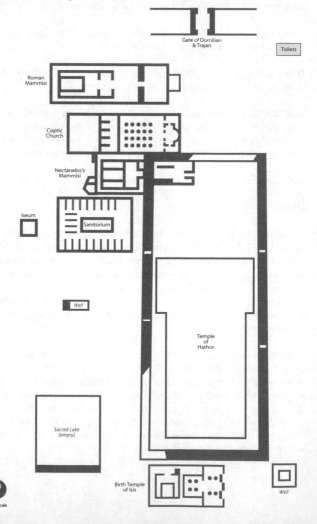

the huge festival held at Edfu (see page 276) when her barque symbolically sailed upstream on her annual visit to Horus to whom she was both wet-nurse and lover. As they reconsummated their union the population indulged in the Festival of Drunkenness which led the Greeks to identify Hathor with Aphrodite who was their own goddess of love and joy.

The **Temple of Hathor**, ■ *daily 0700-1800, E£12, students E£6, use of cameras and video recorders free*, which was built between 125 BC and AD 60 by the Ptolemies and the Romans, is only the latest temple on the site with the first being built by Pepi I in the 6th Dynasty (2345-2181 BC). The enclosing wall of the temple is of unbaked bricks laid alternately convex and concave, like waves of a primeval ocean, perhaps this had some religious significance. The huge well preserved temple dominates the walled Dendera complex which also includes a number of smaller buildings. Even although it was built by non-Egyptian foreign conquerors it copies the earlier pharaonic temples with large hypostyle halls leading up, via a series of successively smaller vestibules and store rooms, to the darkened sanctuary at the back of the temple. There are also two sets of steps leading up to and down from the roof sanctuaries.

At the front, the pylon-shaped façade is supported by six huge Hathor-headed columns and reliefs showing the Roman emperors Tiberius and Claudius performing rituals with the gods. Through in the **Hypostyle Hall** the 18 Hathor-headed columns, capitals of which are sistra-rattles associated with music and dance. These are organized into groups of three, and are identical to those on the façade. The magnificent ceiling, which is illustrated with an astronomical theme showing the mystical significance of the sky, has retained much of its original colour. It is divided between day and night and illustrates the 14 days moon cycle, the gods of the four cardinal points, the constellations, the zodiac, and the elongated goddess Nut who swallows the sun at sunset and gives birth to it at dawn.

Holes at the base of the pillars here were reputedly used as tethering points for animals kept by the Copts whilst in hiding in the temple after Roman times.

The next room, which is known as the **Hall of Appearances** and is supported by six columns, is where the goddess 'appeared' from the depths of the temple as she was transported on her ritual barque for the annual

Temple at Dendera

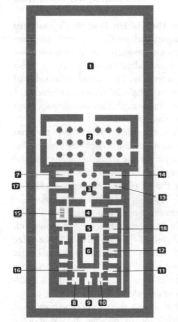

N

Not to scale

1 Court
2 Pronaos/First
Hypostyle Hall
3 Second Hypostyle Hall/
Hall of Appearances
4 First Vestibule/
Hall of Offerings
5 Second Vestibule/
Hall of Ennead
6 Sanctuary
7 Treasury
8 Per-Neser Chapel/
House of Flame
9 Per-Ur Chapel/
Shrine of Egypt
10 Per-Nu Chapel
11 Sacred Serpent
12 Seat of Repose
13 Harvest Rooms
14 Laboratory
15 Stairs to roof
16 Stairs to crypts
17 Nile Room
18 Hathor's Wardrobe

Middle Egypt

voyage to Edfu. On either side of the doorway there are scenes of offerings and the presentation of the temple to the gods.

Around this Hall are six small rooms. The first on the left was the laboratory, used for the preparation of balms and the nine oils used to anoint the statues, which has several inscriptions with the recipes and instructions for their preparation. The next two rooms were used as store-rooms for offerings such as flowers, beer, wine and poultry. On the right of the hall's doorway is the Treasury which has scenes on the base of the walls representing the 13 mountainous countries where the precious minerals were found. The second room called the Nile Room, has river scenes and an exit to the back corridor and the well outside.

Next is the first vestibule which was known as the **Hall of Offerings** because it was there that the priests displayed the offerings for the goddess on large tables. The food and drink was then divided among the priests once the gods had savoured them. On the left a stairway leads to the roof sanctuary. **NB** All the rooms are lit by sunlight from holes in the roof. The second vestibule called the **Hall of the Ennead** contained the statues of the kings and gods which were involved in the ceremonies to Hathor while her wardrobe was stored in the room on the left.

This leads on to the **Sanctuary of the Golden One** which contained Hathor's statue and her ceremonial barque which would be carried to the river each New Year to be transported on a boat upstream to the Temple of horus at Edfu. The south and north walls of the independently roofed sanctuary depict the Pharaoh in various phases of the ceremony. The so-called **Corridor of Mysteries** around the outside of the sanctuary has nine doors which lead to 11 small shrines with 32 closed crypts below the back shrines including the crypt where the temple's valuables would have been stored.

The walls of the stairway from the left of the Hall of Offerings to the **Roof Sanctuaries**, which unlike anywhere else have been completely preserved at Dendera, depict the New Year ceremony when the statue of Hathor was carried up to the roof to the small open **Chapel of the Union with the Disk** pavilion to await the sunrise. The scenes on the left of the stairs represent Hathor going up and those on the right going down. In the northwest corner of the roof terrace is **Osiris' Tomb**, where ceremonies commemorating Osiris' death and resurrection were carried out. In the east corner there are two rooms with the outer one containing a plaster-cast copy of the original **Dendera Zodiac** ceiling which was stolen and taken to the Louvre in Paris in 1820. The Zodiac was introduced to Egypt by the Romans and, although Scorpio's scorpion is replaced by a scarab beetle and the hippo-goddess Tweri was added, this circular zodiac held up by four goddesses is virtually identical to the one used today.

The views from the uppermost level of the roof terrace are superb and provide an excellent opportunity to appreciate the overall scale and layout of the temple buildings, the extensive outer walls and the intensively cultivated countryside surrounding Dendera. From the northern edge of the upper terrace there are good views looking down on to the sanitarium, the two birth houses and the Coptic basilica (see below).

Back downstairs in the temple enclosure on the exterior south wall of the temple there are two damaged reliefs depicting Cleopatra and her son Caesarion and beyond a number of small ruined buildings surround the main temple. This is the only relief, depicting Cleopatra, which survives in all Egypt. At the back is the small **Temple of Isis** which was almost totally destroyed by the early Christians because of the fear that the worship of Isis as the universal Egyptian god might spread. At the front of the main temple to the right is the **Roman Birth House**, or Mammisi, which has some interesting carvings on its façade and south walls.

It was built to replace the older 30th Dynasty **Birth House of Nectanebo** (380-362 BC) which was partially destroyed when the Romans built a wall around the temple. The **Sanatorium** between it and the main temple was where pilgrims, who came to Dendera to be healed by Hathor, were treated and washed in water from the stone-lined **Sacred Lake** to the southwest of the main temple which is now drained of water. Between the two birth-houses is a ruined 5th century **Coptic Basilica**, one of the earliest Coptic buildings in Egypt, which was built using stone from the adjacent buildings.

The only semi-decent hotels are: **D** *Aluminium*, Aluminium, Naga Hammadi, Qena, T/F581320. 72 rooms.

Sleeping

F *Dendera*, Dendera, T322330. Also called *Happy Land*, is on the junction of the main road to Sohag and the turnoff for the temple 1 km away and is probably a much better bet than Qena's grubby hotels. **F** *New Palace*, Midan Mahata, Qena, T322509. 75 rooms, very cheap, behind the Mobil garage near the train station.

Camping Located next to the *Hotel Dendera*, the camp site has hot showers, electricity and a kitchen.

There are a few small cheap restaurants, including the *El-Prince*, *Hamdi* and *Maradona* in and around town, but none of them is particularly good.

Eating

Train: 6 daily trains from the station next to the canal both north to Cairo (11-12 hrs) via Sohag, Assiut, Minya and Beni Suef, and south to Luxor (2 hrs) and Aswan (6-7 hrs). **Bus**: although they are slower and less convenient than service taxis, there are buses to Assiut, Sohag and Cairo, from the bus station on the main street, but the 6 daily buses to Hurghada on the Red Sea coast may be of more use. Also to Quesir at 0700 and 1000, E£6. **Service taxis**: the quickest way to Luxor (1 hr) and other points south is by service taxi from the square just across the canal behind the railway station: 500 m away there are taxis to Safaga and Hurghada. Northbound service taxis along the West Bank to Sohag via Nag Hammadi and El-Balyana, can be caught from the depot which is next to the bus station but one should be prepared for a long wait except in the early morning. Any transport by road is in a convoy controlled by the Tourist police.

Transport

Communications Post Office: open Sat-Thu 0800-1400 and 1800-2000 and is at the canal end of the main street.

Directory

Middle Egypt

Luxor and the West Bank

6

Luxor and the West Bank

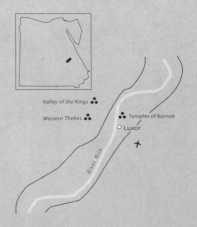

Valley of the Kings

Western Thebes

Temples of Karnak

Luxor

River Nile

The area around Luxor, which was the capital of the New Kingdom (1567-1085 BC), has the largest concentration of ancient tombs and monuments in the country and has been described as the world's greatest open-air museum filled with the most awe-inspiring monuments of ancient civilisations. It has been the focus of Upper Egypt's tourist industry for more than a century. Luxor is more dependent on tourism than any other town in Egypt and its fortunes have therefore fluctuated in recent years.

A no-hassle destination, it has horse drawn transport, a curious souq and its own excellent museums and temples which give access to the wondrous antiquities on the West Bank.

The River Nile offers a scene of constant activity which can be observed in luxurious comfort from land or water. And with all this comes a comfortable climate and friendly people.

Luxor

Ins and outs

Getting there

Phone code: 095
Colour map 4, grid A2
Population: 45,000

Air The airport is 7 km east of the town centre which can be reached by taxi (E£15) or bus. Visas are on sale just before passport control. Taxis are the only means of transport if you are not being met or with a group. Official fare into town is E£10. **Train** Those arriving at the railway station can take a *calèche*, a taxi or walk the 500 m along Sharia al-Mahatta into town. **Road** The bus terminal is on Sharia Television about 10 mins walk from the centre of town, while the service taxi terminal is just off Sharia el-Karnak about 1 km from both Luxor town centre and Karnak temple. The majority of the tourist hotels and shops are located near the River Nile along the Corniche and the parallel Sharia el-Karnak.

Getting around

Luxor is a very comfortable place, easy to get around and impossible to get lost with the River Nile as a marker. Most of the main hotels, shops, tour offices, museums and temples are adjacent to the river on the eastern side. Apart from the outlying hotels like the Hilton and Movenpick which will require the use of the shuttle bus or a taxi to get to town, from everywhere else it is possible to walk, depending on the heat. The market, smaller shops and cheaper hotels are in the streets set back from the river. Access to the West bank is provided by ferries and private hire motor boats or feluccas all along the Corniche.

Tourist offices The official and very well meaning *Egyptian Tourist Authority (ETA)* office, T372215, open daily 0800-2000, is on the Corniche between the Luxor Temple and the *Old Winter Palace Hotel*. It is worth a visit to check the bus, train and road convoy times and current official prices for everything including *calèches*, taxis and other services. The tourist police are isn the same building but also have branches at the airport and the railway station.

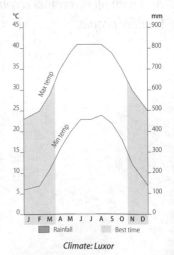

Climate: Luxor

Best time to visit

The best time to visit Luxor is Nov-Mar inclusive. After that it gets too hot for any serious temple and tomb visiting.

24 hours in Luxor

If you only have one day, a sample of major monuments can be seen, preferably in the cooler late autumn, winter and early spring (November-March, inclusive).

First light, approximately 0700, stroll along the corniche from the Old Winter Palace to Hotel Pharaon . Make an early start to get to the West Bank ticket booths (open 0600-1600) to obtain entrance permit to the tombs, taking particular care to buy a ticket for Nefertari's tomb (E£100). Sites open at 0700. By all means rent a guide but be strict in telling him what your targets are – 1. Amenhoptep II; 2. Meneptah; 3. Ramses VI or if closed Ramses

IX; 4. Nefertari;5. Khaemhet;and/or (entry ticket is for two tombs of nobles) Ramoza.

After a long morning on the West Bank return for lunch and a visit to the Luxor Museum, the afternoon opening hours of which are 1600-2200.

Before sun down, take a felucca to catch the wonderful shades of evening and watch the birds fly along the river in squadrons to roost.

Complete your day with the sound and light show at Karnak - this is the best way to view the complex of temples at the site since temperatures will be lower than the day and the area is most attractive under floodlight.

History

On the site of the small present-day town of Luxor, stood the ancient city which the Greeks called **Thebes** and which was described in Homer's *Iliad* as the 'city of a hundred gates'. Later the Arabs described it as 'el-Uqsur' or 'city of palaces' from which it gets its current name.

The town, (676 km south of Cairo, 65 km south of Qena and 223 km north of Aswan), and the surrounding limestone hills had been settled for many centuries but during the Old Kingdom (2616-2181 BC) it was little more than a small provincial town called Waset. It first assumed importance under Menutuhotep II who reunited Egypt and made it his capital but it soon lost its position. It was during the 18th-20th Dynasty of the New Kingdom (1567-1085 BC) that Thebes reached its zenith when, except for the brief reign of Akhenaten (1379-62 BC), it was the capital of the Egyptian Empire which stretched from Palestine to Nubia. At its peak the population reached almost one million. Besides being the site of the largest and greatest concentration of monuments in the world it was, for the ancient Egyptians, the prototype for all future cities.

When the capital later shifted elsewhere it remained a vibrant city and the focus for the worship of Amun ('the Supreme Creator'). Although there is no obvious connection with the Greek city of Thebes the name was subsequently given to the city by the Greeks. It was a shadow of its former self during the Ptolemaic (323-30 BC) and Roman (30 BC-AD 640) periods but, unlike ancient Memphis to the south of Cairo, it was never abandoned and it became an important regional Christian settlement. In the Luxor region a number of temples became Coptic monasteries. For example at both Deir el-Medina and Deir el-Bahri Egyptian monuments have been taken over and converted for Christian use.

After the Muslim conquest in AD 640, the town continued to decline and it was not until the beginning of the 19th century, during Napoleon's expedition to Egypt, that its historical importance began to be recognized. The display of some of its treasures in Paris' Louvre museum (see box, page 117) sparked off considerable interest from the world's archaeologists who still continue to explore the area almost 200 years later. Since 1869, when Thomas Cook took his first party of travellers to Egypt for the opening of the Suez Canal, Luxor has become the most important tourist destination in Upper Egypt. Today, although it has become an important administrative town, the economic livelihood of Luxor is, as the sudden collapse in business during the 1990/91 Gulf war and as the mass exodus of thousands of tourists in November 1997 demonstrated, almost totally dependent on the tourist industry.

Sights

There is so much to see in Luxor that it is best to plan your itinerary carefully. In and around the town on the East Bank of the river the **Luxor Temple** (see page 218), **Luxor Museum** (page 221) and **Karnak Temple** complex (page 221) are essential stops. Although the West Bank is dominated by the **Theban Necropolis** (page 228) and the **Valley of the Kings** (page 230) there are also important temples and monuments to see above ground and the West Bank is certainly worth two days. (See below.)

Who's who in Ancient Egypt: Kings and Queens

It will certainly aid your visit to be able to recognize the personalities which dominate the area. Not all of them can be seen in Luxor but they are all highly relevant to your visit.

Akhenaten Amenhotep IV, who later took the name of Akhenaten, ruled for 15 years around 1379-52 BC. He is remembered for the religious revolution he effected.

The authority of the priests of Amen-Re, the Sun God, the chief god of the Egyptians, had grown so great it almost rivalled that of the pharaohs. The pharaoh was regarded as the son of Amen-Re and was bound by strict religious ritual, part of a theological system understood clearly only by the priests, wherein lay their power.

Meanwhile a small religious cult was developing with the god Aten (a manifestation of the old sun-god Re of Memphis) at the centre, the sole god. This new cult appealed to the young prince Amenophis and after he succeeded his father he changed his name to Akhenaten meaning 'it is well with the Aten' and moved his capital from Thebes to an entirely new city identified with the modern Tell el-Amarna, though no trace remains (see page 179).

This idea of the sole god was new in Egypt, new in the world, and Akhenaten is known as the first real monotheist. There is no evidence that the new religion appealed to the mass of the people for while the King was deeply involved in his worship his empire fell into decay. The new religious ideas were expressed in carvings. While the pharaoh as the son of god could not be portrayed and the queen rarely appeared at all in reliefs

Cartouche of Akhenaten

Cartouche of Cheops

and statues, Akhenaten changed all the conventions and his artists represented him, and his wife and family, as they were, riding in chariots, bestowing gifts to his followers, even kissing.

When Akhenaten died at the age of 41, his half brother, Tutankhaton, a young boy, succeeded him. The Court returned to Thebes, the priests of Amen returned to power, the King changed his name to Tutankhamen (see page 207) and everything possible was done to wipe out Akhenaten's 'heretical' religion.

Cheops

Cheops or Khufu was an Old Kingdom pharaoh, the second king of the fourth Dynasty succeeding his father Snefru. His mother was Queen Hetepheres. He reigned between 2549 BC and 2526 BC . He is well known as the builder of the Great Pyramid of Giza (see page 155). He is recorded as having had four wives. Three names are given – Merityetes, Hen-utsen and Nefert-kau one of whom was his sister/half-sister, and one queen is unnamed. For Merityetes and Hen-utsen there are smaller pyramids built beside his own.

Herodotus records his reign and that of his son Chephren (Khafre) as a century of misery and oppression under wicked and tyrannical kings but in Egyptian history he is considered to have been a wise ruler. There was certainly misery. He shut all the temples and forbade the people to make sacrifices. At the same time he forced them to give up their livelihoods and assist in the construction of the pyramid being part of the team of a hundred thousand men who worked a three month shift. The preliminaries and actual construction took over 20 years. Part of the preparation was the construction of the oldest known paved road. Its purpose was to allow the huge granite facing blocks for his pyramid to be dragged and rolled to the site. Small fragments of the road exist today.

Cleopatra
69-30 BC

In 51 BC at the death of her father Ptolemy XIII she became joint ruler of Egypt with her younger brother. Three years later she was ousted from the throne but reinstated by Julius Caesar. It is related that while Julius Caesar was seated in a room in the citadel in Alexandria two slaves entered bearing a magnificent carpet.

'Cleopatra, Queen of Egypt, begs you to accept this gift' says one and as the carpet unrolls out springs 19-year-old Cleopatra. Dazzled at the sight of such loveliness, so the tale goes, the stern warrior fell in with all her plans, helping her subdue her enemies and permanently dispose of her brother.

When the daggers of the conspirators at Rome removed Caesar's protection she turned her charms on Mark Antony. Called to his presence to answer charges of assisting his enemies she came, not as a penitent, but, in a barge of beaten gold, lying under a gold embroidered canopy and fanned by 'pretty dimpled boys'. This certainly caught his attention and conveniently forgetting his wife and duties in Rome he became, we are told, her willing slave. While Cleopatra had visions of ruling in Rome as Antony's consort his enemies at Rome prevailed on the Senate to declare war on such a dangerous woman. The battle was fought at Actium in 31 BC but Cleopatra slipped away with her ships at the first opportunity leaving Antony to follow her as a hunted fugitive.

Cleopatra attempted to charm Octavian, Antony's conqueror, but he was made of sterner stuff and proof against her wiles. Antony killed himself and Cleopatra,

Cartouche of Cleopatra

Luxor

proud and queenly to the last chose to die by the bite of a poisonous asp (this fact is unsubstantiated), rather than be taken to Rome in chains. Certainly an eventful life for a woman who never reached her 40th birthday.

Hatshepsut   She was the first great woman in history living about 1503-1482 BC in the 18th Dynasty. She had immense power, adopted the full title of a pharaoh and was dressed in the full regalia down to the kilt and the false beard. She ruled for about 21 years.

She was the daughter of Tuthmosis I and Queen Ahmose and was married to her half brother Tuthmosis II who came to rule Egypt in 1512 at the death of his father. He was not very

Cartouche of Hatshepsut

strong and at his death Hatshepsut, who had had no sons of her own, became the regent of his young son Tuthmosis III, son of a minor wife/woman in the harem. She took effective control of the government while pretending to be only the prince's regent and Tuthmosis III was made a priest of the god Amun.

Around 1503 she gave up all pretence of being subservient to her stepson and had herself crowned as pharaoh. To have reached this position and to retain it indicates the support of a number of faithful and influential officials in her government. Her steward Senenmut was well-known and may have been the father of her daughter Neferure.

Determined to expand commercially she despatched (with Amun's blessing, she said) an impressive expedition to Punt on the African coast (now part of Somalia) from which were brought gold, ebony, animal skins, live baboons, processed myrrh and live myrrh trees to decorate her temple and that of Amun in Karnak. Tributes also flooded in from Libya, Nubia and the nearer parts of Asia.

In the name of/to honour the god Amun-Re (the main god of the region and her adopted 'father') she set about a huge construction/reconstruction programme repairing damage caused to earlier temples and building new ones. The chapels to the Thebian Triad behind the Great Pylon of Ramses II at Luxor were built by Hatshepsut and Tuthmosis III. She renovated The Great Temple of Amun, at Karnak where she introduced four huge (30 m+) obelisks made of Aswan granite. At Beni Hasan she built a rock cut temple known as Speos Artemidos but her finest achievement was her own beautiful temple cut into the rock at three different levels.

The wall reliefs in the temple fortified her position of importance, her divine birth which is a very complicated set of scenes involving the god Amun, her mother and herself as a baby; her selection as pharaoh by Hathor; her coronation by Hathor and Seth watched over by her real father, Tuthmosis I.

Her expedition to the exotic land of Punt is depicted in very great detail with pictures of the scenery (stilt houses) and selected incidents from the voyages (some baboons escaping up the rigging). Items brought back are offered to Amun in another relief. She even had depicted the huge barges used to transport the four obelisks she had erected for her adopted father (Amun) in Karnak.

To continue her position as a pharaoh even after her death she had her tomb cut in the Valley of the Kings. It was the longest and deepest in the valley.

Keeping everything in proportion

Production of carved reliefs for the decoration of temple walls or coloured illustrations for tombs had to follow many rigid rules. While the eye and the brain soon get used to the Egyptian representation of human and animal forms mental adjustment has to take place for the Egyptian artist was not permitted to draw what he saw but only to represent what he knew to be there. There was no place for originality. Perhaps the best artists were those who produced illustrations indistinguishable from earlier examples. The grid marked on to the wall gave the parameters and variations were not allowed. All the men in the picture were the same size, only gods or pharaohs were larger while enemies, children and sometimes women were drawn on a smaller grid. On the earlier drawings the grid was made up of 18 squares – from the hairline to soles of the feet, later (from the 19th Dynasty) the figures were slightly elongated using a 21 square grid. Measuring to the hairline gave scope for ornamental head-dresses.

Examine a figure. The head was always drawn profile, more generally facing right (the preferred direction) but the eye with a very dark eyebrow looked out of the picture to the viewer, not forward. The shoulders were square and parallel to the floor while the front of the body, from the armpits, was sideways with a nipple or breast in profile. The navel was placed slightly off centre, so it could be seen. Arms were of equal length but the back of the right hand and the incurled fingers of the left hand were not necessarily on the correct arm.

Female clothing caused a problem as the tunic top hanging from square shoulders did not cover the breasts that were in profile. The legs like the head pointed to the right, the left leg in front, or it could be the right leg because both legs have left feet, feet drawn from the inside,

no toes indicated. Sometimes an instep is drawn but both feet are still the same. The female figures took shorter, daintier steps.

Having produced one figure the rear outline could be repeated to indicate a host of soldiers, hostages, etc. It is interesting that the Egyptians depicted were all without blemish, did not suffer from wrinkles or spots or any deformities.

With animals, conventional depiction was easier to follow. For example if it was in profile it was crocodile, if shown from above a lizard. Fish were always two-dimensional side view but drawn swimming in a square pool.

Use of colour was restricted too, with no change of tone or shading used. Outlining in black or brown was common. Men were dark skinned while the women who were expected to be indoors all day were much lighter in colour.

A sculptor had no greater freedom of expression. The forward facing head of a figure is in almost every case at right angles to the shoulders. All seated statues have their hands on their knees. The smaller figures of children and wives always cling to the legs of their master. A standing statue has the left leg forward – no variation allowed.

Strange as they are these illustrations show us what we are meant to see, and we have no problem in comprehension or appreciating the work of the artists from such distant centuries.

Luxor

📌 ### The Curse of Tutankhamen

Tutankhamen tomb's fame and mystery was enhanced by the fate of those who were directly connected with its discovery. The expedition's sponsor Lord Carnarvon, who had first opened the tomb with his chief archaeologist Howard Carter, died shortly afterwards in April 1923 from an infected mosquito bite. A subsequent succession of bizarre deaths added weight to British novelist Marie Corelli's totally unproven and unhistoric claim that "dire punishment follows any intruder into the tomb". Such alleged curses have, however, done nothing to deter the tens of thousands of visitors who still visit the site despite the fact that most of the treasures are now in the Egyptian Museum!

Late in his reign Tuthmosis III turned against the memory of Hatshepsut and had all her images in the reliefs erased and replaced with figures of himself or the two preceding male pharaohs. In many places her cartouches have been rewritten too. Unfortunately he had all her statues destroyed.

Ramses III   He reigned from 1198-66 BC, in the 20th Dynasty which was noted for the beginning of the great decline of Egypt. He was not part of the decline being known as a worthy monarch. He excelled himself in the earlier part of his reign with victories on land and victories at sea vanquishing the Cretans and the Carians. On land he used the military colonies established by previous rulers such as Ramses II and Seti I to conduct his missions further into Asia. He had little trouble subduing the tribes far into Asia but had problems nearer at home – having to fight to hold his position as pharaoh. A group of invaders made up of Libyans, Sardinians and Italians managed to advance as far as Memphis in the 8th year of his reign but their defeat put him in a much stronger position internally.

Having had his fill of expeditions to foreign parts and no doubt having returned with sufficient booty to have made the trips worthwhile and make him a very wealthy monarch he paid off his troops and set about adding to and constructing temples and other monumental works. Of particular note are the buildings at Medinet Habu. Here there is a magnificent temple with the walls covered in reliefs depicting the engagements on land and sea in which he had been so successful. Even the gate is inscribed with reliefs showing the despatch of prisoners and where a neat design on the pylons shows a cartouche of each vanquished country surmounted by a human head and with bound arms (see Medinet Habu, page 261). This is a valuable historical record of Egypt and the surrounding lands at this time.

In brief he restored law and order within Egypt and provided some security from outside aggression. He revived commercial prosperity. His attentions to the temples of Thebes, Memphis and Heliopolis certainly enriched Egyptian architecture. He was, however, unable to turn the slow ebb of his country's grandeur which was said to be suffering from 'fundamental decadence'.

Cartouche of Ramses III

Cartouche of Tutankhamen

He was assassinated. Four sons, all bearing the his name, succeeded him but their reigns were not distinguished and the decline of Egypt was hastened.

Tutankhamen

He was a pharaoh of the New Kingdom, 18th Dynasty, and reigned from 1361-52 BC. He was the son of Amenhotep III and probably his chief queen Tiy and was married to Akhenaten's daughter. He was too young to rule without a visir and regent. He died in the ninth year of his reign at about 18 years of age, leaving no surviving children, his regent Ay succeeded him by marrying his widow.

He was originally called Tutankhaton but changed name to Tutankhamen to distance himself from Atun and the cult of Atun worship of his half brother Amenhotep IV (Akhenaten). He moved his capital back to Memphis and to eradicate the effects of the rule of his predecessor he restored the temples and the status of the old gods and their priests. His greatest claim to fame was his intact tomb discovered by Howard Carter in 1922, details of which are given on page 240, see also box, The Curse of Tutankhamen, above .

Tuthmosis I – the trend setter

He was an 18th-Dynasty pharaoh who ruled from around 1525-12 BC. He is noted for his expansion of the Egyptian Empire south into Nubia and east into present day Syria. He led a river-bourne expedition into Nubia to beyond the fourth Cataract (he was after the gold there) and set up a number of defensive forts along the route. His foray across the Euphrates was part of his campaign against the Hyksos who caused many problems for the Egyptians. Tuthmosis I used the Euphrates as the border over which he did not intend these enemies to cross.

He is also noted for the building and renovation works he contracted at Karnak. Much of the inner temple of Amun at Karnak is attributed to him. In particular the sandstone fourth Pylon in front of which one of his obelisks still stands, and the limestone fifth Pylon which marked the centre of the temple at the time, and behind which was the original position of the sanctuary of Tuthmosis I.

He was born in the era when burial in a pyramid was 'out of vogue' and being buried in a secret tomb in the rocks of the surrounding hillside was just coming 'in'. (See box below Pyramids out of fashion.) It is suggested that his tomb was the first in the Valley of the Kings and he certainly set a trend. Even so his red quartzite sarcophagus was found in the tomb of his daughter Queen Hatshepsut and is now in the museum in Cairo.

Cartouche of Tuthmosis I

👉 Pyramids out of fashion

By the Fifth/Sixth dynasties the scale of pyramid building diminished at Memphis and elsewhere in the northern kingdom. They were costly to construct, took a long time to complete and were very prone to be robbed. Instead the kings of Egypt built temples – often to the god Re with their available resources. Then in the 11th dynasty (Middle Kingdom) the geographical focus shifted to Thebes where, aided by local geology in the easily worked wadi cliffs, burials were made in rock-cut tomb temples. Pyramid building with few exceptions ceased after this epoch.

Zoser This was a king of the Old Kingdom, the second king of the 3rd Dynasty. It is hard to piece together his history. He succeeded his brother and perhaps reigned for 19 years between 2667-48 BC. Two of his daughters were called Intkaes and Hetephernebti, their names taken from steales in the complex.

His funerary complex at Saqqara (see page 144) is an example of some of the world's most ancient architecture and it was all, not only the Step Pyramid, but also the huge enclosure wall and the subsidiary temples and structures, designed by Zoser, under the charge of his talented architect/chancellor/physician Imhotep. This building was important being the first large scale building to be made completely of stone. In addition it was of an unusual stepped design. Many of the buildings in the surrounding complex were never intended for use but were replicas of the buildings used by the pharaoh on earth so that he could use them in eternity. Eventually he was buried under his Step Pyramid. So what was the other tomb for in the complex? Perhaps it was for his entrails as it was too small for a royal person?

He made Memphis his capital which gave impetus to the growth in importance of this town which eventually became the political and cultural centre.

Travellers interested in seeing his likeness must visit room 46 in Cairo Museum which has the huge seated figure of King Zoser taken from the complex.

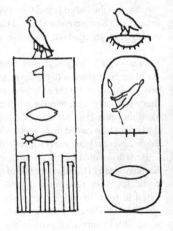

Cartouche of Zoser

Who's who in Ancient Egypt: Deities

There were hundreds of gods and goddesses worshipped by the ancient Egyptians. Over time some grew in favour and others became less important. In addition each district of the country had its own deities. It is useful to have an idea of their role in ancient Egypt and to recognize them on the wall paintings and carvings. Unfortunately they could be represented in more than one way, being different aspects of the same god.

Aker He was an earth god often shown with the head of a lion. He guarded the east and west gates of the afterlife.

Amun He was first worshipped as a local deity in Khmun in Middle Egypt in Hermopolis and later when his cult reached Thebes his importance spread to all of Egypt. He was believed to be the creator of all things, to order time and

the seasons. When he sailed over the heavens he controlled the wind and the direction of the clouds. His name means 'the hidden' or 'unseen one'. At times he was identified with the sun-god Re, hence Amun-Re, and as Amun-Min was the god of fertility. He was often drawn as a human form with twisted rams horns and two tall feathers as a headdress, a sceptre/crook in one hand and a ceremonial flail in the other, an erect phallus and a black pointed beard.

The sacred animals with which he was identified were the ram and the goose (the Great Cackler). As the ram-headed god he renewed the life in the souls of the departed. He was part of the Thebian Triad with Mut his wife and Khonsu his adopted son.

Anubis This god was responsible for the ritual of embalming and looking after the place where the mummification was done. Indeed he was reputed to have invented embalming, his first attempt of this art being on the corpse of Osiris. When Anubis was drawn on the wall on either side of a tomb's entrance the mummy would be protected. He helped Isis to restore life to Osiris.

He was also included in scenes weighing the dead person's heart/soul

against the 'feather of truth', which was the only way to enter the next world.

In the earlier dynasties of the Old Kingdom he held an important position as lord of the dead but was later overshadowed by Osiris. Later he was better known simply as a conductor of souls. He was closely associated with Middle Egypt and some sections of Upper Egypt.

He was depicted as a recumbent black dog/fox/jackal or a jackal-headed god. On any illustration the ears of the creature were alertly up and slightly forward. The association with a fox/jackal was the number of jackals that were to found in the cemeteries. Sometimes he was shown seated on a pylon.

Luxor

Anukis   This was the wife of Khnum and the mother of Sartis, the third member of the Elephantine Triad. She was the goddess of the first cataract area and was depicted wearing a high crown of feathers and carrying a sceptre of papyrus plant.

Apis Bulls   The sacred bulls of Memphis were all black bulls with a white triangle on the forehead and a crescent shape on the flank. A sacred bull was believed to contain the spirit of Ptah and lived in a palace and was present as guest of honour at state functions. When it died it was mummified and buried at the huge underground tomb of the Serapeum at Saqqara and a new younger bull, its reincarnation, took its place. On illustrations it was sometimes shown with a sun disc between its horns.

Apophis   This was a symbol of unrest and chaos in the form of a large serpent. It was kept under control by the stronger powers of good, in particular the cat-goddess Bastet and by Sekhmet the fierce lioness god.

Aten   He was the sun-god depicted as the solar disc emitting long bright rays which often terminated in human hands. For a brief time, under Akhenaton, worship of Aten was the state religion. He was considered the one true god. After the demise of Akhenaton he disappeared into obscurity.

Atum   This was one of the first forms of the sun-creator god. He was originally just a local deity of Heliopolis but joined with Re, as Atum-Re, he became more popular. Re took the part of the sun at the zenith and Atum was identified with the setting sun when it goes to the underworld. As this he was represented as a man, sometimes an old man, indicating the dying of the day.

Bastet   The famous cat goddess of the Delta region was the daughter of Re. She represented the power of the sun to ripen crops and was considered to be virile, strong and agile. Her home city was Bubastis (see page 327) but her fame spread widely. She was initially a goddess of the home but in the religion of the New Kingdom she became associated with the lioness war goddess. She was regarded as a friendly deity – the goddess of joy.

She was represented as a woman with a cat's head, carried an ancient percussion instrument, the sistrum, in her right hand, a breast plate in her left hand and had a small bag hung over her left arm. Numerous small cat figures were used in the home for worship or as amulets. Mummified cats (votive offerings) were buried in a vast cemetery at Bubastis. She was loosely connected with Mut and Sekhmet.

Bes   This was a strange creature, the god of dancing, merriment and music, being capable of playing many musical instruments. He was always portrayed as a jolly dwarf with a large head, a round face, round ears, goggle eyes, protruding tongue, sprouting lion's whiskers, which later became stylized as a fancy collar, under a tall headdress of feathers. He had short bow legs and a bushy tail. He was one of the few gods drawn front face rather than profile.

It is suggested his hideousness was to drive away evil spirits and hence pain and sorrow. As the guardian of women and children he kept the house free from snakes and evil spirits. He was portrayed on vases, mirrors, perfume jars and other toilet articles and even on the pillows of mummies. He was frequently represented in birth houses as the guardian of women in childbirth. It seems that at first he just protected the Royal family but later took on the care of all Egyptians.

This deity, also known as Wadjet, was a cobra goddess whose fame spread from **Buto**
the Delta to all of Lower Egypt. She was known as the green goddess (the colour
of papyrus) and was said to be responsible for the burning heat of the sun.

These members of the Heliopolitan ennead, are frequently depicted together. **Geb/Shu/Nut**
Geb (god of the earth), son of Shu (god of the air or emptiness), was married to

his sister Nut (goddess of the sky).
The sun-god Re was displeased
with this association although
most gods seem to marry their sisters and ordered Shu to keep the
two apart. Hence all three are represented together with Shu
between Geb's green recumbent
form and Nut arching in the sky.

As explained, this was the god of the earth, the physi- **Geb**
cal support of the world. Along with his sister/wife
Nut he was part of the second generation ennead of
Heliopolis. He was usually drawn as a man without
any distinguishing characteristics though sometimes
had the head of a goose which was distinguishing
enough. He could be also be depicted as a bull in contrast to Nut's cow. His recumbent form mentioned
above represented the hills and valleys and the green
colour the plants growing there.

He was the cause of the bitter quarrel between
Osiris and his brother Seth for at his retirement he left
them both to rule the world. Hence the famous myth.
See box, page 503.

He was the god who lived next to the river because **Hapi/Hapy**
he controlled the level of Nile and was responsible for the floods. He was
even responsible for the dew that fell at night. He was represented as a
bearded man with a female breast wearing a bunch of papyrus on his head
and carrying offerings or leading a sacrifice. There was an association here
with Apis.

There was another god Hapi who was one of the sons of Horus, the baboon
headed guardian of the Canopic jar of the lungs.

This was the name given to Horus as a child. In illustra- **Harpokrates**
tions he was a naked child with a finger in his mouth.
The side lock of hair he wore is an indication of youth.

This was the goddess of the sky who was also known **Hathor**
as the golden one. Her name means 'castle of the
sky-god Horus'. She was a goddess of festivity, love
and dance. The original centre of her cult was
Dendera and her importance spread to Thebes and
Memphis. With the increase in her fame and contrary to her earlier nature she became known as a
goddess of the dead and the region of the dead. She
was believed to have been responsible for nearly
destroying all mankind. See myths, page 180. On

illustrations she was represented as a cow or a cow-headed woman or a woman with a headdress of a disc between two horns and large cow-like ears.

Heh This lesser known god can be seen kneeling holding a palm branch notched with the number of the years in a king's life.

Heqet This was a frog goddess who sometimes assisted at childbirth.

Horus This was a very important god, the falcon headed sky god. Horus means 'he who is far above' and the hawk fits this image. Hence he was depicted as hawk-headed or even a full hawk often wearing the double crown of Egypt. The hawk's eyes are thought of as the sun and the moon. Horus' left eye was damaged in his conflict with Seth and this was thought to indicate the waxing and waning of the moon. He probably originated in the Delta region and the cult spread to all of Egypt. It was only later that he became associated with Isis and Osiris as their son.

Imhotep He was a man, one of two mortals (the other was Amenhotep) who were totally deified. He was recorded as the designer of the first temple at Edfu and the official architect of Zoser's step pyramid. When he was later deified it was as a god of healing and made the honorary son of Ptah. He was known, not as a temple builder, but, as a patron of scribes, a healer, a sage and a magician, and was worshipped as a god of medicine. He was considered to have been a physician of considerable skill.

At the time of the Persian conquest he was elevated to the position of a deity. His cult reached its peak in Greaco-Roman times where his temples at Memphis and on the island of Philae in the River Nile were often crowded with unhealthy people who slept there hoping that a cure for their problems would be revealed to them in their dreams. He was depicted on wall illustrations as a seated man holding an open papyrus.

Isis She was one of the most important ancient Egyptian goddesses, the most popular goddess in Egypt from around AD 650 right up to the introduction of Christianity. Originally the cult was in Lower Egypt but it spread to embrace eventually the whole of Egypt and parts of Nubia. Her name means 'throne' and because the word throne is feminine it was depicted by a woman's figure. This made her the mother of the king who sat on the throne. She receives a number of mentions as the grieving widow of Osiris. She was also the sister of Osiris, Seth and Nephthys.

She was held in high esteem as the perfect wife and mother and became the goddess of protection. She was also an enchantress, using her power to bring Osiris back to life again. She was represented as a woman with the hieroglyph sign for a throne on her head, an orb or sun between two horns, and was generally sitting nursing her son Horus, or seen also kneeling at a coffin of Osiris. Her ability to give life to the dead meant she was the chief deity at all funerals.

There are temples to her at Dendera, on Philae and in the Nile Delta. Several temples were dedicated to her in Alexandria where she was the patroness of seafarers. She was guardian of the Canopic jar which held the viscera.

Khepri

He was the sun-god represented as a scarab beetle with a sun disc. As the scarab beetle rolls a ball of dung around so the Egyptians thought this was how the sun was moved. They thought the scarab possessed remarkable powers and used it as an amulet. See box, page 147.

Khnum

He was represented on wall drawings as a man with a ram's head with long twisted horns. The Egyptians believed he made the first man by moulding him in clay from the River Nile on a potter's wheel. Over time his area of responsibility changed. He lived at the first cataract on the Nile where he presided over all the cataracts of the Nile. He had the authority to decide whether or not the god Hapi 'rose' and the River Nile flooded. He was associated with temples at Elephantine and Esna.

Khonsu

He was regarded as the son of Amun and Mut. The three made up the Thebian Triad. He had the ability to cast a range of spells, dispel demons and act as an oracle. He travelled through the sky at night and sometimes assisted the scribe of the gods. As the moon god he was usually represented as a man wearing a disc of the full moon and horns on his head or the head of a falcon. He had a single lock of hair to show his youth.

Ma'at

This well loved deity was the goddess of order, truth and justice. She was the daughter of the sun-god Re and Thoth the goddess of wisdom. She can be seen at the ceremony of judgement, the balancing of the heart of the deceased against a feather. The scale was balanced by Ma'at or her ideogram, the single ostrich feather as a test of truthfulness. The priests with her were judges. She often appears, confusingly, as two identical goddesses, a case of double judgement. She was very popular with the other gods. She was also depicted on wall paintings in the solar barque.

Mertseger

This was the goddess of the west, a cobra goddess from Thebes. She was said to punish those who did not come up to scratch with illness or even death.

Luxor

Min   This was the god of sexual prowess, of fertility and of good harvests. He was depicted bearded, wearing a crown of two feathers, phallus erect, a ceremonial flail in his raised right hand and a ribbon from his headdress reaching down to the ground at the back. He was worshipped at Luxor. His feast day was an important festival often associated with wild orgies. He was worshipped too as the guardian of travellers as he protected the routes to the Red Sea and in the Eastern Desert. The lettuce was his sacred plant.

Montu   The war god Montu who rose to importance in the 11th Dynasty protected the king in battle. He has a temple to the north of the main temple in Karnak. His image was hawk-headed with a sun disc between two plumes.

Mut

She was originally a very ancient vulture goddess of Thebes but during the 18th Dynasty was married to the god Amun and with their adopted son Khonsu made up the Thebian Triad. The marriage of Amun and Mut was a reason for great annual celebrations in Thebes. Her role as mistress of the heavens or as sky goddess often had her appearing as a cow, standing behind her husband as he rose from the primeval sea Nu to his place in the heavens. More often she was represented with a double crown of Egypt on her head, a vulture's head or lioness's head on her forehead. Another role was as a great divine mother. She has a temple south of the main temple at Karnak.

Nefertum   He was one of the Memphis deities most often associated with perfumes. He was represented as a man with a lotus flower on his head.

Neith   This was the goddess of weaving, war and hunting, among other things. She was also protector of the dead and the Canopic jars. She wore a red crown of Lower Egypt and a shield on her head (sometimes held in her hand), held two crossed arrows and an ankh in her hand. She was connected with Sobek and was worshipped at Memphis, Esna and Fayoum.

Nekhbet   In her more important guise she was the vulture or serpent goddess, protectress of Upper Egypt and especially of its rulers. She was generally depicted with spreading wings held over the pharaoh while grasping in her claw the royal ring or other emblems. She always appeared as a woman, sometimes with a vulture's head and always wearing a white crown. Her special colour was white, in contrast to her counterpart Buto (red) who was the goddess of Lower Egypt. In another aspect she was worshipped as goddess of the River Nile and consort of the river god. She was associated too with Mut.

Nephthys   Her name was translated as 'lady of the house'. She was the sister of Seth, Osiris and Isis. She was married to Seth. She had no children by her husband but a son, Anubis, by

Osiris. She wears the hieroglyphs of her name on her head. She was one of the protector guardians of the Canopic jars and a goddess of the dead.

Nut She was goddess of the sky, the vault of the heavens. She was wife/sister of Geb. The Egyptians believed that on five special days preceding the new year she gave birth on successive days to the deities Osiris, Horus, Seth, Isis and Nephthys. This was cause for great celebrations. She was usually depicted as a naked woman arched over Shu who supported her with upraised arms. She was also represented wearing a water pot or pear shaped vessel on her head, this being the hieroglyph of her name. Sometimes she was depicted as a cow, so that she could carry the sun-god Re on her back to the sky. The cow was usually spangled with stars to represent the night sky. It was supposed that the cow swallowed the sun which journeyed through her body during the night to emerge at sunrise. This was also considered a symbol of resurrection.

Osiris This was one of the most important gods in ancient Egypt, the god of the dead, the god of the underworld and the god of plenty. He had the power to control the vegetation (particular cereals because he began his career as a corn deity) which sprouted after the annual flooding of the River Nile. He originated in the Delta at Busiris and it is suggested that he was once a real ruler. His importance spread to the whole of Egypt.

Annual celebrations included the moulding of a clay body in the shape of Osiris, filled with soil and containing seeds. This was moistened with water from the River Nile and the sprouting grain symbolized the strength of Osiris. One of the main celebrations in the Temple at Abydos where he was very popular was associated with Osiris and it was fashionable to be buried or have a memorial on the processional road to Abydos and so absorb the blessing of Osiris. There are temples dedicated to Osiris at Edfu and on Bigah Island opposite Philae.

According to ancient Egyptian custom when a king and later any person died he became Osiris and thus through him mankind had a some hope of resurrection. The Apis bull at Memphis also represented Osiris. The names Osiris-apis and Sarapis are derived from this.

He was shown as a mummy with his arm crossed over his breast, one hand holding a royal crook the other a ceremonial flail. These crook and flail sceptres on his portraits and statues showed he was god of the underworld. He wore a narrow plaited beard and the white crown of Upper Egypt and two red feathers.

Ptah He was originally the local deity of the capital Memphis and his importance eventually spread over the whole of Egypt. He was very popular at Thebes and Abydos. He was worshipped as the creator of the gods of the Memphite theology. Ptah was the husband of Sekhmet and father of Nefertum. Only later was he associated with Osiris. He was the patron of craftsmen, especially sculptors. He was renowned for his skill as an engineer, stonemason, metal worker and artist.

He was always shown in human form, mummified or swathed in a winding sheet, with a clean shaven human head. He would be holding a staff and wearing an amulet. The Apis bull had its stall in the great temple of Ptah in Memphis.

Qebehsenuf The falcon headed guardian of the Canopic jar of the intestines was the son of Horus.

Re This was the sun-god of Heliopolis and the supreme judge. He was the main god at the time of the New Kingdom. His importance was great. His cult centre was Heliopolis and the cult reached the zenith in the fifth Dynasty when he had become the official god of the pharaohs and every king was both the son of Re and Re incarnate.

Re was the god who symbolized the sun. He appeared in many aspects and was portrayed in many different ways. He was found in conjunction with other gods Re-Horakhte, Amun-Re, Min-Re etc. As Amun-Re (Amun was the god from Thebes) he was king of the gods and responsible for the pharaoh on military campaigns where he handed the scimitar of conquest to the great warriors. Re was king and father of the gods and the creator of mankind. It was believed that after death, the pharaoh in his barge joined Re in the heavens.

He was thought to travel across the sky each day in his solar boat and during the night make his passage in the underworld in another boat. He was represented as man with a hawk or falcon's head wearing a sun disc or if dead with a ram's head. See also page 207.

Sekhmet This was another aspect of the goddess Hathor. Sekhmet the consort of Ptah was a fierce goddess of war and the destroyer of the enemies of her father the sun-god Re. She was usually depicted as a lioness or as a woman with a lion's head on which was placed the solar disc and the uraeus. She was also the goddess who was associated with pestilence, and could bring disease and death to mankind but her task also was to do the healing and her priests were often doctors. She was said to have chained the serpent Apophis.

Selket This was one of the four goddesses who protected the sources of the River Nile. As the guardian of the dead she was portrayed often with a scorpion on her head. She was put in charge of the bound serpent Apophis in the underworld.

Seshat Seshat was shown as a woman with a seven point star on her head, and dressed in a panther skin. She was the goddess of writing and of recording the years. She carried a palm leaf on which she wrote her records.

Seth Seth did not begin with such bad press. He was in favour in the 19th Dynasty especially in the Eastern Delta around Tanis but by the Late Period he was considered evil and on some monuments his image was effaced. By the Christian era he was firmly in place as the devil. The Egyptians thought Seth who was the brother of Osiris, Isis and Nephthys tried to prevent the sun from rising each dawn.

As such an enemy of mankind they represented him as a huge serpent-dragon. He was sometimes depicted as a hippopotamus and sometimes took the form of a crocodile as he did to avoid the avenging Horus. More often he was depicted as an unidentified animal, a greyhound, dog, pig, ass, okapi, anteater or a man with the head of an animal. The head had an unusual long down curved snout and the ears were upstanding and square-tipped. The eyes were slanting and the tail long and forked. He was also seen in drawings standing at the prow of the sun-god's boat.

Shu

He and his twin sister and wife Tefnut were created by the sun-god Re by his own power without the aid of a woman. They were the first couple of the ennead of Heliopolis. He was father of Geb the earth god and Nut the sky goddess. He was the representation of air and emptiness, of light and space, the supporter of the sky.

He was portrayed in human form with the hieroglyph of his name, an ostrich feather on his head. Often he was drawn separating Geb and Nut for their union was not approved of by Re.

Sobek

He was known as the crocodile god, a protector of reptiles and of kings. Crocodile gods were very common in Fayoum, mainly at the time of the Middle Kingdom and also at Esna and Kom Ombo. The live crocodiles at the temples were believed to be this god incarnate and accordingly were treated very well. These sacred crocodiles were kept in a lake before the temples. They were pampered and bejewelled. After death they were mummified. Confusingly he was usually depicted with Amun's crown of rams' horns and feathers.

Taweret

This upright pregnant hippopotamus had pendant human breasts, lion's paws and a crocodile's tail. Sometimes she wore the horns of Hathor with a solar disc. She was also known as Apet/Opet. She was the goddess of childbirth and attended both royal births and the daily rebirth of the sun. She was a goddess at Esna.

Tefnut

She was the wife/sister of Shu, the lion-headed goddess of moisture and dew, one of the Heliopolitan ennead.

Thoth

His cult originated in the Nile Delta and was then mainly centred in Upper Egypt. He was held to be the inventor of writing, the founder of social order, the creator of languages, the patron of scribes, interpreter and adviser to the gods, and (in his spare time?) representative of the sun-god Re on earth. He gave the Egyptians knowledge of medicine and mathematics. He possessed a book in which all the wisdom of the world was recorded. In another aspect he was known as the moon god. He was also associated with the birth of the earth.

Thoth protected Isis during her pregnancy and healed the injury to Horus inflicted by Seth. He too was depicted in the feather/heart weighing judgement ceremonies of the diseased and as the scribe reported the results to Osiris. His sacred animals were the ibis and the baboon. Numerous mummified bodies of these two animals were found in cemeteries in Hermopolis and Thebes.

He was usually represented as a human with an ibis' head. The curved beak of the ibis was like the crescent moon so the two were connected and the ibis became the symbol of the moon god Thoth.

Wepwawet He was the jackal-headed god of Middle Egypt, especially popular in the Assiut region. He was know as 'the opener of the ways'.

Sites in Luxor and on the east bank

Luxor Temple

Allow three or four hours to see this in detail and if possible get to see it in the evening – with spotlights it looks stunning. ■ *The temple, in the centre of town on the Corniche, is open daily 0700-2100 in winter, 0700-2200 in summer and during Ramadan 0800-1100 and 2000-2300. E£20, cameras free.*

Like the much larger Karnak Temple it is dedicated to the three Theban gods Amun, Mut and Khonsu. **Amun** is usually depicted as a man wearing ram's horns or a tall feathered Atef crown. His wife **Mut** was considered to be the mistress of heaven and **Khonsu** was their son who was believed to travel through the sky at night assisting the scribe god.

Because it is smaller, more compact and fewer pharaohs were involved in its construction, Luxor Temple is simpler and more coherent than Karnak Temple a few kilometres away. Although the 18th Dynasty (1537-1320 BC) pharaoh **Amenhotep III** (1417-1379 BC) began the Temple, his son **Amenhotep IV**, who changed his name to **Akhenaten** (1379-62 BC) by which he is better known, concentrated instead on building a shrine to Aten adjacent to the site. However **Tutankhamen** (1361-52 BC) and **Horemheb** (1348-20 BC) later resumed the work and decorated the peristyle court and colonnade. **Ramses II** (1304-1237 BC) completed the majority of the building by adding a second colonnade and pylon as well as a multitude of colossi. The Temple subsequently became covered with sand and silt which helped preserve it although salt encrustation has caused some damage. Because the ground level has risen 6 m since its construction the temple now stands at the bottom of a gentle depression. An avenue of sphinxes, a 30th Dynasty (380-343 BC) addition, lines the approach. This avenue once stretched all the way to the Karnak Temple complex.

The entrance to the temple is through the First Pylon. In front of the pylon are the three remaining colossi of Ramses II, two seated and one standing and, to the left, a single obelisk 25 m high.

The **First Pylon** gives an impression of how awe-inspiring the Temple must have looked in its prime. The 22.8 m high second Obelisk, which was given to France by Mohammed Ali Pasha in 1819 and was re-erected in the Place de la Concorde in Paris, and another three of Ramses II's six original colossi have been removed. The reliefs on the First Pylon depict Ramses' victory at the Battle of Kadesh with later embellishments by Nubian and Ethiopian kings.

Passing through the pylon, the **Peristyle Court** is set at a slight angle to the rest of the Temple and encompasses the earlier shrine of **Tuthmosis III**

(1504-1450 BC) which is also dedicated to the Theban triad. The east end of the court has not been fully excavated because it is the site of the **Mosque of Abu el-Haggag**, the patron saint of Luxor and, although another mosque with the same name has been built nearby, this one is still preferred by locals. While most of the mosque is 19th century the northern minaret is very much older. At the south end of the court, the portal flanking the entrance to the colonnade supports two black granite statues bearing the name of Ramses II, but the feathers of Tutankhamen.

The **Colonnade** of 14 columns with papyrus capitals was built by Amenhotep but decorated by Tutankhamen and Horemheb. Beyond it is a

Luxor town

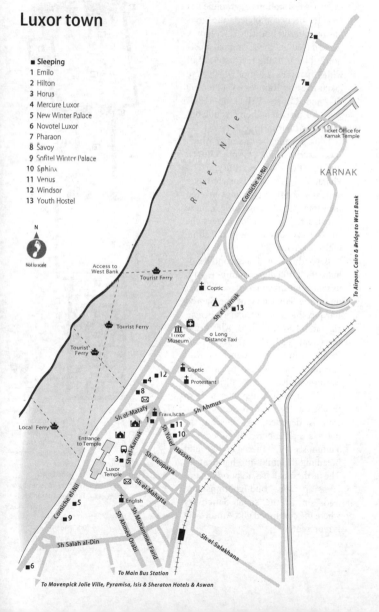

■ Sleeping
1 Emilo
2 Hilton
3 Horus
4 Mercure Luxor
5 New Winter Palace
6 Novotel Luxor
7 Pharaon
8 Savoy
9 Sofitel Winter Palace
10 Sphinx
11 Venus
12 Windsor
13 Youth Hostel

To Movenpick Jolie Ville, Pyramisa, Isis & Sheraton Hotels & Aswan

Luxor

Court of Amenhotep III, which is the second peristyle court with double rows of columns flanking three of the sides. It was built by Amenhotep III for the deity Amun who he claimed was his father. None of the original roof remains, but the columns are well preserved. Because the rising water-table has undermined the foundations of this court, an extensive restoration programme has recently been completed, the floor has been relaid and the 22 columns reassembled in their original positions. It leads to the **Hypostyle Hall** with 32 papyrus columns which were taken over by **Ramses IV** (1166-60 BC) and **Ramses VII** (1148-41BC) who took no part in their erection but still added their cartouches!

Look out for the chamber which was converted into a **Coptic church** during the 4th century. The Pharaonic reliefs were plastered over and early Christian paintings covered the whitewash although little of these remains today. In a few places the stucco has crumbled away and some of the original reliefs are revealed.

Beyond is a smaller second vestibule, the **Offerings Chamber**, with its four columns still in place. Further on, in the **Sanctuary of the Sacred Barque**, the doors were made of acacia and inlaid with gold. **Alexander the Great** (332-323 BC) rebuilt the shrine in accordance with Amenhotep III's original plans. The east passage leads to the Birth Room built because of Amenhotep's claim that he was the son of the god Amun, who is depicted as entering the queen's chamber disguised as Tuthmosis IV (1425-17 BC) and breathing the child into her nostrils. The furthest hall has 12 poorly maintained papyrus bud columns and leads on to the small **Sanctuary** where the combined god Amun-Min is represented.

Temple of Luxor

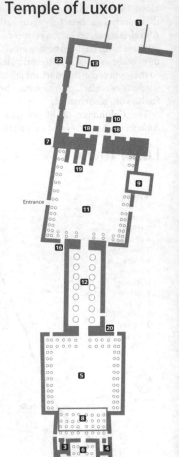

1 Avenue of human-headed sphinxes
2 Birth room
3 Chapel of Khonsu
4 Chapel of Mut
5 Court of Amenhotep III
6 First antechamber or Roman sanctuary
7 First Pylon of Ramses II
8 Hypostyle hall
9 Mosque of Abu el-Haggag
10 Obelisk
11 Peristyle Court of Ramses II
12 Processional Colonnade of Amenophis III
13 Roman shrine to Sarapis
14 Sanctuary to Amun-Re
15 Second antechamber/ offering room
16 Second pylon
17 Shrine of Sacred Barque
18 Statues of Ramses II
19 Temple to Thebian Triad/ triple shrine
20 Third pylon
21 Transverse hall
22 Walls of Roman brick

Luxor Museum

The Luxor Museum is located on the Corniche half way between Luxor and Karnak temples. ■ *Daily – winter 0900-1300, 1600-2100 (last tickets 1230 and 2030) summer 0900-1300, 1700-2200 (last tickets 1230 and 2130). E£30 plus E£10 for New Hall, E£10 for using a camera, 50% discount for students.*

The few exhibits in this modern museum are tastefully displayed, centred around a small garden, with a large ground floor and a smaller upper gallery. The most important and of particular interest are the New Kingdom statues which were found in a cache at Karnak in 1989 but the exhibits range from pharaonic treasures to the Mamluke period (AD 1250-1517).

Of the statues on the ground floor the most striking are the large pink granite head of Amenhotep III (1417-1379 BC), an alabaster crocodile-headed Sobek, and two memorable busts of Akhenaten. A few choice exhibits from Tutankhamen's tomb are also displayed including a gold-inlaid cow's head of the goddess Hathor, a funerary bed and two model barques. The prints showing how the sites looked in the 19th century are also interesting.

On the second floor is the wall of Akhenaten, 283 sandstone blocks found at the Ninth Pylon at Karnak. Here Akhenaten and Nefertiti are shown worshipping Aten.

Museum of Mummification – right on the banks of the River Nile – tells the story of mummification as practised by the ancient Egyptians as an integral part of their religious belief in the after life. This museum, considered to be the first of its kind in the world, contains a comprehensive display. Exhibits include several human, reptile and bird mummies as well as stone and metal tools used in the mummification process. It is well set out and is certainly worth a visit. Note examples of canopic jars for storing the liver, lungs, stomach and intestines. ■ *Daily, summer 0900-1300, 1700-2200, winter 0900-1300, 1600-2100. E£20, student E£10, camera E£10.*

Karnak Temple

Allow half a day to see this in detail and if possible return in the evening for the Sound and Light show. The Karnak Temple complex, 2½ km north of Luxor town, is the largest pharaonic monument in the country after the Giza Pyramids and covers almost 25 ha. ■ *Daily winter 0600-1730, summer 0600-1830, general entry E£20, student entry E£10, cameras free.* The site can just about be covered in two hours. The evening Sound and Light Show ■ *E£33 and E£30 for video cameras* is good with a somewhat overdramatic commentary. See Sound and light, page 266. *Calèches* and service taxis from Luxor town should officially cost about E£5 but you can expect to have to pay double and the ride along the Corniche is very pleasant.

Known in earlier times as **Iput-Isut** 'the most esteemed of places', the extent, scale and quality of the remains is astonishing. The complexes' numerous temples vary greatly in style because they were constructed over a period of 1,300 years. Their only common theme is worship of Amun, Mut and Khonsu who make-up the Theban Triad of gods. In order to see as much of the site as possible, aim to arrive very early or just before sunset when it is relatively cool and less crowded.

At the heart of the complex is the enormous **Temple of Amun** which was altered and extended by successive pharaohs. For example although the heretical **Akhenaten**, who converted to the world's first monotheistic religion and moved the capital from Thebes to Tell el-Amarna (see page 179), replaced the images of **Amun** with representations of **Aten**, these were later erased by his successors and Amun's images were restored! Included in and surrounding the main temple are numerous smaller but magnificent ones including the **Temple of Tuthmosis III**, the **Temple of Ramses III** and the smaller **Shrine of Seti II**.

The **Temple of Amun** is approached via the **Avenue of Ram Headed Sphinxes (1)** which used to link it to the Temple at Luxor. The imposing **First Pylon** is 130 m wide and each of the two unfinished towers are 43 m high and, although incomplete, nothing else matches its enormous scale. Dynasty after dynasty added to it and one might speculate about which ruler oversaw each of the various sections. Moving towards the inner core of the temple, which is the oldest section, one is moving back in time through successive dynasties. The entry towers are thought to have been constructed by the Nubian and Ethiopian Kings of the 25th Dynasty (747-656 BC) while recent work has revealed that several levels were built during the later Greek and Roman eras. For a little *baksheesh* it may be possible to climb the stairs up the north tower and marvel at the fantastic view it offers of the complex.

Arriving through the First Pylon, you come to the **Great Forecourt** which was begun in the 20th Dynasty (1200-1085 BC) but completed somewhat later. Immediately on the left is the very thick-walled rose coloured granite and sandstone **Shrine of Seti II** (1216-10 BC) which was a way-station for the sacred barques of Amun, Mut and Khonsu as they were taken on ritual processions. The west wall had to be subsequently rebuilt because it collapsed when the First Pylon was under construction. The outer façade portrays Seti II making offerings to various deities. In the middle of the Great Forecourt are the 10 columns of **Taharga** which once supported a 26½ m high kiosk or small open temple.

To the right of the forecourt is the small **Temple of Ramses III** (1198-66 BC) which would have stood in solitary splendour in front of the **Second Pylon** when it was first built in honour of Amun. Like the Shrine of Seti II, it was used as another way-station for the sacred barques. Part of an inscription in the interior reads: "I made it for you in your city of Waset, in front of your forecourt, to the Lord of the Gods, being the Temple of Ramses in the estate of Amun, to remain as long as the heavens bear the sun. I filled its treasuries with offerings that my hands had brought."

To the left of the **Second Pylon** is the 15 m high **Colossus of Ramses II** (1304-1237 BC) with his daughter Benta-anta standing in front of his legs. On the right of the pylon is the **Bubastite Portal** named after the 22nd Dynasty (945-715 BC) kings

Karnak

1 Avenue of Ram-
   headed Sphinxes
2 Great court
3 Great Temple of Amun
4 Hypostyle hall
5 Ptolemaic Temple
6 Sacred Lakes
7 Temple of Montu
8 Temple of Mut
9 Temple of Ramses III

from the Delta town of Bubastis. Through the Second Pylon is the immense 5,000 sq m (102 x 53 m) and spectacular **Hypostyle Hall** which is probably the best part of the whole Karnak complex. Its has 134 giant columns, which were once topped by sandstone roof slabs, of which the 12 largest making up the central processional way to the other chambers are 23 m high and 15 m round. The other 122 smaller columns, which have papyrus bud capitals and retain some of their original colour at the higher levels, cover the rest of the hall. They are decorated by dedications to various Gods, but particularly to the many different guises of Amun and the Theban Triad, and are also inscribed with the cartouches of the pharaohs who contributed to the hall. The south side was decorated by Ramses II with vivid but cheap and simple concave sunk-reliefs, while the north is attributed to Seti II whose artists painstakingly carved

Karnak central enclosure - Temple of Amun

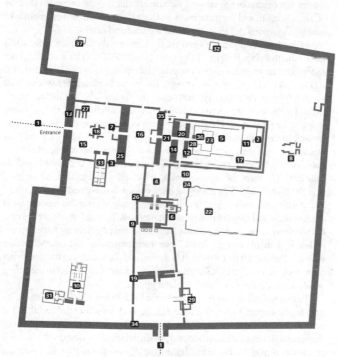

0 metres (approx) 100
0 yards (approx) 100

1 Avenue of ram-headed Sphinxes	8 Eastern Temple of Ramses II	23 Sanctuary of sacred boats
2 Botanical vestibule	9 Eighth pylon	24 Scarab statue
3 Bubastite portal	10 Fallen Obelisk of Hatshepsut	25 Second pylon
4 Cachette court	11 Festival Hall of Tuthmosis III	26 Seventh pylon
5 Central court	12 Fifth pylon	27 Shrine of Seti I
6 Chapel of Tuthmosis III	13 First pylon	28 Sixth pylon
7 Colossus of Ramses II	14 Fourth pylon	29 Temple of Amenhoptep II
	15 Great forecourt	30 Temple of Khonsu
	16 Great hypostyle hall	31 Temple of Opet
	17 Karnak Table of Kings	32 Temple of Ptah
	18 Kiosk of Taharqa	33 Temple of Ramses III
	19 Ninth pylon	34 Tenth pylon
	20 Obelisk of Hatshepsut	35 Third pylon
	21 Obelisk of Tuthmosis	36 Vestibule
	22 Sacred lake	37 White Chapel of Sesostris

LUXOR

delicate convex bas-reliefs on the walls. Ramses is shown, on the south side of the internal wall of the Second Pylon, making offerings before the gods and seeking their guidance, while on the left is a beautiful representation of Thoth inscribing Seti's name on a holy tree.

Seti II is depicted on both sides of the **Third Pylon** but the south wall running along the right of the hall was mainly decorated by Ramses II. He is shown being crowned by Horus and Thoth and then being presented to Amun while the Theban Triad is also pictured.

The **Third Pylon** was constructed by Amenhotep III (1417-1379 BC) on the site of several earlier shrines which were moved to the Luxor Museum and the Open Air Museum within the walls of Karnak. On the inner east face is a text of tribute and a scene showing the gods' sacred boats. Amenhotep III built a small court to enclose four **Tuthmosid Obelisks** in the narrow gap between the Third and Fourth Pylon which at that time represented the entrance to the Temple. Of the four, only one pink granite obelisk (23 m high, weighing 143 tonnes and originally tipped with electrum) built by Tuthmosis II (1512-04 BC) now remains and the stone bases and some blocks from two other obelisks built by Tuthmosis III (1504-1450 BC) are scattered nearby.

Moving towards the earlier centre of the temple is the limestone faced sandstone **Fourth Pylon**, built by Tuthmosis I (1525-12 BC). Texts describing later restorations are recorded on both sides by Tuthmosis IV (1425-17 BC) to the left and Shabaka (716-702 BC) to the right. Just inside is a small **Transverse Hall** which was originally a hypostyle hall before the Temple was extended outwards. Only 12 of the original papyrus bud columns and one of two 27 m and 340 tonne rose-granite **Obelisk of Hatshepsut**, which once stood at the entrance, now remain. In the 16th year of the reign of Hatshepsut (1503-1482 BC), the only woman to rule Egypt as pharaoh, these two obelisks were transported from Aswan where a third unfinished one still remains (see The Unfinished Obelisk, page 299). The tip of the second obelisk, which fell to the ground, is now lying near the Sacred Lake. The surviving erect obelisk is decorated along its whole length with the following inscription – "O ye people who see this monument in years to come and speak of that which I have made, beware lest you say, 'I know not why it was done'. I did it because I wished to make a gift for my father Amun, and to gild them with electrum." Her long frustrated and usurped infant step-son Tuthmosis III (1504-1450 BC), who had plotted against her during her reign, took his revenge by hiding the obelisks behind walls almost to the ceiling which actually preserved them from later graffiti.

The east wall of the Transverse Hall is the **Fifth Pylon** which has been attributed to Hatshepsut's father Tuthmosis I. Beyond is another hall and then the badly damaged sandstone **Sixth Pylon**. The world's first imperialist, Tuthmosis III inscribed it on both sides with details of his vanquished enemies and his victory at the Battle of Megiddo or Armageddon. Past the pylon is a **Vestibule** which is flanked by two courts and is dominated by two granite pillars with carvings showing Tuthmosis III being embraced by Amun, and the lotus and papyrus symbols of Upper and Lower Egypt. A seated statue of Amenhotep II (1450-25 BC) is against the west wall and on the north side are two colossi of Amun and Amunet, although their faces resemble Tutankhamen (1361-52 BC) who had had them built. The Vestibule leads to the Granite Sanctuary built by Alexander the Great's moronic half brother and successor Philip Arrhidaeus (323-317 BC). The ceiling is covered with golden stars on a dark base while the walls depict scenes of Philip with the god Amun. The exterior walls are decorated in a similar fashion.

North of the Sanctuary beyond the granite door is a series of small chambers built by Hatshepsut but later altered by Tuthmosis III. Some of the rooms were

The Brooke Hospital for Animals

Dorothy Brooke arrived in Cairo in October 1930. Twelve years earlier at the end of World War One the British government had tragically sold off some 20,000 cavalry horses to buyers in Egypt. The condition of the surviving horses, still working in the streets of Cairo, so shocked Mrs Brooke she at once set about putting an end to their suffering.

Donations from a single descriptive letter in the 'Morning Post' raised sufficient funds to purchase the remaining 5,000 horses. The vast majority, being over 20 years old and often in the final stages of collapse, had to be destroyed. However, they ended their days peacefully amid the care and attention to which they were all once so accustomed.

Mrs Brooke then turned the attention of her committee to the working conditions and hardship of the other draught animals. Their owners are, for the most part, very poor and so have the greatest difficulty in just feeding and maintaining their families. When their animals become old, lame or need treatment they cannot be released from work and many literally die in harness. This process benefits nobody.

One often hears of cruelty to animals but perhaps not enough of the love the owners feel for their charges. After all their very livelihood depends on them. Choices are very limited for a man whose income is equivalent to US$4 a day. His own life is very harsh and sometimes he has to work his animal beyond what we might consider reasonable limits. This is not malicious cruelty; it is pure survival.

Following on from the first free veterinary clinic set up in 1934 as the 'Old War Horse Memorial Hospital' and now known as the 'Brooke Hospital for Animals' millions of animals and their owners have received assistance.

In Egypt today there are 14 fully qualified veterinary surgeons and 70 veterinary assistants, farriers and supporting staff working at five centres in Cairo, Alexandria, Luxor, Aswan and Edfu. The new centre in Marsa Matruh is almost complete. They provide over 182,000 treatments annually and owners are always instructed in the future care of their animal, a fundamental part of the work. Egypt has the largest network of assistance. The Brooke Hospital for Animals also has centres in Jordan, Pakistan and India.

The ultimate aim is to work until there is no job left to do. In the meantime all animals are treated free of charge; mares brought in for foaling are kept for four weeks after the birth; no animal is discharged until fit for work; all discharged animals are reshod and have their harness refitted; very poor owners receive a small subsistence while their animal is 'off the road'; owners of animals beyond assistance are often given a small contribution towards a replacement.

If the condition of working animals in the concerns you, be practical, send a donation to The Brooke Hospital for Animals, Broadmead House, 21 Panton Street, London SW1 4DR.

walled up by her son to conceal Hatshepsut's influence and consequently the bright colours have been very well preserved although Hatshepsut's face has been cut away whenever it appeared.

Further to the east is Tuthmosis III's **Festival Hall** which, with its central tentpole-style columns symbolizing the tents used during his campaigns, is unlike any Egyptian building. It was built for his jubilee festivals which were intended to renew the pharaohs' temporal and spiritual authority. Access is via a small vestibule which leads to the central columned hall. The columns in the central aisle are taller than the side ones and would have supported a raised section of the roof thereby permitting sunlight to enter. The hall was later used as a Christian church and early paintings of the saints can still be seen on some of the columns.

Off to the southwest is a small chamber where the original stela, or standing block, known as the **Karnak Table of Kings** minus Hatshepsut was found. The original is in the Louvre in Paris, the one on display being a replica. The series of interconnecting chambers beyond is dedicated to the Theban Triad and further north is an attractive chamber known as the **Botanical Vestibule**. Its four columns have papyrus capitals and are carved with the unfamiliar plants and shrubs discovered by Tuthmosis III during his Syrian campaign. Surrounding the small chamber on the far east wall is the small and badly decayed **Sanctuary of Amun**, built by Hatshepsut and originally decorated with two raised obelisks on either side of the entrance – only the bases now remain. The nearby **Chapel of Sokar**, which is dedicated to the Memphite god of darkness, is better preserved.

To the south of the main temple is the **Sacred Lake** (200 m x 117 m), which has been restored to its original dimensions but has become stagnant since the inundation which used to feed the lake by underground channels from the River Nile ceased after the construction of the Aswan Dam. Today the lake is totally uninteresting but it has the Sound and Light Show grandstand at the far end and a café on the north side. A Nilometer is attached to the lake and there is a statue of a giant scarab beetle which childless women walk around five times in order to ensure that they soon bear children.

While the main temple runs from west to east there is a secondary axis running south from the area between the third and fourth pylons. It begins with the **Cachette Court** which received its name after the discovery between 1903 and 1906 of 17,000 bronze statues and 780 stone ones which had been stored in the court during the Ptolemaic period and the best of which are now in the Egyptian Museum, Cairo. The reliefs on the outside wall of the Hypostyle Hall, northwest of the court, depict Ramses II in battle. On the east walls, close to the **Seventh Pylon**, is a replica of a stela now in the Egyptian Museum which shows the only reference to Israel during Pharaonic times. The Seventh Pylon was built by Tuthmosis III and shows him massacring his prisoners before Amun. In front of the façade are parts of two colossi of Tuthmosis and in the courtyard to the left is the small chapel of Tuthmosis III.

Although restoration work continues on the nearby **Eighth Pylon** and others further along, it may be possible to have a quick look in return for a small tip to the guard, either early or late in the day when there are fewer people. The Eighth Pylon was built by Tuthmosis II and Hatshepsut and contains extensively restored reliefs and cartouches. As in so many other places, Hatshepsut's name has been erased and replaced by Tuthmosis II's name while Akhenaten's name was systematically erased by Seti I. The south side of the pylon has four of the original six **Seated Colossi**, two of which are Tuthmosis II and one is Amenhotep I.

The **Ninth Pylon** and the **Tenth Pylon** were built by Horemheb (1348-20 BC) using materials from the demolished Aten Temple. The Tenth Pylon has two colossi of Ramses II and his wife Nefertari

Karnak southern enclosure - Precinct of Mut

Sacred Lake

N

| 0 metres | 100 |
| 0 yards | 100 |

1 Avenue of the Sphinxes
2 Remains of Barque Sanctuary
3 Temple
4 Temple of Amenhotep III
5 Temple of Mut
6 Temple of Ramses III

usurping the original colossi of Amenhotep III. On the south side of the pylon there are two quartzite colossi of Amenhotep III. The pylon is part of the outer enclosure and marks the start of the ram-headed sphinx-lined road to the southern enclosure.

To the south, enclosed by a mud-brick wall are the much over-grown remains of the **Temple of Mut** and associated buildings. They are worth a quick visit. The entrance is in the centre of the north wall. Outside the enclosure and to the east are the ruins of a temple and to the west remains suggested as a barque sanctuary. Inside the enclosure, in a central position between the entrance and the Sacred Lake, and orientated north-south, stands the Temple of Mut, consort of Amun. Little remains of this construction accepted as the work of Ptolemies II and VII except a number of diorite statues of the lioness-headed god, Sekhmet. To the northeast is the Temple of Amenhotep III, later restored by Ramses II. Little remains except the bases of the walls and pillars and the feet on wall decorations which certainly leaves much to the imagination. To the west of the Sacred Lake stands the Temple of Ramses III with some military scenes on the outer walls and a headless colossus on the west side.

Back in the main central enclosure in the far southwest corner are two fairly well preserved temples, but they of limited interest. The **Temple of Khonsu** was built by Ramses III and Ramses IV and dedicated to the son of Amun and Mut. Many of the reliefs show Herihor, high-priest of Amun, who ruled Upper Egypt after Ramses XI (1114-1085 BC) moved his capital to the Delta and delegated power to the high-priest. In the courtyard Herihor's name is inscribed on every pillar and all the scenes depict him venerating the gods and making offerings to them. The **Temple of Optet**, the hippopotamus-goddess, is normally closed to the public.

On the north side of the central enclosure, the **Temple of Ptah** leads on to Karnak's northern enclosure which includes two temples, a sacred lake (now dry) and some chapels. The **Temple of Montu**, the god of war was built by Amenhotep III, some of his cartouches survive, and restored by Ramses IV. He left his mark too. Also in this small enclosure (150 sq m) to the west is a temple to Amun. At the southern wall, six small gateways gave access to six small chapels of which the chapels of Amenortais and Nitocris are the best preserved.

To the east outside the enclosure is the Treasury of Titmosis I, while to the west stand the remains of a temple to Osiris. This precinct does not have the splendours of the more famous temples and is best appreciated by real enthusiasts.

The **Open Air Museum** is situated to the northwest of the complex. It contains 1,300 blocks from the foundations of the Third Pylon and 319 stone blocks reassembled into Hatshepsut's **Sanctuary of the Barque**. Another barque sanctuary built by Amenhotep I is also on

Karnak northern enclosure - Precinct of Montu

Sacred Lake (dry)

Central enclosure

1 Avenue of Human-headed Sphinxes
2 Chapel of Nitocris
3 Chapel of Queen Amenortais
4 Forecourt of Temple of Montu
5 Hypostyle Hall
6 Sanctuary
7 Temple of Amun
8 Temple of Harpre
9 Temple of Osiris
10 Treasury of Tuthmosis I
11 Vestibule

0 metres 50
0 yards 50

Luxor

display, but the most beautiful monument is the lovely 12th Dynasty (1991-1786 BC) **White Chapel** built by Senusert I (1971-28 BC) which is divided into four rows of five pillars and includes some wonderful convex bas-reliefs and an interesting geographic list of the Middle East. The rest of the chapel is dedicated to offerings to a phallic Amun-Min who is embraced by Senusert. ■ *Daily 0700-1800 summer, 0700-1700 winter. E£10, students E£5, tickets sold at museum entrance.*

The West Bank and Theban Necropolis

Direct road access from Luxor to the West Bank is now possible following the opening of the new Nile Bridge approximately 7 km to the south of the town. A transfer time of 35-40 minutes should be expected by tour parties travelling from Luxor by coach. The new bridge has been built well to the south in an attempt to ensure that the main town buildings are restricted, as far as is possible, to the East Bank by not creating a direct crossing at Luxor itself. The authorities are making strong efforts to restrict buildings on the West Bank to ensure that the development of water, drainage and sewerage systems does not

Luxor environs

1 Temple of Ramses III
2 Temple of Tuthmosis III
3 Pavillion of Ramses III
4 Temple of Amenophis III
5 Colossi of Memnon
6 Temple of Tuthmosis IV
7 Temple of Merneptah
8 Temple of Tuthmosis III
9 Temple of Amenophis II
10 Temple of Mentuhotep
11 Temple of Tuthmosis III
12 Temple of Hatshepsut
13 Site of Ramesside Temple
14 Temple of Amenophis I
   & Ahmes Nefertari
15 Temple of Seti I & Ramses II
16 Great Temple of Amun
17 Temple of Montu
18 Temple of Ramses III
19 Temple of Amenophis II
20 Temple of Mut
21 Luxor Temple
22 Nobles' tombs at Dra'a Abul Naga
23 Nobles' tombs at El Asasif & El Khokah
24 Nobles' tombs at Sheikh abd el-Qurna

have a detrimental effect on the condition of the tombs as a result of capillary action and alterations to the water table. Protection of tourists is ever important. While the land is cultivated up to the road edge and much of it sugar cane, notice that no tall crops grow adjacent to the main roads but are set back to reduce cover for terrorists.

An organized tour booked through an agent relieves you of all the hassle but confines you by time spent at the venue and choice of tombs. It is not difficult nor expensive (no more than E£150 a day) to arrange for independent travel from Luxor with a guide. Tickets for the tombs are extra of course. Less expensive, cross by ferry and pick up a guide at each site. You will need some sort of transport to get to the different areas so hire a bicycle in Luxor or on the West Bank or more comfortably hire a taxi (be clear where you want to go and bargain from about E£55) once you have crossed. Access aross the River Nile is by ferry (E£3 single) from beside the Mercure Luxor Hotel and the ticket booths are a long uphill walk away.

Travel to the West Bank

Although so far a total of 62 tombs have been opened many, including some of the most remarkable such as that of Seti I (1318-04 BC) (No 17), are closed to the public because they suffered so badly from mass tourism that they have had to be

Visiting the tombs

Luxor

resealed for restoration work. The combination of long queues and the hot and stuffy atmosphere in some of the most popular tombs make it impractical to try and visit all of the tombs on one visit. In order to avoid the heat and the rush it is best to go as early as possible, particularly during the summer, take a bottle of water and a torch both because there are occasional power cuts and the lighting in some of the tombs is inadequate.

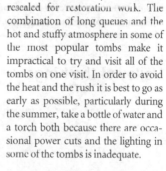

■ *It is very important to note that tickets for all of the sites on the West Bank of the Nile* **must** *be bought in advance at the main booths which are clearly marked. Booths are open from 0600-1600. Sites are open 0700-1800 summer, 0700-1700 winter. Entry for the Valley of the Kings is E£20 for 3 tombs and E£40 extra for Tutankhamen's tomb. Entry for other sites is E£6. Some tombs are individually priced at E£6, others E£6 for 2 or 3 tombs. A system has been devised to reduce wear and tear on the more popular tombs – by closing them at intervals. Always check if you have a particular destination in mind. A list is displayed by the ticket booths. The booths also sell non-refundable photograph permits at E£10 per tomb (flash photography is strictly forbidden because it damages the pigment). The use of video cameras is not permitted in the Valley of the Kings.*

In the Valley of the Queens the tickets for Nefertari's tomb cost E£100 and are limited to 200 sold on the day and one ticket for E£12 will give access to the other three tombs there that are open to the public.

The Tombs of the Nobles are divided into four groups and a separate ticket costing E£12 is needed for each group. The most important group of tombs is 100, 96, 55 and 52: the next important is 69, 56, and 57. Students with a card should always ask for a discount.

The Valley of the Kings

Also known as Wadi Biban el-Muluk. Allow a day to do this in some comfort and a little depth. One of many necropoli in the limestone hills on the West Bank of the River Nile, the area first became a burial site during the New Kingdom rule of Tuthmosis I (1525-1512 BC) in the hope that the tombs would be safe from looters. The kings' tombs are not actually confined to the single valley and it is believed that there may be others still waiting to be discovered. Those already discovered are numbered in the chronological order of their discovery rather than by location. Although some are simple and comparatively crude the best are incredibly well preserved, stunningly decorated and illustrate their intricate craftsmanship. By far, most of the discovered tombs are in the East Valley but the Tomb of Ay in the West Valley (Valley of the Monkeys) is worth a visit.

Valley of the Kings

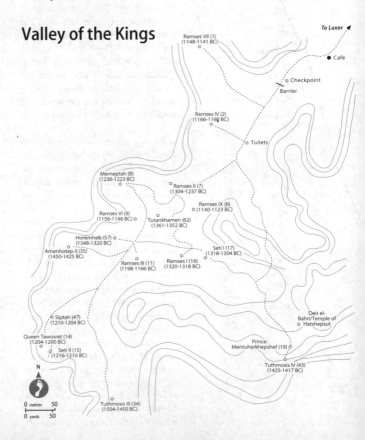

Ramses VII (1) (1148-1141 BC)
To Luxor
Café
Checkpoint
Barrier
Ramses IV (2) (1166-1160 BC)
Toilets
Merneptah (8) (1236-1223 BC)
Ramses II (7) (1304-1237 BC)
Ramses IX (6) (1140-1123 BC)
Ramses VI (9) (1156-1148 BC)
Tutankhamen (62) (1361-1352 BC)
Horemheb (57) (1348-1320 BC)
Seti I (17) (1318-1304 BC)
Amenhotep II (35) (1450-1425 BC)
Ramses III (11) (1198-1166 BC)
Ramses I (16) (1320-1318 BC)
Siptah (47) (1210-1204 BC)
Queen Tawosret (14) (1204-1200 BC)
Seti II (15) (1216-1210 BC)
Deir el-Bahri/Temple of Hatshepsut
Prince Mentuherkhepshef (19)
Tuthmosis IV (43) (1425-1417 BC)
N
0 metres 50
0 yards 50
Tuthmosis III (34) (1504-1450 BC)

There is a small rest house at the entrance to the Valley of the Kings, only just adequate but has drinks, literature and toilets if you are desperate. The tuf-tuf bus from here (cost E£1 per ride) saves some of the tiresome walking in the heat.

The tombs generally follow two designs. The early 18th-Dynasty (1567-1320 BC) tombs are a series of descending galleries followed by a well or rock pit which was intended to both collect any rain water and deter thieves. On the other side of the pit there were sealed offering chambers and then the rectangular burial chamber built at right angles to the descending galleries. The later tombs, from the late 18th to the 20th Dynasties (1360-1085 BC), were built in the same way but the galleries and burial chambers were on the same axis being cut horizontally but deeper straight into the rock face.

This later style, single horizontal plane, and poorly preserved tomb lies in a small valley to the right after the entrance gate and is seldom visited by tourists. Above the outer door Ramses VII's names are displayed with a scabbard and disc. The walls are lined with scenes from the *Book of Gates*. The most interesting area is the Burial Chamber with its granite sarcophagus still in place. The picture on the ceiling portrays the constellations and calendar of feasts while the sky goddess Nut spans the area. The inner chamber contains scenes of Ramses making offerings to the gods.

Ramses VII (1148-41 BC) (1)

Tomb of Ramses VII (1)

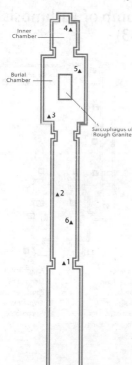

- Inner Chamber — 4
- Burial Chamber — 5
- 3
- Sarcophagus of Rough Granite
- 2
- 6
- 1

▲ **Murals**
1 Names of King
2 Pharaoh dressed as Osiris
3 Constellations on ceiling
4 Pharaoh makes offerings to gods
5 Scene of deity & slaves
6 Book of Gates

0 metres 2
0 yards 2

Luxor

Nearer is the looted tomb but not the body of Ramses IV, although his coffin was reburied in Amenhotep II's tomb. Do not be discouraged by the Coptic and Greek graffiti because the colours of the inner tomb are truly fantastic. The first two corridors contain poorly preserved reliefs of the *Litany of Re*, while the Hall and Burial Chamber are decorated with parts of the *Book of the Dead* and Nut spans the ceiling. The sarcophagus lid shows Ramses IV protected by images of Isis and Nephthys and the pink granite sarcophagus is inscribed with magical texts. This is the only tomb for which the original plans, drawn on papyrus, now in the Turin Museum, still survive.

Ramses IV (1166-60 BC)

The tomb of Prince Mentuherkhepshef was discovered in 1817. Sited in the southeastern extremity of the East Valley is a tomb intended as a final resting place for a king (Ramses VIII) but truncated and occupied by Prince Mentuherkhepshef, one of the sons of Ramses IX. The tomb is made up of an entrance area, a main corridor and a make-shift Burial Chamber, which seems to be no more than the beginnings of a second corridor, though it

Prince Mentuher-khepshef (Son of Ramses IX) (19)

Luxor

Throw some light on the subject

*There was obviously no need, originally, for light in the tombs and today the authorities maintain the lowest possible illumination necessary. **Take a torch** which will enable* *you to read the explanation and diagrams in this book, to admire the outstanding wall decorations and illustrations, to avoid tripping on the uneven ground.*

does have crude side niches. The entrance is remarkable for its width (3.6 m). Splendid mock doors are painted on the walls at the portico together with door jambs decorated with serpents. The walls of the main 3 m corridor each bear seven images of Prince Mentuherkhepshef making offerings to the gods, including Khonsu, Osiris and Ptah. The paintings, particularly of Prince Mentuherkhepshef although sadly now rather damaged, are renowned as among the most technically excellent in the Valley of the Kings and exhibit the Ramsesian school to great advantage.

Tuthmosis IV (1425-17) (43) This large tomb was discovered in 1903 by Carter, but others had been there before and everything moveable had been taken. Many of the walls and pillars are undecorated and the impression is rather austere. The well room has scenes of Tuthmosis paying homage to various gods and receiving the key of life from various deities including Hathor. The antechamber has illustrations of a similar theme and both have a ceiling of yellow stars on a dark blue sky.

Ramses IX (1140-23 BC) Situated immediately to the left of the barrier, it is of the typical later long deep style which became the established style by the end of the New Kingdom. The reliefs on the corridor walls depict Ramses before the gods and this is followed by three chambers. The four pillared Offerings Chamber leads to the richly decorated Burial Room but the sarcophagus is missing. The ceiling in yellow on a dark blue background depicts a scene from the *Book of the Night* with jackals, watched by Nut, drawing the barque through the skies to the after-life.

Tomb of Tuthmosis IV (43)

Not to scale

1 Entrance	7 Antechamber
2 Steps down	8 Store rooms
3 Corridor	9 Burial chamber
4 Well room	10 Crypt (at lower level)
5 First pillared hall	11 Sarcophagus
6 Corridor sloping down	

Set back against the cliff face on the other side of the road is a long steep 80 m tomb with a wonderfully preserved false Burial Chamber. The ceilings of the five corridors are decorated with flying vultures and other forbidding reliefs. Looters abandoned the sarcophagus lid, which portrays scenes taken from the *Book of Gates* and the *Book of Am-Duat* similar to those in the hallway, in the antechamber. Steep steps lead down to the Burial Chamber where the pink granite inner sarcophagus lies, decorated with intricate designs from the *Book of Gates*. It is claimed that Meneptah was pharaoh during the time of the Exodus.

Meneptah (1236-23 BC) (8)

The discovery of this tomb, which was usurped and enlarged from his predecessor Ramses V (1160-56 BC) and is one of the longest in the valley, shed light on some aspects of pharaonic beliefs which were not previously understood. The corridor displays reliefs from unknown and long since lost *Books*. Egyptologists were fascinated at their revelation of Pharaonic concepts, more usually associated with India, of reincarnation birth into a new life. One does not, however, have to be an expert to appreciate the graphic designs and the colours beyond the graffiti drawings in the first two corridors.

Ramses VI (1156-48 BC) (9)

The themes on the corridor ceilings are predominantly astronomical while the walls are largely devoted to the *Book of Gates* and the entire version of the *Book of Caverns*. In the Offerings Hall there is a relief of Ramses making libations before Osiris. The pillars are devoted to the Pharaoh making

Tomb of Meneptah (8)

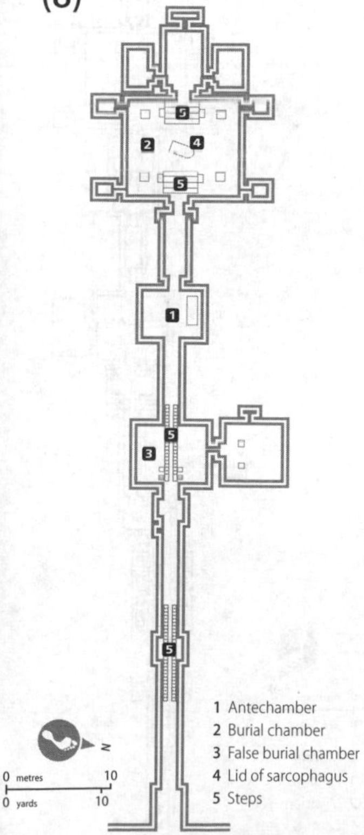

Tomb of Ramses VI (9)

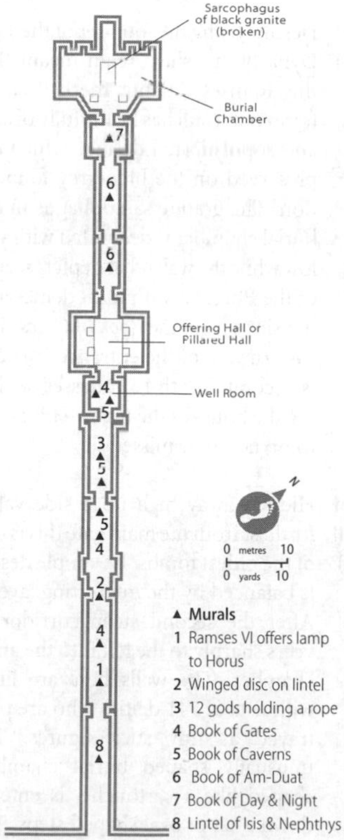

1 Antechamber
2 Burial chamber
3 False burial chamber
4 Lid of sarcophagus
5 Steps

Sarcophagus of black granite (broken)

Burial Chamber

Offering Hall or Pillared Hall

Well Room

▲ Murals
1 Ramses VI offers lamp to Horus
2 Winged disc on lintel
3 12 gods holding a rope
4 Book of Gates
5 Book of Caverns
6 Book of Am-Duat
7 Book of Day & Night
8 Lintel of Isis & Nephthys

offerings to other gods including Amun. Descending deeper within the tomb the passage leading to the Burial Chamber is guarded by serpents of Nekhbet, Neith, Meretseger and Selket. Further on illustrations from the *Book of the Dead* predominate. Just before the entrance to the Burial Chamber, cryptographic texts adorn the ceiling. The Burial Chamber is supported by four pillars but two are damaged. Astronomical scenes from the *Book of Day* and the *Book of Night* cover the ceiling and the sky goddess Nut observes from above. The sarcophagus, shattered by grave robbers centuries ago, lies broken in the centre of the room. At present this tomb is closed.

Ramses III
(1198-66 BC)
(11)

This particularly beautiful and exceptionally large tomb is unusual because, unlike those of most Pharaohs, it illustrates scenes from everyday life as well as a wonderful scene of two harpists from which the tomb's other name is derived. It was originally intended for Sethnakht (1200-1185 BC), but the angle of digging was such that it coincided with another tomb and it was abandoned. Later Ramses III restarted the work by digging into the rock face from a different angle. The lintel with a disc and Re shown with a ram's head accompanied by Isis and Nephthys can be seen at the entrance. 10-side chambers – five to the left and five to the right – which were for storing objects that the Pharaoh would require after his death, lead off from the entrance corridor. Only part of this tomb has lighting. One section of the tomb is closed because of a collapsed ceiling.

Tomb of Ramses III (11)

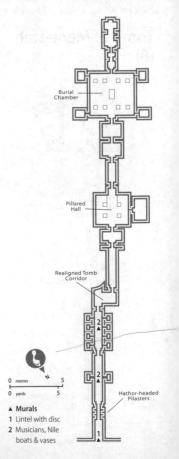

Ramses I
(1320-18 BC)

Despite being the founder of the 19th Dynasty, his short reign meant that this Ramses did not merit a larger tomb but it still has beautifully ornate and sophisticated designs which are preserved on the blue-grey foundation. The granite sarcophagus in the burial chamber is decorated with yellow while the wall relief depicts scenes of the Pharaoh with local deities and divisions from the *Book of Gates*. The eastern wall of the entrance corridor is decorated with 12 godesses depicting the hours of the night. This is one tomb not to be missed

Tomb of
Tuthmosis III
(1504-1450 BC)

Hidden away high up a side valley furthest from the main gate this is one of the oldest tombs. Its simple design is balanced by the interesting layout. After the second steep corridor, it veers sharply to the left into the antechamber. The walls here are lined with lists of 741 deities who are portrayed as tiny stick figures. The unusually shaped burial chamber, shaped like a cartouche, is entered down a set of oval shaped steps. The

Burial Chamber

Pillared Hall

Realigned Tomb Corridor

0 metres 5
0 yards 5

Hathor-headed Pilasters

▲ **Murals**
1 Lintel with disc
2 Musicians, Nile boats & vases

Luxor

Books of the Afterlife

The Egyptians believed that the journey to the afterlife was through Duat the underworld and to combat the monsters and other evils there, a series of prayers and some magic spells were necessary. These were written in the Book of the Dead which also contained a map of Duat. (Was this the first guide book?).

Book of the Dead: – called by the Egyptians 'The Book of Coming Forth by Day'. This is a collection of mortuary texts, a collection of spells or magic formulas which were placed in tombs and intended to be of aid in the next world. They are thought to have been compiled and perhaps edited during the 16th century BC. They included texts dating back to around 2000 BC (Coffin Texts) and 2400 BC (Pyramid Texts). Selected sections were copied on papyrus by scribes illustrated versions cost more, and sold for inclusion in one's coffin Many selections were found and it is estimated that there were approximately 200 chapters. Extracts appear on many of the antechamber walls of the Ramessid tombs. Nearly 12 chapters are given over to special spells – to turn the deceased into any animal shape.

Book of Am-Duat: – called by the Egyptians 'The Book of the Secret Chamber'. It deals with the sun's journey through the underworld during the 12 hours of the night. Selections are found in many tombs. Full versions are inscribed on the walls of the burial chambers of Tuthmosis III and Amenhotep II.

Book of Gates: refers to the 12 gates which separate the hours of the night and first appears on tombs of the 18th Dynasty. The inscriptions in the tomb of Ramses VI give the most complete version. This has the same journeying theme as the book of Am-Duat but the Duat is not comparable other than having 12 segments.

Book of Caverns: A full version of this is found in the tomb of Ramses VI.

Litany of Re: This deals with Re in his 75 different forms.

Books of the Heavens: which describes the passage of the sun through the 24 hours of the day includes the Book of the Day, the Book of Night and the Book of the Divine Cow. These texts were first used during the New Kingdom and there are several pieces inscribed in the tomb of Ramses VI.

For further details refer to book by RO Faulkner, see page 61.

walls here are dominated by sections of the Book of Am-Duat with an abridged version also inscribed on two pillars. The Pharaoh is depicted on one of the pillars with his mother standing behind him in his boat. A beautiful carving of Nut, effectively embracing the mummified Tuthmosis with her outstretched arms, lines the inside of the red granite sarcophagus. His mummy is in the museum of Cairo.

Siptah (1210-04 BC) (47)

This interesting tomb is situated in the East valley of the Valley of the Kings (Wadi Biban el-Muluk). Siptah was a monarch of the late 19th dynasty, probably the son of Amenmesse. He reigned for six years until 1204 BC. The tomb was discovered by Edward Ayrton in 1905. The tomb was constructed from a stair entry leading to a long corridor decorated with formal scenes of the Litany of Re on the right and left, with images of Mut and other scenes such as a fine representation of Siptah before Re-Horakhte. The first corridor, consisting of three linked passages, is plastered and painted to a good standard but both the intermediate pillared hall/stairway and the second corridor with its antechamber are undecorated. The same applies to the third short corridor leading from the antechamber to the burial chamber off which there is a dead-end tunnel on the left hand. The burial chamber is rough cut with four pillars and contains a red granite sarcophagus. The sarcophagus bears jackal and demon figures. The cartouches appear to be reworked. The tomb was disturbed at one time – possibly during the 21st dynasty – and the mummified body of Siptah was found in a cache of royal mummies in the tomb of Amenophis II (35) in 1898, the withered left foot of King Siptah clearly visible.

Tawosret (1204-00) & Sethnakht (1200-1198 BC) (14)

Sited in Wadi Biban el-Muluk, close by the tomb of Tuthmosis I, this is one of the longest (112 m) axial tunnels in the Valley of the Kings – belonging to Tawosret, wife of Seti II from the 19th dynasty. The monument was later taken over by Sethnakht, the first ruler of the 20th

Tawosret & Sethnakht (14)

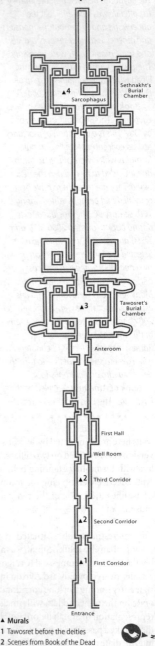

▲4 Sarcophagus

Sethnakht's Burial Chamber

▲3

Tawosret's Burial Chamber

Anteroom

First Hall

Well Room

▲2 Third Corridor

▲2 Second Corridor

▲1 First Corridor

Entrance

▲ **Murals**
1 Tawosret before the deities
2 Scenes from Book of the Dead
3 Sun God Re
4 King & deities

0 metres 10
0 yards 10

Tomb of Siptah (47)

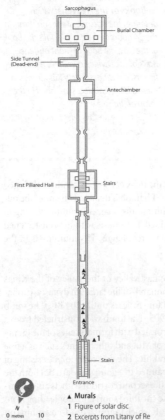

Sarcophagus

Burial Chamber

Side Tunnel (Dead-end)

Antechamber

First Pillared Hall — Stairs

▲2

▲2
▲3

▲1
Stairs

Entrance

N
0 metres 10
0 yards 10

▲ **Murals**
1 Figure of solar disc
2 Excerpts from Litany of Re
3 Siptah before Re-Horakhte

dynasty, who lengthened the tomb and removed the remains of Tawosret, it is suggested, to the cache in Tomb KV35. The ownership of the first corridor of the monument is still apparent, with male deities bearing female designations but many scenes of the owner before the gods were usurped by Sethnakht. There are scenes in the second and third corridors and in the First Hall of passages from the *Book of the Dead*. The Well Room and anteroom to the Burial Chamber by contrast carry images of the deities. In the Burial Chamber of Tawosret itself, comprising an eight section pillared hall, there are scenes from the *Book of the Dead*, the ceremony of the opening of the mouth and the *Book of the Gates* together with a finely drawn scene of facets of the Sun God Re as a disc and ram-headed eagle from the *Book of the Caverns*. Beyond the Burial Chamber of Tawosret is the extended royal tomb of Sethnakht along broad corridors decorated with scenes from the *Book of the Secret Chamber*. The Burial Chamber of Sethnakht has a barrel-domed ceiling with a painted astronomical finish while the walls are decorated with scenes from the *Book of the Caverns* and *Book of the Gates*. The eight pillars of this Burial Chamber carry representations of the king and the deities. The granite sarcophagus is shattered but still in place and has probably been taken over from a previous incumbent.

Tomb of Seti II (15)

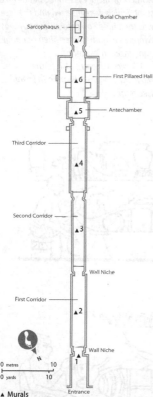

Murals
1 Picture of Ma'at
2 Plaster & painted reliefs - Litany of Re
3 Litany of Re/Book of the Secret Chamber
4 Book of the Secret Chamber
5 Deities/Seti II on panther/King hunting
6 Book of Gates/Shrine of Osiris
7 Nut inscribed above sarcophagus

The tomb of Seti II has been open since antiquity. It is also a hastily completed monument but is important in that it has a number of innovations which became standard practice in subsequent works in the Valley of the Kings. The wall niches in the antechamber to the first pillared hall (the well room) are much more pronounced than in earlier tombs while the entrance is cut into the hill face lacking the previously used wall and stairway. The burial chamber is crudely adapted from what was to have been a passage to a larger room that was never excavated. There are conventional decorations on the entrance doorway of Ma'at, the goddess of truth and beauty (see page 213), and scenes from the *Litany of Re* are shown in a variety of reliefs on both the left hand wall of the first and second corridors. Beyond the first corridor the walls are unplastered and generally painted in an attractive but peremptory fashion. The antechamber to the first pillared hall has an unusual format of figures of deities in which a representation of the king is shown riding on a panther and a picture occurs of the king hunting in a papyrus boat. In the pillared hall itself

Seti II
(1216-01 BC)
(15)

Luxor

Mummification

The ritual of Mummification reached its zenith during the New Kingdom at the same time as the Luxor and Karnak temple complexes were built. It was developed because the Ancient Egyptians believed that in order for a person to reach their heavenly aspect or **Ak** in the after-life, it was essential that both their name and body survive thereby sustaining their cosmic double or **Ka** which was transported from one life to the next. In order to achieve this, the mummification ritual developed into an extremely complex means of preserving bodies. The dead were placed in tombs together with any food and utensils thought necessary to accompany the pharaoh's Ka for the journey to the underworld. Although we know the most commonly used New Kingdom mummification methods, others are still being revealed. For example a recently opened princess' tomb in Giza revealed that the body had been hollowed out and lined with very fine plaster. However, the most common mummification method found in and around the Valley of the Kings is described below.

The brain was removed through the nose and was discarded because the heart was thought to be the centre of intelligence. The entrails and organs were then extracted and stored in jars, known as Canopic jars, while the corpse was soaked in natrun salts for 40 days until it was dehydrated, when the embalming process began. In an attempt to recreate its original appearance the body was packed and then painted red for men and yellow for women, artificial eyes, made of polished stone/jewels were inserted and the face was then made up before the body was wrapped in gum-coated linen bandages and placed in its coffin.

We recommend a visit to the Museum of Mummification in Luxor (see page 221).

there are formal scenes from the *Book of the Gates*. Over the site of the sarcophagus there is a fine picture of Nut, goddess of the sky, with outreaching wings. There is little of the sarcophagus that remains. The mummy of Seti II was among the kings found in the cache of royal mummies at the tomb of Amenophis II (35).

Over 90 steps lead down to the Burial Chamber which is in one of the deepest tombs in the valley. Here for once the tactics of building false chambers and sunken pits actually worked and the mummified body was found in the sarcophagus, together with another nine royal mummies which had been removed from their original tombs for safety's sake, when the tomb was opened in 1898. Amenhotep's mummy was originally kept in the tomb but after a nearby theft it was removed to the Egyptian Museum in Cairo. Steep steps and a descending corridor lead into a pillared chamber where the tomb's axis shifts 90° to the left, after which the walls and ceiling are decorated. Further steps and a short passage lead to the enormous two-level Burial Chamber.

Amenhotep II
(1450-25 BC)
(35)

The entrance passages are rough-hewn and each led down to by flights of stairs, entirely without formal decoration. In the well room – its painting unfinished – there is a shaft to a sunken but plain chamber. The first decoration of note is found in the two-pillared hall with paintings on only two adjacent walls. The Burial Chamber at the end of a short corridor is made up of a six-pillared hall with a sunken area containing the sarcophagus and storage rooms off, the western (right side) areas being where the cache of mummies was found in 1898. The ceiling is coloured blue with an astronomical star design in yellow and the walls delicately decorated with passages from the *Book of the Secret Chamber*. Columns show pictures of the king with deities – Anubis, Hathor and Osiris.

Amenhotep's sarcophagus remains in place, indeed his mummy was found undisturbed by Victor Loret who first found his way into the tomb in the 19th century. Particularly look for the beautiful image of Isis in sunk relief at the end of the highly decorated quartzite sarcophagus, still with its lid in situ. The sarcophagus is still in place in the centre of the pillared chamber.

Tomb of Amenhotep II (35)

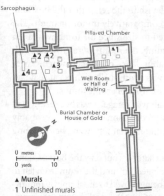

Sarcophagus

Pillared Chamber

▲2 ▲2
▲3
▲4☐

Well Room
or Hall of
Waiting

Burial Chamber or
House of Gold

N

0 metres 10
0 yards 10

▲ **Murals**
1 Unfinished murals
2 Pillars with Amenhotep before the gods
3 Ceiling of stars
4 Image of Isis on sarcophagus

After the long, steep and undecorated descent is the Well Room where the reliefs begin. Colourful scenes portray General Horemheb, who despite lacking royal blood was the effective regent during Tutankhamen's short rule and leader of the Theban counter-revolution against Akhenaten's mono-theistic religion, being introduced to Isis, Osiris, Horus, Hathor and Anubis. The scenes are repeated in the antechamber which is dominated by the huge red granite sarcophagus.

Horemheb
(1348-20 BC)
(57)

Luxor

Luxor

 ### *Howard Carter – discoverer of the Tomb of Tutankhamen*

Howard Carter was born at Swaffham in Great Britain in 1873. When only 17 years of age he was taken on by the Archaeological Survey of Egypt under Flinders Petrie and later became inspector general of antiquities in Upper Egypt in 1899 for the Antiquities Service. Carter was responsible for excavation of the Valley of the Kings and discovered the tombs of Hatshepsut and Tuthmosis IV in 1902 for the American Theodore Davis. After a dispute with Davis he moved to Saqqara in 1903 but then left the Archaeological Service to open a studio in Luxor where in 1907 he met and began his archaeological association with the wealthy Earl of Carnarvon, whose own efforts at excavation had failed. When Theodore Davis gave up his concession to excavate in the Valley of the Kings in 1914, Carter, backed by the Earl of Carnarvon, took it up and continued digging, locating six more royal tombs. In 1922, Carter's last year of sponsorship by Lord Carnarvon, he came across a set of remains of workmen's houses built across a stairway to a tomb. Howard Carter waited for Lord Carnarvon to arrive at the site and then dug

away the remaining rubble to reveal the entrance to the Tomb of Tutankhamen. Eventually Carter's men cleared the way to the ante-room which was found ransacked in antiquity but full of interesting cloths, furniture and other materials. The burial chamber that Carter found was once again packed with valuable objects but none more so than the gold-laden coffins and mummy of Tutankhamen. Carter remained at the site for a further 10 years supervising the cataloguing activity of so great a find. He died in London in 1939.

Howard Carter will be known principally as the discoverer of the Tomb of Tutankhamen. But his imprint on Egyptology went far deeper. He was among the first archaeologists, following Flinders Petrie, to apply scientific principles to the recording of his excavations. Remarkably, the treasure trove of objects found in 1922 has still to be studied in full and, to Carter's great disappointment, there were in any case no parchments or manuscripts to explain historical events surrounding the boy king and the court politics of the day.

Tutankhamen
(1361-52 BC)
(62)

The tomb owes its worldwide fame not to its size or decoration, which is small and ordinary, but to the multitude of fabulous treasures that were revealed when it was opened in November 1922. The scale of the discovery was so vast that it took 10 years to fully remove, catalogue and photograph all of the 1,700 pieces.

The funeral objects in this tomb were lavish in the sense that the boy king reigned for a mere 9-10 years and was a comparatively minor pharaoh. The burial chambers too were relatively limited in size since the tomb was taken over from a private owner so that on opening, the rooms were crowded with items, hence a feeling that there was an abundance of artifacts when Carter broke through into the tomb. The hoard was additionally rich because it had not been significantly robbed – unlike most other pharonic tombs.

If Tutankhamen's tomb was important above average, it was because he had rejected the heresy (monotheism) of his predecessor, though it is probably correct to believe that tombs of more dominant pharaohs were, before being looted, even more lavishly furnished.

The short entrance corridor leads to four chambers but only the Burial Chamber, which is the second on the right, is decorated. Around the room from left to right murals display Tutankhamen's coffin being moved to the shrine by mourners and officials after which his successor Ay (1352-48 BC) performs the ceremony of the Opening of the Mouth and makes sacrifices to sky-goddess Nut. Tutankhamen is then embraced by Osiris and is followed by his black-wigged Ka or spirit. A scene from the *Book of Am-Duat* on the left hand wall depicts the Pharaoh's solar boat and sun-worshipping baboons. The quartzite sarcophagus is still in place, with its granite lid to one side, and inside is the outermost of three coffins.

The 'Lost' Tomb

Explored and looted decades ago, dismissed as uninteresting by Egyptologists and used as a dump for debris from the excavation of Tutankhamen's tomb, Tomb 5 in the Valley of the Kings was about to become a car park. However the final exploration in May 1995 unearthed a major discovery, certainly the largest and most complex tomb ever found in Egypt and possibly the resting place of up to 50 sons of Ramses II. Excavations are expected to take at least another five years, but the tomb's unusual design is already apparent. Instead of plunging down into the steep hillside, Tomb 5 is more like an octopus with at least 62 chambers branching off from the central structure. There may be more chambers on a lower level where it is hoped some of the mummies may still be entombed. No treasure is expected, robbery of the tomb was documented as early as 1150 BC, but the elaborate carvings and inscriptions along with the thousands of artifacts littering the floor, including beads and fragments of jars used to store the organs of the deceased, nevertheless offer a wealth of information about the reign of one of Ancient Egypt's most important kings. Egyptologists have never before found a multiple burial of a pharaoh's children and in most cases have no idea what happened to them. This find thus raises the question of whether Ramses buried his children in a unique way or that archaeologists have overlooked a major type of royal tomb. And where are Ramses' dozens of daughters? Are they buried in a similar mausoleum perhaps in the Valley of the Queens?

Luxor

Tomb of Tutankhamen (62)

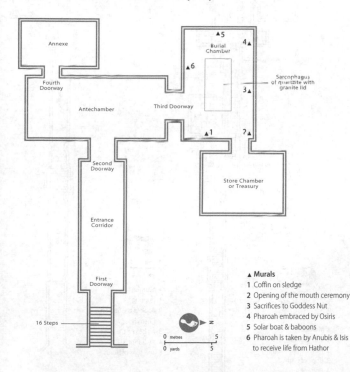

Annexe

Fourth
Doorway

Antechamber

Third Doorway

Second
Doorway

Entrance
Corridor

First
Doorway

16 Steps

▲5

Burial
Chamber

4▲

▲6

3▲

Sarcophagus
of quartzite with
granite lid

▲1

2▲

Store Chamber
or Treasury

0 metres 5
0 yards 5

N

▲ **Murals**
1 Coffin on sledge
2 Opening of the mouth ceremony
3 Sacrifices to Goddess Nut
4 Pharoah embraced by Osiris
5 Solar boat & baboons
6 Pharoah is taken by Anubis & Isis
  to receive life from Hathor

Seti I (17) Seti I is regarded as the most developed form of the tomb chambers in the Valley of the Kings. At some 100 m it is among the longest, though it is closed at present, perhaps permanently for conservation purposes since its decorations suffer from condensation produced by visitors. Throughout the tomb there are paintings/reliefs of fine workmanship on nearly every surface, though not all were completed. In particular look out for the picture of Osiris in the pillared hall and the depictions of tomb furniture in the side chamber. The mummy can be viewed in the museum in Cairo. The sarcophagus is in London.

Ay (1352-48) (23) This monument dates from the 18th Dynasty and was opened up by Bellzoni in 1816, cleared by Schaden in 1972 and opened to the public in recent years. Entry shaft at first has a shallow incline but then after a second flight, steps become steep. Flat shoes are a necessity here on the ramp-like corridors. There is good lighting provided the generator is turned on.

Ay was the counsellor of Tutenkhamen and his successor to the throne. The tomb had probably been built for King Tutenkhamen but was incomplete at the time of that king's sudden death. Ay had no claims to royal descent and was

Tomb of Seti I (17)   # Tomb of Ay (23)

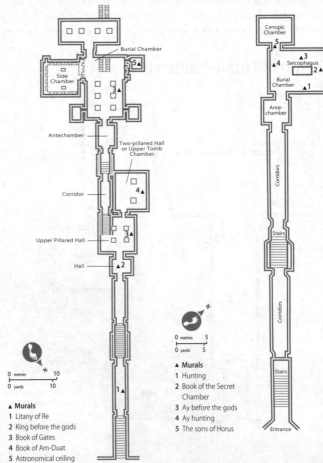

Tomb of Seti I (17)

Burial Chamber
5
Side Chamber
3
Antechamber
Two-pillared Hall or Upper Tomb Chamber
Corridor
4
Upper Pillared Hall
3
Hall
2
1

0 metres 10
0 yards 10

▲ Murals
1 Litany of Re
2 King before the gods
3 Book of Gates
4 Book of Am-Duat
5 Astronomical ceiling

Tomb of Ay (23)

Canopic Chamber
5
4   3
Sarcophagus
2
Burial Chamber
1
Antechamber
Corridors
Stairs
Corridors
Stairs
Entrance

0 metres 5
0 yards 5

▲ Murals
1 Hunting
2 Book of the Secret Chamber
3 Ay before the gods
4 Ay hunting
5 The sons of Horus

Theban Death Rites and the Book of the Dead

In order to fully appreciate the Theban Necropolis in the soft limestone hills opposite Luxor on the West Bank of the River Nile it is important to understand a little about the celebration and rituals of death in Ancient Egypt.

The **Book of the Dead** is the collective name given to the papyrus sheets which were included by the ancient Egyptians in their coffins. The sheets contained magic spells and small illustrations to assist the deceased In the journey through the underworld to after-life. In total there are over 200 spells though no single papyrus contained them all. Some of the papyrus strips were specially commissioned but it was possible to buy ready-made collections with a space left for the relevant name. Some of these spells came from the **Pyramid texts**. They were the oldest written references to this passage from one life to the next. They were found on the walls of pyramids constructed during the fifth to seventh Dynasties (2494-2170 BC). Later the text and descriptions of the rituals which were involved were written on the actual coffins of commoners, not kings. The spells were written in vertical columns of hieratic script. Eventually lack of space on the sarcophagi led to only the ritual prayers and offerings being listed. When papyrus began to be used

during the New Kingdom (1567-1085 BC) written texts were enclosed in the coffin and they became known as the Book of the Dead. Many copies of the writings, including the Book of the Caverns and the Litany of Re, were subsequently discovered.

The ancient Egyptians believed that at sunset the sun-god Re descended into the underworld and voyaged through the night before emerging at dawn to sail his barque (boat) across the heavens until sunset when the whole cycle began again. This journey was believed to be replicated by the dead pharaoh who descended through the underworld and whose heart, which was believed to be the centre of intelligence, would be weighed in the **Judgment of Osiris** to determine whether or not he would be permitted to continue his journey to the after-life.

The burial ceremony was elaborate with priests performing all the necessary rites, including sacrifices, in order to ensure that the deceased had a rapid passage to the next life. The tomb, together with everything the pharaoh might need, including slaves, was then closed, plastered over and stamped with the royal seal. In order to protect the royal tombs from grave-robbers, they were fitted with false burial chambers and death-traps which unfortunately did not work.

not even high ranking in the priesthood. His tomb is important for its unusual pharaonic hunting scene in the burial chamber.

The tomb is constructed with a strong linear alignment as a single corridor with a flight of very steep steps down to the small chamber which leads into a burial chamber. The Burial chamber itself is approximately 7 m by 10 m and about 4 m high but off to the right of the axis of the tunnel. A small canoptic room terminates the tomb.

Only the Burial chamber is decorated but even here there has been extensive damage to the paintings and the roof is just rough hewn rock without decoration. Throughout almost all of the tomb the cartouches have been defaced. On the entry wall to the left of the door is the famous hunting scene with the deceased shown clubbing birds and plucking reeds as if he was an ordinary being rather than a deity. On the north wall is a painting representing 12 baboons (hence the name tomb of the monkeys) or hours of the night from the Book of the Secret Chamber. On the west wall look for the image with Ay before the gods, including Osiris, Nut and Hathor. A well worked but slightly damaged boating scene is shown on the south wall above passages from the *Book of the Secret Chamber*. On the lintel area above the door to the canopic chamber is a fine representation of the four sons of Horus, not to be seen elsewhere in the Valley of the Kings. The sarcophagus is in place, made out of quartzite, and nicely tooled in reliefs of deities, Neith, Nephthys and Selkis. The sarcophagus was formerly in the museum in Cairo and was transported back to the tomb for display to the public in 1994. Its lid is intact and there are wings of four goddesses – one at each corner with wings wrapped round the sarcophagus for protection.

Deir el-Bahri

Meaning 'northern monastery' in Arabic, it derives its name from the fact that during the seventh century the Copts used the site as a monastery. It is now used as the name for both the magnificent **Mortuary Temple of Hatshepsut** and the surrounding area. ■ *E£12, cameras and videos free of charge.*

Queen Hatshepsut was not only the only female Pharaoh to reign over ancient Egypt (1503-1482 BC) but also one of its most fascinating personalities. She was Tuthmosis I's (1525-12 BC) daughter and was married to his successor Tuthmosis II (1512-04 BC) but was widowed before she could bear a son. Rather than give up power to the son of one of her husband's minor wives she assumed the throne first as regent for the infant Tuthmosis III but then as queen. Tuthmosis III, who later hugely expanded the Egyptian Kingdom and was the first imperialist, was only able to assume office when Hatshepsut died 21 years later in 1482 BC. He naturally resented her usurping his position and removed all traces of her reign including her cartouches. Consequently the truth about her reign and the temples she built both here and at Karnak was only fully appreciated by archaeologists relatively recently. As a woman she legitimized her rule by being depicted with the short kilt and the false beard worn by the male pharaohs.

Hatshepsut's imposing temple which was only dug out of the sand in 1905 was designed and built in the Theban hills over an eight-year period between the 8th-16th year of her reign, by **Senenmut** who was her architect, steward, favourite courtier and possibly the father of her daughter Neferure. The temple's three rising terraces, the lower two terraces lined with fountains and myrrh trees, were originally linked to the River Nile by an avenue of sphinxes which was aligned exactly to Karnak. A pair of lions stood at the top and another at the bottom of the ramp which leads from the ground level first terrace over the first colonnade to the large second terrace.

The scenes on the restored left hand south side of the first colonnade columns depict the transportation of the two obelisks from Aswan to Karnak temple. Behind its columns on the right hand north side is a relief defaced by Tuthmosis III in which Amun can be seen receiving an offering of four calves from Hatshepsut whose face has been erased. The original stairs from the second terrace to the second colonnade have now been replaced by a ramp. Hatshepsut's famous voyage to **Punt**, which was known as 'God's Land' by the ancient Egyptians, and various texts to Amun are depicted on the left hand or south side of the second colonnade. Voyages to Punt, now believed to be modern-day Somalia, had been undertaken since the Old Kingdom (2686-2181BC) in order to find the incense and myrrh which was required for temple rituals.

Further to the left is the large **Chapel of Hathor** where the goddess is depicted both as a cow and as a human with cow's ears suckling Hatshepsut. This area was badly damaged because Tuthmosis removed most but not all traces of Hatshepsut and Akhenaten later erased Amun. The reliefs on the colonnade to the right hand or north side of the ramp portray Hatshepsut's apparent divine conception and birth. She claimed that her father was the supreme god Amun who visited her mother Ahmose disguised as Tuthmosis I just as Amenhotep III (1417-1379 BC) made similar claims later on (see Luxor Temple, page 218). Further to the right is the fluted colonnade and the colourfully decorated **Chapel of Anubis**, who is portrayed in the customary way as a man with a jackal mask, but the images of Hatshepsut are once again defaced.

The ramp leading to the smaller and recently restored upper terrace (unfortunately closed) is decorated with emblems of Upper and Lower Egypt with vultures' heads guarding the entrance. There are suggestions that this was originally a Hypostyle Hall and not a terrace. The columns were

Temple of Hatshepsut

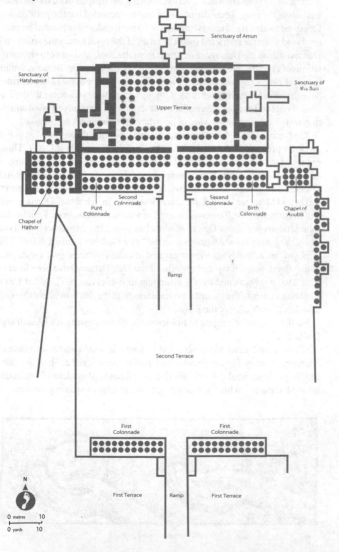

originally round but were squared off by Tuthmosis III in an attempt to replace her name with his own and that of his father Tuthmosis II. Beyond the Osiride portico to the left is the **Sanctuary of Hatshepsut** with its enormous altar and to the right is the **Sanctuary of the Sun**. In the middle at the back of the whole temple is the **Sanctuary of Amun** which is dug into the cliff-face and is therefore connected to the Valley of the Kings which lies on the other side of the hill. Hatshepsut's burial chamber lies underneath but it is unclear whether she was actually ever buried there.

Tombs of the Nobles

While the pharaoh's tombs were hidden away in the Valley of the Kings and were dug deep into the valley rock those of the most important nobles were ostentatiously built at surface level overlooking the temples of Luxor and Karnak across the river. Their shrines were highly decorated but the poor quality limestone made carved reliefs impossible so the façades were painted on plaster. Freed from the restricted subject matter of the royal tombs the artists and craftsmen dedicated less space to rituals from the *Books* and more to representations of everyday life and their impressions of the after-life. Because, unlike the royal tombs, they were exposed to the elements many of the nobles' shrines have deteriorated badly over time. Although some were subsequently used as store rooms and even accommodation others are still in relatively good condition and give a clear impression of how they must originally have looked.

The tombs of the nobles are found at a variety of sites throughout Egypt but no better preserved than on the West Bank of the River Nile at Luxor. Three groups of tombs are worth visiting for their wealth of vernacular paintings – quite as interesting as the formal sculptures of the great tombs of the Kings and Queens. The tombs of Rekhmire, Sennofer, Ramoza, Userhat, Khaemet, Nakht and Mena are located in the area known as Sheikh abd el-Qurna, north and northwest of the Ramesseum and the tombs of Sennedjem, Peshdu and Inherkhau are just above Deir el-Medina (see page 258), an archaeological site where the housing of the workmen on the West Bank has been excavated. The tombs of Dra'a Abul Naga were excavated in valleys scattered over a wide area of the desert. Some forty-eight tombs of the 18th Dynasty have been located here. Two newly opened tombs belonging to nobles can be viewed at Dra'a Abul Naga, cut into the mountainside just north of the junction where the road leads left to the Valley of the Kings.

Further tombs belonging to nobles are open for viewing at El Asasif and El Khokhah.

If time is limited, see the tomb of either Sennedjem or Sennofer for a taste of this form of art. ■ *The entry fee for each pair of tombs is E£12.* There are cafes and shops throughout the area, which also still has local modern village housing – inhabitants sell bric-a-brac and genuine artefacts to passing tourists.

Tomb decoration - offerings of wine

Sheikh abd el-Qurna

Set in the entrance of the tomb is an interesting display of representations of **Tomb of Nakht** the statue of Nakht as originally photographed together with hunting and **(52)** offering scenes and a plan of the tomb. Inside the tomb is well lit and the decoration protected by glass screens. The tomb is small and is best visited early when not many visitors are about.

Nakht was Tuthmosis IV's astronomer, vineyard keeper and chief of his granaries. He and his wife Tawi were buried in this small shrine with its well preserved and colourful antechamber which depicts the harvest in intricate detail. On its west wall in the centre is a painting illustrating what is known of Nakht's life together with the goddess of the west. On the left of the far wall is a depiction of a funeral banquet at which Nakht, his top half having been badly defaced, is shown seated beside his wife with a cat eating a fish at his feet while being entertained by a blind harpist and beautiful dancing girls. Opposite, on the east wall, in one of the most individual of paintings is grape picking where peasants are shown treading grapes while empty wine jars await filling. Here the ceiling is brightly decorated with designs representing woven mats. The marshland scenes on the right-hand, south-facing section of the antechamber are exceptionally fine, with fish wonderfully depicted. In the inner chamber there is a small niche with a replica of a statue of Nakht bearing a stela with a hymn to Re. Unfortunately the original was lost in 1917 when the SS Arabia, which was transporting it to the USA, was torpedoed by the Germans in the Atlantic. There is a deep shaft leading to the inaccessible burial chamber.

Ramoza was Visir and Governor of Thebes at the beginning of the Akhenaten's **Tomb of** heretical rule in 1379 BC and the tomb illustrates the transition in style between the **Ramoza** worship of Amun and Aten (see Tell el-Amarna, page 179). The impressive and **(55)** excellent quality workmanship of the shrine is probably because it was built by Ramoza's brother Amenhotep who was the chief of works at the family's home-town of Memphis. Only the main columned hall can be entered, since the inner hall and false sarcophagus area are separated. This is one of the few tombs where the forecourt is still preserved and the central entrance leads into a broad columned hall. The tomb was carved out of solid limestone and all the decoration carved on polished rock. On the wall to the right are depictions of Ramoza with his wife and opposite on the back wall Akhenaten and Nefertiti stand at their palace windows giving a golden chain to Ramoza. On the left hand wall are scenes of Ramoza and his wife worshipping Osiris. Beyond is an undecorated inner hall with eight columns and the shrine at the far end. There is a second gap on the left of the end wall leading to the actual sarcophagus chamber. Within each hall are the gated entrances to dark and dangerous tunnels which end with a 15 m drop to the burial chamber.

Tomb of Nakht (52)

Statue of Nakht

Inner Chamber

Antechamber

▲3
▲2
▲1

4▲
5▲

N

▲ Murals
1 Harvesting
2 Stele - Life of Nakht
3 Funeral banquet
4 Hunting
5 Wine making

0 metres 2
0 yards 2

Tomb of Userhat Userhat who, in the reign of Amenhotep II (1450-25 BC), was a royal tutor and scribe was buried in a small but pinkishly decorated tomb which was partially damaged by early Christian hermits. At the extremity of the outer hall on the left is a small stela showing the purification by opening of the mouth. At the opposite end of this hall look out for the representation of the double python, a symbol of protection. **NB** The interesting representation of rural life on the left on the way into the hall, the façade of the snake-headed harvest goddess Renehat on the right of the back wall, and a realistic hunting scene in the desert on the left of the inner hall.

Khaemhet (57) Khaemhet, another royal scribe and overseer of the granaries in the period Amenhotep III in the 18th Dynasty, adopted a raised relief system for the carved and painted decoration of his tomb-chapel which is well worth seeing for its variety. The tomb is entered through a courtyard off which there are other tomb entrances largely blocked off. The Khaemhet tomb is made up of two transverse chambers joined by a wide passage. In the outer chamber there are rich reliefs depicting rural scenes, some of the originals now only to be seen in Berlin. The passage has funeral scenes (south wall) and the voyage to Abydos (north wall), while both the transverse chambers, though mainly the far one, have statue niches of Khaemhet and his family. There is a small room annexed to the inner transverse chamber, possibly added later.

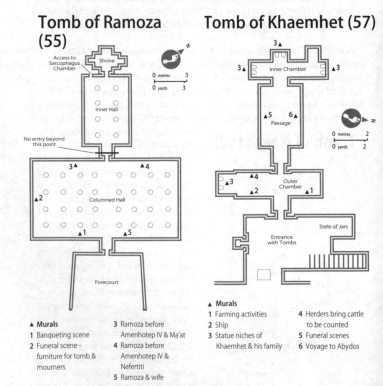

Tomb of Ramoza (55)

Access to Sarcophagus Chamber

Shrine

0 metres 3
0 yards 3

Inner Hall

No entry beyond this point

3▲   ▲4

▲2

Columned Hall

▲1   ▲5

Forecourt

▲ **Murals**
1 Banqueting scene
2 Funeral scene - furniture for tomb & mourners
3 Ramoza before Amenhotep IV & Ma'at
4 Ramoza before Amenhotep IV & Nefertiti
5 Ramoza & wife

Tomb of Khaemhet (57)

3▲

3▲   Inner Chamber   ▲3

▲5   6▲
Passage

0 metres 2
0 yards 2

▲3   ▲4
▲   Outer
▲2   Chamber   1

Stele of Jars

Entrance with Tombs

▲ **Murals**
1 Farming activities
2 Ship
3 Statue niches of Khaemhet & his family
4 Herders bring cattle to be counted
5 Funeral scenes
6 Voyage to Abydos

Antefoker was the Governor of Thebes and his tomb-chapel deserves a visit. The tomb is structured as a main corridor which carries a series of scenes of farming, the life of the marshes and hunting at the time of the 12th Dynasty at the time of Senosert 1. Domestic scenes of servants and gifts for the New Year are all contained within the main corridor. The inner chamber has figures carrying offerings and in front of the niche at the head of the tomb is a statue of Antefoker's wife.

Antefoker (60)

This tomb has been undergoing restoration and, although Mena's eyes have been gouged out by rivals to prevent him seeing in the afterlife, the paintings are in good condition. He was an 18th-Dynasty scribe or inspector of the estates in both Upper and Lower Egypt. In particular, visit this tomb to see the following items: on the end wall on the right hand side of the outer hall is a depiction of a series of gods, notably, Hathor and Isis. On the adjacent wall is a fine painting of Mena and his wife giving flowers. Opposite is as vignette of the younger members of the family making gifts to their father. In the left hand limb of the outer hall note the depiction of Mena's wife in an elegant dress and jewellery as she stands with her husband before Osiris. In the inner hall there is a niche for a statue of Mena and his wife. Elsewhere in the inner hall are well-preserved paintings of the gods, presentation of gifts, funeral and Judgement scenes. Look out for the finely executed paintings of hunting and fishing scenes on the right hand wall close to the statue niche, which are extremely well done with crocodiles, wild cats and fish. The ceilings are brightly coloured and represent woven cloth.

Tomb of Mena (69)

Tomb of Antefoker (60)

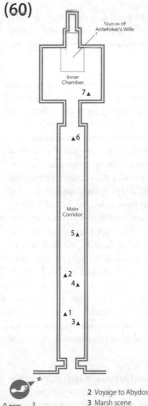

Statue of Antefoker's Wife

Inner Chamber

7 ▲

▲ 6

Main Corridor

5 ▲

▲ 2
4 ▲

▲ 1
3 ▲

Tomb of Mena (69)

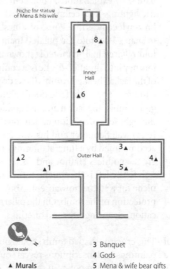

Niche for statue of Mena & his wife

8 ▲

▲ 7

Inner Hall

▲ 6

Outer Hall

▲ 2

3 ▲

4 ▲

▲ 1

5 ▲

0 metres 2
0 yards 2

Not to scale

▲ Murals
1 Grape harvesting
2 Voyage to Abydos
3 Marsh scene
4 Hunting
5 Domestic servants
6 New Year gifts
7 Offerings

▲ Murals
1 Labourers working in fields
2 Mena & his wife stand before Osiris
3 Banquet
4 Gods
5 Mena & wife bear gifts of flowers
6 Funeral
7 Judgement
8 Hunting

Horemheb Horemheb was a scribe of the recruits in the reign of Tuthmosis III-Amenhotep III. His tomb-chapel is made up of a rectangular entrance hall and a main corridor leading to a four-pillared hall. The main corridor of his tomb is decorated with scenes of his official life in the military and decorations in the entrance hall show a concern with funeral affairs.

Ineni Ineni was the architect of Tuthmosis I and in charge of the granary of Amun. His main work is thought to have been building the tomb of Tuthmosis I and the monarch's obelisk at Karnak. The temple-tomb spans the period Amenhotep I-Hatshepsut of the 18th Dynasty. The tomb is constructed with a transverse corridor defined on the southwest by six large

Sennofer & his wife Meryt

square pillars. The corridor is decorated with rural scenes of farming and hunting. The inner chamber has the normal offering, banqueting and funeral procession. Additionally at the northern end it has statue niches for Ineni, his wife and family.

Tomb of Sennofer At the time of Amenhotep II (1450-25 BC), Sennofer among other positions, was Mayor of Thebes, overseer of the granaries and gardens, and chief vintner. In the antechamber of this tomb there is an excellently clear set of diagrams etched on the glass showing the layout of the tomb and its decorations, accompanied by explanations. Look at these first. The entire tomb has discrete electric lighting. The ceiling is covered in illustrations of vines and the tomb is known locally as the 'Tomb of Vines'. The antechamber is rough and irregular in shape. Pass into the pillared main chamber under a low beam. Within the four pillared hall Sennofer is shown making offerings to the deities and on his journey into the after-life he is accompanied by his wife Meryt. A double figure of the jackal-headed Anubis looks down on the whole chamber from above the entrance. There is a false door painted on the east (right hand) wall with the god Anubis, the jackal and the goddess Isis. Facing the entrance arch look to the right for a depiction of Sennofer's wife, son and daughters. On the north (end) wall Sennofer and his wife cross to the west bank of the river by boat, accompanied by a funeral offering of wine, flowers and food. On the west wall are the goddess Hathor and Osiris in dark colours of the dead. On the same wall to the left is the funeral furniture for use in the afterlife. There is a small niche for a statue now absent. Above note the vultures with wings spread for protection of the tomb. On the pillars are formal representations of mummification, cleansing rites and offerings.

Tomb of Rekhmire (100) This crucifix-shaped tomb should not be missed because its highly decorative paintings and inscriptions reveal some of the secrets of Egypt's judicial, taxation and foreign policy at that time. Rekhmire, who came from a long line of viziers and governors, was the visir at the time of Tuthmosis III's death in 1450 BC when he then served his successor Amenhotep II. The tomb is in good order, though lit only by a hand-held mirrors (held by the man at the door who will require a tip), which means that the vision is only fair. Walking left or clockwise around the whole tomb from the entrance wall of the transverse corridor one sees – Egyptian taxes, Rekhmire being installed as visir, foreign tributes being received from Punt, Crete, Nubia, Syria and Kush, then along the main corridor the inspection of the various workshops, the voyage to Abydos, the various gods of the dead, and the end niche which would have contained a statue of Rekhmire. The ceiling has deteriorated but some of the original plaster work remains, with a continuous line down the centre of the main north-pointing chamber. Look out too for the splendid marsh/woodland scene which, with a small lake and trees, has a warmth and realism to it that contrasts nicely with the formal and predictable decoration in praise of the gods (notably Osiris) and Tuthmosis III. On the way out along the other corridor wall are pictures of the after-world and then, back in the transverse hall, illustrations of hunting and fowling, wine-making, Rekhmire's wives and ancestors, and finally more taxes being collected.

Opened to the public in 1999, this finely decorated tomb was prepared for Roy, the royal scribe, steward of the estates of Horemheb (1348-20 BC) and of Amun in the 18th Dynasty. This is a small tomb consisting of an open entry court and a hall from which there is a shaft. It is one of the most beautiful tombs here because its scenes and colours are remarkable. The southern wall is decorated with ploughing, pulling flax and the deceased and his wife worshipping at the tomb with Ennead (the nine gods of the cosmonogy of Heliopolis). Also Horus leading them to Osiris with the weighing scene, a funeral procession, friends and mourners held by Anubis at the pyramid tomb. The northern wall is decorated by offering scenes and a libating scene before the deceased and his wife. There is a niche containing stelae with barque of Re adorned with baboons and the deceased and his wife and a Hymn to Re. **Draa Abul Naga Roy (255)**

On the left side the deceased is adoring western Hathor in the form of a tree goddess with Ba (the soul) drinking. On the right Roy's wife is worshipping.

Tomb of Rekhmire (100)

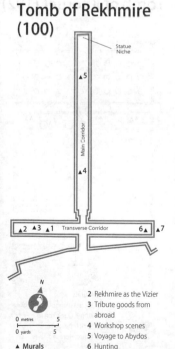

Statue Niche

Main Corridor

▲5

▲4

▲2 ▲3 ▲1 Transverse Corridor   6▲ ▲7

N

0 metres   5
0 yards   5

▲ **Murals**

1 Taxation scene

2 Rekhmire as the Vizier
3 Tribute goods from abroad
4 Workshop scenes
5 Voyage to Abydos
6 Hunting
7 Treading grapes

Also situated north of the road at Dra'a Abul Naga is the tomb of Shuroy, the head of the brazier bearers. The tomb is newly opened and worth a visit since the entry chamber is brightly coloured with many scenes in a good state of preservation – as bright as the day they were drawn. It is well lit and the decoration easy to see. **Shuroy (Suroy, Shoray) (Ramesside 13)**

The monument consists of a court and two halls forming a T shape. The first hall on the left is decorated with sketches of the deceased and his wife adoring divinities, adjacent is the *Book of Gates*. A representation of Zed appears on a pillar. On the right the deceased and his wife adore Macet and Re-Horakhte and there are gates decorated with demons. In

Luxor

the second hall the door jambs carry sketches of the deceased on the right and of his wife on the left. The left side of the chamber is decorated with offerings bearers and a funeral procession including a child mourner before a mummy and the deceased kneeling with braziers before Hathor the cow on a mountain. On the right side there are scenes representing offerings bringers before the deceased and his wife and a banquet with clappers and bouquets.

There is a niche off-set to the right with a squatting woman on the left and on the right the deceased bearing a brazier followed by his wife.

El Asasif & We recommend four tombs open to the public in this area of the
El Khokah West Bank.

Kheruef This tomb made for Kheruef, the Steward of Amenhoptep III's wife Queen Tiye, is
(192) of great interest because it is one of the few tombs at El Asasif which survived the rapacious activities of the tomb robbers largely since it was filled with compacted debris. There is added importance arising from its decoration, which is not only of good quality but also as a rarity illustrates the festivals of the Jubilee, an affirmation of a king's power in the land towards the close of the 18th Dynasty.

The architecture of the tomb is sophisticated, with a short entry tunnel leading into a large square open courtyard at the west side of which is a four-pillared portico over three steps down to a decorated wall. In the centre of the west wall there is a narrow entrance (with locked gate) to the 30-pillared hall, where only one fluted column approximately 3-4 m high is left standing at the extreme left side. This remnant does however give some idea of the original grandeur of this chamber before its ceiling collapsed. A doorway leads to an extension to an unfinished second hall, where two pillars are in place.

The decoration of the tomb is worth some attention. To the right hand after the entrance under a picture of Amenhotep are nine vignettes of nations conquered by the pharoah, each being a representative of a different race and city. On the portico wall (3) is a set of scenes of stick fighting, sports, dancing, men driving cattle as part of the festival of the pharaoh's jubilee in which Kheruef is keen to show his important role. Also there is a picture of the king and priests worshipping Jed, husband of Nut, on a pillar adjacent (4). At the left hand end of the portico is another set of images showing the king and queen (2) sailing at the end of the jubilee festival and decorated large scale figures of Amenhotep and his queen. There are wonderful impressions of ladies clapping, musical instruments such as flutes being played, and ladies dancing during the jubilee celebrations – all very beautifully and graphically done. Look out for Nubian dancing ladies even though some of

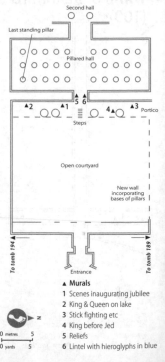

Tomb of Kheruef (192)

0 metres 5
0 yards 5

▲ **Murals**
1 Scenes inaugurating jubilee
2 King & Queen on lake
3 Stick fighting etc
4 King before Jed
5 Reliefs
6 Lintel with hieroglyphs in blue

Luxor

the colouring is now faded. These figures are mainly on the bottom two registers, the high levels scraped and broken and in very bad condition.

At the very end of the blue-ceilinged access tunnel to the pillared hall, on the right hand side, is a large panel of the king and queen in boat crossing to Abydos but this is badly damaged. On the right hand of the corridor, about 2½-3 m from end and about 1 m from ground, is a small cartoon in black of Sinmootè, one of the great craftsmen of the period, and it leads specialists to suspect that this area was used as a trial ground for the workers who built the main Hatshepsut temple.

This 26th-Dynasty tomb in El Asasif was prepared for the chief steward of the **Anch-hor** divine votaress of Amun and Overseer of Upper Egypt. It is much restored **(414)** with the main pieces saved represented by the relief at the entrance and the very deep burial chambers repaired by the Austrian Archaeological Institute in 1971-81. The tomb is cut heavily into the strata. Down a long flight of stairs is a set of ten rooms and an open courtyard. The main chamber or western hall has eight square columns and leads to a deep ante-chamber and thence to a small burial chamber with a niche in the west end.

Two items of interest in the decoration are the change in style of wigs at this late stage as Mediterranean influences penetrated to Thebes. Secondly, there is a unique scene of the art of bee-keeping. (This tomb can become unpleasantly warm.)

This is among some 60 tomb chapels from the Ramesside period at El Khokha. **Nefersekhru** There is a descent down a long ramp of stairs cut in the rock to the entrance of **(292)** the tomb, discovered in 1915 by Mond. Nefersekhru was the scribe of the divine offerings of all of the gods. He married three wives who are represented in the tomb. The monument has a short corridor leading to a single chamber some 2 m x 10 m aligned on a north-south axis. In the west wall of chamber at the north end is a barred entrance with steps to a set of undecorated burial chambers. The main tomb is well lit and the images screened behind glass.

On the entrance corridor walls of this tomb (1) are scenes on the right of Nefersekhru and his wife coming into, and on the left the wife and the deceased coming out of, the main chamber. Inside there is a ceiling of highly coloured panels in geometric designs, probably representing a carpet. To the south of the door on the entrance wall (2) is a formal picture taken from the *Book of the Gates* and scenes of Nefersekhru before deities. On the back wall opposite the entrance are

Tomb of Anch-hor (414)

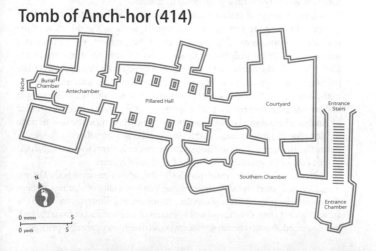

more decorated panels – beautifully coloured and designed. The owner of this tomb is shown in his leopard skin (3) on a panel on the top left. The middle panel on the back wall exactly opposite the doorway has three registers, of which the left one, more or less intact, shows a wife. Of special note are the dominating image of Osiris (4), the king of the dead – sadly scarred – and the statues of Nefersekhru set in niches set in the middle section. On the right inset and slightly damaged is another well detailed female figure.

On the right wall at the end is well executed sculpture of two wives and the deceased sitting on a bench. On the back wall under a lintel (5) is a scene of feasting with the deceased and one of his wives handing out gifts to visitors including flowers. There are agricultural scenes on the left hand side of door on entry to the chamber.

Tomb of Nefersekhru (296)

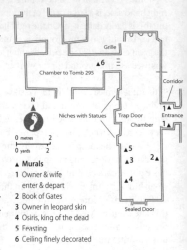

▲ **Murals**
1 Owner & wife
  enter & depart
2 Book of Gates
3 Owner in leopard skin
4 Osiris, king of the dead
5 Feasting
6 Ceiling finely decorated

The western side chamber leads to another Ramesside tomb chapel (295) of unknown ownership with a shaft in its north eastern extremity. The ceiling of this side room (6) has a spectacular carpet design.

In the same cutting are other tombs such as that of the 18th dynasty **Nefermenu (365)**, Overseer of the wig-makers of Amun at Karnak, now firmly closed. Peer in through grill on door to a large but undecorated chamber.

Neferrompet (178) This small but famous tomb temple to the Scribe of the Treasury is open for public viewing in El Khokha. It lies to the right at the bottom of the stairs leading to the tomb of Nefersekhru. Discovered in 1915 by Mond it dates from the time of Ramses the Great. The monument is made up of two chambers joined by a narrow doorway. The first small chamber is 3 m by 2½ m. Lights in the tomb are good. The walls are protected by glass.

Decoration is typical of the Ramesside tomb type. On the centre outer lintel of entrance the door are cartouches of Ramses II, while in the thickness of the entrance door the deceased and his wife are shown, respectively, entering and leaving, worshipping with hymns to Re. In both rooms the frieze represents Hathor's face and Anubis. The first hall, has a ceiling with beautiful carpet-like paintings bearing geometrical designs with flowers. The most interesting decoration, is a representation of 14 scenes from the *Book of the Gates* with Neferrompet and his wife drinking from the pool, a weighing scene with deceased and wife led by Anubis, a harpist singing before Neferompet and Mutemwia and his wife playing draughts. His wife has beautiful hair styles and is wearing attractive dresses. In places the garment appears so fine that the outline of her arm shows through the cloth. Look for the cat with a bone in the far left hand corner!

In the second chamber are five panels showing adoration of the gods. There is a much noted panel showing Neferrompet keeping a tally of/storing offerings given to the temple, which is in excellent condition and illustrates the life in the treasury at that time. On the end wall is a series of four statues cut from the rock and decorated, showing perhaps Mutemwia and daughters or possibly priestesses.

Luxor

Ramses The Great

Known by the Egyptians as Ramses al-Akbar (the great), a name that would no doubt have pleased him, the achievements of Ramses II, arguably Ancient Egypt's most famous king, were majestic. During his 67-year reign, the pharaoh presided over an empire stretching west from present-day Libya to Iraq in the east, as far north as Turkey, and south into Sudan. While his military feats were suitably exaggerated for posterity in the monuments of the day, Ramses also engineered a peace treaty with Egypt's age-old northern rivals, the Hittites, by a strategic marriage to a daughter of the Hittite king in 1246 BC which ended years of unrest. The peace lasted for the rest of the pharaoh's lengthy reign. Ramses II is believed to be the pharaoh of the biblical 'exodus', although Egyptian records make no mention of dealings with Israelite slaves. His massive fallen statue at the Ramesseum inspired Shelley's romantic sonnet Ozymandias, a title taken from the Greek version of Ramses' coronation name User-maat-re. Egypt's most prolific pharaoh (siring at least 80 children), he was also a prodigious builder. He began building soon after ascending the throne at the age of 25 having discovered that the great temple his father Seti I had begun at Abydos was a shambles. During the rest of his reign he erected dozens of monuments including a temple to Osiris at Abydos, expansions of temples at Luxor and Karnak, and the awe-inspiring cliff temples at Abu Simbel. In an age when life expectancy was 40 years at most, Ramses, who lived to 92, must truly have appeared to be a god.

Valley of the Queens

Like the Valley of the Kings, the Valley of the Queens, which is about 3 km south from the tombs of the nobles, can be reached via another road which cuts northwest through the main northeast-southwest escarpment. It was once known as the 'Place of Beauty' and was used as a burial site for officials long before the queens and their offspring, who had previously been buried with their husbands, began to be buried there in the 19th Dynasty (1320-1200 BC). It contains more than 80 tombs but many are still unidentified. The tombs are generally quite simple with a long corridor, several antechambers

Valley of the Queens

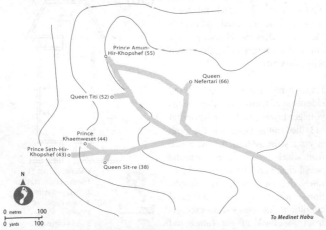

branching off and the burial chamber at the end. The most famous tomb is that of Ramses II's wife Nefertari newly reopened to the public.

■ *At present 4 tombs are open to the public; one ticket costing E£12 will give entry to tombs 44, 52, 55 and separate ticket costing E£100 for tomb 66 (Nefertari). See page 201 for ticket purchase information.*

Queen Sit-re (38) Queen Sit-re's tomb-chapel is situated in the south quadrant of the Valley of the Queens. The tomb is normally closed and official permission must be sought to gain entry. The Queen was the wife of Ramses I and is among the earliest tomb-chapels built in the valley. The elemental structure comprises an outer hall chamber and an unfinished burial chamber. The decorations include in clockwise order in the hall chamber scenes of the sons of Horus, the queen at a shrine, a water scene with gods, gods and Lion-headed god.

Prince Seth-Hir-Khopshef Prince Seth-Hir-Khopshef was a son of Ramses III who died of small pox when very young. He was ceremonial charioteer of the great stables. His tomb-chapel is decorated with a series of scenes of the gods, clockwise from the entrance to the corridor including Ramses III and Seth-Hir-Khopshef in front of Osiris and other deities, the sons of Horus, Osiris enthroned, Ramses III and Prince Seth-Hir-Khopshef offering gifts, Ramses and the prince before a set of deities. At present this tomb is closed.

Prince Khaemweset Although the tomb is dedicated to one of Ramses III's (1198-66 BC) young sons who died of smallpox, it is dominated by the pharaoh himself. The reliefs depict the young boy being led to the underworld by his father who is offering sacrifices and helping his son through the underworld and the judgement of Osiris to the Fields of Yaru.

Queen Titi Queen Titi was the daughter, wife and mother of a succession of the 20th Dynasty (1200-1085 BC) pharaohs called Ramses but it is uncertain to which one she was married. Although the tomb is open to the public the reliefs are faded and damaged. A corridor leads to a square shrine which branches into three antechambers with the badly preserved burial chamber on the left being dedicated to the four sons of Horus and Osiris. The central chamber features the Queen before the gods and the shrine is dominated by animal deities with pictures of jackals, baboons and guardian lions. The right hand chamber is the best preserved and depicts the tree goddess and Hathor as a the cow goddess rejuvenating the Queen with Nile water.

Tomb of Queen Sit-re (38)

▲ **Murals**
1 Scenes of sons of Horus
2 The Queen at the shrine
3 Water scenes with gods
4 Gods
5 Lion-headed god

Prince Amun-Hir-Khopshef (55) Prince Amun-Hir-Khopshef was the eldest son of Ramses III who like his younger brother Seth-Hir-Khopshef (43) died young. Descent to the tomb is via a stairway into the main hall from which there is a corridor to the burial chamber. The tomb is elaborately decorated with fine illustrations which remain in good condition. The scenes show excerpts from the *Book of the Gates* and

Calling on Nefertari

Although this tomb was discovered in 1904 the delicate condition of the tomb walls and fragile nature of the ornate reliefs have prevented Nefertari from receiving visitors. At last the tomb is open but visitors are restricted to 200 per day. Visitors may be asked to wear masks to reduce moisture in the atmosphere and shoe pads to protect the stone from wear and tear. Nefertari was the favourite wife of Ramses II and her tomb was decorated with 430 sq m of the finest wall paintings ever produced. Sodium chloride seeped into the plaster which covered the limestone walls and salt crystals developed. As they grew in the damp atmosphere they forced the painted plaster off the walls and the murals fell to the floor in fragments. With the help of photographs from the museum in Turin and those taken by Ernesto Schiaparelli who discovered the tomb the

carefully cleaned pieces of mural were replaced on the wall, a huge Egyptian jigsaw. Now, after six years of painstaking labour and the outlay of over US$2 mn, Nefertari is fit to entertain.

Tomb of Nefertari (66)

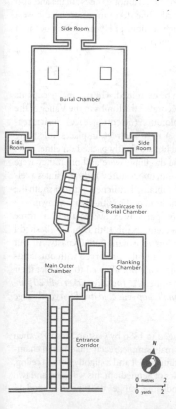

Ramses III leading his son in a course around the stations of the gods. An oddity is the sarcophagus which contained the remains of a foetus, thought to be one of the prince's still born infants. This foetus is displayed in a glass cabinet in one corner of the burial chamber.

The most famous and outstanding tomb is that of Nefertari, the favourite wife of Ramses II, which in November 1995 was opened to the public for the first time since its discovery in 1904. Even the most tomb-resistant visitor to Egypt should try to see this for the bright clear paintings are a sheer delight. One of the most sophisticated pieces of artwork created during the New Kingdom, it stands, like the Taj Mahal, as a final testament to a king's love for his wife. Small compared to the tombs in the Valley of the Kings, its 430 sq m of fine reliefs were nearly completely destroyed by flood damage and leaching of the salt crystals in the tomb's limestone bedrock which caused the plaster to buckle and crack. After a US$6 mn six-year restoration project by the Getty

Nefertari's Tomb (66)

Luxor

Conservation Institute, the tomb is ready for public display. ■ *In order to control humidity levels, only 200 visitors are allowed inside per day. Separate tickets are required from a separate booth (E£100 or E£50 for students).*

The entrance corridor leads to a main outer chamber and a small flanking chamber, the former dominated by the image of a smiling Nefertari holding hands with Horus and being acknowledged by Isis, the vivid colours splendidly preserved. The stress here is on her beauty rather than good works. The staircase descends to the burial chamber and three small side rooms. Among the immensely rich illustrations to be seen are Queen Nefertari bearing gifts and the Queen hand in hand with the goddess Hathor and the god Horus. Unfortunately the downstairs reliefs are badly damaged but it is still possible to see that in the burial chamber Nefertari, offering sacrifices to the gods, becomes solemn and her fashionable clothes are replaced by more sombre attire. The wall texts are chapters from the *Book of the Dead*.

Private Tombs

Qurnat Murai

Amenhoptep (Huy) Amenhoptep (Huy) was the Viceroy of Kush in the reign of Tutankhamen. The tomb-chapel is cruciform with a transverse chamber and an unfinished or damaged inner chamber with four irregular pillars. The decoration of the transverse chamber is very pleasing, showing scenes of Nubians offering gifts to Tutankhamen, and Amenhoptep is depicted among the Nubians and also with Tutankhamen. Almost all the worthwhile decorations are in the west wing of the transverse chamber, although sections of Hymn to Ptah occur in the small corridor between the two chambers.

Deir el-Medina

Here the neat remains of the village can be examined. The original occupants were the workers who excavated and decorated the tombs in the Valley of the Kings. The village is certainly worth exploration (no entrance fee) and it is recommended to begin at the north end. A narrow street, in places little more than a metre wide, runs south with the houses tightly packed on either side. The foundations show how small these dwellings were and often they were subdivided but remains of stairs indicate an upper storey and sometimes a cellar. Some houses were a little larger and contained a kitchen. Further south the street turns to left and right, marking the limit of the 18th-Dynasty town.

Above the site of Deir al-Medina, now partially excavated, there are three tombs open at present, those of Sennedjem, in the 19th Dynasty, Peshedu and Inherkhau, Foreman of a construction team of the 20th Dynasty. All, but especially the tomb of Sennedjem, are beautifully preserved with outstanding paintings to be seen. Normally guides are not allowed to conduct their groups into the comparatively small chambers. ■ *Inclusive ticket is E£20 purchased at the main ticket office, and a small shop sells cold drinks, a good range of cards/books.*

Sennedjem Sennedjem's tomb was found undamaged in 1886 by Gaston Maspero, then head of the Antiquities Service. It is a small, simple, rectangular burial chamber, 6 m by 3 m, with narrow stairs leading into it and a slightly domed ceilng. On discovery it held intact the mummies of Sennedjem, his wife, son and two daughters-in-law. There was a handsome range of funeral materials.

Unfortunately, the mummies and funerary objects were dispersed across the museums of the world so that a compehensive view is no longer possible. The wall decorations shown in the burial chamber and now protected by glass are first rate in colour, style and present condition and are worth travelling to see. The domed ceiling is wonderfully decorated with snakes, pictures of the gods and a golden orb. Clockwise round the chamber are hunting/forest scenes in the lower register and above a mummy on a bier with the goddesses Isis and Nephthys protecting it. On the side wall Sennedjem and his wife stand before the gods and, on the back wall, the masterpiece of the tomb, the body of Sennedjem lying on an ornamental bier is embalmed by Anubis opposite to the entrance. On the east wall is a double painting of the barque of Re above and a view of life in eternity below. The south wall (right of the door) shows Sennedjem and his wife, Iyneferty, facing the Deities of the Gates. The usual offering scenes are shown. Of great appeal is the depiction of the tree of life from which a goddess is appearing bearing an offering table.

Inherkhau

This is another brilliantly painted tomb in excellent order and accessible down a steep flight of steps to a small ante-room with a low ceiling into a chamber with decorated plastered walls bearing coloured paintings, now considerably damaged by efflorescence and exfoliation of the limestone rock. From this chamber are two exits, one into a rough rock-cut burial chamber. The second exit leads down steps under a low lintel to the main decorated chamber itself. This room is vaulted and is approximately 5 m by 2 m. On the left hand side is a painting of a stork, the god Anubis and a fine depiction of the family with hair left down in funeral form. At the north end, slightly damaged is a full-scale representation of Inherkhau and his family with offerings. The right hand side wall also carries more pictures of Inherkhau's family, children naked and with hair curled round their ears to denote immaturity. The ceiling is vaulted and painted in bright colours – ochre, yellow, gold, bearing cartouches and a detailed list of events in the life of Inherkhau.

Peshedu (Ramesside 3)

Peshedu's tomb is highly decorated and in very good condition. It celebrates the life of the "servant in the place of truth" and was opened for visits in 1998.

The tomb is very light and airy, with the coloured scenes protected by transparent screens and a cooling fan. It is entered down a very steep flight of stairs, with a low roof – take care! Eventually a narrow entrance is reached which leads

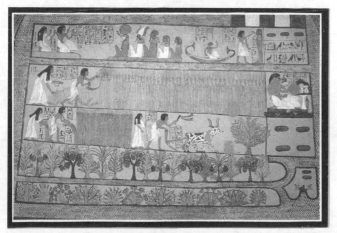

Agricultural scene from Tomb of Sennedjem

to the first large chamber which is not decorated. After about 6 m it narrows down into a low gateway just 1½ m high. This is where the wonderful decorations begin – all in good condition on panels on both sides with hieroglyphics above. On the sides of the entry corridor are images in very good colour of Anubis as a jackal lying on an altar. Within the burial chamber there is a wealth of decoration. Above the doorway the god Ptah-Sokaris is shown as a winged falcon under the eye of Horus. The two human figures are Peshedu on the right and his son on the left. Inside the burial chamber to the left the upper register shows a beautiful image of a female (probably the goddess of the sycamore) carrying water up the tree and below right are rows of Peshedu's attendants in fine detail. The long left-hand wall carries an image of Peshedu and his wife with two children standing before Horus with passages of *Book of the Dead* around them.

The right hand wall of the burial chamber shows Peshedu and his child before Re-Horakhte and three other gods. Surrounding these images are passages from the *Book of the Dead*. Inside the burial chamber to the left is the now famous scene of Peshedu beneath a date palm in fruit by the side of the water.

Other Temples and sites

The Ramesseum While most tourists confine themselves to the two valleys and Hatshepsut's temple there are a number of other interesting West Bank ruins closer to the river. Of these, among the most impressive was the Ramesseum, a 19th-century name for what was effectively a state cult-temple, on the opposite side of the road near the tombs of the nobles. Today only scattered remains and faded reliefs suggest the great temple which once stood there and reportedly rivalled the splendours of the temples at Abu Simbel.

Ramses II (1304-1237 BC) built this mortuary temple, on the consecrated site of Seti I's (1318-04 BC) much smaller but collapsing temple, in order to impress his subjects but he failed to take account of the annual flooding of the River Nile. The result was that this enormous tribute to Amun and himself was less eternal than he expected!

The first two pylons collapsed and only a single colonnade remains of what would have been the First Courtyard. On its south side is a palace where Ramses stayed when he attended religious festivals on the West Bank. In front of the ruins of the Second Pylon is the base of the enormous colossus of Ramses which was originally over 17 m high but it is now much eroded and various parts of his anatomy are scattered throughout the world's museums. The forefinger alone measures more than 1 m in length. The upper part of the body crashed into the second court where the head and torso remain. Three smaller colossi stood next to the three stairways leading to the Hypostyle Hall but only one fragmented one now remains.

Although it is now roofless, 29 of the original 48 columns still stand in the Hypostyle Hall. The centre of the roof would have been higher than the sides in order to allow shafts of sunlight to enter the hall. To the left of the entrance is the famous relief of the Egyptian victory over the Hittite city of Dapur in the battle of Kadesh. Around the base of the west walls some of Ramses' many sons are depicted. At the far end of the hall a central door leads into the Astronomical Room renowned for its ceiling which is illustrated with the oldest known 12 months' calendar. Because the temple was dedicated to Amun it is thought to represent a solar year. Two other vestibules, a library and a linen room, lead to the ruined sanctuary which is the temple's highest point.

The Mortuary Temple of Ramses III (1198-1166 BC), which lies west of the Colossi of Memnon and south of the Valley of the Queens at a place known in Arabic as **Medinet Habu**, was modelled on that built by his forefather Ramses II (1304-27 BC) near by. It is second only to Karnak in terms of its size and complexity and within the enormous enclosing walls are a palace, a Nilometer and several smaller shrines with some pre-dating the temple itself.

When Thebes was threatened, such as during the 20th Dynasty's Libyan invasions, the enclosing walls sheltered the entire population. Although Ramses III named his temple the 'House of a Million Years', the smaller shrine that already occupied the site next to the south enclosure walls was in use long after the main temple shrine had fallen into disuse.

The small temple, which was constructed by Hatshepsut but later altered by Tuthmosis III who, as ever, erased her cartouche, was built on a platform from which there are good views in all directions. Until the 18th century a grove of

Ramesseum site

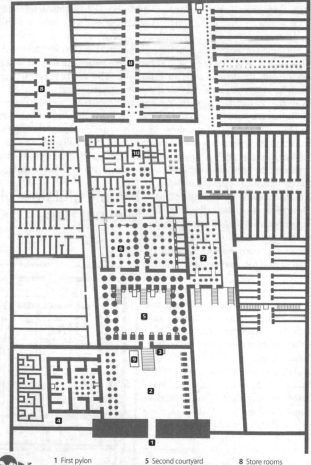

1 First pylon	5 Second courtyard	8 Store rooms
2 First courtyard	6 Hypostyle hall	9 Base of Colossus of Ramses
3 Second pylon	7 Temple of Seti I	10 Sanctuary
4 Palace/temple		

0 metres 20
0 yards 20

acacia trees led to the Colossi of Memnon. The site, known as Jeser Ast or 'Sacred Place', was venerated because it was thought that the waters of chaos had divided and the primeval mound erupted here. During Akhenaten's rule, Amun's images were destroyed but they were later replaced by those of Horemheb and Seti I.

The whole temple complex is entered via the three-storey southeast gatehouse which is built like a fortified Syrian pavilion and was originally 22 m high. Arriving through it into the large forecourt one sees the small temple to the right, the huge main temple directly ahead, and the small Chapels of the Votressess, dating from the 25th Dynasty (747-656 BC) kings of Kush, just to the left.

The remarkable homogeneity of the main temple's structure reflects the fact that it was designed and built by Ramses III alone rather than being expanded and altered by successive pharaohs. The immense and wonderfully preserved First Pylon, which is 65 m long by 27 m high, was originally dedicated to Amun but was also used by Ramses II as a memorial to his Libyan and Asiatic campaigns. It would originally have been larger than the one at Luxor, standing 27 m high and 65 m long, but now the north corner and cornice are missing. The images on the left of the Pylon show Ramses slaying Nubian prisoners watched by Amun and Ptah while Syrians are slain on the right hand side. Although the illustrations are based on genuine wars Ramses III never actually fought either nation!

On the left of the entrance way through the first Pylon, before arriving in the large 48 m x 34 m first court, also known as the palace, Ramses III is shown worshipping the deities Ptah, Osiris and Sokar. The west of the great court is flanked by eight columns and the east by seven Osiride pillars. On the Second Pylon the Pharaoh is depicted marching rows of prisoners, the third row being Philistines (or Palestinians) wearing feathered head-dresses, towards Amun and Mut. The second court is also made up of a combination of Osiride pillars and columns. Eight pillars line the back and front of the hall while the sides are flanked by six columns. One scene depicts the Feast of Sokar while the lower register of the back wall is dedicated to the Ramses III's sons and daughters. At the far right end of the hall is a small entrance which has two interesting illustrations. One shows the Pharaoh before Seth, but this was later defaced to change him into Horus, while above the door Ramses is shown kneeling on the symbol of the united Upper and Lower Egypt.

Temple of Ramses III, Medinet Habu

The west door connects to the ruins of the severely damaged Hypostyle Hall. Above the door the Pharaoh can again be seen kneeling over the symbol of Upper and Lower Egypt and at the base of the entry wall are 13 princesses and 10 princes. The central aisle of the hall would have been raised, in the same way as at Karnak, to allow Re's sunlight to enter.

A multitude of side rooms would originally have led off from the hypostyle hall but little now remains because of the severe damage caused by the major earthquake in 27 BC. The best preserved room is the

The Singing Colossus of Memnon

The northern gigantic sandstone colossus was broken off at the waist by the earthquake in 27 BC after which it was reputed to sing at dawn. This phenomenon, which was most likely caused by the wind or the expansion of *the broken stone in the morning sunlight, attracted many visitors including the Roman emperors Hadrian in AD 130 and Septimus Severus (AD 193-211). The latter decided it should be repaired, after which time it never sang again.*

Treasury to the north where the walls are adorned with scenes of the Pharaoh making offerings of gold to Amun. Another small room shows the Pharaoh wearing the Osiride symbols of the Atef feathered crown, a crook and flail.

The outer walls are better preserved and some of the reliefs are clearly visible. At the far end of the south wall is a calendar of religious feasts which is believed to be the longest such inscription. Further along is a portrayal of all the benefits with which Ramses III was blessed by Amun. The rear west wall is dedicated to the Pharaoh's victories in battle. In the northeast corner of the enclosure near the small temple is a small sacred lake where childless women came to bathe at night and pray to Isis that they might conceive. Close by stand the remains of the Nilometer that was originally fed by a canal which branched off from the Nile.

Colossi of Memnon These two gigantic sandstone colossi, which are located on the main road 1.65 km from the river and next to the student ticket kiosk, represent Amenhotep III (1417-1379 BC). They once stood in front of his mortuary temple which collapsed and was plundered for stone long ago. Although the faces and crowns have been eroded the two colossi make a strange spectacle seated in splendour in the midst of the desert and are well worth a visit (see box, page 263).

On a more modern theme – the **Monastery of St Theodore** lies to the southwest of the Temple of Medinet Habu (see page 261) and is within easy reach. The religious pictures are quite modern. Theodore was one of the many Christian soldiers who fell foul of Diocletian's oppression.

Essentials

Sleeping Because Luxor attracts so many tourists there are numerous hotels, with thousands of beds, covering the widest range of accommodation. Most hotels are located on or close to the River Nile although some are a short bus ride south of the town. Rooms are cheaper if booked as part of a package. In normal circumstances, during the peak season in Nov-Feb there are no spare rooms but during the hottest months there are plenty of cut-price deals to be had if you shop around. Don't be shy to ask for a better rate or an upgrade even at the best hotels.

AL *Luxor Hilton*, New Karnak, T374955, F376571. 261 rooms with twin beds, rather small, but magnificent views from private balcony. Located to north of town with free courtesy bus, unprepossessing exterior hides an excellent interior with reportedly the best hotel management in the town. Sleep may be disturbed by cruise liners which moor alongside and run engines all night, three restaurants provide wide choice of excellent food, coffee shop, heated pool (necessary for comfort in winter) with sundeck which overlooks the River Nile, casino, feluccas to rent E£40 per hr, new mini-gym, billiards. **AL** *Luxor Sheraton Hotel & Resort*, Sharia El-Awameya, PO Box 34, T374544, F374941. 298 rooms in main building with views of River Nile (more expensive) or bungalows in garden (very comfortable). Shopping arcade, hairdresser, disco, tennis courts, heated pool, feluccas to rent E£35 per hr, well managed, caters for tour groups which receive reduced rates, the service is consistently excellent, a pleasure to be a guest and our choice of the **AL** hotels. **AL** *Movenpick Jolie Ville Luxor*, Crocodile Island, T374855, F374936. 320 rooms in 20 bungalow pavilions, the only tourist village in Luxor. Beautiful location 4 km south of Luxor, connected to mainland by bridge and to town centre by a free ferry and more frequent free shuttle bus, under 16s can sleep free in their parents' room. Good restaurants – *Movenpick, Jolie Ville, Garden Terrace, Sharazade Nile Terrace, Crocodile Bar*, and the Sobek Hall for banquets, functions and conferences, good pool. **AL** *Sofitel Winter Palace Hotel*, Corniche el-Nil, T380422, F374087. 110 rooms in the old building and 260 in the new, overlooking the Nile. The oldest and most famous luxury hotel in Luxor whose guests have included heads of state, Noel Coward and Agatha Christie. The old style rooms are unusual but rather basic, 2 restaurants, terrace bar in splendid position overlooking Corniche and river, shared pool. **AL** *Sonesta St George Hotel*, Corniche el Nil just 7 km from the airport. A modern 7 storey building where the lower level terrace overlooks the River Nile. Serapis restaurant, Beban coffee shop, Isadore elegant dining room with excellent food and attentive service; Mikado Japanese restaurant; Nobles pub; Poolside bar with light refreshments; Nightclub and disco; Sport and fitness. T382575, www.sonesta.com

A *Pyramisa Isis Hotel*, Sharia Khalid Ibn el-Walid, T373344, F372923. The largest hotel in Upper Egypt with 520 large, clean, well decorated rooms set in 3 wings round the garden and 2 large pools (one is heated) where non-residents can swim for E£15. Located in extensive grounds to the south of town, courtesy bus, main Italian and sea-food restaurants plus 3 specialists restaurants, 2 bars, excellent facilities but slow service, sports facilities including clay tennis courts and squash. **A** *Akhetaten Village*, Sharia Khalid Ibn el-Walid, T380850, F380879. Run by Club Med with its unique and stylish atmosphere.

B *Mercure Luxor Hotel*, Corniche el-Nil, T380944, F373316. 306 quality rooms with bath, located in town centre on river front, attractive atmosphere, very well run, 2 restaurants with live entertainment. 24-hr coffee shop, most guests are tour groups who are mainly British in summer and German in the winter high season when the hotel is always full.

C *Mercure Inn Luxor Hotel*, 10 Sharia Maabad Luxor, T373521, F580817. 89 rooms, caters mainly for tour groups, reportedly has excellent food. **C** *Novotel Luxor*, Sharia Khalid Ibn el-Walid, T380925, F380972. New hotel, 185 rooms, emphasis on friendly service, 2 restaurants (1 floating), conference and fax facilities, most guests are tour groups.

D *Emilo Hotel* and *New Emilo Hotel*, Sharia Yusef Hassan, T386666, F374884. Roof garden, in town centre, 111 a/c rooms with bath and TV, 2 restaurants, 3 bars, disco, pool, small shop, exchange, international phone lines, friendly service, main guests are German and British tour groups. **D** *New Windsor Hotel*, Sharia Nefertiti, T374306, F373447. 40 rooms, biggest and probably the best 3-star hotel in town. Located just behind the Corniche, roof garden has river view, rooms in the new extension around the small pool are better choice, bar, discotheque below the restaurant, a bank and 2 international telephone lines, food good but unspectacular.

D *Arabesque*, Sharia Mohammed Farid, T372193, F372193. 36 rooms, new, roof garden with impressive view of Luxor temple. **D** *Pharaon*, New Karnak, T374924, F376477. 50 rooms, clean rooms, good pool. **D** *Philippe Hotel*, Sharia Dr Labib Habashi, T372284, F580060. 40 rooms, located in the heart of town, swimming pool, roof garden. **D** *Savoy Hotel*, Corniche el-Nil, PO Box 83952, T580522, F580526. 108 rooms, cheapest of Luxor's classic Victorian hotels.

E *Marwa Palace*, Sharia Television, T380040. 40 rooms, convenient for bus station.
E *Santa Maria*, Sharia Television, T372603. 48 rooms, convenient for bus station.
E *Windsor*, Sharia Nefertiti, T372847, F373447. 112 rooms, clean, family run budget hotel joined to the *New Windsor Hotel*.

F *Abu el-Hagag (4 Seasons)*, Sharia Maabad Luxor and M Farid, T372958. 15 rooms, one of the cheapest hotels in town mainly frequented by long-stay budget travellers, located adjacent to Luxor Temple with excellent views from the top floors. **F** *El-Mustafa Hotel*, Sharia Television, T374721. 20 rooms, new, near bus station and the *Marwa Palace* and *Santa Maria* hotels. **F** *Horus*, Sharia el-Karnak, T372165. 25 a/c rooms. Highly recommended. Centrally located but rather noisy budget hotel with friendly staff, clean a/c rooms (erratic), hot showers and a good breakfast. Recommended. **F** *Mina Palace*, Corniche el-Nil, T372074. 40 rooms, one of the best cheap hotels, excellent location, some rooms overlook Nile/Luxor Temple. **F** *Nobles*, Sharia Yusef Hassan, Midan Ahmose, T372823. 40 rooms, very cheap. **F** *Nour Home*, Sharia Mohammed Farid. Highly recommended. Quiet budget hotel with worn but clean rooms, helpful owner. **F** *Pyramids Hotel*, Sharia Yusef Hassan, 1373243. 20 rooms, cheapest but not cleanest in town. Located near *Nobles Hotel*. **F** *Ramoza*, Sharia Sa'ad Zaghloul, T372270, 48 clean a/c rooms, hot showers, near railway station but about 1 km from the river. **F** *Sphinx*, Sharia Yusef Hassan, T372830. 33 rooms. **F** *Venus*, Sharia Yusef Hassan, T372635. 23 clean, basic rooms with fans or a/c and bath, one of the best small downtown budget hotels. Good laundry service, new rooftop bar and restaurant serves meals and alcohol, popular with young German tourists, discounts for long stay guests, price includes breakfast.

Camping Opposite the youth hostel, the permanently guarded camp site (T382425), which mainly caters for noisy Egyptian families, offers space for tents and hot showers.

Youth hostels Clean, spartan 275 bed *IYHF Youth Hostel* halfway between Luxor and Karnak Temples at 16 Sharia Karnak Temple, T/F372139. 275 beds, meals available, family rooms, laundry, There are many cheap hotels which offer more comfortable and convenient accommodation without the 1000-1400 lockout and 2300-0600 curfew. There has been some attempt to provide accommodation on the West Bank at Habu, Habukah, Pharoah and Sheik Ali but choice is limited and Western tastes are better catered for in Luxor.

The majority of the better hotels have expensive good quality restaurants, which **Eating** serve standard international hotel food, and in some cases interesting Egyptian food. There are, however, a number of comparatively cheap restaurants which are concentrated around the tourist shops on Sharia el-Karnak behind Luxor Temple.

Expensive: *The Class Restaurant*, Sharia Khaled Ibn el-Walid. Excellent food – continental or oriental – and service.

Mid-range: *Amigos Restaurant*, Italian food well presented, Sharia Salah al-Din. *Anubis Restaurant*, open 24 hrs serving European food, the breakfast is recommended and the view of the Nile can be enjoyed any time of the day. Adjacent to Museum of Mummification on Corniche el-Nil. *The Green Palace*, Karnak Temple, offers traditional Egyptian cuisine together with Italian staples. *Tudor Rose English Restaurant,* Sharia el Nil between *Sheraton* and *Isis*. Rather quaint to find such an English restaurant here, warm welcome, good for tourists seeking a bit of home after all the temples and tombs – braised beefsteak with onions, shepherd's pie, no alcohol, selection of English tea. Desserts of the home-made cake variety and ice creams. T371077, open 0800 (for breakfast) to 2300.

Luxor

Cheap: *Ali Baba Café*, offering a view of Luxor temple and Egyptian fare at reasonable prices. *Chicken Hut*, takeaway chicken, adequate but not ethnic, junction of Sharia Station and El-Souq. *El-Fishawy Café*, coffee and *shisha*, Sharia Salah al-Din. *Oriental* adjacent to *Hotel Mercure*, good English food. *Pizza Hum*, spicy Italian cooking, pizza heads the menu, try the seafood soup, lots of pasta. No alcohol served – lots of fruit cocktails.

A number of cheap new restaurants have sprung up on the **West Bank:** *The Tutankhamun*, on the public ferry dock. Highly recommended. No alcohol. The *African Restaurant* next door. The *Valley Bloom* and *Marsam Hotel* all serve decent Egyptian food and possess good Nile views particularly at sunset.

Cruising restaurants *Le Lotus*, at *Novotel*, well organized dinner cruises offering international cuisine, book to get a good seat, also day cruises with high quality lunch while travelling to Dendera and Esna. *Sheraton Nile Cruiser* moored at *Sheraton Hotel* for sunset and dinner cruises, also day cruise with lunch to Dendera. *Vivant-Denon* at *Movenpick*. Breakfast, lunch, afternoon tea and dinner cruises in a 105-year-old sailing boat.

Bars & nightclubs Although some of the major hotels have music and floor shows they are generally mediocre compared with Cairo. Nightlife is largely restricted to promenades through the town and along the Corniche with stops for soft drinks, a water-pipe *sheesha*, and backgammon *thowla*. Discos can be found in some hotels: *Aladin* in *Isis Hotel* open from 2100. *Rababa* in *Luxor Hilton* open 2000-0200 . *Sabil* in *Mercure Luxor Hotel*. *Sukkareya Club* in *Sheraton Hotel*. *Club Med Disco* in *Club Med*, open 2200-0200, *King Tut* in *Winter Palace*, live band from 1830, belly dancer 1900-2000, snake show 2100.

Entertainment **Balloon flights**: *Balloons over Egypt* in British built hot air balloons holding 8 persons, opposite Isis Hotel, Sharia Khalid Ibn el-walid, T/F370638. Leave your hotel at 0500, total excursion time is 4 hrs, flight 45-90 mins, breakfast served in desert or leave your hotel at 1430 and return after a desert 'sundowner buffet'. Insured by Lloyds of London and full refund if weather conditions prevent flight, T370638 F376515 (E£250 per person). Details available at Luxor office of *Balloons over Egypt* T581584, T/F386515 and at all leading hotels and cruise ships. Hat, sunblock and flat shoes recommended.

Casino: *Luxor Hilton* has the only casino in Luxor offering roulette, blackjack and lots of slot machines. Open only to non-Egyptians over 18 years, have your passport available, open 2000-0200.

Sound & light: The sound and light show at Karnak is over melodramatic but certainly worth a visit. Rather than buy an expensive all inclusive 'tour', which can cost E£75 or more, arrange your own transport for a few E£ and pay the normal E£33 entrance at the kiosk. Shows daily at 1900, 2015, 2130 and 2245 (for Fri, Sat, Sun only) as follows:

Mon: English/French/Spanish; **Tue**:French/English/Italian; **Wed**:German/English/French; **Thu**:English/French/Italian; **Fri**:French/English/Spanish; **Sat**:French/English/Italian; **Sun**:German/English/French/Italian. Make sure to see one of these performances, not to be missed, the spotlights accentuate the carved figures and make an unforgettable sight.

Festivals The National Day is in **Nov** and the Nile Racing Regatta is in **Dec**. Both are moveable dates.

Luxor shops are mainly divided between those for tourists found in the hotels and in **Shopping**
the main central tourist bazaar, and the local markets. Many of the shops in the *souqs*
are closed on Sun where the stall holders are Christian. For the independent traveller
good quality fruit and vegetables can be bought in the **Sharia Television Market** on
Tue. Generally the further away from the river the lower the prices and the less the
hassle. Laser printed T-shirts are at Venti on the corner of Sharia Mohammed Farid.
The shawls similar to those worn by the caleche drivers on sale in Sharia
el-Souq/Sharia Cleopatra. Local alabaster carved into vases (E£25 small), clay pots and
tagins are cheap (E£2 medium size). An unusual collection of unpolished precious
and semi-precious stones, many believe to have healing properties can be found at
Zaghloul Bazaar by Luxor Temple.

Bookshops: Bookshops are found at all major hotels such as **Chez George Gaddis** at
the *Hotel Sheraton* open 0830-2330 and **Book and Papyrus Shop** at *Luxor Hilton* open
0900-2300, but better to go to **Aboudi Books** near *New Winter Palace* on Corniche
el-Nil, T373390, for books in English, German and French, also a good selection of
cards and a shelf of second-hand paper back novels in English. Open 0800-2000
except Fri. Internet café upstairs, E£6.25 for 15 mins; **Al Ahram** by the *Museum of
Mummification* on Corniche el-Nil with a good selection of books, also maps and cards
and newspapers. Open 0800-2200; **Gaddis Bookshop** by *New Winter Palace* on
Corniche el-Nil, T372142, has books in English, French and German. Open 0800-2130.
Recommended as the best of the book shops in Luxor. Foreign newspapers are sold in
a kiosk in the middle of the street outside the *Old Winter Palace Hotel*. There is a good
chance that these will also be offered for sale by street vendors along the Corniche
where the cruise ships are moored.

Besides swimming pools, the main hotels have the best sporting facilities including **Sports**
tennis, sailing and a wide range of indooor games. This section of the River Nile is used
for international rowing championships.

Those in the main hotels are generally very good and can arrange tickets for almost **Tour operators**
anywhere in the country. The town's travel agents include **Eastmar Travel**, Corniche
el-Nil, *Old Winter Palace*, T376211, F382151; **Kuoni Travel**, *Sheraton Hotel*, T384544;
Abercrombie and Kent, Sharia Sayed Youssef, T370444; **Thomas Cook**, Corniche el-Nil
T372402; **Misr Travel,** Corniche el-Nil near *Winter Palace Hotel* T383460.

NB check all transport times with great care – timetables are often a printed figment **Transport**
of someone's imagination...

Local Cycle hire: from *Hilton Hotel* or *Mercure Inn Luxor Hotel* for E£5 per hour.
Cheaper and fairly roadworthy cycles can be hired from El-Hussein behind Luxor Temple or adjacent *Emilo Hotel*.

Horse riding: on West Bank has become popular, usually passing through villages
and some monuments towards the mountains (E£20 per hour). Camel and donkey
excursions can also be taken.

Air There are frequent daily flights particularly in the winter high season to Cairo,
Aswan and Abu Simbel and less frequently to Hurghada. *Egyptair* (office in *Winter
Palace Hotel*, T380580-380586) and the privately-owned *ZAS* (in *New Winter Palace*,
T375928), charge identical rates for their flights. There are an increasing number of
charter flights to/from European cities. EgyptAir advertise from Luxor to: Assiut, Tue at
1545; Aswan daily at 0900 and various other times and days; Brussels, Mon at 0200;
Cairo numerous; Hurghada, Wed at 0915, 2230 and Sat at 0915, 2230; Jeddah, Wed at

1130; Kuwait, Tue at 0850, Wed and Thu at 0945; London, Mon at 1115; Manchester, Sun 0815; Paris, Sat 0715, Sun 0915; Sharm el-Sheikh, Thu and Sat at 0915, Tue at 2130; Zurich, Sat at 1005. Airport information: T384655.

Train Foreigners are restricted in their choice of trains from the station on Sharia al-Mahata. (Train information: T372018. Office hours 0900-1400, 1700-2000). The first class service on the Cairo trains is good and it is a pleasant way to see the Egyptian countryside. It is essential, particularly in the high winter season, to reserve your seat at the station a few days before you travel. A/c sleeper daily to Cairo leaves at 2030 and arrives 0630. First/second class to Cairo (E£50/30) (10 hrs) leaving daily at 0815 and 2315 also for Abydos and Minya. First/second class to Aswan (E£20/15) (5 hrs) leaving daily at 0600 and 1715. Train to Kharga leaves each Thu around 0700 (E£10).

Road Bus The buses leave from the station behind Luxor Temple (T372118) and there will be restrictions on the buses foreigners can use. The daily bus to Cairo leaves at 0700 (10 hrs); 6 rather slow buses depart during the morning for Esna, Edfu and Kom Ombo going on to Aswan. The three daily buses to Hurghada (5 hrs) (the left hand seats are cooler) continue on to Suez and there are 2 or 3 early morning buses each week to Kharga (get a right hand seat this journey).

Private taxi: sample charges E£120 to Aswan, E£160 to Hurghada (need to go with the convoy) E£13 to airport. **Service taxi**: from the terminal just off Sharia el-Karnak, half way between the Luxor town centre and Karnak temple, these are quicker and more convenient than trains or buses but only go as far north as Qena (1 hr).

Boat Feluccas: are numerous on this most beautiful stretch of the Nile. Travel is limited to the southward direction, but this also has the most attractive scenery. Sunset is the best time to ride but bring a sweater and protection against mosquitoes (E£20 per hour). Feluccas are available as you walk down Corniche el Nil. For longer trips (which are few and far between due to security concerns) try the hotels or perhaps the tourist office.

Directory **Airline offices** *EgyptAir*, T380581. Luxor international airport, T374855. **Banks** *Bank of Alexandria*, north of Sharia Nefertiti and Sharia el-Karnak intersection on Corniche el-Nil. *Banque Misr* (Sun-Thu 0830-2100), on Sharia Dr Habib Habashy. *Egyptian American Bank* in *Novotel* on Corniche el-Nil. *National Bank of Egypt*, on Corniche el-Nil (open Sat-Thu 0830-1400 and 1700-2000, Fri 0830-1100 and 1700-2000), just south of the *Old Winter Palace Hotel*. **Communications** Internet *Aboudi Books* near *New Winter Palace* on Corniche el-Nil, T373390, 0800-2000 except Fri has internet café upstairs, E£6.25 for 15 mins. **Post Office:** main post office (Sun-Thu 0800-1400) is on Sharia al-Mahata on the way to the railway station, T372037. Hotels sell stamps. **Medical services** Hospital: T382025/372045. General Fever Hospital: T372474. Maged Pharmacy: 24 hr, Sharia Aly Ibn Abi Taleb, T370524, will deliver. **Places of worship** Roman Catholic: The Holy Family Church, 16 Sharia Karnak Temple, holds Mass in Italian with multilingual readings each Sun at 0900 and 1800. **Useful addresses** Passport Office: On Sharia Khaled Ibn el-Walid, just south of and opposite *Hotel Isis*, T380885. **Useful telephone numbers** Fire: T180. Police: T372350. Tourist Police: T376620.

Luxor to Aswan and South of Aswan

7

The majority of tourists travel non-stop from Luxor to Aswan missing en-route a number of interesting and beautiful temples of which Edfu and Kom Ombo are certainly not to be missed. What is so extraordinary about the generally unspectacular road journey is the fact that the strip of cultivated land between the Nile and the desert is so narrow. On one side is lush vegetation and the river and on the other the harsh and arid desert.

For many visitors to Egypt the highlight of their trip is the delightful city of Aswan, Lake Nasser and Abu Simbel which, after the noise and crowds of Cairo and the over-commercialization of Luxor, is wonderfully relaxing. Early travellers, spending uncomfortable days on the river journey, were overcome with the splendour of the temples at Abu Simbel. Today the journey is shorter and generally more comfortable but the awe inspired by these breathtaking reconstructions remains undimmed. They were built to impress visitors and to intimidate by their grandeur and they still do. Don't travel all the way to Aswan and return without experiencing the magic of Ramses' outstanding display.

The combination of these magnificent sites, the reliable weather, the breathtaking sunsets and the friendliness of the indigenous Nubian population make Egypt's deep south an experience which must not be missed. It has been a popular winter resort for cold blooded Europeans since Victorian times.

South of Luxor Aswan and Lake Nasser

The main road follows the River Nile along its East Bank from Luxor, past Edfu (115 km) which is on the West Bank about half way to Aswan, before continuing via Kom Ombo (176 km) to Aswan (216 km). There is an alternative less crowded but less scenic route along the West Bank from the Valley of the Kings to Esna (55 km) and Edfu before having to cross the river to continue the journey along the East Bank to Aswan. Make enquiries at your hotel or car hire outlet about times of the convoys south from Luxor.

Increasing numbers of visitors are now making this journey by river in one of the many floating hotels which moor at the sites along the way (see box, page 282). Egyptian village life, which is often obscured from the road and cannot be appreciated from the window of a speeding car, can be seen on this relaxing journey which is thoroughly recommended.

The **Temple of Montu** at **Tod**, the ancient city of Tuphium, is 21 km south of Luxor on the east side of the River Nile. It appears on the specialist tour itineraries and is best known for the treasure discovered in 1936 now in the museum in Cairo. This was a collection of gold ingots and silver vessels found in the temple during excavations by the French, found in four bronze chests bearing the cartouche of Amenemhat II. This treasure is thought to have been tribute sent from Syria to King Amenemhet II and gives an indication of contacts with Greece and the Near East during the period of the Middle Kingdom.

Cross the railway at the second junction after Armant station. Aim for the mosque, the temple is adjacent. Ticket E£20 purchased in advance from the kiosk at Luxor Temple (the custodian could not be bribed). Taxi return fare plus waiting time E£50.

It is suggested that the original building, a mud brick chapel, was constructed here in the 5th Dynasty. A granite pillar bearing the cartouche of King Userkaf of that time was found here but the main temple to Montu (god of war) was constructed consecutively by Mentuhotep II, Mentuhotep III and Senusert I (2050-1928 BC). Only fragments of this structure remain. Tuthmosis III (1504-1450 BC) erected a barque shrine for Montu which has undergone much rebuilding. Many of the blocks from here were recycled – to build the nearby church to the east of the site.

Ptolemy VIII built the new temple (170-145 BC) and a Kiosk was added later in the Roman period.

Mo'alla Cemetery There are rock-cut tombs in the cemetery of Mo'alla on the east bank 40 km south of Luxor dating from the First Intermediate period. Before visiting this site buy your tickets at the kiosks on the West bank, at the Luxor Museum kiosk or be prepared to pay an informal fee of some E£20 to the guardian.

Travelling along the Nile

There is always a choice. In addition to the hundreds of cruisers on the river between Luxor and Aswan consider a voyage by paddle-steamer. Paddle-steamer SS Karim was built in the UK in 1917 for the then sultan who became King Ahmed Faud I in 1922. It became the property of King Farouk his successor from 1936-52. After the formation of the Arab Republic in 1952 it was the property of the Ministry of Irrigation and was used by presidents Nasser and Sadat. It has been fully refurbished (there are just 17 double cabins) making a careful attempt to evoke the atmosphere of the early 1900s with the comforts of today. Contact Spring Tours, T3415972 for further details.

Motor yachts such as Doma run by the Imaginative Traveller are another option. Fourteen simple cabins with bunk beds, bed linen provided, two bathrooms each with w/c and shower. Comfort levels are lower but the sights/sites are the same.

At the cheap end try the felucca, the traditional sailing boat about 10 m long and 3 m wide, driven by one large triangular sail. Travel is totally dependent on wind and current. The wind is stronger in the winter and blows from the north so helping the sailors against the flow of the river. As progress is at the mercy of the elements particular night stops and destinations cannot be guaranteed. There are cushions to sit on and a canopy for shade over most of the boat leaving the bow end un-shaded for sunbathing. With eight passengers and a crew of two there is room to move about. The luggage is stowed below and only available morning and evening so a daysack is essential.

Traditional meals, soft drinks and beer are available on board, tea and coffee are served with the meals. There are no toilets on these boats – the boat pulls to the bank near a bush if possible and a spade is provided. For the night stops a latrine is dug. Washing is done in the river using eco-friendly soap and shampoo. Germicide soap is provided and we are assured that the utensils are disinfected after being washed in the River Nile.

Travelling from Luxor, after the Nagga Abu Said station take the first turning left, cross the bridge over the canal then take the unsurfaced track which swings left towards the cliffs and the cemetery.

Four tombs are located here, cut into the cliffs. All entrances face the west and the River Nile.

1. **The tomb of Ankhtifi** Ankhtifi was one time governor of the area between Edfu and Armant. He was a very important man of his time, noted for feeding the people in neighbouring areas during a time of famine.

The tomb is of slightly irregular shape and cut directly into the rock. On entry there is a rectangular chamber which originally had 30 pillars in 3 rows of 10. The chamber is 6 m wide and 20 m long and shaped to fit in with the harder veins in the rock strata. Some of the pillars have disappeared though it is clear that a number of pillars were round and others hexagonal in form. Most pillars are decorated with fine plaster work and those pillars near the doors carry the best examples of coloured hieroglyphs.

An amusing fishing scene on the wall immediately to the right of the entrance door shows a huge fish being caught by spear. There is also a small picture of the deceased and his beautiful wife in very good condition about 50 cm square. There are other interesting scenes of daily life, one on the wall facing the entrance with lines of animals carrying food to relieve a local famine and another with a line of spotted cattle to indicate Ankhtifi's wealth. A burial chamber lies at a lower level in the centre rear of the main hall. Much of the roof has been hidden by recent protective material.

Tombs 2 and 3 comprise small chapels cut into the rock. No 3 is about 5 m square with a burial chamber to the left and a little off centre. Very little decoration remains – mind your head as you go down into the chambers!

4. **The tomb/chapel of Sobekhotep** This monument to another regional governor lies a short way to the north in the cemetery. It is entered or seen into via a metal door. There are vestiges of decoration on the door jamb but the best known decoration is seen on the back wall where there are representations of trees and a man taking animals as offerings. The three pits inside the grill have over them on the left a picture of the owner in full size carrying a staff and on the right a scene with eight ladies. The three pits inside are cut some 600 mm x 300 mm x 300 mm deep with burial chambers under the rock face.

Half-way between Tod and Mo'alla on the other side of the River Nile to the edge of the desert is the Convent of St George. It is not easy to miss as the surrounding walls are about 2 m high. The annual feast day is celebrated in November when thousands of pilgrims including the Bishop of Luxor attend. The main church which has 21 domes also has 6 altars dedicated (from north-south) to St Pachom, St Mercurius, The Virgin Mary, Saint George, Saint Paul of Thebes and Saint Michael.

Going through the locks at Esna can be a fascinating experience, well worth the wait. See page 275.

Esna

Phone code: 097
Colour map 4, grid A2 This small market town lies about 55 km south of Luxor on the West Bank of the Nile which, besides its **Temple of Khnum**, is mainly known for the sandstone dam across the river. This was built in 1906 at about the same time as the first Aswan dam and today cruise ships and barges usually have to queue for a number of hours for their turn to pass through its locks. The town and the temple are certainly worth a couple of hour's visit.

Sights The **Temple of Khnum**, lies partially exposed in a deep depression in the centre of town. The excavation began in the 1860s but did not continue because the area above was covered in houses. Over the centuries since its construction the annual Nile flood has deposited 10 m of silt over the temple site so that all that is visible today is the **Hypostyle Hall**. The part of the temple that can be seen today is Ptolemaic/Roman and was built on the foundations of a much older shrine which was also dedicated to the ram-headed deity Khnum. He was believed to have created man by moulding him from River Nile clay on a potter's wheel. Later, when Amun became the principal deity, Khnum's image changed and, in conjunction with Hapy, he came to be regarded as the guardian of the source of the River Nile.

The hypostyle hall's **Outer Façade** is decorated from left to right with the cartouches of three Roman emperors Claudius (AD 41-54), Titus (AD 79-81) and Vespasion (AD 69-79) (1, 2 and 3). Above the entrance, at the very top, on the lintel, is the winged sun disc.

Inside the tall hall 18 columns with capitals of varying floral designs support the **Astronomical Ceiling** which, although once a beautiful and complex spectacle, is barely visible today because it was blackened by the wood fires of a Coptic village which was once housed within the temple. In

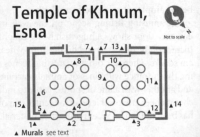

Temple of Khnum, Esna

Not to scale

▲ Murals see text

places various deities and animals, including winged dogs, two-headed snakes and the pregnant hippo-goddess Taweret (see page 217), can be seen intermingled with signs of the zodiac. Enter and turn left passing a tiny enclosed space built into the walls (4), perhaps the doorkeeper's chamber. In the first corner the pillar is decorated with rams (5) and the side wall on the second register Roman emperors Septimus Severus (he is second from the left), Caracella and Greta make offerings to Khnum (6). At the back, opposite the entrance, the walls of the original Ptolemaic temple (7) are incorporated in this hypostyle hall. The hall's columns are inscribed with texts detailing the temple's various festivals. On the lighter side look out for the cross-legged pharoah (8), frogs on top of the capital (9) representing the goddess Heqet (see page 212) and a god being offered a laurel wreath (10) showing Greek influence here. On the right hand wall pharoah with Horus and Khnum netting fowl and demons is illustrated (11) and in the last corner the column has countless crocodiles (12). Around the northern outer walls at the back of the temple are texts of Marcus Aurelius (AD 161-180) (13) while Titus, Domitian and Trajan slay their Egyptian enemies on the eastern and western outer walls (14 and 15). ■ *Daily 0700-1800, E£8. To get there: Service taxis and buses stop about 10 minutes walk from the temple which is in the centre of town. Walk to the river and then south along the Corniche to the ticket kiosk. The railway station is in the centre of town and is a short calèche ride to the temple.*

The **Convent of the Holy Martyrs** lies 6 km to the southwest of Esna. It commemorates 3,600 Christians who refused to sacrifice to the Roman gods and died for their faith c.249-251. The older church in the complex dedicated to the martyrs was first built in 786 but has been destroyed and rebuilt on a number of occasions. It has some interesting wall paintings. The Church of the Holy Virgin Mary is of more recent construction (1931).

F *Haramin* about 1 km south of the ticket kiosk along the Corniche is the best. Also **Al Medina** in the central square and **Dar as Salaam** even nearer the temple but all are best avoided. **Sleeping**

There are a few cafés and stalls in the central square but there are no restaurants. Nothing that we can recommend. **Eating**

Esna style: When the cruise ships reach the locks here the traders appear in a flotilla of small rowing boats and attempt to sell a wide variety of clothing, table clothes etc. Goods are hurled from the small boats in a polythene bag with great accuracy on to the top deck of the ship for the purchaser to examine and then barter over the price by shouting to and fro. Rejected goods are expected to be thrown back, although these are not always dispatched with the same accuracy as they were received! If a price is agreed and a purchase made, a small garment to act as ballast, again in a bag, is then thrown up on deck with the expectation that payment will be placed inside the package and returned to the sender below. **Shopping**

Train: To Luxor and Aswan stop at Esna but only very slow and crowded 2nd and 3rd class service. The station is an awkward 5 km out of town. **Transport**

Road Bus: north to Luxor or south to Edfu, Kom Ombo and Aswan are frequent but crowded in the morning. Make enquiries for the bus east to the Red Sea. **Service taxis**: to Luxor (1 hr), Edfu (1 hr) and Aswan (2-3 hrs) are quicker but marginally more expensive than the buses.

Banks One bank open Sat-Thu 0830-1400, Sun 1800-2100, and Wed 1700-2000. 1000-1330 during Ramadan. **Directory**

Luxor to Aswan

El Kab

Thirty-two kilometres south of Esna the mud-brick walls of El Kab stand on the western bank of the River Nile. The ramparts are very solid and in places measure 12 m thick. The important ruins here are the **Temple of Thoth** (see page 217) built by Ramses II and the later **Temple of Nekhbet** the vulture goddess (see page 214) who was worshipped on this site. The inclusion of stone blocks from earlier periods in the building of these temples is an example of pharaonic recyling! Cut into the hills to the west of the old town are a number of tombs. The keys are held in Edfu so make arrangements to visit in advance.

Edfu

Phone code: 095
Colour map 4, grid B2

Edfu, which is 60 km south along the West Bank and almost equidistant between Luxor (115 km) and Aswan (106 km), is the site of the huge, well preserved Ptolemaic cult **Temple of Horus** which, as the most complete in the whole country, is certainly worth a visit.

The temple is west or inland from the river along Sharia al-Maglis and can be reached by *calèche*, many of which are drawn by emaciated and badly treated horses, or taxis which await the arrival of the tourist cruise ships. Expect, in addition, to be approached by the ubiquitous photographer who will be keen to take a picture of your *calèche* party and to offer the developed photograph for sale as you return to your cruise ship. Taxis and pick-ups to the temple can be caught from the train station, which is just across the Nile bridge, while the service taxi terminal at the town-side west end of the bridge is a 20 minutes walk or short ride to the temple. Inter-city buses drop their passengers on Sharia Tahrir or the parallel Sharia Gumhorriya about half way between the bridge and the temple.

Sights   **Edfu Temple**, is the name given to the enormous **Temple of Horus** which was the focus of the ancient city of Djeba. It was begun in August 237 BC by Ptolemy III and took 25 years to complete, with the decoration taking another five years. Because of a revolt in Upper Egypt it was not until

Temple of Horus at Edfu

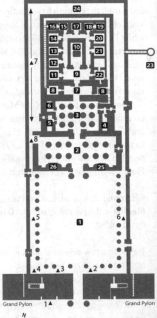

N

0 metres   20
0 yards   20

1 Court of offerings
2 First hypostyle hall
3 Second hypostyle hall/ festival hall
4 Offering hall: liquid offerings
5 Offering hall: solid offerings
6 Laboratory
7 First vestibule/hall of offerings
8 Stairs to roof
9 Second vestibule/ Sanctuary of Horus
10 Main sanctuary dedicated to Horus with altar
11 Chapel of Min
12 Chamber of Linen
13 Chamber of the Throne of the Gods
14 Chamber of Osiris
15 Tomb of Osiris
16 Chamber of the West
17 Chamber of the Victory (Horus)
18 Chapel of Khonsu
19 Chapel of Hathor
20 Chapel of the Throne of Re
21 Chapel of the Spread Wings
22 Sun Court
23 Nilometer & well
24 Passage of victory/ ambulatory
25 Library
26 Chamber of Ungents

▲ **Murals** see text

Horus – The First Living God-King

Horus who was originally the Egyptian sky-god and falcon-god was later identified as the son of Osiris and his sister Isis. He subsequently avenged his father's murder by his uncle Seth in an epic fight at Edfu in which Horus lost an eye and Seth his testicles. It was not until Isis intervened that Horus prevailed as good triumphed over evil. Osiris pronounced his judgment by banishing Seth to the underworld and enthroning Horus as the first living god-king. Each Pharaoh claimed to be an incarnation of Horus and the annual Festival of the Coronation, at Edfu's now destroyed Temple of the Falcon in front of the main temple's grand pylon, followed by a crowning ceremony in the temple's main forecourt, symbolized the renewal of royal power.

February 176 BC that the opening ceremony took place under Ptolemy VII, but there were further additions until Ptolemy XIII. Like Esna's **Temple of Khnum**, it was completely buried except for its huge pylons under silt and sand and its top was covered with houses until the 1860s but, unlike Esna, the whole site has been excavated. It had been severely damaged by the town's inhabitants and it was not until 1903 that the excavation work was finally completed.

The whole complex is entered from the ticket office in the northwest corner at the rear of the main north-south axis temple, which one walks along to reach the entrance at its south end.

Along the base of the enclosing walls look for the images of vultures representing the goddess Nekhbet and falcons representing Horus.

Just to the southwest is the small east-west axis birth house called the **Mammisi of Horus**, which was built by Ptolemy VII and VIII. The inner sanctuary is surrounded by a peristyle of foliage capped columns, topped by pilaster capitals showing the grotesque figures of Bes, god of joy and birth. His frightening appearance was thought to dispel evil and to protect women in labour (see page 210). Each year there is a performance of the miracle play which represents Horus' birth at the same time as the birth of the divine heir to the throne of Egypt. At the southwest corner of the birth house there are reliefs of Isis suckling Horus and an erect Amun. On the pillars of the colonnades in the forecourt Hathor beats tambourine, plays the harp and suckles Horus.

The main **Temple of Horus** is entered through a gateway in the huge **Grand Pylon** on either side of which are grey granite statues of the hawk-god Horus. A tiny Ptolemy stands in front of him. On the left outer wall of the pylon Ptolemy XIII (88-51 BC), who was also known as Neos Dionysus and had usurped the pylon from its original builder Ptolemy IX (170-116 BC), is shown killing his enemies before Horus and Hathor (1). The right wall has the same illustration in mirror image. Above are carved decorations and niches which were cut into the walls, as supports for the flagpoles. On its inner wall in the upper register the barge of Horus tows the barque of Hathor (2) and at the other side (3) the water bourne procession continues in the lower register. No sails are required as the journey is downstream. Celebrations for the gods' arrival are seen at (4).

The pylon contains the usual guardians' quarters and stairs up to the roof.

The giant **Court of Offerings**, at a slightly lower level, is lined with 32 columns with paired capitals behind which on the west side Ptolemy IX makes offerings to Horus, Hathor and Ihy, their son (5), and on the right Ptolemy X appears before the same three (6). At the north end of the court is the **First Hypostyle Hall**, built by Ptolemy VII (180-145 BC), with its 18 once brightly painted columns supporting the roof. There are three different types of capital,

Luxor to Aswan

How to survive a Nile cruise

Selecting a tour operator and cruise ship

The quality of operator and cruise ship will, of course, be largely dependent on the price paid. If the cruise is taken as an all-inclusive package, it is recommended that, if possible, one is chosen where the overall itinerary is under the day to day control of a tour manager who is a direct employee of the travel company. The local management of cruises can be sub-contracted to Egyptian travel agents who, should difficulties arise with the tour, may consider themselves primarily as guides and show marked reluctance to take on any wider responsibility or be fully accountable for solving problems of a more challenging nature. For health and safety reasons it is also recommended that travellers use only the best grade five-star Nile cruise boats (see table on pages 282-285).

Typical cruise itineraries

Most popular is between **Luxor and Aswan**, with the journey sometimes in reverse, or a trip both ways. The itinerary will offer the following typical popular features:

Luxor: visits to the West Bank (Valley of the Kings, Valley of the Queens, Colossi of Memnon, Temple of Queen Hapshetsut), Luxor and Karnak Temples (plus at least one alabaster factory shop!). Option of sound and light show at Karnak.

Esna: Temple of Khnum.

Edfu: Temple of Horus – access by calèche.

Kom Ombu: Temple of Horus and Sobek.

Aswan: Felucca boat outing to Kitchener Island, trip to Nubian village on Elephantine Island, Unfinished Obelisk, High Dam, Temple of Philae (plus at least one papyrus factory shop!). Option of sound and light show at Philae.

Dendera: Temple of Hathor – may not be on all itineraries.

The difference in the educational quality of the cruise will depend heavily on the calibre of the guides, library facilities on board and the availability of the evening lectures. It seems pointless to visit such spectacular historic sites without adequate instruction. Expect early starts to some excursions for example 0700 with opportunities to relax later in the heat of the day.

Esna lock closures

Cruises from Luxor to Aswan can be disrupted by the twice-yearly closure of the lock at Esna for maintenance. Closures usually in June and December and prospective travellers are strongly advised to check these dates beforehand. When the lock is closed, ships are moored at Esna and passengers are transported by coach to those points on the itinerary inaccessible by river. These makeshift arrangements can significantly reduce the pleasure and relaxation of a cruising holiday.

Meals

Expect three good meals per day, often buffet style, although there can be some variation with table de hote menus. Some meals served on covered deck. Meal times likely to operate to a fairly inflexible timetable. Free tea, coffee and soft drinks available at any time. Bar open most of day. Special menus can usually be organized.

Social life and entertainment

Almost inevitably at some stage during the cruise there will be an evening dinner at which travellers will be encouraged to dress in local Egyptian costume – a jallabah party. A local photographer will be on hand to record the event for your family album. Prints are available for purchase within 24 hours. A good range of costumes may be available both for hire or purchase on board ship (expect hire prices in the range E£25-40) but there are also opportunities to buy these cheaply at tourist bazaars on route, for example at Edfu and Kom Ombu. An entertaining alternative to these bazaars may be to buy from the traders who congregate around the cruise ships as they queue to pass through the lock at Esna (see page 275). This is an evening to enjoy.

Other evening entertainment may include discos, live Egyptian/Nubian music and performances by belly dancers, jugglers and acrobats.

Banking arrangements

Access to banks for obtaining local Egyptian currency can be somewhat limited. Whilst moored in Luxor and Aswan, for example, banks in the towns are accessible, although tour itineraries do not always allow convenient spare time during banking hours. Remember, too, that banks are usually closed on Fridays, so plan ahead. Do not forget that banks will want to see your passport unless you are exchanging cash for local currency. Cruise ship operators may make arrangements for a local banker to come on board whilst boats are moored at Luxor and Aswan. Rates of exchange using this facility can be disappointing, however, despite the fact that Egypt is supposed to have a fixed rate system.

Payments on board ship

It is very probable that the ship will operate a system by which all extras, for example drinks, laundry and any purchases from shops on board, can be signed for and the bills settled at the end of the cruise. The advantages of requiring less ready cash should be balanced with the need to keep a reasonable check on items being accurately debited to your cabin account. Although it is likely that payment of this account by credit card, in travellers' cheques or cash (hard or local currencies) will be fully acceptable, personal cheques will almost certainly not be.

Dress code

Shorts and beachwear acceptable on board ship but take note of the advice in Essentials for visits ashore. Casual dress for mealtimes is likely to be acceptable (no beachwear), with something smarter for evening dinner.

Tipping

In an attempt to ease the problem of when and who to tip on board ship, tour managers may suggest paying an amount per traveller (suggestion E£100) direct to the Boat Manager at the end of the cruise for distribution amongst all the staff working on the vessel. Tipping of tour managers (suggestion E£50) and drivers,

porters, temple guards, felucca sailors (suggestion E£35) would be additional to this. Although such systems exist, this does not preclude travellers from ignoring them and dealing with this issue personally as they see fit.

Medical assistance

Most ships have a resident doctor in attendance throughout the cruise. Given that access to pharmacies may be difficult during a cruise itinerary, it is recommended that travellers take a well stocked personal medical kit .

Cabin accommodation

Cabins at water level will offer limited views and, depending on position, may be more affected by engine noise and fumes. A supplement can be paid for a cabin on an upper deck. Top level cabins may have a sun deck as their roof. Obtain a plan of the vessel before you book. Bear in mind that when the ship is moored there may not be a view from the cabin whatever its level. Ships can often be berthed six or seven abreast and access to the shore is gained by walking through one ship after another. Expect to be issued with a boarding pass when going ashore.

Shopping facilities

There are likely to be some limited shopping opportunities on board at reasonable prices for buying postcards, stamps and some souvenirs, jewellery, books and perhaps items of clothing. Other options may include a hairdressing salon.

Telephone and fax

Do not expect these facilities to be as good as those on shore. Availability may be erratic and unpredictable and charges expensive. Minimum fax/phone charges to the UK are around E£50 per call.

Safe deposit boxes

If safety and security of valuables, passports and money is a concern, check whether the ship offers safe deposit boxes for passenger use.

Enjoying the cruise life

One of the great pleasures of cruising on the River Nile is just sitting and watching the landscape glide gently by. The scenery is ever changing, albeit at an undemanding pace which gives a unique

•••

opportunity to take a leisurely look at village settlements which slip in and out of view and the cultivation of the narrow strip of green fertile land close to the river's banks. Dusk brings the contrast of vivid sunset colours and perhaps the graceful sight of felucca boats silhouetted against the water. Useful things to have to hand are a pair of binoculars and perhaps a book to help with the identification of the many birds which can be seen on the islands and river banks.

If enjoyment extends to taking exercise to keep fit, despite the heat, then exercise bicycles and rowing machines may be found on the top deck (no privacy here!). Don't expect swimming pools to be, in effect, anything more than a large plunge bath. With a gentle breeze coming off the river, the heat of the sun can often be misjudged whilst cruising. A ship with a good area of awning on the top deck might be a preferred choice.

•••

repeated on either side of the hall. Before the entrance of the Hall stands another large statue of Horus, in grey granite. At the entrance to the Hypostyle Hall is the small Chamber of Ungents to the left with reliefs of flowers and recipes for consecrations and a small Library, where the names of the guests for the day's festival would be kept, to the right. Here many rolls of papyrus were found. The foundation ceremonies are illustrated on the walls of the hall.

Leading north from the hall is a smaller 12 slender columned hypostyle hall, known as the **Festival Hall**, the oldest part of the building dating back to Ptolemy III (246-222 BC) and completed by his son, where offerings entered the temple and were prepared. Recipes for offerings are found on the walls of the laboratory. These were then carried through into the **Hall of Offerings**, or first vestibule, where the daily offerings would have been made at the many altars and tables bearing incense, juices, fruit and meat. From here there are steps to the east which were used for the procession up to the roof where a **Chapel of the Disc** once stood. The stairs are illustrated with pictures of the priests carrying the statues of the gods to the roof to be revitalized before returning down a separate staircase, not safe to climb, to arrive back on the west side of the Hall of Offerings. Today all the roof offers is an excellent view of the surrounding area.

The Offerings Hall leads to the inner vestibule called the **Sanctuary of Horus**, where engravings show Ptolemy IV (222-205 BC) making offerings to the deities while others show Horus and Hathor in their sacred vessels. The sanctuary holds a low altar of dark syenite on which stood the barque and behind is the large upright shrine of Aswan granite where the statue of the god was placed. The sanctuary is virtually a separate temple within the main temple and is surrounded by a series of 10 minor chambers with doors, then immediately behind the sanctuary containing a lifesize model of the sacred barque. The original is in the British Museum. The chapel of the Throne of Re shows Horus with a serpent, Horus in the sacred tree and Horus with monkeys. These chambers, many of which originally served as vestries and store rooms, are better examined with a torch. Horus' defeat of Seth, who is portrayed as a hippopotamus, is illustrated in the middle of the west wall of the ambulatory (7). Note how the hippo gets smaller and smaller as the tale is repeated to the north. On the same side where the ambulatory narrows to the south the pharoah helped by gods pulls close a clap net containing evil spirits portrayed as fish, birds and men (8). There are some interesting water spouts jutting into this area, some in better repair than others, carved as lions' heads.

On the dimly lit northeast wall of the outer corridor are the remains of a Nilometer. (see Aswan, page 294) and a well.

■ *Summer 0700-1800, winter 0700-1600, general entry E£20, student entry E£10, E£6 charge for cameras or videos used for commercial photography.*

The **Monastery of St Pachom** is in the desert about 6 km to the west of Edfu. It is worth a visit if you are in the area – but not worth a special journey.

Sleeping There are no good hotels in town and most tourists are either only passing through or are staying on cruise ships which moor on the river bank from where *calèches* take them to the temple.

There are a few cheap hotels including the relatively clean **F** *Dar es-Salaam*, near the temple. The friendly but shabby **F** *El-Medina*, just off the main roundabout on Sharia Gumhorriya; **F** *El-Magdi*, further down Sharia al-Maglis.

Eating The *Happy Land Restaurant* is on the Corniche between the bridge and Sharia al-Maglis where the *Zahrat el-Medina Restaurant* is located; neither of these cheap restaurants is very good.

Shopping The main tourist bazaar is next to the Edfu temple complex and offers a colourful selection of cheaply priced goods, particularly jellabahs, scarves, tablecloths and other local souvenirs. Not surprisingly, the *calèche* drivers taking tourists from the cruise ships will drop you and collect you from this area. When bargaining for goods here, as elsewhere, take care to establish whether the price is in Egyptian pounds or UK pounds sterling; local traders are adept at switching between the two and even introducing a fictitious Nubian pound in an attempt to cause confusion!

Transport **Train**: To Luxor and Aswan stop at Edfu but only very slow and crowded 2nd and 3rd class service.

Road **Bus**: north to Esna and Luxor or south to Kom Ombo and Aswan, caught from Sharia Tahrir half way between the bridge and the temple, are slow but very cheap. **Service taxis**: north to Esna (1 hr) and Luxor (1 hr), or south to Kom Ombo (45 mins) and Aswan (1 hr, E£5), can be caught from the west end of the bridge.

Directory **Banks** Sharia Gumhorriya in the centre of town is open Sun-Thu 0830-1400. **Communications** Post Office. located near the temple on Sharia Tahrir on the south side of the main roundabout.

Feluccas on the River Nile

Nile Cruisers

It is recommended for health and safety reasons that travellers use only the best grade Nile Cruise boats. The following list gives the names of Egyptian Government Five-Star grade Nile cruisers. See also Tour Operators in Essentials. Further information can also be found at www. Sherryboat.com.eg, www. Sonesta.com, www.ie-eg.com

Boat	Operator/Owner	No of Cabins
Abercrombie Sun Boats	Abercrombie and Kent, 11 Sh Cleopatra, Heliopolis, T4145602, F4199910	32+
Aida III	Nile Valley Hotels, 8 Midan Halkim, Azbakeya, T5900466, F5933466	92
Alexander the Great	Jolleys Travel & Tours, 8 Sh Talaat Harb, Cairo, T777340, F771670	60
Anni	Sheraton Corp, 5 Sh Shohadaa, Mohandessin, T3055600, F3051330	90
Aton	Address as above, T3055600, F3051330	80
Aurora	European Floating Hotels, 15 Sh Hassen Sabry, Cairo, T3406822, F3410432	42
Cairo	Shalakani Tours, 36a Sh Bahgal Ali, Zamalek, T3412346, F3412624	65
Cheops	International Co for Nile Cruising, 23b Sh Ismael Mohammed, Zamalek, T3400675, F3400706	80
Cheops III	Address as above	68
Citadelle	Sphinx Tours, 2 Behel Passage, Kasr El Nil, T3920704, F3920710	64
Cleopatra	Nile Cruising Co, 30 Sh Baghat Ali, Zamalek, T3416738, F3416739	47
Comfort I	Roward Tourism Co, 15 Sh Mahmoud Talaat, Dokki, T3613680, F3610023	68
Comfort II	Address as above	75
Coral II	Isis Tours Co, 48 Sh Giza, Dokki, T3499326, F3484821	73
Diamond Boat	Egyptian Italian Co, 15 Sh Hassan Sabri, Zamalek, T3406822, F3410432	75
Egelikia	23 Sh Ismail Mohammed, Zamalek, T3400676, F3409922	67
Florence	Florence St Maria Co, 2 Sh El Khalifa El Maamoun, Heliopolis, T4502327, F4503218	70
Giselle	Egypt Hotels, Midan Ramses, Cairo, T5892290, F3416187	60
Giza	Shalakani Tours, 36a Sh Bahgat Ali, Zamalek, T3412346, F3412624	60
Glorey	Inter Egypt Co, 10 Sh Syria, Mohandessin, T3606650, F3490194	55
Helio	Heliopolis Tours, 26a Anower, El Mofty, Nasr City, Cairo, T4837257	56
Horizon	Egyptian Cruise Lines, 21 Sh Giza, Nile Tower, Giza, T5701905, F5701210	105
Hotp	Sheraton Corp, 5 Sh Shohadaa, Mohandessin, Cairo, T3055600, F3051330	90

Boat	Operator/Owner	No of Cabins
Imperial	Travcotels, Sh Sharay El Gezira, Zamalek, T3414290, F3414541	43
Isis	Nile Hilton Hotel, Cairo, T777444, F5780393	48
Jasmin	Wing Tours, 21 El-Oboor Buildings, Sh Salah Salem, Cairo, T2618771, F2618297	62
Kasr el Nil	Cataract Nile Cruises, 26 Sh Adan, Mohandiseen, T3600863, F3613051	50
Lady Diana	Inter Nile, 61 Sh El Marghany, Heliopolis, T4177970, F4187099	60
Leonardo Da Vinci	Tatot Garranah Tours, 15 Sh Mahmoud Talaat, Giza, T3613680, F3610023	70
Le Scribe	Rey Vacances Travel, 229 Sh Pyramides, T5835557, F5835868	44
LTI Excelsior	Seti First Nile Cruises, 16 Ismail Mohammed, Zamalek, T3419820, F3402419	25
LTI Kira	Address as above	65
Marquis II	Song of Egypt Co, 32 Sh Riad, Mohandiseen, Giza, T3446658, F3025538	74
Miriam	Delta Nile Cruises, 21 Sh Oboor, Nasr City, T4016993, F4016989	96
Miss Egypt	N.T.S Cruises, 10 Sh Talaat Harb, T5741264, F770095	70
Miss Universe	Miss Universe Co, 18 Gamet el Dowal, Mohandiseen, T3470107	59
Monatasser I	Inter Travel, 122 Sh El Tahrir, Giza, T3606223, F3607133	76
Moon River	Silver Moon Nile Cruises, 20 Sh Mathal Zerae, Giza, T3602733, F3608630	50
Nephtis	Nile Hilton, Cairo, T777444, F5780393	60
Neptune	Trans Egypt Travel, 37 Sh Kasr El Nil, Cairo, T3924313, F3932118	52
Nile Admiral	Presidential Nile Cruises, 13 Sh Marasshi, Zamalek, T3400517, F3405272	78
Nile Beauty	Flotel Nile Cruises, 17 Sh Ahmad Heshmat, Zamalek, T3403748, F3400894	55
Nile Bride	Nile Bride Cruises, 150 Sh El Nil, Agouza, Giza, T3378459, F3378459	65
Nile Comodore	Presidential Nile Cruises, 13 Sh Maraashi, Zamalek, T3413423, F3405272	78
Nile Crocodile	Travel Ways Egypt, 41 Sh Abdel Khalek Sarat, Cairo, T3914554, F3928153	60
Nile Crown	Isis Nile Cruises, 48 Sh Giza, Dokki, T3499326, F3484821	59
Nile Elegant	Smart Tours, 8 Merry Land Building, Heliopolis, Cairo, T4521300, F4543650	65
Nile Emerald	Nile Sun Cuises, 1 Sh Gezirah El Wosta, Zamalek, T3405371, F3420735	72
Nile Empress	Travcotels, 112 26 Sh July, Zamalek, T3400959, F3403520	31

Boat	Operator/Owner	No of Cabins
Nile Jewel	*Nile Sun Cruises, 1 Sh Gezire El-Wosta, Zamalek, T3420735, F3420735*	*56*
Nile Legend	*Presidential Nile Cruises, 13 Sh Marasshi, Zamalek, T3400517, F3405272*	75
Nile Marquis	*Song of Egypt Co, 32 Sh Riad, Mohandiseesn, Giza, T3025625, F3025538*	74
Nile Monarch	*Travcotels, 112 Sh 26 July, Zamalek, T3400959, F3403520*	45
Nile Plaza	*Presidential Nile Cruises, 13 Sh Marasshi, Zamalek, T3402810, F3405272*	78
Nile Queen	*Sphinx Tours & Cruises, 2 Behle Passage, Kasr El Nil, Cairo, T3920704, F3920710*	50
Nile Ritz	*Presidential Nile Cruises, 13 Sh Marasshi, Zamalek, T3400517, F3405272*	78
Nile Romance	*Flotel Nile Cruises, 17 Sh Ahmad Heshmat, Zamalek, T3403748, F3400894*	35
Nile Sapphire	*Spring Tours, 3 Sh Sayed Bakri, Zamalek, T3415972, F34161877*	54
Nile Secret	*Address as above*	54
Nile Smart	*Memnon Nile Cruises, 49 Sh Nobar, Cairo, T3556711, F3556557*	65
Nile Spirit	*Address as above*	65
Nile Symphony	*Presidential Nile Cruises, 13 Sh Marasshi, Zamalek, T3400517, F3405272*	75
Nora	*Noratel Hotels & Tourism, 4 Sh Mehdi, Heliopolis, T2627348, F2627389*	74
Norma	*Egypt Hotels, Midan Ramses, Cairo, T5892290, F3416187*	60
Oberoi Philae	*Oberoi Investments, 6 Sh Pyramids, Giza, T3833222, F3837777*	58
Oberoi Shehrayar	*Oberoi Corporation, Mena House Hotel, Sh Ahram, Giza*	40
Oberoi Shehrazad	*Oberoi Corporation, Mena House Hotel, Sh Ahram, Giza*	69
Orchid	*Wing Tours, 14 El-Oboor Buildings, Sh Salah Salem, Cairo, T2618771, F2618297*	64
Osiris	*Nile Hilton Hotel, Cairo, T5780391, F5780393*	48
Papyrus	*Rey Vacances Travel, 48 Sh Mossadak, Dokki, T3614796, F3601912*	44
Prince Omar	*Zamalek Nile Cruises, 21 Sh Behgat Ali, Zamalek, T3407726, F3404072*	73
Princess Amira	*Cataract Cruises, 26 Sh Adan, Mohandessin, Zamalek, T3615240, F3600864*	67
Pyramisa Champollion I	*Pyramisa Hotels, 60 Sh Giza, Dokki, T3360791, F3360795*	51
Pyramisa Champollion II	*Address as above*	51
Pyramisa Vittoria	*Address as above*	67
Queen Isis	*Isis Tours Co, 48 Sh Giza, Dokki, T3499326, F3484421*	59
Queen Nefer	*Nefer Tours, 5 Sh Kasr El Nil, T5753225, F762878*	54

Boat	Operator/Owner	No of Cabins
Queen of Sheba	Salakamy & Naggar Tours, 195 Sh 26 July, Giza, T3933999, F3929795	76
Ra	Egyptian Co for Nile Cruises, 13 Sh Kasr El Nil, Cairo, T3403087, F3413230	72
Ra II	Address as above	83
Radamis	Movenpick Nile Cruises, Crocodile Island, Luxor, T2929681, F2929684	74
Ramses Egypt I	Nile Co for Tours & Floating Hotels, 195 Sh 26 July, Giza T3472205, F3462354	40
Ramses Egypt II	Address as above	62
Ramses Egypt III	Address as above	82
Ramses King of the Nile	Address as above	83
Regency	Tavcotels, 112 Sh 26 July, Zamalek, T3404890, F3403520	52
Regina	Address as above	63
Royale	Address as above	52
Royal Orchid	Nile Exploration Co, 21 Ahmed Heshmat, Zamalek, T3412052, F3417873	31
Royal Rhapsody	Address as above	31
Salacia	Trans Egypt Travel, 37 Sh Kasr El Nil, Cairo, T3924313, F3932118	57
Salome	Egypt Hotels, Midan Ramses, Cairo, T5892290, F3416187	40
Serenade	Inter Egypt Co, 10 Sh Syria, Mohandiseen, T3606650, F3490194	64
Sherry Boat	Sherry Nile Cruises, 33 Sh Abdel Khalek Sarwat, T3907221, F3917339	63
Seti III	Seti First Nile Cruises, 16 Ismail Mohammed, Zamalek, T3419820, F3402419	55
Seti the Great	Address as above	65
Sobek	Cataract Nile Cruises, 26 Sh Adan, Mohandiseen, T3615240, F3600864	48
Solaris I	Solaris Cruises, 6 Sh Kasr El Nil, T3356378, F3612782	62
Soleil	Five Star Travel, 49 Sh Mohey El Din Abu El Ezz, T3360244, F3360255	34
Sonesta Nile Goddess	Sonesta International, 4 Sh El-Tayaran, Nasr City, T2617100, F2628765	65
Sonesta Sun Goddess	Address as above	62
Spring I	Spring Tours, 3 Sh Sayed Bakri, Zamalek, T3415972, F3416187	42
Star of Luxor	Tarot Garranah Tours, 15 Sh Mahmoud Talaat, Cairo, T3613680, F3610023	55
Tarot	Address as above	70
Triton	Trans Egypt Travel, 37 Ksar El Nil, Cairo, T3924313, F3932118	20
Tut	Sheraton Corp, 5 Sh Shohadaa, Mohandiseen, T3055600, F3051330	80
Voyageur	Solaris Nile Cruisers, 2 Sh Abdel Azem Rashed, Dokki, T3193451, F2911182	64

Luxor to Aswan

🐦 Easy to recognize – The Pied Kingfisher

The Pied Kingfisher (Ceryle rudis) is very common in Egypt – wherever there is water. Like all kingfishers it is recognized by a larger than expected head with a rather insignificant crest, a long, sturdy, sharp beak and by its short tail and short legs. The Pied Kingfisher, 25 cm long, is found in both salt and fresh water. It is a superb diver, fishing from a hovering position over the water or from a perch on a convenient branch. The sexes are similar in sizes in colouring, being black and white – a white band over the eye reaching to the back of the head, a mottled crest, a white throat and neck. The back is mottled, the feathers being black with white edges. The wings are mainly black with a white central band. It has a white breast and under surface except for two black bands (only one black band on the female). It nests in holes in the river bank.

Kom Ombo

Phone code: 097
Colour map 4, grid B2

Kom Ombo was the ancient crossroads where the '40 Days Road' caravan route from western Sudan met the route from the eastern desert gold mines. It was also the site of the training ground for the war elephants used in the Ptolemaic army. It is 66 km south of Edfu and only about 40 km north of Aswan, and is a small East Bank town known today for its sugar refinery which processes the cane grown in the surrounding area. It is home for many of the Nubians who were displaced by the flooding which followed the construction of the Aswan High Dam. Most tourists stop here to visit the **Temple of Sobek and Horus**, which stands on the banks of the River Nile 4 km from the town.

To reach the temple, leave the service taxi to Aswan at the turnoff 2 km south of Kom Ombo town from where the signposted 'tembel' is only 1½ km away. In the town itself both buses and service taxis stop on the north-south Sharia 26th July but 300 m apart. Cheap pick-ups to the temple can be caught from behind the white mosque which is one block away from the Luxor-Aswan road on the east-west axis Sharia Gamhorriya. These days the vast majority of visitors arrive by coach or by cruise ships which dock on the river bank directly below the temple itself.

Sights **Kom Ombo Temple**, is the more usual name given to the small but beautiful **Temple of Sobek and Horus**. It faces the Nile at a bend in the river. The temple is unusual because it is dedicated to two gods rather than a single deity. Sobek was the crocodile god which, given the fact that the nearby sandbanks were a favourite basking ground for crocodiles until the construction of the Aswan Dam, was particularly appropriate. On its right hand side Sobek-Re, who is identified with the sun, his wife in another form of Hathor, and their moon-god son Khonsu are honoured. The left hand side is devoted to a form of Horus the Elder or Haroeris known as the 'Good doctor', his consort Ta-Sent-Nefer ('good sister') and his son Horus the Younger who was known as Pa-Heb-Tawy ('Lord of the Two Lands'). A healing cult developed and pilgrims who came to be cured would fast for a night in the temple precinct before participating in a complex ceremony with the priest of Horus in the heart of the temple.

The present temple, like many others along this stretch of the River Nile, is a Greco-Roman construction, built of sandstone. Ptolemy VI started the temple, Neo Dionysus oversaw most of the construction while Emperor Augustus added some of the finishing touches. Its proximity to the Nile was a mixed blessing because, while its silt assisted in preserving the building, the flood waters eroded the First Pylon and Forecourt which were falling into the Nile before they were strengthened by the Department of Antiquities in 1893.

Like so many others the temple lies on a north-south axis with the main entrance at the south end. In front of it to the west on the riverbank itself is the **Mamissi of Ptolemy VII** (180-145 BC) which has been virtually destroyed by flooding. To the east of the main temple is the **Gate of Neos Dionysus**, who is believed to have been Ptolemy XIII (88-51BC) and the father of Cleopatra, and the tiny two-room **Chapel of Hathor** which is now used to display mummified crocodiles found near the site.

With the Pylon and much of the **Forecourt** now destroyed by water erosion, one enters the main temple at the forecourt which was built by Tiberius (AD 14-37). Unfortunately only the stumps of the colourful columns, with a high-water mark clearly visible at about 2½ m, and a few pieces of its walls now remain. Continuing the theme from the rest of the temple the twin deities are divided so that the left-hand columns are dedicated to Horus the Elder and the right-hand ones to Sobek-Re. In the centre of the forecourt is the base of a huge square altar which is flanked by two granite basins set into the paving. On the column in the far corner (1) note the eye socket in the relief of Horus. Once this was inlayed for greater decoration. Behind this column, right in the corner (2), a staircase rose up to the roof level. At the north end is the double entrance of the **First Hypostyle Hall** with one door for each deity. On the left wall of which (3) Neos Dionysus undergoes the purification ritual overseen by Horus and on the right (4) the same ritual is overseen by Sobek. The capitals are brightly decorated with floral arrays while the bases are decorated with lilies. The reliefs on the lintel and door jambs show the Nile gods binding Upper and Lower Egypt together.

The five entrance columns and the 10 columns inside the Hypostyle Hall and its wall reliefs are attractively decorated and the curious mixture of the two deities continues. Part of the roof has survived on the east side of the Hall

Temple of Sobek & Horus at Kom Ombo

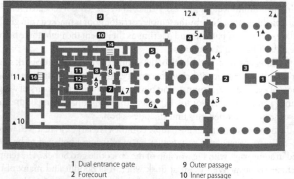

1 Dual entrance gate	9 Outer passage
2 Forecourt	10 Inner passage
3 Altar	11 Sanctuary of Sobek
4 First hypostyle hall	12 Secret chamber or
5 Second hypostyle hall	priest hole
6 Outer vestibule	13 Sanctuary of Haroeris
7 Middle vestibule	(Horus the Elder)
8 Inner vestibule	14 Stairs ▲ **Murals** see text

Luxor to Aswan

and flying vultures are clearly depicted on the ceiling (5). The rear walls leading to the older **Second** or **Inner Hypostyle Hall**, which has two entrances and 15 columns, five incorporated in the front wall, show Ptolemy VII holding hymnal texts before the Nile gods. Inside he is shown offering sacrifices to the god. The most striking relief is adjacent on the left of the north wall where Horus the Elder presents the *Hps*, the curved sword of victory to Ptolemy VII, while Cleopatra II and Cleopatra III, his wife and sister respectively, stand behind him (6).

This is then followed by three double **Entrance Vestibules**, each progressively smaller and higher than the last, also built by Ptolemy VII. The outer vestibule shows the goddess of writing Sheshat measuring the layout of the temple's foundations (7), while the middle chamber served as an **Offering Hall** to which only priests were allowed entrance. Look for the long list or calendar detailing the temple gods' various festivals, one for each day (9). Two small side rooms originally served as the Library for the sacred texts and the other as a vestry for the altar clothes and the priests' robes. As in Edfu, a staircase originally led to the now destroyed Chapel of the Disk on the roof.

The inner vestibule has two doors leading to the two separate **Sanctuaries of Horus and Sobek** and between the doors the gods give a Macedonian cloaked Ptolemy a notched palm branch from which the Heb Sed, or jubilee sign displaying the number of years of his reign, is suspended (9). Khonsu, who is wearing a blue crescent around a red disk, is followed by Horus in blue symbolizing the air, and Sobek in green representing the water. The sanctuaries, built by Ptolemy XIII (88-51BC), are in a bad state and are much smaller than those at Edfu. Within each was an altar upon which a portable shrine would have stood. Beneath the sanctuary are the crypts which are empty but, unusually, are open to the public.

A small secret chamber or priest hole lies between the two sanctuaries, in what would have appeared as a very thick wall. This chamber was connected to the small room behind and to a space above the altars.

On the inner wall of the outer corridor (10) is the first known illustration of instruments, including bone-saws, scalpels, suction caps and dental tools, which date from the second century AD. A seated figure of a god accepts these as offerings. While your guide may tell you that complicated operations were carried out 1,800 years ago it is most probable that these were instruments used in the mummification process. Adjacent to the left is a repeated relief of Isis on a birthing stool. Nearby the temple corridor floor is marked with graffiti which were drawn by patients and pilgrims as they spent the night there before the next day's healing ceremonies.

In the outer corridor, at the back of the temple (11), Horus and Sebek stand either side of a small niche/shrine now empty. Above and around are mystic symbols of eyes, ears and animals and birds each sporting four pairs of wings. Continue round the corridor to (12) where the traditional killing of the enemies scene, much eroded, this time includes a lion.

In the northwest corner of the temple complex is a large circular well which has a stairway, cistern and rectangular basin which are believed to be connected in some ways with the worship of the crocodile god Sobek. The temple is particularly attractive to visit at dusk when it is floodlit and many of the beautiful reliefs are shown at their best, especially in the first and second hypostyle halls. Taking a torch with you at this time of day is essential, however, because the floors are uneven and there are many small steps and depressions waiting to catch out the unwary and footweary traveller. ■ *Daily 0600-1800, E£10, students E£5, E£30 for commercial photography permit.*

The cheap and clean **F** *Cleopatra Hotel* is located near the service taxi depot on Sharia **Sleeping**
26th July.

Besides the small stalls which serve *'ful'* (beans) there is the cheap and clean *El-Noba* **Eating**
Restaurant just to the south of the white mosque on the main Luxor-Aswan road.

There is a small but colourful tourist bazaar in the street below the entrance to the temple. **Shopping**
Scarves seem to be the speciality here and bargaining with the stallholders tends to be a
more relaxed and good-natured experience as you travel further south towards Aswan.

Train: To Luxor and Aswan stop at Kom Ombo station just across the highway but **Transport**
only the very slow and crowded 2nd and 3rd class service.

Road Bus: north to Edfu, Esna and Luxor or south to Aswan, leave the bus terminal
on Sharia 26th July about 350 m south of Sharia Gumhorriya. **Service taxis**: north to
Edfu (1 hr) or south to Aswan (45 mins) can be caught from the terminal on Sharia 26
July just south of Sharia Gumhorriya.

Banks Next to the mosque, open Sun-Thu 0830-1400 but 1000-1330 during Ramadan. **Directory**

Aswan

Aswan, Egypt's southern frontier town, in its delightful river setting is the *Phone code: 097*
highlight of any Nile cruise. It is stunningly beautiful, charmingly romantic, *Colour map 4, grid B2*
and wonderfully relaxing, an escape from the over-commercialization of *Population: 350,000*
Luxor's hordes of tourists and vendors. This is the sunniest city in Egypt, *Altitude: 193 m*
hence the popularity. It is not too large to walk around in the cooler part of the
day, pace of life is slow and so relaxing. From the corniche, observe the tall
masted *feluccas* handled so masterfully by a tiny crew, listen to the Nubian
musicians. In the late evening watch the flocks of egrets skimming the surface
of the Nile as they go to roost, in the early morning watch the sun rise behind
the city and hear the call of the muezzin. Feast on freshly caught Nile fish.

Aswan's indigenous inhabitants are the ethnically, linguistically and culturally distinct **Nubians** who are undoubtedly African rather than Arab. Despite
being frequently invaded and con-
quered by their northern Egyptian
neighbours, the Nubians actually controlled Egypt during the 25th Dynasty
(747-656 BC). Cleopatra was a
Nubian from the modern-day Sudanese town of Wadi Halfa. Indeed, the
term Nubian is equally applicable to
the Sudanese who live along the Nile as
far south as Khartoum. The later
Nubian kingdom of Kush, whose capital was the Sudanese town of Merowe
and which included Aswan, remained
largely independent from Egypt. Having been the last region to adopt the
Christian faith Nubia became a sanctuary for Coptic Christians fleeing the
advance of Islam and it remains a
Christian stronghold today.

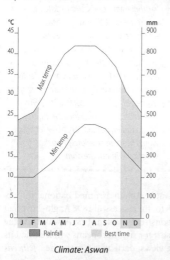

Climate: Aswan

Rainfall   Best time

°C / mm temperature and rainfall axes: Max temp, Min temp; J F M A M J J A S O N D

👉 **The Great Dams of Aswan**

*Although it has since become a cliché, the River Nile really is 'the lifeblood of Egypt' and the combination of a restricted area of agricultural land and an ever expanding population has necessitated the very careful management of what limited water is available. The theory behind the construction of the Aswan dams was that, rather than years of low water levels, drought and famine being followed by years when the Nile flooded and washed half the agricultural soil into the Mediterranean, the flow of the River Nile could be regulated and thereby provide a much more stable flow of water. Unfortunately, although the two dams did control the Nile waters and thereby boost both hydro-electric-power and agricultural production, the mushrooming population outstripped the gains and Egypt now imports almost half of its cereal requirements. At the same time it is now recognized that the **High Dam** was planned and built when the level of the River Nile was particularly high. Whether it is because of climatic change or simply part of an apparent 20-30 year cycle the volume of water reaching Aswan is decreasing and if the trend continues it may be necessary to pipe natural gas from the Gulf of Suez to generate the electricity at the giant 2,100 mw power station at Aswan.*

*The original **Aswan Dam** was built by the British between 1898-1902 and was then raised twice in 20 years to make it the largest dam in the world. Although no longer used for storage or irrigation the dam, which is crossed by the road to the airport, is now mainly used to provide local power. After the 1952 Revolution, the new leaders recognized that massive population pressure meant that a more radical solution was required both to control the waters of the River Nile and generate sufficient electricity for the new*

*industrial sector and bring power to every Egyptian village. To finance the construction of the planned **High Dam**, following the withdrawal of a World Bank loan under US pressure, Nasser nationalized the Suez Canal and persuaded the USSR to help build the dam. Construction started in 1960 and was completed in 1971 after Nasser's death in September 1970.*

*Although it took a number of years to fill, the most visible effect of the dam was the creation of **Lake Nasser** which, covering an area of about 6,000 sq km and being over 180 m deep in places, is the world's largest reservoir. This has enabled Egypt, unlike Sudan or Ethiopia, to save water during times of plenty and have an adequate strategic reserve for times of shortage. The extra water from the dam significantly increased the area of land under permanent irrigation and allowed over one million feddans (about 400,000 ha) of desert to be reclaimed. In addition, the extra electric power facilitated the expansion of the industrial sector not only around Aswan but throughout the country.*

There were, however, major environmental implications of the dam's construction because the rise of Lake Nasser flooded the homeland of the Nubians who were forced to migrate north to other towns and cities: to date they have been offered negligible compensation. Another drawback is that the lake accumulates the Nile's natural silt which used to fertilize the agricultural land downstream from Aswan. Consequently farmers in Lower Egypt are now having to rely heavily on chemical fertilizers which destabilizes the whole food chain. In view of its expanding population, however, Egypt would be in an absolutely hopeless situation without the dams.

For many centuries a sleepy backwater, Aswan assumed national importance when it became the headquarters for the successful 1898 Anglo-Egyptian re-conquest of Sudan. With the 1902 construction of the first **Aswan Dam** the town became a fashionable winter resort for rich Europeans who relished its dry heat, luxury hotels and stunning views, particularly from the *feluccas*

The Souq

The souq or bazaar economy of North Africa has distinctive characteristics. In Egypt a series of large souqs continues successfully to exist while bazaar economies elsewhere are faltering. In Egyptian cities as a whole, such as Aswan (see **Sharia Sa'ad Zaghloul**), Islamic ideas and traditional trading habits have remained strong.

The bazaar originally functioned as an integral part of the economic and political systems. Traditional activities in financing trade and social organizations were reinforced by the bazaar's successful role in running international commodity trade. The bazaar merchants' long-term raising of credits for funding property, agricultural and manufacturing activities was strengthened by this same trend.

There is a view among orientalists that there is an Egyptian/Islamic city of specific social structure and physical shape. The crafts, trades and goods were located by their 'clean' or 'unclean' status in an Islamic sense, and whether these goods could be sold close to the mosque or medersa. Valuable objects were on sale near to the main thoroughfares, with lesser trades needing more and cheaper land pushed to the edge of the bazaar. There was a concentration of similar crafts in specific locations within the bazaar so that all shoe-sellers for example were in the same street. These ground rules do not apply in all Egyptian bazaars but in many cases they are relevant in different combinations. Thus, there is a hierarchy of crafts, modified at times by social custom and Islamic practice, which gives highest priority to book making, perfumes, gold and silver jewellery over carpet selling and thence through a graded scale of commodities through metal work, ceramics, sale of agricultural goods and ultimately low grade crafts such as tanning and dyeing.

sailing on the River Nile at sunset. With the completion of the **Aswan High Dam** in 1970, the Nubian villages to the south of Aswan were submerged by the rising waters of Lake Nasser and many of those who were displaced joined in swelling the population of that ever expanding town. Despite the subsequent construction of a number of heavy industries in Aswan, to take advantage of the cheap hydro-electric power generated at the dam, the town has retained its attractive charm and relaxed atmosphere.

The railway station is at the north end of the town, about five minutes' walk from the Corniche where most of the tourist hotels are found. The inter-city taxi depot is nearby, just one block to the south of the railway station. The inter-city bus station is even more conveniently located in the town centre behind the Corniche on Sharia Abtal el-Tahrir and *feluccas* and cruise boats moor at many places along the Corniche. Aswan's desert airport is 24 km south of the town. There is no bus service connecting the airport and town. A hired taxi will cost about E£30 but bargain like mad.

Getting there

Sights

In the town itself, besides watching the beautiful sunset either from the **Corniche** or from the terrace of the **Old Cataract Hotel**, it is well worth visiting the exotic *souq* which, with the exception of Cairo, is probably the best in the country. Running parallel to the Corniche there are stalls selling food and a wide range of fresh produce, best bought in the morning, as well as jewellery, textiles and a host of oriental herbs and spices which are best bought after sunset.

The recently opened **Nubian Museum** which cost E£30 mn stands on a granite hill to the south of the town on the road to the airport. The construction is of sandstone and incorporates features of Nubian architecture. It covers an internal area of 7,000 sq m and and has an open air display of a further 50,000 sq m.

Luxor to Aswan

There are two storeys where 2,000 artefacts trace the area's history since early times and there is a promise of 1,000 more to be displayed. The colossal statue of Ramses, the remaining part of a temple at Gerf Hussein, dominates the entrance, a reminder of his positive presence in Nubia. There are 86 explanatory panels and a huge diorama. The displays include the oldest skeleton – unearthed in the southern area of Toshka. The pre-history cave depicts the first attempts at rock carvings and the use of tools. Here the animals portrayed include elephant and giraffe. The Pharaonic period demonstrates the importance of this region to the rulers of Egypt, it being the gateway to the south and thus an important routeway. There are sections devoted to the Graeco-Roman, Coptic and Islamic influences to irrigation, and the UNESCO project to save the monuments.

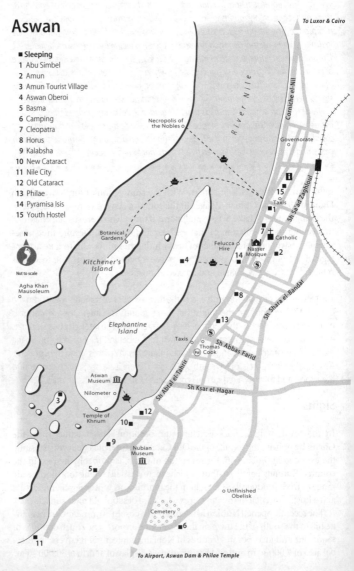

Aswan

■ **Sleeping**
1 Abu Simbel
2 Amun
3 Amun Tourist Village
4 Aswan Oberoi
5 Basma
6 Camping
7 Cleopatra
8 Horus
9 Kalabsha
10 New Cataract
11 Nile City
12 Old Cataract
13 Philae
14 Pyramisa Isis
15 Youth Hostel

To Luxor & Cairo

River Nile

Corniche el-Nil

Necropolis of the Nobles

Governorate

Taxis

Catholic

Felucca Hire

Nasser Mosque

Sh Sa'ad Zaghloul

N
Not to scale

Botanical Gardens

Kitchener's Island

Agha Khan Mausoleum

Elephantine Island

Sh Shara el-Bandar

Taxis

Thomas Cook

Sh Abbas Farid

Aswan Museum

Nilometer

Sh Abtai el-Tahtit

Sh Ksar el-Hagar

Temple of Khnum

Nubian Museum

Unfinished Obelisk

Cemetery

To Airport, Aswan Dam & Philae Temple

The colourful exhibition of the folk heritage emphasizes the individuality of Nubian culture. The most common crafts are pottery and the weaving of baskets and mats from palm fronds. Hand weaving is less well developed.

Outside, the features in the garden can be translated into the journey of the River Nile across desert and cataracts – bringing life to Egypt.

■ *0900-1300 and 1700-2100. E£30, students E£15. No photography permitted. As yet no guide book has been produced.*

Opposite the Corniche and only a short ferry ride away in the middle of the Nile is **Elephantine Island**. Measuring 2 km long and 500 m at its widest point the island which gets its name from the large black rocks off its south tip which look, perhaps, like bathing elephants, is worth visiting. Public ferries run every 15 minutes between 0600-2400 from the landing dock opposite the EgyptAir office and dock just next to the island's **Aswan Museum**, like the *feluccas* which can be hired at negotiable rates (see Transport below). **NB** The free ferry to the *Aswan Oberoi Hotel* does not give access to the rest of the island.

The region's first inhabitants lived on this island long before Aswan itself was occupied. It was reputed to be the home of Hapy, the god of the Nile flood, and the goddess of fertility Satet, who were both locally revered, and the regional god Khnum, who was represented by a ram's head. The **Temple of Khnum** (30th Dynasty) once accounted for over two-thirds of the island's 2 sq km fortress town of **Yebu**, the word for both elephant and ivory in ancient Egyptian and which for centuries was the main trade and security border post between Egypt and Nubia. The ruined temple, at the south end of the island boasts a gateway portraying Alexander II worshipping Khnum which suggests that the Greeks added to this temple complex. The German Archeology Institute are at present excavating the region round the Temple of Khnum and while visits are not permitted there is plenty to see from the sidelines. The island has a number of less impressive ruins, and temples have been built here for 4 millennia. Make time when visiting this site to take advantage of an outstanding high viewpoint from which to enjoy the beautiful panorama of the Aswan corniche to the east, including the picturesque *Old Cataract Hotel*, the islands and the River Nile itself. To the west the **Aga Khan Mausoleum** (see page 295) is clearly visible and to the south, look for the pink fronted *Hotel Amun* set on its own island amongst palm trees and exotic gardens.

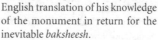

You will be unlikely to visit the ruins of the Temple of Khnum without being intercepted by a local 'custodian' anxious to impart a severely limited English translation of his knowledge of the monument in return for the inevitable *baksheesh*.

The **Roman Nilometer** is reached by taking the pathway southwards to the left of the museum entrance. This fascinating device, rediscovered on the southeast tip of Elephantine Island in 1822, was designed to measure the height of the annual River Nile flood. This enabled the coming season's potential crop yield to be estimated and the level of crop taxation to be fixed. Besides Roman and very faint pharaonic numerals, there are also more recent tablets inscribed in both French and Arabic, on the 90 walled stairs which lead down to a riverside shaft.

Nilometer

Luxor to Aswan

The **Aswan Museum**, was established in order to display relics salvaged from the flooded areas behind the Aswan dams, which is ironic because the villa and gardens originally belonged to Sir William Willcocks, the designer of the first Aswan Dam. Its brief was subsequently expanded to act as a museum of the region's heritage. It offers a spread of exhibits of phaoronic material, Roman and Islamic pottery, jewellery, and funerary artefacts. The arrangement is logical and names are clear. When the Nubian material is transferrred to the newly open Nubian museum there will space to display the wealth of material found on Elephantine island itself. The ground floor is arranged in chronological order with items from the Middle and New kingdoms, including pottery, combs and some jewellery, while the basement displays a series of human and animal mummies and an impressive gold sheathed statue of Khnum. ■*Daily winter 0800-1700, summer 0800-1800, E£10, students E£5 and E£15 for camera. Price includes entrance to the museum, view of ruins and walk down steps of the nilometer.*

Besides the museum, Nilometer and temple ruins in the south and the *Aswan Oberoi Hotel* in the north, there are also three small typical **Nubian villages** in the middle of Elephantine Island. Although it is suggested that the villagers prefer not to become a tourist attraction, visits are organized for foreigners including hospitality in the houses.

Kitchener's Island which lies north of the larger Elephantine Island, originally known as the 'Island of Plants' has a magnificent **Botanical Garden**. The beautiful island was presented to Lord Kitchener, who had a passion for exotic plants and flowers from around the world, in gratitude for his successful Sudan campaign and the gardens have been maintained in their original style. The atmosphere on the island, which is almost completely shielded from the bustle of Aswan by Elephantine Island, is very relaxed and its lush vegetation, animals and birds make it an ideal place to watch the sunset. There is an expensive café at the south end of the island. ■ *Daily from 0800 until sunset, E£10. Can be reached by felucca, start bargaining at E£5 return. The local motorized ferry boat is a bargain. It costs E£1 each way and the company is much more interesting.*

Related map
Aswan, page 292

Aswan environs

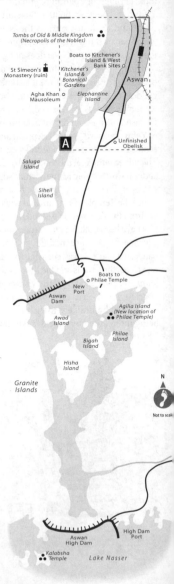

Tombs of Old & Middle Kingdom (Necropolis of the Nobles)

St Simeon's Monastery (ruin)

Boats to Kitchener's Island & West Bank Sites

Kitchener's Island & Botanical Gardens

Aswan

Agha Khan Mausoleum

Elephantine Island

A

Unfinished Obelisk

Saluga Island

Siheil Island

Boats to Philae Temple

Aswan Dam

New Port

Awad Island

Agilia Island (New location of Philae Temple)

Bigah Island

Philae Island

Hisha Island

Granite Islands

N

Not to scale

Aswan High Dam

High Dam Port

Kalabsha Temple

Lake Nasser

Luxor to Aswan

The beautiful **Agha Khan Mausoleum**, which is situated on a hill on the West Bank of the River Nile opposite the town, was built of solid marble for the 3rd Agha Khan (1877-1957) who was the 48th Imam of the Ismaili sect of Shi'a Muslims. He was renowned for his wealth and was given his body-weight in jewels by his followers for his 1945 diamond jubilee. As an adult he visited Aswan every winter for its therapeutic climate, having fallen in love with its beauty and built a villa on the West Bank. His widow, who still lives in the villa every winter, erected the mausoleum on the barren hill above the villa. Its is a brilliant white marble building, closely resembling a miniature version of the Fatimids' mausoleums in Cairo, with virtually the only hint of colour the fresh red rose placed daily on the sarcophagus. Outside, the views of the desert and of Aswan across the Nile are particularly breathtaking at sunset. Unfortunately lack of respect was shown to this monument and it is now closed to the public.

The **Necropolis of the Nobles** at Qubbet al-Hawwa (dome of the wind) is located further north along the West Bank of the River Nile, west being the world of the dead and east the world of the living. The necropolis is illuminated at night by hidden spotlights, magnificent when viewed from the Aswan side of the River Nile. The riverside cliff is lined with tombs from various periods which have been discovered during the last century. ■ *These tombs, open from 0800-1600, E£12, camera E£5, can be reached by ferries, E£1 return, from the Corniche near Seti Tours which run every 30 minutes from 0600-1800 and every hour from 1800-2100.*

Just above the water-line are the Roman tombs, a little higher are earlier ones and in the highest more durable rock are those of the Old and Middle kingdoms. The ceremonial stairways from the river bank to the tomb entrances can be easily seen, but this is not now the access. The majority of the dead are believed to have been priests or officials responsible for water transport between Egypt and Nubia. ■ *Daily between 0700-1700 in summer and 0700-1600 in winter. E£12, students E£6, camera E£5, video camera E£30. The ticket office is above the ferry landing. Wear a strong pair of shoes and take a torch. There is a guide on duty to show the way, unlock the tombs and turn on the electric lights. His services are part of the entry fee but a small tip is recommended.* Most tours begin at the southern end with the tombs of Mekhu and Sabni. Take care in negotiating the terrace from which the rock-cut tombs were mined since the going is uneven and stands above a steep drop. Most of the tombs are numbered in ascending order from south to north with the more interesting ones including the following:

Mekhu (No 25) was a chief overseer in Upper Egypt at the time of the sixth Dynasty and was killed while on official duties. His son **Sabni** mounted an expedition to reclaim his father's body and successfully returned to Aswan to give **Mekhu** a ceremonial burial. The tomb of **Mekhu** comprises two chambers, a narrow antechamber roughly decorated with family and farming scenes (1 and 2). The main chamber is cut out of solid rock leaving 18 slightly tapering columns, themselves decorated with reliefs of the family and fragments of other funeral scenes. The inner wall to the left carries a series of false doors inscribed to **Mekhu**. There is an offering table in the middle of this main chamber.

Also accessed from here (the original entry is blocked) is a memorial to **Sabni** (No 26) son of Mekhu. To the right of the main chamber is a large false door and a depiction of fishing and fowling from river craft.

Sarenput II (No 31), who was governor or Guardian of the South at the height of the Middle Kingdom, has the largest, most elaborate and best

Tomb-temple of Mekhu & Sabni

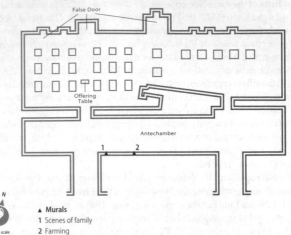

False Door

Offering Table

Antechamber

▲ Murals
1 Scenes of family
2 Farming

N

Not to scale

preserved tomb in this necropolis. It is well lit and comprises two axial chambers, linked by a corridor with niches. The first hall is rectangular with six rock-cut pillars and a small granite offering table. The ceiling is decorated and there is a distinctive stripped, coloured door lintel. Steps lead to a narrow connecting corridor which has six niches with statues of **Sarenput II**. In the inner chamber there are four pillars with the deceased represented on the inward facing sides of each. A niche at the head of the tomb is surrounded by depictions of **Sarenput** and his family. In a small recess at the rear of the tomb there is an elaborate relief portraying him with his wife, son and mother in a beautiful garden.

Harkhuf (alongside No 32) This tomb has no artificial lighting. He was Guardian of southern Egypt and a royal registrar in the sixth Dynasty. He achieved great fame as a noble of Elephantine and leader of diplomatic/military expeditions in the south and west of Aswan. His tomb-temple is modest, being made up of a (now) open entrance area with a doorway centrally placed. On this entrance wall to the main chamber is (right hand side) remains of a verbatim copy of a letter from Pepi II commending **Harkhuf** and (around the doorway) offering scenes. Inside there is a small rock-cut chamber with four columns, inner faces of which carry pictures of the deceased and biographical texts. On the inner wall there are two niches, the left hand

Tomb-temple of Sarenput II

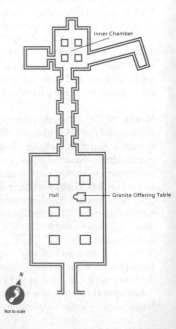

Inner Chamber

Hall

Granite Offering Table

N

Not to scale

side one with a false door bearing offering scenes and the right hand side a false door/painted stela below which is a small offering table. An inclined shaft leads to the burial chamber, while to the left hand side is a second passage, thought to have been used for a later burial.

The tomb-temple of **Pepinakht**, which lies adjacent to that of **Harkhuf** is currently closed while a German excavation is in progress.

Sarenput I (No 36), the grandfather of Sarenput II in No 31, was both Guardian of the South and also the overseer of the priests of Khnum and Satet during the 12th Dynasty (1991-1786 BC). The tomb is one of the largest consisting of three major chambers with joining corridors, but unfortunately the reliefs are badly decayed. The tomb-temple is well lit. Enter through a doorway decorated with excellent reliefs carved on polished limestone, on either side of the doorway are damaged depictions of a seated **Sarenput I**. Pass into an antechamber with six columns in a line close to the inner wall, which originally carried a finely decorated portico. On the right column there are carvings on all faces of a like picture of **Prince Sarenput I**. There are small niches in the side walls of this antechamber which contain representations of **Sarenput I** and his wife. The inner wall carries important scenes in good condition. On the left is a scene of the deceased spearing fish, his wife clutching him, apparently lest he fall and his son on the adjacent bank. Above are farming scenes with oxen. On the right of the inner wall are pictures of **Sarenput**, his wife, mother and family. An inner hall is entered through a narrow doorway, a modest room with four pillars. The pillar decorations have almost vanished in this room and the paintings on the plaster work of the walls have also all but disappeared. Fragments show scenes of fowling, boating and women at work. A narrow corridor has been cut into the west wall rising a little to the small burial chamber with two columns. In this room is a niche and shrine for **Sarenput I**. Two breaks in the rock in the walls of this chamber have no access.

To the north of these tombs is a separate tomb-temple, **Ka-Gem-Em-Ahu**, reached by a sandy path. **Ka-Gem-Em-Ahu** was the high priest of Khnum in the late New Empire. His tomb was discovered by Lady William Cecil in 1902. The outer courtyard measures 10 m wide with a depth of some 7 m. Most of the plaster work has been lost from this six-pillared area but scenes of boats on the Nile can still be made out with one or two residual depictions of funeral scenes such as the weighing of the heart. The main tomb chamber is 7 m square with a low entrance doorway and four pillars. The ceiling is quite ornately decorated with flowers, birds and geometric designs. Although the walls of the main chamber are quite plain, the left hand side inner pillar carries painted plaster with a representation of the deceased and his wife. A sloping passage leads from the main chamber to the burial chamber below which is difficult to access.

The ruined desert **Monastery of St Simeon**, which lies on the West Bank inland from the Agha Khan's Mausoleum, was founded and dedicated in the seventh century to a fourth century monk Anba Hadra,

Tomb-temple of Sarenput I

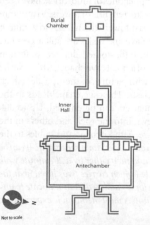

Burial Chamber

Inner Hall

Antechamber

Not to scale

David Roberts – painter of Egypt

David Roberts was a remarkable man whose oriental paintings brought to life Egypt and its heritage for many people in the Western world. His pictures are full of atmosphere and wonderful colour. Among the most famous are the **Temple of Dendera, Island of Philae, Nubia** and **A Street in Cairo** together with his paintings of the **Temple of Ramses II** at Abu Simbel.

Roberts, born in 1796, had a difficult childhood as the son of an impecunious Edinburgh (Stockbridge) cobbler. He eventually became known as a painter of theatrical scenery at the Old Vic and Covent Garden before making his name as a picture painter with items such as **The Israelites leaving Egypt** and scenes of his travels in Spain.

David Roberts arrived in Egypt in 1838 and spent 11 months travelling through the Nile Valley and visiting the Holy Land.

He was a prolific sketcher of sites and left six volumes of lithographs of this visit, including several scenes of Cairo where he terminated his Egyptian travels. Many of these and other scenes were later translated into oil paintings. Roberts returned to Great Britain where, in his absence, he had been made an associate of the Royal Academy. He lived to 69 years and produced many masterpieces based on his travels in Egypt, incidentally providing a wonderful record of the state of Egyptian monuments of the time.

There are many inexpensive cards and books with copies of his illustrations. It is certainly useful to have these with you when visiting the major sites as they show very clearly parts that have disappeared, parts that are now too high to view easily and give an excellent idea of the coloured decorations.

who was later ordained bishop. The monastery was rebuilt in the 10th century. The internal decorations are of interest.

Following an encounter with a funeral procession on the day after his own wedding Simeon decided, presumably without consulting his wife, to remain celibate. He became a student of St Balmar, rejected urban life and chose to become a desert hermit. The fortress monastery stands at the head of a desert valley looking towards the River Nile and from where the dramatic sunsets appears to turn the sand to flames. Until Salah al-Din destroyed the building in 1173 it was used by monks, including Saint Simeon about whom very little else is known, as a base for proselytizing expeditions first south into Nubia and then, after the Muslim conquest, north into Egypt.

Although the monastery is uninhabitable its main feature the surrounding walls, the lower storeys of hewn stone and upper ones of mud-brick, have been preserved. At intervals along the walls there are remains of towers. Visitors are admitted through a small gateway in the east tower which leads to a church with a partially collapsed basilica but the nave and aisles are still accessible. There is a painting of the ascended Christ near the domed altar recess. By him are four angels in splendid robes. The walls of a small cave chapel, which can be entered via the church, are richly painted with pictures of the Apostles which were partially defaced by Muslim iconoclasts. The cave chapel leads to the upper enclosure from which the living quarters can be entered. Up to 300 monks lived in simple cells with some hewn into the rock and others in the main building to the north of the enclosure, with kitchens and stables to the south. ■ *Daily from 0900-1600, E£5. Pay around E£25 for a return trip. It can be reached by felucca (E£30 wait and return) and then either by a 20-minute walk through soft sand or a 10-minute camel ride (which carries two) hired near the landing stage. The guide here is well known for his ability to communicate to any nationality as he practically mimes his account. A most memorable experience in its own right.*

Fishing on Lake Nasser – an old sport in a new area

Lake Nasser is the result of flooding 496 km of the Nile valley with the construction of the Aswan Dam. There are over 6,000 sq km of lake here to fish in – enough space for all. There are 32 species of fish in the lake. The two most popular sport fish are Nile perch and Tiger fish.

Nile perch (Lates niloticus) are found in the River Nile and other rivers in Africa, but grow to their greatest size in large bodies of water like Lake Nasser. They are large mouthed fish, green/brown above and silver below. They have an elongated body, a protruding lower jaw, a round tail and two dorsal fins. They are one of the largest freshwater fish in the world and can be over 1.9 m in length and 1.5 m in girth. The record catch in Lake Nasser is a massive 176 kg.

The most common of the **Tiger fish** caught is Hydrocynus forskaalii. They have dagger teeth that protrude when the mouth is closed. They resemble a tiger in appearance with several lengthwise stripes and resemble a tiger in habit being swift and voracious. They can grow to 5.5 kg.

Catfish are represented by 18 different species in the lake but the two of interest to anglers are Bagrus and Vundu of which the largest caught in Lake Nasser to date is 34 kg.

There are two species of **Tilapia**.

The main methods of fishing are: trolling – restricted on safari to six hours a day which covers a wide area and can result in a bigger catch of bigger fish or spinning or fly fishing from the shore, generally in the cool of the morning, which is a delight and a challenge as it requires more skill as well as a strong line and heavy duty gloves.

All fishing on Lake Nasser is on a catch and release policy, except those needed for the evening meal. Conservation is very important.

Back on the East Bank of the Nile on the outskirts of Aswan about 2 km along the highway south, is the **Unfinished Obelisk**, in the quarries which provided red granite for the ancient temples. The huge obelisk, which would have weighed 1,168 tonnes and stood over 41 m high, was abandoned before any designs were carved when a major flaw was discovered in the granite. It was originally intended to form a pair with the **Lateran Obelisk**, the world's tallest obelisk which once stood in the Temple of Tuthmosis III at Karnak but is now in Rome. When it was discovered in the quarry by Rex Engelbach in 1922 the unfinished obelisk shed light on pharaonic quarrying methods, including the soaking of wooden wedges to open fissures, but shaping and transporting them remains an astounding feat. For those having seen the other wonders of ancient Egypt the Unfinished Obelisk, is a little disappointing and it is probably better combining it with a trip to the Aswan Dams or the Philae Temple. ■ *Daily 0600-1800, E£10, students E£5. Hire a taxi to the High Dam for E£35.*

There are in fact two **Aswan Dams** but it is the so-called High Dam, just upstream from the original 1902 British-built Aswan Dam, that is Egypt's pride and joy and which created Lake Nasser, the world's largest reservoir. In fact the High Dam is so big – 111 m high, 3,830 m long, 980 m wide at its base and 40 m at its top – that it is almost impossible to realize its scale except from the observation deck of the lotus-shaped Soviet-Egyptian Friendship tower or from the air when landing at nearby Aswan airport. It is claimed that the structure of stones, sand, clay and facing concrete give it a volume 17 times that of the Pyramid of Cheops. To help appreciate the scale and consequences of the dam's construction the visitors' pavilion, which includes a 15 m high model of

☞ What colour is a camel?

With a deal of imagination it is possible to distinguish five different colours of camel. The white camel is the most beautiful and the most expensive as it is claimed to be the fastest runner. The yellow version is second best – and slightly cheaper. Looking for a solid, dependable beast to carry the baggage – choose red. A blue camel which is really black but is called blue to avoid the problems of the evil eye is not high in the popularity stakes. A creature which is a mixture of white, red, yellow and black is just another unfortunate beast of burden.

the dam and photographs of the relocation of the Abu Simbel temple, is worth a visit. Occasionally, crossing the dam is prevented for security reasons. The contrast, however, between the view of the narrow river channel looking towards Aswan on the downstream side of the dam and the vast area of Lake Nasser, almost like an open sea, as you look upstream could not be more marked. ■ *It costs E£5 per person to cross the High Dam between 0700-1700 and it may be necessary to show your passport to prove that you are not an Israeli spy. Photography of the snap-shot variety is permitted, but the use of video recorders is prohibited for security reasons. A taxi here from Aswan will cost E£40 return.*

For many tourists the most beautiful and romantic monuments in Aswan, if not in the whole of Egypt, are the **Philae Temples** which were built in the Ptolemaic era (332-30 BC) as an offering to Isis. In fact, the **Temple of Isis** and the rest of the monuments were moved to the neighbouring Agilkia island by UNESCO in 1972-1980 when the construction of the High Dam threatened to submerge Philae forever. They were then reconstructed to imitate the original as closely as possible but the new position no longer faces neighbouring Bigah island, one of the burial sites of Osiris and closed to all but the priesthood, which was the whole raison d'être for the Temple of Isis being on Philae island in the first place.

Although it is possible to catch a bus and then walk 2 km to the lakeside motorboat dock, unless on a organized tour the island is most easily reached by taking a E£10 taxi ride from Aswan to the dock and a motorboat across to the island. They seat eight people and cost E£3 per person or E£20 per boat for the return journey including a one-hour wait at the temple although 1½ hours is preferable. ■ *Summer 0700-1700; winter 0700-1600. E£20, students E£10, permit for commercial photography E£10. There is no charge for video recorders.*

Although there are other smaller temples on the island it is dominated by the **Temple of Isis (8)**. She was the consort of her brother Osiris and eventually became the 'Great Mother of All Gods and Nature', 'Goddess of Ten Thousand Names', and represented women, purity and sexuality. Isis is attributed with reconstructing Osiris' dismembered body and creating his son Horus who became the model of a man and king. In the 3rd-5th century the worship of Isis became Christianity's greatest rival throughout the Mediterranean. There have even been claims that the early Christians developed the cult of the Virgin Mary to replace Isis in order to attract new converts.

Different parts of the Temple of Isis, which occupies over a quarter of the new island, were constructed over an 800 years period by Ptolemaic (332-30 BC) and Roman (30 BC-AD 395) rulers. At the top of the steps where the motorboats arrive is the Kiosk of Nectanebo (1). From here runs a Roman colonnaded Outer Court which leads to the main temple. Its irregular shape gives the impression of greater length. On the west or lake side of the court the **Colonnade of Augustus and Tiberius (3)** is well preserved and contains 31

Temples of Philae, Agilkia Island

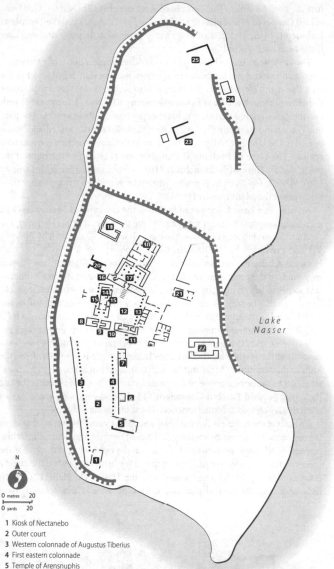

Lake
Nasser

0 metres 20
0 yards 20

1 Kiosk of Nectanebo
2 Outer court
3 Western colonnade of Augustus Tiberius
4 First eastern colonnade
5 Temple of Arensnuphis
6 Chapel of Mandulis
7 Temple of Imhotep

Temple of Isis
8 First pylon (Ptolemy XIII, Neo Dionysus)
9 Entrance to mammisi
10 Gate of Nectanebo II
11 Gate of Ptolemy II, Philadelphus
12 Inner court
13 Second eastern colonnade

14 Mammisi (birth house)
15 Composite columns
   with Hathor's heads
16 Second pylon
17 Hypostyle hall
18 Inner sanctuary

19 Temple of Harendotes
20 Hadrian's Gate
21 Temple of Hathor
22 Roman Kiosk of Trajan
23 Temple of Augustus
24 Roman arch
25 Gate of Diocletian

columns with individual capitals, plant shaped – papyrus in various stages of bud. There are still traces of paint on some of the columns and the starred ceiling. On the right is the plainer **First Eastern Colonnade (4)** behind which are first the foundations of the **Temple of Arensnuphis (5)** (Nubian God), the ruined **Chapel of Mandulis (6)** (Nubian God of Kalabsha) and the **Temple of Imhotep (7)** (the architect of Zoser's step pyramid at Saqqara who was later deified as a healing God).

The Temple of Isis The irregular plan of the temple is due to the terrain. A huge granite intrusion has been incorporated into the right hand tower of the First Pylon and steps to this pylon are also to accommodate hard rock. Enter the temple through the **First Pylon of Ptolemy XIII Neos Dionysus (8)** with illustrations showing him slaying his enemies as Isis, Horus and Hathor look on. The pylon was originally flanked by two obelisks, since looted and transported to the UK, but today only two lions at the base guarding the entrance remain. The **Gate of Ptolemy II Philadelphus (11)**, just to the right of the pylon's main **Gate of Nectanebo II (10)**, is from the earlier 30th Dynasty (380-343BC). On its right is graffiti written by Napoleon's troops after their victory over the Mamlukes in 1799.

Arriving in a large forecourt to the left is the colonnaded **Mammisi (14)**, used for mammisi rituals. It was placed here to the west of and between the First and Second Pylons due to lack of space. It was originally built by Ptolemy VII and expanded by the Romans which explains why images of Isis with Horus as a baby are intermingled with the figures of contemporary Roman emperors. In the inner sanctum of the Mammisi itself are historically important scenes of Isis giving birth to Horus in the marshes and others of her suckling the child-pharaoh. A curiosity to note on the outer western wall of the birth house is a memorial to men of the Heavy Camel Regiment who lost their lives in the Sudanese Campaign of 1884-85. The tablet commemorates the nine officers and 92 men who were killed in action or died of disease. Look carefully at the Hathor headed columns facing into the Inner Court from the walls of the Mammisi. At far end her face is straight but at the near end she is smiling. On the opposite side of the forecourt from the Birth House is the late Ptolemaic **Second Eastern Colonnade (13)** behind which are a number of attractive reliefs and six small function rooms including a library.

The axis of the temple is changed by the **Second Pylon (16)**, set at an angle to the first, which was built by Ptolemy XIII Neos Dionysos and which shows him presenting offerings to Horus and Hathor on the right tower but some of the scenes on the left tower were defaced by the early Christians. Beyond the Pylon a court containing 10 columns opens onto the **Hypostyle Hall (17)**, much reduced in size for normal plan due to lack of space. These columns have

Temple of Isis –
Philae

Worship of the Nile crocodile – Crocodylus niloticus

These huge creatures, the largest reptile in Africa, were worshipped as the god Sobek (see page 217) depicted as a man with a crocodile's head. The Ancient Egyptians kept them in lakes by the temples which were dedicated to Crocodile gods (see page 166) and fed them the best meat, geese and fish and even wine. Special creatures were decked with jewels, earrings, gold bracelets and necklaces. The bodies were embalmed after death. (Some crocodiles live for 100 years). Really they were very ugly creatures to be held in such high esteem. It is suggested that they were worshipped out of fear, in the hopes that offerings and prayers would make them less vicious and reduce the dangers to man and beast.

The problem was these cold blooded creatures needed to come out of the river to bask in the sunshine and they could move at a surprising speed on land. They could stay almost submerged for long periods. The long muscular tail was used as a rudder and on land could be used to fell large animals at a single blow. Small humans were easy prey.

In other regions they were hunted, eaten and considered a protector as they prevented anyone from swimming across the River Nile.

It is fortunate that today these 900 kg creatures can no longer reach the major part of Egypt. They cannot pass the Aswan dam but they exist to the south of this barrier in large numbers.

retained few traces of their original colour although the capitals are better preserved. The ceiling in the central aisle has representations of vultures which were symbolic of the union of Lower and Upper Egypt. The rest of the ceilings have astronomical motifs and two representations of the goddess Nut. On either side of the wall, backing onto the Second Pylon, Ptolemy VII and Cleopatra II can be seen presenting offerings to Hathor and Khnum. The crosses carved on pillars and walls here provide evidence of the Coptic occupation. From the entrance at the far end of the Hypostyle Hall is a chamber which gives access to the roof. The interconnecting roof chambers are all dedicated to Osiris and lead to his shrine. Vivid reliefs portray the reconstruction of his body.

Continuing upwards and north from the chamber, linked to the Hypostyle Hall, are three rooms decorated with sacrificial reliefs representing the deities. The central room leads to a further three rooms linked to the **Sanctuary (18)** in which is a stone pedestal dedicated by Ptolemy III which formerly supported the holy barque (boat) of Isis. Reliefs portray Isis and her son surrounded by Nubian deities. The temple's exterior was decorated at the direction of the Emperor Augustus.

Hadrian's Gate (20), which is west of the Second Pylon, has some very interesting reliefs. The north wall on the right depicts Isis, Nephthys, Horus and Amun in adoration before Osiris in the form of a bird. Behind is the source of the Nile which is depicted emerging from a cavern and Hapy, a Nile god, in human form with a head dress of papyrus is shown pouring water from two jars, indicating the Egyptians' knowledge that the Nile had more than one source. Hapy is crouched in a rocky aperture (encircled by a serpent) under huge boulders representing cliffs, indicating that this is the first cataract. The south wall depicts a mummified Osiris lying on a crocodile together with another image of the reconstructed Osiris seated on his throne with his son Horus.

Smaller shrines can be seen throughout the island dedicated to both Nubian and local deities. East of the temple of Isis is the small **Temple of Hathor (21)**. Two columns depict the head of Hathor at their capital while, in a famous relief, the local deities play musical instruments. Much of the later additions to the buildings on Philae were Roman due to its position as a border post, ie

Luxor to Aswan

extension of walls, huge gates, kiosks. The **Kiosk of Trajan (22)**, built in AD 167, further south has 14 columns with floral motifs and stone plaques on the lintels which were intended to hold sun discs. It was never completed. Only two walls have been decorated and these depict Osiris, Horus and Isis receiving offerings from the Emperor Trajan. It is thought that the Kiosk originally had a wooden roof. From here looking southeast towards the original Philae Island it is possible to see the remains of the coffer dam which was built around it to reduce the water level and protect the temple ruins before they were moved to Agilkia. At the northeast end of the island is the ruined **Temple of Augustus (23)** and the **Gate of Diocletian (25)** which were next to a mud brick Roman village which was abandoned by the archaeologists when Philae was moved because the water had already caused such severe erosion.

Although it is wonderful to visit Philae in the late afternoon, when the light is most attractive, many tourists attend the **Sound and Light Show** which involves a 1 hour floodlit tour through the ruins. As in Karnak and the Cairo Pyramids the visual beauty of the place is more impressive than the historically informative but melodramatic soundtrack. This visit to the temple at sunset in time for the first evening show can be especially memorable. Travelling out from the harbour in a small flotilla of boats, watching the stars come out and tracing the dark shapes of the islands in the river silhouetted against the orange sunset sky is a stunning prelude to the beauty of the ancient floodlit ruins. Tour companies, (see below) obviously keen to sell you a package deal including transport to and from the show, can provide full details of the times of each show which is in a different language. ■ *Inclusive charge from Aswan E£50. Go as an individual, tickets E£33 but boat transfer extra.*

Sound and Light Shows daily at 2000, 2115 and 2230 in summer (end April-end September) and 1800, 1915 and 2030 in winter as follows:

Mon:English/French; **Tue**:French/English/French; **Wed**:French/English; **Thu**:French/Arabic/Spanish; **Fri**:English/French; **Sat**:English/Italian; **Sun**:French/German

Essentials

Sleeping **AL** *Aswan Oberoi*, Elephantine Island, PO Box 62, T314667, F323485. 160 rooms with balcony, excellent location in middle of river Nile, reached by a free ferry which runs to/from the *Isis Hotel*, stunning views particularly at sunset, restaurants offering Indian, Egyptian and continental food, coffee shop, bar, nightclub, health spa, gym, also tennis and pool which non-residents can use. **AL** *Pyramisa Isis Island Aswan Hotel*, T317002, F317405. 382 rooms spread over own island situated to south of town at the 1st cataract, access by private ferry, every facility includes a 9-hole mini golf course, picturesque setting, most relaxing atmosphere, an excellent place to 'get away from it all'. **AL** *New Cataract*, Sharia Abtal el-Tahrir, T323377, F323510. 144 rooms, an unfortunate slab of a building overlooking the Nile about 5 mins walk south from town centre, connected by a series of gardens to and shares many facilities including the pool with the *Kalabsha Hotel*, and the famous *Old Cataract Hotel*, choice of restaurants, 24-hr coffee shop, bar and discotheque. **AL** *Sofitel Cataract Hotel*, Sharia Abtal el-Tahrir, T323434, F323510. 136 rooms, Edwardian Moorish-style hotel, universally known as the *Old Cataract Hotel* and featured in Agatha Christie's book *Death on the Nile*, located opposite Elephantine Island, about 5 mins' walk south from town centre, connected to *New Cataract Hotel* and *Kalabsha Hotel*, opened in 1899, is one of Egypt's oldest and most famous hotels, large a/c rooms, some with river view, friendly service but faults due to age are reported, full range of facilities including classic *1902 Restaurant*, nightclub, lounge bar, shops, tennis, croquet. There are minimum charges for non-residents taking drinks on the terrace (E£25) and in the Elephantine Bar (E£15). Afternoon tea which includes sandwiches and cakes is recommended as better value for these minimum charges than morning coffee.

A *Amun Tourist Village*, PO Box 118, Sahara City, T480438, F480440. 252 rooms, located near airport, about 18 km from the attractions of Aswan and the Nile, less busy in low season, restaurants, pool, tennis. **A** *Basma Hotel*, Sharia El Fanadek, – perched on Aswan's highest hill, commanding breathtaking views – T310901 F310907. 187 rooms. **A** *Pyramisa Isis Hotel*, Corniche el-Nil, T324905. 100 rooms, excellent location between river and Corniche next to *Hotel Oberoi's* landing stage, a/c bungalows, pool, riverside terrace and restaurant.

C *Amun*, Amun Island, T313800, F317190. 56 rooms, excellent location on its own lush island in the middle of the River Nile, opposite *Old Cataract Hotel*, free ferry operates to/from the Egyptair office, a Club Mediterranée resort with excellent standard of food, service and facilities. **C** *Kalabsha Hotel*, Sharia Abtal el-Tahrir, T323434, F325974. 120 rooms, on hill overlooking the Nile, about 5 mins' walk south from town centre, shares many facilities with *New Cataract* and *Old Cataract Hotel*, built in 1963 for Russians working at the High Dam, good reception and public rooms, poorly decorated bedrooms, starkly furnished restaurant serves a good breakfast, friendly and helpful service.

D *Cleopatra*, Sharia Sa'ad Zaghloul, Aswan, T314001, F314002. 130 rooms, located downtown near bus station and *souq*, pool on top floor, restaurant and juice bar.

E *Horus*, T323323, located on Corniche el Nil south of the *Isis Hotel*. 41 pleasant a/c rooms, with balconies overlooking the Nile, daily clean linen and a relaxed atmosphere, many tour groups. **E** *Oskar Hotel*, Sharia Abbas Mahmoud el-Akad, T/F326066. 54 rooms, located in a crowded downtown area with Egyptian life all around it, see the real Egypt! **E** *Philae*, Corniche el-Nil, T322117. 70 small rooms with bath, small fan or a/c, view of the Nile. **E** *Ramses Hotel*, Sharia Abtal el-Tahrir, T324000. 112 rooms with bath, unspectacular but comfortable, small balconies overlooking Nile, friendly staff serve breakfast in the basement restaurant also bar and discotheque.

F *Abu Simbel*, Corniche el-Nil, T322888. Renowned for its reasonable prices, near bus station, 66 a/c rooms have a good view of the Nile, restaurant, bar, discotheque, laundry, bank, garden, oriental dancing and nightclub. **F** *Continental*, Sharia Abbas Farid, T322311. Located near the main police station and close to the Corniche overlooking the Nile is the oldest, cheapest and one of the most infamous fleapits in town, the hotel and café in front are a rendezvous for budget travellers. **F** *Happi Hotel*, Sharia Abtal el-Tahrir, T322028. 60 rooms, located in town centre near the Corniche behind the Misr Bank, Nile views from the rather cramped single and more spacious double rooms with bath on higher floors, has good reputation and serves decent food. For cheaper accommodation try; *Abu Chieleb Hotel*, Sharia Abbas Farid, 20 rooms T322651; *El Salam Hotel*, El Corniche, T322651, 70 rooms; *Hathor, El Corniche*, T314580, 65 rooms; *Nubian Oasis Hotel*, 234 Sharia Saad Zaghloul, T312123, 45 rooms with a/c and private facilities, plus 12 other rooms with fan and shared bath.

Camping Official site with guards is located outside town near the Unfinished Obelisk, rather inconvenient without your own transport. Compound has showers and toilets but almost no shade. At E£5 per car and E£3 per person per night it is probably far more sensible to stay at one of the cheaper hotels unless you are determined to camp out.

Youth hostels 96 Sharia Abtal el-Tahrir, 76 beds, T302313, 3 mins from railway station, overnight fee E£5, free kitchen. Open all year.

Luxor to Aswan

Luxor to Aswan

Eating   **Expensive**: *1902 Restaurant* with classic decor in *Old Cataract Hotel* offers international food spiced with Nubian dancers. *Darna Restaurant* in *New Cataract Hotel*. Excellent Egyptian meal served buffet style in restaurant designed as an Egyptian house. *Orangerie* in *Aswan Oberoi*. Varied buffet, excellent choice. *Tower Restaurant* in *Aswan Oberoi*. Has international cuisine with the most spectacular views over Aswan and the Nile. While in Aswan even the most budget conscious visitors should treat themselves to tea or a drink at sunset on the terrace of the *Old Cataract Hotel*.

Mid-range: besides the hotels there are a number of relatively cheap restaurants which serve good food including fresh fish and some of the local Nubian dishes. They include but are not limited to the *El-Gumhorriya* and *Darwish* near the railway station, *Restaurant Shatti* overlooking river opposite *Hotel Continental*. Highly recommended. *Bonarama* and *El-Nil* on the Corniche and the *El-Medina* near the tourist office.

Cheap: *The Al Masry Restaurant* in the *Souq* is recommended for its authentic local cuisine. *Aswan Moon*, cheap but good.

Entertainment   There are nightclubs in the *Kalabsha*, *New Cataract* and *Oberoi* hotels amongst others which offer Nubian and Western floorshows. There are discos in all the major hotels. In many ways, however, it is both preferable and certainly cheaper to spend the evening promenading along the Corniche and *souq* visiting the riverside restaurants and cafés. During the winter, except on Fri, there are nightly performances (2130-2300) by the Nubian Folk Troupe at the Cultural Centre, T323344, at the north end of the Corniche.

Shopping   Aswan is now a large city and it has shops of every description but the *souq*, which runs parallel to the Corniche probably still has the best selection and the most competitive prices and is much more fun than the tourist shops near the major hotels and cruise ships. There is a departmental store on Sharia Abtal el-Tahrir. Books shops in *Oberoi* and *Isis* arcades. The *souq* sells items from the deeper south – spices and nuts from Sudan, lovely shawls of silk and cotton, table cloths in bright designs, Nubian artefacts, dried hibiscus flowers as a herb tea. The stalls selling fresh fruits and vegetables are an inspiration to castle builders, towering displays.

Sports   The major hotels have good sports facilities but remember that with temperatures as high as 50°C (122°F) in the summer Aswan is not the place to be engaging in very active sports, particularly in the middle of the day. **Horse riding**: on a short or long term basis can be arranged. Try at the large hotels for the safest mounts. **Watersports**: are available at the Rowing Club on the Corniche above the *Isis Hotel*.

Tour operators   There are numerous travel agencies and guide companies throughout the town who are all touting for your booking. *Eastmar Travel*, Corniche el-Nil, T323787. *Misr Travel*, one block behind Corniche on way to railway station, adjacent to Tourist Information.

Transport   **Local Bicycles**: are becoming very popular for short distances. There are many hire shops. Try on the Corniche near Misr Bank at E£5 per hour.

Air   Airport T480307, the easiest way to leave Aswan is by air. (Taxi to the airport E£20.) There are regular daily flights both to Luxor and Cairo which take about 30 mins and 1½ hrs, respectively. Single fare Aswan to Luxor E£280. There are four daily flights to Abu Simbel – usually booked by tour groups. One flight to Paris, Sun 1045. Allow plenty of time. Don't expect any flight announcements. When the gates open for a flight push forward, if it is not your flight you will be turned back.

Train Train information T314754, for long distance travel to Luxor (5 hrs), Cairo (17 hrs) and Alexandria (approximately 24 hrs) train is the most comfortable method. The a/c night train from Aswan to Cairo, E£300, is highly recommended as being safe and comfortable and providing a meal and drinks' service and an early breakfast. The cabins, which have large windows with blinds, are small but easily turn into a room with bunks, a sink and table, and there are clean communal toilets along the corridor. There are restrictions on train travel by foreigners except on the couple of daily express a/c services. Check carefully.

Road Bus: Currently there is no road link to Abu Simbel. The new Aswan-Abu Simbel road will be opened to tourists, travelling in convoy, 'later' in 2000. Police checks and ambulance facilities are to be implemented. Bus station T303225, very regular slow buses and less frequent express buses, stopping only at Kom Ombo (E£2), Edfu (E£4) and Esna, go to Luxor (E£10) which takes 4 hrs. There are also 3 daily buses of very varying quality and price to Cairo (the best at 1530) but, given the distance, the train is a more comfortable option. There is now also a daily a/c bus to Hurghada on the Red Sea coast which continues to Cairo via Suez which is a good stopping off point for travellers to Sinai. All bus journeys are subject to control by the police security. **Service taxis** have security restrictions and it may be easier (more expensive) to hire a private taxi for journeys out of town though they too have to join the convoys.

Boat Feluccas: official prices, regulated by the government, for 1-10 passengers including waiting time from the Corniche are: Kitchener Island and Agha Khan Mausoleum, E£20, 2 hrs; Kitchener Island, Elephantine Island and Agha Khan Mausoleum, E£25, 2½ hrs; St Simeon's monastery and Nobles Tombs, E£35, 3 hrs; St Simeon's monastery and Kitchener Island, E£50, 3 hrs; Nubian village, E£40, 2½ hrs; Elephantine Island only, E£15 per hour, 1½ hrs; Elephantine Island and the Nobles' Tombs, E£50, 4 hrs; Elephantine Island and St Simeon's monastery, E£50, 4 hrs; Elephantine Island, St Simeon's monastery and back via Kitchener island, E£40, 3 hrs. Alternatively a 1 hr tour around the islands costs E£18. Hire your own *felucca* for E£30 per hour and go where you like. The per person prices for long distance *feluccas* from Aswan, which carry a minimum of 6 people and where the group pays for and buys their own food and pays the E£5 pp required to obtain permission to travel are as follows: Kom Ombo, E£25, 1 day and 1 night; Edfu, E£45, 2 days and 2 nights; Esna, E£50, 3 days and 3 nights; and Luxor, E£60, 4 days and 4 nights. The Tourist Office should be able to recommend the best captains and is often a place to meet potential fellow passengers. Feluccas can be found on the Corniche el-Nil, if the men with the feluccas have not found you first!

Directory

Airline offices *EgyptAir*, southern end of Corniche T315000. **Banks** Besides the major hotels which change money, there are numerous branches of most of the Egyptian banks on the Corniche or Sharia Abtal el-Tahrir. No ATM out of banking hours. Recommended are *Bank of Alexandria*, *National Bank of Egypt*, *Bank Du Caire*, open Thu-Sun 0830-1400 with some also open from 1700-2000. American Express, *Old Cataract Hotel*, T302909. Thomas Cook, Corniche el-Nil, T304011, best for TCs. **Communications Internet**: email facilities at all major hotels. *Nubian Oasis Hotel* charges E£1 per minute to send and E£40 per hour to use. **Post Office**: located in the road behind the *Philae Hotel*, open 0800-1400 except Fri. Post restante at the small office on Salah ad-Din (same hours), T323533. It is best to post outgoing mail from the major hotels because they seem to get priority. **Telephone**: office near *EgyptAir*. Business services available at *Isis Island*. **Medical services** German Hospital on the Corniche. **Places of worship** *Roman Catholic*, 89 Sharia Abtal el-Tahir, near *Hotel Abu Simbel*, one block behind the Corniche has services Sat 1800 and Sun 1900. **Tourist offices** Located behind the gardens towards the north end of the Corniche next to *Misr Travel*. Although the official opening times are 0830-1600 and 1800-2000 during the high season it is manned from 0800-2000. **Useful numbers** Emergency Police: T22147. Fire: T303058. Hospital: T322912. Passport Office: T22238. **Tourist Police**: T323163.

Lower Nubia

Colour map 7, grid C4 Sometimes a trip to **Abu Simbel** and other Lake Nasser temples is offered as an 'extra' on a tour or an excursion from the hotel in Aswan. Do not miss the opportunity to see this spectacular site of giant pharaonic statues which have enchanted visitors for centuries.

Abu Simbel, which lies 280 km south of Aswan and only 40 km north of the Sudanese border (virtually closed to all traffic), is the site of the magnificent **Sun Temple of Ramses II** and the smaller **Temple of Queen Nefertari**. With the exception of the temples, hotels and the homes of tourist industry employees, there is almost nothing else in Abu Simbel.

Sights

Temples of Abu Simbel ■ *Daily 0600 until the departure of the last plane. Entrance E£36.* The two temples, which were rediscovered in 1813 completely buried by sand, were built by the most egotistical pharaoh of all, Ramses II (1304-1237 BC) during the 19th Dynasty of the New Kingdom. Although he built a smaller temple for his queen Nefertari, it is the four gigantic statues of himself, which were carved out of the mountainside, which dominate Abu Simbel. It was intended that his magnificent and unblinking stare would be the

Nubian Temples cruise

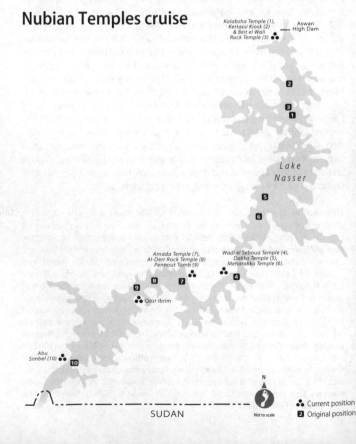

Kalabsha Temple (1),
Kertassi Kiosk (2)
& Beit el Wali
Rock Temple (3)

Aswan
High Dam

Lake Nasser

Amada Temple (7),
Al-Derr Rock Temple (8)
Pennout Tomb (9)

Wadi el Seboua Temple (4),
Dakka Temple (5),
Meharakka Temple (6).

Qasr Ibrim

Abu
Simbel (10)

SUDAN

N

Not to scale

Current position

Original position

first thing that travellers, visitors and enemies alike, saw as they entered Egypt from the south. Behind the statues is **Ramses II's Temple of the Sun** which was originally built to venerate Amun and Re-Harakhte but really is dominated by and dedicated to the pharaoh-god Ramses II himself.

Although it had become the highlight of the trip for the relatively few intrepid travellers who ventured so far south, it was not until the monuments were threatened by the rising waters of Lake Nasser that international attention focused on Abu Simbel. UNESCO financed and organized the ambitious, costly (US$40 mn) and ultimately successful 1964-68 operation, to reassemble the monuments 61 m above and 210 m behind their original site.

Ramses II's Temple of the Sun, Abu Simbel

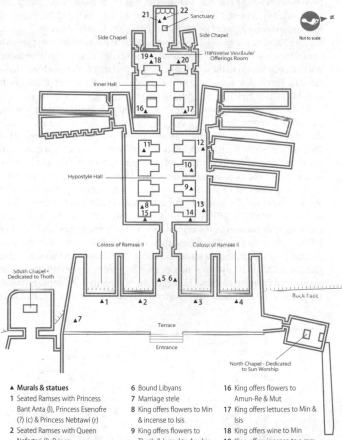

▲ **Murals & statues**

1 Seated Ramses with Princess Bant Anta (l), Princess Esenofre (?) (c) & Princess Nebtawi (r)

2 Seated Ramses with Queen Nefertari (l), Prince Amenhirkhopshef (c) & Ramses' mother Queen Muttuya (r)

3 Seated Ramses with Princess Beketmut (l), Prince Ramessesu (c) & Queen Nefertari (r)

4 Seated Ramses with Queen Mother Muttuya (l), Princess Merytamun (c) & Queen Nefertari (r)

5 Bound Nubians

6 Bound Libyans

7 Marriage stele

8 King offers flowers to Min & incense to Isis

9 King offers flowers to Thoth & bread to Anubis

10 King offers wine to Horus & flowers to Mut

11 King offers wine to Re-Harakhte

12-13 Battle of Kadesh - recruits arriving, encampment, town of Kadesh, enemy chariots

14 Libyan prisoners

15 Nubian & Hittite prisoners

16 King offers flowers to Amun-Re & Mut

17 King offers lettuces to Min & Isis

18 King offers wine to Min

19 King offers incense to a ram-headed Amun-Re

20 King offers bread to Atum

21 King before barque of Amun anoints Min

22 Four (damaged) statues (l-r) of Ptah, Amun-Re, Ramses II & Re-Harakhte

The entrance steps lead up to a terrace, with alternate statuettes of the king and a falcon to mark the edge, where the imposing façade of the main temple (35 m wide by 30 m high) is dominated by the four-seated **Colossi of Ramses II**, each wearing the double crown. Each figure was originally 21 m high but the second from the left lost its top during an earthquake in 27 BC. There are smaller statues of some of the members of the royal family standing at Ramses' rather crudely sculptured feet which contrast with the ornately chiselled and beautiful faces of Ramses. There is graffiti, written by Greek mercenaries about their expeditions into Nubia, on the left leg of the damaged statue.

The sides of the huge thrones at the entrance to the temple are decorated with the Nile gods entwining lotus and papyrus, the plants representing Upper and Lower Egypt around the hieroglyph 'to unite'. Below are reliefs, called the Nine Bows of bound Nubians on the south side (5) and bound Asiatics to the north side (6), representing Egypt's vanquished foes. In the niche above the main doorway is a figure of Re-Harakhte. Lining the façade, above the heads of the four Ramses, is a row of 22 baboons smiling at the sunrise. There are two small chapels at either end of the façade. The smaller chapel with altar to the north was dedicated to the worship of the sun and that to the south was dedicated to Thoth. A marriage stela (7) commemorates the union of Ramses II with Ma'at-Her-Neferure, daughter of the Hittite king.

At the entrance into the temple's rock **Hypostyle Hall** is a door bearing Ramses II's cartouche. Having entered the temple the eye is immediately drawn to eight statues of Ramses, 10 m high and clad in a short kilt typical of the Nubian Osiride form, which are carved in the front of the eight enormous square pillars which support the roof. The four statues on the right bear the double crown and those on the left the white crown of Upper Egypt. Each pillar depicts the kings before the gods. See where he is presenting flowers to Min and incense to Isis (8), wine to Horus and flowers to Mut (9), flowers to Thoth and bread to Anubis (10), wine to Re-Harakhte (11). The hall's ceiling is crowded with vultures in the central aisle and star spangled elsewhere. The reliefs on the walls are colourful and well preserved. The north wall is the most dramatic with four different scenes depicting the Battle of Kadesh against the Hittites in 1300 BC (l and m) which, despite the scenes on the wall, was not an unqualified Egyptian success. The depictions of chariots and camps are particularly revealing of ancient battle methods but, more interestingly, Ramses's

Bound Nubian from entrance to Ramses II
Temple of the Sun

Bound Asiatic from entrance to Ramses II
Temple of the Sun

Burckhardt the Explorer

The Anglo/Swiss geographer and explorer, Johann (John) Ludwig Burckhardt was born in Lausanne, Switzerland on 24 November 1784. He studied at London and Cambridge between 1806-09 and lived in Syria where he learned Arabic and became a follower of Islam taking the Muslim name Ibrahim Ibn Abd Allah. He left Syria, en route for Cairo and the Fezzan (Libya) from where he was to attempt to cross the Sahara. Local Bedouin spoke of the ruins of a 'lost city', located in the mountains. Knowing that the legendary lost city of Petra was in the vicinity of Aaron's tomb on Jebel Harun he persuaded his guides of a

desire to sacrifice a goat in honour of Aaron at his tomb. His scheme succeeded and on 22 August 1812 he was guided through the Siq and into the valley where he saw the Al-Khazneh and the Urn Tomb and thus saw enough to recognize the City of Petra.

When he arrived in Cairo he could find no immediate transport to Fezzan (nothings seems to change). Instead he journeyed up the Nile and discovered the **Temple of Ramses II** at **Abu Simbel**. He next travelled to Saudi Arabia, visiting Mecca. He returned to Cairo where he died on 15 October 1817, before he was able to complete his journey.

double arm lancing a Libyan may have been an attempt at animation. The slaughter of prisoners, generally small in size, is a common theme (14 and 15).

There are also side chambers, probably originally used to store vases, temple linen, cult objects and Nubian gifts, branching off from the hall. Their walls are lined with reliefs of sacrifices and offerings being made by Ramses to the major gods including Amun.

The **Inner Hall** has four columns depicting the pharaoh participating in rituals before the deities. On the far left, Ramses can be seen before Amun (16). Lettuces, considered an aphrodisiac, are being offered to Amun (17). In both these scenes a deified Ramses II has been inserted at a later date. Two sandstone sphinxes, which originally stood at the entrance to the hall, are now in London's British Museum.

Further in and in front of the inner sanctuary is the **Transverse Vestibule** where offerings of wine, fruits and flowers were made. The **Sanctuary** itself, which was originally cased in gold, has an altar to Ramses at its centre behind which are now, unfortunately mutilated, statues of Ptah, Amun-Re, Ramses II and Re-Harakhte. Ramses is deified with his patron gods. Before the temple's relocation the dawn sunrays would shine on all but Ptah, who was linked with death-cults, on 22 February and 22 October. Despite what your guide will say there is no scholastic evidence to connect these two dates to Ramses' birthday and coronation day. A sacred barque (boat) would have rested on the altar and the walls beside the door portray the barque of Amun and Ramses. The adjoining side chapels were not decorated.

Despite its magnificence and beauty for many visitors to Abu Simbel there is a slight tinge of disappointment because of the combination of a sense of familiarity and artificiality. The latter is heightened when at the end of the official tour one is led through a door and into the hollow mountain on which the temple was reconstructed when it was moved. At the same time, however, the combination of Ramses' egoism and the scale of the magnificent feat of saving the temple from the rising waters of the Nile make the trip from Aswan worthwhile.

The **Temple of Queen Nefertari** is situated 120 m north of Ramses II's Temple. Although dedicated to the goddess Hathor of Abshek, like that of her husband, the temple virtually deifies the human queen Nefertari. Unsurprisingly it is much smaller than that of Ramses II but is nevertheless both imposing and very, very beautiful. It is cut entirely from the rock and penetrates about 24 m from the rock face. The external façade is 12 m high and lined with three colossi 11½ m high on either side of the entrance. Nefertari stands with her husband and their children cluster in pairs at their knees. From left to right – Ramses II with Princes Meryatum and Meryre (1), Queen Nefertari shown as Hathor has the solar disc between the horns of the sacred cow with Princesses Merytamun and Henwati (2), Ramses II with Princes Amunhikhopshef and Rahrirwemenef (3). The same groupings appear in reverse order on the other side. The king wears various crowns. To show the importance of Queen Nefertari her statues are of similar size to those of her husband. Just within the entrance are the cartouches of Ramses II and Nefertari. There is one simple **Hall**, with six square pillars. On the aisle side of each is depicted a Hathor head and sistrum sounding box while the other three sides have figures of the king and queen making offerings to the gods. The ceiling bears a well preserved dedication inscription from Ramses to Nefertari. The reliefs on the hall walls are rather gruesome with the pharaoh slaying his enemies while Nefertari and the god Amun look on (8). The walls backing the entrance depict Ramses killing a Nubian and a Libyan.

Three corridors lead from the rear of the hall into the **Vestibule**, the central one passing directly into the **Sanctuary**. The back walls of the Vestibule portray reliefs of Ramses and Nefertari offering wine and flowers to Khnum and Re-Harakhte on the right (18) and to Horus and Amun on the left (17). Vultures protect the Queen's cartouche on the door above the sanctuary (19) which is dominated by the figure of Hathor in the form of a cow watching over Ramses. On the left wall, Nefertari can be seen offering incense to Mut and Hathor (20) whilst on the opposite side Ramses worships the deified images of himself and Nefertari (21).

Other Lake Nasser Temples Originally spread along the length of the Nile, the important Nubian antiquities saved by UNESCO from the rising waters of Lake Nasser were clustered in groups of three to make for easier visiting. Many of the Nubian monuments do not have the magnificence of those north of the High Dam though their new sites are more attractive. A number were erected in haste with little concern for artistic merit, for the sole reason of inspiring awe in the conquered people's of Nubia.

These monuments were previously almost inaccessible. However, *Belle Epoque Travel*, now organizes a relaxing tour of Lower Nubian antiquities aboard its elegant cruiseboat *Eugenie* (see below under Sleeping),

Temple of Queen Nefertari, Abu Simbel

▲ **Murals & Statues**

1 Ramses II with Princes Meryatum & Meryre
2 Queen Nefertari shown as Hathor with Princesses Merytamun & Henwati
3 Ramses II with Princes Amunhikhopshef & Rahrirwemenef
4 Lintel where King offers wine to Amun-Re
5 King offers incense to Horus
6 King offers flowers to Hathor
7 Nefertari offers flowers to Isis
8 Ramses II smites Nubian prisoner before Amun-Re
9 Ramses II receives necklace from Hathor
10 Ramses II crowned by Horus & Seth
11 Nefertari offers flowers & musical instrument to Anukis
12 Ramses II smites Libyan prisoner before Horus
13 Ramses II with offerings
14 Nefertari before Hathor of Dendera
15 Nefertari between Hathor & Isis
16 Ramses II & Nefertari give flowers to Taweret
17 Ramses II offers wine to Horus & Anum
18 Ramses II offers wine to Re-Harakhte & Queen offers flowers to Khnum
19 Nefertari's cartouche between vultures
20 Nefertari offers incense to Mut & Hathor
21 Ramses II worships deified image of himself & Nefertari

constructed in 1993 in the style of a Mississippi paddle steamer. Pampered by the luxurious surroundings, high calibre guides and excellent service, travellers can sit back and appreciate the sheer vastness of desert and lake, a sharp contrast to the lush scenery and teeming villages of the Nile valley. Few more tranquil places exist. The boat's passengers have the monuments almost to themselves. Memorable features include a private sunset tour of Abu Simbel followed by a candlelit dinner on board for which the temples are specially lit.

Kalabsha Temple, the largest free standing Nubian temple and the second largest Nubian temple was also relocated when the High Dam was built and is now semi-marooned on an island or promontory (depending on the water level) near the west end of dam. It is rarely visited by tourists. ■ *Daily 0600-1800*. The easiest way to reach the temple is by taxi from Aswan or possibly as part of a half-day tour which would include the Unfinished Obelisk, the Aswan Dams and Philae. Negotiate with the boatmen with motor launch at the west end of the High Dam near the canning factory if the waters of the lake cover the pathway from the shore. Pay at the end of the return trip after about an hour on the site.

The original site of the temple, which was built in the 18th Dynasty (1567-1320 BC) in honour of Marul (Greek =Mandulis), was about 50 km south of Aswan at Talmis which was subsequently renamed Kalabsha. Mandulis was a Lower Nubian sun god of fertility equated with Horus/Isis/Osiris and usually shown in human form with an elaborate headdress of horns, cobras and plumes all topped off with a sun disc. Over the centuries the later **Temple of Mandulis**, a Ptolemaic-Roman version of the earlier one, developed a healing cult as did those of Edfu and Dendera. It was moved from Kalabsha to its present site in 1970 by West German engineers in order to save it from the rising waters of Lake Nasser.

Leading up to the First Pylon is an impressive 30 m causeway, used by pilgrims arriving by boat, but it is not known why the causeway and first pylon are

Temple of Kalabsha

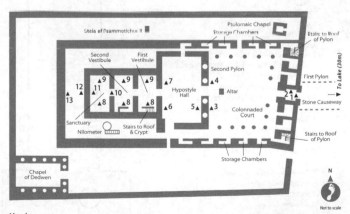

▲ **Murals**

1 Lintel with sundisc
2 Emperor Augustus with Horus
3 King being purified with sacred water by Horus & Thoth
4 Decree in Greek regarding expulsion of pigs from temple
5 Coptic crosses carved on wall

6 Second register - a pharaoh offers a field to Isis, Mandulis & Horus
7 Second register - Amenophis II offers wine to Mandulis & another
8 Procession of gods, the King in the lead, before Osiris, Isis & Horus

9 Procession of gods, the King in the lead, before Mandulis, a juvenile Mandulis & Wadjet
10 Lintel with sundisc
11 King with various gods
12 King with deities - double picture
13 King before Mandulis

Luxor to Aswan

set at a slight angle to the temple. In order to align the structure, the first court is in the shape of a trapezium, with the pillars on the south side grouped closer together. At either end of the pylon a staircase leads up to the roof. Within the thickness of the walls are four storage rooms, two at each side.

The left portico, beside the entrance to the Hypostyle Hall, portrays the pharaoh being purified and anointed with holy water by Thoth and Horus, while on the right is inscribed a decree from Aurelius Besarion who was Governor of Ombos and Elephantine ordering the expulsion of pigs from the temple precincts. The Hypostyle Hall has lost its roof, but the eight columns are still in good condition. The capitals are ornate and flowered, some paintings having been preserved with their original colours, though not all are complete. On either side of the doorway leading to the vestibule is a relief of Trajan making offerings to Isis, Osiris and Mandulis on the left and Horus, Mandulis and Wadjet on the right.

Beyond the hall are the vestibules each with two columns and south access to the roof. Most of the decoration has survived and on the entrance wall the pharaoh can be seen offering incense to Mandulis and Wadjet, and milk to Isis and Osiris. The south wall depicts the emperor making libations to Osiris, Isis, Horus, Wadjet and Mandulis. The statue of Mandulis has long since vanished, though he is pictured on the walls amongst the other deities.

Near the lakeside just south of the Temple of Kalabsha is the Ptolemaic-Roman **Kiosk of Kertassi** rescued by UNESCO from its original site 40 km south of Aswan. It is a single chamber with two Hathor-headed columns at the entrance on the north side. Hathor was associated with miners and quarrymen as patroness. Dedicated to Isis, the temple is undecorated except for one column in the north west whose reliefs on the upper part depict the pharaoh standing before Isis and Horus the child.

Temple of Beit el-Wali, Nubia

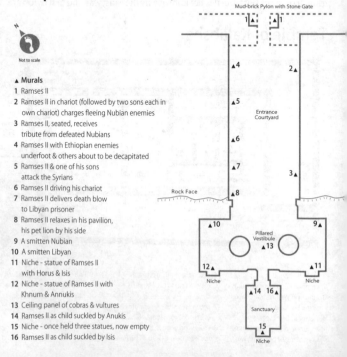

Mud-brick Pylon with Stone Gate

Not to scale

▲ **Murals**
1 Ramses II
2 Ramses II in chariot (followed by two sons each in own chariot) charges fleeing Nubian enemies
3 Ramses II, seated, receives tribute from defeated Nubians
4 Ramses II with Ethiopian enemies underfoot & others about to be decapitated
5 Ramses II & one of his sons attack the Syrians
6 Ramses II driving his chariot
7 Ramses II delivers death blow to Libyan prisoner
8 Ramses II relaxes in his pavilion, his pet lion by his side
9 A smitten Nubian
10 A smitten Libyan
11 Niche - statue of Ramses II with Horus & Isis
12 Niche - statue of Ramses II with Khnum & Annukis
13 Ceiling panel of cobras & vultures
14 Ramses II as child suckled by Anukis
15 Niche - once held three statues, now empty
16 Ramses II as child suckled by Isis

In the hillside behind the Kalabsha Temple stands a small rock temple, **Beit el-Wali** (House of the Governor), again part of the UNESCO rescue mission. This was originally situated northwest of Kalabsha Temple and possessed a long causeway to the river. Built during Ramses II's youth by the Viceroy of Kush it is believed to have been erected in honour of Amun-Re as he is depicted most frequently. The reliefs in the temple's narrow forecourt depict Ramses II victorious against the Nubians and Ethiopians (south wall) and defeating the Asiatics, Libyans and Syrians (north wall). In fact a great deal of smiting and defeating is illustrated. In particular the tribute being offered on the east wall of the entrance courtyard is well worth examination, while on the wall opposite look out for the dog biting a Libyan's leg. The reliefs and residual colours are well preserved making this an interesting visit.

The two columns in the vestibule are unusual in a Nubian monument – being fluted. When this building was used as a Christian church the entrance forecourt was roofed over with brick domes.

The isolated oasis of Wadi El Seboua, 135 km from the High Dam, contains the Temple of Wadi El Seboua, the Temple of Dakka and the Temple of Maharakka. The giant **Temple of Wadi El Seboua** (valley of the lion) is named after the two rows of sphinxes which line its approach. It was constructed between 1279 BC and 1212 BC under Setau, the supervisor of the Viceroy of Kush. It is dedicated to Amun, Re-Harakhte and the deified Ramses II.

Temple of Wadi El Seboua, Nubia

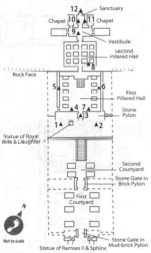

▲ **Murals**
1 King smiting prisoners before Amun-Re
2 King smiting prisoners before Re-Harakhte
3 Various - King makes offerings
4 20 princesses
5 25 princes & 9 princesses
6 28 princes & 7 princesses
7 18 princesses
8 King offering wine ? & incense to three gods
    (colours well preserved)
9 Hathor with a cow's head
10 King before barque of Amun-Re
11 King before barque of Re-Harakhte
12 Remains of Christian mural of St Peter in niche

A huge statue of Ramses II and a sphinx stand on either side of the entrance. The base of each is decorated with bound prisoners, a reminder of Egyptian supremacy.

There are six human headed sphinxes in double crown in the First Courtyard and four falcon headed sphinxes in double crown with small statue of the king in front in the Second Courtyard. Again the bases have illustrations of bound prisoners. Steps lead up to the main part of the temple. The massive statue on the left of the First Pylon is of the wife of Ramses II and behind her leg their daughter Bint-Anath. The corresponding statue from the right of the entrance now lies in the sand outside, damaged when the temple was converted into a church.

The carved reliefs by local artists in poor quality sandstone, are crude but much remains of their original colour. Around the court are roughly carved statues of Ramses II unusually portrayed as a Nubian, holding the crook and flail scepters displayed against the 10 pillars – but most have been damaged. Along the lower register appear a procession of princes and princesses, estimated at a total of over 50 of each.

From the far end of the First Pillared Hall the temple is cut into the rock and this inner section has decorations better preserved – better colours. This section was used as a Christian church – some evidence remains. The Christians who used this as a church covered the reliefs with plaster to permit their own decoration. Fortunately this plaster preserved the earlier work. In the Sanctuary a relief on the wall shows Ramses II presenting a bouquet to the godly triad but early Christians defaced the figures and Ramses II now appears to be offering lotus flowers to St Peter.

Unfortuately a number of the sphinxes have been decapitated and the heads sold to illegal treasure hunters.

Uphill is the Ptolemaic-Roman **Temple of Dakka**, reconstructed on the site of an earlier sanctuary. In fact several rulers contributed to its construction and decoration. It was started by the Meroitic King Arqamani, adapted by the Ptolemies Philopator and Euergetes II and changed again by Emperors Augustus and Tiberius (see key). What a history!

Like many temples it was used for a time by the Christians as a church and in some places fragments of their decorations remain. This is the only temple in Egypt facing north, an orientation preserved by UNESCO, pointing to the home of Thoth but perhaps an error by the foreign-born Ptolemaic builders. The pylon is still in good condition, standing an imposing 13 m in height. The gateway has a curved cornice with a central winged sun disc on either side and a high level niche at each side intended to hold a flag pole while on the left of the doorway is graffiti in Greek, Roman and Meroitic (ancient Nubian). Inside the doorway a king makes offerings to Thoth, Tefnut and Hathor (b). Stairs in either side of the pylon lead to guard rooms and the roof from which a fine view is obtained. Deep incisions in the inner pylon wall were probably made by locals convinced that the stone possessed healing properties. The main temple building is across an open courtyard but before you enter, turn back and admire the view to the north.

There are four interconnecting rooms, many of the decorations being of deities receiving assorted offerings. A staircase leads off the vestibule on the west side up to the roof. Off the sanctury is a small room to the east side leading, it is thought, to a now choked crypt. Here the decorations are in quite good condition, two seated ibises, two hawks and two lions. The lioness being approached by the baboons (6) needs some interpretation. As an animal could approach a lioness without danger except if she was hungry but a human was in danger at any time the humans assumed

Temple of Dakka, Nubia

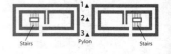

▲ Murals

1 Winged sun disc
2 King before Tefnut, Thoth & Hathor. King offers field to Isis
3 Winged sun disc
4 Sacred cobras
5 King offers gifts to Isis & Osiris
6 Thoth as baboon worships Tefnut as lioness
7 King offers sacred eye to Horus & Hathor
8 Winged sun disc. King receives life from Thoth & Hathor
9 Thoth as ape sitting under sycamore tree. Nile god pours water

animal form to worship in safety. The king is seen worshipping gods including Osiris and Isis (5) and Horus and Hathor (7). The large pink granite casket in the sanctuary once held the cult statue of Thoth.

Less impressive is the unfinished Roman **Temple of Meharakka**, dedicated to Isis and Serapis. This stood on the southern border of Egypt in Ptolemaic and Roman times. Rather plain inside, bar the Roman graffiti from travellers and soldiers fighting Nubian troops in 23 BC, the temple illustrates the union of Egyptian and Roman styles. Isis is depicted full frontal, instead of the more common profile, while her son Horus wears a toga. Other surviving carvings depict Osiris, Thoth and Tefnut. The temple consists of one room – six columns on the north side, three columns on the east and west side and six on the south side joined by screen walls. The capitals (floral?) of the columns were never completed. For stair access to roof, from which there are spectacular views, enter temple and turn right. This is the only known spiral staircase in an Egyptian building. Look east to the pharaohs' gold mines.

Temple of Amada, Nubia

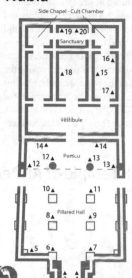

Some 40 km further south in the Amada Oasis, is the oldest temple in Nubia, the sandstone **Temple of Amada**, dedicated to Amun-Re and Re-Harakhte. It was built by Tuthmosis III and Amenhotep II, with the roofed pillared court added by Tuthmosis IV which accounts for the many scenes of Tuthmosis IV with various gods and goddesses on the walls and pillars of this hall. At the left of the entrance hieroglyphics detail the victorious campaigns of Meneptah (3) against the Libyans. Opposite is the cartouche of Ramses II (4). Before entering the next doorway look up at the Berber grafiti of animals high on the wall at both sides (14). Inside turn right. Reliefs show the Pharaoh running the Heb-Sed race (17) (see page 148), cattle being slaughtered and presented as offerings as heads and haunches (16). Opposite (15) are the foundation ceremonies, an interesting depiction of the way a site for a building was marked out, foundations dug, bricks manufactured and the construction eventually completed and handed over to the owner. In the central section are more offering, of pomegranates, very realistic ducks and cakes (18). The stela at the back of the the sanctuary tells of the temple's

▲ **Murals**
1 Tuthmosis III with Re-Harakhte
2 Amenhotep II with Re-Harakhte
3 Hieroglyphs detail Merenptah's successful campaign against the Libyans
4 Cartouche of Ramses II
5 Inscription of Tuthmosis IV as 'beloved of Senusert'
6 Tuthmosis IV & Anukis
7 Tuthmosis IV & Khnum
8 Tuthmosis IV & Khepri
9 Tuthmosis IV & Amun
10 Tuthmosis IV & Atum
11 Tuthmosis IV & Ptah
12 Column with titles of Amenhotep II
13 Column with title of Tuthmosis III
14 Berber graffiti
15 Foundation ceremonies
16 Slaughtered cattle as offerings
17 Pharaoh running Heb-Sed race
18 Offerings of fruit & poultry
19 Inscription of Amenhotep II. Amenhotep dispensing rough justice
20 More rough justice

Luxor to Aswan

foundation during Amenhotep II's time. The holes in the roof allow light in so one can see, also on the back wall, Amenhotep dispensing justice to six Syrian captives (19), a prisoner turned upside down and crucified (20), a grisly reminder to his remote Nubian subjects of pharaoh's treatment of enemies.

Here too is the **Rock Temple of Al-Derr**, built in honour of Amun-Re, Re-Harakhte and the divine aspect of the pharaoh, notable for the excellent colour and preservation of its reliefs. It is the only temple on the east bank of the Nile in Nubia. In the first hypostyle hall the temple's builder Ramses II stands in the Tree of Life and presents libations to Amun. Ibis, the eternal scribe, behind, records the pharaoh's years and achievements. The decorations here are, however, very damaged and only small pieces of these scenes can now be made out. The four large statues of Ramses II as Osiris, guarding the entrance, incorporated in the last row of columns here, are reduced to legs only. The other columns in the hall are very reduced in size too. The majority of the reliefs on the outer walls boast of the pharaoh's military triumphs and warn the Nubians that his might is unassailable. However, inside the second Hypostyle Hall, the pharaoh, depicted as a high priest, becomes a humble servant of the gods. On the right hand wall he gives flowers, offers wine, escorts the barque, receives jubilees from Amun-Re and Mut (4) and further along the Heb Sed emblem is produced nine times (5). On the opposite wall he has his name recorded on the leaves of a tall acacia tree. Entering the sanctuary on the left Ramses is putting in a plea to live for ever (7). In the sanctuary on the back wall there were originally four statues as in the larger temple at Abu Simbel (see page 311), now nothing, but on the wall decorations the king continues to offer perfumes, cake and flowers.

The rock-cut **Tomb of Pennout**, Chief of the Quarry Service, Steward of Horus and viceroy of Wawat (northern Nubia) under Ramses VI, is a rare example of a high official buried south of Aswan. The ancient Egyptians believed that their souls were only secure if their bodies were carried back and buried in Egyptian soil. The tomb's wall paintings rather poignantly reflect this conviction, expressing Pennout's desire to be laid to rest in the hills of Thebes. The walls are decorated with traditional themes, including the deceased and his family. Before entering on the left the deceased and his wife Takha in adulation, on the main wall the judgement scene with the weighing of the heart against a feather and below the traditional mourners pouring sand on their heads. On the end wall Horus leads the deceased and wife to Osiris, Isis and Nephthys for a blessing but the lower register has all disappeared. To the left of the inner chamber representation of the solar cult. There is no entry into the inner chamber but the three badly mutilated statues of

Rock Temple of Al-Derr Nubia

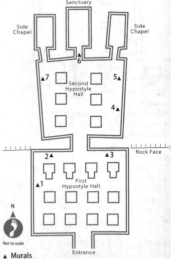

▲ Murals

1 Lower part of Ramses II in horse-drawn chariot
2 King with ka & pet lion smiting enemies before Amun
3 & before Re-Harakhte. Procession of royal children below
4 King as high priest acts as servant to gods
5 Heb-Sed emblem repeated nine times
6 Thoth writes King's name in sacred tree
7 King receives symbol of life from Amun-Re (l) & Re-Harakhte (r)

Scorpions – the original sting in the tail

Scorpions really deserve a better press. They are fascinating creatures, provided they do not lurk in your shoe or shelter in your clothes.

Scorpions are not insects. They belong to the class Arachnida as do spiders and daddy longlegs. There are about 750 different kinds of scorpions. The average size is a cosy 6 cm but the largest, Pandinus imperator, the black Emperor scorpion of West Africa, is a terrifying 20 cm long. The good news is that only a few are really dangerous. The bad news is that some of these are found in Egypt.

They really are remarkable creatures with the ability to endure the hottest desert climates, revive after being frozen in ice, and survive for over a year without food or water. They have a remarkable resistance to nuclear radiation, a characteristic yet to be proved of great use.

Scorpions are nocturnal. They shelter during the heat of the day and to keep cool wave their legs in the air. They feed on insects and spiders, grasping their prey with their large claw-like pincers, tearing it apart and sucking the juices. Larger scorpions can devour lizards and small mammals.

Their shiny appearance is due to an impervious wax coating over their hard outer shell which protects them from any water loss. They have very small eyes and depend on their better developed senses of touch and smell. The sensitive bristles on the legs point in all directions and pick up vibrations of movements of potential prey or enemies. This sensitivity gives them ample warning to avoid being seen by heavy-footed humans.

The oft reported 'courtship dance' before mating is merely repeated instinctive actions. The grasping of claws and the jerky 'dance' movements from side to side are a prelude to copulation during which the male produces spermatozoa in a drop of sticky fluid to which the female is led so that they may enter her body. The male departs speedily after the 'dance' to avoid being attacked and devoured.

Scorpions bear live young. After hatching, the young crawl on to the female's back and are carried there for two or three weeks until their first moult. They gradually drop off after that time and have to fend for themselves.

Most scorpions retreat rather than attack. They sting in self-defence. The sting is a hard spine and the poison is made in the swelling at the base. The sole of the bare foot, not surprisingly, is most often the site of a sting, and the advice in the section on Health in Essentials is not to be ignored. The African **fat-tailed scorpion** (we do not recommend measuring the size) is described as aggressive and quick-tempered. It is responsible for most of the reported stings to humans and most of the human fatalities. The beautifully named Buthus occitanus, the small **Mediterranean yellow scorpion** and Leirus quinquestriatus, the **African golden scorpion**, also have neurotoxic stings that can be fatal.

Pennout, and his wife with Hathor between can be viewed. The actual burial chamber lies 3 m below. Above on the lintel is the sun-god barge and howling baboons. What is left of the decoration on the wall to the right shows Pennout with his wife and six sons while on the end wall Pennout in golden colours is in his illustrated biography which continues on toward the exit. It is very disappointing to note that almost all the wall decorations were intact when this temple was moved here and even more disappointing to note that the damage had been caused by illegal removal from the monument.

☞ Cobras

The Egyptian Cobra occurs on every kingly brow. The Uraeus, the cobra's head and the neck with the hood spread, as worn in the head dress of Egyptian divinities and sovereigns, is a sign of supreme power.

Fortunately this is the only place you are likely to see an Egyptian Cobra although Cleopatra conveniently found one in the environs of the palace.

All cobras are potentially very dangerous although the venom is used to catch prey rather than eliminate humans. Yet these creatures, though infrequently seen are not considered in danger of extinction.

There are other cobras in Egypt. The smaller Black-necked Spitting Cobra sprays venom up to the eyes of its attacker – causing temporary blindness and a great deal of agony. The black refers to the distinctive bands round the neck.

Sightings are confined to the region south of Aswan. The Innes Cobra is exceedingly rare, recorded in particular around St Catherine's Monastery.

The fortress of **Qasr Ibrim** (no access permitted), 40 km north of Abu Simbel is on its original site, once a plateau, now an island. It is noted for an exceptional length of continuous occupation, from 1000 BC to AD 1812. The ancient city included seven temples to Isis and a mud-brick temple built by the Nubian king Taharka, ruins of which are visible in the centre of the island. In the pre-Roman period construction of a massive stone temple, similar to the structures at Kalabsha, turned the garrison city into a major religious centre. A healing cult developed and Qasr Ibrim became 'the Philae of the south'. Footprints, carved by pilgrims to commemorate their visit, are still visible in the temple floor. A tavern, 400 BC, on the north side of the island is recognizable by the large piles of pottery shards. The temple was destroyed by early Christians who built an orthodox cathedral on the site in the 10th century AD in honour of the Virgin Mary, the Christian version of Isis. Three walls remain standing. By the steps to the burial crypt are numerous fragments of red (Roman) and glazed (Ottoman) pottery. Bosnian troops loyal to the Ottoman Sultan invaded the site in 1517 whereupon the cathedral was converted into a mosque, and their descendants inhabited the site for the next 300 years. The fortress was brought under central control in 1812.

Essentials

Sleeping **B** *Nefertari Abu Simbel*, T400509, F400510. 122 a/c rooms, built in 1960s, located near the temples, best hotel in town but has few guests because most tourists only spend 2 hrs in Abu Simbel before returning to Aswan, there is sometimes a problem over the limited choice of food in the restaurant, offers pool and tennis.

C *Nobaleh Ramses Hotel*, T400380, F400381. 40 rooms, good but spartan hotel which sometimes has problems with the limited choice of food.

Floating sleeping – cruise boats on Lake Nasser Since the construction of the High Dam the upper part of the Nile has been effectively cut off to navigation from the lower reaches. The only solution to getting a good vessel on the lake was to set up a shipyard and build one. Vessels on the lake are not hampered by lack of depth as on the River Nile and can be especially designed for these deeper waters.

A *MS Eugenie*, 50 a/c cabins with balcony, 2 suites, pre-Revolution decor, 2 bars, 2 large saloons, 2 sundecks, pool, jaccuzi, health club, excellent food, no enforced entertainment, cabins are US$240 double per night, US$190 single inclusive of meals and sightseeing, peak period supplement of 10%, contact *Belle Epoque Travel*, 17 Sharia Tunis, New Maadi, Cairo, T5169653, F5169646.

The only other cruise boats on Lake Nasser are **Kasr Ibrim** owned by Eugenie Investment Group, 17 Sharia Tunis, New Maadi, Cairo, T202-5169653, F202-5169646, see above, 65 rooms of a similar excellent standard but without the ancient charm; *MS Nubian Sea* owned by High Dam Cruises, 15 Sharia El Shahud Mohammed Tallat, Dokki, Giza T3613680, F3610023 which has 66 cabins and suites; *MS Prince Abbas* launched 1998, 38 standard cabins, 18 junior suites and 4 royal suites; and *MS Tanya*, Sharia 26 July, Zamalek, T3420488, F340520, good quality, 31 rooms, but our last choice.

Camping The *Nefertari Abu Simbel* has a campground where tents can be pitched but camping at the temples is illegal.

Eating Because of Abu Simbel's position in the middle of the desert, most supplies come from Aswan and consequently there are often problems with the range of foods available. Indeed, with the exception of the hotels, there are few if any places to eat and only a few poorly equipped stores.

Shopping Because there are only a few poorly stocked stores it is essential to bring your own supplies if intending to stay in Abu Simbel.

Sports Swimming and tennis at the *Nefertari Abu Simbel*.

Transport **Air** Numerous daily services to Abu Simbel with EgyptAir from Cairo (2 hrs) via Luxor (1 hr) and Aswan (30 mins) during the winter high season and about 3 during the summer low season. It is absolutely essential to book a ticket as early as possible. Most tickets are sold on the assumption that you will return the same day but it is possible to include overnight stopovers. Seats on the left hand side of the aircraft usually offer the best views as it circles the temples before landing at Abu Simbel. See For tourists arriving by plane there are free buses from Abu Simbel airport to the site of the temples.

Road Bus: Currently it is not possible for tourists to reach Abu Simbel by road.

Directory **Communications** Post Office in village centre.

Nile Delta

8

Nile Delta

Beyond Cairo, the two main distributaries of the River Nile continue northwards to meet the Mediterranean near Damietta and Rosetta, respectively. On either side and between the two branches the very flat, green and fertile land fans out to create, with the help of some of the world's oldest and most efficient irrigation systems, the Nile delta, Egypt's agricultural heartland and most heavily populated region. The fertility of this region has enabled this scorched desert country, in which under 4% of its land is cultivatable, to support a huge population and to export large quantities of fruits and vegetables, albeit while having to import huge volumes of cereals. Confusingly, because of its position north rather than south of Upper Egypt, this area was known as Lower Egypt. Because of the lack of hard stone and the very high population density, successive generations plundered old buildings for stone and built new ones on top of ancient sites. As a result there are no outstanding monuments to match the splendours of Upper Egypt. The region personifies Egypt's calm and relaxing but industrious village life fascinating for 'people watching', and is famous for being the region of many moulids or popular religious festivals.

Eastern Delta

The branching of the River Nile divides the Delta into three interlocking areas. The best pharaonic ruins including **Tanis** and **Bubastis** are in the Eastern Delta. The Central Delta includes **El-Mahalla el-Kubra** and **Tanta** which are Egypt's fourth and fifth largest cities, while Tanta is the location of Egypt's largest moulid. If heading for Alexandria, in preference to the more direct desert route, take the more scenic 'agricultural route' on highway H1 from Cairo through the cotton growing region of the Western Delta which includes the coastal town of Rosetta. Although technically in the Central Delta the small coastal resorts of Gamassa and Ras El-Bar can be reached more easily from the Eastern Delta coastal town of Damietta.

Land and sea merge at the fringes of the delta creating a mixture of lagoons and fragile mudflats – so there can be no possibility of a coastal road. The first inland paved route winds its way for over 300 km from Alexandria to Port Said.

The main road (H1) from Cairo to **Damietta** runs north through the Central Delta via **Tanta** before striking northeast through **El-Mansura** but there are other routes which offer more interest to the traveller. Turning east in **Benha**, a road goes through **Zagazig** to the ancient sites of **Nabasha** and **Tanis** from which a minor road continues to the coast or north through the intensive cultivation to El-Mansura. Damietta gives access along the coast either east to **Port Said** (see page 398) at the northern end of the Suez Canal or west to the coastal resorts of **Ras el-Bar, Gamassa** and even the isolated **Baltim**.

The main road is normally very busy with a mixture of agricultural traffic and vehicles bound for the ports. On Fridays and holidays it can be even busier with private cars. Shamut Oranges between Tukh and Benha is a very popular spot for picnics. Pigeon towers of varying designs are common in the delta region. The pigeons provide free fertilizer and are the main ingredient in 'pigeon sweet and sour', a speciality dish.

Benha

Forty-eight kilometres north of Cairo and the first major town on the H1 highway, can be reached by bus which runs every 30 minutes from Cairo's Koulali Terminal (0600-2100). Close by lie the remains of the ancient town of **Athribis** which was once the capital of the 10th Nome and associated with the worship of the black bull. Although it pre-dates the Greeks, its greatest importance was during the Roman period. Its orderly layout, like that of many Delta towns, was built around two intersecting roads. Little remains of the town today except traces of 18th-26th Dynasty temples and an extensive Graeco-Roman cemetery. A cache of 26th-30th Dynasty silver ingots and jewellery from the site is now in the Egyptian Museum in Cairo.

From Benha via Minyet el Qamh the railway lies to north of road. The tall chimney decorated with white bricks and the huge cereal stores indicate you have arrived.

Herodotus – The Historian

Herodotus lived in Greece in the fifth century BC. His great achievement was a history of the Greek wars against the Persian Empire. His origins are obscure but it is believed that he was a Greek born in Asia Minor in approximately 485 BC. He developed the great tradition of Greek historical research in which questions were asked and answers to them sought in the available written evidence. He became an avid collector of information – stories and travel data – which he eventually assembled into his **History** – writings on the wars against the Persians. He travelled widely in Asia Minor, the Black Sea region and the Mediterranean islands.

Perhaps his most famous journey was to Egypt. He began in the Nile delta and voyaged to Memphis, Thebes and the first cataract. He was deeply interested in the topography of the Nile Valley and in the nature of the Nile flood. He is attributed with the saying that, "Egypt is the gift of the Nile". Like all geographer-historians of the early period, he mixed scientific evidence and serious observation with myths, fables and tall tales. His readers were given all the excitement of the grotesque and supernatural wonders of the world, though he rarely entirely gave up rational explanations for historical events he wrote about including those in Egypt. His works were widely accepted in Athenian society and today are regarded as an important development in the establishment of history as an academic study. He was a contemporary and companion of Sophocles. In his later life he moved to a new Greek city colony in Thurii, Italy where he is buried.

Zagazig

The provincial capital, 36 km northeast of Benha and 80 km from Cairo, was founded in 1830 and was the birthplace of the nationalist Col Ahmed Orabi who led the 1882 revolt against the British. It can be reached by bus or service taxi from Cairo and trains to Port Said stop at the local station. The small **Orabi Museum** ■ *daily 0900-1300 except Tue* contains some interesting archaeological exhibits. Most visitors stop in Zagazig to see the large ruins of Bubastis which lie 3 km southeast of the town.

Sleeping Try **F** *Funduk Sharah Farouk*, said to be none better in town.

Eating There are numerous local coffee houses or eat at the *Arak Restaurant* in Sharia Tahrir.

Transport The train takes about 1½ hrs to **Cairo** and shared taxi 1 hr.

Bubastis

This was the capital of the 18th Nome of Lower Egypt and was known to the Ancient Egyptians as Pr Baset (House of Baset). The name is derived from the worship of the Egyptian cat goddess Baset who was believed to be the daughter of the sun-god Re. During the Old Kingdom she was originally associated with the destructive forces of his eye and she was symbolized as a lion. Later, during the Middle Kingdom, this image was tamed and she was represented with a brood of kittens and carrying the sacred rattle. The ancient Egyptians worshipped cats and mummified them at a number of sites including Bubastis because they believed that they would be protected by Baset.

The town was begun during the 6th Dynasty (2345-2181BC) with the granite **Temple of Baset** which was enlarged over the centuries until the 18th Dynasty (1567-1320 BC) and was excavated in the 19th century. Herodotus

Nile Delta

Sacred cats

Cats were first domesticated by the Egyptians and it seems probable that the breed they domesticated was the Kaffir cat, a thin, poorly striped, grey cat common all over Africa. Numerous tomb drawings and mummified bodies have been discovered which date from the very early Egyptian dynasties.

The cat was held in great awe and worshipped in the form of the cat-headed goddess Bast or Pasht from which it has been suggested the word 'puss' is derived. Egyptians believed that all cats went to heaven, a choice of two heavens, the more aristocratic creatures having a better class destination. If a family cat died the household members would all go into mourning and shave off their eyebrows.

described it as the most pleasing in the whole of Egypt but also criticized the antics of up to 700,000 pilgrims who attended the licentious festivals. Near the site is an underground **cat cemetery** where many statues of Baset have survived. You may find a guide to get you in – but unlikely.

El-Mansura

Phone code: 050
Colour map 2, grid A2

About 55 km north of Zagazig, El-Mansura is an attractive River Nile city which was founded comparatively recently (AD 1220) by the great Salah al-Din's nephew Sultan al-Kamil (AD 1218-38) during the Siege of Damietta by the Crusader forces during the 6th Crusade. Despite its name, which means 'the victorious', the Crusaders reoccupied Damietta in 1249 and then, following the death in El-Mansura of Kamil's son Sultan Ayyub (1240-49), which was concealed by his widow in order not to demoralize his troops, the Crusaders captured the town. However when the Crusaders were weakened by a vicious bout of food poisoning, the Muslims counter-attacked and captured not only El-Mansura but also France's King Louis IX before he was eventually ransomed for the return of Damietta.

Today Mansura is better known as the centre of the cotton industry. During harvest time it is interesting to see the activity in the fields but the incredibly overladen carts bring road traffic to a standstill.

Sleeping There are a few cheap and simple hotels in El-Mansura including: **D** *Marshal el Gezirah*, Sharia Gezirah el Ward, T/F36888, 34 beds is the best hotel in town; **E** *Cleopatra*, 13 Souq Toggar, El-Gharby, T341234, 55 rooms; **E** *Marshal*, Midan Om Kalsoum, T324380, 57 rooms; **F** *Abu Shama Hotel*, Sharia Bank Misr, T354227, 31 rooms; **F** *Mecca Touristic*, Sharia el-Abbas, Corniche, T349910, 54 rooms. *Royal*, 40 Sharia El Thawra, T355468, 27 rooms.

Transport **Train, bus & service taxis**: trains to/from **Cairo** there are very frequent buses with *East Delta Co* and service taxis to/from **Zagazig** and **Cairo** to the south and **Damietta** to the north and links to various towns in the Eastern and Central Delta.

Nile Delta

Tanis

While most travellers from Zagazig head north to El-Mansura, those going east towards the Suez Canal might make a detour to the ruins of an Old Kingdom city better known by its Greek name of **Tanis (Djane)**. It is located near the modern village of San el-Hagar, 167 km from Zagazig, and once lay alongside and got its name from the now dry Tanite branch of the River Nile. In the **Second Intermediate Period** (1786-1567 BC) Asiatic settlers to the region, known as the Hyksos kings or 'princes of foreign lands', established the 15th Dynasty (1674-1567 BC) until they were expelled from Egypt and chased back to Asia by indigenous Theban kings from Luxor.

Until earlier this century it was believed that Tanis was Avaris which was the capital of the Hyksos Kingdom but Avaris has now been discovered further to the southwest at the modern day site of Tell el-Dab'a. Instead Tanis was the birth place of Ramses I (1320-18 BC) an ambitious local prince who become pharaoh and founded the 19th Dynasty (see page 234.) The area is dotted with ruins, scattered and broken statues and stones which are the only remnants of the **Temple of Amun**. To the south of the temple is the **Royal Necropolis** which is closed to the public. Six tombs of the 11th and 22nd Dynasties were found here. They were almost intact.

Tell Al-Maskhuta

Another ruined site on the eastern edge of the Delta is **Tell al-Maskhuta** which lies just south of the main Zagazig (70 km) to Ismailia (11 km) road. It has been identified as the site of the ancient town of **Tjehu** which was the capital of the 8th Nome of Lower Egypt and was often known by its Biblical name of **Pithom**. Archaeological excavations have revealed the foundations of the ancient city, a temple structure and brick chambers for single and multiple burials together with children's bodies buried in amporae. A well preserved sphinx and a statue of Ramses II were also uncovered and are now in a museum in Ismailia.

Damietta

Back near the River Nile the easiest way north from El-Mansura is to cross the river to the Central Delta town of Talkha and head up the main H8 highway to the coastal town of **Damietta** (or **Dumyat**). It is located on the east bank almost at the mouth of the Damietta branch of the River Nile and is 191 km from Cairo, 122 km from Zagazig and 66 km from El-Mansura. Furniture making is an important craft, while production of confectionery and fresh fruit and vegetables adds to the economy.

Phone code: 057
Colour map 2, grid A3

The town is in many ways similar to Rosetta, 50 km east of Alexandria (see page 336). Indeed Damietta flourished as a trading port throughout the Middle Ages but suffered greatly during the Crusades. The Christian forces occupied the town in 1167-68 and again in 1218-21 when St Francis of Assisi accompanied the invaders. Sultan al-Kamil's attempts to recapture it followed. (See El-Mansura, page 328.) Worse was yet to come, for the Mamlukes destroyed the city in 1250 and made the river impassable as a punishment for suspected disloyalty and to prevent further invasions. The Ottomans revived the town and, as in the case of Rosetta, many of their attractive buildings are still in good condition. The last Ottoman Pasha here surrendered to the Beys in 1801 before the time of Mohammed Ali. Although the construction of the Suez Canal shifted trade to Port Said, 70 km to the east, Damietta is still a small and successful port although it has little to attract visitors.

Nile Delta

Bird watching in Egypt

Why Egypt? Egypt stands in a special position as a bridge between the continents of Europe, Asia and Africa. Migrating birds, the larger birds in particular like **storks**, **pelicans** and **raptors**, depend on thermals which only occur over land. This restricts their routes and provides birdwatchers in Egypt with some awesome sights. In addition Sinai as the only land link to the east is important.

Egypt is the over wintering quarters for a wide range of birds, visitors such as the **White Stork**, **Spoonbill**, **Greater Flamingo**, **Great Crested Grebe**, **Ringed Plover**. The Nile Delta is a major resting place and the watering holes in the oases are life saving halts.

Egypt is interesting too as the most northern limit for some species which include **Senegal Thick-knee**, **Painted Snipe**, **Kittlitz's Plover**, **Senegal Coucal** and **Nile Valley Sunbird**.

One delightful resident is the Nile Valley Sunbird already mentioned. The male has iridescent purple/green plumage, a yellow breast and a long slender tailfeather. It is only a small bird (10 cm) attracted into gardens by the nectar in flowers. Another attractive resident is the **Purple Gallinule**, sporting red beak and legs along with plumage of blue, purple and green. It is about half the size of a duck. There are many, many more.

Bird watching locations:

1. **Lake Burullus**, a good location for delta birds – thousands of Wigeon, Coot and Whiskered Tern and other water birds. Access can be difficult.

2. **Lake el Manzala** is in the Eastern Delta with access from Port Said. It is an important over wintering area for water/shore birds.

3. **Lake Bardweel** on the north Sinai coast is well known for migratory birds in their thousands, especially in the autumn, and in particular water birds, ducks and herons. Shore birds too like Avocet and Flamingo can been seen here.

4. **Wadi el-Natrun**. Here in the shallow lagoons may be found Kittlitz's Plover and Blue-cheeked Bee-eaters but don't expect an instant sighting.

5. Near Cairo airport at **Gabel Asfar** the recycling plant provides a mixed habitat with opportunities to see Painted Snipe, Senegal Coucal and the White-breasted Kingfisher. The Egyptian Nightjar may be heard but is unlikely to be seen. Cairo Zoo, Giza is recommended – for the song birds in the gardens. In cities, or any settlement for that matter, the Black Kite acts as a scavenger. Near Cairo, at the Pyramids look out for the Pharaoh Eagle Owl.

6. **Suez** in the perfect position for observing migratory birds – for Raptors in particular which pass over in their thousands, also Gulls, Waders and Terns. Look for the Greater Sand Plover and Broad-billed Sandpiper also White-eyed Gull and Lesser Crested Tern more often associated with the Red Sea. All these resident and migratory birds are attracted by the mud flats and conditions in Suez Basin.

7. **Taba** region residents include Namaqua Dove, Little Green Bee-eater, Mourning, Hooded and White-crowned Black Wheatears. Migrants include Olivaceous and Orphean Warblers. White-cheeked and Bridle Tern can be seen off the coast between Taba and Sharm el-Sheikh.

Bee-eater

Painted Snipe

See page 332 for map of birdwatching sites

Nile Delta

8. At **Mt Sinai** look for Verreaux's Eagle which nest in this area. Residents include Lammergeier, Sinai Rosefinch frequently sighted near St Catherine's Monastery, Barbary Falcon, Sand Partridge, Little Green Bee-eater, Rock Martin, Desert and Hoopoe Larks, Scrub Warbler, White-crowned Black and Hooded Wheatears, Blackstart, Tristram's Grackle, Brown-necked Raven and House Bunting. There are special migrants to be observed such as Masked and Red-backed Shrikes, Olive-tree and Orphean Warblers. Look also for Hulme's Tawny Owl.

9. Try the tip of Sinai round **Ras Mohammed** where the Nabq protected area is recommended. Mark up Sooty Falcon seen on the cliffs nest here, Lichtenstein's Sandgrouse further inland near the recycling plant, White-eyed Gull, Bridled Tern, White-cheeked and Lesser Crested Tern (less common are Brown Booby and Crested Tern). Osprey nest in this region too. Migratory birds include White Storks which are very abundant. There is a White Stork sanctuary near Sharm el-Sheikh.

10. **El-Fayoum oasis** is noted for water birds and waders. It has been associated with duck hunting from ancient times. Over wintering duck, Coot and Grebe gather here in great numbers. Lake Qaroun in El-Fayoum oasis is a salt water lake and the area is now protected. In winter it is covered with water fowl. On the north shores of the lake falcons and hawks quarter the ground and in the trees see the Green Bee-eater, Bulbul and Grey Shrike. Note too Lapwing, Swallow and Senegal Thick-knee. Shore birds include Sandpipers, Curlew, Coot (never seen so many) and Grebe.

11. The Red Sea off **Hurghada** is a rich habitat supporting 15 species of breeding birds, both water birds and sea birds. Brown Booby, Western Reef Egret, White-eyed and Sooty Gulls, Crested, Lesser Crested and White-cheeked Terns, Red-billed Tropicbird, Bridled Tern are on the list. The islands in the Red Sea provide a safer habitat for the birds. Such is Isle of Tiran, approach only by boat, not to land. Osprey nest here, in places quite common. Sooty (a few) and White-eyed Gulls (more common) are found on the uninhabited islands further south.

12. Around **Luxor** look for Black-shouldered Kite, Black Kite, Egyptian Vulture, Senegal Thick-knee, Purple Gallinule with perhaps a Painted Snipe or a Nile Valley Sunbird on Crocodile Island where Hotel Movenpick has made an effort to protect the environment for these birds. On the other side of the River Nile in the Valleys of the Kings and Queens are Rock Martin, Trumpeter Finch, Little Green Bee-eater. Desert birds found anywhere in desert are represented here by Hoopoe and Bar-tailed Larks.

13. **Dakhla Oasis** has a large lake called the Fishpond the surface almost obscured by birds, Avocet, Stilt, coot.

14. **Aswan** is one of the best places for herons and kingfishers, best viewed from the river itself. Pied Kingfishers and Egyptian Geese are common. At Aswan try Saluga Island which is a protected area.

15. **Abu Simbel** is important due to its southerly location. After viewing the monuments take time to look for rarities including Long-tailed Cormorant, Pink-backed Pelican, Yellow-billed stork, African Skimmer, Pink-headed Dove and African Pied Wagtail.

16. **Jebel Elba** in the very south-east corner of Egypt has samples of sub-Saharan birds – Verreaux's eagles, Pink headed Doves and perhaps even Ostrich. This region cannot be visited without a permit, which is not likely to be forthcoming.

A study of the birds of ancient Egypt can be done by examining hieroglyphics and carvings . Here they cannot fly away before the glasses are focussed. Sunbird Tours (see page 21) have identified a total of 45 species ranging from the predynastic rock carvings of Ostrich to the Common and Demoiselle Cranes in the Mastaba of Ti at Saqqara. Certainly different.

Nile Delta

Sights As well as looking at the Ottoman buildings, visit the new Coptic church of St Mary opened by Pope Shenuda in 1992. Out of town is the huge **Lake el Manzala** which in winter teems with migrating birds including flamingoes, spoonbills and herons (see box on birdwatching, page 330). On the other side of the branch of the River Nile there are three beach resorts, **Ras el-Bar**, **Gamassa** and **Baltim** which, although technically in the Central Delta, are most easily reached from Damietta.

Sleeping The only government registered hotel is **F** *El-Manshi Hotel*, 5 Sharia el-Nokrashy, T323308. 20 rooms, which is barely comfortable but there are a few other even cheaper hotels along the Corniche.

Transport **Train** Although they are slower, there are trains to **Cairo**, **Alexandria**, **Tanta** and **Zagazig**. **Road Bus & service taxis**: there are hourly buses and service taxis to **Cairo** either down the main H8 highway via Tanta and Benha or the east route via El-Mansura and Zagazig. **Port Said**, 70 km east along the causeway which divides the lake from the Mediterranean, is only easily reached by service taxi.

Ras El-Bar

Located on the west bank of the Damietta branch of River Nile only a few kilometres north of the city at the point where the river meets the sea. It is a favourite resort for middle-class Egyptians who want to get away from Cairo's summer heat. It is an attractive resort, popular without too much bustle. It can be reached very easily either from Damietta or by special a/c buses direct from Cairo's Koulali bus station or service taxis. Al-Jirbi, just 2 km from Ras el-Bar has a therapy centre for the treatment of gout, sciatica, polio and rheumatism. This is only open in the summer months.

Birdwatching sites

See box on previous page for key

Nile Delta

There are lots of cheap beach hotels which cater for the Egyptian tourists. The best of **Sleeping** a mediocre bunch are: **E** *Abu Tabl*, 4 Sharia 17, T528166, 34 rooms; **E** *El Medina El Monawara*, 1 Sharia 29, T527261, 34 rooms and **E** *El-Mina Hotel*, end of Sharia 61, El-Shatee, T529290, 50 rooms. It is impossible to recommended any of the very cheap hotels as the standard changes with staff and management. Choose only after you have inspected the room.

Gamassa

Further west along the coast about 20 km from Damietta, Gamassa is another resort with a long beach, some 25 km, of fine sand. A new development of apartments and new holiday homes has encroached on the beach which could be cleaner. Locals sunbathe here. The sea is dark – with iodine. It can be reached, either by bus from Damietta or directly from Cairo. Alternatively catch a train to El-Mansura or Shirban from where a bus can be caught.

There are a number of hotels which range from those detailed below to unofficially **Sleeping** registered ones with cabin-like chalets. **E** *Amun*, El-Souq area, Gamassa, T760660, located on the beach, best in town. **E** *Beau Rivage*, Gamassa, T760268. 86 rooms. **F** *Hannoville*, Shagaret el-Dor Area, Gamassa, T760750. 50 rooms.

Baltim

This was once the most inaccessible and quietest of the three resorts, actually about half way between Damietta and Rosetta and, although it can be reached from Damietta it may be easier by direct coach from Cairo. Once the playground of the rich and leisured it is now a resort which caters for those who do not expect such high standards of service or cleanliness. Litter is a problem here. Take a Delta East bus or the train to El-Mansura and complete the journey by bus.

There are two officially registered hotels but neither have many Western visitors and **Sleeping** mainly cater for Egyptian summer tourists. Both charge E£10 per night **F** *Baltim Beach*, El-Narguess Area, Baltim, T501541. 30 rooms. **F** *Cleopatra Touristic*, Baltim Beach, Baltim. 28 rooms.

Central Delta

There are fewer sites in the Central Delta but it does include two of Egypt's largest cities and has some of the largest annual *moulids*. Assuming that most tourists to the northern beach resorts will probably either travel to Damietta or take special coaches direct from Cairo it is probably best for visitors to the Central Delta region to base themselves in the centrally situated, large but charming town of **Tanta**, which has excellent communications, and then from there make day trips to the various sites.

Tanta

This town maintains its rural atmosphere despite being the fifth largest city in *Phone code: 040* Egypt with a major university. It is located 94 km north of Cairo and 130 km *Colour map 2, grid A2* southeast of Alexandria on the main agricultural route between the two cities. The H1 highway from Cairo to Benha crosses the Damietta branch of the River Nile and continues northwest via Birket el-Sab to Tanta. In late October the biggest *moulid* of all, attracting up to two million visitors (see page 335) is held here.

Nile Delta

Sights Although it is an interesting city, which is worth visiting to soak up the atmosphere of modern life for most Egyptian without the glories of past eras and masses of tourists, there is little or nothing to see in Tanta itself for most of the year. It really comes alive, however, in October at the end of the cotton harvest during the 8-day festival or **Moulid of Sayid Ahmed el-Badawi** when the population swells to over two million as pilgrims pour in from throughout Egypt and the Muslim world.

Sayid Ahmed el-Badawi (AD 1199-1276) was the founder of one of Egypt's largest Sufi *tariqas* (brotherhoods/orders) which is known as the Badawiya. Born in Fes in Morocco he emigrated to Arabia and then travelled to Iraq where he joined the Rifaiyah brotherhood. He was sent to Tanta in 1234 as its representative but then received permission to establish his own *tariqa* which soon flourished. Although the mosque built by his successor and containing his tomb was demolished in the mid-19th century a large, new, rather undistinguished one was built by pasha Abbas I (AD 1848-54) and is the focus of Badawi's annual *moulid*.

Sleeping There are few facilities for Western tourists here but, unless you are visiting specifically for the *moulid* when it is essential to book well in advance, there should be no problem in finding a room. Although there are many other small establishments there are only 2 officially registered hotels. **D** *Arafa Hotel*, Midan Station, First Tanta, T336952, F331800. 43 rooms, directly outside the station. **D** *Green House*, Sharia el-Borsa, Midan Gumhorriya, T330761, F330320. 30 good a/c rooms, restaurant, splendid central location, parking. Recommended. **Youth hostels** Sharia Mahala el Kobra, T337978. 24 beds, parking.

Eating There are numerous cheap food stalls during the moulids, otherwise eat at the restaurant in *Green House*, which is clean and comfortable.

Directory **Airline offices** *EgyptAir* 321750. **Banks** *Delta Bank* may cash your TCs and *Banque Misr* has an ATM. Both banks are in Midan Gumhorriya.

El-Mahalla El-Kubra

Phone code: 040
Colour map 2, grid A2

The fourth largest city in Egypt, is 25 km northeast of Tanta and 120 km north of Cairo. The only decent hotel is **E** Omar el-Khayyam, Midan July 23rd, T334866, 36 rooms. To the west of the nearby riverside town of **Sammanud** is the remains of the red and black granite **Temple of Onuris-Shu** which was rebuilt by Nectanebo II (360-343 BC) for Tjeboutjes which was the capital of the 12th Nome of Lower Egypt. Further northeast some 10 km from Sammanud along the main H8 highway towards **Talkha** there is the modern town of **Bahbait al-Hagar** and what little remains of the great **Temple of Isis** in the ancient town of **Iseum** or **Pr-Hebeit** as it was known to the ancient Egyptians.

Continuing further along the H8 highway 25 km past Talkha, is the town of **Shirban** which has a bridge to the east bank of the Rosetta branch of the River Nile. Leaving H8 and travelling 12 km west along H7 is **Bilqas** where, 3 km to the north, is the **Monastery of St Damyanah** (Deir Sitt Damyanah). St Damyanah was put to death, along with another 40 maidens, under Diocletian's purges against the Christians. Normally it is isolated and difficult to reach except during the annual **Moulid of Damyanah** between 15-20 May, which is one of the country's largest Christian *moulids*. Thousands of pilgrims flock to the four 19th and 20th century churches on the site in the hope of being healed. Women praying for increased fertility and those who have lost young children are common visitors here.

Moulids – *Festivals in the Delta*

Officially, moulids *are festivals in commemoration of a specific saint when pilgrims obtain their* baraka *or blessing by visiting their shrine. There is usually a parade of devotees, carrying banners and dressed in turbans and sashes in the colours of their saint, which is followed by chanting and dancing that goes on for* hours. *In addition, however, the most important* moulids *are like a giant mediaeval fair where pilgrims meet their friends and eat, drink and have fun together. They stroll amongst the stalls and rides watching the magicians, jugglers, acrobats, snake charmers, animal trainers and other traditional entertainers.*

The only claim to fame of **El-Bagur**, which lies at the extremity of the Central Delta to the south of **Shiban el-Kom**, is that it is President Mubarak's small home town. The only place to stay is E *Nice Tourist Village*, El-Bagur Minufiya, T384073, 25 rooms. Mubarak's predecessor President Anwar Sadat, who was assassinated by Islamic fundamentalists in 1981, came from the nearby village of **Mit Abu el-Kom** which is close to Quweisna on the main Benha-Tanta highway.

Road & train The Central Delta region is well served by public transport and there are buses and service taxis between all the major and most of the minor towns. From Tanta there are very frequent services to Cairo and Alexandria, while the train journeys take 1½ hrs and 2 hrs, respectively. Although they are less frequent there are also train services from Tanta to the other major cities but a service taxi may be easiest given the comparatively short distances. **Transport**

Western Delta

The main H1 continues on to Alexandria and there are many clean roadside restaurants catering for the weekend travellers – strangely there are more on the north bound carriageway. On the outskirts of Tanta going north try the *Pearl* café (where the waiters wear bow ties) for tea or Turkish coffee and a clean toilet.

Abu Qir noted for Nelson's defeat of the French fleet in Abu Qir Bay in 1798 is really now just an extension of Alexandria.

Across the wider Rosetta branch of the River Nile is the **Western Delta** which has fewer ancient remains than either the Eastern or Central Delta. The main attractions are the port of **Rosetta** and a couple of *moulids* held in and around the town of **Damanhur**. This route, like most in the delta, goes through an interesting mixture of scenery: fields of cotton, sugar cane and pocket-sized areas of vegetables, tiny clusters of houses, old fashioned water lifting devices (see delu well in Background) and the whole area is busy with carts, donkeys, and men and women working in the fields. It is an ever-changing scene of rural Egypt, absolutely fascinating, yet most travellers rush straight on to Alexandria. The taming of the River Nile in the late 19th century, changing the water supply from uncontrolled annual flood to perennial irrigation, enables the cultivation of three or four crops a year in this extremely fertile region.

Nile Delta

High Noon at Damyanah – Martyrs' Calendar

Damyanah, who was the daughter of Rome's regional governor in the time of **Diocletian** *(AD 284-305), chose celibacy rather than marriage and took refuge with 40 other virgins in a palace built for her by her father. When her father renounced the worship of the Roman gods and converted to Christianity both he and all of the women were executed on the orders of Diocletian. His persecution of the Christians was so great that the Copts date their era, known as the Martyrs' Calendar, from the massacres of AD 284. The first shrine to Damyanah is believed to have been built by St Helena who was the mother of emperor Constantine (AD 306-337).*

Damanhur

Mid-way between Tanta and Alexandria, Damanhur lies in the middle of the Western Delta, 160 km northwest of Cairo. This sleepy provincial capital and textile town, which was once the site of the ancient city of Tmn-Hor dedicated to Horus, normally has nothing to offer the visitor. In November, however, there is the **Moulid of Sheikh Abu Rish** which follows the more important one in Tanta. Extending over two days in January is Egypt's only **Jewish moulid** at the shrine of a 19th-century mystic called **Abu Khatzeira**. Because of the security problems, non-Jewish Egyptians are kept out of the festival by the police and most of those who attend are Europeans and Israelis who bring sick relatives or bottled water to be blessed at the shrine.

Sleeping **Youth hostels** 9 Sharia el Shaheed Gawad, T3214056. 30 beds, kitchen, station 2 km, overnight fee E£3.

Rosetta

Colour map 2, grid A1 Sixty-four kilometres east of Alexandria on the H18 at the coast on the mouth of the major distributary of the River Nile, stands Rosetta (Rashid). It is famous for the discovery, in 1799, of the **Rosetta Stone**, which was the key to our understanding of Hieroglyphics and, consequently, much of what we know of Egypt's ancient civilization. (See box Breaking the Code page 340). The stone is inscribed, in Greek, hieroglyphics and demotic Egyptian with a proclamation by Ptolemy V Epiphanes. Today the stone is in the British Museum in London.

Rosetta was known as the city of a million palms and dates still form an important industry. Rice cultivation is important too. Once a principle port, a number of the older houses from the Ottoman period have been purchased by the Antiquities department with the intention of repair/restoration and some may be visited. Attractions of these buildings include the external brickwork, overhanging upper floors with white (painted) mortar between, the attractive *mashrabiyya* at windows and balconies. All inclusive ticket for the museum in **Arab Kuli House**, the Qaitbay Fort and the Ottoman Houses is E£12 (cameras E£10) bought at the fort or the museum. ■ *Daily 0800-1600.*

Qaitbay Fort (Fort St Julien) is 5 km out of town and can be reached by taxi (£E6) or boat slightly more. ■ *0900-1600 (closes at 1500 in Ramadan).*

The 18th-century mosque of **Abu Mandur**, 5 km upstream by taxiboat (E£8) or felucca.

Easy to recognize – The Hoopoe

The Hoopoe Upupa epopsis *is like no other bird – it is the only one in its species.*

It is a resident breeder, fairly common especially in the Delta area. The sexes are similar, both 28 cm in length. It is in evidence on lawns and in parks and oases where it disturbs the ground searching for grubs. It also eats locusts, moths, spiders and ants. It nests in holes in old trees or ruins (plenty of scope in Egypt) laying up to six eggs.

In general the colouring is buff/pink with very distinctive black and white bars in a striped pattern (like a zebra) on the wings and tail. It has a long and slender down-curving bill with a black tip, a square tail and broad rounded wings,

striped with black tips. A distinctive, large erect crest runs from front to back of the head, the feathers having quite marked black tips. This crest is raised when it alights and is evident in mating displays.
The call is a distinct Hoo-poo-oo.

The writings of the ancient Egyptians were in hieroglyphs, the word meaning in Greek 'sacred carving' and originally applied only to Egyptian signs though is now used as a general word for all pictorial writing. The evolution of the ancient Egyptian language was complex and more or less continuous from Semitic and other elements. In the Ptolomaic period there was a rapid development of the language through loan-words from Greek leading to the emergence of Coptic, which made use of Greek script. The continuity provided by this transition was a major aid in the ultimate deciphering of hieroglyphs.

There is continuing argument concerning the origins of the hieroglyphs. Some experts believe that hieroglyphs began with a picture writing phase, others that they started as phonetic symbols and never went through a pictorial phase. Certainly, the hieroglyphs became a phonetic alphabet and were designed to enable scribes to distinguish particular dates and events. Kings, important figures of state, time and place were designated with their own sign signature or cartouche. Some objects such as the giraffe or the eye or bread would be rendered by a stylized picture of a giraffe, an eye or a loaf. See examples of pictograms below. By the second dynasty there were whole sentences rather than only key words in use, all phonetically constructed. Words were, however, made up of symbols for consonants only – full vowels sounds were unmarked – and can thus be called 'phonograms', of which there were some 24 signs by 3000 BC. Additionally, there were approximately 700 other signs in use in the classical period though in later dynasties the number of symbols rose considerably as new ones were added to encompass new words and ideas.

Another trend brought groups of words or entire ideas to be represented in script, with the symbols for each word given a picture of general meaning (determinatives) but no phonetic value. In this system the signs for the sounds for example to make up the name of a particular flower would be given,

Hieroglyphs

Nile Delta

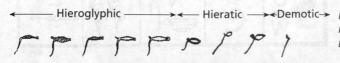

←——— Hieroglyphic ———→◄— Hieratic —→◄Demotic→

Hieroglyphic, Heiratic, Demotic Scripts

followed by a general picture of a flower so that any uncertainty of the meaning would be removed. Similarly, the phonetic signs for prayer would be given follower by the determinative sign of a man with hands raised in supplication.

Hieroglyphs developed into three major forms of writing (see illustration – Hieroglyphic, Hieratic and Demotic Scripts, page 341).

First, traditional hieroglyphs were largely pictorial, with elaborate carving of symbols in representational art. Thus the basket, which was the symbol for 'k' (see illustration – A Hieroglyph Alphabet, see below, was fully lined and unmistakably a basket. Writing hieroglyphs was a time-consuming task either colour painted on smooth surfaces by brush or chiselled into stone.

Second, a shortened or 'hieratic' script, sometimes known as 'cursive' was adopted for sacred texts and for official state manuscripts. Hieratic script read from right to left (though horizontally from 2000 BC) whereas hierglyphs can also occur to be read from left to right and vertically. In both forms the direction of writing can be detected since the symbols for humans, animals and birds always face towards the beginning of a line of script. The cursive script enabled scribes to join up two letters in a single brush stroke.

A third form of script evolved called 'demotic' since it was the common or popular means of writing. It came into use in the seventh century BC. In it a type of shorthand was used with joined up characters though it was mainly applied to symbols carved in stone and was applied to official state papers. Although demotic script was in popular use, in reality it was hieratic script –

Heiroglyph
Alphabet

GM

More a land of buffalo than camels

The conventional view of Egypt is that the camel is king. Far from it. Although no self-respecting tourist will leave without having sampled the riding qualities of the camel, it only makes up a small part of the domesticated animals in Egypt. There are a mere 100,000 camels reported against 3,250,000 buffalo and 3,400,000 sheep. Like the ancient Egyptians, the modern dwellers in the delta and valley prefer birds to animals. Some 39 million chickens and 10 million pigeons populate the country as commercial livestock for eating and egg production. In Egypt's rambling urban areas, where recent migrants from the countryside gather, there are great numbers of sheep, goats and cattle kept for milk and meat by every family that can afford to. The animals scavenge among the refuse tips and graze every available scrap of roadside vegetation, giving even city areas a rustic appearance and a distinctly rural smell! Their value is however undisputed – animal output accounts for as much as 7.5% of gross domestic product (GDP), about half the value of all agricultural production (E£30,000 mn) in 1995.

Stylized camel design common on tribal rugs

easily written using ink on papyrus – which was the principal means of conveying information.

Most visitors to Egypt see hieroglyphs in their various forms on tombs, temple and chapel monuments. These symbols are often repeated in this formal setting, especially the signs for kings, queens, princes and gods. Tutankhamen, for example, carries two names in his cartouche, the first "NB-HPRW-R'" and a second "TWT-'NH-'IMN-HKs-'LWNW RSY" so that he can be distinguished from other kings with similar representational symbols (see illustration – Tutankhamen's Cartouche, page 207).

The gods similarly have symbol signatures, notably the Re, God of the Sun (see symbol of Re on page 216).

Hieroglyphic writing survived at least until the fifth century AD but the Christian period brought change and from the third century AD there was extensive use of Greek script to write the Egyptian language of the time (Coptic) for religious and eventually all purposes. Hieroglyphics fell from use and understanding of it was entirely lost. It was not until Thomas Young in England and, more completely, Jean-Francois Champollion in France deciphered hieroglyphic writing in the 19th century that there was a re-awakening of interest in the ancient Egyptian language.

Sights

Like many towns in Egypt that can claim a flourishing and varied past, there is relatively little to see in Rosetta today. Since ancient times its fortunes have been linked with the ebb and flow of those of it's neighbour Alexandria. When one waxed, the other would wane. Mohammed Ali's Mahmudiya Canal project linking the River Nile to Alexandria marked the end of Rosetta's significance as a port. Whilst Alexandria is now Egypt's second city, Rosetta is little more than a fishing village.

There are some interesting older (early 17th century) buildings in the town, houses of the merchants in this once important trading centre. The Department of Egyptian Antiquities began a programme of restoration

Nile Delta

☛ Breaking the code

Jean-Francois Champollion was born in the village of Figeac in France in December 1790. He was a precocious learner of difficult foreign languages and from an early age became involved with studies of Greek, Latin and the Coptic languages.

*Like other scholars before him, in the 1820s he began deciphering Egyptian hieroglyphs and by 1822 evolved a virtually complete set of hieroglyphic signs and their Greek equivalent, using the information on the **Rosetta Stone**. The Rosetta Stone was found near Rashid in 1799 by soldiers of Napoleon's expedition to Egypt. The huge, irregularly shaped piece of granite weighing 762 kg was embedded in the wall of El Rashid fort, a piece of recycled fortification. It is thought to have been written by one of the high priests of Memphis in the ninth year of Ptolemy V's reign (196 BC) and is originally a decree of Ptolemy V declaring the benefits he, as a monarch, conferred on Egypt. Its importance was not in its content – though it did establish* inter alia *that Ptolemy reunited the country – but in its presentation of three scripts – Greek script below and hieroglyphs, demotic and cursive Egyptian languages above.*

The Swede Akerblad and the Englishman Thomas Young had made some progress in deciphering the Rosetta Stone but it was Champollion, using his knowledge of Egyptology, Greek and Coptic languages, who finally broke the code. He was unique in understanding that individual Egyptian hieroglyphs stood for individual letters, groups of letters and even for entire objects.

Champollion undertook archaeological work in Egypt in 1828 with the Italian Ippolito Rosellini, recording a whole series of sites in the Nile Valley. He died suddenly in 1832 age 42 years having been curator of the Egyptian collection of the Louvre and professor of Egyptian antiquities at the highly esteemed Collège de France. His brother Jacques-Joseph prepared and published his works after Jean-Francois's death.

here in 1985. Many of these houses are made of distinctive red and black brick and incorporate recycled stones and columns from earlier eras. Many too have delicately carved *mashrabiyyas*. In particular are those of El Fatatri just off the main street to the north of the town and Arab Keli (18th century) at the west end of Midan Gumhurriya. The latter is now a museum noted for its delicately handcrafted woodwork. Other buildings to look out for are Thabet House, Mekki House and Abu Shahin Mill. The mosques are worth a visit for their coloured tilework. The huge Zagloul mosque one block north of the main road to Alexandria, is a double mosque, that to the west is brighter and smarter and remembered for its arched courtyard while that to the west (founded around 1600) with over 300 columns is unfortunately suffering from partial submersion. The Mohammed al-Abassi mosque (1809) stands to the south of the town by the River Nile and has a distinctive minaret. A lively market is held in the main street to the north of the town towards the station.

Tutankhamen's Cartouche

Egyptian numbers

The earliest way of writing numbers was by repeated strikes: / for 1, // for 2, /// for 3, etc. This obviously soon became cumbersome so signs for 10 and 1000 and other large numbers were adopted. The Egyptian numbers are shown below. The example drawn out is a great advance on writing and then counting, 1,343 separate strokes.

1   10   100   1,000   10,000   100,000

Example: 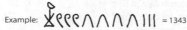 = 1343

The H11 Desert road is a fast dual carriageway and the distance from Cairo to Alexandria (224 km) can be covered easily in three hours. Express coaches of the *West Delta Bus Co* follow this route. It is not busy as most drivers begrudge the E£1.5 toll per car. There is plenty of fuel available and accommodation: try the *Sahara Inn Motel* 117 km before Alexandria for a long or a short rest. Agriculture along here is large scale, comprising huge developments of bananas, dates and deciduous trees all dependent on underground water supplies. There is a large new town, **Sadat City**, off the road to the east.

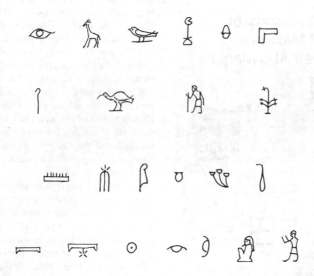

Pictograms

Nile Delta

Wadi El Natrun

Wadi El Natrun is a natural depression of salt lakes and salt flats lying in the desert to the west of the Nile delta. It is a birdwatchers' paradise. The *wadi* is aligned on an axis northwest to southeast to the immediate west of the direct desert road from Giza to Alexandria at approximately Km 100. Access is either from the desert road at approximately 90 km from Giza turning west just before the outskirts of Sadat City, which stands to the east of the road, or from just north of the resthouse at Km 103.

Wadi El Natrun

Wadi El Natrun became the centre of a series of monastic groups principally in the fourth century AD. Insecurity, the plague and attacks by Bedouin led to the decline of some scattered communities but also led to some centralization of Christians into monasteries, of which four remain populated to the present day. The **Monastery of St Makarios** (Deir Abu Maqar) lies 3 km off the desert highway. It comprises the meagre set of remains of a once-great site in which a hasty and not entirely aesthetically pleasing reconstruction programme is under way. Its importance arises from the importance of St Makarios (St Makarios the Egyptian, AD 300-390) the son of a village priest who came to the Wadi El Natrun in AD 330 and became the spiritual leader of the Christian hermits and monks in the area. He was ordained and made his name as a prophet and preacher of the ascetic way of life. He was buried at the monastery in the Wadi El Natrun. Another nine patriarchs of the Church are also interred at the site. This monastery is not open to visitors.

Monastery of St Makarios – Deir Abu Maqar

1 Porch/entrance
2 Store rooms
3 Church of Abu Shenuda
4 Church of St Makarios
5 Cell of the Council
6 Sanctuary of Benjamin
7 Baptistry of St John
8 Pulpit
9 Bakery
10 Cell of the Chrism

■ Original fabric
▭ Recent fabric
■ Fabric under very recent restoration

0 metres 20
0 yards 20

The site itself is made up of several churches, frequently destroyed and rebuilt. The main church, that of St Makarios, is basically a much-restored building on ancient foundations with some small survivals such as the 11th century dome and vestiges of the side chapels which are 7th-9th centuries. Those of St Benjamin and St John are among the most ancient of the original fabric. The main site contains the Cell of the Chrism, the fluid used to embalm Jesus Christ, and there is a belief that some of this original material was stored here at Deir Abu Maqar. A small bakery for making the host is located in a small room still standing in its original form on the north wall. An 11th-century three-storey defensive tower can be found behind the churches. Note the religious paintings in the smaller chapels in the tower.

To the northwest lie two other living monasteries – **Deir Anba Bishoi (Pschoi)** and **Deir el-Suriani**. Deir Anba Bishoi was named after the patron saint who went to the wadi following a divine revelation and lived there in solitude. These two sites are easily reached and offer no problems for visitors who wish to walk around. The buildings at Deir Anba Bishoi are mainly 20th century and are run for a

Monastery of St Bishoi - Deir Anba Bishoi

N

0 metres 10
0 yards 10

1 Entrance porch
2 Nave
3 Footbath
4 Choir
5 Chapel of the Virgin
6 Chapel of St Istkhirun
7 Baptistry
8 Relics of St Bishoi
9 Sanctuary
10 Altar

thoroughly modern community of monks. The layout of the ancient church is cruciform, with a central nave leading to a choir and through doors to the altar sanctuary. Small side chapels (Chapel of the Virgin to the left and Chapel of St Istkhirun or Ischyrion to the right) lie either side of the sanctuary.

Deir el-Suriani (Monastery of the Syrians) is thought to be an 11th-century foundation by orthodox monks who resisted a schismatic movement at Deir Anba Bishoi. The site was acquired by a devout Syrian Christian in the 8th-9th centuries and thus took its now popular name since the schism had ended and the monks had returned to their centre at Bishoi. The Church of the Virgin Mary, the main structure at Deir el-Suriani is built over the cave used by St Bishoi. It is possible to visit this. The church has two main sections – the nave and the choir-sanctuary separated by buttresses and a doorway. The nave has a basin for the washing of feet, a stone screen and houses some religious relics, reputedly including hair from the head of Mary Magdalene, in a niche on the place where St Bishoi lived in ascetic contemplation. In a

Nile Delta

Monastery of the Syrians - Deir el-Suriani

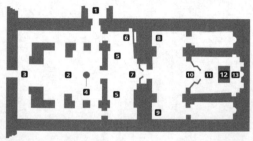

N

0 metres 10
0 yards 10

1 Porch
2 Nave
3 Semi-dome - Ascension
4 Foot bath
5 Stone screen
6 Relics
7 Ebony doors
8 Semi-dome - Death of the Virgin
9 Semi-dome - Annunciation & Nativity
10 Choir
11 Sanctuary
12 Altar
13 Stucco decorative scenes

semi-dome above the west door there is a picture of the Ascension. The altar is a very dark marble.

It is the choir which is most famous, however, for its wonderful 10th-century black wood doors with their ivory inlays. Unfortunately the two three-panel doors between the choir and the sanctuary are in poor condition. There are paintings in the semi-domes in the choir, the death of the Virgin to the left and the annunciation and the nativity to the right. There are interesting stucco decorations behind the central altar. There is a library of over 3,000 books and many valuable manuscripts. There is also a small museum on site which contains a large selection of 16th-17th century icons. Check before visiting as the monastery is closed to the public at times of important religious ceremonies.

Deir el-Baramous also known as the Monastery of the Romans is the fourth monastery of the group, somewhat isolated to the north end of the Wadi El Natrun. Gaining entry is not always possible to this, the oldest of the sites. Legend has it that Maximus and Domitius, two sons of the Roman Emperor Valentinian died young of self-imposed fasting at this place and that St Makarios set up the new monastery to commemorate them. The five churches are dedicated to the Virgin Mary, St Theodore, St George, St John the Baptist and St Michael. The church of St Michael is on the second floor of the keep. There is a drawbridge to the keep held in position by an unusual key/pin known as an Egyptian lock. The now unused refectory has a special table carved of stone, 6 m long and all one piece.

Alexandria and the Mediterranean Coast

9

346

Alexandria (El-Iskandariya), 224 km northwest of Cairo, is Egypt's second largest city and a great cultural centre, rich in classical remains, without the bustle and hassle of the capital city. It extends 20 km along Egypt's northern coast at the western edge of the Nile Delta and has become a popular summer retreat for folk from Cairo. From Alexandria, the Mediterranean Coast stretches 500 km west to the Libyan border, passing the city's local beach resorts of El-Agami and Hannoville, the site of the huge Second World War battle at El-Alamein, and the new beach resorts of Sidi Abdel Rahman and Marsa Matruh from which a road leads inland to the Siwa oasis, before finally arriving at the Libyan border near Sollum.

Alexandria was once an essential port of call for cruise ships but the prohibitive harbour charges have caused itineraries to be changed. Alexandria is a comfortable town in which to stay. Places are not far distant and having the coast to the north locating places and oneself is simple.

Alexandria

Ins and outs

Getting there

Phone code: 03
Colour map 2, grid A1
Population: 3,700,000

The airport is about 10 km from the town centre which is reached by bus No 307 or No 310 to Midan Orabi or No 203 to the nearby Midan Sa'ad Zaghloul. A taxi to the city centre costs E£12. Inter-city buses to Alexandria stop in the heart of the downtown area in Midan Sa'ad Zaghloul while buses from the Delta towns sometimes stop 1 km further south at the huge Midan El-Gumhorriya outside the main Misr railway station. There are at least 12 trains daily from Cairo. Service taxis stop at either of the two squares or at Midan Orabi which is 750 m west of Midan Sa'ad Zaghloul.

Getting around

There is a tram service around the city and taxis abound. **Tourist offices** Open daily 0800-1800 but 0900-1600 during Ramadan, located right in the city centre on south-west corner of Midan Sa'ad Zaghloul, T4807611. There are also tourist offices at the Misr railway station T4925985, the airport, T852021 and the port, T803494. For practical advice visit *Misr Tours. Tourist Friends Association*, offers all services needed by tourists, introduces them to local customs, provides multi-lingual guides, T5962108/5866115.

Best time to visit

This is between June and September.

History

Having conquered Egypt by 332 BC, **Alexander The Great**, who was then only 25 years old, commissioned his architect Deinocrates to construct a new capital city on the coast. He chose a site near the small fishing village of Rhakotis for its natural harbour and its proximity to his native Macedonia, that had significant strategic and commercial advantages over Memphis (near modern-day Cairo). It was the first Egyptian city to be built to the Greek

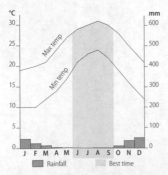

design, with the two major roads running north-south and east-west intersecting in the city centre, and the rest of the town built around them in rectangular blocks, as can be seen in almost any modern North American city. A causeway linking the city to the island of **Pharos** created two huge harbours and Alexandria became a major port.

Alexander never saw his city. He travelled to Asia after instructing his architects and 8 years later he was dead after allegedly drinking from a

Climate:

• •

The Ptolemy Dynasty in Brief

Following the death of Alexander the Great, Ptolemy, satrap (governor) of Egypt soon gained control of the country. He took the title of king and founded a dynasty that lasted from 323 BC to 30 BC. There were 14 monarchs in all, ending with Cleopatra's son. The first three members of the dynasty were the most important.

Ptolemy I 367-283 BC known as Ptolemy Soter (saviour) was a great soldier with administrative ability who built roads and canals, founded the famous Library of Alexandria, wrote a scholarly account of Alexander's campaigns and abdicated at 82 in

favour of Ptolemy II 309-246 BC, surnamed Philadelphus, a cultivated man whose court has been compared to that of Louis XIV at Versailles. He was not a soldier but supported Rome against her foes. Ptolemy III 281-221 BC, like his grandfather, was a vigorous warrior, supreme controller of the eastern Mediterranean who reopened the war against the Seleucids. He was a just ruler and was specially noted for his leniency towards Egyptian religion and customs.

The later members of the dynasty were described as decadent and dissolute, due largely to the convention for the king to marry his own sister.

• •

poison-laced chalice. The priests at Memphis refused him burial, so his body was sent to Alexandria instead.

After Alexander's death his whole empire was divided amongst his various generals. **Ptolemy I Soter** (323-282 BC) started the Ptolemaic Dynasty (323-30 BC) in Egypt, and Alexandria became a major centre of Hellenistic culture, attracting many of the great and good, acquiring significant social, historical, and commercial importance throughout the Graeco-Roman period.

The Greeks integrated well with the Egyptians and created a new hybrid religion known as the cult of Serapis. The Romans, however, were more reserved. The influence of later Ptolemies declined steadily and they relied on the Romans for support. **Cleopatra VII** (51-30 BC), the last of the Ptolemies, seduced first Julius Caesar and then his successor Mark Anthony in order to retain her crown. Mark Anthony and Cleopatra held sway in Egypt for 14 years until they were deposed by Octavian who became the Emperor Augustus.

Tradition has it that the Gospel was first preached in Alexandria by Saint Mark in AD 62. Whatever the accuracy of this date, **Christianity** was certainly established around this time and Alexandria remained the centre of its theology for three centuries. However, its presence was still sufficiently threatening to the Muslim conquerors three centuries later to make them move their administration and theological capital inland to Cairo. Although Alexandria was still important as a centre of trade it's decline as a city was inevitable when the power base, along with the customary baggage of wealth, learning and culture went south.

With the 16th century discovery of America and the sea route around Africa to India and the Orient, which made the land route via Egypt virtually redundant, Alexandria lost its former magnificence. The decline during the Ottoman period was so great that while Cairo continued to flourish, the population of Alexandria fell to a mere 5,000 people by 1800.

Just in time, a saviour was found in the shape of **Mohammed (Mehmet) Ali** (1805-48). He organized the construction of the **El-Mahmudiya Canal** starting in 1819 and linked the Nile and Alexandria's Western Harbour, reconnecting the city with the rest of Egypt, whilst simultaneously irrigating the surrounding land, which had been badly neglected. With a trade route open, the city prospered once more and now it is only surpassed by Cairo itself. Foreign trade grew at a pace with the Egyptian merchant fleet and was later maintained by the

British. Being further north and nearer to the sea, the city is cooler than Cairo in summer and each year the administration moved to the coast during this hot season. The British invested in many building projects including, true to the Victorian obsession, a sea-front promenade. If you half close your eyes, and use a bit of imagination, you could be in an English sea-side resort!

Population growth and industrialization have altered Alexandria since **Nasser's** revolution (see History of Egypt, page 508) in 1952. Today it is a

Alexandria

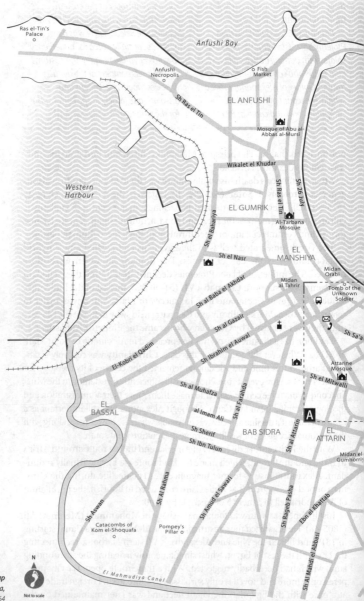

Ras el-Tin's Palace

Anfushi Bay

Anfushi Necropolis

Fish Market

Sh Ras el Tin

EL ANFUSHI

Mosque of Abu al-Abbas al-Mursi

Wikalet el Khudar

Western Harbour

EL GUMRIK

Sh Ras el Tin

Sh 26 July

Al-Tarbana Mosque

Sh el Bahariya

EL MANSHIYA

Sh el Nasr

Midan Orabi

Midan al Tahrir

Tomb of the Unknown Soldier

Sh al Baba el Akhdar

Sh al Gazair

Sh Sa'a

El-Kobri el Qadim

Sh Ibrahim el Auwal

Attarine Mosque

Sh el Mitwalli

Sh al Muhafza

Sh al Farahda

EL BASSAL

al Imam Ali

A

Sh Sherif

BAB SIDRA

Sh al Attarin

EL ATTARIN

Sh Ibn Tulun

Midan el Gumhorri

Sh Al Rahma

Sh Al Aswan

Sh Al Mahdi el Abbasi

Sh Rageb Pasha

Ebn el Khattab

Catacombs of Kom el-Shoquafa

Pompey's Pillar

El Mahmudiya Canal

N

Rleated map Central Alexandria, page 364

Not to scale

Alexandria

modern city with much to recommend it. Although the outer areas have suffered from too rapid rural-urban migration, the busy central area is small enough for the visitor to walk around and become familiar with the main squares and landmarks. Having the coast to the north makes orientation easy. Although Alexandria's opulent heritage is no longer so obvious, the atmosphere of the town which inspired such literary classics as Lawrence Durrell's *Alexandria Quartet* still remains. So don't rush immediately to all

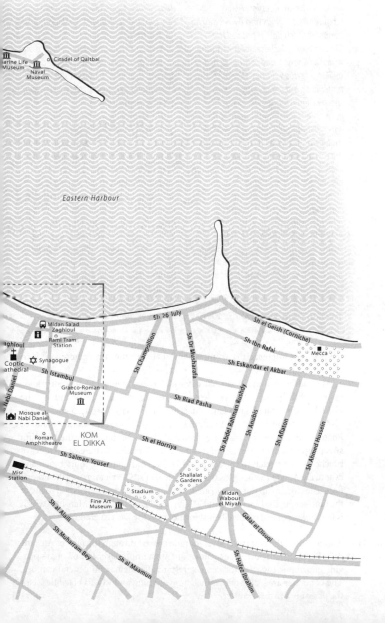

Seeing the Light – Ancient Alexandria

The Mouseion, from which the word museum is derived, meaning Temple of the Muses, was a vast centre of learning standing at the main crossroads of the city. It was commissioned by Ptolemy I, Soter and the important library was collected under the sponsorship of Ptolemy II, Philadelphus.

As well as an observatory, laboratories, lodgings and a refectory for hundreds of scholars, it housed the famous library, Biblioteca Alexandrina, which by Caesar's day contained nearly a million papyrus volumes. Obviously the material on a scroll of papyrus was shorter than a modern book but nevertheless the amount of information was outstanding. There is no evidence that it was destroyed by the Christians mobs – or by any other group – most likely it gradually declined over a period of time due to lack of support.

Recently the international community pledged US$65 mn to rebuild the library which would make Alex once again the centre of the civilized world. It has a huge public and research library, science museum, planetarium and 1000 ancient manuscripts. The phoenix of the Alexandrine Library is due to rise gloriously from its ashes late in 2000.

The Lighthouse of Pharos The fire from this immense lighthouse could be seen from 55 km across the open sea. It was 135 m high and stood at the mouth of the Eastern Harbour where Sultan Qaitbai's fort now stands. The first storey was square, the second octagonal and the third circular, topped by the lantern. At the very top stood a statue of Poseidon, god of the sea, trident in his hand.

It was still in use at the time of the Muslim invasion over 900 years after its construction and was mentioned by Ibn Battuta in 1326 (more than 1600 years after its construction) as being used as a fortress.

The idea for the lighthouse may have come from Alexander the Great but it was actually built in 279 BC by Sostratus, an Asiatic Greek, during the reign of Ptolemy II (284-246 BC). According to popular myth an immense mirror lens made it possible to view ships far out at sea while the fuel to feed the fire is said to have been hydraulically lifted to the top of the lighthouse. Upkeep was a serious problem. Ibn Tulun attempted some repairs but the great earthquakes of 1100 and 1307 destroyed the ancient foundations and the stones lay abandoned until the Ottoman Sultan Qaitbai decided to build the fort on the site in 1479 AD.

the places of interest. It is as important to absorb the atmosphere as it is to view the sights.

Alexandria is a thin ribbon-like city which is 20 km long but only a few kilometres wide because the residential areas are still largely bound by the El-Mahmudiya canal and Lake Maryut. At the city's western end is the El-Anfushi peninsula which now links the mainland and the former island of Pharos and divides the giant functional Western Harbour and the beautiful sweeping curve of the Eastern Harbour and its Corniche. To the east is a series of beaches which stretch to the Montazah Palace and on to Ma'mura beach and eventually Abu Qir which was the site of Nelson's 1798 victory over the French fleet. The city's main downtown area, its main transport terminals and many of the hotels are in the blocks around Midan Sa'ad Zaghloul in El-Manshiya which is in the western end of the city just inland from the Eastern Harbour.

Alexandria – the port About 75% of the country's foreign trade passed through the port of Alexandria, Egypt's main port. The facilities are most impressive. The 62 quays provide enormous capacity for cereals, refrigerated items and general cargoes. The container area, also enormous, has winching and RO-RO facilities. Not the place for a casual wander.

Sights

Historical remains in Alexandria today are such pale shadows of their former glories, chief amongst which were the **Mouseion** and the **Lighthouse of Pharos**, one of **the Seven Wonders of the Ancient World**. For a city with such a magnificent past history there is, unlike Cairo, comparatively little to see today because the modern city overlies the ancient one. Archaeologists continue to search for the tomb of the founder Alexander the Great, supposed to be somewhere under the busy streets, but most Egyptian visitors come to Alexandria for its Mediterranean beaches and cool and cosmopolitan atmosphere, rather than ancient cultures. Future visitors can look forward to an underwater archaeological park in the east side of the harbour where the French and Egyptian archaeologists have uncovered 7,000 artefacts from Alexander's ancient lighthouse and Cleopatra's royal palace – as well as Napoleon's ill-fated fleet. During the next decade a glass-bottomed boat will allow tourists to view the remains, and facilities for organized dives to this site are planned.

The **Anfushi Necropolis** first discovered in 1901, is located to the west of the fort near the sweep of the small Anfushi Bay. This is a set of 2nd and 3rd century tombs in which there are some Roman additions. Of the five tombs only two are fit for examination. The complex is cut into the limestone which is painted to represent alabaster and marble. The main tombs are entered down flights of steps. The right hand stairway is decorated at the turn with scenes of Horus, Isis and Anubis. Below off an open hall lie two principal chambers with vestibules each distinctively decorated. The right hand room bears Greek graffiti and naval scenes while the left hand chamber is more colourful with scenes of deities and a chequer-board pattern above. The burial chamber, with matching wall decoration, is guarded by sphinxes. Inside the left hand group there is an entrance hall off which are two vestibules and tomb chambers. The right hand vestibule has benches and leads to a chamber with a red Aswan

Ancient sites

Anfushi Necropolis, Alexandria

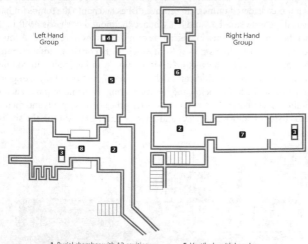

Left Hand Group

Right Hand Group

Not to scale

1 Burial chamber with 12 cavities
2 Hall
3 Sarcophagus
4 Sarcophagus of red granite
5 Vestibule with benches
6 Vestibule with chequerboard decoration
7 Vestibule with Greek graffiti & naval scenes
8 Vestibule with Roman sarcophagi

granite sarcophagus. In the left hand room the layout was modified in the Roman period to take a series of sarcophagi. ■ *Daily 0900-1600, Fri 0900-1130 and 1300-1600, E£12.*

Situated where many of the houses are 120-200 years old are the **Catacombs of Kom el-Shoquafa** (Mounds of Shards), located in Karmouz, originally 2nd century private tombs which were later extended in order to serve the whole community. Three styles of burial are represented here – in sarcophagi, on shelves and as ashes in urns. They have been extensively excavated since their rediscovery in 1900. Another case of the stumbling donkey, (see box page 479). Sadly, water has flooded the lowest of the three levels and caused some deterioration. A large spiral staircase serves as the entrance to the tombs, below which passages lead to interconnecting tomb shafts. Immediately to the left of the entrance is a corridor leading to the more recent tombs. The main passage from the stairwell runs into a large rotunda with a domed roof. Branching from this is a banqueting

Catacombs of Kom el-Shoquafa

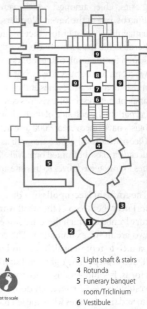

N
Not to scale

1 Entrance
2 Sarcophagus chambers
3 Light shaft & stairs
4 Rotunda
5 Funerary banquet room/Triclinium
6 Vestibule
7 Antechamber
8 Sepulchre Chapel
9 Gallery

room or triclinium for those visiting the deceased! Here in the triclinium the short granite pillars pushed away in the corner once supported the central banqueting table. A burial chamber leads off the rotunda opposite the dining area. As it was considered unlucky to remove dishes taken into the tombs for banquets these were smashed and left – hence the mound of shards. Within the chamber are many niches in which one or more bodies were sealed. A fourth passage leads to another stairway from which further ornate chambers branch off. The mixture of Graeco-Roman decoration with Egyptian – in columns and on wall illustrations indicates the mingling of the two cultures. In places red paint can be found below the niches bearing the name of those encased within. The eerie atmosphere is intensified by the ornate serpents and medusa heads that lurk above doorways and passage entrances. Also on the site is a

Sultan Qaitbai's Citadel

Hypogeum containing over 30 murals. ■ *Daily 0900-1600, closes 1500 in Ramadan, E£12 plus E£10 for camera.*

At the very end of the peninsula, in a most imposing position stands the **Citadel of the Mamluk Sultan Qaitbai**. It was built in 1479 by Sultan Qaitbai (AD 1468-96) on the ancient site of, and probably with the stones of, the Lighthouse of Pharos and stands at the far end of the Eastern Harbour as one of a series of coastal forts. It is one of the city's major landmarks and is now the property of the Egyptian Navy. The Citadel is approached up a wide causeway which ends at the original gateway between two half-round towers, both with interior rooms. Unfortunately today's entrance, further to the east, is less impressive. From the causeway notice the antique granite and marble columns incorporated in the fabric of the west facing wall. Three sides of the enclosed courtyard were given over to storage and accommodation for animals and troops. The north facing wall has emplacements for a score of cannon and the higher look-out tower gives a commanding view over the Mediterranean. The keep houses a small mosque which, unusually for the Delta region, is built in the shape of a cross. The entrance to this mosque is through a huge gateway flanked by pillars of red Aswan granite. Nearby a complex cistern stored water in case of siege. The fort's greatest attraction is the view from the battlements back over the open sea toward Alexandria. ■ *Sat-Thu 0900-1600, Fri 0900-1200 and 1400-1600, Ramadan daily 1000-1430, E£6, students E£3, camera E£10, video camera E£50.*

Alexandria

Citadel of Qaitbai, Alexandria

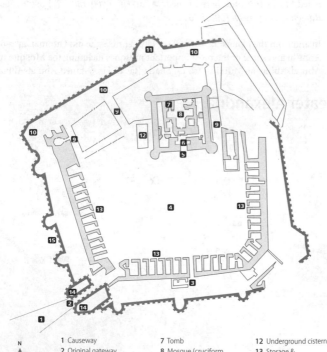

N

0 metres 20
0 yards 20

1 Causeway
2 Original gateway
3 Present gateway
4 Central courtyard
5 Entrance to main tower
6 Anteroom
7 Tomb
8 Mosque (cruciform construction)
9 Access inclines
10 Positions for cannons
11 Outlook tower
12 Underground cistern
13 Storage & accommodation
14 Halfround towers
15 Antique columns in walls

It can be reached from downtown Alexandria by taking the No 15 tram from Raml tram station.

Further southwest on the way to the El-Mahmudiya Canal and Lake Maryut in an area of cheap markets is **Pompey's Pillar**, just to the east of Sharia al Rahman. ■ *Daily 0900-1600, closes at 1500 in Ramadan, E£6.* It is a 27 m high and 9 m thick column of red Aswan granite topped by an impressive Corinthian capital. This pillar, Alexandria's tallest ancient monument, is a rather bizarre spectacle and its origins are the subject of speculation. It certainly does not originate from Pompey and is thought to have come from the **Serapis Temple** (40 km to the west) and to have been erected in AD 300 in honour of **Diocletian** (AD 284-305). It may have supported his statue. Extensive archaeological excavations surround the site. See the three granite sphinxes among a jumble of columns and Coptic crosses and some underground cisterns to the west of the ridge.

To the east of the Nabi Daniel mosque and to the north of the Misr railway station is the **Kom al-Dikkah (Hill of Rubble)**, thought to be the ancient site of the Paneion ('Park of Pan', a hilly pleasure garden), which has been under excavation since 1959. Instead a small semi-circular 700-800 seat **Roman Amphitheatre** or **Odeon**, Kom el-Dikka, behind Cinema Amir was discovered with 12 rows of seats faced with Italian marble focussing on a columned stage which still has the remains of its mosaic flooring. Some of the seats still show their numbers. A residential quarter with Roman baths from the 3rd century is currently being excavated to the north. The site is one of the few in Alexandria to indicate the wealth of the city's heritage and it is well worth a visit. An annex of the Graeco-Roman Museum displays local discoveries such as desalinated blocks from the harbour bed. ■ *Sat-Thu 0900-1600, Fri 0900-1600, Ramadan daily 0900-1500, E£6 .*

Mosques Inland from the peninsula towards the city centre is the old Ottoman area of Anfushi and some of the most important mosques including the **Mosque of Abu al-Abbas al-Mursi** north off Sharia Ras el Tin. Ahmed Abu al-Abbas

Greater Alexandria

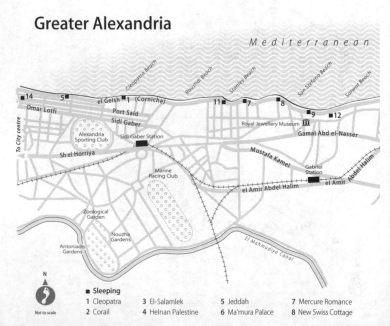

Mediterranean

■14   5■   el Geish ■1 (Corniche)   11■ ■7   ■8   San Stefano Beach   Sarwat Beach
Omar Lotfi   Port Said   Royal Jewellery Museum ▥   ■9   ■12
To City centre   Sidi Gaber   Gamal Abd el-Nasser
          Alexandria   Sidi Gaber Station
          Sporting Club   Mustafa Kamel
Sh el Horriya   Gabriel
                    Marine   Station   el Amir Abdel Halim
                    Racing Club   el Amir Abdel Halim   el Amir
          Zoological
          Garden
               Nouzha
               Gardens   El Mahmudiya Canal
Antoniadis
Gardens

N
Not to scale

■ **Sleeping**
1 Cleopatra   3 El-Salamlek   5 Jeddah   7 Mercure Romance
2 Corail   4 Helnan Palestine   6 Ma'mura Palace   8 New Swiss Cottage

al-Mursi (1219-87) was an Andalusian who came to Alexandria to join and eventually lead the Shadhali brotherhood. He is the patron saint of Alexandria's fishermen and sailors. His mosque and tomb, which is still here, were renovated in 1775 by a rich Maghrebi merchant but was then demolished and rebuilt in 1943 and is now the largest mosque in Alexandria. The current layout is octagonal with Italian granite supporting the roof arches, four decorated domes and the slender 73 m minaret rising in tiers which gives the modern mosque a pleasing weightless aspect. This is one of Alexandria's foremost religious buildings and is well worth a visit but visitors are advised that women are only permitted entry into a room at the back of the mosque.

Further south down the street is the French Cultural Centre where the Mouseion once stood and then the **Mosque al-Nabi Daniel** which is near the main Misr railway station. Although popular myth claims that it houses the remains of the prophet Daniel it actually contains the tomb of a venerated Sufi sheikh called Mohammed Danyal al-Maridi who died in 1497. Excavation works around the tomb have revealed another tomb from a 10th or 12th century Muslim cemetery and also revealed that the site is likely to have been that of the Great Soma Temple which was erected over the tomb of **Alexander the Great**.

Further south in this Ottoman part of the city is the **Al-Tarbana Mosque** which is situated on Sharia Farnaga to the east of Sharia al-Shahid. It has undergone major alterations since it was built in 1685 by Hajji Ibrahim Tarbana. The minaret is supported by two antique columns which stand above the entrance whilst a further eight columns support the ornamental ceiling. The original Delta style façade is almost completely obscured by plastering.

The **Attarine Mosque** dates from the 14th century and stands on the site of the once famous Mosque of a Thousand Columns. It was from here that Napoleon removed the 7 tonne sarcophagus which now is displayed in the British Museum in London.

The **Ibrahim al-Shurbaji Mosque**, to the east of Midan Sa'ad Zaghloul, was built in 1757. The internal layout is similar to that of the Al-Tarbana

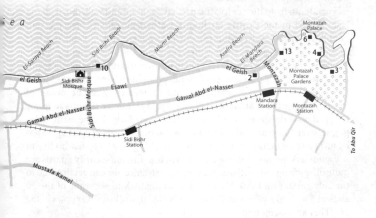

Alexandria

Alexander The Great – Greek King of Egypt

Alexander the Great and his army entered Egypt in November 332 BC. He made a sacrifice to Apis in Memphis, taking at that time the twin crowns of Lower and Upper Egypt. He remained in Egypt for some months setting up control of the Egyptian army and founding the city of Alexandria on the coast of the northwest of the Nile delta. In the spring of 331 he marched along the Mediterranean coast to Paraetonium (present-day Marsa Matruh) and thence through the Western Desert to Siwa.

His visit to Siwa was to consult the oracle of Zeus-Amun. The Temple of the oracle at Siwa (see page 379) is situated to the west of Shali, the new town, at the old site of Aghurmi. There are elaborate stories of Alexander's visit to the oracle temple of Amun but what is clear is that he was received by the priests at Siwa as a pharoah and had a private audience at the oracle. His concern was his expedition against his enemies, the Persians, but he gave no word to his followers on the outcome though in a letter to his mother he promised to tell all when he saw her again (which he never did!). Much later it was reported that Alexander was saluted by the oracle as the son of Zeus which effectively led to his deification and assured him of success in Asia, certainly, Alexander retained a deep belief in the powers of the god Amun and a flow of gifts continued to come during Alexander's lifetime to the temple priests at Siwa.

He went on in 331 to attack Babylon and by 330 had control of the Persian empire and thereafter moved his armies into Central Asia and in 327 to India. Within 10 years he was master of the known world. He died unchallenged in this role aged 33 on 13 June 323. He was buried in the Egyptian city of Alexandria. (See also page 381.)

Mosque. A courtyard to the rear creates a pleasant impression of space. There have been many modifications, but the *mihrab* is still decorated with the original Kufic inscriptions. To complete the examination of mosques don't omit the small mosque in the Citadel.

Turn south from the sea to Midan Sa'ad Zaghloul and walk down Sharia Nabi Daniel to the **Coptic Orthodox Cathedral**. This is a very recent establishment (1950-87), and presented as a large arched vault is a fine example of ecclesiastical architecture. It is dedicated to five saints, in particular St Mark whose head is reputed to be buried at this site together with the remains of early patriarchs of the Egyptian church including St Menas (see page 371). A sunken chapel beyond an interesting recent mosaic of incidents in the life of St Mark gives access to their tombs. ■ *Entry welcome – leave a small donation.* Nearby at 69 Sharia Nabi Daniel is the main **Synagogue**, over 145 years old. The previous building was destroyed by Napoleon. The synagogue which serves the remaining 90-100 Jews who live in Alexandria is not normally open to the public and the security guards are quite off-putting: but with gentle, polite persistence one can get through to the lady curator and into the ornate building. Ask to see some of the 50 ancient 500-1,000-year-old Torah scrolls held in worked silver cases in the arc. They are fascinating.

Palaces To the east of downtown Alexandria lie 17 km of beaches stretching to the beautiful 160 ha gardens of **Montazah Palace** (see gardens, page 363), which is now a state guesthouse. It was constructed in the 19th century by the visionary Mohammed Ali as a palace for the engineers who built the barrages which are so important for the irrigation of the Delta. It was later inhabited by King

Farouk. The original construction had been halted, and was completed later in the century, on a grander scale, by Sir Colin Scott-Moncrieff.

Further west along the peninsula are formal gardens and then **Ras el-Tin's Palace** (Cape of Figs Palace) which overlooks the Western harbour but which is now the Admiralty Headquarters and is unfortunately closed to the public. It was built so that Mohammed Ali (1805-48) could review his fleet and was reconstructed in the European Turkish style by Fouad I (1917-36) to serve as the government's summer seat. It was therefore ironic that his son King Farouk signed his abdication at the palace on 26 July 1952 before boarding a yacht bound for exile in Italy.

In downtown Alexandria is the **Graeco-Roman Antiquities Museum** in Sharia **Museums** Amin Fikri and Tariq Abdel Nasser. ■ *Daily 0900-1600, Fri 0900-1130 and 1330-1600, during Ramadan daily 0900-1500, E£16.* It contains an interesting collection of around 40,000 items, mainly taken from local tombs dating from about 300 BC to AD 300, of relics from the Graeco-Roman period. The most significant cult was that of Serapis which was a hybrid of the Greek god Dionysus and the Nile god Osiris. The Serapis was depicted as a bull and is directly associated with the ancient Egyptian cult of the Apis bull. Take the rooms in chronological order, beginning in **Room 6** with the centrally placed magnificent sculpture of the black granite Apis bull (see Deities, page 210). The inscription dates it at AD117-138. The white marble sculpture of Serapis was, like the bull, found near Pompey's Column. This room has some attractive mosaics.

Canopus, now reduced to rubble, was situated on the coast to the east of Alexandria and the artefacts from there in **Room 7** seem to be a collection

Alexandria

Graeco-Roman Museum, Alexandria

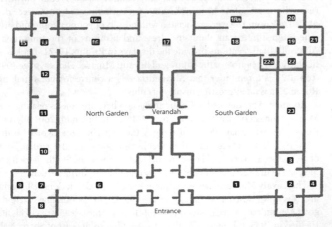

1-2 Coptic earthenware
    & architectural elements
3 Jewellery
4 Textiles
5 Coptic stucco
6 Cult of Serapis
7 Artifacts from
    ancient Canopus
8 Mummies & sarcophagi
9 Crocodile worship in El-
    Fayoum

10 Late Pharaonic - Sir John
    Antoniadis collection
11 Statues & fragments
    from Athribus near
    Benha
12-14 Miscellaneous sculptures
    of Graeco-Roman period
15 Tomb paintings
16-16a Hellenistic sculpture
17 Monolith & sarcophagi
18 Pottery & glass

18a Miniature Tanagra
    terracotta figures
19 Statues, funerary urns
    & pottery
20 Chatby collection
21 Ibrahimeya collection
22 Coloured glassware
22a Bronze & other metals
23 Coins

Not to scale

Twentieth century pirates

Are we likely to see raids with sabres clashing under the emblem of Salah al-Din's golden eagle? Perhaps not. However, while it is hard to believe, pirates do exist in this day and age and Sharon Bailey, anti-piracy manager for Africa, the Middle East and Mediterranean regions has a special interest in activities in Egypt.

It is claimed that pirated software accounts for 88% of software use in Egypt, and Microsoft are not impressed. They estimate that Arabic versions of its software could be produced 20% more cheaply in Egypt than in Europe but plans to contract out the work depend on controlling the pirates.

of headless statues, sandstone sphinxes and basalt goddesses. Ramses II put his name on the huge red granite statue. **Room 8** has mummies differently decorated and an example of a Fayoum portrait (see box, page 168 Fayoum portraits) while **Room 9** has a mummified crocodile and other pieces from the Temple of Pnepheros, all connected with the crocodile worship practised there. **Room 11** – the mixture of Greek and Egyptian influences produced some interesting sculptures excavated from Athribus near Benha in the Central Delta. On the fragments of tomb paintings in **Room 15** is a *saqiya* or waterwheel with jars to collect and lift the water (see section on the Nile and man, page 543). The sculptures in **Rooms 16-16A** are some of the most worthwhile exhibits in the museum. Look particularly at the Persian god, the lion-headed Mithras; the giant eagle from the Aegean; the graceful figure of Aphrodite and the carefully executed male and female torsos. There are six marble sarcophagi in **Room 17**, most with intricate carvings and one with scenes from the Greek myths, keeping company with what is claimed to be the largest statue ever carved in porphyry (even though it has no head). The tiny terracotta figures from Greece displayed in **Room 18a** were associated with burials of young people and provide interesting detail about the dress and fashions of the time. Local Alexandrian excavations provide the displays in **Rooms 19-21**. Look particularly at the figures of the happy god Bes and Min (see Deities, page 209). **Room 22** is a reminder that Alexandria was a centre for glass making. **Room 23** has an interesting display of coins.

Rooms 1-5 are devoted to Coptic artefacts. There are objects relating to St Menas' Monastery (see Abu Mina, page 371), including numerous pilgrim's flasks. The textiles have delightful designs, the Copts being recognized as fine weavers. Take time to examine the larger items displayed in the garden. Some of the statues are very fine. There are rock-cut tombs in the South Garden and the parts of the Temple of Pnepheros (Room 9) in the North Garden.

The **Cavafy Museum** has recently moved from the Greek Consulate building. It is now housed at 4 Sharia Sharm el-Sheikh, in the building where the great Alexandrian poet Constantine Cavafy lived for the last 25 years of his life. He died in 1933. It is marked with a plaque. It lies to the east of Sharia Nabi Daniel in the street parallel to and just north of Sharia el Horriya. Two of the rooms have been arranged with his household furniture, books and manuscripts to give an idea of the place when he was in occupation. ■ *Daily 0900-1400 also 1800-2000 Tue and Thu, closed Mon. Free.*

The **Fine Art Museum** is located at 18 Sharia Menasce. On the ground floor there is a permanent exhibition of 20th century Egyptian painting while the upper floor is dedicated to temporary exhibitions which are generally of modern Egyptian art. It is a venue for concerts and the film club meets here every Wednesday. ■ *Daily 0800-1400, closed Fri, Free.*

Western artists in Egypt

Egypt has rarely been an independent country. The Ottoman Empire lasted until 1805, though the first direct intervention in Egypt began in 1798 with the Napoleonic invasion. A great entourage of scientists, writers and artists accompanied the French occupation of Egypt, which went on until 1801 opening this hitherto largely protected Islamic country to a new and interested audience.

The orientalist artists and writers of the 19th century were confronted in Egypt and elsewhere in North Africa with sights and scenes of what appeared to be a startlingly different culture. They recorded what they saw for an audience at home that was eager to catch glimpses of these unknown lands. By the end of the century, a new breed of artists found their way to the new territorial possessions that their countries had acquired in the great grab for colonial purposes. France was the military power in Egypt and much of the Maghreb and it was from here that inspiration came to many of the great French and other artists – though to indulge their art and their own senses rather than to convey impressions of exotic lands. Some artists such as Baron Gros and Jean-Augustine-Dominique Ingres never actually got as far as Egypt but none the less produced fine paintings of the Napoleonic campaigns (viz The Battle of Nazareth by Gros).

In addition to the French, the British imperial mission was important in 19th century Egypt and brought its own harvest of 'orientalist' works of art. John Frederick Lewis (1805-75) spent 10 years in Egypt and was a prolific British painter of watercolours of ancient monuments such as Edfou, Upper Egypt and scenes of contemporary Cairo life such as A Turkish School in the vicinity of Cairo.

David Roberts (1796-1864) was another British master of the sketch and oil painting who voyaged along the Nile in 1839. His sketches, reproduced as lithographs, are still popular and provide a wonderful catalogue of the major Nilotic sites in the mid-19th century. Temple at Denderah and The Island of Philae are fine examples of his work.

Later comers to Egypt were William Holman Hunt (1827-1910), who was a founder member of the Pre-Raphaelite Brotherhood and who visited Egypt in 1854-56. His paintings were enlightened by his view of the archaeological sites of Egypt and the Levant, with notable pieces such as The Great Pyramid and Entrance to the Temple of Amun. In the 20th century a German modern artist, Paul Klee (1879-1940), was deeply influenced by his travels in Egypt in 1928-29, from which he took not merely symbols into his paintings but ideas of a holistic universe. His Legend of the Nile encapsulated his Egyptian experiences in a single modern picture in pastel.

Today, keen painters can still take advantage of a brilliantly unique Nile landscape and highly individualistic local architecture and dress in Egypt to develop their expertise through an accompanied tour with organisations such as The Prospect Music and Art Tours, 36 Manchester Street, London, W1M 5PE, T0207-4865704, F0207-4865868.

The **Marine Life Museum** and Hydro-Biological Institute near Sultan Qaitbai's Fort on Anfushi Bay houses a rare collection of fish and marine life. ■ *Daily 0900-1400, 10 piastres.* The **Naval Museum,** next to the *Marine Life Museum*, is situated at the end of the peninsula, at the west end of the Corniche. It contains artifacts from Roman and Napoleonic sea battles which are likely to appeal more to specialists than to the casual tourist. ■ *Daily 0900-1500 except Fri.*

Royal Jewellery Museum, 21 Sharia Ahmed Yehia Pasha, Gleem, T5868348 (behind the Governor's residence). The palace, originally belonging to Fatma el-Zahra, granddaughter of Ibrahim Pasha, was formerly one of

Alexandria

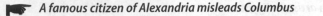

A famous citizen of Alexandria misleads Columbus

Claudius Ptolemy the famous Greeek astronomer and geographer lived in Alexandria. According to the Ptolemaic system the sun and moon rotated round the earth which was believed to be the centre of the universe. In his Geography, *eight books which contained many maps, he greatly under-estimated the distances between continents and left out the Americas altogether. This miscalculation led Columbus, 15 centuries later, to seek a route to India by travelling west from Spain.*

King Farouk's palaces which with its garden covers an area of over 4,000 sq m. It now houses a glittering collection of treasures from the time of Mohammed Ali through to King Farouk. There are jewels on everything in cases clearly labelled in Arabic and English. Statues and paintings are also on display. The mansion in which these are housed is almost of equal interest. It contains 10 stained glass doors and many stained glass windows depicting stories of European history. The bathrooms, cordoned off but on view to the public, are an inspiration. Lift your eyes from the jewels to admire the ceilings. The items in the collection considered the most important include – from Mohammed Ali, a gold plated, enamelled and inscribed snuff box; from King Fuad, a gold knob inlaid with diamonds, gold medals and decorations, a platinum crown inlaid with diamonds and sapphires with other pieces of jewellery to match; from King Farouk, a gold chess set enamelled and inlaid with diamonds, a gold tray inscribed with the signatures of 110 pashas; from Queen Safinaz, her crown of platinum inlaid with diamonds, gold and platinum brooches inlaid with diamonds. This is just the beginning of the catalogue. ■ *Daily 0900-1600, Fri 0900-1130 and 1330-1600, E£20, video E£150.*

Tombs **Tombs** Tombs of Chatby, Sharia Port Said, dates from 3rd century BC. Believed to be the most ancient tombs to be found in Alexandria. Entrance E£6. Tombs of Mustafa Kamel, Sharia Moasker Romani, Rushdi. Here there are four tombs dating from the 3rd and 2nd centuries BC. ■ *E£12.*

The **Tomb of the Unknown Soldier**, about half way round the Eastern Harbour on Midan Obari, is worth noting as a good landmark.

To the east and 5 km along Ma'mura Bay is **Canopus** which bears few traces of the Delta's chief market which flourished before the development of Alexandria and was best known for its Temple of Serapis. Canopic jars were produced here, see box on Mummification on page 238 . The motivation for building a city in the area was the Canopic branch of the River Nile which has long since dried up. The city is claimed to have been built by Menalaeus' pilot Canopus on his return from the Trojan wars who was venerated by the local population after his death from snakebite. Today little remains of the site. The destruction is a recent phenomenon, apparently mainly caused by British occupation during the First World War and the Second World War. The ancient remains which have survived, including several statues of Ramses II, are now in the *Graeco-Roman Museum* in Alexandria. Two abandoned forts to the east of Canopus can be explored. Further east from Canopus, submerged under the waters of the Mediterranean Sea and 2 m of silt are the remains of the ancient cities of Herakleion, the main port of entry into Egypt before Alexandria was founded and Menouthius, the centre for the cult of Isis. Recent elaborate excavations have verified the position and extent of these lost cities and produced some fascinating artefacts.

How plump is the planet?

Eratosthenes lived in Alexandria. He was an eminent astrologer cataloging 675 stars and a mathematician but his fame came from measuring the circumference of the Earth.

At Aswan on the Tropic of Cancer at noon on midsummer's day the sun is directly overhead and casts no shadow. Eratosthenes who was in Alexandria measured the shadow cast there and was able to work out the angle of the sun's rays on the same day at the same time. Using information gathered from travellers he had previously concluded that the distance from Aswan to Alexandria was about 800 km. These two facts he used to calculate the circumference of the earth as 40,000 km, an error of only 75 km. He went on to work out the distance from the Earth to the Sun and the Earth to the Moon. His calculation of the angle of tilt of the axis of the Earth at 23° 51'14" was truly amazing.

Anywhere along the Corniche the beach is very pleasant and there are all the **Beaches** facilities nearby. Ask for Stanley Beach which is one of the best in town. To the east is the beach of the Montazah gardens and another at Ma'amoura. Abu Qir, a small fishing village further east again offers a good beach and the opportunity to sample the extremely fresh fish and shell fish.

The **Antoniadis Gardens** are near the El-Mahmudiya Canal and the zoo. The **Gardens** house, originally owned by a wealthy Greek family is now used for meetings of state. The gardens contain beautiful arrangements of trees and flower beds as well as several marble statues. Well maintained gardens and walkways, several Greek statues. ■ *Daily 0800-1600, 50pt.* The **Montazah Palace Gardens** ■ *E£3*, cover almost 160 ha. A very large area is formal gardens, a welcome respite from the bustle of the city. Originally built in 1892, this palace only dates from 1926 being the summer residence of the Egyptian royal family. The adjacent beautiful beach makes this the most popular of the gardens here. ■ *Open 24 hrs, entrance E£4.* **Nouzha Gardens and Zoo**, Sharia Smouha, Smouha has many interesting birds and animals in the zoo. Adjacent gardens have picnic areas. ■ *Both open daily 0800-1600, 50pt.* **Shallalat Gardens** to east of city centre, varying levels, rockeries and waterways, lovely.

The Yacht Club beside Qaitbai's Fort hires boats, so why not end your tour of Alexandria by seeing it from the sea?

Essentials

Alexandria is Egypt's 2nd largest city and the major domestic resort for Egyptian tour- **Sleeping** ists and has hotels to suit every taste. Besides the main downtown hotels there are others east along the coast to the exclusive El-Montazah area and beyond. **NB** That all hotels on the Corniche suffer from traffic noise – day and night. They include but are not limited to the following officially registered hotels.

AL *El-Salamlek Palace Hotel & Casino*, Montazah Palace, T5477999, F5464408. Built like an Alpine chalet for the Khedive's Austrian mistress, newly renovated. Once a royal guesthouse, now a very exclusive hotel, 6 rooms and 14 suites, 2 restaurants – French, Italian.

AL *Helnan Palestine*, Montazah Palace, El-Montazah, T5474033, F5473378. 184 rooms, also located in the grounds of the Montazah Palace with a lagoon, beautiful gardens and an excellent beach nearby. Very comfortable, charming staff and a most pleasant place to stay, watersports from private jetty into Mediterranean.

AL *Montazah Sheraton*, Corniche, El-Montazah, T5480550, F5401331. 305 rooms, located outside the grounds of the walled Montazah Palace, with excellent sea-views, private beach, for luxury and convenience this cannot be faulted. Highly recommended. **AL** *Sofitel Alexandria Cecil*, 16 Midan Sa'ad Zaghloul, T4807224, F4836401. 86 rooms, guests have included Winston Churchill, Noel Coward and Lawrence Durrell, 5 restaurants and casino open 2000-0400. Pseudo Moorish style. While this has the convenience of being in the centre of town, situated in the former European quarter close to the Old Eastern Harbour, it lacks the peace of the other high quality hotels in El-Montazah. Weigh up the attractions before you decide.

A *Mercure Alexandria Romance*, 313 Sharia el-Geish, Saba Pasha, T5876429, F5870526. 64 rooms, very comfortable. **A** *Plaza,* 394 Sharia el-Geish, Zizinia, T5878714, F5875399. 180 rooms, good standard, modern, sea view. **A** *Ramada Renaissance*, 544 Sharia el-Geish, Sidi Bishr, T5490935, F5497690. 20 suites and 150 very comfortable double rooms, located on coast road 12-15 km from town centre, try excellent restaurant with panoramic view of the Mediterranean. This has all the comforts of a good international hotel and the charm of well-trained staff. Check your room for traffic noise. This is certainly the best choice of the A grade hotels.

B *Landmark*, Midan, San Stefano, T5877850, F5880515. 150 rooms, located about half way between downtown Alexandria and the Montazah Palace. Conveniently situated.

The quality of hotel varies considerably in this price range. A change of management or staff makes a bigger difference here. Always ask to see the room first.

C *Alexandria*, 23 Midan El-Nasr, El-Manshiya, T4801041, F4823113. 108 rooms, family run downtown hotel with attentive personal service. **C** *Delta*, 14 Sharia Champollion, Mazarita, T4825188, F4825630. 63 rooms. **C** *Desert Home*, Sharia Omar el-Mokhtar, King Mariout, T981315, F4914939. 14 rooms, cosy. **C** *Ma'mura Palace*, El-Ma'mura, T/F5473761. 80 rooms, good standard, modern, good views, located in the exclusive El-Ma'mura area to the east of the Montazah Palace. Recommended. **C** *San Giovanni*, 205 Sharia el-Geish, Stanley, T5467774, F5464408. 30 rooms, beach hotel located about half way between downtown Alexandria and the Montazah Palace.

Central Alexandria

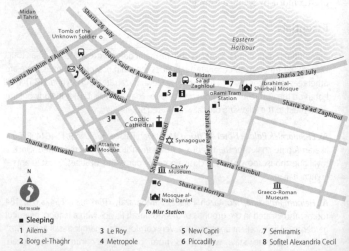

■ **Sleeping**

1 Ailema	3 Le Roy	5 New Capri	7 Semiramis
2 Borg el-Thaghr	4 Metropole	6 Piccadilly	8 Sofitel Alexandria Cecil

D *Amun*, 32 Midan el-Nasr, El-Manshiya, T807131. 120 rooms. **D** *Mecca*, 44 Sharia el-Geish, Camp Caesar, T5973925, F5969935. 120 rooms. **D** *Metropole*, 52 Sharia Sa'ad Zaghloul, Raml Station, T4821466, F4822040. 82 rooms, all with phones and TV, worth staying for the wonderful Art Deco and Art Nouveau décor, a good atmosphere. **D** *New Swiss Cottage*, 346 Sharia el-Geish, Gleem, T5875830, F5870455, on coast road about half way between downtown Alexandria and the Montazah Palace, next door to the original *Swiss Cottage*. **D** *San Stefano*, Sharia Abdel Salam Aref, San Stefano, T5863587, F5865935. 120 rooms, good position, on beach. **D** *Semiramis*, 80 Sharia el-Geish, Raml Station, T4830824. 64 rooms, many with sea view, rooftop restaurant. **D** *Venezia*, 21 Sharia el-Nasr, El-Manshiya, T802322, F4824664. 120 rooms, good value for money.

E *Admiral*, 24 Sharia Amin Fikri, Raml Station, T4831787. 68 rooms, generally clean, some rooms with bath, good value, breakfast included. **E** *Ailema*, 21 Sharia Amin Fikri, Raml Station, T4827011. 38 rooms, rather faded Greek-run downtown hotel. **E** *Borg el-Thaghr*, Sharia Safeya Zaghloul, Raml Station, T4924519. 33 rooms. **E** *Corail*, 802 Sharia el-Geish, El-Mandara, T5480996, F5407746. 28 rooms, beach hotel just to west of Montazah Palace. **E** *Deauville*, 271 Sharia el-Geish, Stanley, T5454804, F5454806. 41 rooms, on beach **F** *Holiday*, 6 Midan Orabi, El-Manshiya, T8014559. 44 double rooms, comfortable. **E** *Jeddulı*, 137 Sharia el-Geish, Sporting, T057643. 69 rooms, just north of the Alexandria Sporting Club.

F *Cleopatra*, 160 Sharia el-Geish, Cleopatra, T852409. 60 rooms, on beach at Cleopatra bay. **F** *Hyde Park House*, 21 Sharia Amin Fikri, Raml Station, T4835667. 58 rooms, rather run down, one floor above the *Ailema hotel*. **F** *Le Roy*, 25 Sharia Talaat Harb, Raml Station, T4833439. 65 rooms, a shadow of its former Art Deco self. **F** *New Capri*, 23 El-Mina, Sharia el-Sharkia, Raml Station, T809310. 32 rooms, downtown hotel located in tourist police building. **F** *Piccadilly*, 11 Sharia el-Horriya, El-Nabi Daniel, T4934802, 32 rooms, a 6th floor exceedingly cheap hotel, near the railway station, a very good bargain.

Camping At Sharia Bahr al-Mait in Abu Qir which is about 20 km from downtown Alexandria about 5½ km east of the Montazah Palace.

Youth hostels 32 Sharia Port Said, Shatbi, Raml, T5975459, 2 km northeast of city centre, 200 beds, meals available, train 3 km, ferry 5 km, family rooms, laundry, facilities for disabled, self catering available.

For the greatest concentration of restaurants and cafés, try the area bounded by **Eating** Sharia Sa'ad Zaghloul, Raml station and Eastern Harbour by Midan Sa'ad Zaghloul. The restaurants in the higher grade hotels are reliable and serve Western and Egyptian cuisine.

Expensive *Alexander's* at the *Ramada Renaissance*, 544 Sharia el-Geish, Sidi Bishr, T866111. Elegant service, excellent fish food, has a panoramic view of the Mediterranean. *Al Farouk*, Montaza Gardens, T5477999. Eat in elegant surroundings. *Chinese Restaurant*, *Cecil Hotel*, T4877173. A pleasure to eat here. *San Giovanni*, on Corniche in Stanley. Excellent fish, sea views, from E£30 per head. *Santa Lucia*, 40 Sharia Safeya Zaghloul, T4824240, excellent seafood, serves wine and beer, open 1200-1600 and 1900-0100.

Mid-range: *Denise*, Sharia Ibn Bassam, off Raml tram station, T4830457. Select your own fish from the freezer, alcohol, open 0900-0100. *Dynasty* 544 Sharia El Geish, Sidi Bishr. A little out of town, worth the journey for the food and the sea views. T5483977

Elite, 43 Sharia Safia Zaghloul, T4823592. Opposite *Santa Lucia*, large helpings, alcohol, open 0900-2400. *New China Restaurant* in *Corail Hotel*, T5470996, 802 Sharia el-Geish. Chinese food, spicy shrimps and beef served in lovely setting, alcohol, open 1200-1600 and 1800-2300. *Seagull*, Sharia el Agami, T4455575. Highly recommended but way out of town to west in industrial area. *Shanghai Chinese Restaurant*, 12 Sharia Mohammed Afifi, San Stefano, T5879334. Open 1400-0200. *Tikka Grill*, T4805119, near Al-Mursi's Mosque. Views overlooking Eastern Harbour, beautifully served, spicy Indian food, salad bar, open 1300-1700 and 2000-0200, from E£40 per head.

Cheap: *Cafeteria Asteria*, T4822293, next door to *Santa Lucia* in Sharia Safeya Zaghloul. Serves a range of tasty, cheap meals, open until 2400. *Fuul Mohammed Ahmed*, 17 Sharia Shakor, near Raml station, T4833576, a block east of Midan Sa'ad Zaghloul, beyond Bank of Alexandria and a block south of Sharia Safia Zaghloul. Very cheap, very tasty, open 0600-2400. *La Pizzeria*, T4838082, 14 Sharia el-Horriya. Filling rather than fancy. *Taverna Restaurants*, T4928189, at Raml station. Greek owned tasty fish dishes and pizzas with salad bar, open 0730-0200. Recommended. For those who can't be without fast food there are **3** *Kentucky Fried Chicken*, **2** *Pizza Huts* and a *McDonalds*.

Cafes 24-hr service in better hotels including *Sheraton*, *Ramada Renaissance*, *Plaza*, *Landmark* and *San Giovanni*. Good atmosphere at *Cecil Hotel* by bus station. Minimum charge E£8 per person, mouthwatering pastries. *Athineos* by the station. Classical décor, gets noisy in the evenings. *Brazilian Coffee Shop* by the Tourist Office on Sharia Sa'ad Zaghloul. Open 0630-1500, excellent coffee and pastries. *Délices*, T4825657, 46 Sa'ad Zaghloul. Faded charm. *Pastroudis*, T4929609, 39 Sharia el-Horriya, behind Roman amphitheatre. Enjoy the atmosphere, watch the crowds and try the excellent cakes. *Trianon*, T4828539, east end of Midan Sa'ad Zaghloul by station under *Hotel Metropole*. Elegant, pricey, excellent coffee. *Welad el Zawat Café*, Sharia Victor Emanuel, Semouha, T5245455.

Nightclubs Most of the large hotels have some evening entertainment, though not with the style of the capital. Try *Aquarius* at *Montazah Sheraton Hotel*. *Crazy Horse*, Midan Sa'ad Zaghloul. *Dolphin Nightclub* at *Palestine Hotel*. Open 2200-0330. *El-Phanar* at the *Montazah Sheraton Hotel*. Open 2230-0300 except Mon. *Monte Carlo*, 34 Sharia el Geish. *Palace Suite* at the *Plaza Hotel*. Open 2200-0430. *Queen's Hall Nightclub* in the *San Giovanni Hotel*.

Entertainment **Cinemas**: *Amir* 42 Sharia el Horriya, T4927693. *Metro* 26 Sharia Safia Zaghloul, T4830432. *Radio* 22 Midan Sa'ad Zaghloul, T4830282. *Rialto* 31 Sharia el Horriya, T4824694. *Rio* 37 Sharia el Horriya, T4929036. Five new American-style cinemas opened in 1999 close to the new Zaharan Mall, another 4 inside the Mall – so Semouha has 9 cinemas with mostly English language, T4245899.

Concerts: *Alexandria Conference Centre*, in Great Hall – contact Les Amis de la Musique et Des Arts, T5862325 for programme.

Theatre *Sayed Darwish Theatre*, Alexandria's old opera house opposite *Cinema Royal* presents plays, concerts and ballets, T4865110.

Festivals **Mar** *International Marathon*, Cairo-Alexandria; **Jul** Jul 26, *Alexandria National Day*; **Sep** International Movie Festival, alternate Septembers World Alexandria Festival; **Nov** *International Yacht Regatta*.

Alexandria has a wide range of shops but lacks the famous specific *souqs* of Cairo. **Shopping**
The main area is south and west of Midan Sa'ad Zaghloul. Leather goods including
shoes are of good quality and recommended as best bargains. Look also for silk and
cotton material and clothes. The public sector chain stores are well represented, for
example Omar Effendi Stores, Haute Couture Co. and Couture Moderne Co. The best
Malls to visit are: El Samalek, El Samalek Palace Hotel, Montazah Gardens; El
Wataneya, Sharia Shaarawi, Loran; Mena, Sharia Bilouz, Ibrahimia; Zaharan, Sharia
Victor Emmanuel, Semouha.

The **Fish Market** further west on Anfushi Bay is easy to find, just follow your nose.
Go early to see this small area teeming with fish and people.

Bookshops: *Al-Ahram*, 10 Sharia el-Horriya. *Book Bazaar* in *Ramada Renaissance*.
Open 0900-2300 daily. *Book Centre*, 49 Sharia Sa'ad Zaghloul. Has best choice of
books in English, French and German. *Dar el-Mostakbal*, 32 Sharia Safeya Zaghloul.
Books and magazines in English, French and German. *International Language
Bookshop*, 18 Sharia Abd el-Hamid El-Dib, Tharwat. *Nile Christian Bookshop*, 4
Sharia Anglican Church, Attarine. *Ramada Bazaar Bookshop* in Ramada Renais-
sance open 0900-1200.

Supermarkets. *Danam* in Zizenia, *Fathalla* in San Stefano, *Assala El Mady* in Manshia.

Beach and watersports facilities are available at all major hotels. Non residents can, **Sports**
with permission, use pools at major hotels like *Sheraton* and *Ramada Renaissance*.
Alexandria Sporting Club has golf, tennis, bowling and horse riding.
Alexandria Yacht Club, adjacent to Sultan Qaitbai's Fort, gives sailing lessons and
holds an annual regatta each Nov, boats available for hire. *Delta Harriers* run or jog
each Fri evening, about 1 hr before sunset, T4847054. It is almost impossible to rent a
self-drive boat in Alexandria – too much red tape. Enjoy being driven. Horse racing at
Semouha, Nov-May on Sat and Sun, starts 1330.

Abercrombie & Kent, 52 Sharia Sa'ad Zaghloul, T4821465. *Atlantic Tours*, 40 Sharia **Tour operators**
Safeya Zaghloul, T4821109. *Egyptian International Travel*, 16 Sharia Talaat Harb,
T4825426. *Fayed Travel*, 7 Sharia el-Fath, Wezarah Station, Fleming, T5870579.
Misr Tours, 28 Sharia Sa'ad Zaghloul, T4809617, F4808776. *Misr Travel*, 33 Sharia
Salah Salem, T4825025. *North African Shipping Co*, 63 Sharia Nabi Daniel, 14830050.
Passant Travel, 164 Sharia el-Horriya, Camp Caesar, T5966091. *Sporting Tours*, 178
Sharia Omar Lutfi, Sporting, T5952778. *Thomas Cook*, 15 Midan Sa'ad Zaghloul,
T4828077 and in hotels *Pullman Cecil*, *Palestine*, *Metropole* and *San Stephano*.

Local Trams and city buses: from Raml station just to the east of Midan Sa'ad **Transport**
Zaghloul there are very cheap but crowded trams from dawn until 2400 including:
east to **Sidi Bishr beach** (No 1-No 4), west to the **Maritime Station** (No 6) in the Western Harbour, north to **Qaitbai Fort** (No 5) via El-Gomruk and El-Anfushi, and south
from Midan Orabi which is west of Midan Sa'ad Zaghloul to **Karmous** and **Pompey's
Pillar** (No 5 and No 15). As a general rule blue trams to middle class areas and yellow
to poorer areas. Local buses, which are fast but very crowded and dirty, operate
throughout the city from the main squares. The main services include the following:
Midan Sa'ad Zaghloul to the **airport** (No 203), Midan Orabi to the **airport** (No 307 and
No 310), Montazah and Abu Qir (No 129), Raml to **Pompey's Pillar** (No 209), along the
Corniche to **Montazah** (No 120, No 220 and No 300), Ma'mura (No 725), Abu Qir (No
729), or to **El-Agami** and **Hannoville beaches** (No 455 or No 500), Misr station to the
Zoo (No 41). **Car hire**: *Avis*, T807532, in *Pullman Cecil*. *Budget*, 59 Tariq el-Geish,
T5971273. A/c Fiat costs E£125 per day including tax and insurance, deposit of E£300
required. *Limousine*, 25 Sharia Talaat Harb T4825253. **Service taxis**: run quick and

relatively cheap services from Midan El-Gumhorriya, which is next to the Misr railway station and about 1 km south of the Corniche, to most places within a few hundred kilometres radius. Drivers call out their destinations. Fares to Cairo E£15, to Marsa Matruh E£10-15. **Taxis and calèches**: metered black and orange city taxis can be caught throughout the downtown and many other areas but a tip will be expected. E£25 to ride full length of Corniche. A ride in a horse-drawn *calèche* along the Corniche or from outside the Misr railway station for a pre-negotiated price is a slower alternative.

Long distance Air The airport, which is southeast of the city on land reclaimed from Lake Maryut off the main Delta road to Cairo, has regular daily flights to **Cairo** at 1225, 1330, 1915, 2200, not Sat or Sun, check the days and times carefully. **Hurghada** and **Sharm el-Sheikh** Mon and Fri at 0845; **Athens**, **Frankfurt** and **Paris** (1 a week). For information T4227808. Considering the time wasted at airports and the travel time to and from it is certainly as quick, and much, much cheaper to travel by road to Cairo.

Bus: *Western Delta Buses* (T4200916) and *Superjet* (T4228566) stop at **Sidi Gaber** railway station. Purchase tickets here before departure. From the town centre (*Cecil Hotel*) catch minibus (No1) for 50pt. Cairo service (E£20-30, 2½ hrs) has a/c with toilets and there are often three buses an hour. The 0100 service goes direct to **Cairo** airport. To **El Alamein** and **Marsa Matruh** (E£15-25, 4 hrs) each hour during daytime, stops at El Alamein; 0830 and 1100 go to **Siwa** (just 1100 in winter); 0930, 1530 and 1800 go to **Sollum**. To **Sharm el Sheikh** via El-Tur daily at 0600. To Hurghada daily at 2000. Non-scheduled buses east along the coast to Rosetta and Damietta can be caught from near the Roman Theatre in Midan El-Gumhorriya.

International: Departures from outside *Cecil Hotel* to Tunisia, Libya, Syria and Abu Dhabi. Payment on these *Superjet* services required in hard currency. Where *Western Delta Buses* have equivalent departure this can be paid for in local currency.

Train The main Misr station in Midan El-Gumhorriya has inter-city services south to **Cairo** via Sidi Gaber, Damanhur, Tanta and Benha (dozen a day, 2½-3 hrs) and some a/c which go onward to **Luxor** and **Aswan**. Express Turbini (non-stop) leave at 0800, 1400 and 1900; calling at **Tanta** at 1100 and 1730; calling at **Banha**, **Tanta** and **Damanhour** at 0600, 0610, 1000, 1210, 1300, 1520, 1700 and 2000. Although less frequent and certainly slower, there are trains west to **El-Alamein** and **Marsa Matruh** at 0645 and 1300. For information T4923207.

Directory

Ambulance: T123
Fire: T180
Police: T122
Port: T4803494

Airline offices *Airport* T4427808. *Air France*, 22 Sharia Salah Salam, T4836311. *Air Maroc*, 15 Midan Sa'ad Zaghloul, T4816638. *British Airways*, 15 Midan Sa'ad Zaghloul, T4821565. *EgyptAir*, 19 Midan Sa'ad Zaghloul, T4838613. *Lufthansa*, 9 Sharia Talaat Harb, T4835983. *Sudan Airways*, 6 Sharia Talaat Harb, T4824834.

Banks There are branches of most domestic banks. The downtown branches of *Bank of Alexandria*, 1 Sharia Mahmoud Azmy, 59 Sharia Sa'ad Zaghloul and 6 Sharia Salah Salam are open Sun-Thu 0830-1400 and 1030-1300 during Ramadan. *Bank Misr*, 9 & 18 Sharia Talaat Harb, T807429/807031, and *Pullman Cecil*. *Banque du Caire*, 16 Sharia Sisostris and 5 Sharia Salah Salam. Foreign banks including *Bank of America*, T4921257, on Sharia Lomomba, *Barclays*, T4921307, at 10 Sharia Fawoteur, *Chase Manhattan*, 19 Sharia Dr Ibrahim Abdel el-Said, *Citibank*, T806376, 95 Sharia 26th July, takes all Visas and Mastercard, as well as money changing outlets in most of the major hotels. *Thomas Cook*, Midan Raml, is recommended for changing TCs.

Communications Internet: New one in the *Zaharan Mall* (one on the 1st floor and one on the 2nd) making a total of 3 in Semouha – an important meeting place for young folk in Alex. Try also *NetServ* T5872269 or *SatNet* T3129985 in Loran. Post Office: open daily 0800-2000 at Midan

Raml, Misr station which has an express mail service, and Sharia Iskander al-Akbar with a post restante service. *American Express* (c/o *Eyeress Travel*, 26 Sharia el-Horriya, Mon-Thu 0830-1300 and 1730-1800, Fri and Sat 0830-1300), also does post restante. **Telephone:** International calls: from the exchange at Midan Raml, open 24 hrs. International calls from hotels are trouble free but slightly more expensive. Cheaper calls 2000-0800.

Cultural centres *American* 3 Sharia Pharana, T4821009. *British Council* 9 Sharia Batalsa, Bab Sharaqi, T4820199. *French* 30 Sharia Nabi Daniel, T4920804. *German* 10 Sharia Batalsa, Bab Sharaqi, T4839870. *Italian* Italian Consulate, Midan Sa'ad Zaghloul, T4820258. *Russian* 5 Sharia Batalsa, Bab Sharaqi, T4825645. *Spanish* 101 Sharia el Horriya, T4920214, open 1700-2000.

Embassies & consulates *Denmark and Norway*, 20 Sharia Lumumba, T4921818. *France*, 2 Midan Orabi, T4827950, Sun-Thu 0900-1400. *Germany*, 5 Sharia Kafr Abdu, Roushdi, T4845443. *Netherlands*, 35 Sharia el-Shaheed Salah Mustafa, T4823999. *Spain*, 101 Sharia el Horriya, T4838346. *Sudan*, Silsila Bldg, Sharia 26th July, Azharita, T483920. *Switzerland*, 8 Sharia Mokhtar Adbel-Hamid Khalifa, T5872978. *UK*, 3 Mena Kafr Abdu, Roushdi, T4847166, open Sun-Thu 0800-1300. *USA*, 110-111 Sharia el Horriya, T4821911, Sun-Thu 0900-1200. Please note Libyan consulate is for Arab nations only.

Medical services Chemists: *El-Issaf*, 55 Sharia el-Sayed Mohammed Korayem. *El-Zahaby*, 157 Sharia Gamal Abd el-Nasser. *Hisham*, 40 Sharia Moharram Bay. *Oxford*, 10 Sharia Kolleyet el-Teb, Rushdi, 423 Sharia el Horriya. Hospitals: *Coptic Hospital*, Sharia Moharam Bey, T4921404. *Egyptian-British Hospital*, Sharia el-Ghatori, Semouha, T4227722. *Egypt Denmark Hospital*, Sharia el-Gaberti, T4913417. *German Hospital*, 56 Sharia Abd el-Salam Arif, T5881806. *International Hospital*, 8 Sharia Mustafah Kamel, Semouha, T4425017. *Italian Hospital*, El-Hadarah, T4921459. *Medical Care Advisory Team*, 97 Sharia Abdel Salam Aref, Glym Beach, T5862323. *Medical Centre*, Sharia 14th May, Semouha, T4202652. *Medical Research Institute*, Sharia el Horriya, T4212373. *Sharia el Horriya*, T4212886. *Poison Hospital*, Downtown T4822244. *University Hospital*, T4820029.

Places of worship *Anglican/Episcopal* in *All Saint's Church*, Stanley Bay, services Sun 1800 (in Arabic) and Fri 1030 (in English) and St Mark's, Midan el-Tahrir, El-Mansheya at 1030 each Sun. *Catholic* at *Sacred Heart Convent*, opposite *Lord's Inn*, Roushdi, Fri 1700 and Sat 0830 and *St Catherine's Cathedral*, Sun 0830 in Arabic, 1200 in Italian and 1800 in French. *Protestant*, interdenominational worship, Schutz American School, details on T5873591. *Seventh Day Adventists*, 10 Sharia Sidi Bishr Sporting, T857535 Sun at 1030. *Synagogue*, 69 Sharia Nabi Daniel, Fri afternoon and Sat morning, T4821426. Please check as temporarily closed. Interdenominational services at Alexandria Community Church, 51 Sharia Schultz, T5862944.

Shipping agencies *Abu Simbel Agency* 3 Sharia Adib, T808935. *Alexandria Agency*, *Amoun Agency and Thebes Agency*, 71 Sharia el Horriya, T4937109. *Egyptian Agency*, 1 Sharia el Horriya, T4920824. *Mena Tours Agency*, Midan Sa'ad Zaghloul, T808407. *North Africa Agency*, 63 Sharia Nabi Daniel, T4830059.

Useful addresses *Archaeology Society*: 6 Shari Mahmoud Mukhtar, behind Graeco-Roman museum. *Passport Office*: 28 Sharia Talaat Harb, T4824366, for registering arrival and renewing visas, open Sat-Thu 0830-1400, Fri 1000-1300 and 1900-2100. *Tourist Friends Association*, introduces tourists to local customs, habits and colloquial Arabic. Provides multilingual guides, T5501581. *Tourist Police*: on Midan Sa'ad Zaghloul, T5473814, and in grounds of Montazah Palace, T863804.

West to Libya

The **Mediterranean Coast** stretches 500 km west to the Libyan border passing through **El-Alamein**, Alexandria's local beach resorts of **El-Agami** and **Hannoville**, and the new beach resorts of **Maraqia**, **Marabilla**, **Sidi Abdel Rahman** and **Marsa Matruh** from which a road leads inland to the **Siwa** oasis (see page 379), before finally arriving at the Libyan border near Sollum.

The first few kilometres are the worst as the road west out of Alexandria is complicated and very badly signposted. There are two roads going west: it is best to take the more scenic coastal route. For the first 30 km a series of developments, more attractive to stay in than to look at, lie between the road and the sea. Petrol is easily available.

Ins & outs Advertised flights to Marsa Matruh do not appear on the Schedule. Check carefully. **Trains** including the express Turbini leave from Ramses Station. **Buses** – *Superjet, West Delta Bus Co, Golden Arrow* from Abd el Mouneem Riyad terminal near *Ramses Hilton*. Some buses depart directly from Cairo Airport. Regular departures too from Midan Sa'ad Zaghloul in Alexandria. **Service taxis** from in front of *Nile Hilton*, near Ramses Station or Ahmed Helmi Station.

Sites **El-Agami** and **Hannoville**, 20-25 km west of Alexandria, are beach resorts which are packed at weekends and during the high season with the result that litter and pollution are a growing problem. They can be reached both easily and cheaply from Alexandria by bus (No 455 from Midan Sa'ad Zaghloul or No 760 and No 600 from Misr Station and Midan Orabi); service taxi; or micro buses which leave El-Gumhorriya every 10-30 minutes.

Abu Sir, 43 km from Alexandria is further along the coast halfway between Alexandria and El-Alamein. Here an important but neglected archaeological site of Taposiris Magna dating back to the 27th Dynasty stands to the south of the road. Remains include that of a necropolis, two temples, a 10th-century church and the **lighthouse**. In the Ptolemaic period a string of beacons lit up the coast from Pharos in Alexandria to Cyrenaica in Libya. The **Burg al-Arab** (Arab Tower) just to the east of Abu Sir, is the sole survivor. The 17 m high lighthouse has the same three-tier construction as Pharos but is just a 10th of the size. The cylindrical top has collapsed but it does give an accurate impression of the appearance, if not the scale, of the Wonder at Pharos. The ancient temple dedicated to Osiris was of Ptolemaic design except for the gate at the east which had a more traditional Pharaonic structure. The series of colonnades were thought to resemble Karnak temple.

A second temple was discovered here at the beginning of the century by Italian archaeologists. This was dedicated to Ibis the sacred bird of Egypt. This was hewn out of the rock and is well enough preserved for the illustrations of birds and animals on the walls to be quite clear today. There is much concern, however, about the continuing deterioration of the buildings due to erosion, the dampness and salt in the atmosphere being harsh enough to make some places critical. There is grave concern too about the stability of the remains of the church. Many damaged stones have been replaced and a safe walkway for visitors has been cleared.

The mound or tell has been excavated – following the discovery during the Second World War of an engraving – and it is here the necropolis is buried, parts dated as Graeco-Roman and others going back to the 27th Dynasty. All the sarcophagi found here were anthropoidal in shape. Abu Sir was once an important coastal town, surrounded by great walls which have long since crumbled, so now only the gates remain. From the top there is a beautiful view over the Maryut marshes to the sea.

Abu Mina lies 48 km westsouthwest from Alexandria and about 15 km inland from Abu Sir, beyond the new town of Mobarak. It is black top all the way. It was once the most important destination in the east for Christian pilgrims as **Deir Mari Mina** is one of the largest Coptic monasteries. Most pilgrims left carrying a small amount of healing water in a small clay bottle – marked with the image of a St Menas and two kneeling camels. These are common enough to appear in your local museum. **St Menas**, who was an Egyptian-born Roman legionnaire, was martyred in Asia Minor in AD 296 for refusing to renounce Christ. He had rather a bad time. Legend says that first they tore off the soles of his feet, then they poked out his eyes before pulling out his tongue. None of these assaults prevented him from standing up to address the crowd. In the end the Emperor himself struck the fatal blow and the body was placed in a lead coffin and sunk out at sea. The coffin was washed ashore, discovered by passing bedouins and loaded on to a camel. He was buried here when the camel carrying his coffin would go no further. When miracles occurred at the site of his tomb the news travelled across Christendom, via the camel trains, that the tomb of Abu Mina and the Holy Waters nearby could cure sickness and suffering, and his sanctity was assured. Successive emperors built temples and basilicas around the shrine but when the waters dried up in the 12th century the town fell into decay. Excavations have revealed the remains of the basilicas and shrines and much of the surrounding pilgrim town. Most pilgrims left carrying a small amount of healing water in a small clay bottle – marked with the image of a St Menas and two kneeling camels. These are common enough to appear in your local museum. Saint Menas' day is now celebrated on 11 November and the town is the site of an austere concrete Coptic monastery which was built in 1959, easily recognized by its two white towers.

At 51 km out of Alexandria is **Maraqia**, built by the public sector Maraqia Co in 1982. There are chalets, villas and small cabins. Units can be rented by the night, week or month. There is a huge shopping area, banks, restaurants and a medical centre. There are four swimming pools and most other sports are catered for. The beach is splendid but not the place for a quiet stay. Stay at **D** *Maraqia Village*, T991313/2 as there is little choice.

Coastal resorts west from Alexandria

Marabilla, also built by Maraqia Co and very similar in style but less strident, is mainly villas and no apartments. The beach is smaller but it is very private, just for those in residence.

Aida Beach located 30 km east of El-Alamein has become very popular despite being 77 km west of Alexandria. Easy access by *Super Jet* bus from Alex or Cairo. (See transport entry, page 374.) **B-C** *Aida Beach Hotel*, Km 77 on Alexandria to Marsa Matruh road, T/F990858 has 100 rooms in the hotel, 40 apartments and 22 villas. Sports equipment and courts to hire, jet skis and windsurfing. Not as close to the beach as the name suggests. Recommended for its high quality service and entertainment facilities. No real competition.

El-Alamein

106 km west of Alexandria, owes its fame to what was, until the 1967 Arab-Israeli war, the largest tank battle in history. In July 1942 the Allies under Britain's Field Marshal Montgomery halted the German-Italian advance towards the River Nile and, in British eyes, if not in those of the Soviet troops at Stalingrad, turned the course of the Second World War. Winston Churchill later wrote, not entirely accurately that, "Before Alamein we never had a victory. After Alamein we never had a defeat". (See The North Africa campaign, page 372.) Unless you are a military historian or have a personal interest in the

Colour map 1, grid A3

Alexandria

The Desert War 1940-43

*Italy, the colonial power in Libya at the outbreak of the Second World War, invaded Egypt in the closing weeks of 1940 thus beginning a long period of fighting between the Axis powers and Great Britain in North Africa. Italian, and later German strategic plans, were the displacement of Great Britain from Egypt, destruction of Britain's imperial communications links through Suez, and the opening up of the Middle East oilfields to Axis penetration. The local Arab and Berber peoples of North Africa played a remarkable small role in events. The damage and disruption of the war were considerable and their negative effects (see Box **Mines peril ever present**) persisted for many years after the end of hostilities.*

The Italians were soon expelled from Egypt and much of eastern Libya but were powerfully reinforced in Tripolitania in February 1941 by the arrival of German troops and armour which rapidly drove the British back to the Egyptian frontier by April. The German formations were led by General Rommel with skill and audacity. Air power favoured the joint German-Italian armies in the earlier part of the campaign. Rommel's eastward advance was slowed by the protracted resistance of the garrisons, first Australian then British and Polish, at Tobruk. Meanwhile, the main armies fought pitched battles around the

Libyan-Egyptian border until Rommel withdrew temporarily in December 1941. He used his improved lines of communications in the west to prepare a counter attack and pushed east again as far as Gazala, near to Derna, in January and February 1942 and, after a pause, into Tobruk and deep into Egypt in June though his advance was finally held at El-Alamein after a fierce battle. Rommel made a final attempt at Alam Halfa east of El-Alamein to push aside British and Commonwealth forces and break through to the Nile Valley in August 1942 but failed in the face of strong defensive effort and his own growing losses of men and equipment.

The balance in the desert war changed in mid-1942 as the allies gradually won superiority in the air and had more freedom of movement at sea. The Germans and Italians began increasingly to suffer from shortages of equipment, while the health of Field Marshal Rommel gave rise to concern. On the allied side General Montgomery took over leadership of allied forces and began a build-up of the Eighth Army sufficient to overwhelm the well trained and experienced Afrika Korps. Montgomery opened his attack at El-Alamein on 23 October 1942 and after eleven days of hard fighting the Axis army was beaten back and retreated by rapid stages to the west to make a last, unsuccessful, stand in Tunisian territory.

battle, there is little to see and it is probably best to combine a visit here with other sights on the journey from Alexandria to El-Alamein.

Ins and outs El-Alamein is only a short car or bus ride away from Alexandria but the trains are slow and it is a 2 hr return journey and then a 2 km walk north from the station to the town. The buses and taxis doing the journey between Alexandria and Marsa Matruh stop at *Alamein Rest House*.

El-Alamein was the site of the battle between Germany's Afrika Korps and the Allied Eighth Army which turned the Second World War in the latter's favour and marks the closest that the Axis forces got to the Nile valley. The results of the encounter can be seen adjacent to the town in the huge **war cemeteries**. about 11,000 were killed and 60,000 wounded. The Greek war memorial is passed first. The **Commonwealth cemetery** ■ *daily 0700-1630, free,* but books of remembrance not available Friday, lies to the east of the town to the south of the road.

Through the arch and beyond the gardens' sombre lines of over 7,000 white headstones commemorate those who fought and died supporting the Allied cause. Despite the sombre surroundings the gardens here encourage migrant birds – and bird watchers. The **German cemetery** lies about 4 km to the west of the town between the road and the sea. Here in a sand coloured building resembling a castle there are 4,200 graves. The man with the key will see you coming. He lives nearby. The **Italian cemetery**, the only one in North Africa, lies a further 6 km west of the town on seaside. The white memorial tower is dedicated to 4,800 Italian soldiers, sailors and airmen of the desert and the sea. Just walk in.

A **museum** to the west of the settlement contains maps of the campaign and some of the uniforms and weaponry used in Egypt by both sides. A clever map/model display with lights and commentary (choose your language) explains the North Africa campaign. There is also information here about the war between Egypt and Israel in 1973. ■ *Daily 0800-1800, 0900-1500 in Ramadan, E£5, E£5 for camera.*

El-Alamein has a fairly good beach but heed the danger signs for unexploded mines!

Essentials

Sleeping

For something a little different try the resort of Marina, just 10 km beyond *Aida Beach*. This is a 3 km stretch of up-market 2-storey villas. Some of these villas are for rent at about E£4,500 a month. The beach is beautiful but the reason the beach is so clean is the strong sea currents – be warned. **A** *Seagull Resort Hotel* overlooking the artificial lake in the middle of the complex rents out jet skis. A very smart place to stay.

B *El-Alamein*, Sidi Abdel Rahman, El-Dabaa Center, T4921228. 209 rooms and villas with own seaside barbecue, very good standard, located on the beautiful white sands of the isolated up-market resort of Sidi Abdel Rahman about 25 km west of El-Alamein, early reservations essential, open Apr-Nov. Prices have been reduced slightly but rooms and general facilities are not really up to price standard. Day use of beautiful beach E£350.

C *Atic Hotel*, Km 90, Alexandria to Marsa Matruh road, T4921349, F4938313. 64 double rooms, located 16 km east of El-Alamein, good standard of service, pool, private beach, mainly Egyptian guests. This hotel is recommended as it has plenty of space – the rooms are large, the beds are large and so are the dining room and the pool and the beach is huge. The sports facilities are not up to the standard of *Aida Beach*. Compensate

Desert War

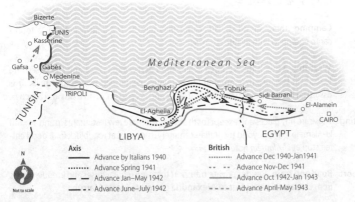

Mediterranean Sea

Bizerte
TUNIS
Kasserine
Gafsa Gabès
Medenine
TRIPOLI
Benghazi Tobruk
Sidi Barrani
El-Aghella
El-Alamein
CAIRO
LIBYA EGYPT
TUNISIA

N Not to scale

Axis		British	
▬▬▬	Advance by Italians 1940	··········	Advance Dec 1940-Jan1941
··········	Advance Spring 1941	– · – · –	Advance Nov-Dec 1941
– – –	Advance Jan–May 1942	▬▬▬	Advance Oct 1942-Jan 1943
– · – ·	Advance June–July 1942	– – – –	Advance April-May 1943

Alexandra

Mines peril ever present

Thirty people die from land mine explosions in Egypt each year on average. There are estimated to be as many as 21 million land mines still in place dating from World War Two or the several Arab-Israeli wars in more recent years. Some 16.7 million lie in the Western Desert, a damaging legacy of the long campaigns in that area in the years 1940-43. Most of the remaining 5.7 million mines are located in the Canal Zone and the adjacent battlefields of Sinai.

Most mines are anti-tank devices but, as they deteriorate with age, become unstable and are quite capable of detonating under the pressure of a human foot. Clearances and minefield marking are going ahead slowly but meanwhile tread with care in the following areas:

1. Thirty kilometres either side of the Alexandria-Marsa Matruh highway and all areas around the el-Alamein battlefields.

2. The area west of the Suez Canal such as Port Said, el-Qantara and Ismailia.

3. The open country to the west of the Red Sea such as in the deserts surrounding Safaga and Hurgada.

4. Gulf of Suez.

5. The remote areas of the Gulf of Aqaba/Sinai hinterlands.

6. North Sinai around sites such as el-Arish.

7. The Sinai passes at Mitla and Giddi.

Best advice is to stay away from locations where there are no signs of previous recent entry and always heed warning markers which are posted in Arabic and English.

---

by enjoying the lively night life, the good food (try the fish food, the pizzeria or the coffee shop in addition to the main Omda restaurant). Used by day guests who are not quite so restrained.

D *Agami Palace*, Al-Bittash Beach, El-Agami, T4330230, F4309364. 56 rooms, located 20 km west of Alexandria, tasteful décor, pool. **D** *Hannoville*, Hannoville Beach, El-Agami, T4303258. 157 rooms, located on rather polluted and crowded Hannoville beach about 25 km west of Alexandria, day-trippers from Alexandria flock here every weekend.

E *New Admiral*, Hannoville, El-Agami, T4303038. 44 rooms, on beach.

F *Costa Blanca*, Sharia Hannoville, El-Agami, T4303112. 36 rooms, on beach, see comment for *Hannoville Hotel*. **F** *Menas Agami*, Agami Beach, El-Agami, T4300150. 55 rooms. **F** *Monoco*, Abu Talaat, Km 25, Alexandria to Marsa Matruh road, T4321100. 33 rooms, on beach. **F** *New Talaat* Hannoville, El-Agami, T4891039. 25 rooms, see comment for *Hannoville Hotel*.

Camping There are no specific camp sites but the *El-Alamein Hotel* has a tourist camp equipped with all necessary services.

Warning As with the Red Sea coast, large parts of the coast and the desert are fenced off because they are still littered with unexploded mines and shells. It is **essential** to obey signs, use common sense and keep to the main roads and beaches.

Eating These are tiny places and except for the hotels there are few restaurants in and around El-Alamein. 8 km beyond the Italian cemetery, turn right at roadblock for a good coffee stop at *El-Alamein* hotel.

Transport **Road and train** Besides private transport there are regular buses and irregular trains from El-Alamein either east to **Alexandria** or west to **Marsa Matruh**.

Marsa Matruh

Marsa Matruh (178 km west of El-Alamein, 288 km west of Alexandria and 512 km northwest of Cairo), has been transformed from a sleepy village noted for sponge fishing and minor port into a popular, low grade, summer resort for domestic tourists with a plethora of tatty beach side tented areas belonging to trade and government groups. Despite the government's attempts, it has not, and is unlikely to be, turned into the new mass tourist Mediterranean beach destination for European tourists. Although there are some good beaches in the area and the lagoon has potential if correctly developed, the dull little town with a population of around 25,000 has few of the holiday facilities and night-life that tourists expect.

Phone code: 094
Colour map 1, grid A2
Population: 25,000

Alexandria

Ins & outs

Marsa Matruh's streets are on a grid pattern with most of the hotels being located on the streets behind and parallel to the Corniche. Buses and service taxis stop at Sharia Cleopatra about 1 km south of the beach and the hotels which can be reached by one of the *carettas*, cheap donkey carts, which are the main type of transport within the town. Airport close to south of town.

Sights

There are really only two reasons for visiting Marsa Matruh, either to travel to the magnificent desert oasis at Siwa (see page 379) or a rest *en route* to Libya. The area's much advertised beaches are a severe disappointment. Except for the *Beau Site* hotel's private beach, almost all beaches are public. Western women can still experience problems from both voyeurs and exhibitionists who are more used to seeing fully-clothed Egyptian women swimming and sunbathing, although the situation is improving as the locals become more used to visitors. No serious attempt has been made to solve the major litter problem on those beaches closest to town.

The beaches in the town's bay are protected by two sand spits which will eventually meet and form a lagoon. The water is shallow and stagnant, NOT a place to swim. **Lido Beach** and **Beach of Lovers** curve around the bay to the west of the town while in the other direction **Rommel's Beach** and its small military museum in a cave hewn in the rock, are beyond the small port and are almost facing the town on the landward side of the east spit. The approach, past rusting pipework which once served as the naval pier, is depressing even in the sunshine. **The Rommel Museum**, ■ *daily in summer 0930-1600*, gives details of this famous field marshal in the the Second World War campaign. Offshore from the beach is a red buoy, 25 m beyond which is a sunken German U-boat, which can be seen if you have suitable underwater swimming gear.

The better and cleaner beaches are those to the west of the town: in order they are **Cleopatra's Bath** (7 km) which is surrounded by cliffs and gets deep very suddenly; **Al-Nasr City Beach** (10 km); **El-Obeid Beach** (20 km) with beautiful white sand and **Agibah Beach** (28 km), best of all, the name means 'a wonder', which is set in the middle of a cove.

The nearby beaches can be reached from town by hiring a bicycle for 24 hrs from the hire shop (open 0600-2400) E£10 or by donkey cart for a negoti-ated price. Donkey carts carry two people and cost E£3 out to Rommel Museum. The more distant beaches to the west can be reached in summer by service taxi, microbus or Tuf-Tuf which shuttle back and forth (0800-1700) from near the bus station. In the winter the seaside areas are dead but the town life continues as normal.

Instruments for navigation in the desert

The Arabs are thought to have been among the great navigators and certainly the Middle East and North Africa were the sources of invention of many means of navigation such as by the stars. Its people invented a fascinating range of instruments for determining locations and directions, most notably the astrolabe. It was the Babylonians who as early as 1700 BC used systems of numbering, algebra and geometry and who combined their mathematical knowledge to develop astronomy to a fine art by 100 BC. Further expansion of mathematics were made by the Greeks, notably in the eighth and seventh centuries BC by individuals such as Pythagoras and, later, Archimedes.

Astrolabe of Esfahan, 1715

The Arabs were very early students of mathematics and algebra (the English name of which was derived from the Arabic al-gebit) was widely developed, a book on the subject by Mohammed ben Moosa being printed in the ninth century AD at the instigation of the Caliph Mam'un. Most importantly the Islamic period witnessed the tabulation of information, much of it of direct value to navigation in difficult or featureless desert terrain. The astrolabe, invented by the Greeks, was developed in Egypt by Ptolemy of Alexandria and was perfected by the Muslims as an accurate fixer of angles. The earliest known astrolabe was manufactured in the Iranian city of

Esfahan in AD 984. The astrolabe was made from a circular brass plate, some as large as 500 mm in diameter, with a movable pointer or finger called an alidade pinned at the centre of the plate. The astrolabe would be suspended from a ring and the angle to a given star or planet fixed from gradations marked on the rim of the plate which could indicate latitude and even time of day. Instruments of this kind were often wonderfully ornate, often those in Egypt imported from Iberia or Persia.

One of the earliest references to use of a magnetic compass in navigation was in the Middle East in the 13th century. The sun compass is still a useful instrument for desert navigation. With this the direction of the sun is picked out on a form of gnomon on a plate that gives an approximation of north.

The arrival of satellite aided navigation and location systems has finally made safe desert travel possible – but not in all cases. The local knowledge of the Arab nomads in desert areas is still invaluable, especially in sand sea areas such as the Western Desert, where electronic devices might tell you where you are geographically speaking but not how to escape the maze of sand.

Egyptian astrolabe, with Zodiac signs

Alexandria

Essentials

There are 28 hotels on the official list but many are closed in winter and fully booked with holidaying Egyptians in summer. Hotels may have a problem of fresh water supplies. There are no really first class hotels and it is best to avoid the very cheap ones near the bus station. This leaves, in addition to a number of cheap and cheerful hotels to the south, away from the beach, a wide range of choice in and around Marsa Matruh including:

B *Badr Tourist Village*, El-Obeid, T945348, F730443. 130 rooms, large hotel located on El-Obeid beach about 20 km west of town. **B** *Beach House Hotel*, Sharia el-Shatee, T4934011, F4933319. 20 suites here sleeping 3/4, very expensive.

B-C *Beau Site*, Sharia el-Shatee, T4932066. 56 rooms, open summer season only. Highly recommended. Located 2 km west of Sharia Iskandariya on the Corniche, the food is still reported as excellent, also rents out chalets for 3-8 persons. **C** *New Beau Site* has 88 rooms and splendid views from the Corniche.

C *Negresco*, Corniche, T4934492. 68 rooms, breakfast included.

D *Miami Hotel*, Corniche, T4935891, F4935892. Rather large with 200 rooms. **D** *New Royal Palace*, Corniche, T4933406. 170 rooms. **D** *Radi*, Corniche, Old Port, T4934827, F4934828. 72 rooms, disco in summer, pleasant staff, lots of hot water, food ok, very warm welcome. **D** *Riviera Palace*, Sharia Galaa, Market Area, T4933045. 32 rooms, a downtown hotel, overpriced restaurant, no alcohol, closed in winter. **D** *Rommel House*, Sharia Galaa, T4945466. 60 rooms, good café, a good standard. **D** *Royal Palace*, Corniche, T4934295. Largish with 126 rooms. **D** *Semiramis*, Corniche, T4934091. 64 rooms, good standard, open all year.

Marsa Matruh

N
Not to scale

■ Sleeping
1 Adriatika
2 Arouss el-Bahr
3 Beach House &
  Beau Site
4 Negresco
5 New Royal Palace
6 Radi
7 Reem
8 Riviera Palace
9 Rommel House
10 Semiramis
11 Youth Hostel

E *Adriatika*, Sharia Galaa, T4945195. 55 rooms with bath and balcony, good, located just north of the tourist office, closed in winter, inexpensive, yet facilities include 24-hr room service, laundry, bar, cafeteria and TV. **E** *Arouss el-Bahr*, Corniche, T4942419. 54 rooms, some bungalows for 4 persons, small hotel, sea views, helpful staff, restaurant. **E** *El-Khalig el-Azrak*, Corniche, T4942981. 57 rooms, recently expanded. **E** *Reem*, Corniche, T4943605. 58 rooms, very cheap, good value.

Camping It is essential to obtain permission to camp on the beach from the Military Intelligence Office on Sharia Galaa because they patrol the beaches at night. There is camping on the beach at *Badr Tourist Village* and on El-Obeid beach.

Youth hostels Behind 4 Sharia Galaa, Sollum Rd, T4932331. 52 beds, kitchen, meals, parking, facilities for disabled, overnight fee E£5, train 2 km.

Eating Besides the hotel restaurants including those at the *Beau Site* and *Riviera Palace*, there are a few cheap downtown restaurants near the Corniche including the *Alexandria Tourist Restaurant*, *Mansour Fish Restaurant*, *Restaurant Panayotis* which serves cheap beer and salads, and the bargain *Hani el-Onda*. Choose carefully remembering the fresh water problems.

Entertainment **Nightclubs**: there are nightclubs in the larger hotels and discotheques at the *Beau Site* and *Radi* hotels, in summer.

Transport **Air** There are flights advertised by *EgyptAir* from Marsa Matruh to **Cairo** which never actually appear on the schedule. Check carefully.

Bus: local transport to the beaches of **Cleopatra**, **El-Obeid** and **Agibah** leave every 15 mins during daylight. The best long distance services are the 3 daily Golden Rocket buses to **Alexandria** (3-4 hrs) and **Cairo** (8 hrs) which should be booked in advance. There are also slower blue buses to **Alexandria** (5 hrs) which stop at Sidi Abdel Rahman and El-Alamein, E£8. There is an early morning non-stop 5 hrs a/c daily service to **Siwa**, E£10, which is better than the afternoon service which, because it originates in Alexandria, is usually very crowded by the time it reaches Marsa Matruh and only operates in summer.

Service taxis: are quicker and cheaper but less comfortable than the express buses to Alexandria. Taxis to **Siwa** (4 hrs), E£15, leave early morning or in the afternoon to avoid the midday heat. It is difficult but not impossible to take one of the service taxis, which carry Egyptian expatriate workers, to the **Libyan** border (230 km east of Marsa Matruh) via Sidi Barrani (150 km) and Sollum (220 km) but it is essential to have a Libyan visa.

Train Although in summer there is a daily train service to **Cairo** (5-15 hrs) it is very slow and is not really worth the effort.

Directory **Airline offices** *EgyptAir*, Sharia Galaa, near Tourist office. **Banks** Most of the town's banks are west of the *EgyptAir* office and are open daily 0900-1400 and 1800-2000. The *Banque du Caire* branch, located east of the main north-south Sharia Iskandariya is open 0830-1430 and 1800-2100. *National Bank of Egypt* to west of town. There are no banks in Siwa so make sure that you have enough or change your money in Marsa Matruh. **Communications** Post Office: on Sharia Galaa to east of Sharia Iskandariya, open daily 0900-1500. **Telephone**: 24-hr telephones are just opposite the post office on Sharia Galaa. **Tourist offices** On Sharia Galaa, open daily 0900-1400 and 2000-2200, has limited material. You are advised to get information from one of the better hotels.

Marsa Matruh to Sollum

This last 215 km has little to recommend it. There are some new developments, the town of 'Agiba at a once lovely beach being an example, and sundry beduoin settlements. Sidi Barrani was the site of fierce battles during the Desert Campaign of the Second World War.

Sollum, the ancient port of Banaris, is the border town with Libya. The British and Commonwealth cemetery at the eastern side of the town has 2,060 war graves.

Colour map 1, grid A1

Buses to and from Marsa Matruh take four hours, E£10 and there are three a day. *Hotel al-Ahram* is for those who get stuck. **Visas for Libya**. These are not readily available at the border and are best obtained in Cairo. They are £20 sterling for UK nationals and are valid for one month, but must be used within 45 days. The border is 12 km west of the town and service taxis, E£4 are available. Service taxis *LDZ* go to Al Bardia. The bus from here goes to Benghazi.

Border crossing

Siwa Oasis

Siwa Oasis, where parts of the film *The English Patient* were filmed, is 82 km long east-west and 20 km north-south at its widest point and includes a number of large lakes. It is just 50 km from the Libyan border and 300 km southwest from Marsa Matruh, a journey by car of four hours along a tarmacked road. Traffic is sparse. The half way stop for tea or coffee is the *Badwy 'hotel'*. Scenery is limited until the escarpment is crossed and the trees of Siwa, 300,000 date palms and 70,000 olive trees come into view below. Siwa is in fact 18 metres below sea level. This magnificent oasis is recommended for those who want a break from the beach and want another type of sand. Comparatively few travellers visit the oasis because of its isolation and very limited facilities, but with the improved road and the encouragement of tour companies, the sense of 'away from it all' has been lost. Some 7,000 tourists visit here each year. Siwa is further from the Nile Delta, the source of Egyptian civilization and the point of contact with those civilizations which superseded it, than any of the oases along the Great Desert Circuit. With Siwa's customs unchanged for centuries, untouched by the world around, and its position on the shores of the

Colour map 1, grid A2

Sexism in Siwa: Female donkeys are not allowed in Siwa oasis!

Siwa Oasis

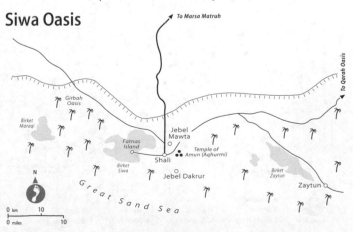

Great Sand Sea, it is geographically and culturally remote, and the closest to every romantic's notion of what a *real* desert should be like. It is not surprising then that there is a potential clash of cultures and visitors would do well to respect local customs by dressing modestly. Siwan married women cover themselves in a voluminous blue shawl. Women visitors are requested to keep legs and upper arms covered. Alcohol and affection are forbidden in public.

Siwans, currently numbering 25,000, have always been fiercely independent, in fact this oasis only officially became part of Egypt in the 19th century. It has been inhabited, with reliance on the 200 or so fresh, salt, warm and cold springs, since Palaeolithic times.

South from Siwa the Sudanese border lies across 700 km of desert. Of this 400 km is **The Great Sand Sea**, which like a frozen storm with waves 100 m high, has rolling sand dunes in every direction. Legend tells of a **lost oasis**, but it has never (obviously) been found. Perhaps the descendants of Cambyses live on! (See box, page 384.)

Permits are no longer required

The main settlement is **Shali**, until recently straddling two low hills within the depression, but now abandoned. The ruins of the old town established in 1203 are still impressive. The minaret of the 17th-century mosque remains. The mud brick walls and towers are floodlit at night, a splendid sight. New stone dwellings, mainly single storey, have been constructed. They are certainly not so attractive but probably much more comfortable. The new mosque of Faud I, a solidly built structure of stone in the pleasant style of the late 19th/early 20th century, is the natural centre of the new town. Adjacent to it is the tomb of Sidi Sliman, a local saint.

The economy is based on agriculture, dates and olives. The Sa'idi date is preferred for eating. Water supply is from natural springs. No pumping is necessary but the springs are capped to provide some control. Surplus water is a serious problem and the water level is rising at about 9 mm annually. New land is taken into cultivation if demand increases, the olives bearing fruit in five years and the

Shali in Siwa Oasis

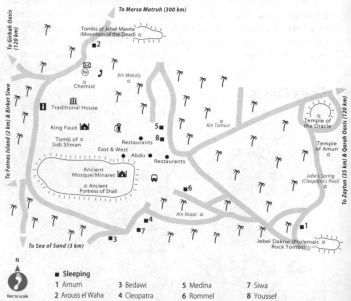

To Marsa Matruh (300 km)

To Girbah Oasis (120 km)

To Fatnas Island (2 km) & Birket Siwa

Tombs of Jebel Mawta (Mountain of the Dead)

Chemist

Ain Makaly

Traditional House

King Faud

Tomb of Sidi Sliman

East & West

Restaurants

Abdu

Restaurants

Ancient Mosque/Minaret

Ancient Fortress of Shali

Ain Tamusi

Temple of the Oracle

Temple of Amun

Juba's Spring (Cleopatra's Pool)

To Zaytun (35 km) & Qarah Oasis (120 km)

Ain Nsaar

Jebel Dakrur (Ptolemaic Rock Tombs)

To Sea of Sand (3 km)

N

Not to scale

■ Sleeping
1 Amum
2 Arouss el Waha
3 Bedawi
4 Cleopatra
5 Medina
6 Rommel
7 Siwa
8 Youssef

Alexandria

A long lost tomb?

First it was, then it wasn't and now it probably isn't – the long lost tomb of Alexander the Great. The recent announcement by Greek archaeologist, Liana Souvaltzi, that she had uncovered at Maraqi in Siwa possibly the most important archaeological find since that of Tutankhamun's tomb created a storm of controversy. Her claim centres around a 50 m above-ground 'tomb' which Souvaltzi says bears the same markings as that of Alexander's father, King Philip of Macedonia, including his royal symbol, an eight-pointed star. Just 18 m away, lies an entrance to a tunnel guarded by two royal lion statues and three stelae. The inscriptions, she claims, describe Alexander's funeral procession to Siwa. The find, if authentic, would rewrite history. According to ancient texts, the

conqueror, who died possibly through poison in 323 BC, expressed a wish to be buried in Siwa, where he was deified in 331 BC, but was finally laid to rest in Alexandria. A team of Greek experts, who flew out immediately to assess the find, concluded that there was "no evidence" of Alexander's tomb: the inscriptions were from the late Roman rather than earlier Hellenistic period, and the 'royal' eight-pointed star was a common theme in Macedonian monuments. Meanwhile, the burial chamber, at 76 cm wide, is too narrow for a sarcophagus to pass through. Excavations are still continuing but so far the only point of agreement is that the tomb, unusually large by Macedonian standards, is an important discovery – but of whom has yet to be decisively determined.

date palms in 10 years. Quarrying, transport, trade (and smuggling) are also important with increasing revenue from tourism. Labour costs are high as labourers have to be brought in and need food and accommodation.

The recent filming in Siwa of the Oscar-winning *The English Patient*, starring Ralph Fiennes, Kirstin Scott Thomas and Juliet Binoche, has drawn tourist attention to this area. There are plans to open to commercial traffic the adjacent military airport which guards the nearby Libyan border. This could increase the visitors, currently about 100 a week, to vast numbers accommodated in planned luxury tourist villages and so damage the very essence of this remote area.

Sights Siwa is such a wonderful place that rather than going to see anything specific most tourists visit Siwa simply to soak up the experience and the atmosphere of life in the oasis which is totally surrounded by the majesty of the desert. Its isolation from the rest of Egypt is increased by the fact that the inhabitants speak Siwa, which is a Berber dialect, rather than Arabic, and have their own festivals and customs.

Birket Siwa salt lake and **Fantis Island** reached by a newly built causeway are a popular picnic spot and on all itineraries. Recommended for an afternoon swim and later for the spectacular sunsets. Take precautions against the many mosquitoes.

Temples of Amun There are two temples to Amun here, both at the deserted village of Aghurmi 3 km to east. The **Temple of the Oracle** (see box, page 384) is built on a large rock amid the remains of the village. The ascent is quite steep and in summer when temperatures reach 44 °C almost impossible. The Temple which dates back to the 26th Dynasty is fairly well preserved and some attempts have been made to clear the debris and reveal the original façade. There are views to the adjacent Temple of Umm 'Ubayda, Jebel Matwa and across the palm groves to the shimmering salt lakes. The site of the second temple **Umm 'Ubayda**, from the 30th Dynasty, is marked by an area of fallen blocks in which one wall, all that survived the 1877 earthquake, carefully inscribed, still stands.

☛ The 'sacred aunt' of the Arabs – the date palm

Egypt produces about half a million tons of dates each year, though only a small portion of the total is made up of top quality dessert fruit. Even so, dates are important parts of the Egyptian rural diet and each year some 62,000 tons of dates are produced from scattered palmeries in the Delta and valley areas, though principally in the commercial plantations of the true desert or the oases such as Siwa. The date palm is among the longest established orchard trees in Egypt and was a favoured symbol on monuments from pre-dynastic times.

The prophet Mohammed called on the Islamic faithful to protect the date palm, which he called their 'sacred aunt' because of its many uses as a food, building material and provider of shade (see below). The Swedish naturalist Carl Linnaeus rendered homage to the beauty and generosity of the palm tree when he classified it in the order of Principes, 'The Order of Princes'. The green and yellow foliage of the date palm is also a fine decoration in the otherwise vegetation-less squares and avenues of many Egyptian cities. In the western oases of Egypt, the palm is the tree of life, its fruit, leaves and wood the basis of the local economy. The Latin name of the date palm, Phoenix dactylifera, may be translated as "the Phoenician tree with fruit resembling fingers". Egypt's top variety of date from the Western desert is the sa'idi, which has a delicate translucent appearance. Other favourite dates are the ghazali, known in Siwa for its energy giving properties, and the frihi, a succulent date with a good flavour. The izzawai date is a low grade crop used as human food but also for feeding to animals and for making into alcoholic beverages.

The date palm is a close relation to the grasses. The tree has neither branches nor twigs. Its trunk is in fact a stem: it has no bark; being simply covered by the base of the old fallen leaves. A cross-section of a palm trunk reveals a multitude of rigid tubes containing sap bearing vessels, rather than the annual growth rings of a true tree. Due to the activity of a single bud hidden at the heart of the palm leaves, this trunk grows continuously.

The phoenix dactylifera grows to 23 m. The top delicate, pinnate leaves grow to some 5 m long. Flowers spring from the axils of the leaves and today most cultivated palms are hand pollinated. The date fruit (trees bear fruit at five years of age) is a berry – with one long seed or pit and an individual palm can have up to 1,000 dates in one bunch. The dried fruit contains by weight 50% sugar and a little protein and fat. Date palms can live for up to 100 years, though the older trees become ragged in foliage and gradually yield less fruits.

In the wild state, the young palm tree tends to resemble a hedgehog due to the uncontrolled development of buds at the base of the initial trunk. If severed with skill, these buds can be planted elsewhere. There are both male and female trees. Broadly speaking, a male tree can pollinate some 50 female trees. To ensure maximum fruit production, the farmer will place a sprig of male flowers next to the female flowers – or should he have only a small orchard, he will not grow any male trees at all, preferring to buy male sprigs at the market.

In March or April, the tiny green date is round like a marble. Its future is uncertain: if the hot winds from the south are too fierce, it may be blown

Juba's Spring, also called Cleopatra's Pool although it has nothing at all to do with the lady, was mentioned by Heroditus. It is supposed to change temperature during the day but the reality is the relative difference between air temperature and the temperature of the person dipping in, and many people do. On a practical note, the spring produces enough water to irrigate 121 ha every 14 days.

Tombs of Jebel Mawta or Mountain of the Dead is a conical hill about 1½ km north from the centre of Shali. It is honeycombed with tombs from 26th Dynasty to the Roman period, varying from small chambers to large

from the tree before its time. During the summer, the date reaches full size, becoming smooth and yellow, rich in vitamins but bitter to taste. In the heat of the summer and autumn, the fruit slowly matures on the tree, softening and turning an amber colour, deep brown or black, depending on the variety. The date sugars change as well and, little by little, the date dries out and becomes a preserved fruit if left on the tree.

For the oasis dwellers, the date is so precious that they have a name for each stage of its growth. The date palm may produce up to 100 kg of dates annually for a whole century. However, in order to do this, it needs manure and a lot of water, anything up to 300 litres a day!

The palm tree provides many essentials for its owner. The trunks are used to support roofs of houses, strengthen walls and in slices are used to make doors. One or two trunks make an adequate bridge over an irrigation channel, and with pieces cut out can be used as steps. The fibres on the trunk are removed and used as stuffing for saddles while the base of the palm frond, stripped of its leafy part, makes a beater for the washer woman and a trowel for the mason. Palm fronds are used to make baskets and a variety of mats such as the famous margunah or covered basket of Siwa. Midribs have enough strength to be used to make crates and furniture. Leaf bases are used for fuel and fibre for packing. The sap is drained and consumed as a rough but intoxicating beer laghbi or even as a distilled liqueur. This practice is banned for Muslims, who are forbidden alcohol and in any case drawing the sap can also kill the tree and is therefore discouraged by the authorities. The flesh of fruit, which is rich in sugar and vitamins is eaten by man and the stone is eaten by the camel. Date stones can even be ground and used to supplement coffee. Best quality fresh dates are a delicacy for the rich. Dried and pressed dates stay edible for long periods and can be taken on journeys or used to sustain the nomads in their wanderings.

It is possible to buy fresh dates in Egypt or special packs for the tourist trade. Date purchased from an open market stall, must be washed thoroughly before they are eaten.

composite excavations complete with columns and wall paintings. Anything worth stealing has long since been removed. During 1940 many items were 'sold' to the visiting troops by Siwans who had moved into the tombs for security. Splendid views from the summit. ■ *0900-1400, closed Fri. No photographs allowed inside.* Tombs open to visitors: that of Si-Amun is the most important with wall paintings of the Si-Amun and his family, of Nut the goddess of the sky, and a very recognizable maple tree; Tomb of Mesu-Isis; Tomb of the crocodile; and Tomb of Niperpathot which is in very poor condition.

The Oracle of Amun

*It was **The Oracle of Amun** which brought Siwa to the attention of the world, from the 26th Dynasty (664-525 BC) onward. **Alexander the Great** is known to have consulted the Oracle in 331 BC after wresting control of the country from its Persian rulers in order to ask it if, as he suspected, he was indeed the son of Zeus. His arrival with a large party of friends and an even larger number of soldiers must have caused*

quite a stir in sleepy Siwa. Unfortunately posterity does not record the Oracle's response. Nearly 200 years earlier, Egypt's Persian ruler Cambyses (525-522 BC) is said to have carelessly lost an army of 50,000 men who were dispatched from Aïn Dalla near the Farafra Oasis to Siwa in order to destroy the Oracle. The army was simply never seen again having been either buried by a sandstorm or snatched by aliens.

Traditional Siwan House, exhibition financed by Canadians, shows in great detail the artefacts and decorations used until very recently in the houses of the oasis. ■ *0900-1200 on request – best to give some notice – visitors' book is almost as fascinating as the house. Take time off in the small garden by the house. No entrance fee, just a tip.*

Olive press This old press, driven by donkey power, is in operation only at the end of the olive season around the first week of December. Arrangements can be made at the Tourist Office. ■ *No fee but do tip as it is the man's livelihood.*

Siwa water bottling plant is run by an Italian company on the outskirts of Shali. It produces over one million bottles annually. Safi water, of equal quality, has a smaller output. An excellent way to exploit an area with too much water.

Sulphur Springs and **Oasis Garden** in desert, contact Ahmed in *Café Abdou*. Cost E£35 day trip.

Essentials

Sleeping The *Safari Paradise* is the best accommodation, in huts and bungalows, a/c, satellite TV, with prices from E£30-E£200. There are small cheap hotels too. Price for double rooms give range of comfort. All basic facilities, tiled floors, a/c of sorts. Always ask to see the room. Except for Oct festival it is not hard to find a room. An ecolodge is under construction about 30 mins away with huts for sleeping, plumbing but no electricity. *Amun Hotel*, government run, E£8. *Arous el Waha*, rather run down, all rooms bath and balcony, hot shower, E£40. *Bedawi Hotel*, hot showers, E£6. *Cleopatra*, front view over ruins of Shali with shower, E£15-20, rear view with shower, E£10, dormitory E£5 each, roof E£1, hot showers, clean spartan rooms, friendly staff. Recommended. *Medina Hotel*, E£6. *Palm Trees Hotel*, E£6. *Rommel Garden Hotel*, under construction. *Siwa Hotel*, E£6. *Youssef Hotel*, in the market square, E£10.

Camping This is a sensitive area close to the Libyan border, so despite the good relations, don't camp out without permission from the tourist office. Hotels are so cheap camping is really unnecessary but is allowed at the springs called Cleopatra's Baths. *Hotel Cleopatra* permits sleeping on the roof for E£1 per night.

Eating The only places to eat in town are 2 or 3 small cafés in the area around the market and new mosque in the centre of town. *Abdou*, which is cheerful and welcoming, is considered 'one of the best' but there is not much competition. Prices cheap, omelette and chips with Pepsi E£4. *Restaurant Alexander* serves a version of Indian food while the *East-West Restaurant* is a no better/no worse alternative.

Siwa Festival in Oct just before date harvest, lasts 3½ days and over 3,000 people come to celebrate with prayers and sing some religious songs. **Festivals**

Market: every Fri. Siwan handicrafts of note include carpets woven from local wool, in thick bright stripes of red, yellow and blue; traditional wedding gowns in black – equally eye catching but less popular as a purchase; Siwan jewellery, is in limited supply. **Shopping**

Local Most places are within cycling distance – *Youssef Hotel* and *Cleopatra Hotel*, hire cycles at E£3 per hour or E£5 per day. *Abdou Café* or your hotel can organize a donkey cart. **Transport**

Bus: The bus station and taxi halt are in the south of the town only a short walk from the centre. Besides a reliable private car, the only way to and from the oasis are the 2 daily buses from Siwa to **Marsa Matruh** at 0700 and 1000 (summer only), costs E£12, goes on to **Alexandria** (extra E£6.50). **Service taxis**: there are service taxis back to the coast which leave mid-morning and late afternoon.

It is possible to approach **Siwa** from Bahaiya but a reliable 4WD vehicle is required as only part of the road is surfaced.

Communications Post Office: located with the police station just south of the *Arous el-Waha Hotel*. **Banks** There is no bank in town. **Tourist offices** Located to the west of the new mosque, the tourist office (open Sat-Thu 0900-1300, Fri 1800-2000), is a very helpful first stop for any information. A guide for the main sites of Siwa will cost around E£25. **Directory**

Alexandria

386

The Suez Canal Zone

10

The Suez Canal Zone

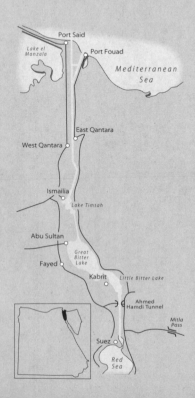

Although the Suez Canal Zone may not be the most attractive or interesting region in Egypt, it is certainly worth a detour to Ismailia when crossing between Sinai and the rest of Egypt. We may live in an age when it is difficult to be impressed by something as mundane as a canal but it should not be forgotten that the Suez Canal was as great a feat of engineering in the 19th century as the Pyramids were in their day. The convoys of vessels through the canal are an inspiring sight and viewed from the comfort of a hotel window in Port Said become a fascination which is almost addictive. Into the night the riding lights of the container vessels mark the line of their movement. Only one thing can improve on this – a journey through the canal itself.

The Suez Canal Zone

Most visitors who head east from Cairo cross the desert and go under the Suez Canal through the Ahmed Hamdi Tunnel, 12 km north of the town of Suez. which connects Africa to Asia. It is 3 km long and costs E£10 each way. From there they go into the Sinai peninsula, ignoring not only Suez itself which is not a pleasant town but also the relatively tedious journey north past the Great Bitter Lakes to Ismailia and El Qantara and to Port Said on the Mediterranean. Although these towns may not have the attractions of either Cairo or the Sinai resorts, the route is used by those travelling overland to Israel or to catch the ferry to Cyprus and Greece.

Suez

Phone code: 062
Colour map 2, grid B4
Population: 458,000
Altitude: 11 m

At the southern end of the Suez Canal, just 134 km from Cairo, Suez was known as Klysma during the Ptolemaic period. It was the spice trade and the pilgrims travelling to Mecca that made the walled city, then known as Qulzum, so prosperous in the Middle Ages. In the 15th century it became a naval base and the opening of the Suez Canal in 1869 ensured its survival and development. It was almost totally destroyed during the 1948 and other wars with Israel, after which it was rebuilt with Gulf funds. Today it is one of Egypt's largest ports and an important industrial centre producing cement, fertilizers and petrochemicals using domestic oil from the offshore fields in the Gulf of Suez. Besides a new ferry terminal for pilgrims bound for Mecca it is also linked to Port Tawfiq and its other docks and ferry terminals. Suez has been unable to cope with its litter problem and is, in places, decidedly unpleasant.

Ins & outs
Buses and service taxis arrive at the Arba'in Terminal just off the main Sharia el-Geish which leads left to the nearby railway station and right to the main hotels and then the causeway to Port Tawfiq. There is a *Tourist Friends* booth at the bus station manned by friendly volunteer students who want to be helpful while improving their English. The **Tourist Information** T223589, is right across by the canal on Sharia Sa'ad Zaghloul.

Some of the streets are too dirty to walk through but the coastal area and the garden in the newly reclaimed area east of the stadium is worth visiting. An evening stroll along Sharia el-Geish and across the causeway towards Port Tawfik is recommended. Wander as far as the monument made of four captured US-made Israeli tanks. Port Tawfiq is worth spending time in. It is

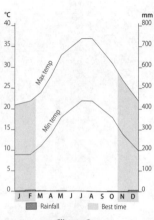

Climate: Suez

amazing how much of the European influence remains, neat privet hedges, pavements to walk on, relative absence of litter.

Excursions are organized from here to the Monasteries of St Anthony and St Paul. (See page 447.)

D *Green House*, Sharia Port Said, T331553, F331554. 48 rooms, like most of the hotels in Suez the majority of the guests are Egyptians and oil company workers. **Sleeping**
D *Red Sea Hotel*, 13 Sharia Riad, Port Tawfiq, T334302, F334301, 81 rooms, TV a/c, comfortable, good choice in restaurant (open 24 hrs). **D** *Summer Palace*, Port Tawfiq, T224475, F321944. 90 rooms, good views, pool, restaurant.

F *Misr Palace*, 2 Sharia Sa'ad Zaghloul, T223031. 30 rooms. **F** *White House*, 322 Sharia el-Geish, T227599, F223330. All rooms are clean and have bath, a/c, TV.

Youth hostels *Sharia Tariq el-Horriya* (nr sports stadium), PO 171, Suez. 105 beds, kitchen, station 2 km, T339069.

There is a decent fish restaurant on Sharia el-Geish near the bus station. Beer can only **Eating**
be found in 1 or 2 of the hotels and the average *El-Magharbel Restaurant* near the *White House Hotel*. Try also the cheaper *El-Tayib* on Sharia Hoda Sharawi.

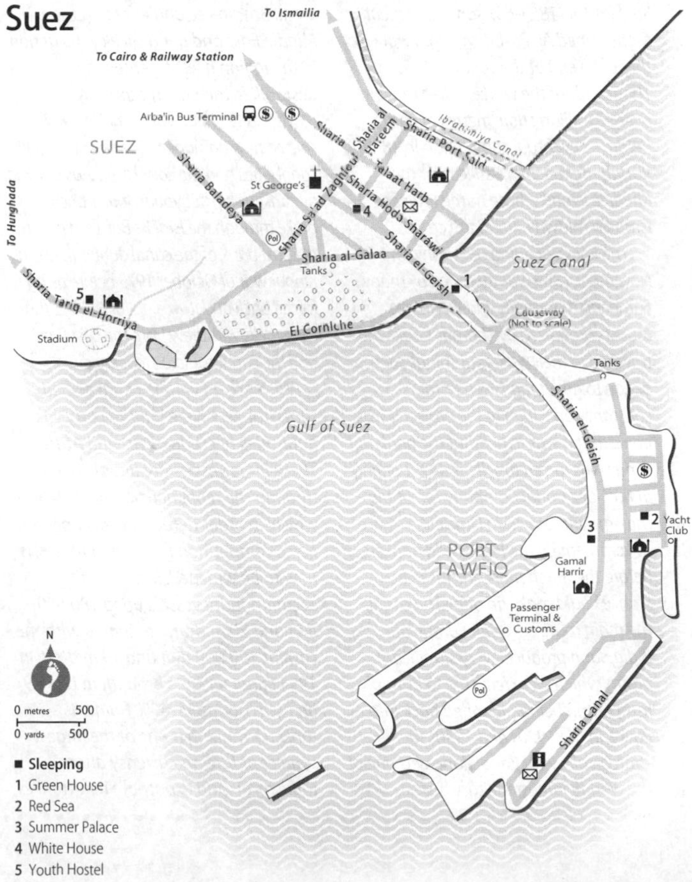

The Suez Canal

Suez

■ **Sleeping**
1 Green House
2 Red Sea
3 Summer Palace
4 White House
5 Youth Hostel

The Suez Canal

Since its completion in 1869 the **Suez Canal**, which at 167 km is the third longest in the world, has enabled ships to pass from the Mediterranean to the Indian Ocean via the Red Sea without sailing around the southern tip of the African continent. There had been many previous attempts to build a canal including those in the 26th Dynasty by Necho II (610-595 BC) and the Persian Emperor Darius I (521-486 BC). Napoleon's engineers vetoed their own plan to build the canal after calculating (incorrectly) that the sea level in the Red Sea was 10 m lower than in the Mediterranean. Although it was the British who discovered their error in the 1840s it was **Ferdinand de Lesseps**, a young French vice-consul in Egypt, who finally persuaded the Khedive Said Pasha (1854-63), son of the great Mohammed Ali Pasha, to begin work at the north end of the canal in 1859. Thousands of the workers died moving over 97 million cubic metres of earth, before its eventual completion in 1869 during the rule of his successor the Khedive Ismail whose name is given to Ismailia midway along the canal.

The lavish opening ceremony on 17 November 1869 was attended by many European dignitaries and a party of tourists organized by Thomas Cook who travelled in their wake, but things soon began to go wrong. Given Britain's constant opposition to the project it was ironic that it was to her that the bankrupt Ismail was forced to sell his 44% holding in the Suez Canal Company for £4 mn, the amount loaned to Disraeli's government by the Rothschild bankers, before the much more enthusiastic France could make an offer. The canal, the main route between Europe and India, soon produced very significant profits which were remitted to Britain rather than being ploughed back into Egypt. In the 1920s and 1930s the strategically vital Canal Zone was one of the world's largest military bases.

Since 1945 the canal has been the subject of both important political disputes and serious armed conflicts. Britain reluctantly agreed to remove its troops in 1954 but refused to give a larger share of the revenues to Egypt. The West vetoed World Bank loans to help finance the construction of the Aswan Dam because of the Soviet Union's offer to rearm Egypt after its 1948 defeat by Israel. In reply Colonel Gamal Abdel Nasser nationalized the Suez Canal on 26 July 1956. Britain and France used the pretext of an agreed and pre-planned Israeli invasion of Sinai in October 1956 in an attempt to reoccupy the Canal Zone but were forced to withdraw when the US, opposed to imperialism but wanting to break Britain's stranglehold on the Middle East and get a slice of the action in the region itself, threatened to destabilize the British economy.

The Six Day War with Israel in 1967 caused new damage to the recently rebuilt canal cities and the canal itself was blocked by sunken ships. Egyptian forces briefly broke through the Israeli's Bar-Lev Line on the east bank of the canal during the Yom Kippur war of October 1973 before being forced back and it was not until 1982 that the Israelis withdrew from the East Bank and the canal could be reopened.

With access via the canal denied, super-tankers were built to carry vast quantities of crude oil around Africa. These huge vessels are unable to pass through the reopened Suez Canal which, in order to face increasingly fierce competition from other routes, is now to be widened. It will accommodate vessels up to 180,000 dwt and 20 m draft compared with the current 150,000 dwt and 19 m draft. In 1994 canal receipts brought in US$1.9 bn (with about 35-40% from oil tankers), making it one of the largest sources of foreign currency after tourism, oil and expatriate remittances.

Train Trains run to/from **Cairo** (Ramses railway station) but it is better to take the direct express (3 hrs) train which runs 4 times a day rather than the much slower ones via Ismailia.

Road Bus: buses leave the terminal every 30 mins between 0600-2030 for the 2 hrs journey for **Cairo** (near Ramses railway station) and north along the canal to **Ismailia** and **Port Said**. Other buses include 2 a day east to **Sharm el-Sheikh** and **Dahab**, **St Catherine's monastery** and **Nuweiba**, and **Taba**, and north to **Alexandria**, 5 a day south along the Red Sea coast to **Hurghada** and on to **Luxor**. Buses from Suez; **El-Tur**, 0830, 1600; **Sharm el-Sheikh** 1100, 1330, 1500; **Dahab** 1100; **St Catherine** 1400; **Nuweiba** and **Taba** 1500. **Service taxis**: from the main Arba'in terminal off Sharia el-Geish travel to all of the same destinations as the buses. Foreigners may be requested not to travel in these taxis – for their own protection. Besides the very frequent services to Cairo and north along the canal, travellers going east and south to more remote destinations must split the pre-arranged cost of the journey.

Boat Ferry: the vehicle ferry service, taking 2-3 days, from Port Tawfiq to **Port Sudan** is supposed to be weekly but because of both operational and political problems it is often less frequent, if it runs at all. Ferries shuttle instead to and from **Jeddah** in Saudi Arabia, contact *Mena Tours* T220021 for information. Don't attempt this journey during the Hadj.

Transport

Banks Both the *Bank of Alexandria* and *Bank Misr* are on Sharia el-Geish just east of the bus station. **Communications** Post Office: on Sharia Hoda Sharawi which is 1 block away from the main Sharia el-Geish, near the causeway to Port Tawfiq. Open Sat-Thu 0830-1400. The telephone office is further south on Sharia Sa'ad Zaghloul. **Useful addresses** Passport office: for registration or extending a visa is on Sharia Tariq el-Horriya.

Directory

Suez Canal

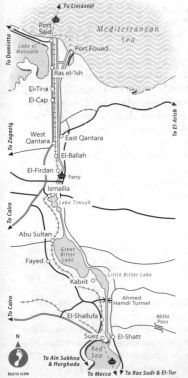

Aïn Sukhana

This is a region of hot springs, hence its name, on the Gulf of Suez about 55 km south of Suez on route 44. It is a very attractive area, popular with bird watchers as it is on the raptor migration route. These natural springs at a temperature of 35°C have become the centre of a popular weekend resort for the people of Cairo which is only 110 km away. There are some fine beaches (quieter during the week), a coral reef close to shore, fishing and opportunities for most watersports. Three or four buses daily from Suez.

A *Stella Di Mare* (part of Swiss Inn chain) T06225000, F06225001. A quality resort, a new touristic village, open air restaurant, watersports, bowling centre, commercial centre, 700 m of beach, lagoons. **B** *Al-Sukhna Portrait Hotel*, Km 59, Suez/Zafarana Rd, partly time share so

Sleeping

higher standard, T325560, F322003. 63 quality rooms with sea view, pool, all water sports, tennis. **B** *Palmera Beach*, T410818, F410825, offers further quality accommodation. **B** *Three Corners Amigo Resort*, 54 rooms, 24 family units, pools, restaurants. **C** *El Aïn el Sukhana village*, T775226, F5783642, 72 rooms.

Directory The bus from Suez is E£6. Taxi from Suez is E£15-25.

Fayed and Abu Sultan

Small beach resorts located just to the west of the Great Bitter Lakes about 60 km and 70 km north of Suez.

Sleeping **B** *Helnan Morgan Village*, Km 54, Ismailia/Suez Rd, Fayed, T661718, F661719. 92 good double rooms, excellent views, good pool and beach, a real 'find' in this area. Recommended. **C** *Six Corners Resort*, Km 32, T400232, F400849. 70 good standard rooms. **C** *Shamoussa*, Km 59, Suez Canal Rd, Great Bitter Lakes, T661525, F661009. 54 rooms of good standard. **D** *Bonita Village* is a new resort hotel in Kabrit, T6604341. 60 rooms, a/c and good choice in restaurant. **E** *El Safa Hotel*, Farana, T661659. 30 rooms, cheapest place in town.

Transport **Road Buses and service taxis** running between **Suez** and **Ismailia** stop at **Fayed**.

Ismailia

Phone code: 064
Colour map 2, grid B4
Population: 600,000

Ismailia is 120 km east of Cairo, 90 km north of Suez and 85 km south of Port Said, and is the largest and certainly the most attractive of the three main Canal Zone cities. It was named after Ismail Pasha, Khedive of Egypt. It was built as a depot by the Suez Canal Company in 1861 on the west shore of **Lake Timsah** (Crocodile Lake), one of Egypt's largest lakes. It is divided by the railway track with the attractive and calm Garden City, which was built for the company's European employees to the south towards the Sweetwater Canal and the lake, and the poorly constructed apartment blocks, which were financed with Gulf money, and slums to the north. Lake Timsah covers 14 sq km. The calm waters make it suitable for international water sports championships, the many beaches are popular especially at weekends as are the small lakeside settlements. The land is very low-lying, only 10 m above sea level. The Sweetwater Canal was dug from its source in Lake Timsah to provide fresh water during the construction of the Suez Canal. Desert weary travellers find the orchard gardens and trees a delight. There is very little night life but blissful days can be spent sitting on the beach on Forsan Island watching the ships go by.

Ins and outs

Getting there Foreign visitors to this area will have the company of the police, for their own protection (from the first check point on the freeway from Cairo, from the outskirts of Port Said or from the border with Palestine) for the whole of their sojourn. See box – coping with police protection.

Travellers arriving by public transport from the Canal Zone and the Delta will be dropped at the depot on Sharia Gumhorriya on the wrong side of the railway tracks. Cross the line to reach the decent end of town and head for the railway station on Midan Orabi. Buses from Alexandria and Cairo drop passengers at the terminal on Midan Orabi. Sharia Ahmed Orabi outside the station runs straight down to the lake and most of the hotels are to be found to the north or left of the street in the Garden City area.

The Suez Canal

Islamic dietary laws

Islam has important rules governing what things may be eaten by the faithful. The Koran specifically forbids the eating of the flesh of swine and the drinking of wine. Other rules dictate how an animal may be slaughtered in proper Islamic manner and ban the consumption of meat from any carcass of an animal that perished other than in the approved way. Any food made of animal's blood such as black pudding or boudin is strictly excluded from the diet of a good Muslim. Non-muslim visitors are not included in these controls and international food is provided in all quality hotels.

The ban on wine has been interpreted as a total outlawing of all alcohol. In practice, local traditions have led to relaxations of the ban from place to place. Some areas, such as much of Turkey forbade Muslims from trading in alcohol but not necessarily from drinking it. Indeed sufi poets used wine as a metaphor for liberty and the ecstasy of truth – and perhaps often as a real stimulant to freedom of the soul! As the poet Hafez wrote:

"From monkish cell and lying garb released,

Oh heart of mine,

Where is the Tavern fane, the Tavern priest,

Where is the wine?"

In Egypt sufism was a road to spiritual understanding, but the tradition of wine imbibing was never well developed here. Wine is produced in Egypt though the quality varies round the 'only fair' standard.

Fasting is a pillar of Islam, as originally of Judaism and Christianity. It demands that Muslims desist from eating, drinking and smoking for the month of Ramadan during the hours of daylight. The Ramadan fast, always followed by the faithful in Libya and Egypt, is now rigorously enforced by social influence.

Travellers are unlikely to be disconcerted by Islamic taboos on food and during Ramadan meals will be provided at normal times. However, the Ramadan fast can be very inconvenient for the uninitiated western traveller. Quite apart from a rising tide of irascibility in some of the Egyptian population, the break of fast in the evening can mean that service in transport, hotels and restaurants can be discontinuous or erratic. The holidays that follow the fast have a similar impact as most local people meet with their extended families and leave their places of work for several days. Check the calendar on page 50 with care.

The Suez Canal

In summer hire a horse drawn carriage to see the sights. The tourist office is open Sat-Thu 0800-1400. It is upstairs in the new Mahefezah building, the district authority head office. Very helpful.

Getting around

Ismailia is located in Mallaha Park, with over 200 ha of trees, flowers and grass. In this attractive Garden City is situated the huge Suez Canal University opened in 1997, the attractive Catholic church built in 1930 to a unique architectural design and the El Rahman mosque to the west of town constructed post 1973. Also some 7 km south of Ismailia on the west bank is the memorial to the unknown soldier, recalling the First World War, and an unusual memorial of 6 October, 1973 is located on east bank of the canal near the ferry crossing – a fixed bayonet.

Sights

A number of minor sites which, although comparatively unimportant, are worth visiting while in town.

The **Ismailia Regional Museum** near Fountain Park (established 1932) in the north of the Garden City. ■ *Sat-Thu 0900-1600, Fri 0900-1100, 1400-1600 daily during Ramadan 0900-1400, E£6, E£3 students, labels in French.* Although it has some minor ancient Egyptian pieces it is the mosaics and other pieces amongst its collection of 4,000 Graeco-Roman artifacts which are the museum's highlights. Permission is necessary from the museum to visit the Garden of Stelae nearby which holds a number of pharonic artefacts and obelisks, mainly from the period of Ramses II.

Left off Sharia Ahmed Orabi on Mohammed Ali Quay next to the Sweetwater Canal is the **House of Ferdinand de Lesseps** which, although officially a museum, is sometimes used as a government guesthouse at which times it is closed to the public. It displays many of his personal possessions, his diaries and his private carriage. ■ *Wed-Mon 0900-1600.*

About 7 km north of the city is the main car-ferry across the Suez Canal to Sinai and the **Bar-Lev Line** which is the impressive 25 m high embankment built by the occupying Israelis to stall any Egyptian advance across the canal and into Sinai. Although Egyptian forces managed to break through the line at the beginning of the October 1973 war, by using the element of total surprise and high pressure water hoses, the Israeli counter-attack across the Great Bitter Lakes virtually succeeded in surrounding the Egyptian army and, under pressure from the super-powers, both sides were forced to the negotiating table.

Bicycles can be rented from the streets off Mohammed Ali Quay. Picnic in the park between Lake Timsah and Sweetwater Canal.

Beaches There are some pleasant beaches located around Lake Timsah.

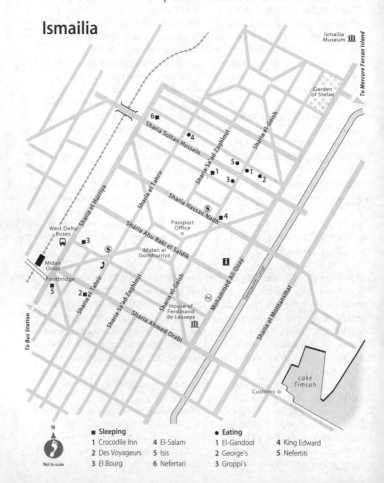

Ismailia

■ Sleeping
1 Crocodile Inn
2 Des Voyageurs
3 El Bourg
4 El-Salam
5 Isis
6 Nefertari

● Eating
1 El-Gandool
2 George's
3 Groppi's
4 King Edward
5 Nefertiti

N
Not to scale

Essentials

B *Mercure Forsan Island*, PO Box 77, T765322, F338043. 152 rooms, the best in Ismailia, **Sleeping**
located on the lush Forsan Island to the northeast of town, good views of Crocodile
Lake, private beach, tennis and watersports, a lunchtime buffet on Fri and Sat and a
nightly barbecue, all facilities available to non-residents for E£20 per day, excellent
value. **B** *Palma Abu Sultan Village*, Abu Sultan, T400421, F400862. 98 rooms.

C *El-Salam Hotel*, Sharia el-Geish, T324401, a/c, TV, clean, includes breakfast.

D *El Bourg Hotel*, off Midan Orabi, T226327. Large colonial style hotel, rooms a/c,
friendly service.

F *Crocodile Inn*, 179 Sharia Sa'ad Zaghloul, T222724. 20 rooms, small restaurant and
bar/coffee house open 24 hrs. **F** *Hotel des Voyageurs*, 22 Sharia Ahmed Orabi,
T228304. 25 rooms, atmospheric but cheap colonial style hotel. **F** *Isis*, 32 Sharia Adli,
Midan Station, T227821. 51 rooms, façade more impressive than service, favoured by
Egyptian honeymoon couples, rather rundown. **F** *Nefertiti Hotel*, 41 Sharia Sultan
Hussein, T322822. 32 rooms, excellent value with good rooms and facilities.

Youth hostels *Sea Scout's Building*, Timsah Lake, Ismailia, T/F322850. 266 beds, meals
available, family rooms, kitchen, laundry, parking, station 5 km. A very high standard.

Although there are many other places to eat, besides the hotels, the best restaurants **Eating**
are the *King Edward* on Sharia Tahrir just off Sharia Sultan Hussein. *George's Restau-*
rant and Bar, 11 Sharia Sultan Hussein, T337327 (open daily 1100-2300), is famous for
its seafood. Across the road is the cheaper family-owned *Nefertiti Restaurant*
(T220494, open daily 1200-2400), which also specializes in seafood. If looking for a
snack or takeaway *Zahran*, Sharia el-Geish, T229037, has an outdoor barbecue grill
and rotisserie and often cheap decent kofta, lamb chops and chicken. Across the road
from *George's* is *Groppi's Patisserie*, a branch of the famous Cairo Café, where coffee
and sticky cakes are good. At the other extreme are the kebab and other food stalls
around the bus terminal but there are also a few cheap restaurants such as the
El-Gandool off Sharia Sultan Hussein. *Pizza Inn*, El Gomhurriya, T340245.

The International Folklore Dance Festival takes place each Aug and the International **Festivals**
Festival of Documentary Films each Jul.

El Ghamri Travel 211 Sharia El Hurriya, T321726, F225567   **Tour operators**

Train There are 7 daily trains to **Cairo** (3-4 hrs). **Transport**
Road Bus/service taxis: There are regular buses and service taxis to towns in the
Canal Zone and Delta which can be caught from the depot in Sharia Gumhorriya to
the west of the railway tracks. Those to **Cairo** (every 30 mins, 0630-2000, E£8, 2½ hrs),
Alexandria 2 per day (E£10 for 4½ hours) and **El-Arish** on the Sinai coast can be
caught from outside the railway station.

Communications **Post Office:** located beside the railway station, open Sat-Thu 0900-1500, **Directory**
T228179. **Medical services** The huge *Suez Canal University hospital*, opened in 1993, has 350
beds and all the latest equipment. **Useful telephone numbers** **Police**: T270008.

Carry on up the Suez

Ships transit the canal, the longest in the world without locks, in three convoys daily. Pilotage is compulsory. It can accommodate tankers up to 575 tonnes dwt, maximum draft is 18 m.

Speed limit in the canal itself is 13-14 km per hour according to category and tonnage. In southern sector this varies between 11-15 km per hour depending on wind velocity and direction of tidal current. On average it takes 15 hours to do the journey.

El Qantara, East and West, lies to the north. Two unattractive settlements with poor refreshment facilities. Movement of visitors is restricted to getting off and on their transport. The free ferry across only takes 18 small vehicles and it can get busy with delays from 30 minutes to two hours. Foreign visitors with the police escort are saved the wait. Neither side of the canal is attractive, lots of people just waiting.

A hanging bridge over the Suez canal to link Africa and Asia is nearly complete. It stands just south of the ferry crossing. It will have the highest clearance point of any bridge in the world – when it is complete. Date of opening is scheduled for April 2001 and 6,000 vehicles a day are expected to use this bridge.

Port Said

Phone code: 066
Colour map 2, grid A4
Population: 526,000

Port Said, 225 km from Cairo and 85 km north of Ismailia on the Mediterranean coast at the nothern end of the Suez Canal, was founded in 1859, as a harbour, and named after Said Pasha (1854-63) who began the construction of the canal. It used to be synonymous with smuggling, drugs and every vice under the sun, but today it is a slightly seedy beach resort, predominantly for Egyptians, and a free port since 1976. It is Egypt's second port after Alexandria and Egypt's fourth largest city.

Although it has few sights, because of the lack of Western tourists it is a relaxing place to sit on the beach for a few days. As this is a duty free zone have passports ready to enter and leave.

Ins and outs

Getting there   Most visitors arrive either at the bus terminal in the centre of town near Ferial Gardens or at the railway station and service taxi depot near the Arsenal Basin. The city's main streets are Sharia Filistine (Palestine) along the water-front and the parallel Sharia Gumhorriya which are only a few minutes walk from either transport depot.

Getting around   It is easy to walk around. Most places are easy to access and services are on the main street. The Tourist Office is at 43 Sharia Filistine, T23868.

Sights

There are one or two landmarks/buildings to note. See the Abd el-Rahman mosque on the main street, El-Salam Mosque by the *Helnan* and *Sonesta* hotels, the base of de Lesseps' statue, and the Obelisque memorial in front of the Government Building. The three shiny green domes of the Suez Canal Authority Building on the canal side on Sahria Mostafah Kamal are another landmark in the town. Like the other Canal Zone cities there is less to see compared with the major tourist attractions. The many Egyptian and few Western visitors stroll around the main shopping streets by day and promenade along

Building the Suez Canal

Ferdinand de Lesseps was a French citizen through whose vision and perseverance the Suez Canal was constructed. He was born in France in 1805 and served as a senior diplomat in the French Foreign Service. His first visit to Egypt was in 1832 when he was the French consul in Alexandria. At this time he became acquainted with proposals for a canal across the Isthmus of Suez by a French engineer, Le Père, with whom he had served in Egypt during the Napoleonic invasion. De Lesseps was deeply convinced of the economic and strategic utility of a Suez Canal and was encouraged to press the scheme's merits by the then ruler of Egypt, Mohammed Ali. De Lesseps transferred to Cairo as French consul in the years 1833-37 when he became a friend of the ruler's eldest son, Said Pasha. Said Pasha in 1854 invited de Lesseps back to Cairo to pursue the Suez Canal scheme, granting him a concession for construction of the canal in that same year.

Within two years de Lesseps had engineering designs prepared, raised the necessary capital and overcome British political reservations. On 25 April 1859 the project for the Suez Canal (Qanat es-Suways) was begun. The canal ran for 168 km from Port Said to Suez, using the path of Lake Menzala and the Bitter Lakes.

It was 8 m deep and 22 m wide with passing places every 25½ km. The project saw the excavation of great volumes of material and the building of port and ship handling facilities at sites along the canal. Although de Lesseps had hoped to finish the scheme in six years, it took 10 years to complete, delayed by environmental difficulties, labour problems and disease.

The Suez Canal came into full use in 1869 run by the Suez Canal Company which had a 99-year concession to manage it. The new company was 52% French, 44% Egyptian and 4% internationally owned. In 1875 financial troubles of the Egyptian government led to its holding being bought out by the British. De Lesseps welcomed the British involvement and kept a close interest in the affairs of the company. De Lesseps sponsored the construction of the Panama Canal but his company was caught up in engineering and commercial problems and failed. Despite this shadow, de Lesseps remains a monumental figure in Egyptian history for his foresight and determination in creating the Suez Canal which still contributes generously to Egypt's foreign exchange earnings, employs thousands of workers and which brings prosperity to the entire zone along its banks.

the canal and sea-front in the evening. There is a free ferry 15 minutes across the canal to Port Fouad and its yacht basin. It is one of Port Said's suburbs, located on the eastern side of the Suez Canal – and thus being part of Asia. It still retains some of the colonial feel, fairly quiet residential areas with green spaces, a number of sports clubs and a popular beach.

The **Port Said National Museum**, is located near *Nora's Floating Restaurant* on Sharia Filistine in a brand new and cool, uncrowded building. Its collection is well presented. The ground floor is dedicated to early history and pharaonic times including sarcophagi, statues, and two well preserved pharaonic mummies beside utensils and pots. The second floor is Islamic and Coptic material, textiles, coins and manuscripts. The coach used by Khedive Ismail during the inuaguration ceremonies of the Suez Canal in 1869 is also on display. Our favourite, a handworked shroud, a tunic decorated with images of the apostles. ■ *Sat-Thu 0900-1600, Fri 1200-1400, T237419, E£12, students E£6.*

The **Military Museum**, is located on Sharia 23rd July near the Corniche and displays exhibits from the various conflicts fought along the length of the Suez Canal. These include not only the 1956 Suez crisis with some very lurid paintings and daioramas (look for the headless figures in the scene of Nasser at Al-Azhar), but also the successive wars with Israel: the 1973 storming of the

Bar-Lev line receives pride of place and is on display in a separate room. ■ *Daily 0800-1500, E£2.*

The base of the statue of **Ferdinand de Lesseps** stands on the quay by the canal he constructed. The statue was pulled down in 1956 – no way to treat the person who brought prosperity to the region. Take a Port Cruise T326804 to see the ship convoys going through De Lessep's canal, from the jetty opposite the museum.

Port Said is the access point for Lake el Manzala, an excellent spot for fishing and watching migrating birds and those that overwinter on the shores.

Beaches The beach looks good but it is safer to swim in the hotel pool.

Cemeteries These lie to the west of town, Muslim, Christian and one maintained by the Commonwealth War Graves Commission with over 1000 graves from the First World War.

Christian monuments Church of St Eugenie founded 1869, Sharia Ahmed Shawki; Roman Catholic Cathedral founded 1931, Sharia 23rd July. Church of St George (Mari Girgis), founded 1946, Sharia Mohammed Ali. The Christian cemetery is to the west of town opposite the army officer holiday camp.

Essentials

Sleeping There are expensive hotels and cheap hotels, but no happy medium. If possible, for comfort's sake, go up-market.

A *Helnan Port Said,* Sharia el-Corniche, PO Box 1110, T320890, F323762. 2200 good rooms, restaurant, 2 pools, private beach overlooking the Mediterranean, best hotel in town. **A** *Nora's Beach Hotel*, Sharia el-Corniche, T329834, F329841. 384 rooms, the first tourist village in Port Said and still very good. **A** *Sonesta Port Said Hotel*, Sharia Sultan Hussein, T325511, F324825. 91 rooms yet another high quality hotel. **A** *Panorama Hotel*, Sharia Gumhorriya/Sharia Tarh el Bahr, T325101-2, F325103. 40 rooms. **A** *Wahman* Sharia Sa'ad Zaghloul/Sharia Akka, T322072, F325595. 58 rooms.

D *Holiday*, 2/3 Sharia Gumhorriya, PO Box 204, T220713, F220710. 81 rooms. **D** *New Concord*, corner of Sharia, Salah Salam & Sharia Mustafa Kamel, T235341, F235930. 60 a/c rooms. **D** *New Regent Hotel*, 27 Sharia Gumhorriya, T223802, F224891. 36 rooms. **D** *Palace Hotel*, 19 Sharia Ghandy, T239490, F239464. 84 a/c rooms, near the governorate building just off the main coast road and good access to the beach.

F *Akry Hotel*, 24 Sharia Gumhorriya, T221013. 26 rather shabby rooms, with shared facilities and very little hot water. **F** *Crystal*, 12 Sharia Mohammed Mahmoud, T222747. 70 a/c rooms. **F** *De La Poste*, 42 Sharia Gumhorriya, T224048. 46 rooms. **F** *New House*, 128 Sharia Orabi, T220515. 40 rooms. **F** *Regent*, 27 Sharia Gumhorriya, T223802. 16 rooms, TV. **F** *El Riviera*, 34 Sharia Ramses, T328836, 48 rooms. **F** *Savoy Tourist Hotel*, Sharia Mohammed Ali, El-Shohada, T222197. 44 a/c rooms, oriental & European menus, business centre.

Youth hostels *El Nasr Hostel*, Sharia el-Amin and El-Corniche (near sports stadium), T228702, F226433. 145 beds, family rooms, kitchen, meals available, parking, train 2 km, bus 3 km, overnight fee E£5 includes breakfast. Also *Port Said Hostel*, T228702.

Eating There are numerous restaurants serving fairly decent if unspectacular Western food with the best being on Sharia Gumhorriya and the Corniche coast road, such as the *Seahorse* which serves good seafood. *Al Bagaa Restaurant* , seafront, splendid seafood, T334334. *El Borg Restaurant* on the seafront, seafood, T323442. *Kastan Restaurant* – seafood especially shell fish, open 24 hrs daily, in season, Sharia el Corniche T235242. Medium-priced *Maxim*, T234335, is upstairs, adjacent to the *Sonesta*. The reasonably priced lunch and dinner cruises on the *Nora's Cruising Restaurant*, T326804, which operates from Sharia Filistine in front of the *National Museum*, provide a good view of the Canal, leaves at 1400 and 2000. El Shamandoura is another floating restaurant. The most fashionable place in town is the *Pizza Pino*, Sharia Gumhorriya, T239949, serving standard Italian fare, which is nearby just behind the National Museum on Sharia Gumhorriya. Further south along the street is *Popeye's Café*, T224877, which is really a burger bar, past which is *Reana House* which serves large helpings of Korean food.

Shopping

As Port Said is a free port, visitors, excluding ship's passengers, are supposed to pass through customs when entering and leaving and it is therefore necessary to declare all valuable items on arrival to avoid being charged a hefty tax when leaving. The shops offer many imported goods at very competitive prices. **Places to visit** are: *Sharia El Togary* which is organized like a typical Egyptian market but sells a wide variety of goods; *Sharia Filistine* where the Shopping Centre has a wide range of high quality imported goods. This is a European style shopping centre with parking, restaurant and café; *Sharia Gumhorriya* and *Sharia El Nahda* further west are important commercial streets with some shops.

Port Said

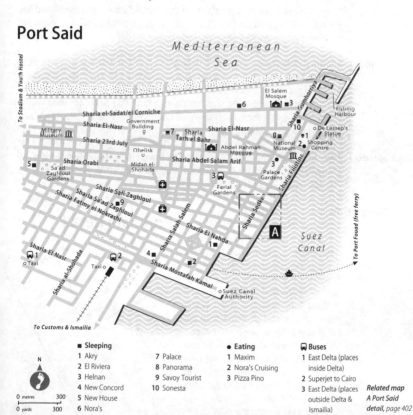

Related map
A Port Said
detail, page 402

■ Sleeping		● Eating	🚌 Buses
1 Akry	7 Palace	1 Maxim	1 East Delta (places inside Delta)
2 El Riviera	8 Panorama	2 Nora's Cruising	2 Superjet to Cairo
3 Helnan	9 Savoy Tourist	3 Pizza Pino	3 East Delta (places outside Delta & Ismailia)
4 New Concord	10 Sonesta		
5 New House			
6 Nora's			

0 metres 300
0 yards 300

The Suez Canal

The Suez Canal

Recipe for Basboussa

This Oriental dessert is served as a delicacy during Ramadan.

180 gm of unsalted butter
250 gm of sugar
600 gm of semolina (fine grade)
2 medium size eggs
250 gm of yoghurt
1 teaspoon of vanilla essence
1 teaspoon of baking powder.
Split blanched almonds
Prepare a greased shallow baking tray (20x30 cm)

Beat the butter, sugar and vanillas essence together until light and fluffy. Beat in the eggs one at a time. Add the yoghurt.

Sieve semolina and baking powder and fold into mixture. Spead the mixture on the tray with almonds evenly distributed. Bake for 30-40 mins at 180 C.

Syrup
500 ml of water
400 gm sugar
1 tablespoon lemon juice.
Dissolve the sugar in water over a medium heat, add lemon juice and boil rapidly for 10 mins.

Spoon the cooled mixture over the cooked cake, allow to cool then cut into diamond pieces or squares and serve with whipped cream.

Items on sale of Egyptian origin of interest to visitors include oriental dresses and fine scarves, silver and gold jewellery, leather work and paintings on papyrus. Avoid the ivory items which cannot be imported into Europe or USA.

Sports **Sporting clubs**: Large Stadium to west of town. *El Uonani Club*, by Yacht Club, T240926. *Fishing Club*, north end of Sharia Gumhorriya, T236870 (Places to fish – Al-Jameel bridge, Hagar Said, Lake el Manzala, Al-Tafri'a and Port Fouad bridge, pre-pare for the National Fishing Competition each Oct). *Port Said Club*, west end of Sharia 23 July by stadium, T221718. *Yacht Club*, Sharia El Tirsana/El Baharia, across canal in Port Fouad, T240926.

Tour operators *EgyptAir*, Sharia Gumhorriya, T220921. *Misr Travel*, 16 Sharia Filistine Mondial, 16 Sharia Filistine, T338853/226610. *Port Said Tourist*, Sharia Filistine, T329834. *Thomas Cook*, 43 Sharia Gumhorriya, T227559.

Transport **Train** Bear in mind the restrictions placed on foreign travellers – for their own safety. There are 5 slow and dirty trains a day to and from **Cairo** which take 4-5 hrs via Ismailia (details T221861), 40 Sharia Gumhorriya. Buses and service taxis may be preferable.

Road Bus: there are both regular express and normal a/c buses from the bus station at Ferial Gardens to **Cairo** (3 hrs) and **Alexandria** (7 hrs) (details T228793 for superjet and T226883 for regular buses). There are also buses south along the canal, west to the **Delta** and east to **El-Arish**.

Service taxis: regular and quick ser-vice taxis can be caught to **Cairo** and **Alexandria** from the depot on Sharia El

Port Said detail

Sbah, near the railway station as well as to other destinations in the Canal Zone, Delta and across the canal to El-Arish.

Boat Ferry: Free ferry crosses to **Port Fuad**, a smarter suburb of Port Said founded in 1920s. It leaves every 10-15 mins – and then returns! Princess Marissa provides a weekly ferry service to **Limassol, Cyprus** usually leaves Port Said on Tue while its sister ship sometimes goes on to **Athens** via **Rhodes** (details T223783).

Banks There are numerous banks: *Bank of Alexandria*, *Central Bank*, *Bank of Cairo* or **Directory** *Thomas Cook* all on Sharia Gumhorriya, open 0900-1800.

Embassies & consulates A number here as it is an important port: *Belgium*, in main shopping centre, T238513. *France*, in main shopping centre, T322875. *Greece*, 52 Sharia Gumhorriya, T222614. *India*, 12 Sharia El Gisr, T226865. *Italy*, Sharia Salah Salem, T223755. *Norway/Sweden/Denmark*, 30 Sharia Filistine, T336730/224706/336740. *Spain*, 19 Al-Gabarty/El Geish, T233680. *UK*, in main shopping centre, T226963. *USA*, 11 Sharia Gumhorriya, T222154. Passport office in Government Building (closed Fri).

Communications **Post Office**: T225918, the main post office, with International Telex and Fax, open daily 0700-1700, is on the corner of Ferial Gardens near the bus station.

Shipping agents. All on Sharia Filistine: *Aswan Shipping Company*, T220662; *Canal Shipping Company*, T220790; *Damanhour Shipping Agency*, T220351; *El Menia Shipping Agency*, T220351; *Assuit Shipping Agency*, T2203551. For *Arab Express Shipping Co* contact head office in Alexandria T4939142.

Useful numbers. **Passport office** in Government Building, T226720 (closed Friday). **Passport office** in Port Police Building, T224811. **Port Said Harbour Authority**, Sharia Filistine, T223783.

West of Port Said towards Bahra el Manzala by way of El Maatariya is no problem for foreigners. Unfortunately there is little to see, the beach is very dirty, the flat land is under the control of the military who access the area by helicopter. The sea to the north is hidden by a series of poor quality settlements, Egyptian holiday homes and a refinery. The lake here has been reclaimed and some areas are cultivated, others marked out for industrial use. The journey on to Damietta records similar scenery.

The ring road around Port Said, route 5, is a different journey. This is a new dual carriageway, with lake on both sides, no adverts, no litter. here the people fish by walking in the water, quite fascinating, and from small dingies. Very interesting for bird watchers too.

The Suez Canal

The Sinai Peninsula

11

The Sinai Peninsula

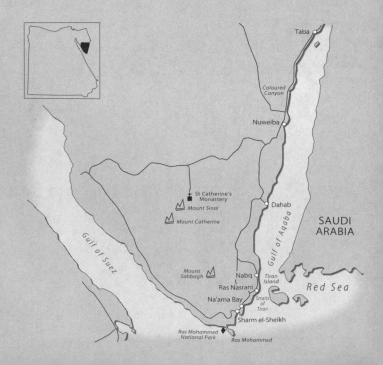

Although some hardy travellers wish to encounter the isolation of the harsh but stunning landscapes of the desert interior, most tourists come to the Sinai peninsula to visit the remote St Catherine's Monastery and experience some of the world's finest diving and snorkelling grounds off the Gulf of Aqaba coast around Sharm el-Sheikh. Others are part of the rapidly expanding sector of sun, sea and sand tourism that the region is trying so hard to promote. The government has succeeded in encouraging the private sector to invest in this area and it is now Egypt's major tourist destination outside the Nile Valley.

Accommodation and activities here and along the easily accessible eastern coast cater for every possible demand and there is enough space for everyone although some of the more popular sites both on land and under the sea are being overworked.

Northern Sinai is harder to access, and the accommodation provided on the coastal strip, while more than adequate, does not reach the same international standards but is certainly improved since the Children of Israel travelled across here in the 13th century BC.

The Sinai Peninsula

Sinai is a very sparsely populated 62,000 sq km desert peninsula which throughout history has acted as both a land bridge linking, and a hostile but spectacular wilderness dividing, Africa and the Middle East. It was the route by which the Israelites reputedly reached the Promised Land and Islam arrived in Africa. It is divided from the rest of Egypt both literally, by the geographical barrier of the Suez Canal and Gulf of Suez, and metaphorically, by successive Israeli occupations between 1948 and 1989 when the dispute over the ownership of the Taba enclave was finally resolved in Egypt's favour. While many tourists still travel overland, either from Cairo or Israel, or by ship from Hurghada or Jordan, the majority now fly to Sinai direct to Sharm el-Sheikh airport.

Warning Never allow your driver to stray off the tracks in the desert because in the National Parks it is illegal and because many areas still have mines. Maps of mined areas are unreliable, mines are moved in flood waters and remain hidden. This is a general warning for all desert-border areas of Egypt and the Western Desert but is especially pertinent in the Sinai.

The East Coast

The east coast of Sinai from Ras Mohammed to Taba boasts the most attractive shoreline coral reefs in the northern hemisphere. The climate, tempered by the sea, varies from pleasant in winter to hot but bearable in summer. There are white sand beaches, rugged cliffs and views east to Saudi Arabia and Jordan while to the west lies the barren interior.

Sharm El-Sheikh

Phone code: 069
Colour map 3, grid B6

This is the usual name given for the twin resorts of Sharm el-Sheikh and Na'ama Bay (some 7 km further north) which lie about 470 km from Cairo. The area has developed very rapidly in recent years. It has become an international resort with the development of a spectacular and now exceedingly popular diving area. There are over 60 km of reef providing dramatic drop offs and breathtaking formations claimed to be unparalleled anywhere else in the diving world. The location takes advantage of the coasts for the divers, the

	Abu Rudeis	Cairo	Dahab	El Shatt	El-Tur	Nuweiba	Ras Sudr	Sharm el-Sheikh	St Catherine's Monastery	Taba
	272									
	459	570								
	161	111	459							
	104	376	194	265						
	367	639	69	528	263					
	98	174	396	63	202	465				
	200	472	98	361	66	167	298			
	149	412	361	301	167	430	247	263		
	431	703	133	592	327	64	529	231	404	

Distances in Sinai in kilometres

beaches for the holiday makers and the interior for the more adventurous. Being in the lee of the desert highlands the site is protected from the winds most likely to disturb the waters for divers. One of the great advantages to visitors is the lack of hassle on the beaches. There are no hawkers on these carefully controlled stretches of sand.

Sharm itself, which existed pre-1967 as a closed military zone was used by the Israelis. This small town, which is rapidly shedding its previous dilapidated image, has a new bus station, marina and docks, three banks, post office, telephone exchange, hospital, police station, supermarket, garages with repair facilities, a row of souvenir shops, in an upgraded souq, and a number of small restaurants. More high quality hotels have been built and while Sharm cannot compete with its neighbour for beach access and general leisure facilities it has the advantage of being an Egyptian town rather than an international playgound.

Purely a tourist resort, **Na'ama Bay**, which gets its name from the Arabic for 'God's Blessing', is considered more attractive than Sharm and has an excellent sandy beach, good quality modern hotels, an attractive vehicle free Corniche and some of the best diving facilities in the world (see **Sports**, page 415). There are restaurants and shops for divers and other tourists but little or no indigenous Egyptian life. Indeed the vast majority of the hotel workers come not from Sinai but from elsewhere in Egypt. There are spectacular views across the clear blue waters of the Red Sea to the mountains of Saudi Arabia. It is an excellent place for relaxation and for the variety of watersports available. You don't have to be interested in diving but it helps.

Eastern Sinai

Ins and outs

Getting there Individual travellers must rely on service taxis (around E£30) into town from the airport, about 10 km north of Na'ama and 17 km north of Sharm. Package tours lay on a bus to the hotel from Sharm el-Sheikh airport. Buses from Cairo (470 km) to Sharm via Suez (336 km) and the rest of Sinai can be caught from Cairo's Sinai Bus Terminal, and terminate in the new bus station behind the Mobil Petrol station half way between Sharm el-Sheikh and Na'ama Bay. You will need a taxi from here (E£10). South bound buses from Dahab (98 km), Nuweiba (167 km) and Taba (231 km) stop on request at some of the major Na'ama hotels. There are also frequent cheap bright-coloured minibuses called Tuf-Tufs which run between the two resorts (50 piastres one way, 0630-2400). While a taxi will cost E£10 (tourist rate E£20!) for the same journey. Ferries from Hurghada arrive at Sharm el-Sheikh port.

Getting around Take a Tuf Tuf or taxi, but walking around is easy as it is quite compact. A peripheral hotel would require a taxi into town otherwise it is no distance to walk from the shopping area and restaurants to the beach or even to the marina. The bus station is now out of town and would require transport. There are shuttle buses from the major hotels down into Na'ama Bay either free or for a nominal sum which normally will carry any visitor. The *Egyptian Tourist Authority* (ETA) office is at the top of the hill near the youth hostel in Sharm el-Sheikh, T768385. In addition all the major hotels can provide detailed tourist information. EgyptAir, Sharm el-Sheikh, T661056.

Sights There is very little to see in Sharm el-Sheikh or Na'ama Bay and tourist life revolves around the diving and typical beach life.

Dive sites **Straits of Tiran**: Jackson, Woodhouse, Thomas and Gordon (wreck of Loulica lies here). Reefs, currents can be strong here. Wrecks of Sangria and Laura. Coral reef at 10-15 m, large pelagic fish and perhaps shark. Hushasha south west off island, shallow with sand floor and sea grass. Ras Nasrani (The Light): 40 m drop off, large pelagic fish, watch the currents. Ras Nasrani (The Point) hard coral boulders. Tower: steep wall, 60 m, large caves. Ras Nasrani (End of the Road Reef). Amphoras: Unnamed Turkish wreck, cargo of mercury still evident, sandy floor at 25 m.

Shark Observatory: wall with vertical drop to 90 m.

Shark Reef: sandy slope with two submerged islands, open sea and pelagic fish, sharks.

Quay: steep slope, pelagic and reef fish, sharks.

Liveboards available at Sharm el-Shiekh: Recommend *M V Sea Surveyor* – 18 divers in 9 rooms, with a/c and wash basins. 7 toilets and shower. Tutors for underwater photography and dark room facilities. Very comfortable. Was a Danish oceanic research vessel – equipped for serious diving – long range cruises. Small boats available at Sharm el Sheikh, *Freedom II*, *Freedom III* and *Seagull* – from 18 m-24 m long, holding 8-14 persons, limited a/c.

Essentials

Sleeping There is accommodation to suit all pockets. A few hotels are in Sharm el-Sheik but most are in Na'ama Bay and in the newly developed areas east towards the airport – Ras Nasrani, Gardens Bay, Om el-Seid Hill etc and it is advisable to make advance bookings for all but the winter season. Rooms are much cheaper if they are booked as part of a package. Attempts are being made to popularize Sharm Maya Bay offering cheaper accommodation plus the traditional shopping area of Sharm el-Sheikh which provides lots of local colour. Good value for money restaurants. Lies 6.5 km south of Na'ama Bay, on a cliff top area.

The hotels in **Sharm el-Sheikh** (with the more expensive ones offering all the usual facilities), itself are: **A** *Riu Palace*, T661111, something for everyone at a very high standard, free shuttle from airport, wonderful views from position on cliff top, extensive landscaped grounds, nearby sandy beaches, easy walk to town centre. Junior, Executive and Royal suites available, terrace or balcony, casino and disco. International restaurant, Italian and Grill restaurants, Terrace café, beachside barbecue. Private beach, large outdoor pool, indoor pool, children's pool, sports centre with extensive watersports, volley ball, snooker, 2 floodlit clay tennis courts, health club, fitness room, children's club for the over 4's, baby sitting. Rooms overlooking pool can be noisy. **A** *Seti Sharm Beach*, T660870-9, F660147. Brand new, 231 rooms, beach location, 5 restaurants, 2 swimming pools, tennis courts, watersports and diving centre.

B *Aida Beach Hotel*, T660719, F660722. Hilltop location, wonderful views, overlooking Sharm el-Maya Bay, 147 large split-level rooms, restaurants, coffee shop, bars, shops, pool, tennis and squash, snooker and pool, bowling alley, free transport to hotel beach about 5 mins away. **C** *Helnan Cliff-Top Hotel*, T660251, F660253. 30 rooms, part of *Sinai Hotel & Dive Club*. **C** *Marine Sporting Club*, T660450, quiet comfortable, popular with Egyptians. **C** *Palermo Hotel*, very new, good pool, use of beach nearby, T661561, next to **C** *Sun Rise Hotel*, Om el-Seid, very new, T/F661721, 120 rooms. **D** *El-Kheima Village*, T660167, F660166. 33 rooms of which 20 double rooms have a/c, near harbour.

The number of hotels in **Na'ama Bay** continues to grow rapidly. They include: **AL** *Jolie Ville Movenpick Golf Hotel and Resort*, T603200, F603225, on Om Merikah Bay is 5 km to west of airport and within walking distance (in the heat?) of the 18 hole Championship Golf Course. 9 restaurants and bars and a unique water theme park. No pets, shuttle to airport, golf and Na'ama Bay. **A** *Ghazala Hotel*, T600150, F600155. Smart modern hotel, main restaurant, also Grill Room, Franco's Pizzeria, Tam Tam (Egyptian cuisine) and Ice Cream corner, bars in lobby and by pool which is said to be

The Sinai Peninsula

Dive sites

the largest in the region, separate children's pool, easy access to beach and all facilities, restaurants, beach location. **A** *Hilton Fayrouz Village*, T600137-9, F770726. 150 double bungalow rooms, in lovely gardens, private beach location, bar, choice of restaurants, excellent meals, first class watersports, yacht, glass-bottom boat, pool, tennis, minigolf, volley ball, horse riding, massage, aerobics, disco, games room, play area for children, bus (E£1) to and from Na'ama Bay every hour until midnight. **A** *Iberotel Palace Om el-Seid*, 254 rooms 2 outdoor pools, indoor pool, floodlit tennis, 3 restaurants, snooker, spacious, by beach so safe for families. 15 mins to airport, use of beach at adjacent hotel. **A** *Marriott Beach Resort*, spacious, modern hotel, large free-form pool, connected by wooden bridges and surrounded by sun terrace and gardens. All mod cons, dining room, restaurant, 2 bars, pub, health club, gym, volley ball, horse riding, being greeted by a spectacular waterfall in the central courtyard is a wonderful experience, refreshing and very impressive, modern, spacious, comfortable, on sandy beach approximately 10 mins from airport (ie 10 mins from town centre), choice of cuisine, pool dive centre, watersports (pay locally) fully equipped health club. **A** *Movenpick Hotel Jolie Ville*, T600100-9, F600111. Very large low level building, spreads on both sides of desert road, most extensive hotel in Na'ama Bay so not suitable for those with walking difficulties, 337 rooms and 10 suites, the cheaper rooms on far side of desert road are 5 mins to walk from beach. Large circular pool, children's pool, children's club. excellent service, good food, modern facilities but soulless. **A** *Sofitel Coralia*, T600725-7, F600733. A beautiful, sophisticated hotel, large pool, children's pool, diving centre for beginners and advance level skills, health club with gym, aerobics, sauna, jacuzzi, Turkish bath and massage, table tennis, archery (pay locally) and mountain bikes for hire. Shows and entertainments provide by in-house professional team, has the coral gardens called Nir Gardens just off shore. Not recommended for the elderly. **A** *Sonesta Beach*, T600725-7, F600733, just 10 km from airport and 10 mins from centre, at north end of the bay. A cool collection of white domes in extensive gardens, attractive and spacious, 3 pools of which one salt water, diving centre, shops and boutique. 228 split level rooms decorated in bedouin style with either balcony or patio. Selection of cuisine, main dining room known as the Citadel plus La Gondola Italian restaurant, 3 cafés, 3 bars, children's club 5-12 years runs daily 1000-1600, tennis, squash, spa, 24 hr baby sitting service.

Sharm el-Sheikh

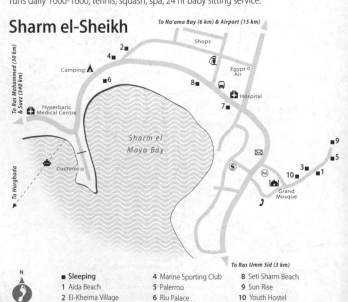

■ **Sleeping**		
1 Aida Beach	4 Marine Sporting Club	8 Seti Sharm Beach
2 El-Kheima Village	5 Palermo	9 Sun Rise
3 Helnan Cliff-Top	6 Riu Palace	10 Youth Hostel
	7 Safety Land	

Not to scale

B *Novotel Aquamarine Hotel*, T600178, F600193. 152 rooms, with terrace or balcony, central position, landscaped gardens, choice of restaurants (*Al Dente* is recommended), tennis, pool, Aquamarine Diving Centre in complex, all watersports. **C** *Helnan Marina Hotel*, T600170-1, F600170. 150 rooms, the first hotel here, beach location, good sea views, helpful and efficient staff, bar service, clean rooms, buffet. **C** *Tiran Village*, T600221, F600220. 150 seat restaurant open to non-residents, bank, shops, diving centre, snack bars, pleasant open air areas, mainly European tourists in winter and Israelis in summer.

D *Gafi Land Tourist Village*, T600210, F600216. Beach restaurant open to non-guests, special dinners, loud disco, relaxed, friendly, clean, welcoming, credit cards accepted, plans for pool. **D** *New Tiran Village*, next to *Tiran Village*, T600225, T600220, shares the facilities and slightly cheaper. **D** *Kanabesh Hotel*, T/F600185. 64 double rooms with a/c, restaurant, café, snackbar, bar, live music, small kiosks, travel agent, dive club (see **Sports**, page 415). **D** *Rosetta Hotel*, T601888 about 10 mins from airport. Owned by same management as *Tropicana*, friendly, high standard, main restaurant, pizza, Egyptian tent, bank, doctor, 3 pools, laundry. **D** *Red Sea Diving College* run by the *Sinai Hotel & Dive Clubs*, has 12 rooms; but only for divers taking their courses. **D** *Sanafir*, T600197, F600196. 90 rooms, all creditcards accepted. Highly recommended by all the guests of whom about 80% are divers. Relaxed, friendly authentic Egyptian atmosphere, *Divers Den* bar, Egyptian, fish and South Korean restaurants, snackbar, own private beach.

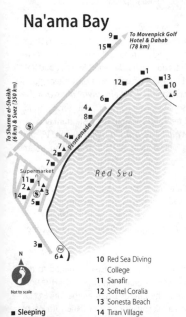

Na'ama Bay

*To Movenpick Golf
Hotel & Dahab
(78 km)*

*To Sharma el-Sheikh
& Suez (350 km)
(6 km)*

Red Sea

N

Not to scale

■ **Sleeping**
1 Gafi Land Tourist
Village
2 Ghazala
3 Helnan Marina
4 Hilton Fayrouz
5 Kanabesh
6 Marriott
7 Movenpick Hotel
Jolie Ville
8 Novotel Aquamarine
9 Pigeon House
10 Red Sea Diving
College
11 Sanafir
12 Sofitel Coralia
13 Sonesta Beach
14 Tiran Village
& New Tiran Village
15 Tropicana

Diving centres/clubs
1 Aquanaute
2 Camel
3 Colonia
4 Novotel Aquamarine
5 Oona
6 Red Sea
7 Sinai Divers

E *Emperor Diving Village*, forms part of the newly built *Rosetta Hotel* with which it shares facilities, at Na'ama Bay purpose built for divers. 18 small rooms and 16 slightly larger. Pool is central and built for diving training, a very basic, quite ugly hotel. **E** *Pigeon House*, 5 mins' walk to beach, small, basic, **A** rooms have a/c, bath, double bed (small) and single bed, mini bar and terrace, **B** rooms in the main hotel complex have fan and share wc and showers, **C** grade in straw huts have 2 beds and cupboard and share the same WC and showers. Use of beach at Sonesta. For the laid back budget conscious diver. **E** *Tropicana*, Tivoli, T600652, just 5 mins walk from beach. 60 rooms built in Moorish citadel style, white with domes, small, friendly, pool has slide, but is deep and has no shallow end – not suitable for children, restaurant, billiards, all watersports available nearby. 20 mins by bus from airport, and 15 mins by hourly free shuttle bus into Na'ama Bay. Used by divers who rent the cheaper rooms, some with windows and some with skylights. All rooms a/c, studio rooms are larger with balcony.

Camping *Safety-Land*, large, cheap camp site next to Sharm el-sheikh's *Tentoria Diving Centre*, T60373, F660334. It is particularly popular with young

The Sinai Peninsula

Israeli tourists, US$12 per person. Divers should be warned that, although cheaper than the Na'ama Bay clubs, the diving safety record is generally not so good at Sharm el-Sheikh. 38 bungalows for 2-4 people at about E£25 per person for half board and 60 large army tents sleeping 4 at the same price, an indoor winter and outdoor summer restaurant with a E£5 breakfast and a E£12 lunch/supper. Nearby *Sharks Bay* camp, T600942, 5 km to north of Na'ama Bay, about 10 mins from airport by taxi, offers very basic accommodation, Bedouin style huts (bamboo cabins) with communal toilet/showers. There is a diving centre (US$45 a day; liveaboard US$100)Meals are taken in the Shark's Bay open air restaurant where the speciality is sea food or in a Bedouin style tent by the beach. Friendly and informal, coral garden for diving or snorkelling is directly off the beach, dive centre on site with diving programme, very popular, run by Bedouin. Recommended for budget travellers.

Youth hostels *Sharm el-Sheikh*, PO 46619, T/F600317. 120 beds in a/c dormitories, with double bunks, no lockers, open 0600-0900 and 1400-2200, kitchen, food available, laundry, parking, members E£15 per night, including breakfast.

Eating Pick from the multitude of restaurants, which cater for all pockets and tastes, both along the Na'ama Bay beach-front and in all the major hotels which are open to non-residents. Most serve huge buffet meals.

Expensive *Wings and Things*, at *Oonas Divers Inn* for a special occasion meal.

Mid-range *Al Dente Restaurant* in *Azur Aquamarine Hotel*. Open 1200-1600 and 1800-2200, also does takeaways. *Bedouin Restaurant*, T600826, at foot of Ras Umm Sid light house, 1 km from *Hilton Residence*. Offers charcoal grill, Bedouin entertainment and torchlight camel rides. *Franco Pizzaria*, at *Ghazala Hotel*. Serves good Italian food. *The Ship Restaurant* in Sharm El Maya is actually on a grounded ship – how about that for local colour and the sea food is excellent. *Viva La Vista* at the *Divers College* (Sultana). Serves reasonably priced, no nonsense, food. *Viva Restaurant*, beach location, friendly, new and spacious a/c restaurant and bar which serves good quality French food. *Wadi Restaurant* in *Hilton Fayrouz Village*. Lunch E£40, restaurant dinner E£46, with belly dancer at 2100. *Yong Jong*, South Korean restaurant at *Sanafir Hotel*.

Cheap In addition there are beach-front stalls serving most varieties of takeaway food. The *Tam Tam*, in front of the *Gazala Hotel* is still on our highly recommended list, also *Sinai Star*, T660393, in market area of Sharm which offers cheap, decent fish and *Safsafa*, in the same area, excellent seafood, although only 8 tables and no alcohol, meals starting at around E£25.

Bars & nightclubs Oriental floorshows, which are open to non-residents, are largely confined to the major hotels but new independent bars and restaurants are being opened all the time in Na'ama Bay. *Pirates Bar* in *Fayrouz Hilton*. The *Cactus Disco* at the *Movenpick*. *Bus Stop* at the *Sanafir*, E£20 entry includes a drink and is open until 0400 with lots of noise, dancing and billiards down stairs. *Salsa* same house and admission as above is mainly 80s music but lots of fun. The *Spot American Bar*, dark (dingy) but popular with the local youth looking for excitement.

Entertainment **Filmshow**: every Fri evening at *Spot* at the *Gazala Hotel*, entry E£15, first drink free.

Folk music: The traditional *El Fishawy Café* in Sharm Mall has lively Egyptian folk music.

Most shops in Na'ama Bay are linked to the hotels and are small but well stocked with **Shopping**
provisions for a beach or diving holiday. Two shopping malls offer a variety of fashionable shops including *Adidas*, *Benetton*, *Next* and *Naf Naf*. With expansion of the town
the services have expanded too and shops have a wider selection of fresher produce.

Bookshops: bookshops in *Sharm Mall*, *Movenpick*, *Sanafir*, *Ghazala* and *Fayrouz
Hilton* hotels.

Photography: hire an underwater camera at *Hilton Fayrouz Village*. *Sanafir Hotel* has
a shop where film can be developed within 1 hr. *Movenpick*, *Fayrouz Hilton* and *Tiran
Village* all have photo shops.

Bowling: the *Aida Beach* has a bowling alley.   **Sports**

Diving: watersports in general, and diving in particular, are the main attractions in
south Sinai. The reefs off the Gulf of Aqaba coast are acknowledged as some of the
best in the world with incomparable coral reefs and colourful marine life. The main
dive centres, which are based in Na'ama Bay but which organize dive trips to all of the
region's major reefs, including the following: *Aquanaute Diving Center*, T600187,
F600019, located in Na'ama Bay next to the *Kanabesh Hotel*, comes **very** highly rec
ommended by our correspondents, 11 instructors, 3-6 boats, good underwater photo
facilities. Aquanaute has lots of return customers. Backpackers are welcome and
helped with accommodation while booked groups receive discount rates. Bookings
through *Regal Diving*, Station Rd, Sutton in the Isle, Ely, Cambridgeshire CB6 2RL,
T01353-778096, F01353-777897. *Colonia Dive Club* in *Kanabesh Village*, T600184,
recommended as friendly and efficient. *Camel Dive Club*, Na'ama Bay, T600700,
F600601, which claims to be the largest in town, slick and friendly service. In winter
the majority of the divers are Italians, Swiss and Germans while British and French predominate in summer. The club runs 4-7 boats, has 10 European instructors who provide a flexible range of CMAS, PADI and NAUI courses. Provides free camping for
divers who should bring their tents and sleeping bags. Operates dive safaris to Sudan
for a maximum of 12 passengers at US$140 a night. *Novotel Aquamarine Diving Cen-
ter*, Na'ama Bay, T600178-182, F600193, is hidden away in the *Novotel Aquamarine
Hotel* from where its 9 instructors operate friendly PADI, NAUI and CMAS diving
courses using 4 boats. *Oona Diving Centre*, Na'ama Bay, T600581, F600582. Residential diving club whose guests come exclusively via tour operators, accommodates up
to 48 divers in self-catering room over diving centre, which has full equipment and
repair facilities, at about US$20 a night. Oona runs land safaris in 2 Mercedes trucks at
US$90 a day and sea safaris for 6-8 people at US$100 a day. Mainly European instructors and divers. Egyptian office at 32 Sharia Baron, Heliopolis, Cairo, T02668747,
F02674153, overseas bookings which include flights can be made through
Oonas Divers UK, 23 Enys Rd, Eastbourne, Sussex, T01323-648924, F01323-738356.
Red Sea Diving College, Na'ama Bay, T600145, F600144, located in the centre of the
beach next to *Kanabesh Hotel*, is a PADI 5-star fully equipped IDC centre joint project
between Sinai Hotels & Diving Clubs and Scubapro Europe. Opened 1991, 10 multi-lingual PADI instructors from a good pur-
pose built facility. Courses which include
all the gear but excludes certification fees
are US$40 for an introductory dive,
US$265 for a standard open water course,
US$360 for a 3 days underwater photog-
raphy course and US$550 for a dive mas-
ters' course. The college caters for up to 40
divers. *Sinai Divers Club*, Na'ama Bay,

Blacktail Butterfly Fish

The Sinai Peninsula

Animal, vegetable, mineral

The Sinai has been a new experience for Egypt's tourism industry which has previously orientated around the nation's rich cultural heritage. When travellers started coming to the Sinai in greater numbers during the 1980s they were looking for something different, something that they found in the wilderness of the desert and the abundance of life along the coast. Although the concept of eco-tourist was as yet unheard of, the Egyptian authorities were sufficiently far-sighted to start planning the protection of the area, so that people could visit in great numbers and yet still experience a largely untouched area of natural beauty.

This protection has taken the form of a network of protected areas along the coast from Ras Mohammed National Park to the Taba Managed Resource Protected Area, and St Catherine's National Park covering a huge swathe of the southern mountains. The Department of Protectorates has responsibility for conservation and natural resource management, education and the enforcement of environmental planning law for all developments in the area of their control.

It is of course, the fringing coral reefs that line the Gulf of Aqaba that make Sinai, especially Ras Mohammed designated in 1983, so popular with divers. As well as the stunning variety of forms and colours in the corals and reef fish, areas such as the Straits of Tiran and Ras Mohammed are also famous for shark, manta ray and turtle. Two of the reefs in the Straits of Tiran, which falls under the Ras Mohammed National Park, are the

permanent residences of Hawksbill Turtles and there are also turtle nesting beaches within the restricted areas of the National Park. Particularly good fossil reefs dating back 15,000 years can be found all around Ras Mohammed but especially vivid around the mangrove channel and the visitors' centre.

Ras Mohammed is also remarkable too for its rare northerly mangroves which lie in a shallow channel at the tip of the peninsula, in an area with many rock pools and crevices in the fossil reef which hold shrimp – and much stranger creatures too. The famous Hidden Bay confuses visitors, because it appears and disappears with the changing tide, and the Saline or Solar Lake is also interesting for the associated salt loving plants.

Although the land appears to be barren and hostile it is in fact home to a variety of life, from insects to small mammals, Nubian ibex and Desert foxes. The foxes are often seen near the main beaches and cubs can be seen at sunset in late spring. They are harmless if approached but should not be fed. The Park is an important area for resident bird populations including four heron species – Grey, Goliath, Reef and Greenback, gulls, terns and ospreys and during the late summer for migrating birds, especially White storks.

Nabq, to the north of Na'ama, is also an outstanding area designated in 1992, containing a dense area of mangroves, at the mouth of Wadi Kid the most northerly in the world and also rare sand dune habitats. As well as the birds of the area, ibex and gazelle can be seen. The Hyrax, a small

T600140-4, F600158, in *Ghazala Hotel*. Claims to be the largest diving centre in Na'ama Bay and handles 40-110 divers on 2 dives a day. Germans make up half the divers in summer (May-Oct) while about 60% of the winter divers are British. Book in advance in the winter high season. Sinai runs 8-day boats and 2 live aboard boats, has 10 qualified instructors, runs a full range of courses, has daily excursions and dive cruises for the keen diver with everything under one roof and trips to all the major reefs. **Umbarak Diving Resort** (Umbarak was the first bedouin to learn to dive) – local style architecture, right on beach, very basic, very laid back, bamboo bungalows sleep 2, shared shower and facilities, fish restaurant, the only PADI dive centre with its own private jetty, ideal for the more adventurous who can live without today's luxuries. There are many other watersports.

rodent-like mammal which is actually the closest living relative to the elephant, can be found here in Wadi Khereiza. The diving here is superb, though little is done these days as the reefs lie at some distance. Naqb has 134 plant species.

Much of the 600 sq km of Nabq is a restricted area to prevent critical damage by four-wheel drive vehicles but there is much to see here for the careful viewer. A small bedouin settlement lies on the coast where the tribesmen continue to fish in a traditional manner. The Parks make a sincere effort to involve the bedouin in their work and to protect their traditional lifestyle currently under much pressure from the rapid development in the area. Near the settlement is a more modern establishment, a shrimp farm that supplies much of the produce for the hotels and restaurants in Sharm el-Sheikh.

Ras Abu Galum, designated in 1992 which lies between Dahab and Nuweiba, has yet no entry fee or visitors' centre, although one is planned to the north of the protectorate. This is an area of stunning scenery, with high mountains and long winding valleys running right down to the sea. Safaris with camels and bedouins can be arranged to visit these areas where wheeled vehicles cannot venture. It is strongly recommended not to visit without a guide and certainly never to leave the marked trails. Although the Protectorate is valued mainly for its rare plant life, the diving here is superb. It should be noted, however, that access to the underwater cave network at Ras Mamlah is strictly forbidden. Many divers have died here and their bodies remain unrecovered, as the caves which exceed 100 m in depth are very unstable.

Taba is the newest and largest in the network of coastal and inland protected areas (declared January 1998). It lies south and west of Taba and includes the Coloured Canyon. Already known are the wealth of ancient writings and carvings on rock walls in the area that span the history of Sinai as the crossroads between Asia and Africa. The scripts include Arabic, Semetic, Greek, Nabatean and other, unknown, languages.

The largest single protected area in Sinai is St Catherine's National Park designated in 1987, which covers a roughly triangular area of the mountains from the monastery south. As well as containing the cultural sites of the monastery of St Catherine and Mount Sinai, a site holy to Christians, Muslims and Jews, the Park also contains ibex, gazelle and hyena, hyrax, leopards and possibly cheetahs. Bedouin have been recruited as community guards to help the Rangers patrol this immense expanse of mountains, wadis and desert. Although the Park has not been long established, it has already had noticeable success, particularly in cleaning the area of the previously abundant rubbish and providing information and nature trails.

Although the ecosystems of the Sinai are being subjected to the effects of rapid development due to its success as a tourist destination, it is hoped that the National Parks will preserve the natural beauty of the area for interested visitors.

The Sinai Peninsula

Horse riding: the *Sanafir* offers horse riding excursions including sunset rides. Lessons E£10 per hour; hire E£20 per hour and E£70 per day and good stables at *Sofitel*.
Ice skating: yes, believe it or not, a new rink has opened in Na'ama Bay. **Parasailing**: the *Movenpick* offers parasailing. **Quadrunners** (4-wheel drive bikes for short desert rides): available at most hotels. **Snorkelling**: is practised in many places but the headland of Ras-um-Sid has possibly the best snorkelling drop-offs in the world.
Watersports: on the beach outside the *Marina Sharm Hotel* you can rent masks and fins (E£16 per day), windsurf board (E£31.5 per day), jetski (E£150 per hour, E£75 per 30 mins, E£40 per 15 mins), glass-bottom boat E£20 for 30 mins. At *Fayrouz Village* snorkelling equipment E£15, motor boat E£30 for 15 mins, windsurf board E£30 per hour, pedal boat or canoe E£15 per hour. Glass bottom boat trip E£20 for 30 mins.

Tour operators There are travel agents attached to almost all the major hotels, as well as a few independent ones (see below under Excursions), which can book transport, hotels, sight-seeing and other excursions.

Transport **Local Car hire**: *Avis* from *Sonesta Hotel*; *Europe Car* from *Fayrouz Hilton* or *Ghazala* hotels; *Hertz* from *Movenpick Hotel*. **Taxi**: T600357.

Air Ras Nasrani Airport, T601140, F600416, is further along the coast 10 km north of Na'ama Bay with direct flights to and from an increasing number of European cities as well as internal flights to **Cairo** (daily at 0645), **Hurghada** and **St Catherine**.

Bus The bus station in Sharm el-Sheikh, T660660, is at the bottom of the hill. Buses to **Cairo** cost E£40-E£65, and take 6 hrs. Other destinations include: **Suez** (E£25) very frequent about one an hour, takes 5 hrs; **Dahab** six buses a day (E£10, takes 1½ hr), of which the early morning bus goes on to **St Catherine** (E£25, takes 4 hrs,) and of which two go on to **Nuweiba** (E£25, takes 2½ hrs) and one of these to **Taba** (E£35, takes 3½ hrs). Shared **taxis** cover all these routes on a leave when full basis – cost more but take much less time, avoiding the tedious stops in each town.

Sea **Ferry**: ferry to **Hurghada** (Sun, Tue and Thu at 0900), takes 5-10 hrs, costs E£90 – 121, depends on the type of vessel, T544702. Harbour Master in reply to a query of when the ferry would run, "this week, if God wills it", so do check.

Private vessels: Entry procedures for Sharm el-Sheikh port. Visas may be obtained for boats and crews from Egyptian consulates in country of origin. It is possible but more hassle to get one in Sharm el-Sheikh. It is as well to give clear advance (at least 1 week) notification of your intention to berth. The Port Commander must be notified upon arrival. The course of the vessel, in national waters, must be filed and approved by the Port Authority.

Directory **Airline offices** *Egyptair*, *Hotel Movenpick*, T660409. Sharm market area, T661057, airport, T660408/664. The office of the local independent airline *ZAS* is in the Gafi Mall, T661909. **Banks** In Sharm el-Sheikh there are three banks and two banks in the Na'ama Shopping Mall (Mon-Sat 0800-1400 and 1800-2100, Sun 1000-1200). Most hotels have banking facilities exchanging money at the normal rate. **Communications** **Internet** The local internet service, T661090, can provide a short term connection for your own computer or rent theirs at hourly rates. **Post Office**: at the top of the hill in Sharm el-Sheikh (Sat-Thu 0800-1500) but all the major hotels have mail services. Telephone The main telephone exchange is up on the Hataba, opposite the Grand Mosque.

Medical services Ambulance: Sharm, T660425. The Egyptian Army operates a 'flying ambulance' to take serious cases to Cairo, T02-665663/668472. Doctors *Movenpick Hotel* runs a daily clinic (1900-2000) and their doctors are on 24-hr call, reached through hotel reception. *Fayrouz Hilton* has a doctor living on the premises. The *Red Sea Diving Club* has 2 doctors, T660343. *The Hyperbaric Medical Centre*, T661011/660922/3 (very modern facilities) deals with diving accidents and also with emergencies needing cardiology, intensive care and minor surgery. *Air Medivacs* can be arranged by helicopter at Cessna, open 0900-1800, T660922/3, F661011, Room 2012 or 3008. *Sharm Hospital*, T660425, near the bus station (which looks like a glass pyramid), has very limited facilities but will help in an emergency. Better medical care is available from *Dr Adel Taher* at the *Hyperbaric Medical Centre* or for non-emergency cases there are doctors on call at the larger hotels. Pharmacy In Sharm Mall: *Towa Pharmacy*, T660779; In Sharm town: *Dr Sherif Pharmacy*, T660388.

Useful telephone numbers Fire: T660633; **Police**: T660415; **Tourist Police**: (Na'ama) T600517 (Sharm), T660311.

Excursions

To see Sinai's desert interior, take an organized day trip to **St Catherine's Monastery,** (10 hours) (see page 432), which is breathtaking. A tour usually includes a visit to a bedouin village and perhaps the oasis of Feran for a visit to a convent. Price varies with content US$80-100. Include a visit to Mount Sinai to climb to the summit (see page 435). There are many boat trips on offer out to the coral reefs or arrange a desert safari to Wadi el-Aat for E£200, which includes a camel ride and possibly supper under the stars at a bedouin encampment. A helicopter or a glider can be rented for a tour of the area from Cessna or the *Siag Travel Agency* offices in Sharm, T600860 (helicopter, five-seater, US$70 an hour), or through the *Movenpick Hotel* (glider). *Spring Tours*, office at Sharm port, offer daily boat trips, except Friday, between Sharm el-Sheikh and Hurghada. Day trips to Luxor 0600-2130 are organized by *Sonesta Hotel*.

A visit to nearby **Ras Mohammed** Egypt's only **National Park,** a terrestrial and marine area covering 480 sq km, is well worth the effort. It is just 20 minutes from Na'ama Bay. Ras Mohammed is a small peninsula which juts out from Sinai's most southerly tip and is the point where the waters of the shallow (95 m) Gulf of Suez meet the deep waters (1,800 m max) of the Gulf of Aqaba. The result is that, while the land is barren desert, the waters teem with exotic marine life. Besides the huge variety of brightly coloured fish which live on the coral reef, normally deep water species such as sharks, tuna, barracuda and turtles come to the reef to feed. Ras Mohammed has clean, shallow beaches, some sheltered but others very windy, from which the snorkelling is excellent, but beware the strong currents.

Ras Mohammed National Park

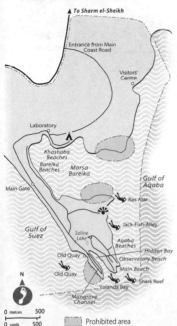

Diving is possible here for those with a licence and equipment can be hired for diving and snorkelling but it is better to take gear with you. Bird watchers will find this a delightful spot though shaded places from which to view are hard to find and some transport is necessary. Don't expect to find isolation – there are over 100,000 visitors annually here.

■ *The national park is open from sunrise to sunset while the visitors' centre, which includes a restaurant, audiovisual presentations, first aid, shops and toilets, is open from 1000 to sunset. US$10 equivalent plus US$10 per car. Also crude toilets between Main Beach and Observatory Beach. Bring your own water bottles from Sharm el-Sheikh. Taxis to Ras Mohammed from Sharm el-Sheikh cost E£60 one way but it is advisable to keep the taxi for the day – around E£150 – as there are no taxis at Ras Mohammed. A four-wheel drive vehicle is a better bet – cannot go off road but greater purchase on the poor road* surfaces. Vehicles pass through UN checkposts. Passports are scrutinized at the Egyptian checkpost where *Israelis or any non-Egyptians who came in through Taba may experience delays. Beyond deserted Israeli trenches are the gates of the national park and nature reserve.*

Camping is permitted in designated areas (US$5 per person per night) but numbers are strictly limited to preserve the environment. Permits are available from the park office at Sharm el-Sheik. Booking: T600559, F600668.

Collection of or damage to any natural resource, hunting, driving on vegetation or in a prohibited area, spear fishing or fish feeding are prohibited. Rules are strictly enforced by the park's English-speaking Rangers.

The **Nabq Protected Area** 35 km north of Sharm el Sheikh though popular with safari groups is less crowded. There are two permanent Bedouin settlements, Ghargana on the coast and Kherieza, inland from the main coastal valley Wadi Kid. ■ *Free. Taxis from Sharm E£60-80 one way but it is advisable to keep the taxi for the day at around E£200.* The wildlife is outstanding, storks, kites, ospreys and raptors are quite common but mammals like foxes and gazelles are much rarer.

Nabq Protected Area

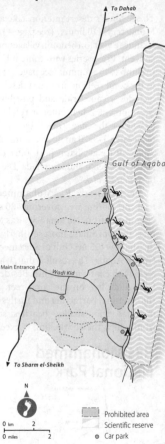

To Dahab

Gulf of Aqaba

Main Entrance Wadi Kid

To Sharm el-Sheikh

N

0 km 2
0 miles 2

Prohibited area
Scientific reserve
Car park

North from Sharm El-Sheikh

The road journey north from Sharm el-Sheikh to Dahab (98 km) takes 1-1½ hours and passes the airport before turning inland through beautifully rugged scenery past a bedouin school, a water drilling camp, a manganese quarry, the tomb of an Israeli general and the remains of his bombed out vehicle before entering Dahab.

Dahab

Dahab, which means 'gold' in Arabic, made its name as Egypt's hippy capital after Israeli troops started visiting the bedouin village for rest and recreation on its golden beaches in the 1960s. Palm trees, turquoise sea, rugged mountains, brilliant sunshine by day, and the brightest stars by night, have made this Sinai spot a timeless attraction. It is a higgledy piggledy stretch of beach cafes, bazaars, mosques, satellite dishes, Bedouin huts, crumbling concrete camps, smarter hotels and bizarre shops mingled with, rubbish, goats, camels, Bedouin, touts, tourists, divers lugging tanks and tangling themselves around you, girls selling bracelets, cats, chickens and bicycles.

Phone code: 069
Colour map 3, grid A6

Although it is a rather commercialized shadow of its past it is still a primary destination for backpackers and those wanting to take time out for a while. Travellers from all over the world congregate at the beachside cafes, and drink copious amounts of tea amid the bright coloured rugs and cushions. In recent years the government has tried to clean up Dahab's image, by cracking down on drugs and discouraging backpackers and turning it into a more conventional resort. (As with most places, drugs are available, but in Egypt the penalties are severe.) There is a splendid coral garden along the shore line and excellent wind conditions due to its position in a wide *wadi* mouth, making it an important windsurfing centre.

Dahab, which is 98 km north of Sharm el-Sheikh, 82 km from Sharm el-Sheikh airport, 133 km from Taba and 570 km from Cairo, can be divided into two distinct areas. The bedouin village, **Assalah**, and adjacent areas Masbat and Mashraba (although the area is described as Assalah), are where travellers hang out. However, many campgrounds are now upgrading to simple hotels. About 3 km south and 1 km inland from the beach is the little administrative town of Dahab which has been 'improved' with some new facilities. Meanwhile the totally self-contained resort on the beach to the south (Golden Beach Resort) is deliberately isolated from the two other parts of the town.

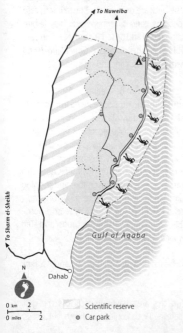

Abu Galum
Protected area

To Nuweiba

To Sharm el-Sheikh

Gulf of Aqaba

N

Dahab

0 km 2
0 miles 2

Scientific reserve
Car park

The Sinai Peninsula

Ins & outs   There are daily buses north from Sharm el-Sheikh (E£10) and south from Taba and Nuweiba, or shared taxis can be hired from the main towns in Sinai. Because of Dahab's split site, make sure you know where you want to be set down. To get to the campgrounds and hotels of Assalah – if you arrive by service taxi you will be dropped in Masbat by the mosque. Buses arrive in the bus station in Dahab in the south and a pick up taxi (which will be waiting) will transport you for US$1.

Getting around   A taxi costs E£5 from one section of town to the other.

Sights   Dahab is primarily a diving and relaxation destination. For diving information see 'Sports' page 425. Camel trips can be organized to one or two bedouin villages in the beautiful interior. Jeep and horseback safaris can be taken into the mountains. The protected area of **Ras Abu Galum** lies to the north and Nabq to the south of Dahab and consists of both terrestrial and marine environments. An aerial tour can be taken by helicopter or cessna, through *Siag Travel* in the *Novotel*, T640301.

Sleeping   The options are the self-contained resort – (the Golden Beach Resort), the hotels in the bedouin village of Assalah or the numerous campgrounds along the beach in the bedouin village.
Hotels near Dahab (the Golden Beach Resort):

AL *Hilton Dahab Resort*, T640310. Whitewashed dome shaped rooms, with all the usual 5-star facilities, recommended dive centre. **A** *Helnan Dahab Hotel*, T640425, F640428. 80 rooms, a/c, private beach, 2 swimming pools, 2 restaurants, café, bar, tennis, squash, pool hall, watersports; stands separate to the south. **A** *Swiss Inn Golden Beach Resort*, T640471, F640470. 126 rooms another new 5-star resort. **A-C** *Novotel Dahab Holiday Village*, PO Box 23, Dahab, T/F640301-5. 141 a/c rooms with private terrace, including 40 divers' cabanas, very attractive, excellent beach, **A** rooms are on the beach are larger and have a sea view, **B** rooms in the middle of the village, have a garden view and **C** rooms at the back are more basic, 2 restaurants, café, bar, disco, bank, windsurfing, a glass boat, pedalos, canoes, tennis courts, bicycle hire, volley ball, jet skis, speed boats, horseback riding, safari and desert trips, shops, non-residents can enjoy the facilities for E£40. NB pool has no shallow end. **C** *Ganet Sinai Hotel*, T640440, F640441. 57 rooms, chalet style, with seaviews, windsurfing school.

Assalah   After the luxury of the above hotels the contrast could not be greater. In Assalah to the north along the beach front there are numerous camping grounds varying from basic to pleasant. These start in the south in Mashraba, followed by Masbat, and then Assalah. Camp/camp hotel quality varies though all, or parts of all, have electricity, sit toilets, hot water, fans and even a/c. For the sake of security it is best to opt for padlocked rooms. There are generally three categories: basic bamboo huts or concrete rooms, rooms and rooms with private bathroom. Some camps only have hot water in winter. Check also for additional charges for fans and breakfast and keep in mind mosquitoes and peeping toms. Don't drink the tap water – it's brackish and makes for interestingly un-soapy showers! Prices are negotiable and better deals can be made in the low season. Some campgrounds/hotels have less than desirable reputations relating to drugs, and staff who are over friendly to women. Ask other travellers for their opinion.

C-D *Lagona Hotel*, T640352, located on the beach between Dahab City and Assalah. With pool and dive centre.

Mashraba area   Most camps and hotels in this area have views across the gulf. **B** *Dyarna Hotel*, T640120, clean rooms with satellite TV, balconies, beach and reef access.

C *Nesima Hotel*, T640320, nesima@intouch.com, quality hotel, breathtaking views across the Gulf, 51 spacious rooms with a/c, private facilities, some are designed for wheelchair access, popular restaurant and bar, pool, beach and reef access, and dive centre. First class snorkelling. Doctor on call.

C-E *Christina Beach Palace*, T640390, new with beach access and rooms have balconies. **D** *Inmo Hotel*, T640370 FT640372, inmo@inmodivers.com Long established quality hotel owned by German-Egyptian couple. Discounts for divers using their centre. Pool, beach and reef access. **D** New Sphinx, T640032, more upmarket than *Sphinx*, but same owner. With pool and beach access. **D** *The Sphinx*, T640032. Offers cheaper rooms without en suite bathroom, close to centre.

E-F *Auski/Bedouin Lodge*, T640474. Popular camp with beach access. Camel, snorkelling and jeep trips can be arranged. Bike rental US$4. **E-F** *Dolphin*, T640018. A tradtional-styled camp conveniently located for the centre while maintaining the peace of a non-central position. Beach and reef access, cushioned seating area with additional wicker seating outside some rooms. Also has bamboo huts boarded inside (which should reduce most visitors). Buffet breakfast and tours organized by Magdi, the owner, who speaks fluent English. **E-F** *Happyland & Musa Camp*, an old established camp, reasonably popular. Not very smart, being more in the old style, but its bonus being the traditional beach setting with palms and reef access. Rooms are basic, but clean. A/c available. **E-F** *Jasmine Hotel and Restaurant*, beach access and some rooms have sea view. **E-F** *Seth Ville Hotel*, no beach access, but it's not far. Lounge area and billiards, very clean, some rooms with sea view. **E-F** *Star of Dahab*, has reef access and a beach with traditional seating where one can truly gaze at the stars of Dahab. Unfortunately the rooms are not of such good quality, but there's hot water and the shared bathrooms are reasonably clean. Candelight only in bamboo huts. Most repellent needed. **E-F** *Sunsplash Camp*, M012333577O, anita.sun@t-online.de This camp is trying to maintain the old Dahab atmosphere. Peacefully located on the edge of Mashraba you can relax on traditional seating or within a few strides, snorkel the house reef. A clean camp, including brightly-coloured wooden huts, restaurant, ladies-only sun roof, table tennis and gift shop. Anita, the owner, speaks English, German and Arabic and can organize trips into the desert away from the crowds.

F *Bishbishe*. Although located on the roadside away from the beach, the camp is clean and its courtyard is attractively arranged with young palms. There's a cushioned seating area, soft drink sales and guest kitchen. Snorkelling, St Catherines, jeep and camel trips can be arranged. Snorkel and fin hire, US$1. **F** *New Life*. Popular camp with a good reputation with local workers, but located away from the beach. Central cushioned seating area. Trips arranged. **F** *Penguin*, T640117, penguindivers@crosswinds.net Has lost much of its traditional atmosphere, but maintains a traditional beach seating area with reef access. Penguin projects a trendy, young image with continuous music, coffee shop and café, so if you are looking for peace and quiet this is not the place to be. There are a few bamboo huts on the roof for US$1. A/c available. **F** *Venus*. Traditional style camp with café and basic rooms. Clean around the edges only, quiet.

Masbat area D *Bamboo House*, T640263, new, rooms with TV, fridge.

F *Youth Hostel/Sinai Tours*. Not an IYHA, basic rooms, bracing cold showers, communal seating and tea, close to lighthouse reef. Owner Mohammed speaks reasonable English and can arrange tours. **F** *Seventh Heaven*. In the centre of things, but not living up to its name. Communal bathrooms and concrete box with wooden roof, clean. Some rooms with balcony, but no view.

Assalah area C-D *Bluebeach Club*, T640411, bbeach@intouch.com, pool, billiards, table tennis, horseriding, rooftop restaurant. **C-D** *Mirage Village*, T640341. A former camp with courtyard and sunken BBQ, good view, beach access, breakfast additional. Apartments available. These camps are accessed from the dirt road in front of the *Lighthouse* camp. **E-F** *El Dorado*, M 0123549198, last camp to the north near the eel garden dive site. Beach and reef access, café and pigeon coop. **E-F** *Sinbad*. Basic rooms, bathrooms not particularly clean, beach and reef access. Cushioned seating area and café. **F** *Marine Garden*. Old style, very basic rooms, some with corrugated roofs. Bathrooms clean.

Between Assalah and Blue Hole dive site D-F *Bedouin Moon*, T640695, bedouinmoon@menanet.net, dorm rooms available. Dive centre, *Reef 2000* attached. **E** *Blue Hole*, next door to *Bedouin Moon*, very new and empty. Balcony and mountain views available. Unattractive decor. **E** *Canyon Dive Resort*, next to dive site of the same name, 8 km north of Dahab.

Eating   The traditional places to eat and chill out in Assalah are at the beach side cafés, with bright coloured cushions and rugs draped over palm trunks. While shading under their umbrellas or palms, travellers can indulge in Dahab's favourite pastime – talking to people from all corners of the globe. There area also places to eat in the Golden Beach Resort.

Golden Beach Resort: **Expensive**: *Zeitouna*, main restaurant. **Mid-range**: *Aqamarina*, diving centre cafeteria. *Bar-A-Cuda*, bar, Bedouin Corner; *Lagoon*, beach café and all the main hotels provide a good selection.

Assalah area: *Ali Baba*, which include vegetarian dishes, a Chinese restaurant; *Dolphin Café*, next to *Dolphin* camp. Includes Indian and vegetarian dishes for under US$3, and has a beach seating area. *El Hosain*, near the pickup/taxi drop off in Masbat. Less touristy with typical Egyptian food such as a chicken meal. *Lakhbatita*, on the beach at Mashraba. Interestingly decorated with doors and oddments from the Delta. *Neptune's*, Egyptian food. *Nesima Hotel* restaurant serves alcohol, good standard of more expensive food in a more intimate atmosphere, if you choose the right seat. Try also *Jays*, M 0123353377, great food with an extensive menu, budget options. Reservations are sometimes necessary. Run by English-Egyptian couple. *Sharks*, run by an Australian-Egyptian couple is friendly, popular, vegetarian available, budget options, also has seating next to the sea. *Jays* and *Sharks* are at the northern end of Masbat and serve dinner only. They are best for food quality and cleanliness in the budget range. *Tarabouche*, next to the mobile tower in Masbat. Recommended and has fish dishes for around US$7. Booking is necessary, M 0122356338. *Tota* is the most highly recommended eatery. *Trattoria Pizzeria*, near the Police Station with terraces overlooking the sea. Serves thin crust pizzas and fish for around US$6.

Bars &   Nightlife mainly revolves around the restaurants and cafés in Assalah which are open
nightclubs   until around midnight. *Nesima Hotel* bar is popular, particularly with divers and has a happy hour from 7-9pm. There is a DJ there on Fri evenings. Also popular are *Tota* (the boat) and *Crazy House* next door. Both are having a price war and sell Stella at US$1. The *Elzar* disco next to *Dolphin Restaurant* is a non-starter. The *Golden Beach Resort* has belly dancing shows and the *Where-Else* disco and bar.

Shopping   In Dahab town, and a few very small supermarkets in Assalah, which are open 0730-2400. They stock most of the basics including bottled water. Fresh fruit and veg are hard to come by – there's a shop on the road next to *Lighthouse* camp and sometimes a stall near *Bishbishe*.

Responsible diving

There has been a great deal of unnecessary damage caused to the beautiful coral reefs around the coast. Divers taking trophies, anchors being dropped on to the living corals, rubbish being thrown into the water. The regulatory bodies set up to prevent this damage to the environment have had little effect – it is up to those who delight in this area to preserve it for the future.

Code of responsibility for reef divers

1. Check you have the correct weights. As the Red Sea is a semi-enclosed basin it has a greater salt content than the open ocean. The extra salinity requires heavy weights thus bouyancy checks are essential.

2. Avoid all contact with coral. These living creatures can be damaged by the slightest touch. Many reef fish are inedible or poisonous – but the reef needs them to survive.

3. Remove nothing from the reef. Shells and pieces of coral are an integral part of the reef. In Egypt this is taken so seriously that boat captains can lose their licence if either shells or pieces or coral are brought on board.

4. Move with care. Careless finning stirs the sand and can smother and kill the softer corals.

5. Do not feed the fish. Introducing an unnatural imbalance in food chain can be fatal and is thus prohibited.

6. Air bubbles trapped in caves can kill the marine creatures who extract their oxygen from the water.

7. Do not purchase souvenirs of marine origin. Aid conservation, do not encourage trade in dead marine objects which is illegal in Egypt.

8. Take back only memories and photographs.

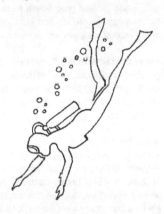

Necklaces, tie-dyes, skirts and bags etc, the hallmark souvenirs of Dahab are available in the small bazaars on the main bay and by the taxi drop off. Don't shop when the Sharm el-Sheikh tourists are in town – everything doubles in price. Bedouin girls sell cotton bracelets in the beach cafes, but barter hard. Henna tattoos are available along Masbat and Reiki healing with US/British qualified lady (Maha) for women only.

Diving Although the reefs are not as good as in Na'ama Bay there are diving centres **Sports** in the Golden Beach Resort and in Assalah which rent equipment and run PADI diving courses. Overnight trips to see the nocturnal lobsters at the Blue Hole, 2 km north of the village, and possibly eat one the next day are recommended. **Be advised the Blue Hole is difficult and dangerous and is only for very experienced divers.** The Golden Beach Resort also offers a wide range of sporting activities including windsurfing, a glass boat, pedalos, canoes, tennis courts, free bicycles, volley ball.

Dive centres at Dahab. The coral is so close here that the dive sites have shore access. There are more than 40 diving centres, of those only a handful are considered to be safe. Accidents occur on a daily basis and every year there are a number of deaths.

There are many stunningly beautiful and interesting dive sites most with the advantage of being closely located to Dahab, generally less crowded than Sharm el-Sheikh and Hurghada, and shore dives which keeps the price down slightly. The following list are recommended centres, but remember managers and instructors do change and with them the quality of the centre. Prices range from US$40-60 for one day's diving with full equipment. PADI Open Water courses are in the region of

US$280-310. These centres generally have instructors catering for a number of languages which gives them an advantage over the Hurghada area for English speakers:

Inmo at *Inmo Hotel and Dive Centre*, Mashraba, Dahab, T640370, inmo@inmodivers.com; **Red Sea Scuba,** *Hiton Hotel*, Golden Beach Resort, T640310, redseascuba@sinainet.com.eg; **Lagona,** *Lagona Hotel* between Dahab and Golden Beach Resort, T640358, CMAS (French), catering mainly for the German market; **Fantasea** located at the northern end of Masbat bay, central Dahab, T640043, ide@intouch.com; **Nesima,** *Nesima Hotel*, Mashraba, Dahab, T6400320, Nesima@intouch.com; **Reef 2000,** Bedouin Moon Hotel, between Dahab and Blue Hole, T6400087, catering mainly for the British market.

Dive sites include: **North from the lighthouse**: Lighthouse, by lighthouse in Dahab Bay Eel Garden; north of lighthouse, off Assalah; north again is Small Canyon; Canyon, opposite Canyon Dive centre, north of Small Canyon – one of the deep sites to be dived appropriately; Blue Hole – another deep dive to treat with respect; The Bells – north of Blue Hole. **South from the lighthouse**: Off *Lagona Hotel* is The Islands, a very beautiful location. The Caves, some 5 km south of the lighthouse Gabr el Bint south of the Caves, access from road to be arranged by camel.

Horse and camel riding. Camel treks can be arranged, going into the desert for a genuine bedouin meal. You are advised to tell someone where you are going and not to pay until you get back. Horse riding is generally of a local nature, hire from your hotel, *Novotel* is recommended or at a pinch on the beach from a wandering arab leading a horse.

Transport **Road Bus**: the bus station, T640250, is outside the *Bank of Egypt* in Dahab and there are five daily buses south to **Cairo** (E£40-70, takes 9 hrs) via Na'ama Bay and Sharm el-Sheikh (E£12, takes 1½ hrs), north to **Nuweiba** (E£8) and **Taba** (E£20), and east to **St Catherine** (E£15). **Taxis**: are a necessary expense for getting between Dahab town and the beaches and unfortunately tourists are usually charged more than Egyptians. Minibus/Taxis usually meet the service bus – to take travellers to Assalah.

Directory **Banks** *Bank of Egypt* (open daily 0830-1400 and 1800-2100), near the bus station, in Dahab town accepts TCs. There is also a bank in the Golden Beach Resort. **Communications** Internet Service in *Snapper Photo* in Dahab. **Post Office** in Dahab town centre is open Sat-Thu 0830-1500. **Telephone**: Office near bus station. **Useful numbers** Tourist Police near *Novotel*. Drivers should be warned that there is only one petrol station on the 81 km route between Dahab and Sharm el-Sheikh which also has the nearest hospital.

Nuweiba

Phone code: 062
Colour map 3, grid A6

This town, 69 km north of Dahab and 64 km south of the Israeli border at Taba, and its Moshav or cooperative village, used to be a major destination for Israeli tourists during its occupation, but it has long since been surpassed by Na'ama Bay and has now lost most of its tourist business. Nuweiba is divided between the tourist village with its fine white sandy beaches, and the small town around the port, some 8 km south used both for fishing and as a port for boats which ferry Saudi Arabia-bound Egyptian expatriate workers and pilgrims to the Jordanian port of Aqaba. From Nuweiba you can see Saudi Arabia across the water as the Gulf of Aqaba narrows towards the north. There can be strong southerly winds but not sandstorms for a few

Parrot Fish

days in January, February, April and October. Guests of Nuweiba hotels entering from Israel must pay Israeli departure tax locally, US$17, and Egyptian Tax US$6 on leaving. Access time from Ovda 2½ hours.

All the buses arrive at Nuweiba port and most continue on to the tourist village or vice versa. Arriving at the port – the only means of transport is taxi. Bargain hard – don't pay more than E£5-10.

Ins & outs

Apart from the beachlife there is little to see or do in Nuweiba which is a boring little town. Enterprising locals, however, organize camel treks and jeep safaris from the resort to the magnificent Coloured Canyon and elsewhere in the interior. Many take short trips to Petra in Jordan via the ferry to Aqaba. Swimming with a wild dolphin which has adopted a local Bedouin has become a tourist attraction (E£5 for 15 minutes), by the beach front *Abdullah's Café* in the Bedouin village at the entrance to Nuweiba. It is important not to wear any suntan lotion or cream as this can harm the dolphin.

Sights

Nuweiba has a range of hotels and camp sites mainly in the tourist village but also in the port and further along the coast towards Taba.

Sleeping

A *Nuweiba Hilton Coral Village*, T520321-6, F520327, on the beach just north of the port. Choice of restaurants, spread over 115,000 sq m of beach front, watersports, camel and horseriding, safaris, bicycles, squash, tennis, children's facilities, 2 heated pools, diving centre, travel agency, disco. A stylish resort, very relaxing, ideal for recuperating, rather isolated from rest of Sinai resorts. Excellent snorkelling just 30 m off shore where there is a coral garden. *Aquasport Dive and Watersport Centre* on the beach.

B *Helnan Nuweiba Hotel* T500402, F500407. 127 bungalows, disco, private beach, dive centre, mainly package tours, comfortable, restaurant, sports facilities.

C *Bawaki Beach Hotel*, 18 km north of Nuweiba, T500470-1, F3526123. 36 rooms, beach location, 1 km from Nuweiba-Taba road and 47 km from Taba, attractive, well built chalet hotel, friendly and helpful staff, cheap restaurant, bar, beach café, seawater pool, mainly European guests in winter and locals in summer, some problems with fresh water, power and telephone facilities, hire of fishing boat, cruise boat (E£100 per hour), speed boat for water skiing (E£40 per hour), windsurfing, and good snorkelling with submerged coral reef just offshore.

D *El-Sayadeen Touristic Village*, south of the port, T520340, F2476535. 99 a/c twin bed chalets with bath, poorly located near (but outside) the port, adequate but rather old and spartan, restaurant, pool, pebbly beach with windsurf boards and pedalos, European guests in winter and locals in summer. **D** *El-Salam Village*, Nuweiba, T500441, F500440. 89 rooms; on private beach north of Tarabeen, own coral reef, 2 pools, rooms with a/c and bath, bar and restaurant. **D** *La Sirene*, T500701/2, just down the road from *Hilton*. Simple, no pool, but right on the beach with excellent snorkelling on the coral reef.

Other places to consider are: **D** *Aquasun* T530391. 60 rooms on road out to Taba; *Barracuda*; *BasataVillage* T500481, 15 rooms, on road out to Taba; *Bawaki Beach*; *El Khan*; *El Waha Touristic Village*, T/F500420 38 rooms, just south of *Helnan* with wooden bungalows, a dozen large tents and space to sleep on the beach, restaurant; *Safari Beach*.

E *Sally Land Tourist Village*, Taba-Nuweiba Rd, Nuweiba, T530380, F530381, located off coast road half way between Nuweiba and Taba (36 km). Highly recommended. Tastefully planned, 68 attractive chalets, beautiful white sandy beach, courteous and efficient staff, mainly European guests, restaurant, café, bar, shop and beach snack bar, snorkelling and windsurfing equipment for hire.

Camping: *Nuweiba Helnan Camp*, bamboo cabins allow breezes to flow (and sand and hot air) comfortable interiors, dive centre, use of facilities at *Helnan Hotel*.

The Sinai Peninsula

Nuweiba Camping located next to *Nuweiba Holiday Village*, simple huts with 3 beds, a mirror, cupboard, table and chairs (E£24 pp), E£12 to pitch your own tent or E£3 to sleep on the beach, large clean communal cold showers, self-catering facilities and also near to a range of restaurants, cheerful staff who will organize camel and other trips.

Eating The *Nuweiba Holiday Village's* main restaurant provides adequate but unspectacular breakfast (E£8), lunch (E£21) and dinner (E£23) as well as a special barbecue (E£25), and fish restaurant dinner (E£23). At *Bawaki Village* restaurant the prices are slightly less. Besides the hotels there are a number of places to eat such as the average *Macondo's* fish restaurant next to the Holiday Village and the cheaper *Sharkawi* which is one of 3 cheap restaurants near the former Moshav and along the beach towards the village of Tarbeen, 2 km north of the resort.

Bars & nightclubs Nightlife in Nuweiba is very limited and revolves around the hotel beach bars. *Pool Cave Bar* with live music and darts at *Nuweiba Hilton Coral Village* is the most popular.

Shopping There are a few small stores and bakeries in and around Nuweiba town and the tourist resort.

Sports Although the Holiday Village has some facilities including tennis courts, bicycles for hire and horse riding (E£150 for 8 hrs), sports are otherwise limited to watersports with equipment being hired out at the hotel.

    Diving The *Nuweiba Diving Centre* is run by good European divers who are recommended as being particularly helpful for beginners. Nuweiba itself is not the best site on the coast for diving but, because it is quiet, it is ideal for beginners and a 45 mins introductory course costs US$40 while a full diving course costs US$240 pp. Trips to other and better dive sites can also be organized. *Aquasport Dive and Water Sports Centre*, T520329 has a 'Hobycat' at Nuweiba. Learning to dive for 12 years and over is just US$185.

Tour operators *Hilton Coral Village*, Nuweiba; also *Abanoub Travel*, T520201, F520206.

Transport **Road Bus**: T520370-1. There are various daily buses from **Cairo**, **Suez**, **Sharm el-Sheikh** and **Taba** which call at the port and the tourist village. Buses leave for **Sharm el-Sheik** at 0700 and 1500. **Service taxis**: with passengers sharing the cost of the journey, are available from **Nuweiba port** to **Taba** and other towns in the region and prices should be negotiated before setting off.

    Sea Ferry: there are 2 ferries a day (except on Sat, when there is one) between **Nuweiba port** and the Jordanian port of **Aqaba** which is 4 hrs further up the coast. Although there are some tourists the service is mainly used by Egyptian expatriate workers and also pilgrims who have to queue for hours outside the port during Ramadan, when a third sailing is often added to the schedule. Having checked their passports, foreigners are usually encouraged to jump the queue and proceed into the port to the ticket office and through customs. 2 weeks or 1 month Jordanian visas (£23 equivalent) are issued on board or immediately on arrival in Aqaba, with charges varying according to nationality.

Directory **Banks** There is a bank inside Nuweiba port, but you need your passport to get into the port, and the tourist village will change cash. **Communications** Post Office: in the tourist resort.

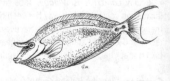

Longnose Unicorn Fish

Taba

Phone code: 062

This town has a special place in the hearts of most Egyptians because, although it is only tiny, it was the last piece of territory which was occupied by the Israelis. The fact that the luxury *Sonesta hotel*, one of Israel's best and most popular hotels, was located in the Taba enclave no doubt complicated the dispute. Despite having to pay compensation to the Sonesta's owners, before handing the hotel over to the Hilton group to manage and despite the very small size of the area in dispute, Cairo had been determined to retrieve every centimetre of Egyptian land and was satisfied at the outcome.

Taba is unusual, an international border town between an empty desert and the bright lights of Eilat. The coastline is attractive but although shelter from the wind is sought by sunbathers, windsurfers have no complaints. Besides the hotel there is little else in the tiny enclave except barracks and facilities for the border guards and customs officials. There are, however, major plans for the area and a danger of too much development. Land is very cheap at only E£5 per sq metre to be paid over a 10 years period. The result is that at **Taba Heights** just 9 km southwest of Taba five beach side hotels are under construction with plans for an international airport there. Having won Taba back from Israel, the government is now concentrating tourist development in the region and is building power stations and other infrastructual facilities to support the planned tourist influx.

The easiest way to reach Taba, which is 390 km from Cairo and 260 km from Sharm el-Sheikh, is via Israel's Eilat airport which is only 15 km across the border. However, few flights come directly here, most come in through Ovda. Time from Ovda to Taba Hilton at least 1 hr depending on border controls. Guests of the Taba Hilton and Nelson Village do not have to pay Israeli Departure Tax. These hotels will provide a pass to allow free movement through the border during time of stay. Taxis and buses run to the border and the hotel is just a few steps on.

Sightseeing in Taba is limited to trips to the beautiful interior, **Pharaoh's Island**, with the ruins of Salah al-Din's (Saladin's) fortress (the most important Islamic remains in Sinai), and across the Israeli border to Eilat. A visit to the island, which is a short boat ride (400 m) from the *Salah el-Din* hotel, where refreshments are available, is well worth the trip especially around sunset when it is particularly beautiful. The fortress was originally built by the Crusaders to guard the head of the Gulf of Aqaba and protect pilgrims travelling between Jerusalem and St Catherine's monastery. It was also used to levy taxes on Arab merchants travelling to and from Aqaba. Although Eilat, which is Israel's main holiday resort

Sights

The Sinai Peninsula

Pharaoh's Island

has many obvious attractions, it should be remembered that a visit could cause passport problems in other Arab countries (see Border crossing to Israel, page 432). There are helicopter rides available from Taba (also Dahab and Sharm el-Sheikh), maximum five passengers, range 600 km. For information *Siag* at *Taba Hilton*, T530300-1, also Sharm el-Sheikh, T600860.

Sleeping **A** *Taba Hilton*, Taba Beach, Taba, T530300-1, F5787044 (address via Israel which is far more efficient is PO Box 892, Eilat 88107, Israel, T059-79222, F059-79660). 10 storey hotel, private beach, pool, watersports, a 150 hp motorboat, a diving yacht with 14 berths for extended trips, 5 floodlit tennis courts, volley ball, table tennis, billiards room, games room, and video games, use of facilities at the sister hotel *Club Inn* just across the border in Eilat, there are 5 restaurants and 3 bars – the *Taba Lounge*, *Papo's Pub*, *Fantasy Island*, pool bar and *Nelson Village* bar, in addition there is the *End of the World* nightclub and a gambling casino attracting cross-border business from Israel, a variety of shops, bank, travel agency and car rental service. There is an excellent coral reef just off the shore with *Aquasport Dive and Watersport Centre*, T520329, on the site, Aquasport has a 'Hobycat' at Taba – learning to dive available for those over 12 years old for just US$180.

B *Nelson Village*, T530140, F530301. Designed using natural materials to blend in with the surroundings. An extension of the Taba hotel, with a private beach, garden and sea view. Lounge and coffee bar, restaurant offers Tex/Mex cuisine, also more standard fare. Guests have use of facilities of *Taba Hilton*.

C *Salah el-Din Hotel*, Taba, T530340-2, F530343. 50 double well equipped chalets, located 5 km south of Taba, view of Pharaoh's Island, large portions of simple food, friendly staff.

Camping **F** *Basata Camping*, at Ras al-Bourg, T500481 or 3501829, beach location 42 km south of Taba. Peaceful, well run, caters for a maximum of 300 people in single/double/family huts but 80-90 is normal, especially popular with Germans, Israelis, Egyptians, Dutch, British and French including many diplomats from Cairo embassies, strict policy of no drugs, alcohol or loud music, only natural food, no diving which would damage the coral, communal evening meal (E£7-E£10), clean and well run communal kitchen, facilities including a small desalination plant, showers, snorkelling, safari trips by camel and jeep, and 2 taxis for hire.

Eating Expensive but good standard in the *Taba Hilton* restaurants – **Palm Court**, **Marhaba Oriental**, **Casa Taba Italian**, **Surfer's Deck**. Average at the *Taba Hilton*, outdoor **Nelson Village Grill** and cheap and cheerful meals in the **Salah el-Din**.

Bars & nightclubs The **End of the World** and gambling casino at *Taba Hilton*. **Nelson Village Disco** under the stars, also at *Taba Hilton*.

Shopping Except for a few local food shops the only other ones are in the hotel.

Sports *Aquasport Dive and Watersport Centre*, T520329. See *Taba Hilton* above for more sports available.

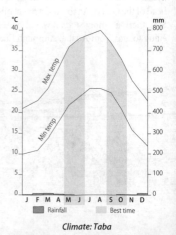

Climate: Taba

Taba tug of war

Taba is an enclave of land of no more than 1 sq km on the Gulf of Aqaba seized by the Israelis in the war of 1956 but, unlike the rest of Sinai, not returned to Egypt. Assuming that the Taba strip would be forever Israeli, an international hotel complex was built there (now the Taba Hilton). In 1986 agitation by Egypt for a final settlement of the international border at Taba led the dispute being put to arbitration.

This revealed that the border post at Ras Taba, 1 of 14 put in place after the 1906 Anglo-Turkish agreement, had been moved by the Israeli side.

In one of the oddest of cases concerning the delimitation of an international border this century, it was found that the Israeli army had cut away part of the hill at Ras Taba to enable Israeli artillery to have a good sweep of the Sinai coast road as it approached the port of Eilat. At the same time the Israeli military engineers removed the border post which rested on the top of Ras Taba. This gave the Israeli government the excuse to claim that, despite Israeli maps to the contrary, the old border had always run south of the Taba strip. In 1989 the arbitrators returned Taba to Egypt, though it remains virtually an enclave with border posts on all sides.

The *Taba Hilton* is very efficient and can arrange onward travel and provide car hire. **Tour operators**

Air Nearest airport is Eilat (15 km) with direct daily flights to major European cities. (No **Transport** problem at Egyptian border but customs officials at airport are very thorough.) By comparison the local Ras el-Naqb airport 39 km away only has a few flights a week from Cairo. *Orascom* has plans for more frequent flights as the new hotel complex develops.

Road **Bus**: *East Delta Bus Co* runs daily buses to and from **Cairo, Sharm el-Sheikh** via Nuweiba and Dahab, and **Eilat** across the border in Israel. **Service taxis** are more frequent than the buses, more comfortable, quicker – but marginally more expensive.

Banks *Taba Hilton* in Taba open 24 hrs, only bank in Egypt that changes Israeli money. **Directory** **Communications Post Office**: use *Taba Hilton* which sends mail via adjacent Eilat rather than distant Cairo.

The Ahmed Hamdi Tunnel The road journey across the centre of the Sinai peninsula from Taba to the Ahmed Hamdi tunnel under the Suez Canal takes about 4 hrs. The turnoff just to the south of Taba is the main road, which is good except for the first 17 km which is very steep and suffers from regular flooding, to the tunnel 270 km away. Ras el-Naqb airport, 20 km further on, serves Taba and Nuweiba which is 80 km away but only has a few flights a week from Cairo. From the airport the road proceeds onto a flat plain and to both UN and Egyptian checkpoints. About 190 km from the tunnel there is a small, dirty site which includes a petrol station, mosque, restaurant, radio mast and semi-finished houses. Further along the route there are pillboxes, burnt out trucks from the fleeing Egyptian army in 1967, and lots of road building. At **Nakhl** there is a petrol station, police post, garage, mosque, as well as cafés and stalls which have fresh fruit. At a crossroads 126 km from the tunnel there are turnoffs to El-Arish (151 km) and El-Hasana (63 km). The maximum speed limit is 90 km per hour for cars and 80 km per hour for buses. About 70 km from the tunnel there is turnoff for Ras Sudr one way and El-Hasana the other way. Further on is the **Mitla Pass** and its trenches, pillboxes and other war debris, which was the site of one of the largest tank battles in history. Closer to the tunnel there are turnoffs for Ras Sudr, Wadi

The Sinai Peninsula

el-Giddi, El-Tur and El-Qantara. The tunnel under the Suez Canal costs E£1.50 for cars and E£3 for buses.

Immediately after the Ahmed Hamdi Tunnel there is a crossroads to Ismailia, Suez and Cairo where there are some rather dirty cafés and a petrol station. The road to Cairo across a empty featureless desert plain passes lots of quarries, a coal stockpile and army camps, including one with candy striped huts, and follows the railway line from Suez to Cairo. After a major traffic police checkpoint the dual carriageway is a very good road. About 100 km from Cairo there is a Red Crescent station. The east of Cairo has some very large industrial works and the air becomes noticeably more polluted.

Border crossing to Israel Although the checkpoints are always open it is better to cross between 0700-2100 and to avoid crossing on Friday just before the Israeli sabbath when almost all businesses close and transport ceases. Free one-month Israeli entry visas are available for most Western tourists. **NB** Make sure that your **entry card** and **not** your passport are stamped because an Israeli stamp, and even an Egyptian entry stamp from Taba, may disqualify you from entering some Arab countries. Once on the Israeli side of the border you can catch a service-taxi or No 15 bus into Eilat.

The Interior

St Catherine's Monastery, despite its location in the heart of the Sinai wilderness, is one of the most important tourist sites in the country. This Greek orthodox monastery located at the base of **Mount Sinai**, where God is believed to have revealed the Ten Commandments to Moses, has attracted pilgrims and visitors for centuries. From Cairo it is 450 km, Sharm el-Sheikh, Dahab 140 km, Nuweiba 110 km, Taba 188 km, and Ras Sudr 260 km.

The **Burning Bush**, through which God is said to have spoken to Moses, holds religious significance for Jews, Christians and Muslims and in AD 337 **Empress Helena**, mother of **Constantine**, decreed that a sanctuary was be built around what was thought to be the site of the bush. It became a refuge for an increasing number of hermits and pilgrims who sought the wilderness of the Sinai Valley over the following centuries. Between 537 and 562, **Emperor Justinian** expanded the site considerably by building fortifications and providing soldiers to protect the residents and adding the **Church of the Virgin** and the **Basilica of the Transfiguration**. The monastery and its community which then, as today, was controlled by the Byzantine Church was tolerated by the subsequent Muslim conquerors.

The number of pilgrims dwindled until a body, claimed to be that of the Egyptian born St Catherine, was 'discovered' in the 10th century and was brought to the monastery which attracted many pilgrims during the period of Crusader occupation (1099-1270). The numbers of both pilgrims and monks, who are now restricted to Greeks mainly from the Mt Athos area, subsequently waxed and waned until today there are only 25 monks, but the thousands of international pilgrims and tourists actually make the monastery too crowded in the high season.

The road journey from Dahab to St Catherine, which is generally very good with little traffic, takes about 1½ hours. On the way, at the top of a very steep hill there is a breathtaking view over the desert. The coaches and taxis stop here and bedouins attempt to sell fossils, sand-roses and other souvenirs. You then pass through one UN and then two Egyptian checkpoints. There is a small rundown cafeteria 55 km from St Catherine, trenches (25 km), the *El-Salam Hotel* (15 km), *Green Lodge camping and restaurant* and Masr petrol station (10 km), *Morganland camping* (8 km) and a bedouin village and encampment just before arriving in St Catherine.

St Catherine's Monastery

While all of the organized tours to St Catherine stop at the monastery itself, the normal buses services stop in the small village of St Catherine about 2 km below the monastery. **NB Climate**: St Catherine's is very cold in winter with a metre of snow a few times a year and snow sometimes until Mar but it is very hot in summer. Despite the environment there are no problems with water or electricity.

Although an official tour guide, who will explain the history and symbolism of each part of the monastery, is a bonus he is not essential if you buy the monastery's guide book in the small bookshop near the entrance.

The ancient gate on the western face has been walled up (but the funnel above, for pouring oil on unwary attackers, remains) and a newer entrance constructed alongside. Visitors now enter through the north wall. The outer wall, constructed of local granite by Justinian's builders, is 2-3 m thick and the height which varies due to the uneven topography is never less than 10 m and in places reaches 20 m. The southern face has some interesting raised Christian symbols.

The highlight of the walled monastery, which includes the monks' quarters and gardens which are not open to the public, is the highly decorative and incense-perfumed **St Catherine's Church** which includes **St Helena's Chapel of the Burning Bush**. The church was built between AD 542-551 in memory of **Emperor Justinian**'s wife. The building is of granite in the shape of a basilica. It has a wide central nave and two side aisles reduced by the construction of side chapels and a vestry. Its 12 enormous pillars, six in each side, each a single piece of granite, are free standing decorated with beautiful icons representing the saints which are venerated in each of the 12 months of the year. A candle is lit below the relevant icon on each saint's day. Examine the capitals for their Christian symbols. The walls, pillars and cedar-wood doors of the church are all original.

Monastery of St Catherine

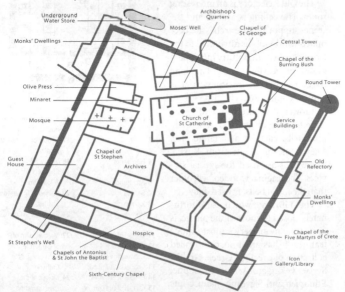

The Sinai Peninsula

In the church – the ancient roof is hidden above a more recent (18th century) ceiling. The ancient cedar wood doors at the entrance to the church are 1400 years old. Observe the reliefs of animals and plants. Above them the inscription (in Greek) reads – "This is the gate to the Lord; the righteous shall enter into it." By comparison the 11th century doors made by the Crusaders are new. The gable window in the western end of the church is made in the form of a cross. This, with the palm tree reliefs on either side, is better observed from outside.

The *iconostasis* is dated at 1612. In the apse is one of the delights of this building, a magnificent mosaic illustrating the Transfiguration. It is the earliest and one of the finest mosaics of the Eastern Church. The theme is taken from St Matthew's gospel. Christ is in the centre with Moses and Elijah one at each side and Peter, James and John at his feet. Around these are further figures identified as the twelve apostles, the twelve prophets, the abbot in church at the time of the mosaic's construction and John of Climax, the deacon. At the far side of the north aisle is **St Helena's Chapel of the Burning Bush** which, although it was the site of the original sanctuary, was not included in Justinian's original building but was only enclosed later on. A silver plate below the altar marks the site where the bush is supposed to have stood.

West of the church is a small 11th century **Mosque** which, originally a guesthouse, was converted apparently in order to placate the Muslim invaders and to encourage them to tolerate the monastery. The detached minaret which faces the church is 10 m high. Significantly, however, the church steeple is considerably taller.

The Old Refectory is an interesting room. The ceiling is arched and the stones supporting the arches are decorated with symbols attributed to the Crusaders. A 16th century mural decorates the eastern wall. The long refectory table has intricate carvings worth examination. The three-tiered bell tower at the western end of the church was built in 1871. There are nine bells, each of a different size. They came as a gift from Russia. These bells are used for special services. The original wooden bell, older than the metal bells, is used daily.

The **Library**, which is unfortunately closed to most of the public, is one of the monastery's most unique features. It has an almost unrivalled collection of precious Greek, Arabic, Syriac, Georgian, Armenian Coptic, Ethiopian and Slavonic manuscripts reputedly second only to that of the

Church of St Catherine

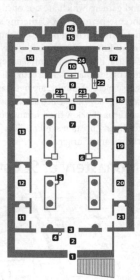

1 Fatimid Crusader doors
2 Narthex
3 Justinian doors
4 Holy water
5 Pulpit
6 Archbishop's chair
7 Basilica
8 Iconostasis
9 Holy altar
10 Apse
11 Chapel of St Marina
12 Chapel of Sts Constantine & Helena
13 Chapel of St Antipas
14 Chapel of St James
15 Chapel of the Burning Bush
16 Site of the Burning Bush
17 Chapel of Martyrs of Sinai
18 Vestry
19 Chapel of Sts Anna & Joachim
20 Chapel of St Simeon Stylites
21 Chapel of St Cosmas Damian
22 Marble coffin of St Catherine
23 Sarcophagi of St Catherine
24 Mosaic of the transfiguration

Vatican. There are over 5,000 books and over 3,000 manuscripts, most in Greek including the famous Codex Syriacus, a fifth-century translation of the gospels. An extra US$8 is charged to see the library and refectory. The icon gallery contains 2,000 priceless icons in the collection, of which 150 are unique and date from 5th-7th centuries. Some are on display in the narthex of the church. Look out for the icons which show Moses receiving the commandments and Moses taking off his shoes before the **Burning Bush**.

The monastery's small **Museum** contains a collection of the gifts presented to the monastery over the centuries. The treasures were randomly scattered throughout the monastery until their accumulated worth was calculated by Friar Pachomius who then carefully gathered and preserved them in one place but many of the more interesting items have been lost over the ages.

Because the monastery's **Cemetery** in the gardens was so small the custom was developed of storing the overflow of monks' skeletons in the crypt of the Chapel of St Tryphon. This serves as the Ossuary of the **Charnel House** which is in the monastery gardens. When a monk died his body was buried in the cemetery place of the oldest body which is then removed to the Charnel House. The remains of the archbishops are kept separate in special niches. Visitors can visit this rather macabre room which is full of skeletons and skulls.

The monastery gardens are small. All the soil was carried here by the monks who also constructed the water tanks for irrigation. It contains olive and apricot trees, plums and cherries with vegetables growing between. Immediately to the right of the monastery's main entrance at **Kleber's Tower**, which is about 15 m high and 3 m thick, is **Jacob's Well** which it is claimed has never dried up. It is supposed to be the site where the 40-year-old Moses, who was fleeing from Egypt, met one of Jethro's seven daughters called Zipporah whom he subsequently married. Just around the corner to the left of Kleber's Tower is a rather unimpressive overgrown thorny evergreen bush which is claimed to be a transplanted descendant of the **Burning Bush** from which God allegedly spoke to Moses.

■ *Mon-Thu and Sat 0900-1200, but closed Fri, Sun and public holidays, free. Visitors to the interior of the Monastery must dress modestly. Shorts are not allowed – for either men or women. There is no dress code for outside visiting.*

Mount Sinai

If time permits, climb Mt Sinai (Jebel Musa), 2,285 m, where, according to Christian tradition, Moses received the tables of Law known as the Ten Commandments. The view is particularly spectacular at sunset and sunrise. The shortest way with access from immediately behind the Monastery is up 3,700 steps, tough going and very difficult in the dark. The alternative, an easier way, is indirect but can be done on donkey or camel back. The stiff walk or ride up the steep camel track, which takes about 2½ hrs, is quite rough and stout shoes and warm clothing are essential. Camels can be hired from behind the monastery for E£35. One way takes you three parts of the way up in 1½ hours. The last 700 steps you must walk takes 30 mins. Although there are refreshment stalls on the way up, which get more expensive nearer the summit, it is advisable to take at least 2 litres of water per person if making the ascent during the day but it is best to start the ascent at about 1700, or earlier in winter, in order to arrive at the summit at sunset. On Mt Sinai is a chapel where services are performed some Sundays by the Monks and a mosque where those of Islamic faith sacrifice a sheep once a year. Camping is possible (see Sleeping below).

Blazing Bushes and Catherine Wheels

Mount Sinai marked the half way point of the flight of the Jews from Egypt to the 'promised land'. Moses was clearly an inspirational leader for the incident of the burning bush led him to return to Egypt to lead his people to the land of milk and honey. Despite calling down from God the 10 plagues (frogs, lice, locusts, hail and fire among them), he failed to persuade the Pharoah to release them from their slave labour. Finally the 80-year-old Moses asked God to strike the Egyptians with the pass-over when the Jews marked their houses with lamb's blood and were spared the massacre of all first born children. As a result, the Pharoah banished the 600,000 Israelite men, women and children from Egypt. Their epic journey is related in the Book of Exodus in the Bible. They were pursued by the Egyptians (drowned after the Red Sea divided to allow the Israelites across), faced starvation (rescued with manna from heaven) and thirst (saved when a spring flowed from a rock Moses had struck with his staff) and defeated an attack by the Amaleks.

On Mount Sinai, Moses received the wisdom of the Ten Commandments which have formed the code of practice for human behaviour for centuries.

The supposed site of the burning bush was developed into a monastery and in the 10th century named after Saint Catherine. According to legend Saint Catherine, who was born in AD 294 and was from a noble family in Alexandria, was a Christian convert who was martyred in the early fourth century for refusing to renounce her faith. She herself converted hundreds of people to Christianity and accused Emperor Maxentius of idolatry. When he tried to have her broken it was claimed that she shattered the spiked (Catherine) wheel by touching it, so Maxentius resorted to having her beheaded in Alexandria. After her execution her body vanished and according to legend was transported by angels to the top of Egypt's highest mountain, (2,642 m) now named after her. Three centuries later this body was 'discovered', brought down from the mountain and placed in a golden casket in the church where it remains to this day.

Mount Catherine

Phone code:
The area has a split phone code 062 & 069

At 2,642 m Mount Catherine or Jebel Katrinahht is Egypt's highest peak. It is about 6 km south of Mount Sinai and is a 5-6 hours exhausting climb.

Enroute you pass the Monastery of the Forty Martyrs. On the summit there is a small chapel dedicated to St Catherine with water, a two-room hostel for overnight pilgrims and a meteorological station. The path up to the summit was constructed by Monk Moses who is said to have laid the granite staircase up Mount Sinai.

B *St Catherine Tourist Village*, Wadi el-Raha, St Catherine, T/F470288, in the Wadi el-Raha or 'Valley of Repose', unrestricted views of the monastery 2 km up the road. 100 clean twin-bed chalets of local stone, the shape of a Bedouin tent, mainly European, US and Japanese guests who stay 1 night, normally full in high season, restaurant, coffee shop, gift shop, library, video hall, tennis, billiards, and table-tennis.

C *Daniella*, T69 470379, F69 3607750, St Catherine. 54 rooms, nice grounds, simple, comfortable but not enough blankets in winter, overpriced, provides good packed lunch for climbing mountains! **C** *El-Salam*, St Catherine Airport, St Catherine, T471409, F2476535. 35 rooms, expensive 2-star hotel. **D** *El Wadi El Mouquduss*, T69 470225, F2632021. 58 rooms.

Ful for all

Ful has been an important dish for Egyptians since banquetting scenes were painted on the Pharonic tombs. Ful is nutritious and cheap and is the staple diet for low income and strong stomached locals. In Cairo a meal from one of the 25,000 (illegal) street vendors will start the day. At 25 p per sandwich and E31 per plateful it fills an empty space, provides protein and carbohydrates. Ful is also considered 'in' and the smart set frequent luxury outlets such as El Gahsh, Akher Saa, El Tabei and El Omda buying the ful with onions, pickles, lemon and fresh bread to eat in or take away.

The ful bean is grown in most agricultural areas of Egypt, as a follow on to the major crop - the best is said to come from Minya. Imports are necessary to supply consumption demands and have been responsible for the rise in price.

Recipe – ful
Ful bil zeit el harr - with hot oil
Ful bil samna - with ghee (clarified butter)
Bisara – with oil, onion, garlic and coriander
Ful is also the main ingredient in Ta'ameya and Felafel.

Enjoy your meal

Cheaper accommodation at **E** *Morgan Land*, T62 470331, 92 rooms each sleeping 3/4 and at **E** *Zeitouna Camp*, T69 470404, 50 double rooms.

Camping There is no specific camp site at St Catherine but it is possible to spend the night on **Mt Sinai** to see the sunrise but, because of the altitude, its sub-zero night-time temperatures for much of the year make a torch, sleeping bag and warm clothing absolutely essential.

Hostel The hostel at the monastery, E£30+ a night for a bed in a simple and cramped dormitory, communal showers, including simple breakfast. Reserve a room by asking at the monastery between 1700-1900, T470333, F470343.

Besides the more expensive hotel restaurants like *El-Safsafa* at *St Catherine's Tourist Village* there are 2 cafés serving decent food in town and the *El-Monagah snack bar*. **Eating**

In the town there is the *Supermarket Katreen* and another supermarket, a grocery store, bakery, bazaar and petrol station. **Shopping**

Mainly limited to tennis and a few indoor games at the tourist village. **Sports**

Air Reservations must be made well in advance for the direct Air Sinai flights between St Catherine airport, 15 km from the town, and Cairo (2 flights a week), Hurghada and Sharm el-Sheikh which offer in addition spectacular views of the Sinai peninsula. **Transport**

Road Bus: there are direct buses for the 8 hrs journey between St Catherine town and Cairo's Sinai terminal via Suez and others to Dahab, Nuweiba and Sharm el-Sheikh. **Service taxis**: travellers can share the cost of hiring a 7 seat service taxi to Dahab, Sharm el-Sheikh, Taba, Suez or other towns in the peninsula, but the prices almost double once the last bus has left St Catherine.

Banks *Bank Misr* branch on the main street in St Catherine town is open daily from 1000-1400 and 1800-2100. **Communications Post Office**: is opposite the bank in town, open Sat-Thu 0800-1400. **Telephone**: there is an international telephone exchange in town open from 0800-2400 near the post office. **Directory**

The Sinai Peninsula

Keen travellers/campers could extend the journey westwards from St Catherine taking the minor road to the Oasis of Feiran where Moses left his people when he went to collect the Ten Commandments. Further west is **Serabit El-Khadim** which, in the Pharaonic period was an area well known for the mining of the semi-precious stone, turquoise. Here on the summit of Jebel Serabit (850 m) are the ruins of the Temple of Hathor which they erected to the 'Lady of Turquoise' with a small chapel to Sopdu, who was guardian of the desert ways. The views over the desert region from here are outstanding. Other turquoise mines in the area include Jebel Maghara.

The West Coast

The west coast of Sinai on the Gulf of Suez is far less attractive than the Gulf of Aqaba coast. It has been spoilt by the oil industry which, while being one of Egypt's sources of foreign exchange, has transformed this region into a mass of oil rigs and gas flares and made it unsuitable for another foreign exchange earner – tourism. The largely featureless coast has become polluted with oil industry debris and is far more interesting to the industrialist than to the tourist.

El-Tur Although it is the administrative capital of south Sinai the seedy and dilapidated coastal town of El-Tur, which is 108 km from Sharm el-Sheikh and 170 km from Suez, has little to commend it. The best hospitals are located here as it was the quarantine stop for pilgrims from Mecca. El-Tur airport handles small planes. The port which has always been of some significance can accommodate medium size ships.

If you stop here, look at the Fortress of El-Tur, built by Sultan Selim I in 1520AD and the Temple of Sarabit al-Kahadim which stands on a small hill to the north of the town. To the east are several caves such Cave of Hathor built during reign of King Snefru and Cave of Souidu, the God of War. During the 3rd and 4th centuries El-Tur was an important Christian centre with a monastery built by Justinian (now just ruins).

Sleeping & eating E *Jolie Valley Hotel*, by Port El-Tur, T(062) 771111. 43 rooms. **E** *Lido Hotel*, Moon Beach, T771700/Cairo, T2906496, F771780. 32 rooms. Only the restaurants in the hotels can be recommended.

Transport Road Bus: T770029. The most important information about El-Tur is how to get out of town. There are daily buses to **Sharm el-Sheikh** and **Suez**.

Directory Medical Services Ambulance: T770350. **Hospital**: T770320, (0900-1400).

Ras Sudr Near the northern end of the Gulf of Suez, Ras Sudr is both an oil company town and the site of a noxious oil refinery but also a year-round destination for middle class Egyptian tourists. From Cairo it is 190 km, Sharm el-Sheikh (290 km), Nuweiba (365 km), Dahab (385 km), St Catherine (250 km), and Taba (433 km).

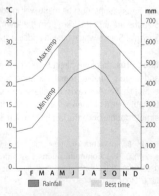

Climate: El-Tur

Sights Nearby sites include **El-Shatt point** (41 km), **Ayoun Moussa** (31 km), the 494 m high natural pyramid at **Hammamat Pharaoun** (50 km), and the rock temple at **Sarabit el-Khadem** 'Heights of the Slave' (130 km). Ayoun Moussa – the springs of Moses mentioned in the Bible – as the place where the Hebrews rested after their exodus from Egypt and God provided honey dew and quails. Seven of the springs still exist and plans are afoot to make this into a new tourist resort.

Sleeping B *Helnan Royal Beach Resort*, just to south of town, T(062) 400101-3, F400108. 82 beds – most expensive hotel in town. **C** *Mesalla Beach Resort*, T400427, F4154054. 150 rooms. **D** *Moon Beach Resort*, about 40 km south of Ras Sudr. All 72 bungalows now have a/c and a fridge. Tuition for windsurfing available, T/F3365103. **E** *Ras Sudr Tourist Village*, T/F400402. 12 villas, 100 chalets, and a 20 rooms hotel, 2 restaurants, shops, watersports, tennis, squash and volley ball, childrens' playground, video hall, billiards, chess and table tennis, information/reservations from Misr-Sinai Tourist Company, *Misr Travel*, Tower Building, Abbassia, Cairo. **E** *Sudr Beach Inn*, PO Box 119, Cairo, T770752 or Cairo, T2828113, F770752. 20 rooms with bath and balcony, good accommodation overlooking the Gulf of Suez, restaurant and gift shop. **E** *Banana Beach Village*, T400698. 64 rooms. **F** *Daghash Land Tourist Village*, T777049. Located 19 km from Ras Sudr, often space available, restaurant, café, table tennis, video hall and private beach with 2 bars, information/reservations, Cairo, T609672. **Eating** Only the restaurants in the hotels are recommended.

Sports Some facilities at the tourist village.

Transport Bus: the daily buses between Suez and Sharm el-Sheikh stop at Ras Sudr.

Northern Sinai

Although the majority of tourists only visit the Gulf of Aqaba coastline and St Catherine's Monastery, the northern part of the peninsula has a number of attractions both in El-Arish and along the 210 km Mediterranean coastline which stretches from Port Said to the border at Rafa. Unfortunately, while the region is beginning to be appreciated by Egyptian tourists, most foreigners only see the area from the bus window as they speed to or from the Israeli border.

Non-Egyptians are not permitted to travel anywhere in north Sinai without an armed escort. This is provided by the Tourist Police for car, minibus or coach and although at first it is quite restricting it is possible with a little determination to follow one's planned programme of sightseeing. (See box on coping with Police protection) At times, like crossing the canal at El Qantara, it has positive advantages.

North coast of Sinai

The Sinai Peninsula

Access from the west is across the Suez Canal at **El Qantara** where an impressive new bridge will, on completion in 2001, eradicate the usual long delays at this point of the journey. There is nothing to stop here for, except a cup of coffee. Access from west but further south is through the Ahmed Hamdi Tunnel.

The main beaches on the north coast of Sinai are at El-Arish, Oruba, further east, beside Rafa near the border and Lake Bardweel really a lagoon on the central north coast famous for its fishing.

If you have your own transport visit the Roman ruins of **Pelusium** also known as Tel el-Farame. The site covers a wide area, lots of rubble, stone, bricks and columns. This ancient city was situated on a now dry distributary of the River Nile. It guarded the access from the east and acted as a customs post. It is mentioned in the Bible as "the stronghold of Egypt". The Persians came through while both Pompey and Baldwin I ended their days here in tragic circumstances. Measure carefully 15 km from junction of the road from El Qantara with the road from the Ahmed Hamdi Tunnel. There is no road sign but the walls are very ornate. Turn north. The road is surfaced until it crosses a small canal. Turn left on to the next (unsurfaced) road. This road is not passable after rain so be prepared to walk from the tarmac. ■ *The site is open 0900-1600 daily.*

Lake Bardweel (66,500 ha) is important for fish such as mullet, seabass, etc and migratory birds but access to the shore is often difficult. At the eastern end is the El-Zaraneek preserve where over 200 species of migrating birds have been recorded. Take the track north at the hamlet of al-Sabeka. **The sign says keep to the road but forgets to mention the landmines.** This area is of such significance that it has been preserved as a wetland under the auspices of UNESCO.

El-Arish

Phone code: 068
Population: 65,000

This town, population 65,000, 180 km east of the Suez Canal is the governorate capital of North Sinai and was noted for its 30 km of palm-lined beach of fine white sand. From the bus and taxi station in Midan Baladiya it is a 2-3 km walk or minibus ride up the main road north to the beach which is the site of most of the hotels. This area is very popular at weekends. Al-Nakheel to the east is the best beach at El-Arish with famous but depleted palm trees extending the length of the beach.

There is an Egyptian General Authority for the Promotion of Tourism office in El-Arish, T341016, in the same office as the Tourist Police station, T341016, which is located just before the beach on Sharia Fouad Abu Zakry. There is a small, helpful Tourist Information on the dual carriageway to the west about 12 km out of town.

Sights

You can visit the Thursday market (**Souq el-Khamees**) bedouin market in the oldest part of town selling north Sinai embroidered cloth, plants, produce, bedouin handicrafts. This is best reached from the coast road turning south just by the *Semiramis*. **El-Arish Fortress**, is located on a plateau to the southwest of the town on the remains of an ancient pharaonic castle. Follow signs to Souq el Khemees and beside the pieces of aqueduct, and hidden behind wooden walls (absolutely no entry) where excavations are taking place, are the ruins of the fort rebuilt by the Turk Sultan Sulayman Al Qanouni in 1560 and demolished in World War One by British bombardment. Otherwise life in town revolves around the beach.

Out on the Rafa road there is a small **museum** of handicrafts and stuffed Sinai wildlife but its opening hours are very irregular and the exhibits disappointing. There is a small zoo, also on the east side of town, T320921, but not recommended. Situated between Abi-Sakl to the west and the zoo to the east is the harbour of El-Arish, used mainly for fishing vessels. Fishing permits may be granted.

Hotels along the beach range from the luxurious **A** *Hotel Egoth Oberoi*, T351321/7, **Sleeping**
F352352. 219 rooms, most with sea view, Sharia Fouad Abu Zakry, sports and recreation facilities including health spa, tennis and squash courts, windsurfing, pedal boats, private beach, which is the only place in town which sells alcohol to a number of more simple tourist hotels. During the Jul-Sep high season it may be difficult to find a room without booking but during the winter most hotels are very quiet. **C** *Semiramis Hotel*, Sharia Fouad Abu Zakry, T344166, F344168. 170 rooms, on both sides of the coast road. **D** *Sinai Beach Hotel*, Sharia Fouad Abu Zakry, T/F341713. 30 rooms some with sea view. **D** *Sinai Sun Hotel*, Sharia 23 Juyl, T341855. All 54 rooms with a/c and shower. Note the cheaper hotels are used exclusively by Egyptians. **E** *Mecca Hotel*, Sharia Fouad Abu Zakry, T344909. 36 rooms.

Youth hostel adjacent to Governorate Building, **Camping**: It is possible to camp on the beach with permission from the police. *El-Arish Camping*, about 7 km west of the town has 2-man tents or you can pitch your own.

Besides the hotels there is an outdoor restaurant near the *Egoth Oberoi* and a number **Eating** of cheap restaurants and sheesha (water-pipe) cafés in and around Midan Baladiya such as *Maxim's* on the beach or *Sammar Basata* and *Aziz* at the coast end of Sharia 23 July, T340345. Highly recommended.

Besides the main hotels there is almost no nightlife except the cafés in Midan Baladiya. **Entertainment**

There are some rather sleazy tourist shops on Sharia 23rd July but for quality items it is **Shopping** better to bargain at the bedouin market on Thu.

Misr Travel Office, T41241/41049. **Tour operators**

Air There are two Air Sinai flights a week from **Cairo** on Sun and Thu, takes 1 hr, **Transport** only in summer and very unreliable. The airport is along the Bir Lahfan road to the south of the town. **Road Bus**: *East Delta Bus Co* runs frequent daily buses between El-Arish and Cairo (6 hrs), which should be booked the day before, and others to the Suez Canal cities of **El Qantara** and **Ismailia**. Bus station off Midan Baladiya near the mosque. **Service taxis**: to/from **Midan Koulali** Terminal in Cairo (takes 5-6 hrs, E£30); **Midan el Gomhurriya** in Ismailia (takes 3 hrs, E£15) or by the Suez Canal in Qantara (takes 2½ hrs, E£12). Taxis to **Cairo** leave early morning. **Taxis**: run from here to the beach.

Banks *Bank of Alexandria*, T40169, *Misr Bank*, T40036, *National Bank of Egypt*, T40414, and *Sinai* **Directory**
National Bank for Development, T40952, in town and the main hotels will also change money. **Communications Post Office**: the post office and the international telephone exchange are located off Sharia 23rd July between the *Sinai Sun Hotel* and Midan Baladiya. **Medical services** Ambulance: T340123. Hospital: *El-Arish General Hospital*, Sharia el-Geish, T340010. Pharmacies: *Pharmacy Fouad*, T341541, open 0800-2400 except Fri. **Useful addresses** The main **police station** is on Sharia el-Geish on the way to Rafa. Police: T340049 and T340202.

The Sinai Peninsula

Border crossing to Palestine & Israel There are very frequent buses and service taxis east to the international border (known as the Gate of Salah al-Din) at **Rafa**, 41 km from El-Arish, open winter 0900-1700 and summer 1000-1800. It is best to avoid crossing on Friday. Whenever you cross it is advisable to leave El-Arish in the morning to avoid getting caught in the Gaza Strip during the 2000-0400 curfew. There is a free 1 month Israeli visa for most Western tourists. **NB** Make sure that your **entry card** and **not** your passport are stamped because an Israeli stamp, and even an Egyptian entry stamp from Rafa, disqualifies you from entering some Arab countries. Occasionally there are major luggage searches of tourists but this is usually reserved for Arab travellers. Once on the Palestinian side of the border you can catch a service-taxi into the Israeli side of the divided town of Rafa and then on to Khan Yunis and Gaza City's Palestine Square from where there are service taxis to Jerusalem and Tel Aviv. Entry into Egypt at Rafa – be sure to have a visa in your passport as they are not granted on arrival here.

The Red Sea Coast and
Eastern Desert

12

The Red Sea Coast and Eastern Desert

The Eastern Desert lies in a belt between the River Nile and the Red Sea which stretches for about 1,250 km from the southern end of the Suez Canal to the Sudanese border. The slowly widening major fault line running along the whole length of the Red Sea has created the Red Sea Mountains, including Jebel Shaayib el-Banat (2,184 m), which are the highest in Egypt outside the Sinai peninsula. Most visitors simply traverse this scorchingly hot, inhospitable and virtually uninhabited region to get to the Red Sea Coast which is one of the fastest growing tourist regions in the country. The mountain region is very remote and the occasional ibex and gazelle can still be seen. The red colour of these mountain ranges is said to have inspired the name for the adjacent sea.

As the closest tropical sea to Europe the Red Sea is the perfect choice for migratory birds, divers and snorkellers. The tropical waters offer an amazing variety of marine fauna – with over 1,000 species of fish feeding on the coral. The species of flora, though less in number, are no less in interest. This is indeed an underwater paradise. The comfortable temperatures of the sea all year round encourage such visitors.

The Red Sea Coast and Eastern Desert

This part of the Red Sea coast has exceptional winds almost all the year round with perfect conditions for wind surfing – sunshine, warm water and well equipped centres.

There is very little rainfall and the temperatures in this tropical region remain high all year round. While air temperatures can reach 30°C in summer the water can be an incredible 28°C. In the winter the water temperature falls to a chilly 21°C and a 7 mm wetsuit is required.

No rivers flow into this sea to disturb the crystal clear waters and the corals increase. This exceptional coral growth is due to many factors – the limited tidal range, the clear water which allows penetration of the sun's light (down to 45 m) and suitable water temperature. Some coral grows at a surprising rate – as much as 35 cm in a year but the damage caused by over diving and over fishing and the proximity of considerable development along the coast is causing a serious imbalance.

There are one or two points to bear in mind. This is the most popular coast for windsurfing – the breezes are always just right. However if you do not intend to take advantage of the wind for surfing it still continues to blow, and blow and blow. Finding shelter from this relentless breeze for a little peaceful sunbathing can be a problem. In addition, due to the increasing popularity of the Red Sea for holidays, coastal resorts have problems providing sufficient accommodation. Building work is evident at every turn but the hotels and facilities included here are complete and fully operational.

Nevertheless this region is not completely isolated and trips are available westward to the Luxor region of the River Nile or north to the monasteries of St Paul and St Anthony and even to Suez and Cairo.

Zafarana is 62 km south of Aïn Sukhana on H44 at the junction to Beni Suef. This is best known as the access point for visits to two neighbouring isolated monasteries hidden in the folds of the Red Sea Mountains. These are **St Anthony's** and **St Paul's**, the oldest monasteries in Egypt. Pilgrim tours to these monasteries are organized through the YMCA in Cairo, T5917877, and by the Coptic Patriachate in Cairo, T2825375. Day tours there with lunch are offered by a number of Hurghada travel agents including *Misr Travel*. Otherwise a group can negotiate a single price with a local taxi in Hurghada. Provided it is not too hot and you take enough water and only light luggage it is also possible to get out of Beni Suef to Zafarana by service taxi or the Hurghada to Cairo or Suez bus at the turn offs for the respective monasteries, and then hitch or walk the remaining distance. For St Paul's turn off the north-south desert road approximately 24 km south of Zafarana at the small blue and white signs indicating the monastery and follow the rough track for about 13 km. For St Anthony's drive inland from Zafarana and after 32 km turn left at the blue and white sign which indicates the monastery. There are still 15 km more to go. Please note that advanced booking is required for accommodation at St Paul's. Ring Cairo 5900218.

St Anthony's Monastery known locally as Deir Amba Antonyus is the more important. It has recently reopened to the public having been closed for a year for cleaning and restoration of the ceiling and entrances to the church. In particular the fabulous wall paintings and icons have been carefully preserved.
■ *Daily 0900-1700, except during Lent and between 25 Nov-7 Jan.*

St Anthony, (AD 251-356), was born in the small village of **Koma al Arus**. He became a hermit after he was orphaned at 18 just before the height of the persecution against the Christians by emperor Diocletian (AD 284-305). By AD 313 not only was Christianity tolerated but it had also been corrupted by becoming the state religion. This led to increasing numbers of hermits following Anthony's example and seeking isolation in desert retreats (see St Catherine's monastery, page 432 and El-Fayoum, page 161). After his death, at the reported age of 105, the location of his grave was kept secret but a small chapel was erected which became the foundation of the monastery. St John the Short sought refuge at the monastery 200 years later and died there.

In the course of its history it has been subject to attacks from the bedouin tribes in the 8th and 9th centuries and the Nasir al-Dawla who destroyed it in the 11th century. It was restored in the 12th century by monks from throughout the Coptic world, only to be attacked again in the 15th century when the monks were massacred and the buildings badly damaged by rebellious servants. Syrian monks were sent to rebuild it in the mid-16th century and it was then inhabited by a mixture of Coptic, Ethiopian and Syrian monks. Its importance rose and many 17th-19th century Coptic patriarchs were chosen from amongst its monks: by the 18th century it was receiving increasing numbers of European visitors. The result has been that the 5-church monastery has developed into a large and virtually self-sufficient modern village which draws water from an ancient spring and grows most of its own food, mills its own grain and bakes its own bread. The whole complex is enormous with the outer walls spanning 2 km. Rituals observed here have hardly changed in the last 16 centuries.

St Anthony's Church, parts of which date back to the 13th century, is the oldest church in the complex. It consists of a central nave, two side chapels and an antechamber. While inside try to identify the apostles in the picture on the south wall! There are four other churches in the complex. **St Mark's Church** dates from 1766 and is reputed to contain the relics of St Mark the Evangelist in a chest on the north wall.

Cave of St Anthony, 276 m above and 2 km northeast of the monastery, is a steep 1-2 hours walk but the view alone from the cave, 690 m above the Red Sea, justifies the climb. The cave, where St Anthony is supposed to have spent the last 25 years of his life, consists of a terrace, chamber, tunnel and balcony. The decorations on the walls are mediaeval graffiti often complemented by more recent additions in the shape of supplications stuck into the cracks of the walls by visiting pilgrims.

The smaller **Monastery of St Paul**, which lies to the southeast of St Anthony's monastery, and is reached via the main coastal road, was built around the cave where St Paul the Theban (AD 228-348) spent his life. Although the dates do not actually match, he is supposed to have fled the persecution of **Decius** (AD 249-251) and arrived in the eastern Desert from Alexandria at the age of 16. He is the earliest hermit on record and was visited by St Anthony to whom he gave a tunic of palm leaves. St Paul apparently acknowledged him as his spiritual superior and St Anthony's Monastery has always overshadowed that of St Paul both theologically and architecturally. ■ *Daily 0900-1700 except during Lent and 25 Nov-7 Jan.*

The larger of the two churches is dedicated to St Michael and there are two sanctuaries. The south one is dedicated to St John the Baptist where a strange 18th century gilded icon depicts the saint's head on a dish. The **Church of St Paul** contains the actual cave where he lived and what are claimed to be his relics which were preserved during the many raids on the monastery. On the third floor of the keep is the **Church of the Virgin** which is unfortunately closed to the public because its wooden floor is dangerous.

El Gouna

Phone code: 065
Colour map 3, grid B5

This is a new up-market resort, with a very attractive coastline, situated just 25 km (40 minutes in a taxi) north of Hurghada. Compared with the bustle of Hurghada this is a very peaceful place to visit. The coastline is a series of lagoons giving privacy for the hotel developments and private villas all of which have been constructed in a style best described as Nubian/Arabesque. There are many uninhabited islands and coral reefs which are exposed only at low tide. The development boasts its own private airport for small planes, a post office, a museum, an observatory, an aquarium and an amphitheatre. There is also a fully functional marina and another planned, a casino, a hospital including a very

El Gouna

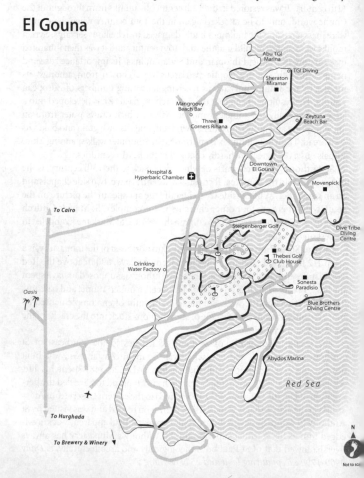

important hyperbaric chamber. Shuttle buses marked Downtown 1 and 2 run from hotels to heart of El Gouna to shops and restaurants.

A *Movenpick*, T/F545160, shuttle bus 30 km from airport. Private airfield, hotel built in terracotta, in tropical gardens with tropical plants and palms framed by the desert behind and the lagoon in front. There are 2 large pools, health club, Turkish bath, disco, a selection of bars and restaurants including El Sayadin on the beach, children's club, children's pool, baby sitting. Associated within the hotel complex is *Nautic Dive Centre* with the latest facilities. Non-divers may join the day boats at US$22 per day. Parasailing, pedalos, snorkelling and water skiing. **A** *Sheraton Miramar*, T545606, F545608. 282 rooms, beach front on 9 separate islands in the lagoon, diving centre in the hotel, health club, beauty salon, choice of restaurants, golf course. **A** *Steigenberger Golf Hotel*, T580141-6, F580147. Set in a golf course, between the lagoon and the mountains retaining a cosy, warm atmosphere. Built round the central pool area. The interiors have been decorated with detail, old golfing prints, and beautiful carpets. Health club fully equipped. Golf course first nine holes open, rest open later in 2000. Club house has outdoor terrace and a la carte restaurant with breathtaking views. **B** *Sonesta Paradisio*, T547934/9, F547933. A sprawling beach-front resort 20 mins from the airport at Hurghada, own private strip for small planes, 3 restaurants, 2 lounges, private beach, 3 pools, watersports, tennis, horse riding. **B** *Three Corners Rihana Resort*, de luxe Nubian style architecture, 1 main restaurant, shuttle bus to beach. 183 rooms, 14 for handicapped, 15 suites with kitchenettes. Low building – just 2 floors, constructed 1999, T580025-9, F580030. Freshwater pool, children's pool. All watersports here, other sports in village eg horseriding and go karting. No pets allowed. **B** *Dawar el Omda*, T545060; **C** *Sultan Bey*, T545600 all domes and arches and **C** *El Khan*, T545060.

Sleeping

No expensive restaurants here – unless you choose unwisely from a menu. *Club House*, located Downtown opposite Dawar El Omda. Try at lunch time the selection of Italian food, freshly prepared. Join an evening beach party. *Kiki's*, Italian food, top floor of museum building just reopened after a total refurbishment, increased seating area but just as cosy. *Paradisio Bakery and Café*. Downtown. For the early bird or very late night snack – sugar coated Danish pastries, muffins and croissants. Open at 0600. *Shahr Zad* – opposite Rihana Hotel, open from 1800-0300. A traditional bedouin tent complete with camel rides and live Egyptian music. Oriental food. Even a belly dancer. *Tamr Henna Food Court*, outdoors only – so dress accordingly. Mixture of Turkish, Egyptian and Italian dishes. Something for everyone. *Horror Pub*, serves the usual Italian cuisine, pizza, tortellini, gnocci while the TV provides entertainment. Take away provision. Stays open later than anyone else. *Café de Paris,* situated on the beach front, considers itself to be the most elegant and romantic restaurant in El Gouna. Good French cuisine. For

Eating

The Red Sea Coast & Eastern Desert

El Gouna downtown

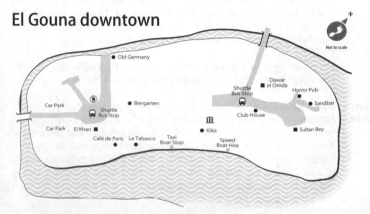

Diving in the Red Sea

Diving here was pioneered in the 1950s by Dr Hans Hass and Jacques Cousteau. Today the popularity of this sport means more and more people can experience the wonders of this special environment and that greater and greater numbers threaten this fragile habitat.

A mixture of deep water fish and surface coral giving a total of over 1,000 species of fish to observe, some 500 species of coral and thousands of invertebrate reef dwellers. The clear waters ensure that the fish can be 'caught' on film.

Sites to visit include sheer drop-offs, sea grass meadows, coral encrusted wrecks, gullies and pinnacles, a new world.

Water temperatures vary. A 3 mm or 5 mm wetsuit is recommended for all year but something thicker for winter wear (18°C) or a prolonged series of dives may be needed.

Liveboard

This method of accessing the dive sights permits divers to reach more remote locations in smaller groups so, in theory, less disturbance is caused at these locations. It provides the diver with accommodation and the opportunity for unlimited dives a day with limited travel.

Most liveboard agents extend all year over the northern waters from Sharm el-Sheikh and Hurghada to Ras Mohammed, Gulf of Suez, Tiran Straits and Port Sudan. In summer they chart south from Marsa Alam to the more isolated reefs and islands. Summer is the best time to dive in the south when the winds and currents are not so strong and the water temperature (here at the Tropic of Cancer) reaches about 30°C.

Boats from Hurghada tend to head northwards to Abu Nawas and Thistegorm, eastwards to Ras Mohammed or southwards to Safaga.

Sleeping

Emperor Divers – 20-25 m long, limited facilities, civilized and comfortable with tolerance.

Emperor Pegasus – 24 m by 7 m, max 16 persons in twin cabins.

Golden Diver – 22 m by 6.5 m, 14 persons in twin cabins.

Crusade Travel – VIP One which has seven cabins, with private facilities, professional crew and PADI Advanced courses available – departs from Sharm el Maya – to Straits of Tira, Straits of Gubal, Abu Nuwas and Thistlegorm and to Ras Mohammed marine park.

Mermaid – wooden hull, built 1998, 16 divers in twin berthed, a/c, en suite rooms, 9 crew.

Miss Nouran – 28 m by 7 m, wooden hull, built 1997, high standard, 16 divers in ensuite cabins (6x2 and 1x4), 8 crew. Full

reservations call ext 4444-4405. **Biergarten**, varied menu from wurst and sauerkraut to spaghetii. Dancing on Wed. **Old Germany**, German-run restaurant provides a hearty meal and traditional desserts of mousse and Weckel pudding. Take aways available. Open 1700 for an early start to the evening. **El Tabasco**, situated on the beach front, noted for its fillet steak and irresistible chocolate souffle. Open very late 7 days a week. Weekends are advertised as big, loud, smoky party nights.

Tower Café; *Zeytuna Beach Bar*; *All Seasons*, T547934; *Morgan Fish*, T547934; *Chez Pascal*, T545162; *Palavrion*, T545160; *Piazza Terrace*, in *Movenpick*.

Bars & nightclubs *Gallery Bar* at *Movenpick*. *Zeytuna Beach Bar*. *Lobby Bar* at *Sonesta Paradisio*, the *Patio Bar* at *Dwar el Omda* or *Sand Bar Pub* – next to *Sultan Bey Hotel*, small in size but great for fun, draught beer, good selection of wine and tasty bar snacks, cold beer and hot music, very popular with divers. *Mangroovy Beach Bar*, special seafood diners with dancing round the bonfire at weekends in season. Access by shuttle bus. Enquire in town. *Movenpick*, *Jazz Bar* next to *El Khan*; *El Arena* – open-air, built in Greco-Roman style, dancing Thu and Fri nights; *Desires* in *Paradiso Sonesta*.

Nitrox and rebreather facilities. Sails in the Straits of Gubal.

Royal Emperor – 29 m by 7 m, steel hull, 14 divers in twin berthed ensuite cabins. Concentration on underwater photography with lab and processing facilities on board. Built specifically for journeys to Marine Park Islands.

Cyclone – 30 m by 7 m, wooden hull, built 1998, 20 divers in 10 twin a/c, ensuite cabins. Cruises to the Straits of Tiran.

From Sharm el-Sheikh – Cyclone, Ghazala I, Ghazala II and Freedom II.
From Hurghada – Emperor Fleet, Golden Diver, Alexandria, Sabrina, Miss Nouran, Amira and Loveman.
From Marsa Alam – Shadia. Sailing out of Marsa Alum gives speedier access to the southern area.

Diving Prices
6/12 days diving US$200-400
5/10 days diving   US$175-350

Diving courses
The prices quoted for PADI diving courses (for which the minimum age is 12 years) should include all diving equipment and materials for the course which should take just five days, three days of theory and work in confined

water/deep swimming pool to put the theory into practice and two days in the ocean completing four open-water dives. After which a new underwater world waits you.

There are three main sections:
    theory – written test after reading the manual and watching a training video
    pool work – confined water training
    open water qualifying dives – in the sea

Courses requiring certification are an extra US$30 per certificate for which you will require two passport photographs. You will also need a log book (on sale in diving resorts) to record your dives (US$8).

Open Water Certification	US$180-300
Advanced Open Water Certification (2 days)	US$190-210
Medic First Aid (1 day)	US$100
Rescue Diver Certification (3-4 days)	US$300-320
Dive Master Certification	US$530-580
Also Under Water Naturalist	US$50
Night Diver	US$60
Multi-level Diver	US$65
Reef Diver	US$65
Wreck Diver	US$100

Entertainment

Cinema: at El Arena twice a week, also theatrical performances. *Cinema Renaissance* has 3 screens with films in Arabic and English.

Sports

Diving: this location provides for the visitor some flora and fauna not normally found any further north and gives opportunity for day boats to reach dives normally accessed only by liveboards. Dives may include the 2 wreck sites as well as the coral gardens and pinnacles. **Diving Clubs in El Gouna**: include *Blue Brothers Diving Centre*, Divers' Lodge, T545161; *The Dive Tribe* at *Movenpick*, *TGI Diving*, T549702; *Subex Paradisio*, T547934. Try also windsurfing, sailing, parascending and power boats (T580580). Other than watersports there is horse riding, tennis and an international grade 18-hole golf course.

Go-Karts, El Gouna T549702

Transport

Air: Orascom fly turbo prop to **Cairo** on Sat evening and return Thu afternoon at US$125 return.

Directory

Bank. There is a bank open for normal business hours. Money may also be changed in the hotels.
Useful telephone numbers Emergency numbers as for Hurghada. See below.

The Red Sea Coast & Eastern Desert

Hurghada

Ins and outs

Getting there
Phone code: 065
Colour map 3, grid B5

Most visitors arrive at Hurghada from the airport, 6 km southwest of the town centre which can be reached by taxi (E£15-20), or by bus or service taxi which stop on the main north-south 'highway' at the south end of the town. This newly improved airport is now 'international' standard with an increased capacity. Public transport will drop you in Dahar. If you arrive by service taxi you will be centrally located (just off El Nasr Road), you can walk to the central hotels from here. Arriving at either bus station you will need to take a short minibus ride unless you stay at the hotels near the Upper Egypt Station. Expect to pay 25pt-1£E, possibly 50pt-1£E for baggage, especially if it takes up seating. The main town and most of the hotels lie to the west and north of the area's main physical feature, a barren rock outcrop known as Ugly Mountain to the east of which is the public beach and the Red Sea. About 2 km south along the main highway is Hurghada's port after which is a number of the major holiday villages. There is a road all the way south to the Sudanese border.

Getting around

Although it is easy to walk around the relatively compact town it is necessary, when trying to get to the port or the holiday villages to the south of town, to take cheap local buses and minibuses or the town's taxis which are among the most expensive in the country. Alternatively cars and bicycles can be hired from some of the hotels. The tourist office, open daily 0830-1500, T444420, is the once-smart new building opposite the *Marine Sports Club* on the west side of the main road. But it now falls far short of its glossy beginnings. Given the intense competition between travel agencies and dive centres, there is probably little additional information that this office can provide.

Hurghada lies on the Red Sea about half way between Suez and the Sudanese border. It extends along the coast for 25 km. It is 506 km southeast of Cairo, 395 km south of Suez and 269 km northeast of Luxor.

In some ways it is an ideal location for a new tourist development because it is in a virtually uninhabited region, its origins a small fishing village, and a long way from the Islamic fundamentalist strongholds. This means that the hotels and their guests do not overburden the local infrastructure or offend the sensibilities of the local population. Instead hotels and holiday villages have been built which, with the exception of fresh water which is supplied from the Nile valley, are largely self-contained. They employ workers from the major cities. Unfortunately, although there are many very good hotels, in its dash for growth the government has allowed the 'get-rich-quick' private sector to erect some less attractive accommodation. In truth the area has been developed too quickly since the first constructions in 1992 and frequently without adequate controls and has thus repeated the mistakes of some resorts on the northern Mediterranean shores, but with maturity the region has gained its own character.

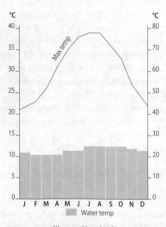

Climate: Hurghada

Diving in Hurghada - tales and tips

A majority of diving centres in the area cater for the German market, so if you want to take any qualifications make sure your instructor can speak your mother tongue. You can't be safe if you cannot understand the instructor. "We all speak the same language underwater," is a sign you should be looking elsewhere.

Be careful in choosing your dive centre – safety, environmental impact and price should be on your agenda.

Make sure you are insured to dive.

Bargain basement prices could mean that short cuts are being made.

Fly-by-night operators do exist. Always be on your guard. Go to an approved operator and watch out for scams, eg non-PADI centres flying PADI flags.

The best options are those centres which have regular guests on dive holidays flying in from abroad.

Common tricks include: cheap deals, making you feel guilty or rude if you refuse, sudden loss of understanding of your language, free desert/restaurant trips,

offers of marriage! Also talk of donations to the decompression chamber, Sinai National Parks and Giftun Islands – these are virtually all compulsory and it is the diver that pays. (The government has introduced a US$1 a day charge for the decompression chamber and a US$2 tax for the Giftun Island Reef).

HEPCA (Hurghada Environmental Protection and Conservation Association), T065-446674, hepca@hepca.org, is concerned about environmental destruction. It organizes clean ups at various Red Sea sites. Some dive centres are members, but this is not necessarily a guarantee of safety.

Membership of the Red Sea Diving and Watersport Association *and the* Egyptian Underwater Sports Association *is not proof of safety either. Membership is a requirement of law.*

Contact PADI, BSAC, CMAS and SSI while at home for advice and check out the international diving press.

Check if dive centres pick you up or you have to arrange your own transport.

While Hurghada's facilities undoubtedly offer good cheap beach holidays it has been partially achieved by removing any trace of local Egyptian culture. The Egyptian government has pledged considerable investment to create further leisure facilities here. Hurghada itself has about 50,000 permanent residents employed in tourism and its related activities, in fishing and in boat construction and repair. There are two harbours, one for the local fishing boats and in the other, the marina, boats associated with sporting activities, excursions and the ferry to Sharm el-Sheikh.

Sights

This is not just another place to toast on the beach. It is now an international resort for watersports – if you can do it in the water, you can do it here. A few hotels have very fine coral gardens actually on their site and there are plenty of coral islands offshore from which to study the hidden life below the warm blue waters. The best hotels with coral gardens are *Safir*, *Arabia Beach*, *Three Corners* and *Shedwan*. In Hurghada life revolves around the beach, watersports and nightlife.

The Red Sea Coast & Eastern Desert

Diving Some of the best diving sites are **Um Gamar,** 1½ hrs north. It is a plateau of beautiful soft and hard corals with a good drop off and cave. **Sha'ab al Erg**, 1½ hrs north. Coral plateau including table coral and if you are lucky, manta rays and dolphins. The **Careless Reef**. Here you may see shark. There is a spectacular drop off and ergs. For advanced divers, due to the currents. **Giftun Islands**, close to Hurghada and thus very popular. Fortunately they possess a number of reefs still with plenty of fish including moray eels. **Fanadir**, popular and close to Hurghada. A pretty reef wall and drop off with nice soft corals. **Sha'ab Abu Ramada**, 40 mins south with a good drop off, lots of fish and coral. Usually a drift dive.

Further afield are a series of islands such as **Shadwan Island**, **Tawlah** and **Gubal**, around which there are less spoiled dive sites with chances of seeing pelagic fish and dolphins.

Excursions All-day boat excursions to **Giftun Island**, now often overcrowded with boats anchored offshore, are available from most hotels which usually add a 20-25% commission to include rental of snorkelling equipment. Expect your tour to include a fish barbecue and perhaps a trip in a glass bottomed boat. The same operators, including *Flying Dolphin Sea Trips*, *Nefertiti Diving Centre* and *Sunshine Sea Trips* also organize longer boat trips including three-day trips to **Gobal Island**, overnight excursions to Giftun, and expeditions to the deeper reefs such as the **House of Sharks** (20 km south) where the experienced divers can see hammerheads and tiger sharks and other exotic marine life. To view marine life and keep dry there is the Finnish-built a/c 44 seat **Sinbad Submarine** offering a two hour round trip including 1 hour underwater which should be booked the day before. Transfer by boat 30 minutes, out to submarine, goes down to 22 m with diver in front attracting fish with food (not a recommended procedure). Carries 44 passengers. Reservations on T444688-90. Trips every hour between 0900 and 1600. Price US$50 for adults and US$25 for children under 12. **Aquascope** has a deep hull with glass sides. Transfer to it from the *Marine Sports Club* near the *Grand Hotel*. It travels to Magawish Island and back. Operates 1000-1400 and each trip takes two hours, costs US$40, reservations necessary, T548249.

The **Marine Museum** is about 7 km to the north of the town centre (take a taxi) and is associated with the *National Institute of Oceanography and Fisheries*. A good place to start to learn about the marine life of the area with stuffed examples of coral reef fish, shark, manta rays and associated bird

Hurghada islands, reefs & dive sites

Dive sites
1 Abu Ramada North
2 Abu Ramada South (The Aquarium)
3 Careless Reef
4 El Aruk
5 El Fanadir
6 Erg Abu Ramada
7 Erg Sabina
8 Erg Somaya
9 Fanous East
10 Fanous West
11 Giftun Police
12 Gota Abu Ramada
13 Little Giftun
14 Sha'ab Disha
15 Sha'ab Eshta
16 Sha'ab Farasha
17 Sha'ab Sabina
18 Sha'ab Tiffany
19 Sha'ab Torf
20 Sha'ab Rur
21 Stone Beach
22 Turtle Bay
23 Um Gamar North
24 Um Gamar South

life as well as samples of coral and shells. ■ *Daily 0800-1700, E£5 for the museum and its adjacent* **Red Sea Aquarium**. The *Aquarium* on Sharia el Corniche adjacent to *Three Corners Village* is quite small but has live specimens in well marked tanks and is well worth the E£5, camera E£2, video E£5. ■ *Daily 0900-2300*.

There are public beaches which are rather dirty at Dahar near Three Corners, near the Port at Sigala and after the V junction on Sharia Sheraton Sigala. (E£1). At all three, and in particular the first two it is socially unacceptable, and inadvisable to wear a bathing costume or less. In any case you will invite unwelcome attention. These beaches are really for Egyptians and you will notice the women sit in a proper manner on upright chairs and if they do venture into the sea, they are fully clothed. Men can wear shorts.

Beach news & etiquette

If you are not staying at a hotel with beach access, the only option is to pay to use one of the resorts' beaches. This will cost between £E10-40 daily. Don't feel tempted to bathe at what looks like a building site or a bit of derelict beach as you will invite unwanted attention.

Time can be spent wandering around the **bazaars** of Dahar even if you don't intend to buy. In the short term it's an interesting experience for all your senses. Touts trying every line you can imagine, the noise and jostle of people, bikes, donkeys, cars. Bright tempting souvenirs, tired white donkeys, men in jallabahs and flip flops, women in pink nighties (jallabah) next to scantily clad tourists, the smell of shisha pipes, herbs, carpets, dead chickens and bad drains.

If you want to observe a bit of the real life of Hurghada residents take a stroll around the "Egyptian areas" behind the *Three Corners Empire* Hotel, near the "mountain" behind Sharia Abdel Aziz, various other side streets in Dahar or by the ferry port in Sigala. The housing is pretty crumbly and the street strewn with litter. Here you will find women staying at home. They are traditionally dressed (well covered), scruffy children play in the dirt of the streets, boys are bold and loud and girls in hejabs wander from school in demure, giggly groups. It's always noisy from cockerels to car horns and with cart vendors continuously calling to sell their wares. There's been a bit of a move to clean up these areas because of the tourists but you can still get a bit of a glance of life as it really is in the rest of Egypt.

You can make an interesting stroll around the old harbour area and see the bright coloured fishing vessels, boat construction yards and small shops catering for Egyptians. In the autumn there are some spectacular sunsets so try and head for a view of the mountains.

Essentials

There are many officially registered hotels and many other non-registered ones and new ones are being erected all the time. Although most visitors pre-book their accommodation as part of a package with their flight there should be no problem, except perhaps during the winter high season, for independent travellers to find a room. All of the hotels have roof tanks to store fresh water which is piped in from the Nile Valley but, depending on their capacity and electricity supplies, there can be problems with the water provisions at certain times. If the promised tourist developments along the coast towards Safaga do go ahead it will be necessary to build at least one desalination plant because the water supply is the main obstacle to any major expansion in tourist numbers in the area. There are more than 100 good quality hotels listed in the latest tourist literature. Much confusion arises when the buildings are purchased by another international hotel chain and names are changed, for example the *Sheraton* becoming the *Meridien*. This is becoming more frequent – stay calm the beds are still there. Single female travellers should always be on their guard, when staying at budget hotels.

Sleeping

The Red Sea Coast & Eastern Desert

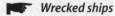 ## Wrecked ships

Satellite images indicate over 180 wrecks on the bed of the Red Sea. By far the most wrecks are to be found around the dangerous Straits of Gubal at the mouth of the Gulf of Suez. Access easiest from Hurghada or Sharm el-Sheikh.

Thistlegorm, was a 126 m long, 5,000-tonne English cargo ship which was damaged on 6 October 1941 by a long range German bomber and sank without firing a defensive shot or delivering her goods to the awaiting British troops fighting in the North Africa campaign. Nine of the crew lost their lives. She lies on the massive Sha'ab Ali reef, on the northern edge of the Straits of Gubal, under 30 m of water just as she went down complete with an incredible cargo of armaments. There are jeeps, trucks, motorbikes, tanks, train cars, a locomotive and an 'explosive' collection of ammunition ranging from rifle bullets to mortar shells, along with uniforms and regulation boots. She was 'discovered' by Jacques Cousteau in 1956 but visits by casual divers only began in the last eight years to this war grave.

Dunraven, a 82 m sail-equipped steam ship has been lying on the reef of Sha'ab Mahmood just south of Beacon rock since 1876 and is now covered with soft corals and sponges and each year looks more attractive. She lies bottom up with the bow 15 m and the stern (propeller still in place) 28 m below the surface. Her journey from Bombay to Newcastle on Tyne remains incomplete. This English merchant ship carrying a cargo of spices and exotic timber is now home to lion fish and other colourful inhabitants.

Carnatic, once a 90 m luxurious Greek steamship is a sad tale. With a passenger list numbering 230 and a cargo of gold reported to be then worth £40,000, she hit the reef at Shab Abu Nuas on 13 September 1869. The conditions were calm, the ship remained upright and life for the passengers remained as normal until the vessel snapped in two without warning. Survivors were taken to Shadwan island but 27 people were drowned. £32,000 worth of gold was rescued, but where is the rest? Perhaps it is still there waiting for the lucky diver. The abundance

AL *Conrad International Resort*, T443250-6, F443258-9, just 10 mins from airport and 15 mins from downtown areas, has shuttle bus to centre. Many restaurants – *La Palma* for breakfast and buffet dinner; Chinese menu in *Ginger House*; El Khan for local flavour and colour; Sunrise pool-side bar; *Café Trottoir* a French style coffee house overlooking gardens and sea; *Poseidon* recommended for fish and seafood, disco bar and *Trocadero* piano bar for relaxation. Sports including volleyball, a huge pool, billiards, 2 all-weather tennis courts, basketball, health club, with all usual facilities, money exchange, shops. same day laundry, medical clinic. Also diving centre. Very friendly staff. **AL** *Hurghada Hilton Resort*, T442116-8, F442113, 10-15 mins from airport and from town centre. Good range of high standard facilities, 161 rooms located round the main pool and near the beach, 40 garden rooms in the hotel block on the desert side of the road all with a/c, bath/shower. All Hilton facilities, free day time shuttle to town centre, 2 pools, private marina, tennis, squash, health club, dive centre. Selection of restaurants, bars, tennis, pool. Good service one would expect from this chain of hotels. **AL** *Intercontinental*, T443911, F443910. Highly recommended as the best in town – and one of the best in Egypt. Very new, opened 1996, secluded bay, large pool, 3 restaurants, bars, health club, 3 floodlit tennis courts, 2 squash courts, billiards, medical centre, horse riding, shops, diving centre. – sheer luxury. **AL** *Marriott*, T446950, F443970. Tranquil and relaxed, large pool, 3 bars, shops, watersport and dive centre, health club, 2 floodlit, tennis courts, 2 a/c squash courts. **AL** *Royal Palace Hotel*, PO Box 18, T443660-6. 120 rooms, new, private beach, 3 restaurants, good food, guests are 80% German and 20% British tour groups, *Sonesta Diving Centre* with 8 instructors, easy access to beach for disabled, recommended as one of the best hotels in Hurghada.

of sponges and corals and the favourable light conditions make this a popular for underwater photography.

Giannis D was another Greek vessel, 99 m long and full of cargo. She ran aground on the reef at Shab Abu Nuas on 19 April 1983 and later broke in two and sank. The shallowest remains are just 8m under the surface allowing easy access to the bridge and the engine room in the stern. Giannis D which is now covered with soft corals is considered one of the best wreck dives.

Aida II was sunk in 1957 to the northwest of Big Brother Island. The stern section of this supply ship, all that now remains, is encrusted with hard and soft corals and is gradually becoming part of the reef that caused it to sink. At between 30 m and 70 m it makes an interesting dive, but only for the experienced diver, and the schools of barracuda add to the interest.

Chrisoula K was a 106 m Greek cargo ship carrying Italian tiles which struck the northwest corner of Shab Abu Nuas reef at full speed. The wreck remains upright but at an angle with the bow nearer the surface. The hull and much of the superstructure can be visited with safety but the badly damaged bow section should be avoided in rough weather. Adjacent to the Chrisoula K is an unnamed wreck sloping down from the lighthouse.

Other wrecks:

Off El Quseir, at Brothers Islands, are two wrecks. One is an unnamed freighter at the depth of about 80 m with its stern firmly wedged into the sea bed. There are strong currents and viewing the corals on this wreck is only for experienced divers.

Further offshore, between Golbal Island and Tawila lies a British 4000 ton steamer which was sunk on 8 October 1941 (see date for Thistlegorm above). The cargo of coals being carried from Cardiff remains with the wreck which lies at a depth of 50 m, the deck at 30 m and the funnel at 18 m.

Hurghada port has its own wreck, an Egyptian minesweeper sunk in 1973 during the Arab-Israeli war, by friendly fire. It is at a depth of 28 m.

A *Grand Hotel*, T443748/9, F443750, just 10 mins drive from airport, on own sandy beach. 549 rooms, all have balcony/terrace, standard rooms have shower, superior rooms are larger and have bath and shower, several restaurants, coffee shop, bars, disco, tennis, health club, watersports on beach, very comfortable and lively beach resort. **A** *Hilton Plaza*, off Corniche, T549745, F547597, 217 quality rooms, own private beach and marina, professional diving centre, 4 restaurants: *La Gondola* serving Italian food, *Sea Grill* on the beach, *Coral Café* in Lobby and *Terrace Grill* by the pool. **A** *Magawish Tourist Village*, south of the airport, T442620-2, F442759. 314 rooms, excellent standard, private bay and beach to south of port, offers all the normal facilities plus a wide range of watersports and children's activities. **A** *Meridien*, T442000-2, F442333. 130 rooms, to south of town, 8 km from airport, 65 rooms in distinctive circular main building, 9 pool-side cabanas and 10 2-storey 4 room chalets on 2 very good beaches, all luxury facilities, 3 restaurants, bars, large pool, tennis, watersports, boat cruises, glass bottomed boat, fishing trips and barbecue. **A** *Sofitel Club*, T447261-69, F447260, El Corniche, directly on beach, just 20 mins drive from airport. 312 rooms with balcony, many interconnecting, most have sea view, all facilities, various restaurants, bars, disco, fitness club, spa with jacuzzi and steam bath, tennis, squash, shops, outdoor amphitheatre for entertainments, kids club, pool, horse riding. Free activities including archery, gymnastics, kayaking, water gym. To pay – water skiing, wind surfing, catamaran sailing, ideal for families, very cosmopolitan. Restaurants including *The Terrace* with German food, German music and German beer, also *O'Reilly's Irish Pub* with Irish beer (Guinness) and Irish food.

The Red Sea Coast & Eastern Desert

B *Arabia Beach Tourist Village*, T548790, F441792, 9 km from centre, very large, well equipped, new, mainly German guests, saltwater pools, tennis, squash, courts, jetski and water-skiing, fitness centre, *Nautico Diving Centre* with 6 instructors.
B *Hilton Villas* on desert side of the road opposite main Hilton. 22 2-storey villas with 4 bedrooms, 3 bathrooms (shower) and 2 lounges and a kitchen sleeping up to 12 people, built round the second pool, bar plus full use of all facilities at *Hilton Hotel*, excellent value for groups. See *Hurghada Hilton* for more details.
B *Sinbad el Mashrabia*, Sharia Sheraton, T443330-1, F443344. 140 rooms, very good Moorish style 4-star hotel, located to south of port, 3 pools, parasailing and excellent watersports, guests 75% German. **B** *Safir*, El Corniche, T442901-3, F442904, on its own beach-front lagoon, 10 mins drive from airport. 123 rooms with usual facilities,

Hurghada

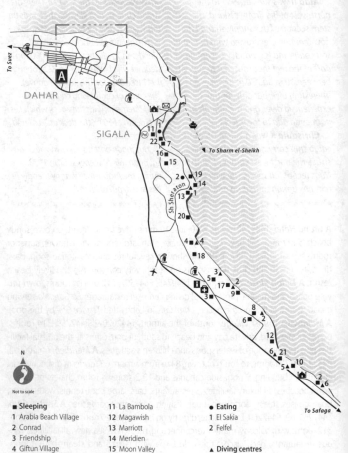

■ Sleeping

1	Arabia Beach Village
2	Conrad
3	Friendship
4	Giftun Village
5	Grand
6	Hilton Villas
7	Helnan Regina
8	Hurghada Hilton Resort
9	Intercontinental
10	Jasmine
11	La Bambola
12	Magawish
13	Marriott
14	Meridien
15	Moon Valley
16	New Ramoza
17	Princess Club/Palace
18	Royal Palace
19	Safir
20	Sinbad el Mashrabia
21	Sofitel Club
22	White House

● Eating

1 El Sakia
2 Felfel

▲ Diving centres

1 Diving World
2 Emperor Divers
3 Euro Divers
4 James & Mac
5 Jasmine Diving Centre
6 Sub Aqua

Related map
Dahar, page 460

To Suez
DAHAR
SIGALA
To Sharm el-Sheikh
Sh Sheraton
N
Not to scale
To Safaga

variety of restaurants, bars, shops, billiards, pool with sun deck and a marina with aqua sports centre, a lively hotel, comfortable. **B** *Three Corners Hotel*, deluxe, downtown adjacent Khan El Khalili shopping centre and bars, hence lively atmosphere also hospital and Sharia Sayed Karim, T549200-9, F549212. 366 rooms, 3 restaurants – international, seafood and oriental. Diving at Khan El Kjalili shopping centre and windsurfing and snorkelling at *Three Corners Village*, airport 7 km, 2 outdoor freshwater pools, beach at 200 m is pebble here, bank, laundry. No pets.

C *Giftun Village*, T442666-7, F442666. 391 comfortable bungalows set in a vast private sandy beach a little out of town, pool, squash, tennis, all watersports are free except diving, windsurfing and tennis lessons, main restaurant provides buffet meals and there are bars and discos for evening entertainment. *Barakuda Dive Centre* within the hotel. **C** *Jasmine Holiday Village*, 6 km south of airport, T446442, F442441. 362 rooms, good standard, so large that it is a long walk from the main building to the beach, has own diving centre. **C-D** *Three Corners Empire*, 82 rooms, central, 2 pools, near hospital on Shari Sayed Karim, T549200, F3369049. A bar and 2 restaurants, no pets, 200 m to the beach. Use of facilities at *Three Corners Village*. **C-D** *Three Corners Village*, El Corniche, T547816-7, F547514. Belgian management, central location, situated on a beautiful sandy beach, 136 rooms with magnificent views and good facilities, 2 restaurants, 2 bars, freshwater pool, dive centre, windsurfing centre, volley ball, minigolf, No pets allowed

D *Gezira*, off Sharia El Bahr, T447785, F443708. 30 good rooms built around a courtyard, located in northeast of town near the poor public beach, restaurant, bar and discotheque. **D** *La Bambola*, El Corniche, T44085. 56 en suite rooms with balconies, clean, good, up-market. Highly recommended budget hotel, located in town centre, 200 m from beach, restaurant, rooftop bar, pool, barbecue, discotheque. **D** *Moon Valley*, Sharia Sheraton, T442811, F443830. 30 rooms, former backpackers' retreat which moved up-market, located to south of port, private beach, diving courses around a small coral reef. Recommended. **D** *Princess Club/Palace*, T443100, F443109. 160 spacious rooms, 2 separate parts directly opposite one another about 3 km south of town, *Palace* offers better accommodation than the cheaper *Club*, both offer good service, cool, relaxing atmosphere, main building has European and Egyptian buffet restaurants, eat also at hotel's private beach or by main swimming pool. The *Fox and Hounds* serves drinks and the *Vienna* serves snacks, bar, shops, bank, squash, tennis, (floodlit), gym, pool, private beach, windsurfing with instruction, hire of jetskis, waterskiing, pedalos, British managed *Red Sea Scuba School* located in Princess Village, *Emperor Divers* located within the complex. **D** *Shedwan Golden Beach*, T447044, F448045. 152 rooms, reasonable standard, town centre location, restaurant, bar, disco, banking, private beach, pool, tennis, squash, dive centre, guests mainly French, Belgian and German.

E *Friendship Village*, T443100-2, F447800. 129 rooms, budget hotel, use of facilities at *Princess Club*, large open-air restaurant, pizzeria, shop and laundry service, clean and spacious rooms, buffet breakfast, 2 tennis courts, pool table, use of beach and facilities across the road at *Princess Palace*, doctor on call. **E** *Mena House*, T442303. 20 rooms, budget hotel which caters mainly for students, restaurant, bar, oriental cabaret and belly dancing, private beach, windsurfing, diving with multi-lingual instructors, and day trips to Giftun Island.

F *California*, Dahar, T549101, good location for reaching downtown or the sea on foot. Some rooms have balconies, some with sea view. Reasonably clean. Breakfast available. **F** *Casablanca*, near public beach, generally the rooms are quite large and clean. **F** *Happy Land Hotel*, El Sheik Sebak St off 23rd July St, a dismal place, but rooms with bathroom are clean. Shared facilities, reasonable. **F** *New Ramoza*, Hurghada. 43 rooms with a/c or fans and balconies, good value, popular with students, small private beach,

TV lobby, and disco. The **F** *Old Ramoza*, just next door, has 24 rooms with fans, communal showers, guests are students or Egyptians. **F** *Pharaohs*, around the corner from *California*. Rooms vary in quality, best are on top floor where a sea view is available. **E-F** *Ramses Hotel*, on dirt road fro Sharia Arab el Dahar. Best in the area, rooms are quite clean, toilets not so. A/c available in some rooms. **F** *Shakespeare Hotel*, T546256, on the edge of the Three Corners area by the roundabout on Sharia Sayyed. Large, but dingy rooms. Some rooms better than others, communal lounge areas with fridge. **F** *St George Hotel*, off Sharia El Nasr, off 23rd of July St, from where it's signposted, T548246, rooms dingy, but hotel is pleasant with roof view. **F** *White House*, Sheraton, T443688, near old harbour. Very clean, up-market budget hotel, German owned, 45 comfortable a/c rooms with bath and balconies, decent restaurant, TV lounge, guests can use facilities of *Giftun Village* which is a short taxi ride away – for divers this transfer is free. There are numerous small, cheap, unclassified hotels too.

Youth hostels *New Tourist Centre*, T442432. 42 beds, kitchen, overnight fee E£5 includes breakfast, parking. *International Hostel* (only one in country of this higher grade), beside *Aquarium*. T/F544989. 160 beds, family rooms, meals, kitchen, laundry, parking, fee of E£25 per night.

Camping: There are so many cheap hotels that camping is unnecessary. The site most recommended is the *National Youth Camp*, 5 km north of town, E£5 per night. **BEWARE If camping on the coast, large areas of shoreline are still mined, enter fenced-off areas at your peril**.

Dahar

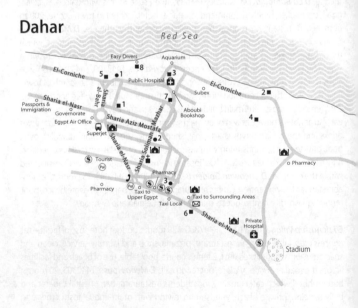

■ Sleeping			● Eating
1 Gezira		5 Shedwan	1 Chez Pascal
2 Hilton Plaza		6 Sunshine	2 Portofino
3 International Hostel		7 Three Corners Empire	3 Red Sea
4 Panorama		8 Three Corners Village	

Besides the hotels there are a number of places to eat in Hurghada.

Eating

Expensive: *Lacost de Mirette*, beach restaurant.

Mid-range: *Chez Miky* for excellent seafood, T441715. *Chez Pascal*, Belgiun-run restaurant, fresh lobster, seafood gourmet and vegetarian dishes, pizza and pasta and home made ice cream. *El Sakia*, off Sharia Sheraton, Sigala. Beach bar, restaurant and fish market restaurant. If you eat at the latter you pay per kilo, otherwise you pay E£11 plus for fish or poultry and E£35 for a seafood platter, T442497. Fish specialities – choose your own from the pond, oriental meals too. Highly recommended for the atmosphere. Does excellent BBQ. *Lagoona* at *Hilton Resort*. A fish restaurant and international dishes, open aspect gives breathtaking views, open daily 1930-2330, T443567. *Portofino* Italian seafood and pasta specialities, by General Hospital, Downtown, T546250. *Jocker Fish Restaurant* on Midan Sheraton, has a long-standing reputation. Frequented by tourists and locals.

Cheap: There are several restaurants, cafés and food stalls in the centre of town of which the best are probably the *Red Sea Restaurant*, with roof terrace, for good fish dishes; *Nefertiti* at the south end of Sharia Abdel Aziz Mustafa and *Golden Spur Restaurant*, steaks and burgers and Mexican food, opposite *Marriott Hotel*, T444414. *Tamar Hena Café* is a good place to watch the bikes and donkeys, located under the *Golf Hotel* in Sigala. Fast food outlets include: *Rossi Pizzeria*, Sigala, T446012; *Pizza Hut* and *KFC* on village road beside *Sindbad*. In Dahar there is *Pronto*, up the dirt road opposite the supermarket near *Papas 2*. Used by Egyptians. A typical meal is a'aish (like pitta bread), small salad and a meat (kofta, chicken, pigeon or fish). Also fruit juices from US$1-4. *Café Cheers* near *Papas 2*, used by tourists and locals. Has pizzas, burgers, billiards and email facilities. *Amon Grill* by trees on Sharia Sayyed has burgers and shishtawook for under US$1.50. Take away available. *Restaurant Riviera* on Sharia Abdel Aziz opposite Pizza Tarboush. Authentic and friendly. *Pizza Tarboush* opposite has student discount. *Quick Cook*, Sharia al Horreya, where you can sit and watch the chaos of the bazaar has shawerma for US$1. *Felfela*, Sharia Sheraton, T442410, popular, modestly-priced Egyptian food, overlooking the sea. A little out of town, but worth it for the view, and the good quality food. *Pharaohs*, on 23rd July St, fish, meat and kebabs.

At the last count there were over 100 bars in Hurghada. They include: *Cheers* open 24 hrs at the *Shedwan Hotel*; *Papas 2* on the v junction of Sharia Sheraton and El Hadaba in Sigala, very popular with the diving fraternity; *Peanuts Bar* next to *Empire Hotel*; *The Pub*, *Hilton Resort* with a variety of draught beers, and local drinks, open 1700-0200, T443567; *Daoud's Pub and Indian restaurant* – authentic Indian food, many vegetarian dishes; *Fisherman's Pub* in *Giftun Village*. If you want somewhere by the sea try the *Chill* near *New Ramoza Hotel*, *Le Sakia* and *Felfela* in Sigala. The *Chill* has BBQs, a dance night, full moon party and diver/tourist volleyball matches.

Bars & nightclubs

As a major tourist resort there is less concern about offending Islamic sensibilities. As a result, besides the main hotel restaurants which serve beer, there are many clubs in town including the *Cha Cha Disco*, next to *Shedwan*, which is open until 0300, and those at the major hotels. These include *Kalaboush* in *Arabella Hotel*, which claims the first karaoke bar, and is popular.

There are plenty of belly dancing shows, at all the big hotels on a nightly basis, mostly performed by Russian women.

If you want the real thing visit the tea shops found around Dahar. There are a number by the small mosque in the centre. Strictly speaking they're for men only, but as foreigners you'll be allowed to sit, sip tea and watch the world go by, just as the locals do. (if the men seem hostile choose another). There are also numerous tourist cafés

Cafés & tea shops

including those mentioned here as restaurants and bars. You could also try sugar cane juice E£1, fresh orange E£3, or whatever fruit is in season, at the only juice shop in Hurghada on Sharia Sayyed, next to *Supermarket Rashidy*, 3 corners. A pleasant café to visit is **Grand Café** on Sharia Sheraton Sigala, just after the v junction. Here at last you can relax and contemplate the stars. The café with dim light and a fountain almost has a Mediterranean feel and overlooks the beach and sea. You can also eat fish here from about £E15. Whilst you're enjoying the lack of hassle you could ask owner Kelal to tell you tales of how it used to be in Hurghada before major tourist expansion. *La Torta* coffee shop, Sharia Sheikh Sabak, has nice cakes and icecream and Ramadan biscuits.

Entertainment **Casino**: at *Intercontinental Hotel*. **Cinema**: There's one in Sigala near *McDonalds* and one in El Gouna.

Shopping Hurghada has very few local shops although all of the major hotels and holiday villages have shopping arcades which cater for the tourists' requirements. You name it and in the souvenir field you can buy it in Hurghada. T- shirts, towels, carpets, jewellery, scarabs, Shisha pipes, papyrus, pyramids, stuffed camels - the list is endless. If buying gold or silver make sure it's stamped and you get a certificate of authenticity. Remember trade in coral and some animals and fish is illegal. Herbs should be much cheaper than at home. Look around the bazaar area, or find the *Red Sea Restaurant* and go straight at each junction - these stalls may have better bargains. Duty free goods can be bought at the Pyramid at the roundabout in Sigala and next to the *Royal Palace* and *Ambassador* hotels. Your passport stamp for duty free is now only valid for one day. There are supermarkets on Sharia Sayyed, 3 Corners and Sharia Abdel Aziz. Small shops, selling limited provisions, such as *Andalus* shop on Sharia Sayyed can be found throughout Dahar. Fruit and veg is easy to get in the Mosque square and by *Quick Cook* in the center. It is now possible to obtain most toiletry and feminine requirements although, as these are imports, they are considerably more expensive than in Europe. If you are travelling further south this is your last chance to stock up on products such as shower gel, moisturizer, tampons, contact lens solution and hair conditioner.

Bookshops: *Aboudi Bookshop*, near *Three Corners Empire*. Good selection of European books, maps and guides. *Al Ahram* in *Hotel Intercontinental* with daily newspapers in Arabic and English (sometimes just 1 day old). *Jetline* in *Arabia Beach* with a good selection of books on the Red Sea. *Pyramid Bookshop* in *Jasmine Village* with international newspapers.

Sports **Ballooning** over the desert, $180 per person for 5-6 hr trip including one hour in the air, breakfast with the bedouin and a jeep ride across the desert. *Cast Ballooning* T444928.

Diving: visitors come to Hurghada for the diving as the Red Sea has a high world ranking for this sport. **Diving Clubs in Hurghada**: this is a selection of the better diving clubs available, choose with care, diving is a dangerous sport, check the qualifications, see what safety precautions are in place. Cheap may not be best. *Dive Point* at *Coral Beach*, T447162, hurghada@dive-point.com; *Diving World*, *Le Meridien*, T442000; *Easy Divers*, *Three Corners Village*, T548816, easydive@intouch.com, has good reputation, caters for all levels with instructors speaking numerous languages; *Emperor Divers*, T442119, info.hurghada@emperordivers.com at *Princess Palace*, T443100 and *Hilton*, T/F443751; *Euro Divers*, *Grand Hotel*, T443751; *James and Mac*, T442665, info@james/mac.com, *Giftun Village*, good reputation; *Jasmine Diving Centre*, *Jasmine Village*, T446455, info@jasmin-diving.com; *Orca*, T444150, orcaredsea@hotmail.com, *La Pacha Hotel*, opposite *McDonalds*, German run, but instructors speak French and English; *Rudi Direkt*, T442960, German-run, will collect divers; *Sub Aqua* at *Sofitel* and *Conrad*, T/F442473, sofiedive@hurghadaie-eg.com, www.subaqua-diveteam.de;

Subex, T547593, redsea@subex.org, office opposite *Sandbeach Hotel*, has very good reputation. (See boxes page 450 and page 453 for details about diving.)

Horseriding At *Hotel Intercontinental*. **Quad Bike** For a short, but expensive desert trip, *Friendship Village*, T0101567571. **Volleyball** At most of the beachside hotels and the *Chill Bar*.

Windsurfing is particularly good at Hurghada because of the gusty winds usually 4-8 on Beaufort Scale and equipment of varying weights can be hired from a number of outlets. Many hotels offer equipment but much of it is outdated. Check your choice of centre has a rescue boat that works. The best equipment is found at centres offering windsurf holiday packages. Try *Planet Windsurf* at *Three Corners Village*, *Happy Surf* (German-run) at *Magawish*, *Jasmine Village*, *Giftun Village* and *Sofitel*. Expect to pay about E£50 per hr, E£150 for one day and E£610 for a week. **Jet skiing** and **water skiing** Jet skis can be hired for E£200 per hour and waterskis from E£220. **Snorkelling** Boats with motors to tow or for fishing or snorkelling can be hired from E£800 per hour depending on size. *Three Corners*, *Arabia* and *Shedwan* hotels all have house reefs, but the best reefs are offshore. A day's snorkelling including lunch can set you back US$20-40. It is cheaper to take your own lunch and water if that is an option. Good snorkelling sites include Giftun Islands, Fanadir, Um Gamar.

Sailing boats are available too. Catamarans and Toppers are best found at the windsurf schools. Pedalos and banana boats can be found at the larger hotels. **Fishing** contact the *Marine Sports Club*, next to the *Grand Hotel*, T442974. Remember spear fishing is illegal in the Red Sea.

Watersports

Besides the independent travel agents there is at least one in each major hotel. *Eastmar,* 12-13 Shopping Centre, T444581; *EgyptAir Offices*, at Tourist Centre, T443591-4; *Emco Travel City Centre*, 2 Talaat Harb St, Down Town, T5756022, F5782692; *Isis Travel*, Grand Hotel Hurghada, T443748; *Misr Travel* at Tourist Centre, T442130; *Nefertari Travel Service*, opposite the *National Bank of Egypt*; *Seti First Travel*, beside *Shedwan Hotel*, T548547.

Tour operators

Check times and destinations with care.

Transport

Local Minibus/microbuses. These make regular circuits of Dahar. A ride from Dahar to Sigala and the resorts should cost E£1-2. **Taxi** Minimum charge would be E£5-10 within Dahar. Bikes can also be rented from the street next to *Bank Misr* and on Sharia Abdel Aziz.

Air International flights go to **Dusseldorf**, **Frankfurt**, **Geneva**, **Milan**, **Munich**, **Rome**, **Vienna** and **Zurich**. There are regular daily flights from **Hurghada** to **Cairo** at 0845 and a frequent service on other days during the week. Flights are advertised to **Luxor** leave Tue at 0030, Wed at 0800 and 1845, Sat at 1650 and 2200. To **Sharm el-Sheikh** on Fri, Sat and Sun at various times. Times and numbers of flights change daily so it is best to visit *EgyptAir* in person, (on Sharia Sheraton) as the phones are rarely answered. Flights to Cairo and Sharm El Sheikh are approximately E£500. Airport: T442831/442594.

The Red Sea Coast & Eastern Desert

Emperor Angel Fish

Lunartail Grouper

Road Bus: the new bus station (T548782) is on the main north-south road to the south of the main town. Bus companies include *Upper Egypt*, T547582 and *Superjet*, see below. Regular daily buses north go to **Suez** (6-8 hrs, E£20) and **Cairo** (6-12 hrs depending on the service, E£50), and southeast to **Luxor** (4-5 hrs, E£15) and **Aswan** via Qena (7-8 hrs) which are very full in the winter high season. Buses to **Cairo** 1000, 1300, 1500, 1900, 2130, 2200, 2400; *Superjet* to **Cairo** 1200, 1430, 1800 contact T546768; to **Luxor** 1200, 2400, returning at 0600, 1100, 1430, 1900. There are also buses to **Safaga**, and **El Quseir**. **Car rental**: *Budget* in *Sofitel*, T442261 and *Marriott* T446950; *Eurocar* in *Royal Palace* T443660; *Hertz* near *EgyptAir*, T442884; *Lease a Car* in *Helnan Regina*, T443811; *Eurocar* in *Sonesta Beach*, T443660 plus many more along Sharia Sheraton. **Service taxis**: Service Taxis (or Peugot) operate to destinations south, north and west, although as a foreigner you may not be allowed in those travelling to the Nile valley. You need to go to the service taxi station located across the roundabout from the Telephone Centrale. You can't get a service taxi on the street, those are *specials* and considerably more expensive. Again, at the station ensure you say "no" to requests for *special*. Service taxi fares are approximately E£3-5 to **Safaga** (1hr) , E£15 to **Marsa Alam** (3 hrs), E£30 to **Cairo** (5-7 hrs), £E20 to **Suez** (4 hrs), **Luxor** (4 hrs)and **Aswan** (6 hrs). You may have to wait some time for the car to fill up (7 people, minibus 14). If you're in a rush, you can can pay for empty seats in order to leave sooner. For long distances, fares and travel times are less than the bus but more dangerous as drivers speed like there is no tomorrow.

Sea Ferry: ferry to **Sharm el-Sheikh** on the Sinai peninsula (1½-10 hrs depending on the weather and the boat), booking is essential through your own hotel or *Spring Tours* on Sharia el-Nasr, T548151. **Hurghada** to **Sharm el-Sheikh** single fare costs E£160 on fast vessel (1½-2½ hrs) and E£110 on slow vessel (7 hrs). Fast Sat and Thu 0800, and possibly Sun, Mon 0500, Tue 0400, returning from Sharm el-Sheikh at 1800 the same day; slow ferry leaves Tue, Thu, Sat 0900; contact in Hurghada T444003/546282 and in Sharm el-Sheikh T544702. Take food and water for the journey. The best idea regarding the schedule is to ask at travel agents and *TRAVCO* T069-661111/065-442231 and take an average of your results! Avoid *AMCO* by *Sand Beach Hotel*, they're decidedly unhelpful, especially to females.

Directory **Airlines** *EgyptAir*, T443591/4 (open 0800-2000) and *ZAS*, T440019 (open 1000-2100) have offices almost next to each other in the square with the new mosque. *EgyptAir*, Sharia Sheraton, T447503/442831.

Banks *Commercial International Bank* in front of *Grand Hotel*. Other banks on the main road in Hurghada are *Bank of Alexandria*, *Banque Misr*, *Islamic Investment Bank* and *National Bank of Egypt*, Sharia Sheraton. Only *Banque Misr* and *National Bank of Egypt* offer cash advances on Visa/Mastercard and only the *National Bank of Egypt* has an ATM. Banks open from Sun-Thu 0900-1300, 1800-2100, Fri and Sat 0900-1330. Money transfer can be arranged through *Thomas Cook* and *Western Union*, T442772, both in Sigala shopping centre.

Communications Internet: Try to go to internet cafes when the locals are at work. Expect connections to be slow and unreliable. *Internet Egypt* in Sigala behind the Pyramid, Yellow sign on balcony. *Aboudi Bookshop* on Sharia Aziz Mostafa near *Three Corners Empire*. New internet café at *Papas Bar* in Sigala. Business services available at *Hilton Resort*. **Post Office:** is located next to the tourist police on Sharia al-Central to the south of the new mosque. Open 0800-1400 daily except Fri, T546372. Special post by Federal Express – T442772, in Sigala shopping centre. Telephone: it is quite easy to make international telephone calls from most hotels. However, it is much cheaper to use phone cards which you can buy at the Telephone Centrales on the main roundabout on Sharia El Nasr, Dahar, and Sharia Sheraton and Midwan Shedwan, Sigala. There are also many *Menatel* phone boxes everywhere. Their cards can be bought in shops and supermarkets.

• •

Who sells sea shells?

The answer is nobody should sell shells because nobody wants to buy.

The sale of shells and coral is illegal, large fines and long prison sentences can be the result if prosecuted. Removing anything living or dead from the water in Protected Areas is forbidden. Fishermen are banned from these areas. Continuing to plunder the

marine environment will cause permanent damage.

The Environmental Protection Association, along with operators of dive centres and hotel are desperately trying to educate the visitors. Unfortunately they know they have a better chance of educating the tourists not to buy than the locals not to sell.

• •

Medical services *Safa hospital*, *Al Salam hospital* and the Public Hospital at turning on Sharia Aziz Mostafa to El-Corniche. **Ambulance**: T546490. *El Gouna Hospital* 1580014, Decompression chamber El Gouna T580011, Decompresson chamber at naval hospital T449150.

Places of worship *Coptic Church*, Fri and Sun 1000, at El-Anba Shenouda.

Useful telephone numbers Fire: T549814. **Public Hospital**: T546/40. **Police**: T546723. **Tourist Police**: 1546765. Visa extensions at Passports and Immigration Office to extreme north of the town on Sharia el-Nasr, open 0800-1400, closed Fri, T546727. *VHF Channel 16*

Excursions from Hurghada

By boat. A trip to **Tobia Island** with sandy lagoons and untouched (for how long?) corals in turquoise water. A sea cruise via **Shadwan Island**, Gulf of Suez, and even Ras Mohammed. Takes at least 6 hrs and costs about E£200 – check with local travel guide.

By land. Hire suitable transport, take sensible provisions and hire a local guide. A day trip to Roman ruins of **Mons Claudianus** near Jebel Fatira (1,355 m). Evidence of Roman military presence, a Roman road and columns. A Roman settlement with houses, stable and temple to Serap and the Roman Fortress of Om Dikhal. A mixture of quarry and fortress – see remains of the cells used to house the workers/prisoners who quarried the stone. An excursion to **Mons Porphyritis**, 55 km northwest of Hurghada at foot of Jebel Abu Dukhan (1641 m), ruins of a Roman temple and ancient quarries for porphyry, a popular stone for sarcophagi and facing walls.

A new tourist complex is under construction just 48 km, 45-minute drive, south of Hurghada on the peninsula of Abu Soma. Thirteen luxury hotels are planned. The 18-hole golf course covering 400,000 sq m and designed by Gary Player, is situated on the highest point of the peninsula, almost 22 m above sea level and offers good views. The first nine holes are already complete. The intention is to attract 'well to do' visitors, such as Japanese who love golf, into their 60 room club house. Other activities are provided by a fresh water swimming pool and the seven coral reefs in the vicinity. A 4 km long promenade is planned and a marina to accommodate 50 vessels. This could be a splendid place to stay. **Ras Abu Soma**

AL *Sheraton Soma Bay*, T545915. Constructed in Pharoanic style, looks like the first pylon of a huge temple, white sandy beaches, 277 rooms, 35 suites, all with quality facilities and sea view, rooms for disabled, 18-hole golf course, 4 pools, 3 restaurants, 6 bars, tennis, squash, even desert safaris. Also under construction at same high quality *Robinson Club* with 300 rooms, T549854 and *The Cascades*. *Diving World's* newest dive centre is established here.

The Red Sea Coast & Eastern Desert

Safaga

Safaga stands a long 567 km from Cairo but just 65 km (45 min by taxi) south from Hurghada airport, where the coastal road meets the main road across the Eastern Desert to Qena. This region does not rely totally on tourism. It has local phosphate mines and the mineral is exported from the small port which imports grain, much of it US food aid, which is currently trucked inland to the Nile Valley, although a disused freight railway line to Qena may soon be reopened.

There is less pressure of people but more hotels are planned. The stiff breezes which favoured the trading vessels along these shores now provide excellent conditions for wind surfing, generally cross-shore in the morning and side-shore in the early afternoon. The Windsurfing World Championships were held here in 1993. Good for diving with noted (recommended) sites of Panorama and Abu Kafana. The prolific marine life is an underwater photographer's dream. There are frequent sightings of dolphin, ray, barracuda, reef and leopard shark.

Most travellers simply pass through in a convoy on their way between Hurghada and the Nile Valley. There is very little to visit other than a small fort which overlooks the town and offers good views. Tourist information: T451785.

Sleeping   The officially registered hotels all addressed as Safaga, Red Sea, are: **A** *Holiday Inn*, T252821/3, usual facilities associated with this hotel chain, spacious, well tended gardens, perfect for sports enthusiasts, health club, tennis, volleyball, large pool, 2 restaurants, bars, shopping arcade. Most expensive hotel in town. **B** *Lotus Bay Beach Resort*, T251040. Whitewashed clusters with gardens between, all rooms have sea view, usual room facilities, choice of restaurants, tennis, squash, volley ball, freshwater pool, cycle hire, horse and camel riding, watersports facilities, *Barakuda International Diving Club*. **B** *Menaville Village*, T251761/4, F251765 is a better choice, about 5 km north of Safaga port. 100 hotel/villa rooms, 48 chalets and 33 suites, villas in gardens, by pool or adjacent to the very good beach, all rooms a/c, telephone, minibar and terrace or balcony, villas sleep 4/5 and have lounge and small kitchen. Shops, bank, laundry, clinic. TV lounge, 24-hr cafe, private beach, cycle hire, billiards, table tennis. Our choice. Has own *Barakuda Dive Club* (German management) with private jetty. Unlimited shore diving from hotel reef and boat dives available with all equipment for hire. **C** *Safaga Paradise Village*, T251633, F251630. 244 rooms, similar to *Menaville* but larger and less cosy. **C** *Shams Safaga Village*, T251783, F251780. Designed and built in local style, 135 bungalow rooms and 150 hotel rooms with a/c, bath, terrace/balcony, TV, private sandy beach within a protected, secluded, natural bay, and spacious, well tended gardens, restaurant, 3 bars, tennis, squash, mini golf, health club, para sailing, all watersports, large pool, small children's pool, play area and baby sitting. Shams diving

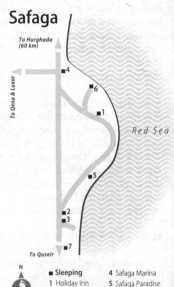

Safaga

To Hurghada
(60 km)

To Qena & Luxor

Red Sea

To Quseir

N

Not to scale

■ **Sleeping**
1 Holiday Inn
2 Lotus Bay Club
3 Menaville

4 Safaga Marina
5 Safaga Paradise
6 Shams
7 Tobia

centre on site. Club Mistral for windsurfing with full range of instruction from beginners to slalom stylists. A rescue boat is on hand. Advantage for disabled is flat access to beach. **D** *Paradise Beach Resort*, on beach, freshwater pool, 190 rooms, laundry shops, very bleak. **E** *Cleopatra Hotel*, T251544. 48 rooms, more than adequate, has a bar. **F** *Abu Gabr* and *Eleez* in central area near port. **F** *Sea Land Village*, Sharm el-Naga, T3545756, F3545060. 15 rooms, value for money.

The resort is so new that really all the best places to eat are in the hotels, as are the only bars. Try *Layalina*, *Lord's Pub* and *Splash Bar* in the *Holiday Inn*; *Moon & Sun* and *Beach Bar* at *Menaville*; *Omar Khayam* in *Safaga Paradise* or the *Dolphin Bar* at *Shams*. **Eating**

Clubs: *Albano* in *Menaville*. *Black Cat* in *Holiday Inn*. *Serpent* in *Shams*; *Paradise* in *Safaga Paradise*. **Bars & nightclubs**

Diving clubs: *Barakuda* at Lotus Bay T251041 and *Menaville* T251763. *Duck's Diving Centre* in *Holiday Inn*, T251760. *El Okby Village* (with some **F** grade accommodation for divers) T252116. *Orca Red Sea Diving*, T342357. *Safaga Divers* at *Safaga Paradise Village* and *Safaga Marina* T257631. **Sports**

Safaga islands, reefs & dive sites

Check all times and destinations with care. **Road** Buses via Hurghada (E£3-5) to Suez (E£20-40) every 1-2 hrs of which 5 go on to **Cairo** (E£50). Buses to **Qena** (E£10), **Luxor** E£15-20) and **Aswan** (E£30-40) 4-5 times a day, currently at 0100,1100,1330,1630, 2330. Buses to **El Quesir** (E£8) and **Marsa Alam** (E£10) are also advertised. Bus station: T4251253. **Service taxis** follow all these routes – change at Suez for Cairo. Taxi: T4251349. **Transport**

Note that the convoys leave from Safaga daily at 0600, 0915 and 1800 with a short stop half way. There is no petrol between Safaga abd Qena

Sea Passenger boats leave here for **Saudi Arabia** during the *haj* (not advised) and occasionally at other times. Check at *Telestar* office in town.

Banks *Banque Misr*, El Quseir-Hurghada Road, T541552. **Communications Post Office:** T451206. **Useful telephone numbers** Fire: T451227. Hospital: T451549. Tourist police: T451208. **Directory**

Dive sites
1 Abu Kefan
2 Gamul Kebir
3 Gamul Soraya
4 Hal Hal
5 Middle Reef
6 Panorama
7 Ras Abu Soma
8 Sha'ab Humdulla
9 Sha'ab Shaer
10 Tobia Arbao
11 Tobia Hamra
12 Tobia Kebir
13 Tobia Soraya

N

Not to scale

El Quseir

Further south is **El Quseir**, 650 km from Cairo and 80 km south of Hurghada (two hours by road), an old Roman encampment and busy port. This is popular for the slightly more adventurous, those wishing to escape the crowds of Hurghada and Sharm el-Sheikh, and for serious divers.

It has had a long history as a major port of the Red Sea. It was from here that Queen Hatshepsut departed on her famous expedition to the Land of Punt (see page 204). This was also once the most important Muslim port on the Red Sea. In the 10th century it was superseded first by Aydhab, which is the ancient name for the Halaib in the currently disputed triangle on the Egyptian-Sudanese border, and then by Suez after the canal was opened in 1869. The port has recently been reopened, its main function for the export of phosphates. The 16th century fortress of Sultan Selim (rebuilt by the French in 1798) which still stands in the centre of the town (see below) indicates its earlier importance. Today the influx is of tourists and fortifications are not required. All the activity here is based on diving, scuba diving or serious snorkelling.

It is a very peaceful place located in a small inlet sheltered by a coral reef. The road inland from El Quseir to Qift, which is just south of Qena, a distance of 164 km, follows the ancient pharaonic road which was built at a time when almost a hundred small but very rich gold mines operated in the region. Some of these mines have been reopened using modern technology.

Diving off El Quseir
Shallow dives Off the shore at *Movenpick's* Subex Dive Centre is El Qadima Bay with a variety of topography and fauna; about 10 km further south is the more sheltered El Kaf.

Deep dives The islands Big Brother and Little Brother are about 1 km apart, 67 km off the shore to the northeast of El Quseir. This region has been recently reopened by the Egyptian government as a Protected Marine Park. They are two exposed parts of the same reef. Access by liveboard. The walls are a vertical 900 m. On the larger island, Big Brother, is a stone built light house constructed by the British in 1883 (and still working) and to the northwest of Big Brother are two wrecks. The unnamed cargo vessel with its shattered bow can be reached at 5 m (and then deeper as it is at an incline). The other wreck is Aida II (see Box on Wrecks).

These two dives offer a wealth of corals and an impressive range of fish. *Subex Diving Centre* very expensive at US$100 per dive including equipment rental. *Daly Dive Resort* is more basic with dives made at the resort from US$15 per dive, US$44 per day. *Coral Cove* offers two dives for E£240 including equipment rental.

Sights
Visit the fort of Sultan Semil. The partly ruined fortress was built by Sultan Selim to protect the Nile Valley from attacks from the sea – until 1710. At that time it became the main departure point for Egyptian pilgrims on their annual journey to Mecca.

There was conflict here too at the end of the 18th century – during the French campaign. Also between the British Indian Army coming in from Bombay and the Egyptian campaign to the Arabian Peninsula headed by Ibrahim Pasha in 1816. (See box on Mohammed Ali and family page 505.) During the Ottoman era it had been used as an administrative office and today the ancient structure is sufficiently repaired to be used as a police station. Some of the inscribed verses from the Koran can still be read. There are other buildings from this earlier period including the mosques of Al-Faroah,

Recipe for Falafel

These tiny chick pea pancakes served with tahini sauce have been served at meals in Egypt since the time of the Pharaohs.

250 gm dried chick peas
1 small onion finely chopped
25 gm of soft bread crumbs
2 cloves of garlic, crushed
25 gm chopped parsley
large pinch of ground coriander
large pinch of ground cumin
olive oil for frying
The chick peas must be soaked overnight, rinsed in fresh water and drained. Blend the chick peas, bread crumbs, onion and crushed garlic with 50 ml of water in the mixer until quite smooth. Add the spices and parsley into the bowl and knead

together. Make the mixture into small balls the size of a date, flatten with the hand and deep fry in batches until golden brown – about four minutes. Drain off excess oil. Serve with the tahini sauce.

Sauce
50 ml of tahini (sesame seed paste)
juice of a lemon
1 clove of garlic, crushed
5 gm chopped parsley
pinch of ground cumin
pinch of salt
pepper to taste
Mix the ingredients with water to a smooth creamy paste.
Both the pancakes and the sauce can be frozen.

Abdel-Rehim Al-Qenay and Al-Sanussi and a number of tombs, mainly by the fortress, of holy men considered important by the inhabitants.

Jeep and horseback safaris can be taken into the mountains to visit nearby oases and a number of ghost cities created when the mines were abandoned.

Sleeping Sample of hotels officially addressed as El Quseir, Red Sea, are: **A** *Movenpick Serena Beach*, El Quadim Bay, T432100-120, F4321290. Unbeatable value with a coral reef running the entire length of the private beach. You can almost snorkel from your room, Moorish style, lovely gardens, beautiful beach, large pool, 3 restaurants of which Orangerie is recommended, 4 bars especially *Jolie Bar*, 2 floodlit tennis courts, squash, archery ranges with coach, gym, mountain bikes to hire, horse and camel riding. Children's pool, children's club, supervised play area. All 175 rooms have usual facilities from sea view to hair dryer. Close by, but completely isolated, is the *Utopia Beach Club*. Also *Pensee* – the Nile cruise boat used as a hotel ship. Excellent diving but no nightlife. *Subex Diving Centre*, see **Sport**. Often windy, spotless, friendly service, good food, fitness centre, wide variety of sports available.

B *Fanadar Beach Hotel*, T430861. 50 little bungalows just 1 km south of town. **B** *Mangrove Bay Resort*, T3486748, 29 km south of town. 48 rooms. **B** *Utopia Beach Club*, a bus is needed to get into El Quseir, 20 km away but taxis are available. New – right on the beach, restaurant, pool with snack bar, lobby bar, disco, billiards, volleyball, tennis, table tennis, windsurfing and pedalo hire, children's pool and small size tennis court, play area, cots and pens free, mini kids club, doctor on call. Some spectacular dives just off the beach, others reached by jeep.

D *Daly Dive Resort*, El Hamrawein, 20 km north of town, T430039, F430720. 54 rooms with bath, sea views, beach site, clean, basic. **E** *Flamenco Beach Resort*, T333801. **E** *Sea Princess Hotel*, beyond traffic island to south of town.

Eating The resort is so new that the best places to eat are at the restaurants in the hotels.

Entertainment No nightlife except in hotels, so try *Jolie Bar* in *Movenpick*.

Tour operators *Movenpick* offers escorted excursions to Luxor and Hurghada.

The Red Sea Coast & Eastern Desert

Transport   Please check all times and destinations.

Buses to **Cairo** take 11-12 hrs (E£55) via Safaga (E£5-8), Hurghada (E£10-15) and Suez. To **Luxor** and **Qena** (E£5-10) via Qift. To **Marsa Alam** (E£5) leaving around noon and midnight. **Service taxis** go to all these destinations, change at Suez for **Cairo**. Journeys to the west are via Safaga to join the security convoys.

Directory   There is a bank in town, a post office and a 24-hr telephone office. **Useful telephone numbers** Fire brigade: T430067. **Hospital**: T430070; **Police**: T430017

Excursions   Pharonic graffiti - Heiroglyphic inscriptions. When travelling from El Quseir to Qift - half way on this journey (about 100 km) and to north of the road, including the names of Pepi, Sesostris, Seti, Cambyses and Darius.

Marsa Shagra

This remote bay located 113 km south of El Quesir and 13 km north of **Marsa Alam** has become a small village well known to divers. It has good opportunities for a variety of coastal shore dives, day and night. There is a very extensive cave system which can be explored and some outstanding coral formations. It is near to a group of offshore reefs with walls such as the Elphinstone Reef.

There is just one accommodation complex known as Marsa Shagra set back from the beach to the west of the coast road (so as not to spoil the view). The construction in local red sandstone is very sympathetic. A central domed area containing all the main facilities is surrounded by separate villas with lots of space. Prices around £800 a week for the diver and £700 for non-diver including full board. This is the first complex to be constructed here and it is to be hoped that the precedent of style and position is copied so that this tranquil area is not spoilt. This is also an excellent spot for fishing.

Live-board dive locations south from Marsa Alam: Elphinstone Reef, 12 km off shore; Daedalus Reef, 96 km off shore; Sha'ab Sharm; Dolphine Reef, 15 km to the northwest of Ras Banas; Zabargad Island, 45 km southeast of Berenice.

There are flights to Hurghada or Luxor – plus 3-hour coach journey. There is also a fairly good surface, direct road from the River Nile at Edfu, 280 km. You would need to hire a taxi.

Berenice

This was a very ancient city – named by Ptolemy II. It became a trading port around 275 BC. The ruined temple of Semiramis is near the modern town and inland there are remains of the emerald mines of Wadi Sakait which were worked from Pharonic to Roman times. Berenice is noted for both quantity and quality of fish and having a climate noted for promoting health.

The coast is lined with mangrove swamps and there are some beautiful coves which are completely isolated.

Offshore is the **Zabargad**, a most unusual volcanic island. Evidence of its origin is found in the (olive-green) olivine mined as a semi-precious gem stone. Mining which has not long been discontinued has been active here on and off since 1500 BC. Peridot Hill (named after another semi-precious stone) offers breathtaking views of the surrounding area. A wonderful place to watch the dolphins and, in season, the migrating birds. Recommended as a place for remedial tourism. Zabargad Island has recently been reopened by the Egyptian government as a Protected Marine Park.

Berenice is 908 km from Cairo, 400 km from Hurghada and 258 km from El Quseir. Access is by road only. The nearest airports are Hurghada and Luxor. Sometimes a permit is required for this area. Permits are available from the Transit Police, Sharia al-Tahrir, T546765.

The small harbour of **Marsa Alam** about 135 km south of El Quscir and best **Sights** reached from the Nile Valley by the paved road from Edfu, is also destined for development. This is a beautiful area. The coast is lined with rich mangrove swamps which encourage bird and marine life. These mangroves are protected and any development must preserve the existing environment.

There is one interesting excursion possible from here into the interior, but a guide is essential. The restored tomb and mosque of Sidi Abul Hassan Al-Shazli lies some distance inland. The track/road is a distance of 110 km southwards off the main road west towards Edfu. Al-Shazli (1196-1258) was an influential sufi sheikh originating in the northwest of Africa but spending much of his life in Egypt. He had a large and important following and was noted for his piety and unselfishness. He travelled annually to Mecca for which Marsa Alam was convenient. His moulid is popular despite the isolation of the site. The buildings are modern, being last restored on the instructions of King Farouk after his visit in 1947.

Sleeping Try *Kahramana Resort* or *Alexander the Great* T4141929, F4181164. **Camping** at *Coral Cove*, Sharia Marsa Alam, T02-3647970, beach location 8 km north of Marsa Alam. Tents for 2, 3 or 10 persons, peaceful, clean, popular with divers. *Red Sea Diving Safari* about 20 km north is a semi permanent campsite for divers.

Transport: Bus to Aswan (E£11) via Edfu (E£9) leaves early morning. Buses to El Quseir for connections north and west.

Directory South of the T-junction a small settlement boasts a pharmacy, telephone.

The Red Sea Coast & Eastern Desert

The Western Desert and the Great Desert Circuit

13

The Western Desert and the Great Desert Circuit

This section concentrates on the journey along the 'great desert circuit' rather than on individual towns, because it is the journey itself and not the oases towns which is of greatest importance. Wherever you are in Egypt, the desert is not far away, and its presence can always be felt. The Western Desert alone constitutes two-thirds of Egypt's total area. Its significance in any travel itinerary depends upon how much of a traveller you are and how much a tourist. Desert travel presents its inconveniences and its hazards, but the rewards are beyond measure.

Highlights of your visit here would include experiencing the seemingly infinite space, the absolute silence of the desert, the absolute blackness of the desert night, the awesome desert sunrise, the incredible desert distances measured in hours rather than kilometres, the eerie windshaped rocks in the White Desert of Farafra, the surprise of the bright green oasis gardens, the flocks of migratory and resident birds, the desolate, windswept abandoned temples and tombs and the almost overwhelming friendliness of the local people continuing to live a lifestyle little changed over centuries.

The Western Desert and the Great Desert Circuit

"It is not easy to conceive the sterile grandeur of the scene ... I may truly say, I never enjoyed myself more, despite the thermometer at 105 degrees, and the numerous petty inconveniences I was necessarily obliged to submit to. Certainly, no fine lady, who could not do without her everyday luxuries and comforts, should attempt the desert ... but I was born under a wandering star ..."
Anne Katherine Elwood 1830.

Depending upon the time available and personal preference there are various choices. They range from a day trip from Cairo to **El-Fayoum** (see page 161) or to **Wadi El Natrun** (see page 342), to **The Great Desert Circuit** of **Bahariya, Farafra, Dakhla** and **Kharga Oases**, or **Siwa** (see page 375) and **The Great Sand Sea**. Although it is undoubtedly part of the Western Desert, the wonderful oasis of **Siwa** is dealt with in the section on Alexandria and the Mediterranean because it is most easily accessible from Marsa Matruh and is not linked directly to the Great Desert circuit.

Many areas in the vicinity of the oases are set aside for military use, so for detours from the main road a **permit** may be necessary. The **Travel Permits Department** (T3556301/3548661) at the Ministry of the Interior in Cairo in the Abdin district is open Saturday-Thursday 0900-1400. In order to get your permit, which can take anything from 1-7 days, it is essential to take photocopies of the important pages of your passport and the Egyptian entry stamp and two passport photos.

Spring is the best time to visit the desert, when the daytime temperatures are still bearable and the nights are cool but not cold, and the summer desert winds and sand storms, which can be very uncomfortable, have not yet arrived. Take enough money with you. Credit cards will *not* do, indeed, you will be lucky to find a bank. When planning a drive NEVER underestimate the potential dangers of the desert. It is said that in 524 BC Cambyses, the Persian conqueror of Egypt, managed to lose an entire army of 50,000 men without a trace! Always carry more than enough fuel, food and water. There are no service stations between towns. You need the right type of vehicle, and the necessary driving skills to handle it in this terrain. See Desert Travel in Essentials and read further on the subject before you throw yourself into a potentially lethal environment. Other options include service buses and organized desert safaris. The latter could be the most rewarding if you are anything but meticulously prepared and equipped.

Locusts by the swarm

Plagues of locusts were problems encountered long before the Children of Israel struggled to escape from Egypt. One locust can eat its own weight of plant material every day. Thus a large swarm containing millions of these insects will eat all available vegetable matter, destroy fields of crops, defoliate trees and cause general devastation and despair. Attempts have been made to control the spread of locusts with little measurable result. Dusting and spraying from the air, spread of poisonous bait, trench digging to prevent the dispersion of young hoppers have all been tried to little effect.

The locust and the familiar European grasshopper belong to the same family Acrididae. Species found in Egypt are Schistocerca gregaria the desert locust, the migratory Locusta migratoria and Dociostaurus maroccanus which causes havoc much further afield than Morocco.

Nevertheless locusts are fascinating creatures able to fly considerable distances at speeds of up to 35 km per hour especially with the wind behind them. Locusts use their strong back legs to leap up into the air so that once airborne they can open their wings and fly. The stronger and tougher front wings fold over the more delicate rear pair when the inect settle on the ground. Colouring varies from dark orange and black to light green but what ever the colour and what ever the species the chew, chew, chew of the jaws has the same devastating effect on any vegetation.

The Great Desert Circuit

The Great Desert Circuit became accessible in the 1980s, when a road was built linking the oases of **Bahariya**, **Farafra**, **Dakhla** and **Kharga**. These are all situated on a dead branch of the River Nile, and depend, for their livelihood on the massive fossil water reservoirs beneath the Libyan Desert. The area was designated as the **New Valley** in 1958 with a scheme to tap this subterranean water-source and relocate landless peasants from the overcrowded Nile Valley and Delta. However the lack of resources and a reassessment of the long-term viability of the water supply led to the virtual abandonment of the project and to the area's inevitable stagnation.

Coming from Cairo, the natural choice is an anti-clockwise journey round the circuit beginning by going into the desert past the Pyramids at Giza on Route 341. This gives the option of a refreshing last leg of your journey back down the River Nile. Driving conditions are not ideal, with pot-holed roads and few opportunities for petrol, food or water. You may have to stand for hours waiting for and on crowded buses, and accommodation along the route is pretty basic. Lacking the time or the inclination for all this you can fly direct from Cairo to New Valley Airport at Kharga, where you can get a taste of the desert, but you will be missing far more than you experience. It may be true that Kharga has more interesting monuments than some of its neighbours, but the desert itself is the star of this piece and Kharga, with it's sprawling modern town, is undoubtedly a disappointment.

Depending on the level of security precautions taken by the Egyptian authorities you may find yourself accompanied by armed guards for part of your journey. Generally these concern themselves with travellers in self-drive vehicles or cars with hired drivers. They cause no problems though the effectiveness of their protection may be questioned. Use it as an opportunity to educate, take them into the museums and round the monuments.

The Western Desert

The Western Desert

Chameleonic camels

There are two kinds of camel, Camelus Dromedarius, the Arabian camel with one hump and Camelus Bactrianus, the Bactrian which has two. Arabian camels, introduced into North Africa in the fifth century BC, though only as domestic animals, are about 3 m long and about 2 m high at the shoulder. They range in colour from white to black.

They are not the most attractive of creatures, looking particularly ragged and scruffy at the spring moult. Large bare leathery areas on legs and chest look like some serious skin complaint but are normal and act as cushions when the animal kneels down.

Interesting physical characteristics which allow these animals to survive in the desert include hairs inside the ear opening as well as the ability to close the nostrils between breaths, both preventing sand penetration; thick eyebrows to shade the eyes from the sun's glare; a pad of skin between the two large toes on each foot forming a broad, tough 'slipper' which spreads the animal's weight over a larger area and prevents sinking in the loose sand; the ability to store a reserve of fat in the hump and to go for days without water. Each eye has three eyelids, the upper and lower lids have very long eyelashes to protect the eyes from sand whipped up by desert winds, while a third, thinner lid blinks away dust from the eyeball. The skin inside a camel's mouth is so tough that cactus thorns do not penetrate, hence a camel can eat anything, 'even its owner's tent'.

Camels can go for many days without food as the hump can store up to 35 kg of fat as emergency rations. They can go without water for even longer, depending on the weather and the kind of food available. As camels do not sweat but instead function at a higher body temperature without brain damage, their demands of fluid are less. At a water hole they drink only enough to balance their body moisture content.

Less pleasant characteristics include a most unpredictable nature, especially in the mating season, which includes nasty habits like using its long sharp teeth to bite people and other camels, viciously kicking with the back legs, spitting and being generally awkward. When a camel stands up it moves in a series of violent jerks as it straightens first its hind legs then its front legs. When a camel walks, it moves both the legs at one side at the same time, giving a very rolling motion which can give the rider travel sickness.

Camels are unwilling beasts of burden, grunting and groaning as they are loaded and generally complaining at being made to lie down or stand up. Once underway though, they move without further protest.

These large, strong beasts are used to pull ploughs, turn water wheels and carry large loads for long distances across difficult terrain. They can carry up to 400 kg but usually the load is nearer 200 kg. Despite moving at a mere 6-7 km an hour, camels can travel 100 km in a day. They also provide their owners with hair for cloth, rich milk and cheese, dried dung fuel and eventually meat, bones for utensils and hides for shoes, bags and tenting.

The Arabian dromedary, bred for riding and racing, is of a slighter build but can cover 160 km in a day and reach speeds of up to 15 km per hour.

Watch how you go

A stumbling horse played a significant part in Carter's discoveries in the Valley of the Kings. He was returning to the rest house on the West Bank when his horse fell and a shaft was exposed. The shaft led to a sealed chamber containing an empty coffin with no name inscribed on the lid. The tomb is still known as the Tomb of the Door of the Horse. Inside the tomb he found a statue wrapped in linen beside the coffin. This statue is now on show in the museum in Cairo and is named as Mentuhotep II.

A donkey's legs played an important part in discoveries in Alexandria too. As Ahmed Kasbara rode along on his donkey, it stumbled in a hole in the path. This led to the discovery of the underground tunnels known as the Catacombs of Kom el-Shoqufa (see page 354).

In August 1990, another horse stumbled. This time it was one ridden by a woman in the area near the Sphinx. The horse fell to the ground after tripping over

a small brick structure. This was the first discovery of a series of tombs of the builders of the pyramids, considered now to be the largest cemetery ever found.

And as recently as 1996 another donkey stumbled into a small hole in the desert floor. This donkey was ridden by an antiquities guard near the Temple of Alexander and its fall brought to light the golden mummies of Bahariya.

The Western Desert

Bahariya

The journey to Bahariya, 310 km west of the Pyramids of Giza, along Route 341 *Colour map 1, grid A3* takes 6-7 hours by bus, with one stop *en route*, 5-6 hours by service taxi or 4-4½ hours in a four-wheel drive vehicle. This is the closest oasis to Cairo in distance and the furthest in historical time, dating back to the Middle Kingdom. At 2,000 sq km it is the smallest of the four depressions and has the great advantage of having water just 7 m below the ground, not 700 m as is common in the other oases.

After taking the turn to October 6th City the dual carriageway becomes a new black top 3-lane highway. A new oil rig – Santa Fé rig no 94 – stands on the right and new road signs, big yellow markers, give distances from Cairo. Running parallel to the road is a private railway which takes iron ore from the country's most important mine at Managum to the giant Helwan steelworks near Cairo. This was the catalyst for Egypt's industrial development in the 1950s.

At 155 km from Giza is a resthouse with petrol. The bus and service taxis stop here. No soft drinks, just tea. Thirty-one kilometres after the resthouse is the new road north to El-Alamein marked by five signs – of the petrol companies involved.

Eighty-one kilometres from the resthouse the road becomes narrower, the surface rougher and the railway swings away to left. The telegraph poles march alongside the road – but there are no wires between them! As the road begins its descent towards the oasis the first huge black topped inselburgs appear, protruding through the yellow sands. The Managum mines are announced by a sign at 150 km from the resthouse but it is a further 10 km before houses for

☞ Asses, donkeys and mules

There is a certain amount of confusion when naming the normally overladen and generally undernourished beasts of burden found in the countries of North Africa. While there can be no confusion as to what is a **horse**, Equus caballus, or even an **ass**, Equus asinus, despite the fact that it is most commonly called a **donkey**, a **mule** requires some definition.

The term **mule** can refer to any hybrid but as a beast of burden it is the offspring of a male donkey (jack) and a female horse (mare), while the offspring of a male horse (stallion) and a female donkey (jenny) is correctly termed a **hinny**.

A mule is a horse in the middle with a donkey at either end. It has longer ears, and a thinner mane and tail than its mother and carries the typical 'cross' markings on the shoulders and back. The hinny is less popular, being nearer the size of a donkey and has the shorter ears and thicker mane and tail of its father.

A mule is stronger than a horse, has a much longer working life under the right circumstances, can withstand extremes of temperature without long-term ill effects, is less vulnerable to sickness and can survive on a very limited diet. Mules are noted for being surefooted and for being fast and accurate kickers. Mules are generally considered to be infertile though instances of offspring are recorded.

The Algerian wild ass originally roamed the Atlas Ranges. The Romans carefully preserved them on mosaics but are held responsible for their demise. The Nubian wild ass, of a distinctive reddish hue, roamed the semi-desert areas between the River Nile and the Red Sea shores. It survived into the 20th century.

The Egyptians used asses. Illustrations from 2500 BC show us that even then these domesticated beasts were carrying loads and passengers out of all proportion to their size. They also had mules which are thought to have first been bred around 1750 BC. Models of this hybrid were found in the pyramids and a mule drawing a chariot is depicted on a vase found in Thebes.

The Romans placed heavy reliance on the mule, for riding, to draw carts and farm implements and to carry equipment. To assist copulation they devised a wooden cage with a ramp to enable the shorter jack ass to reach the taller mare.

the workers appear on the right. The head office of the mines, down the road to the left is reported to have a museum but getting beyond the guard at the gate could prove very difficult.

Pause at the top of the scarp for a really magnificent view of the Bahariya depression, the smallest of the four depressions, with 33,000 inhabitants. **Bawati** is the main settlement. The farmed areas are owned by small landowners. The main crops are dates, olives and wheat. Problems of falling water tables in the oases were solved by tapping the subterranean aquifers held in the Cretaceous sandstones, but the interesting underground water channels (similar to those found as far afield as Morocco and Iran) formerly used in Bawati are dry and a very depressing sight.

Throughout their history the people of the oasis have prevaricated between independence and co-operation with the current régime. They converted to Islam soon after the Muslim invasion but returned to a Berber Emirate during the 10th century before being incorporated once more into the Islamic state by the Fatimids a century later. In the last few centuries they have co-operated fully with the ruling régimes but have maintained a slightly independent stance. They are generally very welcoming to visitors.

The small settlements are all worth visiting to see how these sturdy people combat the elements. Once on the floor of the depression take the track to the south of the road which continues beyond **El Harrah** (rock cut tombs) and

The Golden mummies of Bahariya oasis

It is widely reported that the 'recent' find of these mummies in 1996 was in fact discovered almost four year earlier and that in that time the discovery was supressed to allow some 'private' excavations. Be that as it may these golden mummies are as an exciting find as Tutankhamen's Tomb. It seems this cemetery was in use from the construction of Alexander's Temple to the fourth century AD.

The mummies are all different, representing individual men, women and children. The mask and upper bodies of many were coated with gold, others decorated with painted scenes, Each mummy has, unusually, a painted smile. It will be some long time before this site is open to the public and then it is unlikely that the mummies will be on view. In the mean time five mummies will to be put on display in the Inspectorate of Antiquities when suitable facilities are prepared. There are three kinds of mummies: The first is wrapped in linen without a sarcophagus The second is laid to rest in a pottery coffin The third is characterized by its decorations – pasteboard made of linen or papyrus, from the head to the waist on which artists have depicted scenes or those wearing gilded masks and often surrounded by funerary artefacts.

its ponds which are used by the locals for duck breeding to the gardens round the spring of **Fïn Yousef**. Further west along the main road the ruins of **Muhrib** are out of bounds at present but a tarmacked road opposite on the right leads to **Gabala** where the encroaching sands have been spreading over the oasis gardens for the last 20 years and have covered the rest of the road. Approaching closer to Bawati, again on the right, is **Eïn Hemma** with **Mandesha** beyond, also fighting a losing battle against the encroaching sand. The last turn right before Bawati leads to **Agouz**. A guide from the village is an asset when visiting these small settlements. Ask for school teacher Badry Macpool.

Sites now open in Bahariya oasis (in 2000) include at Qarat Hilwa the tomb of Amenhotep-Huy, mayor of Bahariya oasis in the 18th-19th Dynasty. Also now open is the Temple of Ain El-Moftella, built in the 26th Dynasty by the mayor of that time in the reigns of Kings Apries and Amasis (Ahmose II), the Greco-Roman period. The temple has chapels decorated with scenes of the king presenting offerings to the gods.

At al-Qasr Allam the Temple of Alexander the Great built in 332 BC and occupied perhaps until the 12th century AD, stands at the northern end of the site where the mummies were discovered (see box). The temple is unique – being built to honour a living person. It consists of two chambers within an enclosing wall. Behind the temple the priests' houses were built. The administrator lived to the east of the building and to the front were 45 store rooms made of mud brick where a small statue of the priest to Re was found. The temple itself is constructed of local sandstone. The front faces south and the stone gateway in the enclosing wall is here. A granite altar over 1 m in height was erected to the south of the entrance. The altar is inscribed with Alexander's name and can be viewed in the museum in Cairo. In the inner sanctuary Alexander, with the mayor who built the temple, is shown making offerings to Amun-Re and other gods.

In Bawati itself are the tombs of Banentiu, a wealthy merchant and Zed-Amon-Iuf-Ankh, his father, both from the 26th Dynasty.

Bawati
Colour map 1, grid A3

Bawati is built along the main road and the parallel oasis road to the south. South of the village in a dominant position stands Jebel Hafuf, Bahariya's highest mountain, made of dolerite and basalt.

Tourist Information on the main street opposite Ansari Mosque, has erratic opening. Try between 0800 and 1400.

A circular walk along the main road and the oasis road through the gardens, by Ain Bishmu, the Roman springs, where the hot water is used for bathing and washing clothes and by the shafts to the now dry underground water channels will take an hour. Cultivation of fruit takes place in these gardens, apricots, dates, figs and melons. In some places oranges struggle to survive. The women work in the gardens and also contribute to the household finances by selling embroidery which is of high quality. The hill to the southwest of the town is known as the Ridge of the Chicken Merchant as here in underground passages are small recesses, burial sites of a great many mummified ibis and hawks, dating from the 26th Dynasty and clearly relating to worship of Thoth and Horus.

Sights Oasis Heritage Museum at entrance to village by artist Mahmoud Eed is well worth a visit. An opportunity to learn more about the bedouin and their way of life. Here the traditional handicrafts and artefacts from a typical bedouin home are on display. In fact the main hall of the display is set up as the principal living area of the family – a low bench, a bread oven and some associated implements. Here one can purchase embroidered dresses and locally made pieces of silver jewellery. Opening times erratic, leave a donation.

Sleeping The hotel provision is not constant. The government closes those 'not up to standard' but they reopen very soon. Accommodation includes: **F** *Alpenblick Hotel*, T802184. 22 double rooms with shower E£50, budget room E£16.5, breakfast E£5, lunch E£8, dinner E£12, are based on large helpings of bread, evening tea round the fire in the courtyard makes it a special place. **F** *Aïn Bishmo*, T/F802177. 20 rooms with fans, shared facilities, breakfast included and **F** *Paradise Hotel*, T802600. 6 rooms are slightly cheaper and even less comfortable.

Camping *Pyramid Mountain Camp*, at Bir al-Ghaba, 17 km from Bawati. Hot water spring of 42°C, huts, guard, E£6 per person per night includes mattress and blankets, ask at *Alpenblick Hotel* for details. Take all your own supplies. *Safari Camp* T802090 is included on tour itineraries; 20 double rooms some in reed huts – prices range from E£50 for double with bath to sleeping under the stars for E£2.

Bawati

To Cairo

New Popular Housing

Esso

Tyre Repairs

Oasis Heritage Museum

To Oasis Gardens

To Oasis Gardens & Roman Springs

Shops

To Aïn Bishmu

Antiquities Office

Sh Aïn Dorf

Ansari

Cemetery

3

Chemist

2

1

Butcher

Baker

El Fatah

To Siwa (420 km) & Safari Camp

To Farafra (185 km)

N

0 metres 200
0 yards 200

■ **Sleeping**
1 Alpenblick
2 Paradise

● **Eating**
1 Hamid
2 Paradise
3 Popular

Eating There are small shops and small cheap places to eat. *Popular Restaurant,* only popular because there is none better. None is outstanding.

Tour operators Tours of the White desert are organized by *Alpenblick Hotel*.

Transport Bus: buses from Bawati to **Cairo** (6 hrs) leave daily at 0700. Buses coming through from Farafra leave Bawati any time after 0900 on Sun, Tue and Thu. E£15. Buses for Farafra leave at 1330 on Mon, Thu and Sat. E£20. Enquire at *Popular Restaurant* for current times for these and any additional services. The ticket kiosk (hours very uncertain) is by the telephone office but only sells tickets for journeys originating in Bawati. Otherwise pay on the bus if you can get a seat. **Service Taxis**: leave for Cairo daily in the afternoon; leave for Farafra but not on a daily basis. Ask at the *Popular Restaurant* from where you might catch a microbus. Taxi is the only way to get to Siwa, fare about E£600.

Directory Banks National bank – changes cash – closed Fri and Sat, open 0800-1400. **Medical services** A doctor lives beside the post office.

Al-Qasr lying west on the road to Siwa, is Bawati's sister village, beneath which lies Bahariya's ancient capital. Here you will see stones from a 26th Dynasty (664-525 BC) temple reused for house building and the remains of a Roman triumphal arch which stayed intact until the 19th century.

A much improved but still fairly uncomfortable track leads west from here to **Siwa** (see page 379). A four-wheel drive and guide are recommended. Check at Tourist Information, main street, opposite Ansari Mosque, before you leave.

Before moving on from Bahariya, drivers must fill up with fuel and water as the nearest service station is in Dakhla which is 490 km away. The 180 km road between Bahariya and Farafra is in a very bad state. At best it will take four hours to travel so it is a good opportunity to admire the scenery. Just 12 km beyond the outskirts of Bawati is the Runi shrine of Rene Michael, the Swiss explorer who lived in the village for seven years, rediscovered the area and was so enchanted by the beauty of the place that he wanted to be buried there in the desert. Beyond lies the **Black Desert**, the pebbles of dolerite darkening the land. The road begins to rise out of the Bahariya depression through a colourful 'Rainbow' canyon and a checkpoint at el-Hayz. El-Hayz is a collection of hamlets rather than a specific place, about 35 km to the south. Some Roman finds have been reported including a church dated fifth/sixth century BC, a military camp and evidence of dwellings. A second checkpoint is just beyond the village of **Eïn el Izza**, a place to stop for a drink. On the plateau are numerous erosion features known locally as *lions*. Of special note are the small mountains of calcite. One just 10 m to the left of the road is called *Jebel el Izza* or Crystal Mountain and it is worth spending some time here. The road cuts through the escarpment and descends towards the Farafra depression. Of the flat topped outliers, two are particularly prominent to the east of the road, and are known as Twin Peaks.

Beyond is the fabled **White Desert** where many travellers stop and camp for the night. By moonlight, the eerie windshaped landscape has been compared to the Arctic wasteland, and sunrise here could be the highlight of your

Landforms in White Desert

The Western Desert

trip. These strange shaped rocks have caught the imagination of countless travellers – intrigued by them and inspired by them. Geologists will delight in the huge calcite crystals, the chalk fossils and the accumulations of pyrites. To the north of Jebel Gunna a road goes west to Eïn Della (Spring of the Shade). An extra permit is required for this journey and rarely provided.

Farafra Oasis
Colour map 2, grid B3

This is the smallest and most isolated of the oases in the Western Desert but the deep depression in which it lies suggests that it was once larger. To the northwest steep cliffs rise dramatically out of the desert while to the south there is a gentle incline. In spite of its isolation the residents of the region, who now number about 2,500 and are mainly from two extended families, have been involved in trade and contact with the Nile Valley since earliest times. The village of Qasr el-Farafra had a large 116-room mud brick *qasr* (fort, or castle) from which it got its name. This was used by all the villagers when they were under attack until it collapsed in 1958. The village is generally pleasing with palm-lined roads and decorated houses, although some less attractive concrete buildings are now being constructed.

Sights There are no ancient sites to visit in this oasis

Badr's Museum with its eccentric displays must not be missed. The small oases to the east of the village are intensively cultivated and pleasant to walk through. Open when owner decides! Leave a tip.

Sleeping *Al Badawiyya Hotel*, book in Cairo T3458524. Clean, rooms range from E£150 for large double with bath and TV to E£10 per person in shared room with shared facilities. *New Resthouse*, 5 rooms each with 3 beds, E£10 per bed, shower with warm water, no flyscreen, no curtains, electricity erratic, take your own sleeping bag and a torch and use their blanket to cover the window.

Camping Campsite at Bir Setta, 6 km from village has a hot spring, straw shacks in compound, used by '*Explore*', (see Specialist tour operators in Essentials) etc.

Eating *Hussein's Restaurant* serves *fuul*, omelette or tinned tuna with chips or bread with Coca Cola or tea. Residents at the *New Resthouse* have similar menu with tinned fig jam. *White Desert Restaurant* and *Sa'ad Restaurant* keep very irregular opening days. There is a small bakery and goods like eggs are sold from dwellings.

Tour operators Ask at *Sa'ad Restaurant* for excursions into the desert.

Transport Road Bus: Buses and service taxis board at south of village. A/c bus to **Cairo** (10-11 hrs) is supposed to leave daily each morning and late evening with an extra bus just some days of

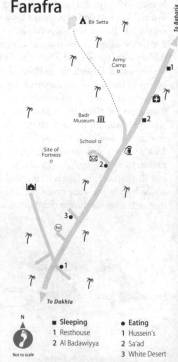

Farafra

To Bahariya

Bir Setta

Army Camp

Badr Museum

School

Site of Fortress

Pol

To Dakhla

N
Not to scale

■ Sleeping
1 Resthouse
2 Al Badawiyya

● Eating
1 Hussein's
2 Sa'ad
3 White Desert

the week. (Fare E£25): bus to Dakhla (4-5 hrs) leaves daily around 1300 and 0100 (fare E£12). Check the latest timetables. Buy your ticket on the bus. **Microbuses** to Dakhla leave when full, fare E£15. Rarely to Cairo. **Service Taxis**: to Cairo are very irregular – depends on a returning vehicle (fare E£15). To Dakhla daily, very early.

Directory Useful information There is no tourist information, and no bank. There is no petrol station but fuel from cans is available. Post office is open 0900-1430, closed Fri. The adjacent telephone office (national calls only) is open daily 0600-1200.

Dakhla Oasis

Moving on southeast from Farafra, the much larger **Dakhla** oasis, with a population of around 70,000 in 14 settlements, is 310 km from Farafra, and buses make the journey in 4-5 hours and a car in 3-4 hours.

Colour map 1, grid B3
Population: 70,000
Altitude: 111 m

The first 100 km of the journey are through unoccupied oases and open areas of sand which in places extend over the road. The check point at Abu Minguan has a resthouse offering tea. Beyond, the sand dunes increase in size and after a huge vegetation filled *wadi* crosses the route and then the check point stands at Maghoub, sheltering under Jebel Edmonstone.

Just 1 km directly south of Maghoub is **Deir el Haga**, a small sandstone temple dating from the Roman period which was built in honour of the triad of Thebian gods, Amun Ra', Mut and Khonsu. It is a remote and very tranquil location. The site, surrounded by a wall, is well preserved due to being enveloped by the sand for much of its more recent history and may have been rebuilt during the reigns of Nero (AD 54-68) and Titus (AD 79-81). This ancient wall, just the mudbrick capping is new, is designed to deflect the drifting sand, and is fairly effective.

The temple consists of a two-columned court and a hypostyle court with four columns, a vestibule and a sanctuary. Each of the columns in the hypostyle hall has inscriptions to Emperor Titus, the columns in the sanctuary to Domitian and to Vespasian and Nero in the sanctuary itself. There are some interesting inscriptions representing religious life. It was officially closed to visitors while Canadian specialists did renovations under the Dakhla Oasis Project. The responsibility for the site now lies in the hands of the Supreme Council of Antiquities, who are actively encouraging visitors. In the corner of the surrounding windbreak was the site workshop, now converted into a simple but instructive visitors' centre. Here there are nine framed panels. The central bilingual (English and Arabic) panel describes the site before restoration. The four to the right (in English) and the left (in Arabic) show a plan, describe the history, introduce the gods and emperors and explain the conservation process. The route is not direct but the temple can be seen from Maghoub or from the Muzawaka tombs and reached across country in the right kind of vehicle. The Roman period **Muzawaka Tombs** (Hill of Decoration), the larger one of Petosiris (AD 54-84) and the other of Sadosiris, his wife, are clearly signed to the south of the road, access by normal vehicle along piste to car park, but everything here is firmly shut. One is thus unable to see neither the murals depicting contemporary myths relating to the afterlife, nor the zodiac ceiling.

The Western Desert

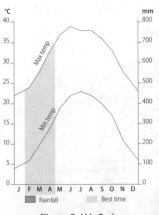

Climate: Dakhla Oasis

Mut

Colour map 1, grid B2 **Sights** Set in a striking landscape, **Mut** (pronounced moot), the capital, is pretty in a shabby faded way. It is a lively town and the people are very friendly. The Tourist Office, Sharia el Tharwa, on road to Al-Qasr, is open Sunday-Thursday 0900-1400, T940407. Ask here for trips into the desert, and overnight stays.

Ethnographic Museum, displays of Oasis life. ■ *0800-1400 and 1800-2100 except Fri.*

Sleeping **D** *Dakhla Muhariz Hotel* on Sharia el Tharwa, T941524. Organized for package tours, quite clean, avoid taking a room over TV lounge or kitchen if you want some rest, large double room, hot shower, netting and shutters on window, 2 restaurants, but little choice.

E *Garden Hotel*, T941577, near to bus station. Clean and fairly comfortable for budget travellers, rent a bike here.

F *Government Rest House*. **F** *Dar el Wafdeen Hotel* has 9 rooms, perhaps a last resort. **F** *Hot Spring Resthouse* at El Douhous has 6 chalets for E£5 each and 6 rooms in resthouse, all have private bathrooms.

Camping At *Hot Springs Resthouse*. Mosquitoes can be a problem here.

Eating Everywhere is cheap, some just cheaper than others. *Dakhla Hotel*, most uninspiring and highest prices. *Hamdy's Restaurant*, popular with tourists and locals. *Alhag Restaurant* noted for shish kebab. *Garden Hotel* for a good range of tasty dishes. *Abu Mohammed* comes last on our list.

Mut

To Farafra

To Qasr

To Kharga

Sh el Tharwalla-Khadra
Industrial Area
Fish Pond
Tyre Repair
Midan Tahrir
Sh 10th of Ramadan
Ethnographic Museum
Chemist
Cinema
el-Jedid
Sh Al-Ganeim
Midan Bakry
Sh Mohammed Mansour
Sh al-Wali
Ancient Muslim Cemetery
New Mosque
Midan al-Gamaa
Sh 23 July
Sh Gumhuria
Exhibition Centre
Sh Khgriba

N
Not to scale

■ **Sleeping**
1 Dakhla Muhariz
2 Garden
3 Government Resthouse
4 Hot Springs Resthouse
5 Dar el Wafdeem

● **Eating**
1 Abu Mohammed & Bike Hire
2 Alhag
3 Anwar Desert Paradise
4 Dakhla Café
5 Hamdy's

The Western Desert

Local Bicycles: can be hired from *Abu Mohammed's Café*, E£5 or *Garden Hotel* for **Transport** E£8. **Bus and service taxis**: run to Al-Qasr, 50 piastres, and a crowded local bus 4 times a day.

Long distance Air: to Cairo, Wed 0835; from Cairo, Wed 0600. **Bus**: from Dakhla (Mut) to **Cairo** taking 8-10 hrs (E£45) via Kharga (E£8) and Assiut (E£15) leave daily at 1700 and 1900; with 3/4 more buses daily just as far as Assiut and one on to Luxor leaving very early on Sun, Tue and Fri. To Cairo (E£35) via Farafra (E£10) and Bahariya (E£15) at 0600 and 1800. Check the latest timetables. **Taxi**: there are also service taxis from the bus station to all the above destinations, generally leaving early in the day. Fares Kharga E£7; Farafra and Assiut E£15.

Banks *Misr Bank*, open 0830-1400 and 1800-2100 each day, takes TCs and cash. **Directory** **Communications Post Offices**: both open Sat-Thu 0800-1400. **Telephone**: international calls are best made from the *Dakhla Muhariz Hotel*. **Medical services** *General Hospital*, T941333. **Useful telephone numbers Police**: T941500/941100.

Travelling northwest from Mut, the Hot Springs are on the left. Here water **Excursions** temperatures reach 43°C and the well is 1,224 m deep. After 1 km are the lakes known as the **Fish Pond**, a haven for water fowl and at times the surface is crowded with birds. Continuing north for 3 km is Rashda where there are Roman ruins at the east end of the village. As the villagers don't call them Roman, or indeed anything in particular, asking directions leads to a great deal of amusing confusion and disagreement. Ezbet Abu Asman has a white mosque and Deir Abuf Matta has Deir el Seba'a Banat Monastery of the Seven Virgins on the left. Look out for the Sheik's tomb and a single tree. Bud Khulu is an agricultural village with an old minaret on the left and the new village further on the right.

The next village is Ezbet Fiteima. Beyond this Bir el Gebel is signposted. This is about 5 km off the main road to the resthouse and well/spring.

Oasis cultivation

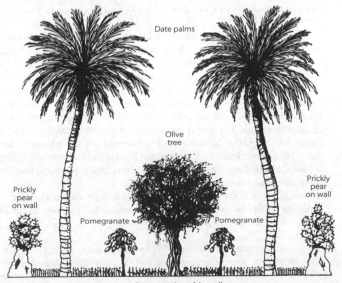

Date palms

Olive tree

Prickly pear on wall

Pomegranate Pomegranate

Prickly pear on wall

Peppers, wheat & broadbeans

The Western Desert

✏ *It must have been a mirage*

For a fascinating optical illusion try the mirage, a feature of all romantic travellers' adventures in the desert. Most commonly they occur in hot desert regions where the distant and most welcome pool of water perhaps reflecting swaying palm trees turns out, much to the disappointment of the thirsty traveller, to be another area of parched sand.

A mirage is caused by the bending of rays of light as they pass through layers of air which vary in temperature and density. The rays of light that come to the eye directly from the swaying palm fronds are interpreted by the brain in their correct position. Those rays that travel nearer to

the hot ground surface move faster through the warmer, less dense air as they meet less resistance. They change their direction as they travel, bending closer to the ground. The brain, however, assumes the rays have travelled in a direct line and records the blue sky as a pool of water and the trees as reflections. This illusion of wide expanses of inviting, shimmering "water" is favoured by film producers and novelists.

The rays are misinterpreted by the brain but they do exist so the mirage can be photographed. That does not, alas, make the water available to quench a thirst.

Mirages

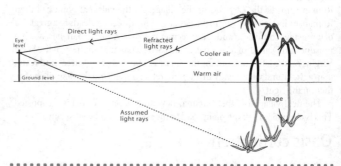

Al-Qasr was a Roman settlement and Dakhla's fortified mediaeval capital. The narrow streets, covered as protection from the sand and sun, found in the old quarter reflect the antiquity of the area. Ancient wooden lintels at doorways are decorated with carved inscriptions from the Koran. It is possible to see inside these houses. The houses of Abu Nafri and Abu Misid are commonly used by guides. An ancient mosque no longer in use dates back to the Ayyubid period, and alongside is Nasr el Din, a three-storey wooden minaret 21 m high. The *saqiya*, an ancient water wheel, near the two high pigeon towers and the sheikh's tomb, is a disappointment. No longer in use due to falling water levels it stands in a litter filled ravine and is rapidly falling to pieces. *El Kasr Hotel*, T876013, and restaurant on the main road is the only comfortable place to stay or eat.

Beyond Al-Qasr the road turns south and a large site on the right is **Amheidah** where the tombs date from 22nd century BC. The road continues by the Ottoman village of Qalamun back to Mut.

Dakhla to Kharga The journey from Dakhla to Kharga, 195 km in a generally easterly direction, takes about three hours. The road, good surface, passes the villages of Sheikh Wali and Masara, Asmant (Smint) a fortress town at 11 km, at 16 km Sheikh Mufta can be seen from the road on the right and at 20 km Qasr el Kassaba. To reach the ruins of Asmant el Khorab (**Kellis**) turn right off the road at the sign which says Kharga 170 km and drive directly into the desert for 1 km.

Balat, an interesting village with narrow covered streets and fertile gardens with vines and palms, dates back to the Turkish period. There are tombs from the 6th Dynasty and a Greek cemetery, but fresh supplies from the bakery at the west side of the village or refreshment at the tea shop are perhaps more attractive!

Bashendi, on a huge arch at its entrance, describes itself as a model village. To see the internal decorations of the Roman period 1st century BC Tomb of Kitnes you need to ask around for the key. The Tomb of Bash Endi has a Roman base and a much more recent Islamic dome.

The French have been working at **Aïn Asil** for 14 years. To reach the site turn towards Bashendi through the triumphal arch, swing left before the mosque and then right at the next through-way into the desert. The track turns off to the left to a brick hut, the excavations are behind the hut, ie going back towards the main road. **Qila el Dabba** visible from the Aïn Asil site with 6th Dynasty pyramids is also being worked by the French. Approaching these excavations from Aïn Asil avoids checks for permits.

Immediately beyond **Tineida** and its tombs on the left of the road is a checkpoint. Look out now for the sandstone outcrops very near the road and on the closest, to the south, are a number of inscriptions – some purporting to be very old.

Forty-five kilometres west of Kharga a new town is being constructed by the road to the phosphate mine. Your next point of interest is a single tree! The road into Kharga for the last 20 km has been replaced at intervals with another to the south due to the contiuing march of the dunes. There is a very poor entrance to Kharga from the west, through a rubbish tip.

Kharga Oasis

Pre-industrial Kharga was very different from the city of today. At that time the water level was considerably higher and the route was vital for the caravan trade. The New Valley scheme has converted this attractive oasis into a modern concrete town thereby removing almost all traces of its former charm. Nevertheless, two sites of interest remain in the surrounding area. **Tourist office**, opposite *Kharga Oasis Hotel*, open Sun-Thu 0800-1400, Fri 1400-2200, T900728.

Colour map 1, grid B4

Alwadi Algadeed Museum on Sharia Gamal Abdel Nasser opened 1993. ■ *Daily 0800-1500, £E20 for foreigners, E£10 students*. In particular look at the mummies, the painted sphinx and the selection of gold coins upstairs. This is a very good museum, well laid out and most of the items are named in English or French.

Sights

The **Temple of Hibis**, dedicated to Amun, at about 2 km to the north of the town, was begun in 510 BC at the beginning of the Persian occupation, under Darius and completed under Nectanebo II. It is one of the few remains from that period. It is dedicated to the triad of Thebian gods, Amun Ra', Mut and Khonsu. Unfortunately it was built on clay and suffers from subsidence. Several attempts have been made to restore the planks and reinforce the foundations. From the outer to the inner gate was an avenue of sphinxes and beyond the inner gate two obelisks of which just the bases remain. A wall, also made of local sandstone, surrounds the main temple with an entrance at the southeast into the portico of Nectanebo I and II. The first Hypostyle Hall has sixteen columns in four rows and the second Hypostyle hall four transverse columns. A third Hypostyle has four columns 2x2. Around this hall are small chambers, one with stairs to the roof. The sanctuary is at the far end.

The remains demonstrate the prevailing influence of the Pharaonic era on the later empires. The ornamentation and designs within the temple are mainly animals, showing vultures, dogs and serpents intertwined with Persian and Egyptian deities. On the walls of the sanctuary is a relief of Seth overcoming a serpent. ■ *E£16, students E£8.*

The **Necropolis of El-Baqawat**, covering an area 500 m x 200 m and situated approximately 5 km north of the town, can be reached by taking a dirt track from the Hibis Temple road through a palm grove and a short distance into the desert.This was once so far from civilization that hermits came for the seclusion it offered. In 490 the Christian theologian St Athanasius was banished here. About 500 baked brick tombs, originating from an early Christian burial site, and dating from 3rd-7th centuries lie crumbling in the desert. Small chapels cover some of the tombs. The most interesting features of the burial ground are the vivid wall paintings of biblical scenes. Some are fairly crudely executed and others were defaced by the ancient Greeks. The chapels are known by the illustrations they contain which are mainly of Old Testament scenes depicting Adam and Eve, the Exodus, Daniel in the lion's den, Noah's Ark, Abraham and Isaac. Look out for Jonah being vomited out of the whale's

The Western Desert

Kharga

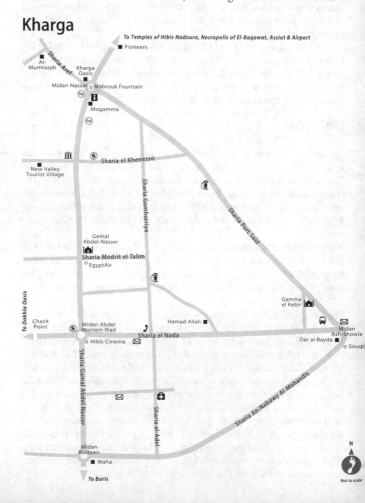

stomach. From the New Testament, the Virgin Mary and St Paul feature most often. Takla Hamanout, an Ethiopian saint, (see page 74) is shown here with St Paul. Some of the best preserved paintings are in locked chapels but, by negotiating with the guard, you may be allowed in to see them.

In the centre is a church dating from the fifth century AD – one of the oldest in Egypt. ■ *Daily 0800-1800 summer, 0800-1700 winter. E£20, students E£10.*

Temple of Nadoura, go north from town and turn right at the triumphal arch. This small temple of sandstone was built by Antonius Pius in AD 138 and commands a splendid view of the Temple of Hibis.

Sleeping

A *Pioneer* on road out to Assiut, T927982, F927983. A little out of keeping with the oasis but clean, comfortable and everything works, even the satellite TV. Bar and restaurant.

D *El Kharga Oasis*, Sharia Gamal Abdel Nasser, T901500. 30 rooms, rooms with a/c are more expensive, food very dull. **E** *Hamad Allah Hotel*, T900638, F925017. 54 rooms with phone and shower, restaurant, bar, shop, garden, lunch E£15, dinner E£20.

F *Dar al-Bayda,* T921717. A new place to stay in old town near Midan Ash-Showla is still being built but the lower floors are occupied. Most rooms have fans and a bathroom. Very noisy. **F** *Waha*, T900393. Cheap, fairly comfortable, hot water supply is erratic.

Government guest houses providing cheap accommodation like *Al-Mumtazah* and *Mogamma* are not always easy to access as occupation is restricted.

Camping At *El Kharga Oasis* where use of hotel facilities is permitted, E£7 per night. *Nasr Wells*, south of Kharga, is in a beautiful site. Although there are only a few official camping areas there is no problem camping along the route. Indeed one of the highlights of the trip, albeit for properly equipped campers with sufficient water, is a night spent under the stars.

Eating

Besides the hotels and the few local cafés the choice is limited.

Transport

Air There are direct flights on Wed (0740) and Sun (0825) to Cairo, takes 50 mins. Airport is 5 km northeast of town on road to Assiut. Airport: T901695.
Road Bus: from Midan Ash-Showla to **Cairo** each day (10 hrs). The evening bus has a/c and costs more. The morning bus is cheapest. There are three buses daily to Dakhla, taking 3 hrs, costing about E£8. Buses to **Luxor** leave on three days a week. Going via Assiut take about 4 hrs longer. There is a more frequent service just to Assiut. *Upper Egypt Bus Co*, T900838. **Service taxis**: usually caught from near the bus station are marginally more expensive than the bus but are quicker, taking 5 hrs to Assiut. Some only travel at night when it is cooler – this means missing the searing heat and the magnificent scenery which are the two things which make the Great Desert Circuit the great experience that it is! **Taxis**: which are supposed to cover the whole of the area, T900029.

Directory

Banks *Misr Bank*, open Sun-Thu 0800-1400 and 1700-2000, Fri-Sat opens at 1030. **Medical services** *General Hospital*, T900777. **Useful telephone numbers** Police: T122. **Tourist police**: T901502.

Excursions south

To the south of Kharga, on the road to Darfur is the Nasser Resthouse and Tourist Wells with campsite; Bulaq village with wells/springs with temperatures reaching 39°C and a primitive resthouse; Qasr el-Ghueita with a 25th-Dynasty Ptolemaic Temple of Amun. Mut and Khonsu; Qasr Zaiyan with a Ptolemaic and Roman Temple again to Amun and Qasr Dush southeast of Baris with a Roman Temple dedicated to the Gods Serapis and Isis, also a mud-brick Turkish fortress, an ancient church and some Coptic pottery. Service taxis and buses operate on this route. The road to Luxor (another 225 km) turns off at Jala.

Excursions north

To the north excursions can be made to Ain Umm Dabadib with ruins of ancient settlements and a Roman castle; Qasr el-Labeka which is one of the largest forts in this oasis and boasts Roman tombs and a temple; and El-Deir where walls and towers still stand. If time is limited visit El-Deir with access by car to within 1 km of the site, but take a guide as the route is unclear.

The cliffs here dominated the route to Assiut, and the mud brick ruins of the Monastery of Mustapha Kachef (Mustapha the taxman) to the west of the road just beyond the airport indicate good use was made of this position.

Assiut

Arriving back in the Nile Valley at **Assiut** (see chapter Middle Egypt page 184) one can either continue the circuit back to Cairo or take the opportunity to travel south (security permitting) via the Abydos and Dendera temples to the wonders of Luxor and the Valley of the Kings.

Transport

Transport is certainly no problem. **Air** There are direct flights to **Luxor** (Tue 0730), **Cairo** (Tue 1715, Sun 0720) and Kharga (Sun 0720) from the airport 10 km northwest of the town. **Train** Trains run 12 times a day to **Cairo** (7 hrs) via Mallawi (2 hrs) and Minya (3 hrs), but less frequently to Luxor (6-7 hrs) via Sohag (2 hrs) and Qena (4-5 hrs). Remember that foreign visitors are restricted to designated trains. **Road Bus**: there are 7 daily buses to Cairo (7 hrs) as well as buses every 30 mins between 0600-1800 north to Minya (2 hrs) and south to Sohag. **Service taxis**: where permitted run to every town between Minya and Sohag and are easy to catch from the main depot in the mornings but are less frequent later in the day.

Background

14

494

Background

History

"There is no country which possesses so many wonders." Herodotus, 450 BC.

The River Nile has been the key influence on life in Egypt since the beginning of civilization many thousands of years ago. This vast supply of sweet water permitted the creation of a society which produced the many wonders of ancient Egypt. Today no less than in the past modern Egypt depends on the river to support its huge population. The River Nile continues to be the lifeblood of Egypt as it was in the time of Herodotus.

The Sahara began to dessicate some 10,000 years ago and divided the Caucasoid populations of North Africa from the Negroid populations of West and Equatorial Africa. The original agricultural mode of production which had been the basis of settlement there was gradually replaced by nomadic pastoralism which, by around 4000 BC, had become the preserve of two groups, the Libyan-Berbers in the east part and the ancestors of the modern Touareq in the west. North African populations, all classified as part of the Hamito-Semitic group which stretched east into Arabia, soon became sub-divided into the Berbers in the west, the Egyptians in the east and the Nilo-Saharians and Kushites to the south in what today is Sudan.

The key to the development of a complex civilization lay in the water and soils of the Nile valley. By 3000 BC, the Nile was supporting a dense sedentary agricultural society which produced a surplus and increasingly allowed socio-economic specialization. This evolved into a system of absolute divine monarchy when the original two kingdoms were amalgamated by the victory of King Menes of Upper Egypt who then became the first Pharaoh. Pharaonic Egypt was limited by an inadequate resource base, being especially deficient in timber. Although it was forced to trade, particularly with the Levant (Eastern Mediterrean), it never became a major seafaring nation. Equally, the growing desertification of Libya meant that its influence never extended west. Instead, the Egyptian Empire sought control up the Nile valley, towards Kush (or Nubia) which it conquered as far south as the Fourth Cataract (between Khartoum and Wadi Halfa in Sudan) by 1500 BC. It also expanded east into the Levant, until it was restrained by the expanding civilizations of the Fertile Crescent (the arc of territory lying between the rainfed east Mediterranean coastlands/Syria/Mesopotamia) after 2300 BC.

By 1000 BC, Pharaonic Egypt was being pressured from all sides. The Hyksos (the shepherd kings of Egypt (2000-1700 BC) who migrated to Egypt from Asia) threatened the Delta from the Mediterranean, whilst the Lebu from Libya began to settle there too. They eventually created the 21st (Sheshonnaq) dynasty of the New Kingdom in 912 BC which, for a short time, extended its power east as far as Jerusalem. In the 7th century BC, however, Egypt was conquered by its Kushitic imitators to the south in the Nubian kingdom under King Piankhy who founded the 25th Pharaonic Dynasty.

The Nubians were expelled some years later by the Assyrians, but their conquest marked the end of the greatness of Pharaonic Egypt. Thereafter, Egypt was to be a dependency of more powerful states in the Middle East or the Mediterranean. The rulers of Nubian Kush in their turn, having been expelled from Egypt, looked south from their new capital at Meroe – to which they had moved as a result of the subsequent Persian conquest of Egypt in 525 BC and later Persian attempts to conquer Kush. Kush became, instead, the vehicle of transmission of iron-working technology and of Egyptian concepts of divine political organization southwards as well.

Dynasties in Egypt up to 30 BC

(with rulers as mentioned in text)
Dates of dynasties and individual reigns are as precise as possible.

Ruler	Date
Early Dynastic Period *(3100-2686 BC)*	
First Dynasty	*3100-2890 BC (Memphis established)*
Menes	
Second Dynasty	*2890-2686 BC*
The Old Kingdom *(2686-2181 BC)*	
Third Dynasty	*2686-2613 BC*
King Zoser	*2667-2648 (Step Pyramid in Saqqara)*
Huni	
Fourth Dynasty	*2613-2494 BC (Pyramids of Giza)*
Snefru	
Cheops (Khufu)	
Chephren (Khafre)	
Mycerinus (Menkaure)	
Shepseskaf	
Fifth Dynasty	*2494-2345 BC*
Unas	
Pyramids of Abu Sir	
Sun Temples of Abu Gharub	
Sixth Dynasty	*2345-2181 BC*
South Saqqara necropolis	
Teti	
Pepi I	
Pepi II	
First Intermediate Period *(2181-2050 BC)*	
Seventh Dynasty	*2181-2173 BC*
Middle Kingdom *(2050-1786 BC)*	
Eleventh Dynasty	*2050-1991 BC*
King Menutuhotep II	*Creation of Thebes (Luxor)*
Twelfth Dynasty	*1991-1786 BC*
Amenemhat I	*1991-1961*
Senusert I	*1971-1928*
Senusert II	*1897-1878*
Amenemhat III	*1842-1797*
Queen Sobek-Nefru	*1789-1786*
Second Intermediate Period *(1786-1567 BC)*	
Fifteenth Dynasty	*1674-1567 BC (capital Avaris)*
New Kingdom *(1567-1085 BC) based on Thebes*	
Eighteenth Dynasty	*1567-1320 BC (Temples of Luxor & Karnak)*
Amenhotep I	*1546-1526*
Tuthmosis I	*1525-1512*
Tuthmosis II	*1512-1504*
Hatshepsut	*1503-1482*
Tuthmosis III	*1504-1450*

Ruler	Date
Amenhotep II	1450-1425
Tuthmosis IV	1425-1417
Amenhotep III	1417-1379
Amenhotep IV (Akhenaten)	1379-1362
Tutankhamen	1361-1352
Ay	1352-1348
Horemheb	1348-1320
Nineteenth Dynasty	**1320-1200 BC**
Ramses I	1320-1318
Seti I	1318-1304
Ramses II	1304-1237
Seti II	1216-1210
Siptah	1210-1204
Tawosert	1204-1200
Twentieth Dynasty	**1200-1085 BC**
Sethnakht	1200-1198
Ramses III	1198-1166
Ramses IV	1166-1160
Ramses V	1160-1156
Ramses VI	1156-1148
Ramses VII	1148-1141
Ramses IX	1140-1123
Ramses XI	1114-1085

Late Dynastic Period (1085-332 BC)

Twenty-second Dynasty	**945-715 BC**
Twenty-fifth Dynasty	**747-656 BC**
Shabaka	716-702
Twenty-sixth Dynasty	**664-525 BC**
Necho II	610-596
Twenty-seventh Dynasty	**525-404 BC (Persian occupation)**
Cambyses	525-522
Darius I	521-486
Thirtieth Dynasty 380-343 BC	
Nectanebo I	380-362
Nectanebo II	360-343

Late Period (332-30 BC) (Macedonian Kings, capital Alexandria)

Alexander III (The Great)	332-323
Philip Arrhidaeus	323-317
Ptolemaic Era	323-30 BC
Ptolemy I	Soter 323-282
Ptolemy II	282-246
Ptolemy III	246-222 (Edfu Temple)
Ptolemy IV	222-205
Ptolemy V	205-180 (Kom-Ombo Temple)
Ptolemy VII	180-145
Ptolemy VIII	170-145
Ptolemy IX	170-116
Ptolemy XIII	88-51
Cleopatra VII	51-30

Background

The Jews in Egypt

Jewish involvement in Egyptian affairs has long historical roots. Twelve tribes of Israel were forced by famine to migrate to Egypt where they remained as an underprivileged minority until led out by Moses 13th century BC, eventually to move to Canaan in today's Palestine. During the period of dominance of Egypt by Greek and Roman cultures, the Jews became scattered around the major lands of the respective empires in the Diaspora. At that time Egypt was a major destination for the Jews in exile. It is estimated that as many as one million Jews lived in Egypt, with important centres of Jewish activity in Alexandria (see page 358), Leontopolis (north of Cairo in the eastern delta) and even in Lower Egypt as far south as Elephantine Island.

The Jewish population in Egypt declined with the passing of the Hellenistic tradition and the imposition of a less tolerant Roman government. During the Islamic era, the Jews, though subject to some social constraints and dealt with separately for tax purposes, thrived as traders and bankers in addition to their role as skilled craftsmen in the **souqs**. Occasional violence occurred against the Jews, who tended to be associated in the Egyptian popular mind with the foreign community and thus attacked at times of anti-British or anti-French riots in the major cities, as for example in 1882, 1919, 1921 and 1924. In general, however, it was true that Jews in Egypt fared far better and were more tolerated than Jews in some countries of Europe.

This all changed dramatically with the rise of Zionism in the period from 1890 and the return of Jews to Palestine. Even before World War Two the scale of Jewish migration to Palestine provoked fears in the Egyptian body politic and there were serious riots against the Jews in eight cities, most importantly in Alexandria and Cairo in 1938-39. Foundation of the State of Israel in 1948 brought an inevitable outbreak of rioting in which the Jews were a principal target. The Arab-Israeli wars of 1948, 1957, 1968 and 1973 added to the problem. Some 29,500 Jews left Egypt for Israel alone in the years 1949-72, in the latter years in official expulsions. Under pressure from both the flight to Israel and migration elsewhere, the Jewish population in Egypt fell from approximately 75,000 in 1948 to a few families by 1998.

A return of diplomatic relations between Egypt and Israel after President Anwar Sadat's visit to Jerusalem in 1977 improved official links and economic contacts between the two sides (albeit put in jeopardy by Israel's break of faith with the peace process in 1997), but the Jews have never returned as a community to Egypt.

Pharaonic Egypt

About 3100 BC, **King Menes** succeeded in uniting Upper and Lower Egypt into a single kingdom. His new capital at **Memphis**, about 15 km to the south of modern-day Cairo, was deliberately located on the border of Upper and Lower Egypt. Despite this the rivalry between the two parts of Egypt continued until the end of the Early Dynastic Period (3100-2686 BC).

The **Old Kingdom** (2686-2181 BC) began with the 3rd Dynasty and ushered in a major period of achievement. A series of strong and able rulers established a highly centralized government. The 'Great House', per-aha from which the word pharaoh is derived, controlled all trade routes and markets. The calendar was introduced and the sun-god **Re** was the most revered deity. Until then it was common practice for leaders to be buried in underground mausoleums (mastabas).

Symbol of Sun-god Re

The Three Crowns of Egypt

The king was a reincarnation of a god – Re, Aten, Amun or Horus. He was addressed by the god as "my living image upon earth".

A king was recognized on illustrations by his garments and paraphernalia. The most important of these was his crown. The earliest kings wore the white bulbous crown of Upper Egypt. The red crown of Lower Egypt was even more distinctive with a high back

and forward thrusting coil. A king wearing the double crown was thought to symbolize his control over all Egypt.

The ultimate sign of kingship however was the uraeus on his forehead, a rearing cobra with an inflated hood – generally in gold.

Other items of importance associated with kingship included the hand held crook and flail and the false plaited beard.

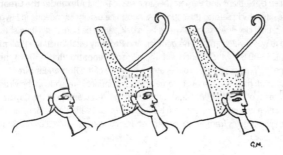

Crown of Upper Egypt known as the white crown or Hedjet *Crown of Lower Egypt known as the red crown or Deshret* *Crown of both Lower and Upper Egypt of Sekhemti*

In the 27th century BC **King Zoser** and his chief architect **Imohotep** constructed the first **step pyramid** in Saqqara, the huge necropolis across the river from Memphis, and pyramids became the principal method of royal burial for the Pharaohs during the next millennium. The scale of organization required to mobilize the resources and manpower to build these phenomenal pyramids is testimony to the level of sophistication of this period. The three 4th Dynasty (2613-2494 BC) giant pyramids of Cheops, Chephren and Mycerinus erected on the Giza plateau still awe the world.

By the end of the Old Kingdom, the absolute power of the Pharaohs declined. Local leaders ruled their own *nomes* (provinces) and a second capital emerged at Heracleopolis. Few great monuments were built in this very unstable **First Intermediate Period** (2181-2050 BC).

During the 11th Dynasty **Menutuhotep II** reunited the country and created a new capital at **Thebes** (Luxor). Remains from this era, the **Middle Kingdom** (2050-1786 BC), demonstrate its prosperity.

During the five dynasties of the **Second Intermediate Period** (1786-1567 BC), central authority again disintegrated and Egypt was controlled briefly by Asiatic kings known as the **Hyksos** (foreign princes), rulers who introduced horses and chariots to Egypt.

The **New Kingdom** (1567-1085 BC), spanning the 18th-20th Dynasties and based at Thebes, ushered in a period of unparalleled wealth and power. During these 400 years the kingdom prospered and expeditions led to the creation of a huge empire. Military campaigns in Western Asia by **Tuthmosis III**, now known as the Napoleon of Ancient Egypt, brought Palestine, Syna and Nubia into the empire and their wealth and cheap labour poured into Thebes. The temple complex of **Karnak** and the **Valley of the Kings** are but two of the astounding remains of the era. During this period (1379-62 BC), **Akhenaten** renounced the traditional gods in favour of a monotheistic religion based on the sun-god Re but his boy-king successor **Tutankhamen** immediately reverted to the former religion and its principal god Amun. In 1922 archaeologists discovered Tutankhamen's undisturbed tomb and its treasures are displayed at the Egyptian Museum in Cairo. After the military dictatorship of Horemheb, a general who seized the throne, royal power was restored by **Ramses I**. **Ramses II**, a most prestigious builder, reigned for 67 years. Following the death of **Ramses III**, the last great pharaoh, effective power moved increasingly into the hands of the Amun priests and the empire declined. The pharaoh's power diminished through intra-dynastic strife, decline in political grip on the levers of power and loss of control of day-to-day administration.

During the **Late Dynastic Period** (1085-332 BC), the succession of dynasties, some ruled by Nubians and Persians, became so weak that **Alexander the Great** had little difficulty in seizing the country. Although he did not spend long in Egypt his new capital city of Alexandria where he is believed to be buried, still flourishes. His empire was divided among his generals and **Ptolemy** established the Ptolemaic Dynasty (332-30 BC) which ended with the reign of **Cleopatra VII** (51-30 BC), the last of the Ptolemies, before Egypt became a province of the **Roman Empire**.

The division of power between Rome and Constantinople resulted in the virtual abandonment of Egypt. Egypt's autonomy led to the development of the **Coptic church** which was independent from both the Byzantines and the Romans, and whose calendar dates from AD 284 when thousands were massacred by the Roman emperor Diocletian.

Greeks and Phoenicians

In North Africa, Egypt's failure to expand westward permitted other developments to occur. The coastal area became the arena for competition between those Mediterranean civilizations which had acquired a naval capacity – the Greeks and the Phoenicians. Indeed, this became the future pattern and resulted in the history of the region being described in the terms of its conquerers.

We do know, however, that the Greek and Phoenician settlements on the coast provoked a response from the nomadic communities of the desert such as the Garamantes around the Fezzan in Libya. These communities appear to have specialized in warfare based on charioteering and they began to raid the new coastal settlements. At the same time, they also controlled trans-Saharan commerce – one of the major reasons why the Phoenicians, at least, were so interested in North Africa. As a result, they also engaged in trade with the new coastal communities, particularly those created by the Phoenicians. Other invasions also took place, this time of Northeast Africa from Southern Arabia, bringing Arab tribes into Africa. The new Arab invaders spread rapidly into modern Ethiopia and Eritrea.

The Greeks had begun to colonize the Egyptian and eastern Libyan coastline as part of their attempt to control Egyptian maritime trade. Greeks and Phoenicians competed for control of the old coastal areas in Libya and eventually created an uneasy division of the region between themselves. The Greeks took over Egypt after the creation of the Ptolemaic Kingdom on the death of Alexander the Great in 323 BC and incorporated Cyrenaica into the new kingdom. The Phoenicians, by now being harried in their original Lebanese home base of Tyre by the Assyrians and Persians, created a new and powerful maritime commercial empire based on Carthage, with outlying colonies to the west, right round to the Atlantic coast at Lixus (Larache).

Coptic Monasteries in Egypt

Cairo

Convent of St George, page 73.

Convent of (Abu Seifein) St Mercurius.

Saqqara – remains of the Monastery of St Jeremias, page 149.

Giza – Monastery of (Abu Seifein) St Mercurius, page 160.

El-Fayoum

Deir al-Adhra (Monastery of the Virgin), page 168.

Deir Malak Ghobrial (Monastery of the Angel Gabriel), page 168.

Deir Anba Samwail (Monastery of St Samuel), page 168.

Deir Mari Girgis (Monastery of St George), page 168.

Deir Hammam, page 168.

Northern Egypt

Abu Mina near Mobarak – Deir Mari Mina (St Menas), page 371.

Wadi el-Natrun – Deir el-Baramous (of the Romans), page 344.

Deir el-Suriani (of the Syrians), page 343.

Deir Anba Bishoi (St Bishoi), page 343.

Deir Abu Maqar (St Makarios), page 342.

El-Mansura – Deir Sitt Damyanah (St Damyanah), page 334.

Red Sea

Monastery of St Anthony, page 447.

Monastery of St Paul, page 447.

Middle and Upper Egypt

Dirunka near Assuit – Deir Dirunka (Convent of St Mary the Virgin), page 185.

El-Qusiya – Deir el-Muharraq (St Mary) (Burnt Monastery), page 185.

Sohag – Deir al-Abyad White Monastery (St Shenuda), page 186.

Sohag – Deir al-Ahmar Red Monastery (St Bishoi), page 186.

Akhmim – Deir al Adra (Convent of the Holy Virgin), page 187.

Akhmim – Deir al Shuhada (Monastery of the Martyrs), page 187.

Nag Hammadi – Monastery of St Palomen, page 191.

Luxor – St Theodore, page 263.

Esna – Convent of St George, page 274.

Esna – Convent of the Holy Martyrs, page 275.

Esna – Deir al Shuhada (Monastery of the Martyrs), page 187.

Edfu – Anba Bakhum al Shayib Monastery of St Pachom, page 281.

Edfu – St Pachom, page 281.

Aswan – St Simeon, page 297.

Kharga

Necropolis of el-Baqawat, page 490.

The Roman Empire

Control of Egypt and North Africa passed on once again, this time to the rapidly expanding city-state of Rome. Control of the Ptolemaic Kingdom of Egypt passed to Rome because of Roman interest in its agricultural produce and Egypt became a province of Rome in 30 BC.

The difficult problem of border security for Roman administrators was solved by creating the limes, a border region along the desert edge which was settled with former legionaries as a militarized agriculturalist population. Thus, although the border region was permeable to trade, resistance to tribal incursion could be rapidly mobilized from the resident population, while regular forces were brought to the scene. The limes spread west from Egypt as far as the Moroccan Atlantic coast.

Christianity

Egyptian Christianity became the major focus of the development of Christian doctrine. The Coptic Church became the major proponent of Monophysitism (the belief that there is only one nature in the person of Jesus Christ (not a three-in-one-being) after the Council of Chalcedon in AD 451; Donatism (direct giving, official largesse) dominated Numidia (an area approximately the size of present day Algeria). At the same time, official Christianity in Egypt – the Melkite Church (Christians adhering to the rulings of the Council of Chalcedon that there are two natures to the person of Christ. Take their name as "monarchists" or "supporters of the Byzantine emperor") – combined with the Coptic Church to convert areas to the south of Egypt to Christianity.

The Islamic Period

In AD 642, 10 years after the death of the Prophet Mohammed, Arab armies, acting as the vanguard of Islam, conquered Egypt. To secure his conquest, the Arab commander, Amr Ibin al-As, immediately decided to move west into Cyrenaica (a part of Libya) where the local Berber population submitted to the new invaders. Despite a constant pattern of disturbance, the Arab conquerers of Egypt and their successors did not ignore the potential of the region to the south. Nubia was invaded in AD 641-42 and again 10 years later. Arab merchants and, later, bedouin tribes from Arabia were able to move freely throughout the south. However, until AD 665, no real attempt was actually made to complete the conquest, largely because of internal problems within the new world of Islam.

The Muslim seizure of Egypt was, despite the introduction of Islam, broadly welcomed by the Copts in preference to remaining under the Byzantine yoke. Islam slowly prevailed as did the introduction of Arabic as the official language although there remained a significant Coptic minority. Cairo became the seat of government and emerged as a new Islamic city. Whilst the seeds of Islam itself strengthened and blossomed there were centuries of political instability which led to the creation of countless dynasties, mainly ruled by foreign Muslim empires. The new faith was only fleetingly threatened when the **Christian Crusader** armies attacked Cairo and were repelled by **Salah al-Din** (AD 1171-93).

The Great Dynasties and their successors

The Fatimids The first of the great dynasties that was to determine the future of North Africa did not, however, originate inside the region. Instead it used North Africa as a stepping stone towards its ambitions of taking over the Muslim world and imposing its own variant of Shi'a Islam. North Africa, because of its radical and egalitarian Islamic traditions, appears to have been the ideal starting point. The group concerned were the Isma'ilis who split off from the main body of Shi'a Muslims in AD 765.

The Fatimids took control over what had been Aghlabid Ifriquiya, founding a new capital at Mahdia in AD 912. Fatimid attention was concentrated on Egypt and, in AD 913-14, a Fatimid army temporarily occupied Alexandria. The Fatimids also developed a naval force and their conquest of Sicily in the mid-10th century provided them with a very useful base for attacks on Egypt.

After suppressing a Kharejite-Sunni rebellion in Ifriquiya between AD 943 and AD 947, the Fatimids were ready to plan the final conquest of Egypt. This took place in AD 969 when the Fatimid general, Jawhar, finally subdued the country. The Fatimids moved their capital to Egypt, where they founded a new urban centre, al-Qahira (from which the modern name, Cairo, is derived) next to the old Roman fortress of Babylon and the original Arab settlement of Fustat.

The Fatimids' main concern was to take control of the Middle East. This meant that Fatimid interest in North Africa would wane and leave an autonomous Emirate there which continued to recognize the authority of the Fatimids, although it abandoned support for Shi'a Islamic doctrine.

Myths

Myths have always played a very important part in the religion of ancient Egypt and it is not possible to separate the myths from the religious rituals. The story of Isis and Osiris, one of the chief Egyptian myths was written on papyrus some 5,000-6,000 years ago. That certainly makes it ancient.

The story of Isis and Osiris

According to the story Osiris was the son of Geb, the earth-god and was therefore descended from the sun-god Re. He was known to have been a great and good king and was particularly concerned with agricultural techniques, growing crops to provide the essentials, bread, beer and wine. He ruled wisely and when he travelled abroad Isis, his sister and wife, most competently took charge.

Now enters the bad guy. His brother Seth was filled with jealously and hatred for his brother Osiris and was determined to be rid of him. This he did with the help of the Queen of Ethiopia and another 72 conspirators. Seth had constructed a most magnificent chest, which exactly fitted the measurements of Osiris. At the feast all the guests tried the chest for size and when Osiris took his turn the conspirators (surprise, surprise) nailed down the lid and sealed it with boiling lead. Well Isis had warned about the dangers of going to that particular party.

The sealed chest was carried to the river bank and thrown into the Nile where it floated out to the sea and came to land at Byblos in Syria. There a tamarisk tree grew up immediately and enclosed the chest. The size of this magnificent new tree caught the eye of the king of Byblos, his name was Melcarthus, and he had it cut down to make a pillar to support the roof of his palace.

Isis, distressed by the disappearance of her husband's body and aware that without funeral rites he could never rest in eternity, went out to search. It took some time to trace the route to Byblos, find the chest still encased in the trunk of the tree but now supporting a main room in the king's palace and even longer to persuade them to part with that pillar and the chest.

She made her way back to Egypt with the body of Osiris still in the chest. Here she was a little careless for leaving the chest hidden but unguarded, she went off to be reunited with her young son. By some mischance Seth, hunting by the light of the moon, stumbled on the chest. He immediately recognized the container and in his rage cut the body into 14 separate pieces.

Seth, determined to rid himself of his brother once and for all took the pieces and scattered them through all the tribes of Egypt. Undaunted Isis set out again, this time in a papyrus boat, to retrieve the separate pieces which she did with the help of her sister Nephthys, the gods Thoth and Anubis and some magic. At every place where she found a part of her husband she set up a shrine. The severed parts where brought together and Osiris was restored to eternal life.

Horus, the son of Isis and Osiris, was brought up in secret to protect him from harm (no doubt his uncle Seth). When he reached manhood he swore to avenge the wrong done to his father and mother. The myth describes his victory over Seth after one or two setbacks and how he was declared by the tribunal of gods to be Osiris's rightful heir.

Background

The Hillalian invasions

Despite Fatimid concerns in the Middle East, the caliph in Cairo decided to return North Africa to Fatimid control. Lacking the means to do this himself, he used instead two tribes recently displaced from Syria and at that time residing in the Nile Delta – the Banu Sulaim and the Banu Hillal – as his troops. The invasions took place slowly over a period of around 50 years, starting in AD 1050 or 1051, and probably involved no more than 50,000 individuals.

The Hillalian invasions were a major and cataclysmic event in North Africa's history. They destroyed organized political power in the region and ensured the break up of the political link between Muslim North Africa and the Middle East. They also damaged the trading economy of the region. There was a major cultural development too for the Hillalian invasions, more than any other event, ensured that Arabic eventually became the majority language of the region.

Egypt after the Fatimids

Fatimid power in Egypt did not endure for long. They were forced to rely on a slave army recruited from the Turks of Central Asia and from the Sudanese. They found it increasingly difficult to control these forces and, eventually, became their victims. In 1073 AD, the commander of the Fatimid army in Syria, which had been recalled to restore order in Egypt, took power and the Fatimid caliph was left only with the prestige of his office.

What remained of the Fatimid Empire was now left virtually defenceless towards the east and the Seljuk Turks, who were already moving west, soon took advantage of this weakness. They were spurred on by the growth of Crusader power in the Levant and, after this threat had been contained, Egypt soon fell under their sway. Control of Egypt passed to Salah ad-Din ibn Ayyubi in AD 1169 and, for the next 80 years, the Ayyubids ruled in Cairo until, they in their turn, were displaced by their Mamluk slaves.

The Mamluks

The Mamluks were a class of Turkic slave-soldiers. The **first Mamluk Dynasty**, the Bahri Mamluks, were excellent administrators and soldiers. They expanded their control of the Levant and the Hijaz and extended their influence into Nubia. They cleared the Crusaders out of the Levant and checked the Mongol advance into the Middle East in the 1250s. They also improved Egypt's economy and developed its trading links with Europe and Asia. Indeed, the fact that the Mamluks were able to control and profit from the growing European trade with the Far East via Egypt was a major factor in their economic success.

In AD 1382, the Bahri Mamluks were displaced from power by the Burgi Mamluks. Their control of Egypt was a period of instability and decline. The Ottoman Turks, in a swift campaign in 1516-17, eliminated them and turned Egypt into a province of the Ottoman Empire.

The Ottomans in North Africa

The arrival of the Ottomans in North Africa was the last invasion of the region before the colonial period began in the 19th century.

The Ottoman Occupation

The Ottomans emerged with some strength from the Northwest heartlands of Anatolia in the 15th century. By 1453 they controlled the lands of the former Byzantine Empire and 65 years later took over Syria and Egypt before expanding deep into Europe, Africa and the Arab Middle East. The Syrian and Egyptian districts became economically and strategically important parts of the empire with their large populations, fertile arable lands and trade links.

Administratively, Palestine west of the Jordan Rift Valley was split into the *wilayat* (province) of Beirut along the northern coastal strip and the Sanjak (district) of Jerusalem in the south reaching down towards the Gulf of Aqaba. The east bank of the Jordan River fell within the *wilayat* of Syria and included Aqaba. Egypt was also a valued part of the Ottoman Empire, ownership of which provided the Sublime Porte (the Ottoman Court at Constantinople) with control over the Nile Valley, the east Mediterranean and North Africa. Power was exercised through governors appointed from Constantinople, but over the centuries an Egyptian, mainly Mamluke (Caucasian-origin) elite imposed themselves as the principal political force within the country and detached the area from the direct control of the Ottomans. In most areas of the empire, the ability of the sultan to influence events diminished with distance from the main garrison towns and a great deal of independence of action was open to local rulers and tribal chiefs outside the larger towns.

Mohammed Ali and his successors

Mohammed Ali, the founder of the Khedival Dynasty, was born in Macedonia in 1769, came to Egypt in 1800 as an officer in the Turkish army, and was made governor under the nominal control of the Ottoman Sultan in 1805. He remained in post as a vigorous and development oriented ruler until 1848. Mohammed Ali died in 1849 having begun the modernization of Egypt and the creation of an Egyptian national identity. He is buried in the eponymous mosque in the Citadel in Cairo.

Ibrahim Pasha, eldest son of Mohammed Ali, was trained as a political leader as well as a soldier. He acted very successfully as his father's right hand man but in his own right ruled for just four months in 1848. See his imposing statue erected in Midan Opera by his son.

Abbas Pasha (1848-54) was the son of Mohammed Ali's third son, Tusun. He organized the laying of a railway from Cairo to Alexandria with British support and encouragement. In other respects he was reactionary, closing schools of advanced studies and slowing down the modernization process.

Sa'id Pasha (1854-63), second son of Mohammed Ali, served as an admiral in the Egyptian fleet and gave permission for the Suez Canal to be constructed. Sadly a large foreign debt was left as a legacy to his successor.

Khedive Ismail (1863-79), son of Ibrahim Pasha, was considered one of the builders of modern Egypt, being responsible for the building of the Suez Canal, the Opera House, Ras el-Tin Palace and Abdin Palace. He was a man of great energy and vision. He expanded Egyptian influence in the south and east but eventually led the country deeper into debt and into subservience to French and British power.

Khedive Tawfik (1879-92) was the son of Ismail, during whose reign Egypt's financial problems led to foreign take over of her affairs and, finally, the beginning of the British occupation in 1882. Manial Palace, his dwelling in Cairo, houses an important museum (see page 120).

Khedive Abbas Hilmi II (1892-1914), son of Tawfik, was noted for his interest in preservation and conservation of the country's ancient monuments. His attempts to develop a nationalist political movement came to nothing. He was deposed by the British in 1914.

Sultan Hussain Kamal (1914-17) was the second son of the Khedive Ismail. He owed his throne to the British and, despite the hardships of the war period 1914-18, he ruled without challenging British power in Egypt.

King Fuad (1917-36) was another son of the Khedive Ismail, though much more an Egyptian nationalist than his brother Hussain Kamal. Egypt became more politically active and was given a form of independence in 1922 as a constitutional monarchy. However, Fuad was unable to create an acceptable political role for himself and was caught up in the political battles between the British and the nationalist politicians.

King Farouk (1936-52) was Fuad's son and the penultimate Khedival ruler of Egypt. He became, like his father, unable to manage an increasingly radical nationalist community in Egypt and the British occupiers distracted by the demands of World War Two and its legacies of change. Farouk had few political friends and he was forced to abdicate in 1952 in the face of the revolution by the Young Officers led by Gemal Abdel Nasser. Farouk's infant son, **Fuad II**, was nominally successor to the throne but lost all rights in the new constitution of 1953.

The great benefit of the Ottoman Empire was its operation as an open economic community with freedom of movement for citizens and goods. Traders exploited the Ottoman monopoly of land routes from the Mediterranean to Asia to handle the spice, gold and silk from the East, manufactures from Europe and the slave and gold traffic from Africa. Ottoman tolerance of Christian and Jewish populations led in Palestine/Syria to the growth of large settlements of non-Muslims. Arabic continued as the local language and Islamic culture was much reinforced. Elaborate mosques were added to the already diverse cultural heritage. Outside the larger towns, however, pastoralism, farming and parochial affairs remained the major occupation of the people and cultural and other changes were slow to occur.

Until the late 18th century the Ottoman Empire was wealthy, its armies and fleets dominant throughout the region but after that date a marked decline set in. European powers began to play a role in politics and trade at the expense of the sultan. The empire began to disintegrate. During the 19th century Egypt under the Khedives, the famous Mohammed Ali and his successor Ismael, were only nominally under the sultan's control. Egypt adopted Western ideas and technology from Europe and achieved some improvements in agricultural productivity. The cost was ultimate financial and political dominance of the French and British in this part of the empire. In Palestine, too, colonial interventions by the French in Syria and Lebanon reduced Ottoman control so that by the time of World War One the collapse of the Ottoman Empire was complete and the former provinces emerged as modern states, often under a European colonial umbrella.

The Ottoman occupation of North Africa was a by-product of Ottoman-Venetian competition for control of the Mediterranean, itself part of the boundless expansionism of the Ottomans once they had conquered Constantinople in 1453. The Ottoman attack was two-pronged, involving their newly acquired maritime power to establish a foothold and then backing it up with the janissary, land based forces that formed the empire's troops. The decrepit Mamluk Dynasty in Egypt fell to the Ottomans in 1517 and a new, centralized Ottoman administration was established there.

Egypt & Sudan In Egypt, the Ottoman administration soon found itself struggling against the unreconstructed remnants of Mamluk society, with the province frequently splitting into two units, each controlled by a different section of the Mamluk Dynasty. By 1786, the Ottomans had destroyed the Mamluk factions and restored central control. In 1798, **Napoleon's** army conquered Egypt, delivering a profound cultural shock to the Muslim world by demonstrating, in the most graphic manner, the technological superiority of Europe. In 1805 Mohammed Ali was appointed governor and lost no time in breaking away from the Ottoman Empire to found a new dynasty, the *khedivate*, which remained in power until a revolution in 1952.

Mohammed Ali sought to modernize Egypt and to expand its power. He brought in European military advisers, destroyed the remnants of the old political elite in Egypt and instituted wide-ranging economic reforms. In the Sudan, Mohammed Ali's Egypt was more successful; after the initial invasion in 1820, some 40 years were spent consolidating Egyptian rule, although, in 1881, the experiment failed (see box, page 505).

By that time, Egypt itself had succumbed to the financial pressures of its modernization programme. Borrowings from Europe began, with the inevitable consequence of unrepayable debt. In addition, Britain realized the potential importance of Egypt for access to its Indian Empire, particularly after the Suez Canal was opened in 1869. A debt administration was instituted in 1875, under joint British and French control. In 1881, a nationalist officers' rebellion against what they saw as excessive European influence in the *khedivate*, provoked a British take-over which lasted until 1922. Following British military commander General Gordon's death in Khartoum and the consequent British campaign against the Mahdist state in the Sudan, which culminated in the Battle of Omdurman in 1898, Britain instituted an Anglo-Egyptian condominium over Sudan.

Papyrus

This word was the name given to the plant *Cyperus papyrus* which grew alongside the River Nile. Later it was also given to the writing material made from the plant. Papyrus is a straight, tall, reed-like plant. Its leafless triangular stems rise to 5 m above the water being as 'thick as a man's arm' at their lower part. It is topped by drooping spikelets of insipid flowers and long thin leaves like soft ribs of an umbrella.

To produce writing paper the pith from the stem was cut into narrow strips and arranged in alternate layers at right angles to each other. The sheets were pressed together and dried in the sun, the natural juice of the plant making the pieces stick together. The sheets were pasted together to form rolls which varied in length. An example in the British Museum is 30 m long. On the inner side of the roll the fibres went across and the writing usually went the same way as the fibres. Paper made this way was cheap. The Egyptians are recorded as using it soon after 3000 BC and the Greeks around 500 BC.

The more slender stalks were woven into baskets (Miriam made a basket for Moses out of papyrus before she hid him in the same plants by the water's edge) and the thicker ones were tied into bundles and used to construct cheap, light boats, the earliest craft on the Nile. Isis went to search for the several parts of Osiris in a papyrus boat. The fibre used to make ropes, matting, awnings, sails and the pith, in addition to its important use for paper, was actually used as food by the less fortunate. The dried root of the papyrus plant was used as fuel and being a harder substance, the manufacture of utensils. The papyrus plant no longer grows in Egypt but can be found in the Sudan.

See the displays at the papyrus museums by the Nile at Cairo, Luxor and Aswan.

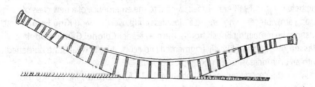

Colonialism

The British occupation of Egypt introduced a régime which, as the well known historian Ira Lapidus said 'managed the Egyptian economy efficiently but in the imperial interest'. Railways were built and widespread irrigation was introduced; the population virtually doubled inside 35 years; private property was increasingly concentrated in the hands of a new elite; and the foreign debt was repaid. Industrialization was, however, neglected and Egypt became ever more dependent on cotton exports for revenue.

Social and political relations were not so smooth. The British occupation of Egypt coincided with a wave of Islamic revivalism. At the same time, a secular nationalist tradition was developing in Egypt which crystallized into a political movement at the end of the 19th century and was stimulated by Egyptian resentment at British demands on Egypt during World War One.

After 3 years of agitation Britain granted limited independence in 1922. It retained control of foreign affairs, foreigners in Egypt, the Sudan and the Egyptian army although some of these controls were abandoned in 1936.

At the beginning of World War One, the potential vulnerability of the Suez Canal (see Box page 392) and the strategic implications of the Turkish-German alliance

President Mubarak – a four times winner

Hosni Mubarak's victory in the presidential referendum held in September 1999 won him a fourth six-year term. It might have been seen as a foregone conclusion. Voters were asked to either vote 'yes' or 'no', though there was no opposing candidate. To stand against the incumbent president an opponent needs the approval of at least two-thirds of the People's Assembly. In most circumstances Egypt's electoral system is designed to ensure that the National Democratic Party (NDP), which Hosni Mubarak leads, commands a majority in the Assembly and prevents any opposition from making a serious challenge.

There is an electoral register of 24 million, of which 19 million voted in 1999. With suspicious alacrity, it was officially announced less than 24 hours after the vote took place that 94% of voters had cast a 'yes' to a fourth term for President Mubarak. There was some skepticism about the scale of the turnout in a nation known for its political apathy. The government encouraged people to vote by offering free rail transport on the day of the election, and, for the first time, the electorate could cast their votes by email. But a four times presidential winner can afford to ignore the criticism and take credit for a well managed political survivor.

led **Britain** to increase its control over Egypt by declaring it a Protectorate. This led to the emergence, over the following 20 years, of both Arab and Egyptian nationalist movements which eventually procured nominal independence for Egypt in 1936, although Britain reserved the right to protect the Suez Canal and defend Egypt. By the end of World War Two, this complex political system had outlived its usefulness. In 1950, Egypt unilaterally abolished the Canal Zone Treaty.

In 1952 the constraints of the **British Mandates,** and the frustration following the defeat in the 1948 Arab-Israeli war, led to the emergence of a new class of young army officers who staged a bloodless coup overthrowing **King Farouk** and ousting the remaining British troops. The new leader, **Colonel Gamal Abdel Nasser**, inherited a politically fragmented and economically weak state burdened with an ever-increasing demographic problem.

When the World Bank, at the behest of the USA, refused to help finance the construction of the new Aswan High Dam in 1956 Nasser nationalized the Suez Canal in order to raise the necessary revenues. This led to shock waves throughout the world and to the **Suez crisis** in which an Anglo-French force invaded and occupied temporarily the Canal zone. Nasser's dreams of development were hampered by Egyptian/Israeli tensions including the shattering Egyptian defeat in the 1967 war. He died in 1970 and was succeeded by **Anwar Sadat**. Sadat was aware that Egypt could not sustain the economic burdens of continual conflict with Israel so, despite the partially successful October 1973 war which restored Egyptian military pride, sought peace with his neighbour. In 1977 he made a historic trip to Jerusalem and laid the foundations for the 1979 **Camp David Peace Accords** which enabled Egypt to concentrate on her own economic development and firmly allied Egypt with the USA. While he was applauded abroad he was considered a traitor in the eyes of the Arab world and Egypt was diplomatically isolated. His assassination by Islamic fundamentalists in October 1981 brought vice-president **Hosni Mubarak** to power.

Egypt in a nutshell

Official name	Jumhuriyah Misr al-Arabiyah (Arab Republic of Egypt)
National flag	Equal horizontal bands of red, white and black with a central emblem of Salah al-Din's golden eagle clutching a panel bearing the country's name in its claws.
Official language	Arabic
Official religion	Islam
Egypt statistics	Population: 63.2 million. Urban population: 43%. Religion: Muslim (mainly Sunni) 90%, Christian 10%. Birth rate: 28 per 1,000. Death rate: 9 per 1,000. Life expectancy: 65/69. GNP per capita: US$790.

Modern Egypt

Government

Egypt became a republic in 1952 with a presidential system of government. The current president is Hosni Mubarak who has effective control of the armed forces and the cabinet and can convene or dissolve the single tier People's Assembly virtually at will. President Mubarak is also head of the ruling National Democratic Party (NDP). There have been efforts to introduce an element of democracy into government with general elections for the People's Assembly. The cabinet is led by Atef Sedki but the principal influence on the membership of the cabinet is the president. The Assembly has worked well but, until recently, was seen as a puppet organization for the régime. The speaker of the Assembly, Rifat Mahjub, was assassinated in October 1990. There was an attempt in 1991 to improve local administration with the appointment of a new minister. Regional government is carried out through four groups of administrations – the governorates for the Desert, Lower Egypt, Upper Egypt and the urban areas. Sub-districts operate from regional capitals and separately for the cities of Port Said, Alexandria, Cairo and Suez. The administration is very bureaucratic and slow. There have been generally fruitless attempts to reform the civil service but, with 22% of the work force in public administration and defence, progress has been slow. Travellers should not have high expectations of officials and official agencies, though there are some institutions, mainly military, which function well. Personal influence is a key element in making the system work.

The government is only partially representative of the people and there are major dissident groups whose activities could affect the traveller. The **Muslim Brotherhood** – a form of fundamentalist Islamic organization – has flourished in Egypt for many years. While the Muslim Brotherhood is now the leading opposition group and is generally tolerated by the government the more extreme splinter groups, which have resorted to terrorism, are pursued by state agencies. In addition to attacking members of the government, often successfully, the extremists are opposed to corrupt foreign influences, of which the excesses of the tourist industry, including the country's 20,000 belly dancers, are seen as a key part. Opposition groups are suppressed by severe laws such as the detention regulations and by an ever-present security service, the **mokhabarat**.

Background

☞ *Turning back the clock – modern landlordism*

Egypt set the pace in land reform in the Arab world in the 1950s, abruptly removing many of the landlords on large estates and reorganizing the basis of farmland ownership by creating a new co-operative structure in which the government played the leading management role. Rural bureaucracy did no better in raising productivity in commercial cropping than the system before land reform.

In 1997 the landlords in farming areas were free from state-imposed (and up-dated) rent controls and security of tenure for tenant farmers was removed. This change led to a threefold increase in rentals for tenants and liberty for landlords to remove tenants on one-year's notice. It is thought that 420,000 out of 905,000 tenant farmers lost their farms in

the period 1997-2000. Many others accepted increased rental payments or remained on fragments of land they owned in their own right. Government schemes to provide new farms on which to re-settle displaced farmers have so far made only 12,000 new farms available. Rural unrest has inevitably followed this turning back of the clock in land tenancy. It is estimated that more than 85 people have died in clashes between displaced tenants and landlords with many injuries and a mass of legal complaints that are slowly being tackled by the courts.

The effects of the new tenancy law are partly beneficial. Productivity appears to be rising in traditional farming areas. But the social and economic collateral damage of the reform is very high for many poor Egyptian families in the villages.

Heritage Egypt's natural assets in the form of her skills and her fabric are at risk. There is now a clear need for the advanced industrialized countries to understand the basis of Islamic science and technology. Certainly this would help to bridge the growing cultural divide between themselves and their more numerous neighbours to the east. In particular, appreciation of the way in which Islamic culture has matured over the long-term is required so that the valuable skills and technologies of Egypt are not wastefully discarded for short-term gains. The rapid pace of 20th century modernizations might all too quickly sweep away the remains and the folk memories associated with traditional culture.

There is also a risk that rapid technological change forced on a developing Egypt by the industrialized nations could lead to the indigenous technology being unnecessarily discarded instead of being used and, in the future, being deployed with advantage. The urgency of the problem of conservation or rescue of traditional Islamic technologies is acute. War and strife are depleting physical assets such as buildings and other works. Quite apart from man-made disasters, the processes of weathering on mud brick, from which many Islamic traditional constructions are made, is considerable. The comparatively recent abandonment of traditional villages, old mosques and underground water cisterns in Egypt has exposed traditional technology/material culture to destruction by natural erosion.

There is a real threat that the existing stock of examples of traditional Egyptian and Islamic technology of this kind could vanish with little trace in less than a generation.

New lands – mega-developments

Egypt hopes to increase the area of land under cultivation by 40% in the next decade, cutting into the 96.5% of the nation's territory that is unused desert. The cultivated area will, it is expected, rise from 3,000,000 ha to 5,000,000 ha – representing an explosion of farming activity such as the country has not seen since the 19th century phase of dam building on the Nile. At the same time, there will be a vast expansion in new urban developments on lands reclaimed from the desert.

Foremost of the new projects is the South Valley Project at the Toshka, a large site close to Lake Nasser. Here 500,000 ha of farm land will be brought into use by private venture capitalists, including Saudi Arabian investors. In all it is estimated that the Toshka scheme will cost US$88 bn in the period 1999-2017.

The initiatives at Toshka and other parallel agricultural/industrial locations are a huge gamble which will need enormous foreign financial backing and great ecological care if they are to be successful. Egypt, with a population growing at 2% per year, needs every opportunity for employment and hectare of land to grow food that it can manufacture. The new projects thus carries immense implications for the country's future prosperity. Success is an imperative.

Economy

Agriculture

Agriculture is the basis of the Egyptian economy accounting for 16% of total national output and 35% of employment. Despite very rapid urbanization, farming and the rural community remains at the cultural heart of the country. Current land patterns show the vital importance of the Nile Valley and Delta because the rest of the country is little better than waste land. Unfortunately even this very limited arable area is being reduced by the encroachment of Cairo and other urban areas.

Traditional Agriculture The great mass of Egyptian farmland is under traditional forms of agriculture and worked by the *fellahin*, the Egyptian peasantry. Farming is based on use of the waters of the River Nile for irrigation which are now available, theoretically, throughout the year from Lake Nasser. In fact, approximately 65% of Egypt's agricultural land is under perennial cultivation and the remainder carries only one crop each year and/or is under a cultivation/fallow rotation. There has been a gradual increase in production of commercial crops but self-sufficiency is an important aim of small farmers. Wheat, rice, vegetables and fodder are the main crops, the latter to support the considerable number of draught (3.18 million buffalo), transport (two million asses and 200,000 camels) and other animals (3.23 million cattle, 3.3 million goats, 4.41 million sheep and 87 million chickens) kept mainly on farms. It is estimated that six million people are engaged directly in the traditional farming sector.

Land tenure Until the 1952 land reforms, 1% of Egypt's land owners possessed 90% of the farming land. The reform stripped the former royal house of its lands and the state took the estates of the great families who had controlled rural Egypt. In their place the revolutionary authorities established centrally controlled co-operatives which substituted civil servants for the former landlords, a move which did little to alter the agricultural system or indeed benefit the peasants. At the present time the peasantry is either landless or has tiny fragments of land which are mainly uneconomic. The

Background

🐾 Agricultural Output 1999

	(Tonnes)
Cotton	800,000
Maize	5,500,000
Oranges	1,525,000
Rice	5,900,000
Sugar cane	14,500,000
Tomatoes	5,900,000
Wheat	6,350,000
Source: FAO	

average availability of land per cultivator is put at 0.35 ha. Attempts to reclaim land in the desert regions using underground water and high technology irrigation systems have, at best, been of marginal use in resolving Egypt's shortage of agricultural land. Many Egyptian farmers now emigrate to adjacent countries and travellers in North Africa will come across large numbers of Egyptian *fellahin* (peasants) working the land and undertaking manual labour in Libya.

Modern Agriculture Modern farming is principally a matter of the operations of the centrally managed co-operatives on reformed land and the activities of the mixed farms on recently reclaimed land in the rimlands of the delta and the newlands in the desert interiors (see Box New lands – mega-developments). The co-operatives are still managed with a large participation by the government, which controls cropping within the central rotation and handles credit and technical matters. These farms have been turned over to commercial crops for the most part – cotton, sugar cane, maize and rice, some destined for export. The newland farms specialize in exploiting the opportunities for early cropping for the supply of fruit and vegetables to the European market. The new farms stand out in the landscape with their contemporary buildings and rectangular field patterns.

Potential Egypt's potential is hindered by its paucity of natural resources which, besides oil and natural gas produced in large enough quantities to meet domestic demand and some exports, are limited to iron, phosphate and a few other non-hydrocarbon minerals. The principal difficulty for Egypt, however, is its meagre area of fertile land and its reliance on the waters of the Nile. The growth of irrigation and hydro-electric schemes in the Upper Nile countries is putting Egypt's water supply at risk and there is no available substitute. Industrialization has some scope for expansion but the past record here is not encouraging.

Ultimately it seems that Egypt will have to continue to rely on its current principal sources of foreign exchange – oil, tourism, Suez Canal fees, and expatriate remittances – for its economic salvation. Unfortunately all four are dependent on stable political conditions in Egypt and the rest of the Middle East

The final problem for Egypt is that economic growth has to exceed its 1.9% annual population increase which implies no mean rate of development simply to stand still. For some years Egypt has relied, and will have to continue to rely, on predominantly US and European foreign aid for the 50% of food supplies needed annually from abroad to enable it to feed itself.

Energy/ Petroleum Egypt has made major strides in the petroleum industry in recent decades without, however, joining the league of principal oil-exporters. Reserves of crude oil are put by the Egyptian authorities at a modest 8.2 billion barrels, with Egypt expected to become a net energy importer by the turn of the century. Production of crude oil ran at 760,000 barrels per day in 1999. Crude sales abroad are important, accounting for 49% of all exports. Natural gas resources are more significant than oil with reserves of 120 trillion cubic feet and output at 2.5 billion cubic feet per day in 1999. The oilfield areas are widely distributed among the Suez/Sinai zone to the east and the more recently discovered Western Desert fields. Western oil companies play a key role in oil development in Egypt. The Aswan High Dam now supplies less than 10% of the country's total electricity of 49 billion kwh per year.

Axis to Africa

Egypt is re-developing its links in trade and economy with the African continent. It is spurred on by the need to establish new markets for its manufactured goods and by the need to compete with the growing political intervention by neighbouring Libya into Africa south of the Sahara. The Egyptian government also sees it as an important objective to compete with South Africa for leadership of the African countries as a whole. Above all, Egypt needs to consolidate its strategic control over Nile water resources by constructing strong diplomatic links with those African states such as Sudan, Ethiopia that lie upstream astride the River Nile. Egypt will be helped considerably in future negotiations for increased supplies of Nile water if it has close and well established relations with its southern neighbours.

Egypt has joined COMESA, a 21-member Common Market of East and Southern Africa, and is fast expanding other formal links into the sub-Sahara area to mitigate the effects of drought and encourage regional security.

The Egyptian engagement with Africa is important but will never displace the Arab world in its emotional attachment and is unlikely to out-perform growth in Egyptian commercial links with the EU under a new trade partnership accord.

Economic plans

Egypt was an early devotee of development planning, reinforced by the desire for a socialist centrally controlled economy under Gamal Abdel Nasser, the first president after the 1952 revolution. The plans were taken seriously and great efforts were made to use national resources to beat the twin difficulties of shortages of domestic natural resources and a burgeoning population. Some successes were won but the constant involvement of the country at the forefront of the Arab-Israeli wars diverted attention, funds and materials away from the economy. Under President Sadat the dedication to centralized control was gradually watered down and the plans became little more than indicative long-term budgets. Strategies were set at the top – development of the Suez Customs Free Zone under Sadat and privatization under Mubarak. The latest development plan continue emphasis on growth of the private sector including the transfer to it of some state assets. The government has limited means at its disposal to promote economic expansion given the high costs of debt repayment and defence, together representing 25% of the budget in most years.

Since the time of the 1952 revolution, there has been a growing tendency to turn to industrialization as a means of achieving faster economic growth and providing for the needs of an expanding population. Most industries were then state-owned, carried very large work forces and were inefficient. The country did nonetheless lay the basis for iron and steel, automobile and petrochemical sectors. Industry was concentrated around Cairo and its outliers such as Helwan. In recent years Egypt has industrialized steadily through a growth of small, private and/or foreign funded plants producing consumer goods, textiles, arms and processed foodstuffs. These factories are often highly efficient. Egypt has still however to diversify effectively into industry. Oil, mining and manufacturing together accounted for a quarter of the value of national output and employ 13% of the work force. The country is a long way from achieving its ideal of being the manufacturing centre for the Arab world.

Industry

Background

● ●

☛ *Industrial output 1996/97*

	(tonnes)
Cement	17,200,000
Cotton yarn	275,000
Fertilizers	7,354,000
Iron ore	2,430,000
Sugar	1,131,000
Automobiles	6,800 units
Source: Central Bank of Egypt	

Economic structure

	(%)
Trade, Finance, Insurance	25
Industry, Mining	27
Agriculture	16
Electricity etc	2
Transport, Communications	11
Construction	5
Public Admin. & Defence	8
Total incl others	100
Source: Central Bank of Egypt	

● ●

Trends in the economy

Economic growth has been erratic, but mainly too low to enable the economy to reach a level of self-sustaining development.

Part of the problem is the heavy foreign debt burden – US$29 bn – on the economy. Egypt continues to borrow overseas and the trend towards external dependence, which includes $US2 bn per year in aid, has not been fully reversed.

Recent policies, enforced by the IMF, are designed to rid the state of its ownership of economic assets, to expand the private sector and remove distortions in the economy arising from subsidies and restrictive practices. Domestic food production has steadily risen in response to the gradual removal of heavy state control on crops. Tourism recovered after the Luxor massacre 1997 to more than US$3 bn in 1999 (three million visitors) but the activities of militant Islamist group continue albeit unwarrantedly to deter many visitors. The use of the Suez Canal increased to a transit of 386 million tonnes in 1997 with revenues at more than US$2 bn. Moderately good flows of water in the upper Nile catchment area in recent years have improved the reserves in Lake Nasser and offer some certainty for future agricultural output.

The changing international context for Egypt

The political economy of Egypt and that of the Middle East as a whole is in course of rapid adjustment to the effects of the implementation of the Middle East Peace Process and the realities of the situation following the demise of the USSR. The two elements are, of course, closely related. A third influence is at work for Egypt in particular – the new inclination of the country towards Africa (see Box Axis to Africa), the Mediterranean Basin and the EU, while the end of the UN sanctions on Libya in 1999 is also accelerating the growth in regional trade.

The removal of many barriers between the Arab states and Israel, signified in the renewal of diplomatic relations and the Jordan-Israel peace agreement indicates that, whereas some frictions will remain, the over-riding trend in the area is towards reconciliation and the beginning of a new era. The openings for Egypt in the new market zone of the Eastern Mediterranean comprising Jordan, Israel, Lebanon and (eventually Syria) are considerable, although there will be competition. But for Egypt to be a principal neighbour of an expanding new economic region will represent a welcome change in the country's situation.

In this historic change, all the factors at work contain far more positive than negative components and Egypt finds itself for the first time since the Second World War with clear opportunities for both internal and regional economic expansion. Indeed, Egypt, which suffered for its early and far-sighted agreements with Israel at Camp David, has now begun to reap some rewards from its pioneering role in the Sadat era. Egypt is also helped in the political

East of Port Said: A new Egyptian port

It has been officially decided to name the giant Shark al-Tafrea (east of Tafrea) hub port and free zone scheme the "East of Port Said Project" since the area is geographically linked to this zone. Construction of the port is moving ahead as scheduled, with the East of Port Said Development Company working on its development plans. Plots of land have also begun to be allocated to new steel, pharmaceutical and building material plants at the site.

The Egyptian Company for Port Said Region Port Development, capitalized at $440 mn, has to present detailed plans for the new hub port including the possibility of linking the new container port with the existing terminals at Port Said and Damietta. The port will be built by P&O Ports, a subsidiary of Australian/Dutch P&O Nedlloyd.

This is one of a number of massive infrastructure projects initiated to transform Egypt into an export oriented, private-sector-led economy. Local and international studies on Egypt's highly inefficient and dilapidated ports have been unanimous in concluding that exports will not grow unless a major reorganization gets under way. The public sector monopoly must be opened up to cheaper and more imports and lower freight costs are needed to encourage efficient private sector operators.

It currently costs twice as much to discharge a container at Egypt's main port in Alexandria as in Cyprus and three times as much as in Lebanon. If full storage charges are also taken into account the costs are as much as six times as high. But the 30-year state monopoly in maritime services was abolished in the latter part of 1997 and privatization of state maritime companies has already begun. The effect has been immediate and now a number of major international shipping lines have begun to look afresh at Egypt's potential.

The new East of Port Said port, estimated to cost US$10 bn to build, is intended to serve as a transshipment hub for the eastern Mediterranean. Egypt hopes it will become the major port between Singapore and Rotterdam. To coordinate Egypt's attempt to get a share of the transshipment trade, the government formed the East of Port Said Development Company. It has the brief to develop Shark al-Tafrea but will also oversee the development of Egypt's existing container ports at Damietta and Port Said.

The army has finished clearing mines from the site of the new port. It is to be established on 2,000 feddans of land on the east bank of the eastern bypass channel of the Suez Canal. An estimated 200,000 people are eventually expected to service the area. The deep water port will be able to accommodate larger container vessels than Port Said and Damietta.

Egypt clearly has a new thrust in its ports policy with East of Port Said but whether it can compete with other ports in the Eastern Mediterranean has yet to be seen.
Source: Egypt Focus

Background

arena by hard-won acceptance as a long-term and valued ally of the USA and the EU.

The EU initiatives towards the Mediterranean Basin are recent but in truth the outcome is for a well established and steady trend in Egypt to look as much westwards as to the Arab heartlands to the east. In North Africa Egypt's aim is to support political stability among its neighbours. More importantly, the Egyptian government sees that the continuing emergence of the EU as a major market on its immediate doorstep offers great possibilities for trade and development.

On grounds, therefore, of a slightly erratic but certain advance of the Middle East Peace Process, an end to great power (cold war) rivalry in the region, and the construction of an economic axis into Europe and the Mediterranean, the international and regional strategic structures within which Egypt has newly begun to operate are politically helpful and economically well timed.

Fundamentalism

Islam has been marked over the course of history by the emergence of rigorous revivalist movements. Most have sought a return of the faithful to the fundamentals of Islam – the basic doctrines of the Prophet Mohammed – uncluttered by the interpretations of later Islamic jurists and commentators. Behind the movements was generally the idea that Muslims should go back to the simple basics of their religion. Some, like the Wahhabi movement in Saudi Arabia were puritan in concept, demanding plain lives and an adherence to the tenets of Islam in all daily aspects of life. Others, imposed a rigorous schedule of ritual in prayer and avoidance of the 'unclean' in public life. A good example of this type of reformist tendency was the Senusi Movement in Libya which in the period from the close of the 19th century to 1969 created an educational, commercial and religious society throughout eastern Libya and northern Chad.

Until recent times the fundamentalist movements inside Islam arose from a desire to cleanse the religion of unnecessary ideology and to make all Muslims observe the basic pillars of the Islamic religion – prayer, belief and actions on a consistent and demonstrable basis. In the last 100 years there has been a growing tendency in the Islamic world for revivalist movements to be reactions to political, military and cultural setbacks experienced at the hands of the Western industrialized world. The aim of the reformers has been to make good the disadvantage and backwardness of the Muslim states in contrast with the powerful countries of Europe, America and the Far East. The matter is varied and complex, depending on the particular cases involved but the clear linkage between an increasingly dominant Western culture and economy and the growth of reactive Islamic movements is inescapable. In Egypt, the Muslim Brotherhood was an early form of revivalist movement of this kind. Founded by an Egyptian schoolteacher, Has al-Banna in 1928, it initially tried to take Islam back to its roots and therefore to its perceived strengths but was later taken over by extremists who used its organization for political ends. The development of the Muslim Brotherhood as a clandestine political group and the harnessing of religious fervour to political objectives, including the assassination of political enemies, set the pattern for most later movements of the kind.

In Egypt the Muslim Brotherhood remained the main organization though other smaller sects were also founded. Fundamentalism in Sudan has been adopted as a system of government and many of the attributes of the Iranian revolution have been copied, some with Iranian assistance. Libya has not been threatened by Islamic fundamentalism on the scale experienced elsewhere in the region.

Politically, the Egyptian government has struggled to find ways either to repress or co-opt the extreme Islamist movements which have been responsible for the murder of and injury to foreign tourists and Egyptians (including the 83-year-old novelist Naguib Mahfouz) over recent years.

This lack of any understanding between the government and the Islamist opposition gives Egypt's political system an unneeded air of fragility. President Mobarak has responded as a soldier – with violence against violence – to armed political attacks on his régime. The attack on the state by the Islamists has diminished but remains as serious and likely to be protracted unless ended by a political solution – unlikely at the present. But for the foreign tourist, there is much less to fear. They now seem to be out of the direct firing line from the Islamists and the situation is very much improved on the previous position. For the first time since they took up arms against the government in 1992, the militants have ceased to dominate the political scene. The unilateral ceasefire, announced by the Gamaa Islamiya has largely held. The head of the Gamma's military wing is believed to be in Afghanistan, cut off trom local officials. Brutal police repression, public hostility, and the large-scale release of Islamist prisoners by the interior ministry make the return unlikely. Gamaa leaders abroad might well find that they are now incapable of reactivating the organization should they so wish.

*** *** *** *** *** *** ***

The Kosheh affair – a damaging confrontation 👈

Events in the village of Kosheh in Upper Egypt have, since August 1998, revealed an extraordinary conflict between extremist Muslims and local Copts that has led to loss of life and bad publicity abroad.

There seems to have been widespread police abuse, including torture and the victimization of over 1,000 people – nearly all Christians, to force a confession to the murder of two Coptic Christians from Kosheh. Egyptian publications, both English and Arabic, had reported the story as an act of unprecedented police brutality. The consensus was that police had concentrated on the Coptic Christian inhabitants of the village because, ironically, of fears of sectarian strife if the murderer turned out to be a Muslim.

In Western Europe the position was described as "ritual persecution" of Copts which was a sad misrepresentation of the case as prominent Christians in Egypt were first to point out. The response of the government did not help. In a clumsy attempt at damage control Egyptian newspaper editors were obliged to follow the official line, reporting that no more than two dozen people in Kosheh, if anyone, received "inappropriate" treatment at the hands of the police. The Interior ministry meanwhile denied that anyone was mistreated at all.

The real issue was lost in the publicity fracas: over 1,000 Egyptians suffered gross violations of their human rights, and Egypt is plagued by a deep-rooted problem of police brutality that touches Muslims and Christians alike.

Source: Egypt Focus

*** *** *** *** *** *** *** *** ***

Egypt's regional partners currently involved in the bi-lateral and multilateral peace talks are Jordan, Israel, Syria and, implicitly, any notional Palestine entity. In economic terms and in other dimensions, too, Egypt is in a very strong competitive position vis-"-vis the East Mediterranean area (see Box East of Port Said – a new Egyptian Port). Egypt, as with other Arab states has, however, a great distance to go to catch up Israel.

To Egypt's advantage, the Eastern Mediterranean area is now showing a markedly improving performance after an extended period of poor economic growth. Jordan's specific difficulties as a result of the outcome of the Iraqi invasion of Kuwait have begun to evaporate and the economic dividend of peace with Israel is already being felt. Lebanon is undergoing a positive rebirth from the ashes of the civil war, while even Syria is experiencing a more rapid rate of economic change than formerly. Most importantly, Israel meanwhile is growing expansively in the high income group affiliated to OECD. It attracts considerable foreign investment and offers a local source of financial expertise. The hope is that the now unrestrained economic multiplier effect will spread from Israel to the other local states, including Egypt, to give some prospect for raising themselves from the ranks of the Third World. Overall, therefore, the economic prospects for Egypt and its neighbours affected by the Peace Process are looking bright.

The Regional Base – The Eastern Mediterranean

Egypt was a notable participant at the Casablanca Peace Summit in October 1994, encouraged by the incentive of the establishment of a US$10 bn regional development bank. The summit examined the ways in which economic gains could be made from the Middle East Peace Process. A bonus for Egypt was the proposal emerging from Casablanca that Egypt should affiliate itself to the existing United Maghreb Association (UMA), which includes Morocco, Tunisia, Algeria and Libya (aggregate GDP worth US$150 bn). Egypt's aims here are mainly political and designed to contain the problem of the extreme Islamist parties in the region. There are economic benefits even here for Egypt as a transit state between North Africa and the Eastern Mediterranean as transport/communications systems are reopened. In so far as Morocco is in the vanguard of North African-EU special economic relationship, Egypt might in the long run benefit from an association with Moroccan successes in respect to its links to the EU.

The regional base – North Africa

Egypt modernizes – slowly

The much talked about modernization of Egypt in the face of the trend internationally towards globalization is happening but slowly.

The government has promised to accelerate the pace of privatization. This has become a necessity because of the need for more foreign capital and to enable the regime to keep at least some of the government's social promises. There are high foreign exchange costs of the very large development projects now in hand. Egypt belatedly is trying to improve management, technology and quality in the economy to permit Egyptian industry to survive international competition.

In particular, there is a need to demonstrate to the outside world that Egypt means business. However, forays into possible sale of state-owned telecommunications and regional electricity companies has been delayed. Only the railways have been actually offered for privatization and even then it will take three years to reach the market. Focus initially will be on the sale of 70 intermediate size public sector companies including the ailing and labour-intensive textile sector.

Entrenched vested interests oppose reform and institutions such as the public sector banks and insurance companies are important tools of government policy, too valuable for the government to lose control of.

Trade liberalization, another critical part of the modernization programme, also remains a thorny problem. The government is committed to reform by international agreements with the World Trade Organization but is held back by the need to protect local industry from foreign competition. However, the pressing need to boost exports should mean that trade liberalization eventually goes forward. It is promised that duties on raw materials will be reduced but that taxes on finished goods imports will be maintained.

The ministry of economy is in the process of implementing a scheme aimed at reducing customs delays but no radical shake-up of Egypt's notorious customs administration will be easy to implement.

Egypt is negotiating free trade agreements with the Arab world, Africa and the USA. An EU partnership agreement, a precursor to the Euro-Med free trade zone by 2010, is complete. Whether Egypt really intends to step into the 21st century and keep its international agreements is unclear – modernization has been tried before and failed on each occasion. Success now might prove just as elusive.

Political constraints The dramatic improvement in Egypt's Middle East regional and international opportunities are only partially strengthened by consideration of the domestic scene. Politically, the government has now found a way successfully to repress and marginalize the extreme Islamist movements which have been responsible for the murder of and injury to foreign tourists and Egyptians over recent years (see Box Fundamentalism) . At the same time, legitimate opposition groups have found it difficult to operate in the political atmosphere of state control and extremism.

This lack of a working arrangement between the government and the opposition gives Egypt's political system an unneeded air of fragility. President Mubarak has responded as a soldier – with violence against violence – to armed political attacks on his regime. The attack on the state by the Islamists is still not entirely over and could re-surface unless terminated by a permanent political solution – unlikely at the present. Despite the damage done by the extreme Islamic fundamentalist groups, not least to the important tourist sector and the flare up in sectarian violence (see Box The Kosheh affair – a damaging confrontation), the country carries a comparatively modest risk factor. This is in acknowledgement that although as assassination of individuals within the government is always possible, and the president himself is a prime target of dissidents, the regime as a whole is very solidly based. The army, the security services, most of the bureaucracy, the

Egypt looks for prosperity

The outlook for the Egyptian economy is sound. Egypt's positive economic situation contrasts well with circumstances in the 1980s with strong international reserves, low inflation and sustained fiscal discipline among the accomplishments of the economic reform programme over recent years. Growth in national income has averaged 5% over recent years and foreign reserves stood at about US$19 bn at the end of June 1999, which would pay for 13 months' worth of imports at current levels. In 1998/99 the government budget deficit was US$1.2 bn, equivalent to 1.3% of GDP.

Egypt weathered recent global financial turmoil well. Foreign exchange earnings were on an upward trend in tourism, oil and gas sectors. Room occupancy rates in hotels were at an all-time high. Egypt benefited from high oil prices and the recovery in Far Eastern economies lead to increased Suez Canal receipts, worker remittances and exports.

Egypt is not short of challenges if it is seriously to capitalize on positive trends. First, structural reform must continue if Egypt is to achieve its long-term objective of export and private sector-led sustainable growth of 7-8% annually. This scale of growth will be needed if the country is to beat its 1.9% annual population growth, a 3.2% increase in persons seeking work and unemployment levels of more than 20%.

Critically important to the prospects for growth is Egypt's privatization programme and a rapid reduction in the size of the civil service, without which the share of private sector will not expand and investment and savings rates will stay low. The programme aims by 2002 to privatize one of the four public sector banks and one of the three public sector insurance companies.

There is an acute need still for the government to improve the business climate by cutting transaction costs and reducing red tape. A modernized and opaque regulatory environment for business is also required. Meanwhile, Egypt's key sources of foreign exchange, which include tourism, petroleum exports, Suez Canal receipts and worker remittances, remain vulnerable to external shocks. Export growth is not as strong as it could be.

A number of trade-related decrees over past years, setting new requirements for the imports of consumer goods and automobiles, have led to concern in the business community regarding the government's commitment to continuing economic reform. The Central Bank's rationing of foreign exchange has disrupted business and sent a confusing policy message to local and international investors.

Background

private sector and a large proportion of the population firmly support the political status quo. While these props remain to support the regime, its troubles will be well advertised abroad but its domestic stability undamaged.

Egypt is at the beginning of a second stage of a far-reaching reform of its economy, urged on by the USA. The main planks for the new phase of change are:
* Deregulation of the business environment.
* Privatization of government industrial and commercial holdings.
* Improved efficiency of public institutions.
* Streamlined judicial practices affecting business.
* Provision of more credits to businesses.
* Reform of the educational system to provide appropriate supply of trained labour.
* Establishment of confidence in the long-term business climate.

Economic development – steady progress is envisaged

Other important elements underpinning the economic reform programme are the acquisition of improved technology. The USA-Egypt partnership for growth agreement was an important step in this process. Egypt's priorities lie in the industrial field, which offers the only realistic area for absorbing available labour and

● ●

☛ *Economic indicators*

Fiscal years	1995/96	1996/97	1997/98	1998/99*
GDP (current prices)	67.	75.5	82.4	89.77
GDP real growth rate (%)	5.0	5.3	5.0	6.8
GDP/capita (US$)	1,140	1,260	1,310	1,430
Government spending as proportion of GDP	27.9	26.1	25.3	24.4
Fiscal deficit as proportion of GDP	7.33	6.2	4.2	4.0
Unemployment (%)	9.2	8.8	8.3	na
Foreign exchange reserves (US$ bn)	17.5	20.2	20.3	19.3
Average exchange rate: US$1.00=	3.39	3.39	3.39	3.41
Total foreign debt as % of GDP	46.1	38.4	34.0	33.2
US assistance (US$ bn)	2,115	2.115	2.115	2.075

Trade (US$ mn)				
Fiscal years	1995/96	1996/97	1997/98	1998/99
Total exports	4,608	4,930	5,128	2,111
of which: petroleum	na	2,449	1,236	483
Total imports	14,106	14,718	16,899	8,287
of which: petroleum	na	1,588	1,123	na
Trade deficit	9,498	9 788	11,770	6,176

Source: Egypt Focus, Menas Associates, UK.

● ●

for lifting living standards. The long-term limitation of water supply gives little hope that agriculture can do the same job. Underwriting of the stability of the Egyptian pound is important. The country is eager to keep the pound steady but pressures are developing, including a severe shortage of US dollars, that might bring an other devaluation crisis. There is a need to support an expanded export promotion programme through preferential interest rates and for the development of commercial linkages to the Eastern Mediterranean and European markets for the Egyptian private sector. Some encouragement is wanting to get more foreign investment in Egyptian industry. Vigilance will be required in protecting Egyptian rights to Nile waters and managing the reallocation of water in Egypt from agriculture to industrial and municipal sectors.

Egypt's performance in economic change has been good. Foreign debt has continued to decline and most other key indicators of economic welfare remain unexciting. Optimism on this score is moderated only by the obstruction of reform by vested interests, especially in the bureaucracy, where change comes very slowly. There is political opposition against and apathy/passive resistance to the regime. Non-participation by the population at large is dimming popular enthusiasm for and acceptance of economic reform. (See Box Egypt modernises – slowly.)

The outlook It is apparent that the Egyptian economy is poised for steady growth in the near future. (See Box Egypt looks for prosperity.) Rapid growth of GDP at more than 6% per year is feasible but will depend heavily on the effective implementation of the reform programme. This in turn will require Egypt to co-operate with the IMF and the World Bank to ensure that structural changes to the economy are consistent and internationally acceptable by scale and pace affecting:

Sainsburys stores in Egypt

UK food retailer Sainsburys opened a store in Egypt in January 2000. The supermarket on Giza's Pyramids Road is the first to be opened by a global retailer in Egypt. Sainsburys is said to be "delighted" with the public's response.

The Pyramids Road store is processing over twice as many customers as an equivalent store in UK. It is being visited by around 7,500 customers each day, whereas the average number of customers in a UK store is only 3,000. And even though the store is offering discounts as big as 15%, it is recording a higher revenue than comparable UK stores.

The Pyramids Road store has become a victim of its own success and is too crowded. Sainsburys are trying to relieve the pressure on the store by converting 36 smaller existing supermarkets in different areas in Cairo into satellites of Sainsburys'

main store. A "freeway" store, stocking a full range of food but no family products, was opened in Heliopolis in April 2000. Meanwhile, the ABC supermarket in the wealthy Cairo island of Zamalek has been converted into a second Sainsburys supermarket, containing a large family section with Early Learning Centre toys, children's products and Sainsburys' Homebase products.

Sainsburys' home delivery service has also proved more popular in Egypt than in the UK, and already the service has attracted twice the volume it has in Sainsburys' home market. Sainsburys is acquiring land and is intending to build its own stores. Eventually it intends to cover the whole country and become a mass retailer in Egypt.

The Egyptian market is still relatively unexploited despite being larger than that of Belgium and the Netherlands combined.

Background

*   Trade liberalization through the elimination of protective tariffs notably the customs users fee.
*   Harmonization of energy prices through removal of subsidies.
*   Privatization, which has gone too slowly over too limited a field for the taste of the World Bank.

In the meantime, key indicators of future economic activity rates mainly look encouraging. Egypt's foreign debt is falling and will come down further by approximately US$1 bn per year as debt is paid off. An improved debt position would make Egypt more credit-worthy and relieve strains on the balance of payments where charges of US$1.5 bn per year are currently incurred on interest payments alone.

The Government will continue to do a good job in holding down the budget deficit. There is a continuing trend to remove subsidies on products but only slowly and the trend does not necessarily go hand in hand with liberalizing prices for manufacturers. Tax reforms will be pursued, with an emphasis on higher indirect taxation. Inflation is being curbed and should stabilize at some 2% annually.

The government's strong pound policy (£E3.4=US$1) seems likely to persist. In effect, the currency has been partly de-dollarized. Reserves at the Central Bank will stay high, probably over US$19 bn, but these could be rapidly eroded if the pound has to be defended. The Central Bank will remain firmly committed to a comparatively uncontrolled exchange mechanism following the liberalization of controls in the recent past.

Privatization will be continued but not rapidly in the teeth of ministerial lack of conviction and professional obstruction at all levels of the civil service. It is probable that the contentious system of private bidding will increasingly be replaced by public auction of stock. It still has to be proved that privatization can be applied to the many and often languishing state-owned industries nationalized by President Nasser in the 1950s.

Egypt's ambitious 16-point economic agenda

Egypt's government set out its major economic policy goals in 2000. Prime minister Atef Obeid made ambitious and costly promises to the nation that the government would work to diminish social inequalities and to achieve high economic growth. The prime minister stressed that his government was not, as is popularly perceived, a government of big business interests, solely focused on selling off state enterprises, but has the welfare of the mass of the lower income population at heart. The main promises he made include:

1. The creation of 650,000 jobs a year. The government later said that the donor-financed Social Development Fund will create 150,000 jobs annually, by helping university graduates establish small-scale enterprises, while 500,000 jobs will be found in government ministries and enterprises.

2. The monthly £E50 pension will be doubled and extended to destitute families without a breadwinner. Some one million families will be eligible.

3. The government will repay investors who lost money in the Islamic investment companies that went bankrupt in the late 1980s taking with them many people's life savings. An initial 10% repayment will be followed by the remainder over the next five years.

4. The government will continue to subsidize homes for the young and plans to build 100,000 housing units yearly and facilitate access to soft loans for younger families.

5. The government will continue to subsidize basic food supplies, water and electricity, public transport, low-cost housing and free education.

6. Bureaucracy is to be cut to the minimum.

7. Slum areas are to be developed, action will be taken to relieve Cairo of its rubbish accumulation problem and tenders put out for the upkeep of roads and lighting of new areas.

8. The government will improve the working conditions of its employees. All government employees and their families will be offered attractive health insurance packages. The new health insurance system will cover 10 million additional people. Twenty five million are already covered.

9. Interest-free loans of up to £E1,000 will be extended to impoverished students. Repayment of the loans will be scheduled over 40 years.

10. Seasonal workers in both rural and urban areas will be offered soft loans to develop income-generating activities

11. Loans will be extended to non governmental organizations to establish productive small-scale enterprises.

12. To raise the annual economic growth rate to 7% during the next decade.

13. To raise exports by 10% annually to ensure a greater supply of foreign exchange.

14. To keep the Egyptian pound at the same value relative to other currencies.

15. To strike hard against corruption, dumping, tax evasion and the smuggling of sub-standard goods into the country.

16. To reduce the volume of foreign and domestic debt. To achieve this, the budget of the economic and public service sector authorities will be separate from the state budget in future so that expenditure can be rationalized.

Trade liberalization will slowly make progress but will be constrained in scope by the need to protect the large scale and inefficient state industries which cannot survive even slight external competition.

The matter of intellectual property rights will be sensitive for Egypt. The balance of trade in intellectual property rights favours the highly developed states rather than countries like Egypt. Deals affecting high tech ventures, especially in sectors such as pharmaceuticals, are seen as adverse for Egypt where patent fees and royalties have to be paid. However Egypt cannot afford to be excluded from the import of key technology given the strategic emphasis on industrialization within the programme for economic development.

Background

In the realm of deregulation of the business environment, optimism for rapid future change must be limited. Little has so far been achieved by the government as a result of passive resistance and obstruction throughout the bureaucracy. There are, however, opportunities in the immediate future for a more flexible labour law, which would greatly assist all – local and foreign – businesses.

The outlook for investment is set fair. Although there is a pervasive air of wariness and uncertainty concerning the progress of economic reform and the political stability of the regime, there is enough confidence to give a steady if unspectacular flow of funds. Growth of fixed investment in the next year is expected to grow.

At the heart of the modern economy is the petroleum sector. Despite the levelling off of the oil industry, natural gas production and export seem set for an expansion as new fields come on stream in the Mediterranean coast, Red Sea and Eastern desert zones. Egypt's strength in gas is shown, for example, by the planned export of natural gas to Israel by 1997. Egypt will also continue to gain enormous benefits from employment of its nationals in the Middle Eastern oil industry, worth US$6 bn per year. The country's income from Suez Canal dues, valued at over US$2 bn, will come principally from oil tanker movements (total vessels in 1998 13,472).

The overall picture of the economy (see Box Economic Indicators) thus contains a growing range of positive factors, although problems are not wanting:
* The declining natural resource base in hydrocarbons in which Egypt could in the near future become marginally import-dependent for oil.
* The need for higher expenditures on job creation and on the military.
* Defending the currency will mean higher interest rates than the 11%, which might deter new borrowing and investment in productive enterprise. IMF will also not be pleased with a high exchange rate for the Egyptian pound.
* Tourism will recover despite the publicity given to terrorism against foreign nationals. With one job in 10 dependent on tourism recovery here is vital to the health of the economy.
* Long-term economic problems will cure only slowly – ie unemployment at 13.5% of work force and low productivity of employed labour.
* Manufacturers in Egypt will face a greater governmental policy emphasis on environmental protection. A new law is expected and there will be a need for all new projects to undergo environmental impact assessments.
Despite this list of caveats, there is a useful and growing economy to be found in an economically buoyant Egypt. Disposable incomes are at last beginning to rise appreciably in what after all is a large and youthful country. Egypt looks to be more favourably placed for economic growth than several of the larger Middle Eastern oil-exporting economies because of its diversified base.

The opportunities for Egypt to make negotiated inroads into the EU market through attachment to a Mediterranean oriented policy are very considerable and will grow exponentially over time. It is early days yet but it is clear that the EU needs to coopt Egypt if it is to succeed in the political stabilization of its southern flank in the face of the threat of extreme Islamism. The EU too officially now sees North Africa as a natural prolongation of its interests in the Mediterranean (see Box Sainsburys stores in Egypt).

Beyond the EU, Egypt has another powerful political and economic patron – the USA. Favourable treatment of Egypt by the USA in defence, technology and investment does no harm to Egypt's economic prospects and has the bonus of guaranteeing a steady commitment to reform within the country which might otherwise be very much neglected.

The question of political stability of the State as a context for economic growth has obvious thorny aspects. But they are generally overstated by the media (see Box President Mubarak – a Four Times Winner). The regime has its brittle aspects and is less legitimate in a democratic sense than most Egyptian intellectuals would like. Reliance on a single charismatic leader with powers concentrated in his hands is to an extent outdated in a global though not in a Middle Eastern context. But beyond individuals in power, the Egyptian ruling elite and the regime that represents it have as deep a stability now as at any time since 1970. Thus the prospects for steady growth should not be undermined by significant political upheavals in the immediate future.

Egypt fights to develop a new structure

Egypt is classified by the International Bank as a poor third world country, in 1997 rating 48th in the bank's league table. Intriguingly, Egypt fails by only a short margin to rank as a middle income economy and leaping this gap is critically important to the Egyptian government as it seeks to accelerate the economy into sustained growth. For this to happen the International Monetary Fund (IMF) estimates that every year the Egyptian economy must grow by 7% in order to outstrip the rate of increase in population numbers and provide the financial sinews for new investment.

In recent years Egypt has lifted its growth rate to some 5% per year, which is a major achievement given the domestic problems of the massacre of tourists at Luxor in November 1997 and the turn down in the Middle Eastern and Asian economies. But, whatever the difficulties, more economic miracles are now needed including: greater efficiency within the country's rigid and slow-moving bureaucracy, modernization of traditional industry and agriculture which have scarcely been touched by the revolution in management that has affected urban services, higher investment by Egyptians and foreigners, create 500,000 new jobs every year, and privatize the inefficient state industries. (See Box Egypt's ambitious 16-point economic agenda.)

Additionally, there is a need to mobilize general support for economic change which will only come when political reform is introduced and the deadening hand of the security services is mitigated. And progress in this sphere is imperceptible. Indeed, the dilemma of keeping the country on an even political keel yet releasing the energies of the people into pursuing economic growth has not begun to be solved.

If the country fails in the current effort to prosper, the IMF foresees that Egypt will relapse back to a moribund third world status where another opportunity to break the shackles of mass poverty might be a long time in coming.

Culture

Architecture

The development of the Egyptian architectural tradition is both complex in so far as many influences affected it over the country's long history and discontinuous because of alien invasions and the impact of internal economic decline. In Egypt, even more than in other states of the Middle East, the extant pre-Islamic heritage in architecture is considerable – readily visible in the pyramids, temples and tombs throughout the length of country. The Egyptian showcase reflects almost all styles from the dawn of history because Egypt lay at the cross-roads of the known world for so long, across the rich and desirable nodal point of African, Mediterranean, European, Turkic, Arab and Persian influences. Even after the coming of Islam, Egypt experienced a diversity of architectural styles, as dynasty succeeded dynasty bringing new fusions of imported and local building techniques. In Egypt, Orthodox Islamic, Shi'ite, Ottoman and many other ruling elites brought in their own ideas of the function and design of public/religious buildings, often together with the craftsmen to construct them, but always interacting with local architectural traditions in a way that gave innovative results in mosques and other great building projects.

In Egypt there are not only local variations on the Islamic theme but also continuities in existing vernacular building styles and Coptic church architecture of the Romano-Greek basilica models as at St Barbara (see page 75).

Background

It must be remembered that the early Islamic conquerors were soldiers and often migrant pastoralists in lifestyle. The nomadic tradition, for all its emphasis on a minimum of light, transportable materials has, over time, produced exciting artifacts in the form of tents, particularly the black tent which survive still in the desert outposts of Egypt. Immediately after the conquest of Egypt by Amr Ibn al-As in the **seventh century**, the Islamic armies used the existing Egypto-Roman stock of citadels, forts and housing at Fustat (see page 67), which enabled some of the historical legacy of the area to survive.

The transition from felt to stone

But is was the remarkably rapid development of science and technology in the construction of Islamic buildings – especially the mesjid al-jami (Friday Mosque) – from a primitive model in Madinah built by Mohammed In **AD 622** – to the building of the original city of Baghdad on the instructions of Caliph Al-Mansur in the **eighth century** and the contemporary expansion of Cairo. Notable in this growth of technology was the codification of knowledge by the great ninth century engineer Al-Karaji, who laid down the scientific principles on which urban water supply works should be undertaken. In the same way, the sciences developed by the Islamic surveyors of the **eleventh century** such as Al-Biruni were also important. It is worth recalling the architectural excitement of the technological and material innovations that stirred invention and development in Egypt in the early Islamic period.

Rapid development in Islamic technologies

At the heart of Islamic architecture is the mosque. The elaboration of Islamic architecture centring on the mosque took place despite the men of the Arab conquest being essentially unlettered nomads and warriors. To redress the shortcomings of the Arab armies, their rulers imported skilled architects, masons and tile workers from established centres of excellence in the empire – Persians, Armenians and others. Together these itinerant teams of artisans and their Islamic

The mosque

patrons evolved a wonderful and distinct style of building form and decoration which are among the great legacies of Islam, especially in its early innovative period.

The mosque was the first and main vehicle of spectacular Islamic architecture, because it was a form based initially on the prayer building constructed by the Prophet himself and was important in enabling Muslims to conform with a need to pray together on Friday. In the Madinah mosque the worshippers faced north towards the holy city of Jerusalem but changes brought about in the first century after the death of Mohammed saw the qibla – direction of prayer – moved to face Mecca and other elaborations.

Key parts of the early mosques which were enduring elements of all mosques built since that time include:

the entrance, normally large and ornate, in the north wall,
the *mihrab*, or niche in the *qibla* wall,
the *sahn*, or open courtyard,
the *minbar*, or pulpit,
the *maqsurah*, or wooden screen
the *liwanat*, or covered arcades
the *koubba*, or dome, which was adopted as a roof form in the Dome of the Rock at Jerusalem, from whence Mohammed ascended to heaven.

As the caliphate extended and grew wealthy, so the architecture of the main Friday mosques, made for mass worship by the faithful on the holy day, became more magnificent as exemplified in the Great Mosque of Damascus, built in the **8th century AD**, which also had a square *ma'dhana*, or minaret outside the main building for the *muezzin* to call people to prayer.

The minaret of the Great Mosque of Kairouan in Tunisia, constructed in the 8th century, is the oldest minaret still standing while in Egypt the Ahmed Ibn Tulun Mosque (**876-879**) near the Cairo citadel has the only original standing minaret tower with an external spiral staircase in Africa.

Local mosques In addition to the great mosques used for public prayer on holy days, there are many local mosques of plain construction, many with architectural modifications to suit regional conditions of climate, culture and the availability of building materials

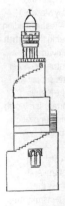

Minaret of Ibn Tulun Mosque, Cairo

Minaret of Medersa Sangar Al-Gawr, Cairo

Minaret of Sultan Al-Zahir Barquq Mosque, Cairo

Background

in Egypt. The basic layout even here is uniform, though the ornamentation and wealth in carpets in the *sahn* many well vary.

The non-Muslim traveller in Egypt is greatly blessed. They are allowed into nearly all mosques albeit with some restrictions on times for public access.

For a traveller to make sense of a visit to a mosque, the following principles and guidelines might be useful. Remember that the mosque serves as a centre for congregational worship in Islam. The word *mosque* implies a place of prostration and this is borne out in the plan of every mosque. The architecture of mosques, like that of traditional Christian churches, was designed to induce quiet and contemplation, above the noise and bustle of everyday life – to induce a subjection of the individual to God, *Allah*.

Understanding the mosque

Muslims pay particular attention to this solemn sanctity of the mosque. Behaviour is muted and decorous at all times, particularly during services, of which the main ones are Friday Prayers. Women are not forbidden from taking part in public services at the mosque but very rarely do so.

Most important is prayer and the *mihrab* is the niche in the mosque wall, known as the *qibla* wall, which indicates the direction of Mecca and hence the direction in which to pray. The main prayer hall is the *sahn* which can be a simple square, though more often it has (usually four) arcaded porticoes the longest and most decorated of which is the sanctuary or *liwan*. In the main Friday Mosques the porticoes can be elaborate and reminiscent of transepts in a church. A pulpit, *minbar*, is sited to the right of the *mihrab* and opposite the lectern from which readings are made from the Koran. In larger mosques there can be a screen, *maqsurah*, normally made as a wooden grill, in the sanctuary to protect the officiating *imam* from the congregation.

An outer courtyard or *ziyada* is generally found or a recess with flowing water or water jugs where people gather and perform their ritual ablutions before prayer. In the teaching mosques the *liwan* or specially created cloisters or side rooms served as classrooms or hospital sick-rooms.

Thus, while all mosques vary in detail of lay-out and decoration, the basic floor plan remains more or less uniform.

Egyptian mosques in particular show great variety of decoration and some differences in ground plan. Even to the untutored eye, five principal styles of mosque can be seen in most Egyptian cities; Fatimid (967-1171), Ayyubid (1171 1250), Mamluk (1250-1516), Ottoman (1516-1905) and modern (1905-present).

The Egyptian contribution to the mosque

The Fatimids left as their monument the great Mosque of Al-Azhar in Cairo, square in plan with a roofed and clestoried sanctuary borne on twin pillared colonnades. There were two side cloisters.

The Ayyubid buildings After the overthrow of the Fatimids by Salah al-Din (**1171 AD**) a new mosque style grew up in Egypt, reflecting the mosque as a major public building by scale and ornamentation. A good example of this style is the Medersa of Sultan al-Salih Ayyub. Unlike all previous mosques, it provided a separate teaching room for the four great schools of Orthodox Islam in a pair of mosques, each with a double *liwan*. Look out for the windows at ground level and for the discordance between the alignment of the adjacent street and the *liwans*, resulting from the need to set the *qibla* facing Mecca.

Legacy of the Mamluks The legacy of the Mamluks includes the Medersa of Sultan Hassan, built in 1356-60. It is an Islamic building on a giant scale with the tallest minaret in Cairo. Architecturally, it is also distinct for its simplicity and for the separate *liwans*, entrances to which are all offset from the magnificent *sahn*.

The Ottoman intervention The Ottomans ruled for many years (**16th century-19th century**) during which Egypt experienced a flood of new architectural ideas – the use of light as a motif, and the deployment of slender pillars, arches and minarets of Turkish origin. The Mosque of Suleyman Pasha dated to 1528 was the first Ottoman mosque to be built in Cairo exhibiting these features, that of Mohammed Ali Pasha, one of the last, with its tall octagonal minaret and fine Ottoman dome.

The modern period The modern period is represented by the Al-Rifai Mosque, completed in 1911, which blends Mamluk with contemporary architecture and by the standard village mosque, small, block built, neat but uninspired.

Features of the mosque Each architectural feature of the mosque has undergone development and change. For example, the minaret (*ma'dhana*) evolved to provide a high point from which the prayer leader (*muezzin*) could call (*adhan*) the faithful to their devotions five times each day. Construction of minarets to give a vantage point for the muezzin began in Damascus at the end of the **7th century AD**. The earliest minaret that has survived is the one at the Great Mosque in Kairouan, Tunisia, built in the years 8-9th centuries. The minaret of the Ibn Tulun Mosque in Cairo with its external spiral staircase is dated to 876-879. There is some belief by scholars that the three-part form of the Egyptian minaret was taken from the 135 m Lighthouse of Pharos at Alexandria, of which the extant Abu Sir lighthouse 43 km west of Alexandria is a small scale copy.

The minarets of the Egyptian mosque are quite distinct despite reflecting influences from elsewhere in the Islamic world. There is great variety in the shape and architectural effects of Egyptian minarets as may be seen from the illustration of three fine minarets in Cairo, the minaret of the Ibn Tulun Mosque has an external stair-way and octagonal third section while the minaret of Sanjar al-Gawli Medersa carries an extended square base with short and delicate second and third sections. In contrast, the splendid early 15th century minaret of the Sultan al-Barquq mausoleum displays great variety as it evolves from square to modified cruciform to circular to octagonal. Yet there is an underlying general tendency for the Egyptian minaret to have three separate levels including a base of square section, overlain by a multifaced column usually octagonal in shape surmounted by a circular tower, itself terminating in an elaborate miniature pavilion. The finial is provided by a small gilded spire carrying a crescent.

The original brick-built minarets in Egypt used finely worked panelling and line work as on the Ottoman minaret of Sultan Hassan Medersa (**1356-62BC**) near the Cairo Citadel. The passage of time saw the expensive kiln brick medium dropped in favour of stone and finally rough random stone covered with a plaster rendering. These painted towers have been augmented in the recent past both in Egypt and other Muslim countries by what has become a standard modern equivalent, reproduced in new urban and country settlements, alike. It is plain and repetitive – scarcely a description of the more traditional and characterful minarets – but serves its purpose (See Box The Call to Prayer, page 99), and remains a principal topographic marker in the Egyptian landscape.

The Islamic college Closely linked to the mosque in both religious and architectural form is the *medersa* which is a college of higher education in which Islamic teachings lead the syllabus. It was an institution originated in Persia and developed in the West in the Thirteenth century. The construction of places of advanced learning was a response by orthodox Sunni Islam to the growth of Shi'ite colleges but they soon became important centres in their own right as bastions of orthodox Islamic beliefs. Subjects other than theology were taught at the *medersa* but only in a limited form and in ways that made them adjuncts to Sunni teachings and acceptable to a very conservative religious hierarchy. Unfortunately, therefore, the *medersa* became associated with a rather uninspired and traditional academic routine in which enquiry and new concepts were often excluded. Muslim scholars believe that knowledge and its transmission sadly fell into the hands of the least academic members of the theological establishment. The poor standards of science, politics, arts and ethics associated with the Arab world in the period since the 13th century is put down by some Arab academics to the lack of innovation and experiment in the *medersa*, a situation which has only very recently begun to break down in Sunni Islam.

It can, however, be argued that formal Islam needed firm basic teachings in the face of rapidly expanding popular Islam and its extravagant sufi beliefs.

The short-comings of the *medersa* in creative teaching terms were in part compensated for by the development of the college buildings themselves. The Egyptian style before the beginning of the tenth century was based on norms borrowed from Syria and Iraq but after that time was mainly modelled on a more Mediterranean tradition with use of a high domed roof as in the mosque of al-Guyushi in the military area above Sharia al-Mokatam in Cairo. The small courtyard is separated from the *sahn* by a vaulted transect. The Al-Azhar Mosque complex in old Cairo began life as a principal congregational mosque but become a great teaching university for Islam, much added to and altered and thus at the apex of the *medersa* form.

Medressa, were until quite recently widely used for student accommodation and teaching. Visitor entry is restricted to specific times but fairly free access is allowed to the building. Other fine architectural works can be seen at the Sultan Barquq Medersa in Cairo with its marbled entry and wonderful four-liwan courtyard and the Medersa of Tatar al-Higaziya with its ribbed stone dome.

The rise in awareness of Islam among the young signalled by the high tide of Islamism in Egypt has given the *medersa* an added political interest and social vitality in recent years.

The Cairo scene has one eye-catching feature, visible even as the traveller comes into the centre of town on the Heliopolis road – the City of the Dead, where 15th century tombs and later additions offer an unparalleled range of Islamic funerary architecture. There are also some separate tomb-temples of the Islamic period which are now parts of larger mosque and medersa complexes such as the finely worked Tombs of Amir Salar and Sangar a-Gawli in Sharia Saliba.

Mausoleums – a very Egyptian celebration of death

Although there was some inertia in the architectural style/practices and building techniques in Islamic Egypt, aided by the Ottoman imperial practice of adopting local building types without change, the private houses belonging to great families and powerful individuals showed much individuality but did at the same time contain strong elements of continuity. All houses had a central courtyard or *waset al-dar*, with perhaps a columned area, fountain, water basin and even trees which was reached indirectly through a corridor from the street. The house entrance was usually via a studded door to a lobby or pair of small rooms designed to ensure that no-one from the street could either view or easily enter the inner courtyard or rooms. Around the central courtyard were clustered all the principal rooms, including in large houses a collection of family rooms set around a main living space or an area to give family privacy to visitors. These groups of rooms had a small courtyard and may be seen as the successors to the peri-styles of Romano-Greek houses in North Africa or to the Perso-Ottoman *haivans*. Libraries were important in the houses of public figures, while some great houses had internal *hammam* or bath areas.

The private house

Naturally, there was a large staff and housing for it in establishments of this kind to service the kitchen, the daily needs of the resident family and the transport/

guard functions necessary for a public figure. The harem was kept distant from the public rooms and often near the baths. Kitchens, stores, water well/storage, stables and accommodation for servants took up considerable space. Egyptian great houses of the 18th and 19th centuries rarely had a developed upper storey, though roof areas were accessed by stairways and used for laundry, the drying of fruits and for water gathering for the cistern below. Open space within the house was often generous in scale. A fine example of the classical Egyptian house can be seen at the House of Zaynab Khatun in Sharia Mohammed 'Abduh near the Al-Azhar Mosque. This building was first laid out in 1468 for Mithqal al-Suduni, a minister of Sultan Jaqmaqis, and has Ottoman additions. It was restored in the 1950s and is open to the public. There are many fine historic houses in various states of repair in Cairo which are rarely seen by visitors simply because they are over shadowed by so many wonderfully attractive public buildings. As a sample of early housing, visit the *Gayner-Anderson Museum* entered from the southeast corner of the Ahmed Ibn Tulun. The museum is located in what are two restored houses of the **16th century** and **17th century**, respectively, with a number of fine features such as a screened balcony (mashrabiyyah) and marbled sitting room. Sadly many of the older grand houses in diverse styles borrowed from France, Greece and Italy of the **18th** and **19th century** have been demolished and few examples remain for which there is public access. In Ismailia look out the house of de Lesseps on Mohammed Ali Quay as an example of "colonial period" housing.

In lower class dwellings this same formula was repeated but on a smaller scale and without the baths and libraries. Many larger houses at the present day are laid out often using an offset entry system just like the older Islamic houses, though only few modern dwellings benefit from total family privacy, thick walling, a generous central courtyard and ornamental gardens. Finding mud-brick for construction purposes is getting difficult as a result of prohibitions on brick-making so that low rise houses are roughly constructed in cement blocks. Increasingly, better off Egyptians are in any case abandoning the traditional house for apartments in tower blocks.

Art and crafts

Jewellery The dynamic history of the region has produced imaginative traditional designs mixed with foreign elements leading to a range of decoration few regions in the world can rival. Influences from the Phoenicians, Greeks and Romans, Arabs and Andalusians have each contributed subtly to the immense range of jewellery found in this part of the world.

Although some urban dwellers have adopted Western attitudes to dress and decoration, at times of festivals and especially for marriage ceremonies, traditional dress and elaborate jewellery that has changed little since the Middle Ages is still worn. The increase of tourism, while in some cases destroying traditional values, is in fact promoting and preserving crafts, especially jewellery making, by providing an eager and lucrative market for ornaments that

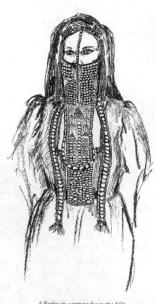

A Bedouin woman from the Nile

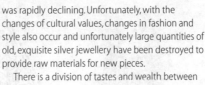

Ankh (Cross of Life)

Nefertiti's head

Silver pendant
Lizard, a talisman against the evil
eye on a Hand of Fatima

was rapidly declining. Unfortunately, with the changes of cultural values, changes in fashion and style also occur and unfortunately large quantities of old, exquisite silver jewellery have been destroyed to provide raw materials for new pieces.

There is a division of tastes and wealth between towns where gold is favoured and the countryside where silver predominates. Basically, traditional styles continue to be popular and jewellery tends to become more traditional the further south one goes. A general shift can be discerned away from silver towards gold, especially in Egypt, where it is now believed to be a better investment.

Despite a whole field of inspiration being forbidden to Muslim jewellers, that of the human form, they developed the art of decorating jewellery in ways that eventually merged to become a distinctive 'Islamic' style. Using floral (arabesque), animal, geometric and calligraphic motifs fashioned on gold and silver with precious and semi-precious gems, coral and pearls they worked their magic.

According to Islamic law, silver is the only pure metal recommended by the Prophet Mohammed. For the majority of Muslims this sanction is felt to apply only to men who do not, as a rule, wear any jewellery other than a silver wedding ring or seal ring.

Every town has its own jewellery *souq* with larger centres providing a greater range of jewellery. There is almost always a distinction between the goldsmiths and the silversmiths and there are also shops, designated in Egypt by a brass camel over the door, which produce jewellery in brass or gold plate on brass for the cheap end of the market.

The tourist industry keeps whole secions of the jewellery business in work, especially in Egypt where designs which have a historical base – the Scarab, the Ankh (the symbol of eternal life), the Eye of Horus, Nefertiti's head and heiroglyphic cartouches – predominate. The jewellery spans the entire range of taste and quality from the very cheap mass-produced pendants to finely crafted very expensive pieces. Jewellers also sell a great number of silver items at the cheaper end of the tourist market which is very popular as 'ethnic' jewellery. Gold and silver jewellery is usually sold by weight and, although there might be an additional charge for more intricate craftmanship, this means the buyer must judge quality very carefully.

Background

Siwan earring

Bracelet from Egypt

One of the many styles of Khamsa or hand of Fatima

The **earring** is by far the most popular and convenient ornament. It appears in an infinite variety of styles with the crescent moon shape being the most common. The earring from Siwa is a particularly fine example. This is closely followed by the **bracelet** or **bangle** which is also very much part of a woman's everyday wardrobe.

Most of the jewellery is worn both as an adornment and as an indication of social status or rank. It generally has some symbolic meaning or acts as a charm. Jewellery is usually steeped in tradition and is often received in rites of passage like puberty, betrothal and marriage. Women receive most of their jewellery upon marriage. This is usually regarded as their sole property and is security against personal disaster.

Many of the **symbols** recurrent in jewellery have meanings or qualities which are thought to be imparted to the wearer. Most of the discs appearing in the jewellery represent the moon which is considered to be the embodiment of perfect beauty and femininity. The greatest compliment is to liken a woman to the full moon. Both the moon and the fish are considered as fertility symbols. The crescent is the symbol of Islam but its use actually predates Islam. It is the most common symbol throughout the region and acquires greater Islamic significance with the additon of a star inside. Other symbols frequently seen are the palm and the moving lizard both of which signify life and the snake which signifies respect.

Amulets are thought to give the wearer protection from the unknown, calamities and threats. They are also reckoned to be curative and to have power over human concerns such as longevity, health, wealth, sex and luck. Women and childen wear amulets more frequently as their resistance to evil is considered to be weaker than that of a man.

North African anklets or Khul-Khal (always worn in pairs)

The Talisman

The use of amulets and other charms was well developed in ancient Egypt when magic charms were worn like jewellery or put into the wrappings round a mummy – to ward off evil. Among the most sought after charms was the Eye of Horus illustrated here or the ankh (see page 490), the cross of life. Protective necklaces were particularly treasured and among the beads would be small carvings of animals representing gods – a hawk for Horus, or a baboon for Thoth. In the same way stelae (marker stones) or house charms stood at the door begging the gods to protect the family from danger.

The 'evil eye' is a powerful force in the contemporary local societies of Egypt and North Africa. It is believed that certain people have the power to damage their victims, sometimes inadvertently. Women are thought to be among the most malignant of possessors of the 'evil eye', a factor associated with the 'impurities' of the menstrual cycle. Even a camera can be considered as an alien agent carrying an 'evil eye' – so only take photographs of country people where they are comfortable with the idea and be exceptionally careful in showing a camera at weddings and above all funerals. Envy too is a component of the 'evil eye' and most conversations where any praise of a person or object is concerned will include a mashallah or 'what god wills' as protection against the evil spirits that surround human kind.

Major victims of the 'evil eye' are the young, females and the weak. Vulnerability is seen to be worst in marriage, pregnancy and childbirth, so that women in particular must shelter themselves from the 'evil eye'. Uttering the name of Allah is a good defence against the 'evil eye'. Alternatively amulets are used, this practice originating from the wearing of quotations from the Koran written on to strips of cloth which were bound into a leather case which was then strapped to the arm. The amulet developed as a form in its own right, made of beads, pearls, horn or stone brought back from a pilgrimage. Amulets also have the power to heal as well as to protect against the occult.

In contemporary Egypt and North Africa, medicine, superstition and ornament combine to give a wonderful array of amulets worn for both everyday and specific use.

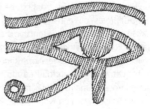

Eye of Horus

Background

The most popular amulets are the *Hirz*, the Eye and the *Khamsa* or hand. The *Hirz* is a silver box containing verses of the Koran. Egypt in particular has a preoccupation with the Eye as an amulet to ward off the 'evil eye', usually modelled on the Eye of Horus which, as with most symbols in Ancient Egyptian jewellery, has always had mystical connotations. The *Khamsa* is by far the most widespread of the amulets. It comes in a multitude of sizes and designs of a stylized hand and is one of the most common components of jewellery in the region. This hand represents the 'Hand of Fatima', Mohammed's favourite daughter. Koranic inscriptions also form a large section of favoured pendants and are usually executed in gold and also heavily encrusted with diamonds and other precious stones.

Coins or *mahboub* form the basis of most of the traditional jewellery, from the veils of the bedouins of the Nile Delta to the bodices of the women from the Egyptian oases. Spectacular ensembles are worn at festivals and wedding ceremonies. Each area, village or tribe has its own unique and extraordinary dress of which jewellery, be it huge amber beads as in Sudan or hundreds of coins, forms a fundamental part.

Among the more interesting items are **anklets** called *khul khal*, worn in pairs and found in a great variety of styles. In Egypt they are mostly of solid silver fringed with tiny bells. Fine examples are expensive due to their weight. They are losing popularity among the younger generation as they are cumbersome to wear with shoes and because of their undertones of subservience and slavery. It is still possible to see them being worn by married women in the remoter villages of Egypt.

Today the main jewellery bazaars are Khan el-Khalili in Cairo (see page 81). Jewellers in all main cities will sell you modern versions of traditional jewellery.

Dress First time visitors will be fascinated by the variety and colour of the garments worn as 'everyday' wear. This section sketches in the background and attempts an explanation of what is being worn and why.

The dress traditions are striking and colourful evidence of a rich cultural heritage. Here, as in all societies, dress is a powerful form of cultural expression, a visual symbol which reveals a wealth of information about the wearer. Dress also reflects historical evolution and the cumulative effects of religious, ethnic and geographical factors on a society.

It is hardly surprising that the many influences which have shaped Middle Eastern history have produced an equally diverse dress culture in which elements from antiquity, the Islamic world and Europe are found. The heritage from earlier times is a rich blending of decorative motifs and drapery. Carthaginian material culture drew upon local tradtions of colourful geometric ornament, which is still seen in Berber clothing and textiles, and luxury goods from Egypt. Greek and Roman fashions have survived in the striking dress of the inhabitants of the deserts and mountains. The Arabs introduced a different dress tradition, influenced by the styles of Egypt and Syria. Here the main features were loose flowing robes and cloaks, wrapped turbans and headcovering which combined a graceful line, comfort and modest concealment. The establishment of Islamic cities encouraged a diverse range of professions and occupations – civil and religious authorities, merchants, craftsmen – all with their distinctive dress. Within cities such as Cairo specialist trades in textiles, leather and jewellery supported dress production. Widening political and commercial relations stimulated new elements in dress.

The Ottoman Turks introduced another feature into city dress, in the form of jackets, trousers and robes of flamboyant cut and lavishly embroidered decoration. Finally European fashion, with emphasis on tailored suits and dresses entered the scene. The intricate pattern of mixed dress styles reflects an adjustment to economic and social change.

The widest range is seen in urban environments where European styles mingle with interpretations of local dress and the clothing of regional migrants. Men have adopted European dress in varying degrees. The wardrobes of civil servants, professional and business men include well-cut sober coloured European suits, which are worn with toning shirts, ties and smart shoes. Seasonal variations include fabrics of lighter weight and colour and short-sleeved shirts and 'safari' jackets. Casual versions of this dress code, including open-necked shirts, are seen in more modest levels of urban society. Blue jeans, blouson jackets, T shirts and trainers may be worn equally by manual workers and students.

Turban

Men's city dress alternates between European and local garments according to taste and situation. Traditional dress is based on a flexible combination of loose flowing garments and wraps which gives considerable scope for individuality. One of the most versatile garments is the *jallabah*, an ankle length robe with long straight sleeves and a neat pointed hood, made in fabrics ranging from fine wool and cotton in dark and light colours to rough plain and striped homespun yarn. Elegant versions in white may be beautifully cut and sewn and edged with plaited silk braid. A modern casual version has short sleeves and a V-shaped neck and is made of poly-cotton fabric in a range of plain colours. Professional men may change from a suit into a *jallabah* at home, while working class men may wear a plain or striped *jallabah* in the street over European shirt and trousers.

The more traditional interpretation of dress can be seen in the medinas. Here the *jallabah* is worn with the hood folded at the the back or pulled up and draped over the head. In the past a fez or turban was worn under the hood and a white cotton high-necked shirt with long sleeves and loose white trousers gathered just below the knee were worn under the *jallabah*.

A handsome and dignified garment worn by high ranking state and religious officials is the *caftan*, another long robe with very wide sleeves and a round neck. The cut and detail, such as the use of very fine braid around the neck and sleeves and along the seams, are more formal than those of the *jallabah*. The modern *caftan* has narrower sleeves and is worn in public by men of an older and more conservative generation. Traditional dress may be completed with the addition of drapery. Examples include the selham or burnous, a wide semicircular cloak with a pointed hood and the *ksa*, a length of heavy white woollen cloth which is skilfully folded and wrapped around the head and body in a style resembling that of the classical Roman toga.

Headcoverings are a revealing indication of status and personal choice. A close fitting red wool felt pillbox cap, a *fez*, *tarboosh* or *chechia*, with a black tassle can be seen more often on older men both in traditional and European dress. The distinctive, often checked, headsquare (*kiffiyeh*) of the Bedouin is secured by a heavy double coil

(*igal*) of black wool. The ends of the cloth may hang loose or be wrapped around the face and neck for protection against heat or cold. The more traditional loose turban of a length of usually white, less commonly brown, cotton is widespread in Egypt, worn by a wide selection of the working men.

Kiffiyeh and igal

Jallabah

Background

Women's town dress is also a mixture of traditional and modern European forms and depends on wealth, status and personal taste. In the larger cities where women are employed in business and professions, European clothes are worn, cleverly accessorized with scarves and jewellery. Longer skirts and long-sleeved blouses are worn, being a more modest form of European dress.

Traditional dress is remarkably enduring among women of all classes. The most important garments are the *caftan* and *jallabah* of the same basic cut and shape as those for men. The *caftan*, as worn in the past by wealthy women, was a sumptuous garment of exaggerated proportions made of rich velvet or brocaded silk embroidered with intricate designs in gold thread. The modern *caftan* is usually made of brightly coloured and patterned light-weight fabric and edged with plaited braid. The shape is simple and unstructured with a deep slit at each side from waist to hem. Variations can be found in texture and colour of fabric, changes in proportions of sleeves and length of side slits. The *caftan* in its many variations is always worn as indoor dress and can suit all occasions. Traditionally it is worn as an everyday garment belted over a long underskirt. A light shawl may be draped around the neck and the hair tied up with a patterned scarf. Women who normally wear European dress to work often change into a *caftan* at home. Very chic versions of the *caftan*, combined with modern hairstyles and accessories, are worn as evening wear at private and official functions.

Literature

Early Egyptian
literary roots

Egypt is literature-rich. Champolleon's and his academic successors' work on the ancient languages of the pharoanic period have opened up official state and private stores of written materials on which much work remains to be done. The pre-Islamic Egyptian tradition was preserved through to the present day to an extent in Coptic liturgies and there is hope for a renaissance in a broader literature now that Coptic is again being taught in religious schools.

Arabic has been the overwhelmingly most important language in Egypt since the **17th century**. Classical Arabic had been perfected long before the Prophet Mohammed but its use in the Koran, the oldest existing book in Arabic, has made it the basis of Muslim texts and liturgies, and of the Arabic exemplified in the literatures of the several Arab nations. Among the very earliest of Arabic writing is a tablet dated 512 AD found at Zabad in Syria. A considerable body of oral literature in Arabic is also known to have existed before that time – mainly poetry. In the early centuries of Islam, there was a flowering of religious, philosophical and scientific texts that in translation had an impact well beyond the boundaries of the Muslim world.

Egypt as a
literary
powerhouse

Cairo in the **19th century** witnessed a remarkable expansion of literary activity under internal pressures of embryonic nationalism and the impact of western cultural and scientific influences in the so-called "modernist" movement. Expansion was greatly assisted by the exploitation of machine printing presses. Poetry, biography and history became the staple element in Arabic literature of the **20th century**. There was also an explosion of interest in political affairs as literacy spread and anti-colonial attitudes deepened. New literary forms were adopted such as the novel, the most influential of which was *Zaynab* by **Husayn Haykal** published in 1914 dealing with human relations and the pastoral theme. By the **21st century** the book stands and book shops in Egypt carry a growing weight of publications. Much is ephemeral, a great number of school and university text books are translated from western languages but there is also a goodly proportion of imaginative, religious, social science and technology writing by Arab authors. The international success of Naguib Mahfouz's novels (see illustration) is an indicator of

قصة السر

*Dust jacket of book
by Naguib Mahfouz*

the great strength of contemporary Egyptian literature. Meanwhile, the rising tide of literacy and education makes Arabic literature universal within the greater Arab world so that an Egyptian knows that his/her potential audience is some 100 million or more readers other than those in Egypt. Although the bulk of serious writing concerns Islam, ethics and politics, new literary effort is apparent in areas as diverse as electronics, to serve the growing revolution in communications, and an expandingly active women's press (though taking its roots from the 1890s) with books, journals, magazines and newspapers as their product. Among the most influential women writers is **Nawwal el-Saadawi**, who is revered among leading female writers as a feminist and political radical. Her book *Woman at Point Zero* is available in English and many other languages. She operates under constraint of the censor in Egypt. Look out for books by **Ahdaf Soueif**, who, although Egyptian, writes in the English language. Her best known work is *In the Eye of the Sun*, a novel based on her own up-bringing in Cairo.

Reflections of Egyptian literature in the West

Of course, the number of non-Arab Arabic readers is limited and most educated people outside the Muslim world come into contact with Egyptian literature in translation. The novels of Nobel Price winner Naguib Mahfouz are a case in point, reaching an enormous international readership. Mahfouz ran foul of the conservative religious establishment in Egypt and was very badly hurt in 1994 by an Islamist assassin responding to a judgment issued against him by a fundamentalist cleric. He has not written since that time but many more of his prolific output of novels remain to be published in translation.

There were also foreign residents in Egypt who were authors of international standing and who brought Egyptian society and environment to the attention of an external audience. Notable in English was **Laurence Durrell** with his *Alexandria Quartet*, a series of novels that take as their subject the Alexandria of the expatriate Europeans. Lesser known is **Constantine Cavafy** (1863-1933), a poet whose home can be visited in Sharia Sharm el-Shaikh in central Alexandria.

Overall, Egypt is a rich mine of literary veins of many different kinds. Fortunately, the repressive activities of government and Islamists have far from extinguished a vibrant intellectual tradition in factual and imaginative writing.

Egyptian popular music

Egypt is the recording centre of the Arab world, although Lebanon is beginning to become a rival once more. Egyptian popular music dates back to pharaonic times, but it is influenced much more by the country's Arab and Islamic heritage. While Western music is popular with the cosmopolitan upper class, the vast majority of Egyptians prefer their own indigenous sounds. Arabic music is based on quarter notes rather than the Western half tone scale.

Classical Arabic Music is the traditional music of the upper class with its roots in the court music of the Ottoman empire. Sung in classical Arabic, it is highly operatic, poetic, and stylized in form. It is characterized by a soloist backed by mass ranks of violinists and cellists and a large male choir. Its most famous singer by far, and the Arab world's first singing superstar, was Umm Kalthoum who died in 1975. During her five-hour concerts, her endless melodic variations could ensure that one song lasted up to 2½ hours.

This tradition was lightened and popularized in the 1960s by Abdul Halim Hafez, the other 'great' of Egyptian music, whose romantic croonings in colloquial Arabic also dominated the Arab musical scene.

By contrast, **Shaabi**, or 'popular' music, is that of the working classes, particularly the urban poor. Like Algerian Rai, it has retained a traditional form but through stars such as Ahmed Adawia it broke convention by speaking in plain and often raunchy language about politics and the problems of society.

Al-Musika al-Shababeya or 'youth music' is highly popular with the middle and upper classes and is sometimes imitated in the *Shaabi*. First appearing in the late 1970s, it is a mixture of Arabic and Western influences, taking typical Arabic singing and Arabic instruments such as the *dof* drum and *oud* lute and underpinning this with a Western beat of melodies. The seminal album is Mohamed Mounir's Shababik (Windows) which, in partnership with Yehia Khalil, revolutionized Egyptian pop music in 1981 by introducing thoughtful lyrics, harmonies and a jazz-rock influence into still authentically Arabic music.

In the late 1980s Hamid al-Shaeri pioneered the offshoot **al-Jil** or '(new) generation' wave of sound whose fast handclap dance style glories in its self-proclaimed

Egyptian-ness. It has spawned a new clutch of stars such as Amr Diab and Hisham Abbas but its disco style and safe lyrics have brought criticism that Egyptian pop music has become stagnant and repetitive.

Much less popular is Egyptian **ethnic music**, although it has its adherents particularly in the countryside. Of particular note are **Simsimmeya** music, named after its dominant guitar-like stringed instrument, which comes from Ismailia and around the Suez Canal zone; **Saiyidi** or Upper Egyptian music the rhythms of which are based on the wooden horn, *mismar saiyidi*, and two-sided drum nahrasan; the **Delta Fellahi** or peasant music which is calmer and less sharp; and **Nubian** music, which possesses a more African feel, and, unlike Arabic music, uses the pentatonic scale. The pre-eminent Nubian folkloric singer is Hanza Alaa Eddin, who counts among his admirers Peter Gabriel and The Grateful Dead.

Cassettes of Egyptian music are available in all major cities either from small roadside kiosks (often bootleg), market stalls, or from record shops. Try the English speaking Jet Line, 20 Sharia Mansour Mohamed, Zamalek, T3400605 or California, 2 Sharia Taher Hussein, Zamalek, T3412619.

People

The Arab Republic of Egypt had a population of 64.6 million in mid-1999. The growth rate of Egypt's population remains a sensitive matter given the difficulties of the government in providing jobs and feeding the people. It had seemed in the 1970s that the annual rate of increase was tailing off at 2.1% per year but there was a spurt again in the mid-1980s to 2.9% per year before falling again in the 1990s to 1.9%. The population at this latter rate will double every 37 years. In the recent past there were high levels of emigration to the oil-exporting states of the Persian Gulf. Meanwhile, the crude death rate has fallen over the last 25 years and life expectancy at birth has gone up to male 60 and female 64, thus adding to the growth of the population size.

Racial origins Egyptians living in the Nile Valley between Aswan and the sea have ancient origins. It is speculated that the people of the Nile Valley were of Berber origin with some Arab and Negroid admixtures. The people of the Delta had a slightly different early history and thus had distinct racial origins in which Armedoid and Arab elements were fused with the other peoples of the Nile Valley. Other racial additions were made from invasions from Libya, then from the desert lands of Arabia and Persia in the east, and finally the Mediterranean connections which are most graphically illustrated by the Alexandrine conquest and the Roman establishment in northern Egypt. Present day Egyptians see themselves as having common racial and cultural origins which increasingly are not identified absolutely with the Arabs and Arab nationalism as a whole.

Distribution/ density The Egyptian population is concentrated in the Nile Valley and Delta where 98% of people are found. Average densities are put at 65 people per sq km but in Cairo and the irrigated lands densities of many thousands per sq km are recorded.

Age groups The population is youthful with 36% under the age of 15, 58% in the working age group 15-59, and 6% over 60. Literacy is high at 51%, with males at 64% being better placed than women at 39% literate.

Income per head Egyptian income is put at US$1,200 per head of population. UN sources suggests that there was a modest level of growth of 2.5% per year in real personal incomes in the 1990s, during which labour productivity has grown slowly and labour market conditions have tended to harden.

Background

● ●

☞ The practice of Islam: living by the Prophet

Islam is an Arabic word meaning 'submission to God'. As Muslims often point out, it is not just a religion but a total way of life. The main Islamic scripture is the Koran or Quran, the name being taken from the Arabic al-qur'an or 'the recitation'. The Koran is divided into 114 sura, or 'units'. It is for Muslims the infallible word of God revealed to the Prophet Mohammed. In addition to the Koran there are the hadiths, from the Arabic word hadith meaning 'story', which tell of the Prophet's life and works. These represent the second most important body of scriptures.

The practice of Islam is based upon five central tenets, known as the Pillars of Islam: Shahada (profession of faith), Salat (worship), Zakat (charity), saum (fasting) and Haj (pilgrimage). The mosque is the centre of religious activity. The two most important mosque officials are the imam (leader) and the khatib (preacher) who delivers the Friday sermon.

The Shahada is the confession, and lies at the core of any Muslim's faith. It involves reciting, sincerely, two statements: 'There is no god, but God', and 'Mohammed is the Messenger [Prophet] of God'. A Muslim will do this at every Salat. This is the prayer ritual which is performed five times a day, including sunrise, midday and sunset. There is also the important Friday noon worship. The Salat is performed by a Muslim bowing and then prostrating himself in the direction of Mecca (Arabic qibla). In hotel rooms throughout the Muslim world there is nearly always a little arrow, painted in the ceiling – or sometimes inside a wardrobe – indicating the direction of Mecca and labelled qibla. The faithful are called to worship by a

mosque official. Beforehand, a worshipper must wash to ensure ritual purity. The Friday midday service is performed in the mosque and includes a sermon given by the khatib.

A third essential element of Islam is Zakat – charity or alms-giving. A Muslim is supposed to give up his 'surplus' (according to the Koran); through time this took on the form of a tax levied according to the wealth of the family. Good Muslims are expected to contribute a tithe to the Muslim community.

The fourth pillar of Islam is saum or fasting. The daytime month-long fast of Ramadan is a time of contemplation, worship and piety – the Islamic equivalent of Lent. Muslims are expected to read 1/30th of the Koran each night. Muslims who are ill or on a journey have dispensation from fasting, but otherwise they are only permitted to eat during the night until 'so much of the dawn appears that a white thread can be distinguished from a black one'.

The Haj or Pilgrimmage to the holy city of Mecca in Saudi Arabia is required of all Muslims once in their lifetime if they can afford to make the journey and are physically able to do so. It is restircted to a certain time of the year, beginning on the 8th day of the Muslim month of Dhu-I-Hijja. Men who have been on the Haj are given the title Haji, and women Hajjah.

The Koran also advises on a number of other practices and customs, in particular the prohibitions on usury, the eating of pork, the taking of alcohol, and gambling.

The application of the Islamic dress code varies. It is least used in the larger towns and more closely followed in the rural areas.

● ●

Background

Religion

The population of Egypt is made up of 94.12 % Sunni Muslims and 5.87 % Coptic Christians.

Religious practices in the Coptic church

Baptism of infants takes place when the child is about six weeks old, with three immersions in consecrated water in the plunge bath. Confirmation takes place at the same time. Men and women are segregated during church services (to left and right) and while men must remove their shoes before moving through the screen from the nave to the altar women are forbidden to enter that part of the church.

The most important celebration in the church's calendar is Holy Week, culminating with the Resurrection on Easter Day. This is preceded by a fasting time of 55 days during which no animal products may be eaten, nor wine or coffee drunk. Like the Muslims no food or drink is permitted between sunrise and sunset (without special dispensation). Holy Week is a time of special prayers beginning with a mass on Palm Sunday, after which family graves are visited and decorated with palm fronds and flowers, as are house doors and rooms where visitors are entertained. These very cleverly crafted decorations of palm fronds are offered for sale in Coptic Cairo. On Good Friday altars are draped with black and many candlelight processions take place at dawn – commemorating the entry of Jesus into Jerusalem. Easter Sunday is a day of celebration, a time for special food, new clothes, visiting relations but also of giving to the less fortunate. As in other Christian communities coloured hardboiled eggs and chocolate eggs are consumed.

Christmas is preceded by 43 days of fasting (see above), ending on 6 January (Christmas Eve) with a midnight service and a celebratory meal. Christmas Day, after church, is a time for visiting relations and friends. Other times of fasting occur during the year.

Background

Land and environment

Egypt lies at the crossroads of Africa and the Middle East as well as having extensive borders on the Mediterranean and Red Sea. The narrow green ribbon of the Nile cuts its way from south to north through the seemingly endless desert. There is an additional 2,000 km of Red Sea where off shore the area is fringed with teeming coral reefs. And to complete these rich offerings is the Mediterranean Sea coast.

Geography

The overall area of the country is 1,002,000 sq km, which is over twice the size of Morocco.

Egypt's location in Northeast Africa gives it great strategic importance arising from its position at the junction of the land routes joining Africa to the Near and Middle East and the sea routes from the Atlantic/Mediterranean and the Indian Ocean/Red Sea. Its borders abut in the north on to the Mediterranean coast and for much of the east on to the Red Sea. These two coastal reaches are separated by the isthmus of Suez, a 150 km land bridge linking the eastern outliers of the Nile Delta with Sinai. The international frontier with Israel runs northwest across the Sinai peninsula from the Taba strip at the head of the Gulf of Aqaba, to the coastal plain of the Negev with a deviation to take account of the Gaza strip.

Travellers coming into Taba from **Israel** intending to stay in northern Sinai and people going to Israel from Taba only need border permits. Travellers crossing from Israel into Egypt or vice-versa can expect two frontier checks one at either end of the Taba strip. People intending to visit most Arab countries should avoid passport stamps at either Egyptian or Israeli border posts here. The border area is clearly marked and the area is monitored by UN forces. Off-shore in the Gulf of Aqaba care is needed not to stray across undemarcated frontiers because the Israelis are particularly sensitive about the possibility of terrorists crossing by sea from the three neighbouring Arab countries just across the water.

Egypt's 1,000 km southern border is with **Sudan**. There is a dispute over ownership of land and economic rights in the Halaib area immediately adjacent to the Red Sea which travellers should avoid. Egypt's 1,300 km long border with **Libya** on the west is one where there have always been periodic tensions. Nomads often smuggle goods across the border in the area between Siwa/Al-Jaghbub and the coastline in the territory of Ulad Ali tribe. The only easy and official crossing point is in the north on the coast road near Sollum. There is some dispute in the Egyptian-Libyan offshore zone about the alignment of the boundary but this does not currently affect either land or sea transport.

Main regions

Egypt is correctly said to be "the gift of the Nile" and Egypt's two most important regions, the Delta and the Nile Valley are both clustered close to its water supplies. The Delta lies north of Cairo and is a vast, low, flat triangle of land through which the tributaries of the Nile pass to the sea. South of Cairo the Nile is contained within a rich and fertile but narrow 2-3 km incised valley which eventually reaches Lake Nasser which is a 425 km ribbon of water extending up to and beyond the border with Sudan. The Delta and the Nile Valley contain almost 99% of the country's cultivated land and approximately the same proportion of the population. East of the Nile Valley is the Eastern Desert and the narrow Red Sea coastline. To the east of the Delta lies the formerly isolated Sinai peninsula which now has international airports and harbours and is traversed by major roads. West of the River Nile is the Libyan Desert which is often referred to as the Egypt's Western Desert. It is broken up by the occurrence of the Al-Uwenat Heights in the southwest which extend in an elongated plateau towards the lowlands of Dakhla Oasis, which has larger

Slope of the River Nile from Lake Victoria to the Mediterranean

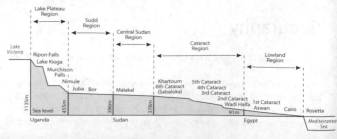

parallel formations in the north as the Qattara and Siwa depressions which, together with Dakhla, form the eastern edge of the Sirtican embayment. The long coastal plain between Alexandria and Marsa Matruh gets narrower towards the west as it approaches the Libyan frontier in the Gulf of Sollum.

Egypt is a country of lowlands and low-lying plateaux of which 60% is less than 400 m above sea-level. The few areas of high relief are the Al-Uwenat Heights in the southwest and in the Eastern Desert adjacent to the Red Sea coast where mountains rise to over 1,000 m. The highest mountain in the country is Jebel Katrinah next to St Catherines Monastery (see page 432) which reaches 2,228 m at its summit.

Egypt has the **River Nile** as its only but vital river. The total annual flow down the Nile, from the **Blue Nile** and **River Atbara** which both start in the Ethiopian highlands and the **White Nile** which begins in East Africa's Lake Victoria, is normally 55 cubic km. Under the 1959 Nile Waters Agreement, Egypt is entitled to take 37 cubic km but, because Sudan so far does not use its full allocation, has been able to take more. There is now growing pressure in all the upstream states for more water and another water crisis is looming.

Egypt has undertaken extensive engineering projects on the River Nile over the centuries which reached a peak with work by the British authorities in the 19th and early 20th centuries. In the modern period the Aswan High Dam, (see page 299) which was designed to give Egypt both water storage facilities and hydro-electric power for its new industries, was built with Russian assistance in the 1960s. In fact the low level of the River Nile in the late 1980s led to a major crisis and precipitated a crash programme to build power stations dependent on locally produced natural gas.

The construction of the Aswan High Dam also reduced the deposition of silt on Egyptian farmlands in the Nile Valley and the Delta. This has necessitated the use of large quantities of fertilizer and led to a decline in the offshore fishing production. Despite some initial success in the search for sub-surface water reservoirs under the deserts, the River Nile remains the very lifeblood of Egypt. There are no other perennial streams, although *wadis* run elsewhere after heavy rain as brief but dangerous spates.

The Nile and man

The River Nile runs for 6,435 km and drains one fifth of the entire African continent. It rises as the White Nile in Lake Victoria close to Jinja in Uganda and flows as the Victoria Nile through the tropics to Lake Albert. The Nile then begins its course through The Sudan as the Bahr el-Jebel eventually reaching the central plains of Sudan and becoming sluggish and ponding up during the annual flood in the marshy papyrus swamps of the Sudd (Arabic for 'dam'). Tributaries such as the Bahr el Ghazal and the Sobat enter the Nile and north from that point the river for its next 800 km is called the White Nile. The Sobat, which takes its source in the Ethiopian Highlands, is an important water supply for the White Nile system. It joins the Blue Nile at Khartoum. The Blue Nile drains an area deep in the Ethiopian Highlands and, like the Atbara which also joins from the east bank, provides run-off from the Northeast African monsoon. Between Khartoum and Aswan the river passes over six cataracts. The cataracts are wide rapids which make navigation impossible, the steepest of the cataracts, the sixth, is at Sababka 80 km north of Khartoum.

The River Nile in Egypt is entrenched in a narrow valley below the surrounding land and has only one cataract at Aswan. In its last 325 km before entering its Delta the River Nile tends to keep to the east bank with the main cultivated zone of the valley on the west bank. Most irrigation requires water to be lifted from the river by traditional means such as the *saqiya*, *shadoof* or by mechanical pumps.

The Nile Delta is the heartland of Egypt. It covers a great silt plain built up by the river over centuries. The Delta stretches 160 km from the vicinity of Cairo north to the Mediterranean coast and 250 km across the Mediterranean end of the wedge. The main distributaries in the delta are the Western Rosetta and Eastern Damietta 'mouths', which are the axes of intensive irrigation networks.

The flow of the River Nile has been influenced by fluctuations in rainfall in the countries where the river has its sources. It is possible that long term climatic change is involved, indicating that the flow in the river might never recover to the average of 84 cu km in the period 1900-59 from the 1984-87 level of less than 52 cu km. The water flow during floods has always varied, as we know from inscriptions in pharaonic times, but recent trends are worrying for the states that rely on the river.

Division of Nile waters is governed by the international agreements of 1929 and 1959, which ultimately gave 48 cu km to Egypt and 4 cu km to Sudan but the arrangement involved only Egypt and Sudan and excluded Ethiopia and the East African states. Argument over allocation of Nile waters continues, with Egypt's rights as the downstream state most at risk. Egyptian governments have felt so strongly on the issue of maintaining their share of Nile waters that they have threatened to go to war if the traditional division was changed against Egyptian interests. A master plan for the future use of Nile waters seems to be a distant prospect.

Finding the source of the River Nile

The ancient Egyptians believed that the waters of the River Nile came from a mystical paradise of plenty. Early exploration by the Greeks and Romans established that the River Nile ran at least from the site of modern day Khartoum. In the 17th century there began a steady stream of European explorers and adventurers seeking the source of the River Nile. Most notable was James Bruce, a Scotsman who in 1769 began a trip which led him to the head waters of the Blue Nile. He was followed by the Englishmen Richard Burton, John Speke and James Grant, who traced the River Nile back to the Lake Victoria connection and, finally, Sir S W Baker, who went further south to Lake Albert. Full mapping of the Nile Basin as a whole went on until the 1960s. The 1980s film *Mountains of the Moon* captures the discovery of the source of the Nile.

Traditional irrigation in Egypt

In Egypt a basic problem for farmers was lifting water from the River Nile up the river banks which enclosed it. Simple systems of lifting water included windlasses and pulleys were used initially to enable humans or animals pull up leather bags full of river water (see Delu Well, page 545). Some mechanization followed in which flow-turned wheels were used. These were driven by the current of the river and had pots or wooden containers to carry the water to be deposited at a higher level as at El-Fayoum (see page 166). In much of the country where irrigation canals have little or no flow an animal powered wheel is exploited. Perhaps the classic and oldest water lifting device in Egypt is the *shadoof*, a weighted beam which is swung into the water by its operator and swung up and on to land with the help of a counter balance on the other end of the beam. In recent times water has been led to the fields by diesel and electric pumps.

The water supply system of Egypt has been much improved. Even before the construction of the Aswan Dam and the later High Dam (see The Great Dams at Aswan, page 299) much had been done to improve the water storage and flow control of the River Nile. Below the river works at Aswan is the Esna barrage, a masonry dam which acts as an enormous weir to raise the height of the River Nile so that water can be led off in side channels to serve the lands lying under the canal. Downstream at Assiut a diversion dam was constructed to send water throughout the year into the existing Ismail Pasha Canal. A second diversion dam was built at Nag Hammadi between Assiut and Esna. In the delta, the replacement Mohammed Ali barrage was erected on the Rosetta branch. Other dams exist at Edfina and at Sennar in Egypt and Jebel Awlia in Sudan.

The use of the River Nile for navigation has been limited by the narrow, gorge-like nature of some stretches of the upper valley, by the Sudd of Sudan and the existence of the six cataracts in the river bed downstream of Khartoum. In Egypt

The delu well – traditional well of North Africa

In the traditional oases of Egypt's Western Desert – and still in evidence today – water was lifted from shallow water tables along the coast or from depressions in the desert by means of a device called a delu. The name is taken from the word for a hide, which is made into a bag comprising an entire goatskin. Strung on a line, this is dipped into a well and drawn up full of water for both household and irrigation purposes.

The mechanism is simple and effective. A shallow 1 or 2 m diameter well is hand dug to about 2 or 3 m below the water table and lined with stone work or cement. Above ground an often ornate gantry is made of two upright stone or wooden pillars rising from the side of the wellhead. A cross beam between the top of the two pillars acts as an axle to a small pulley wheel which carries a rope tied to the mouth of the goatskin bag. The rope is drawn up or let down by the ingenious use of a ramp to ease the task of lifting water to the surface. An animal travels down the ramp when pulling up the goatskin from the bottom of the well and moves up the ramp to return the bag into the bottom of the well. Most delu wells have a secondary rope attached to the bottom of the goatskin bag which can be used when the full bag is at the top of the gantry to upend it and tip out the water.

The rate of water lifting by the delu method is obviously limited. The capacity of the bag is about 20 litres. Working from dawn to dusk, however, enough water could be raised to irrigate up to 3 or 4 ha of land – enough to feed a family and leave a small surplus for sale in the market. Most wells were equipped with a storage basin adjacent to the wellhead so that water could be raised and stored for household use and to give a reserve of water for irrigation.

The creak of the wooden pulley wheel of the delu was one of the characteristic sounds of the Western Desert oases until the 1960s. After that time diesel and electric power pumps became available and the delu system has mainly fallen into disuse. A few delu gantries remain, some as museum pieces, and only the observant traveller in the deepest south of the Saharan oases will come across this splendid and environmentally friendly technology in day-to-day operation.

Delu Well

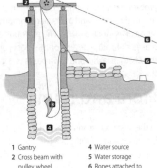

1 Gantry	4 Water source
2 Cross beam with	5 Water storage
pulley wheel	6 Ropes attached to
3 Goat-skin bag	working animal

the River Nile unites the country and local and long-distance craft ply the waterway on a scheduled basis. A large fleet of passenger vessels transport tourists on the River Nile particularly from Luxor to Aswan to serve the great monuments of ancient Egypt (see Nile Cruisers, page 282).

One of the most splendid sights on the river is the local *feluccas* under sail. The *felucca* is a lanteen rigged sailing vessel for inshore or river work. It has very shallow draught so that it can safely cross shoals and can be easily rowed if the wind is absent or unfavourable. Most *feluccas*, once for transporting produce up and down the Nile, are now available for hire by tourists by the hour or the day for a suitably bargained price which will depend on the season and other factors.

The *felucca* is much smaller and less magnificent than the Nile boats of the ancient Egyptians. These ancient craft developed from bundles of papyrus reeds,

Feluccas

woven or bound together to make a buoyant crescent-shaped hull for carrying light loads. Later in the Old Kingdom wood was the principal raw material for constructing larger vessels whose shape followed that of the papyrus craft. Most wood was imported to make a keelless craft with a sail and steering gear made up paddles at the stern. By the Middle Kingdom boats took on a more crescent-shaped silhouette, while a cabin was added to the deck immediately before the stern deck. In the New Kingdom boats on the River Nile were longer and more sophisticated, with deckhouses sited round the mast and ceremonial daises both stern and aft. The sail on the New Kingdom vessels was rigged between top and bottom spars and was much wider than earlier types of sail. An example of an Old Kingdom (4th Dynasty) boat was found at the Great Pyramid at Giza. It was 43.6 m long and 5.9 m beam and when found was still unbuilt kit. The ship was made to be constructed with boards bound to ribs and to carry a small deckhouse and a single steering paddle. It is lodged in a store near the Cheops pyramid.

Climate

Egypt is a desert country. Even its frontage to the Mediterranean offers only a modest tempering of Saharan conditions in the vicinity of the coast in the Alexandria region. Here rainfall is at a maximum with an average of 188 mm per year with summer maximum temperatures averaging 30°C and diurnal ranges rarely more than 10°C. Moving inland brings a rapid decline in rainfall. Cairo, some 150 km from the sea, has an annual average rainfall of 25 mm, a maximum temperature of 35°C and average diurnal ranges of temperature of up to 15°C. Progression southwards brings even greater extremes. At Aswan rainfall drops away to 1 mm per year and average maximum temperatures rise to 37°C with a diurnal range of as much as 18°C. The profound aridity of Egypt outside the Nile Valley makes it absolute desert for the most part, relieved only where water occurs such as the Kharga, Dakhla and Siwa oases (see pages 489, 485 and 379).

Flora and fauna

In the desert environment, annual plants have a very short life span, growing, blooming and seeding in a few short days, covering the ground, when moisture content permits, with a patchy carpet of low-lying blooms. Desert perennials are sparse, tough and spiny with deep root systems. Desert animals are rarely seen, being generally nocturnal and/or underground dwellers to avoid the heat. With water from the River Nile, an oasis or precipitation in the south, the plants are tropical and subtropical and the wildlife becomes more obvious in the form of small and medium size mammals like rats and the Egyptian mongoose. Bird life proliferates by the water, with roosting egrets, herons, kingfishers and hoopoes all very common. The birds of prey range in size from kestrels to black kites and Egyptian vultures. The number of Nile fish is decreasing but the coasts continue to teem with fish.

The area covered by this *Handbook* is predominantly desert yet there are many sub-regions providing a wide variety of habitats. The northern coast of Egypt is influenced by the Mediterranean but the scrub vegetation soon gives way to semi desert; the Nile Delta area includes coastal wetlands and salt marsh; inland lakes and reservoirs provide saltwater and freshwater sites for migrating and resident birds. The limited areas of arable agriculture along the narrow Nile valley and in the extensive delta contrast with the vast expanses of scrub. The mountain ranges of Sinai provide their own climate, delaying flowering and shortening the growing

Prickly pears or barbary figs

Opuntia Vulgaris *is the Latin name for the prickly pear cactus, with large flat spined leaves, which is used for boundary hedges or less commonly shelter belts to deflect wind from delicate plants.*

The attractive flowers of yellow or cyclamen occur on the rim of the leaves from May onwards and provide a bright splash of colour. If your visit occurs in July or August do not hesitate to try the delicacy, the fruit of the Barbary fig. Obtain them ready peeled from roadside sellers and certainly **do not** *pick them yourself as they are protected by a multitude of fine spines, almost invisible to the naked eye, which can only be removed, painfully, by an expert.*

Consume these fruits in moderation as more than two or three can cause constipation.

season. Even the desert areas which cover so much of this region provide contrasts, the sands (*erg*), gravels (*reg*) and rock (*hammada*) being interspersed with the occasional flourishing oasis. The Red Sea provides a colourful and unusual selection of sea creatures.

Many of the habitats mentioned above are under threat, either from pollution, urbanization, desertification or advanced farming techniques. Fortunately the conservation movement is gaining pace and many National Parks and Nature Reserves have been created and programmes of environmental education set up. However, regrettably, wildlife is still regarded as a resource to be exploited, either for food or sport.

In desert regions, wildlife faces the problem of adapting to drought and the accompanying heat. The periods without rain may vary from four months on the shores of the Mediterranean to several years In some parts of the Sahara. Plants and animals have, therefore, evolved numerous methods of coping with drought and water loss. Some plants have extensive root systems; others have hard, shiny leaves or an oily surface to reduce water loss through transpiration. Plants such as the broom have small, sparse leaves, relying on stems and thorns to attract sunlight and produce food. Animals such as the addax and gazelle obtain all their moisture requirements from vegetation and never need to drink, while the ostrich can survive on saline water. Where rain is a rare occurence, plants and animals have developed a short life cycle combined with years of dormancy. When rain does arrive, the desert can burst into life, with plants seeding, flowering and dispersing within a few weeks or even days. Rain will also stimulate the hatching of eggs which have lain dormant for years. Many animals in the desert areas are nocturnal, taking advantage of the cooler night temperatures, their tracks and footprints being revealed in the morning. Another adaption is provided by the sandfish, which is a type of skink (lizard) which 'swims' through the sand in the cooler depths during the day. Perhaps the most remarkable example of adaption is shown by the camel (see box, page 478). Apart from its spreading feet which enable it to walk on sand, the camel is able to adjust its body temperature to prevent sweating, reduce urination fluid loss and store body fat to provide food for up to six months.

Background

Mammals   Mammals have a difficult existence throughout the area, due to human disturbance and the fact that the species is not well adapted to drought. Many have, therefore, become nocturnal and their presence may only be indicated by droppings and tracks. Mammals represented here include the Red fox which is common in the Delta, the Sand fox, a lighter coloured hare, the shrew and two species of hedgehog, the Long-eared and the Desert. The appealing large-eyed and large-eared Desert fox or Fennec is less common and is often illegally trapped for sale. Despite widespread hunting, wild boar survive. Hyenas and jackals still thrive particularly in Sinai while wild cats are found in Sinai and the Delta. The leopard, formerly common in North Africa, is now extremely rare, but is occasionally seen in some isolated regions in Sinai, to the panic of the local people.

There are three species of gazelle, all well adapted to desert conditions; the Dorcas gazelle preferring the Western Desert, the Mountain gazelle inhabiting locations above 2,000 m in Sinai and the Desert gazelle locating in the *reg* of the northern Sahara. The latter is often hunted by horse or vehicle, its only defence being its speed. There are over 30 species of bat in the area, all but one – the Egyptian Fruit bat – being insectivorous. Recent ringing has shown that bats will migrate according to the season and to exploit changing food sources. Many species of bat have declined disastrously in recent years due to the increased use of insecticides and disturbance of roosting sites.

Rodents are well represented. They include the common House rat and the Large-eyed Sand rat, the gerbil and the Long-tailed jerboa which leaps like a tiny kangaroo. Many gerbils and jerboas, sadly, are found for sale in pet shops in Europe.

Weasels are common in the Delta region, even in urban areas such as Cairo, where they keep down the numbers of rats and mice. The snake eating Egyptian mongoose with a distinctive tuft on the end of its tail is frequently sighted but sightings of porcupines are rare and then only in the far south. The ibex too is only found in the south.

Reptiles &   The crocodile, treated as a sacred animal by the Egyptians (see El-Fayoum) who kept
amphibians   them in tanks by their temples, is no longer found north of the Aswan Dam. A few remain in Lake Nasser and in Sudan. Tortoises are widespread. Terrapins are less common. Both tortoises and terrapins are taken in large numbers for the pet trade. There are over 30 species of lizard in the area, the most common being the Wall lizard, which often lives close to houses. Sand racers are frequently seen on dunes, while Sand fish and Sand swimmers take advantage of deep sand to avoid predators and find cooler temperatures in the desert *reg*. Spiny lizards have distinctive enlarged spiked scales round their tails. The waran (or Egyptian Monitor) can grow to over a metre in length. Geckoes are plump, soft-skinned, nocturnal lizards with adhesive pads on their toes and are frequently noted running up the walls in houses. The chameleon is a reptile with a prehensile tail and a long sticky tongue for catching insects. Although basically green, it can change colour to match its surroundings.

Snakes are essentially legless lizards. There are some 30 species in Egypt but only vipers are dangerous. These can be identified by their triangular heads, short plump bodies and zig-zag markings. The Horned sand-viper lies just below the surface of sand, with its horns projecting, waiting for prey. The Saw-scaled Carpet viper, which is of variegated dark camouflage colours, is twice the size but don't stay to measure, it is considered the most dangerous snake in Egypt. The Sinai or Desert Cobra, up to 2 m long, was the symbol of Lower Egypt. It too is deadly. Sand boas stay underground most of the time. Most snakes will instinctively avoid contact with human beings and will only strike if disturbed or threatened. For what to do if you are bitten by a snake, see Health in Essentials.

There are over 190 varieties of fish in the River Nile, the most common being the Nile bolti with coarse scales and spiny fins and the Nile perch, frequently well over 150 cm in length. Bolti are also found in Lake Nasser. Other fish include the inedible puffer fish, lungfish which can survive in the mud when the waters recede, grey mullet and catfish which are a popular catch for domestic consumption but some species can give off strong electric shocks. Decline in fish numbers is blamed on pollution, over-fishing and change of environment due to the construction of the Aswan Dam. Marine fish such as sole and mullet have been introduced into Lake Qaroun which is becoming increasingly saline.

River, lake & marine life

The Mediterranean Sea has insufficient nutrients to support large numbers of fish. The numerous small fishing boats with their small mesh nets seriously over-exploit the existing stock. The catch is similar to the North Atlantic – hake, sole, red mullet, turbot, whiting. Sardines occur off the Nile Delta but in much reduced quantities due to pollution. Tuna, more common to the west, are caught off Libya too. Grey mullet is fished in and off the Nile Delta while sponges, lobsters and shellfish harvested.

The fish of the Mediterranean pale into insignificance against 800 species of colourful tropical fish in the Red Sea. Tiger and Hammerhead sharks, Moray eels, Slender barracudas and Manta rays, all thriller material, occur. Here, while sport and commercial fishermen chase after tuna, bonita and dolphin, scuba divers pay to explore the fringing coral reefs and view the paint box selection of Angel, Butterfly and Parrot fish and carefully avoid the ugly Scorpion fish and the even more repulsive Stone fish.

There are a number of insects that travellers might not wish to encounter – bedbugs, lice, fleas, cockroaches, sand flies, house flies, mosquitoes, wasps and ants. By contrast there are large beautiful dragonflies which hover over the river, the destructive locusts fortunately rarely in swarms, and the fascinating Black dung beetles, the sacred Scarab of the Egyptians, which roll and bury balls of animal dung as food for their larvae (see box, page 147).

Insects

Scorpions, not insects, are all too common in Egypt. See box, page 319.

The bird life in the region is increased in number and interest by birds of passage. Four categories of birds may be noted. Firstly, there are 150 species of **resident** birds, such as the Crested lark and the Sardinian warbler. Resident birds are found mainly in the fertile strip of the Nile Valley and in the Nile Delta. There are surprisingly few in the oases. Secondly, there are the **summer visitors**, such as the swift and swallow, which spend the winter months south of the Equator. **Winter visitors**, on the other hand, breed in Northern Europe but come south to escape the worst of the winter and include many varieties of owl, wader and wildfowl. **Passage migrants** fly through the area northwards in spring and then return southwards in increased numbers after breeding in the autumn. Small birds tend to migrate on a broad front, often crossing the desert and the Mediterranean Sea without stopping. Such migrants include the Whitethroat, plus less common species such as the Nightjar and Wryneck. Larger birds, including eagles, storks and vultures, must adopt a different strategy, as they depend on soaring, rather than sustained flight. As they rely on thermals created over land, they must opt for short sea crossings following the Nile Valley, Turkey and the Bosphorus.

Birds

There are a number of typical habitats with their own assemblage of birds. The Mediterranean itself has a poor selection of sea birds, although the rare Audouins gull always excites 'twitchers'. Oceanic birds such as gannets and shearwaters, however, over-winter here. The Red Sea coast hosts the indigenous White-eyed Gull and White-cheeked Tern, migrant pelicans, gregarious flamingos and, near Hurghada, Brown boobies. Ospreys breed on the nearby Isle of Tiran.

Wetland areas attract numerous varieties of the heron family such as the Night heron and Squacco heron, while spoonbill, ibis and both Little and Cattle egrets are common. Waders such as the avocet and Black-winged stilt are also typical wetland birds. The species are augmented in winter by a vast collection of wildfowl. Resident ducks, however, are confined to specialities such as the White-headed duck, Marbled teal and Ferruginous duck. On roadsides, the Crested lark is frequently seen, while overhead wires often contain Corn buntings, with their jangling song, and the Blue-cheeked and Green Bee-eaters. Mountain areas are ideal for searching out raptors. There are numerous varieties of eagle, including Bonelli's, Booted, Short toed and Golden. Of the vultures, the griffon is the most widely encountered. The Black kite is more catholic in its choice of habitat, but the Montagu's harrier prefers open farmland.

The desert and steppe areas have their own specialist resident birds which have developed survival strategies. Raptors include the Long-legged buzzard and the lanner, which prefer mountain areas. The Arabian rock pigeon of Sinai is a protected species. Among the ground-habitat birds are the Houbura bustard and the Cream coloured courser. Duponts lark is also reluctant to fly, except during its spectacular courtship display. The Trumpeter finch is frequently seen at oases, while the insectivorous Desert wheatear is a typical bird of the *erg* and *reg* regions.

Special mention must be made of the **Nile Valley**. Essentially a linear oasis stretching for hundreds of kilometres, it provides outstanding bird watching, particularly from the slow-moving cruise boats, which are literally 'floating hides'. Apart from the wide range of herons and egrets, specialities include the African skimmer, Egyptian geese, Pied kingfisher and White pelican. Even the tombs and monuments are rewarding for the ornithologist, yielding Sakar falcons, Levant sparrowhawks and the Black shouldered kite.

Lake Nasser provides a good habitat for over 100 species of birds (see box, page 330).

Footnotes

15

Footnotes

Language for travel

It is impossible to indicate in the Latin script how Arabic should be pronounced so we have opted for a very simplified transliteration which will give the user a sporting chance of uttering something that can be understood by an Arab. An accent has been placed to show where the stress falls in each word of more than two syllables.

Numbers

0	sífr	*Please*	min fádlek
1	wáhad	*Thank you*	shukran
2	tnéen	*OK*	kwáyes
3	taláata	*Excuse me*	ismáh-lee
4	árba		
5	khámsa	**Days**	
6	sítta	*Sunday*	al-áhad
7	sába	*Monday*	al-itnéen
8	tamánia	*Tuesday*	at-taláta
9	tíssa	*Wednesday*	al-árba
10	áshra	*Thursday*	al-khemées
11	ahdásh	*Friday*	al-júma
12	itnásh	*Saturday*	as-sébt
13	talatásh		
14	arbatásh	**Food**	
15	khamstásh	*banana*	mouz
16	sittásh	*beer*	bírra
17	sabatásh	*bread*	khubz
18	tmantásh	*breakfast*	futóor
19	tissatásh	*butter*	zíbda
20	ishréen	*cheese*	jíbna
30	tlaatéen	*coffee*	qáhwa
40	arba'éen	*dessert*	hélwa
50	khamséen	*dinner*	ásha
60	sittéen	*drink*	mashróob
70	saba'éen	*egg*	baid
80	tmanéen	*fish*	sámak
90	tissa'éen	*food*	akl
100	mía	*fruit*	fawákih
200	miatéen	*lemonade*	gazóoza
300	tláata mia	*lunch*	gháda
1,000	alf	*meat*	láhma
		menu (fixed price)	ká'ima
Greetings		*milk*	lában
Hello!	assálamu aláikum	*olive*	zeitóon
How are you?	keef hálek?	*restaurant*	restaurán
Well!	kwáyes	*salt*	méleh
Good bye!	bisaláma	*soup*	shórba
Go away!	ímshi, barra	*sugar*	súkar
God willing!	inshállah	*tea (tea bag)*	shay (shay kees)
Never mind	ma'lésh	*water (bottled)*	móyyah (botri)
Thank God!	hamdulilláh!	*wine*	khamr
Yes/no	naam, áiwa/la		

Travel

airport	al-matár
arrival	wusóol
bicycle	bisiclét/darrája
birth (date of)	youm al-meelád
bus	autobées
bus station	maháttat al-autobées
car	sayára
car hire	sayárat-ujra
customs	júmruk/gúmruk
departure	khuróoj
duty (excise)	daréebat
duty free	bidóon daréeba
engine	motúr
fare	ujrat as-safr
ferry (boat)	má'diya
garage	garáge
here/there	héna/henák
left/right	yesáar/yeméen
left luggage	máktab éeda al-afsh
map	kharéeta
oil (engine)	zeit
papers (documents)	watá'iq
parking	máwkif as-sayyarát
passport	jawáz
petrol	benzéen
port	méena
puncture	tókob
quickly	sarée'an
railway	as-sikka al-hadeedíya
road	trik
slowly	shwai shwai
station	mahátta
straight on	alatóol
surname	lákab
taxi	taxi
taxi rank	maháttat at-taxiyát
ticket	tázkara
ticket (return)	tázkara dhaháb wa-eeyáb
what time is it?	is-sa'a kam?
train	tren
tyre	itár
visa	fisa, ta'shéera

Common words

after	bá'ad
afternoon	bá'ad az-zohr
Algeria	Aljazáyer
America	Amréeka
and	wa
bank	bank
bath	hammám
beach	sháti al-bahr
bed	seréer
before	qabl
big	kebéer
black	áswad
blue	ázrag
camp site	mukháyyam
castle	kál'ah
cheap	rakhées
chemist shop	saidalíya
church	kenéesa
closed	múglaq
cold/hot	bárid/sukhna
consulate	consulíya
day/night	youm/lail
desert	sahra
doctor	tebeeb
Egypt	Masr
embassy	sifára
England	Ingiltérra
enough	bás
entrance	dukhóol
evening	mássa
exchange (money)	tabdéel
exit	khuróoj
expensive (too)	kteer
film	feelm
forbidden	mamnóoh
France	France/Francia
full	melyán
Germany	Almáni
good (very good)	táyeb, kwáyes
great	ákbar
green	khádra
he/she	húwa/híya
house	mánzel
hospital	mustáshfa
hostel	bait ash-shebáb
hotel	fúnduq/hotéel
how far to..?	kam kilometri...
how much?	bikám
I/you	ána/inta
information	malumát
is there/are there?	hinák
Italy	Itálya
key	miftáh
later	ba'déen
Libya	Líbiya
light	nour
little	sghéer

market	sook	small	sghéer
me	ána	Spain	Espánya
money	flóos	square	maidán
more/less	áktar/akál	stamp	tábi'
morning	sobh	street	shári
Morocco	al Maghreb	Sudan	as Sóodan
mosque	mesjéed	Switzerland	Esswízi
near	karéeb	synagogue	kenées
newspaper	jaréeda	telephone	teleefóon
new	jedéed	today	al-yóom
not	mush	toilet	tualét
now	al-án	tomorrow	búkra
oil (heating)	naft	tower	qasr
open	maftooh	Tunisia	Toónis
pharmacy	(see chemist)	United States	al-wilayát al-
photography	taswéer		muttáhida
police	bulées/shurta	washbasin	tusht
post office	máktab al-baréed	water (hot)	móyya (sukhna)
price	si'r	week/year	usboo'/sána
red	áhmar	what?	shenu?
river	wádi, wed	when?	ímta?
roof	sat'h	where (is)?	wain?
room	górfa	white	ábyad
sea	bahr	why	laih
shop	dukkán	yellow	ásfar
shower	doosh	yesterday	ams

ARABIC NUMERALS

١	1	١٠	10	١٩	19	٨٠	80
٢	2	١١	11	٢٠	20	٩٠	90
٣	3	١٢	12	٢١	21	١٠٠	100
٤	4	١٣	13	٢٢	22	٢٠٠	200
٥	5	١٤	14	٣٠	30	٣٠٠	300
٦	6	١٥	15	٤٠	40	٤٠٠	400
٧	7	١٦	16	٥٠	50	١٠٠٠	1000
٨	8	١٧	17	٦٠	60		
٩	9	١٨	18	٧٠	70		

Glossary

A

Abbasids Muslim Dynasty ruled from Baghdad 750-1258
Agora Market/meeting place
Aïd/Eïd Festival
Aïn Spring
Almohads Islamic Empire in North Africa 1130-1269
Amir Mamluk military officer
Amulet Object with magical power of protection
Ankh Symbol of life
Apis bull a sacred bull worshipped as the living image of Ptah
Arabesque Geometric pattern with flowers and foliage used in Islamic designs

B

Bab City gate
Bahri North/ northern
Baladiyah Municipality
Baksheesh Money as alms, tip or bribe
Baraka Blessing
Barbary Name of North Africa 16th-19th centuries
Basha see Pasha
Basilica Imposing Roman building, with aisles, later used for worship
Bazaar Market
Bedouin Nomadic desert Arab
Beni Sons of (tribe)
Berber Indigenous tribe of North Africa
Bey Governor (Ottoman)
Borj Fort
Burnous Man's cloak with hood – tradional wear

C

Caid Official
Calèche Horse drawn carriage
Canopic jars Four jars used to store the internal organs of the mummified deceased
Capital Top section of a column
Caravanserai Lodgings for travellers and animals around a courtyard
Cartouche Oval ring containing a king's name in hieroglyphics
Chechia Man's small red felt hat
Chotts Low-lying salt lakes
Colossus Gigantic statue

D

Dar House
Darj w ktaf Carved geometric motif of intersecting arcs with super-imposed rectangles
Deglet Nur High quality translucent date
Delu Water lifting device at head of well
Dey Commander (of janissaries)
Dikka Raised platform in mosque for Koramic readings
Djemma Main or Friday mosque
Djin Spirit
Dólmenes Prehistoric cave
Dour Village settlement

E

Eïd see Aïd
Eïn see Aïn
Erg Sand dune desert

F

Faqirs Muslim who has taken a vow of poverty
Fatimids Muslim dynasty 909-1171 AD claiming descent from Mohammed's daughter Fatimah
Fatwa Islamic district
Fellahin Peasants
Felucca Sailing boat on Nile
Fondouk/Funduq Lodgings for goods and animals around a courtyard
Forum Central open space in Roman town
Ful/Fuul Beans

G

Garrigue Mediterranean scrubland – poor quality
Gymnasium Roman school for mind and body

H

Haikal Altar area
Hallal Meat from animals killed ascending to Islamic law
Hamada Stone desert
Hammam Bath house
Harem Women's quarters
Harira Soup
Hypogeum The part of the building below ground, underground chamber

I

Iconostasis Wooden screen supporting icons
Imam Muslim religious leader

J

Jabal see Jebel
Jallabah Outer garment with sleeves and a hood – often striped
Jami' Mosque
Janissaries Elite Ottoman soldiery
Jarapas Rough cloth made with rags
Jebel Mountain
Jihad Holy war by Muslims against non-believers

K

Ka Spirit
Khedivate The realm of Mohammed Ali and his successors
Kilim Woven carpet
Kif Hashish
Kissaria Covered market
Koubba Dome on tomb of holy man
Kufic Earliest style of Arabic script
Kuttab Korami school for young boys or orphans

L

Lintel Piece of stone over a doorway
Liwan Vaulted arcade
Loculus Small compartment or cell, a recess

M

Mahboub Coins worn as jewellery
Malekite Section of Sunni Islam
Malqaf Wind vent
Maquis Mediterranean scrubland – often aromatic
Marabout Muslim holy man/his tomb
Maristan Hospital
Mashrabiyya Wooden screen
Mastaba Tomb
Mausoleum Large tomb building
Medersa (pl Medressa) School usually attached to a mosque
Medina Old walled town, residential quarter
Mellah Jewish quarter of old town
Menzel House
Mihrab Recess in wall of mosque indicating direction of Mecca

Minaret Slender tower of mosque which the muezzin calls the faithful to prayer
Minbar Pulpit in a mosque
Mosque Muslim place of worship
Moulid/Mouloud Religious festival – Prophet's birthday
Moussem Religious gathering
Muezzin Priest who calls the faithful to prayer
Mullah Muslim religious teacher
Murabtin Dependent tribe

N

Necropolis Cemetery
Noas Shrine or chapel
Nome District or province

O

Oasis Watered desert gardens
Obelisk Tapering monolithic shaft of stone with pyramidal apex
Ostraca Inscribed rock flakes and potsherds
Ottoman Major Muslim Empire based in Turkey 13th-20th centuries
Ouled Tribe
Outrepassé Horse-shoe shaped arch

P

Papyrus (papyri) Papers used by Ancient Egyptians
Pasha Governor
Phoenicians Important trading nation based in eastern Mediterranean from 1100 BC
Pilaster Square column partly built into, partly projecting from, the wall
Pisé Sun-baked clay used for building
Piste Unsurfaced road
Pylon Gateway of Egyptian temple
Pyramidion A small pyramid shaped cap stone for the apex of a pyramid

Q

Qarafah Graveyard
Qibla Mosque wall in direction of Mecca

R

Rabbi Head of Jewish community
Ramadan Muslim month of fasting
Reg Rock desert
Ribat Fortified monastery
Riwaq Arcaded aisle

S

Sabil Public water fountain
Sabkha Dry salt lake

Saggia Water canal
Sahel Coast/ coastal plain
Sahn Courtyard
Salat Worship
Saqiya Water wheel
Sarcophagus Decorated stone coffin
Sebkha See Sabkha
Semi-columnar Flat on one side and rounded on other
Serais Lodging for men and animals
Serir Sand desert
Shadoof Water lifting device
Shahada Profession of faith
Shawabti Statuette buried with deceased, which when required, would work in the hereafter for its owner
Shergui Hot, dry desert wind
Sidi Mr/Saint
Souq Traditional market
Stalactite An ornamental arrangement of multi-tiered niches, like a honeycomb, found in domes and portals
Stele Inscribed pillar used as gravestone
Suani Small walled irrigated traditional garden
Sufi Muslim mystic
Sunni Orthodox Muslims

T

Tagine/Tajine Stew
Taifa Sub-tribe
Tarīqa Brotherhood/Order
Thòlos Round building, dome, cupola
Triclinium A room with benches on three sides
Troglodyte Underground dweller

U

Uraeus Rearing cobra, sign of kingship

V

Vandals Empire in North Africa 429-534 AD
Visir Governor

W

Wadi Water course – usually dry
Waqf Endowed land
Wikala Merchants' hostel
Wilaya/Wilayat Governorate/district

Z

Zaouia/Zawia/Zawiya Shrine/Sennusi centre
Zellij Geometrical mosaic pattern made from pieces of glazed tiles
Zeriba House of straw/grass

Footnotes

Index

Shorts

Footnotes

Maps

Diagrams

Footnotes

Footnotes

Footnotes

Footnotes

Footnotes

Footnotes

Footnotes

Conversion tables

Weights and measures

Weight
1 kilogram = 2.205 pounds
1 pound = 0.454 kilograms

Length
1 metre = 1.094 yards
1 yard = 0.914 metres
1 kilometre — 0.621 miles
1 mile = 1.609 kilometres

Capacity
1 litre = 0.220 gallons
1 gallon = 4.546 litres
1 pint = 0.863 litres

Temperature

°C	°F	°C	°F
1	34	26	79
2	36	27	81
3	38	28	82
4	39	29	84
5	41	30	86
6	43	31	88
7	45	32	90
8	46	33	92
9	48	34	93
10	50	35	95
11	52	36	97
12	54	37	99
13	56	38	100
14	57	39	102
15	59	40	104
16	61	41	106
17	63	42	108
18	64	43	109
19	66	44	111
20	68	45	113
21	70	46	115
22	72	47	117
23	74	48	118
24	75	49	120
25	77	50	122

Sales & distribution

Footprint Handbooks
6 Riverside Court
Lower Bristol Road
Bath BA2 3DZ England
T 01225 469141
F 01225 469461
discover
@footprintbooks.com

Australia
Peribo Pty
58 Beaumont Road
Mt Kuring-Gai
NSW 2080
T 02 9457 0011
F 02 9457 0022

Austria
Freytag-Berndt Artaria
Kohlmarkt 9
A-1010 Wien
T 01533 2094
F 01533 8685

Freytag-Berndt
Sporgasse 29
A-8010 Graz
T 0316 818230
F 3016 818230-30

Belgium
Craenen BVBA
Mechelsesteenweg 633
B-3020 Herent
T 016 23 90 90
F 016 23 97 11

Waterstones
The English Bookshop
Blvd Adolphe Max 71-75
B-1000 Brussels
T 02 219 5034

Canada
Ulysses Travel Publications
4176 rue Saint-Denis
Montréal
Québec H2W 2M5
T 514 843 9882
F 514 843 9448

Europe
Bill Bailey
16 Devon Square
Newton Abbott
Devon TQ12 2HR. UK
T 01626 331079
F 01626 331080

Denmark
Nordisk Korthandel
Studiestraede 26-30 B
DK-1455 Copenhagen K
T 3338 2638
F 3338 2648

Scanvik Books
Esplanaden 8B
DK-1263 Copenhagen K
T 3312 7766
F 3391 2882

Finland
Akateeminen Kirjakauppa
Keskuskatu 1
FIN-00100 Helsinki
T 09 121 4151
F 09 121 4441

Suomalainen Kirjakauppa
Koivuvaarankuja 2
01640 Vantaa 64
F 09 852751

France
FNAC – major branches

L'Astrolabe
46 rue de Provence
F-75009 Paris 9e
T 01 42 85 42 95
F 01 45 75 92 51

VILO Diffusion
25 rue Ginoux
F-75015 Paris
T 01 45 77 08 05
F 01 45 79 97 15

Germany
GeoCenter ILH
Schockenriedstrasse 44
D-70565 Stuttgart
T 0711 781 94610
F 0711 781 94654

Brettschneider
Feldkirchnerstrasse 2
D-85551 Heimstetten
T 089 990 20330
F 089 990 20331

Geobuch
Rosental 6
D-80331 München
T 089 265030
F 089 263713

Gleumes
Hohenstaufenring 47-51
D-50674 Köln
T 0221 215650

Globetrotter Ausrustungen
Wiesendamm 1
D-22305 Hamburg
T040 679 66190
F 040 679 66183

Dr Götze
Bleichenbrücke 9
D-2000 Hamburg 1
T 040 3031 1009-0

Hugendubel Buchhandlung
Nymphenburgerstrasse 25
D-80335 München
T 089 238 9412
F 089 550 1853

Kiepert Buchhandlung
Hardenbergstrasse 4-5
D-10623 Berlin 12
T 030 311 880
F 030 311 88120

Greece
GC Eleftheroudakis
17 Panepistemiou
Athens 105 64
T 01 331 4180-83
F 01 323 9821

India
India Book Distributors
1007/1008 Arcadia
195 Nariman Point
Mumbai 400 021
T 91 22 282 5220
F 91 22 287 2531

Israel
Eco Trips
8 Tverya Street
Tel Aviv 63144
T 03 528 4113
F 03 528 8269

For a fuller list, see www.footprintbooks.com

Italy
Librimport
Via Biondelli 9
I-20141 Milano
T 02 8950 1422
F 02 8950 2811

Libreria del Viaggiatore
Via dell Pelegrino 78
I-00186 Roma
T/F 06 688 01048

Netherlands
Nilsson & Lamm bv
Postbus 195
Pampuslaan 212
N-1380 AD Weesp
T 0294 494949
F 0294 494455

Waterstones
Kalverstraat 152
1012 XE Amsterdam
T 020 638 3821

New Zealand
Auckland Map Centre
Dymocks

Norway
Schibsteds Forlag A/S
Akersgata 32 - 5th Floor
Postboks 1178 Sentrum
N-0107 Oslo
T 22 86 30 00
F 22 42 54 92

Tanum
Karl Johansgate 37-41
PO Box 1177 Sentrum
N-0107 Oslo 1
T 22 41 11 00
F 22 33 32 75

Olaf Norlis
Universitetsgt 24
N-1062 Oslo
T 22 00 43 00

Pakistan
Pak-American Commercial
Hamid Chambers
Zaib-un Nisa Street
Saddar, PO Box 7359
Karachi
T 21 566 0418
F 21 568 3611

South Africa
Faradawn CC
PO Box 1903
Saxonwold 2132
T 011 885 1787
F 011 885 1829

South America
Humphrys Roberts
Associates
Caixa Postal 801-0
Ag. Jardim da Gloria
06700-970 Cotia SP
Brazil
T 011 492 4496
F 011 492 6896

Southeast Asia
APA Publications
38 Joo Koon Road
Singapore 628990
T 865 1600
F 861 6438

In Hong Kong, Malaysia,
Singapore and Thailand:
MPH, Kinokuniya, Times

Spain
Altaïr
C/Balmes 69
08007 Barcelona
T 933 233062
F 934 512559

Altaïr
Gaztambide 31
28015 Madrid
T 0915 435300
F 0915 443498

Libros de Viaje
C/Serrano no 41
28001 Madrid
T 01 91 577 9899
F 01 91 577 5756

Il Corte Inglés – major
branches

Sweden
Hedengrens Bokhandel
PO Box 5509
S-11485 Stockholm
T 08 611 5132

Kart Centrum
Vasagatan 16
S-11110 Stockholm
T 08 411 1697

Kartforlaget
Skolgangen 10
S-80183 Gavle
T 026 633000
F 026 124204

Lantmateriet Kartbutiken
Kungsgatan 74
S-11122 Stockholm
T 08 202 303
F 08 202 711

Switzerland
Office du Livre OLF
ZI3, Corminboeuf
CH-1701 Fribourg
T 026 467 5111
F 026 467 5666

Schweizer Buchzentrum
Postfach
CH-4601 Olten
T 062 209 2525
F 062 209 2627

Travel Bookshop
Rindermarkt 20
Postfach 216
CH-8001 Zurich
T 01 252 3883
F 01 252 3832

Tanzania
A Novel Idea
The Slipway
PO Box 76513
Dar es Salaam
T/F 051 601088

USA
NTC/ Contemporary
4255 West Touhy Avenue
Lincolnwood
Illinois 60646-1975
T 847 679 5500
F 847 679 2494

Barnes & Noble, Borders,
specialist travel bookstores

Will you help us?

We try as hard as we can to make each Footprint Handbook as up-to-date and accurate as possible but, of course, things always change. Many people write to us – with corrections, new information, or simply comments.

If you want to let us know about an experience or adventure – hair-raising or mundane, good or bad, exciting or boring or something special - we would be delighted to hear from you. Please give us as precise information as possible, quoting the edition number (you'll find it on the front cover) and page number of the Handbook you are using.

Your help will be greatly appreciated, especially by other travellers. In return we will send you details about our special guidebook offer.

email Footprint at
egy3_online@footprintbooks.com

or write to Elizabeth Taylor
Footprint Handbooks
6 Riverside Court
Lower Bristol Road
Bath BA2 3DZ
England

Footprint travel list

Footprint publish travel guides to over 120 countries worldwide. Each guide is packed with practical, concise and colourful information for everybody from first-time travellers to travel aficionados . The list is growing fast and current titles are noted below. For further information check out the website **www.footprintbooks.com**

Andalucía Handbook
Argentina Handbook
Bali & the Eastern Isles Hbk
Bangkok & the Beaches Hbk
Bolivia Handbook
Brazil Handbook
Cambodia Handbook
Caribbean Islands Handbook
Chile Handbook
Colombia Handbook
Cuba Handbook
Dominican Republic Handbook
East Africa Handbook
Ecuador & Galápagos Handbook
Egypt Handbook Handbook
Goa Handbook
India Handbook
Indian Himalaya Handbook
Indonesia Handbook
Ireland Handbook
Israel Handbook
Jordan Handbook
Jordan, Syria & Lebanon Hbk
Laos Handbook
Libya Handbook
Malaysia Handbook
Myanmar Handbook
Mexico Handbook
Mexico & Central America Hbk
Morocco Handbook
Namibia Handbook
Nepal Handbook
Pakistan Handbook

Peru Handbook
Rio de Janeiro Handbook
Scotland Handbook
Singapore Handbook
South Africa Handbook
South American Handbook
South India Handbook
Sri Lanka Handbook
Sumatra Handbook
Thailand Handbook
Tibet Handbook
Tunisia Handbook
Venezuela Handbook
Vietnam Handbook

In the pipeline – Turkey, London, Kenya, Rajasthan, Scotland Highlands & Islands, Syria & Lebanon

Also available from Footprint
Traveller's Handbook
Traveller's Healthbook

Available at all good bookshops

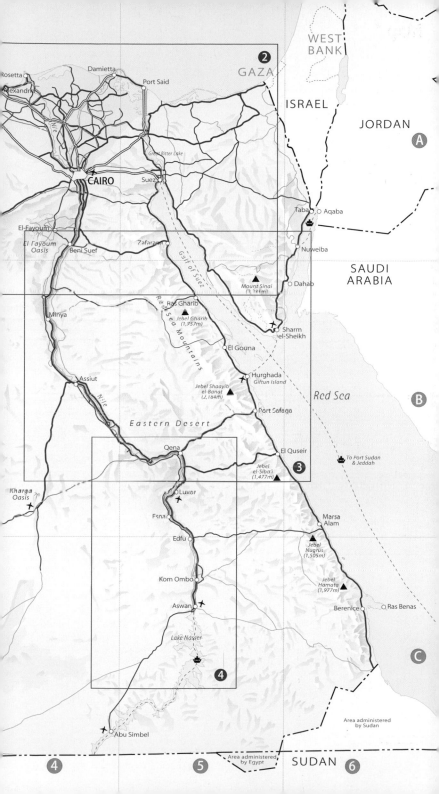

Map 2

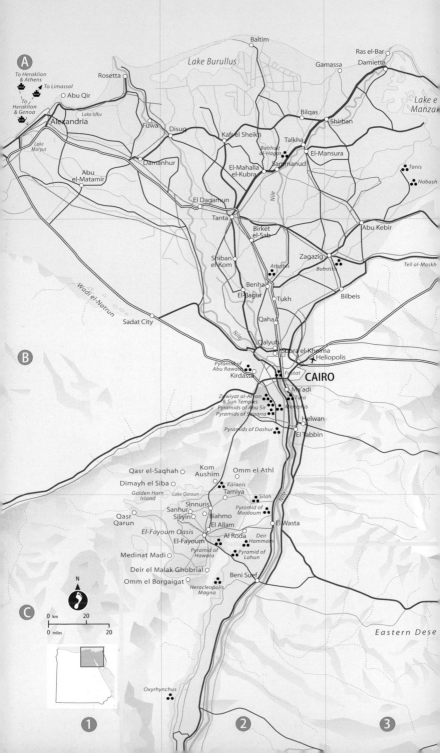

Map 3

Deir el Malak Ghobrial
El-Fayoum
Deir Hammam
Pyramid of Lahun
Beni Suef
Omm el Borgaigat
Heracleopolis Magna

Zafarana
Monastery of St Paul
Monastery of St Anthony

Eastern Desert

A

Oxyrhynchus

Minya

Beni Hassan
Hermopolis
Tuna el-Gabel
Mallawi
Tel el-Amarna
Dairut
El-Qusiya
Burnt Monastery

Nile

B

Assiut

C

N

0 km   20
0 miles   20

Red Monastery
Sohag
White Monastery
Akhmin
Al-Munshaa

Girga
Necropolis of Abydos, Temple of Seti
Dishna
Nag Hammadi

1　　　**2**　　　**3**

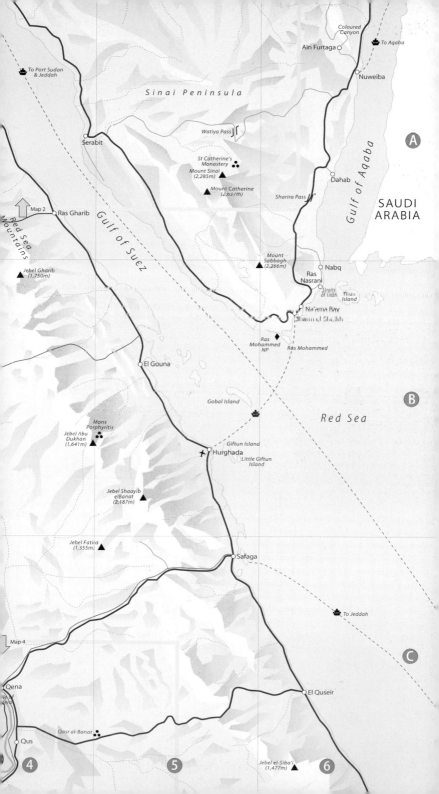

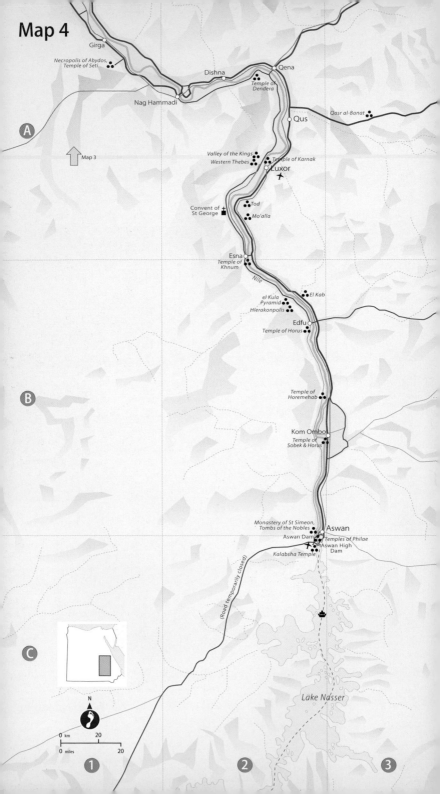

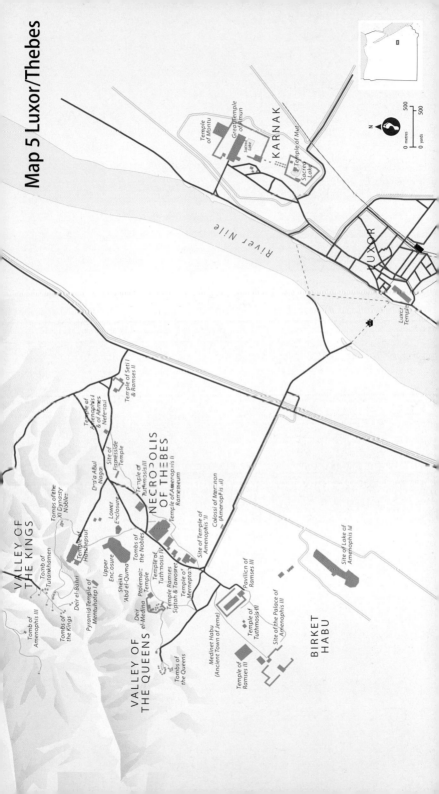

Map 5 Luxor/Thebes

River Nile

KARNAK
- Temple of Montu
- Great Temple of Amun
- Sacred Lake
- Temple of Mut
- Sacred Lake

LUXOR
- Luxor Temple

NECROPOLIS OF THEBES

VALLEY OF THE KINGS
- Tomb of Amenophis III
- Tombs of the Kings
- Tomb of Tutankhamen
- Tombs of the XI Dynasty Nobles

VALLEY OF THE QUEENS
- Tombs of the Queens

- Pyramid Temple of Menthuhotep
- Temple of Hatshepsut
- Deir el-Bahri
- Sheikh Abd el-Qurna
- Upper Enclosure
- Lower Enclosure
- Dra'a Abu'l Naga
- Temple of Amenophis I & of Ahmes Nefertari
- Site of Ramesside Temple
- Temple of Seti I & Ramses II
- Temple of Tuthmosis III
- Tombs of the Nobles
- Deir el-Medina
- Prolemaic Temple
- Temple Ramses Siptah & Tawosret
- Temple of Tuthmosis IV
- Temple of Amenophis II
- Temple of Merneptah
- Ramesseum
- Site of Temple of Amenophis II
- Colossi of Mer-non (Amenophis II)
- Medinet Habu (Ancient Town of Jeme)
- Temple of Ramses III
- Temple of Tuthmosis III
- Pavilion of Ramses III
- Site of the Palace of Amenophis III

BIRKET HABU
- Site of Lake of Amenophis III

N

0 metres 500
0 yards 500

"If 'the essence of real travel' is what you have been secretly yearning for all these years, then Footprint are the guides for you."
Under 26

"Footprint can be depended on for accurate travel information and for imparting a deep sense of respect for the lands and people they cover."
World News

"Footprint Handbooks, the best of the best."
Le Monde, Paris

"Intelligently written, amazingly accurate and bang up-to-date. Footprint has combined nearly 80 years' experience with a stunning new format to bring us guidebooks that leave the competition standing."
John Pilkington, writer and broadcaster

Mail order
Available worldwide in bookshops and on-line. Footprint travel guides can also be ordered directly from us in Bath, via our website **www.footprintbooks.com** or from the address on the imprint page of this book.

Acknowledgements

Special thanks to Janet Johnson, who has lived in Egypt during the past two years, and updated the sections on Dahab and Hurghada.

Geoff Moss for illustrations and Marie-Claire Baker for the text and some illustrations for the Jewellery and dress section in Background.

Mrs Adriana Ruiz, Germany; Miss Vivienne Sharp, Kent; Mr G M Nicholson, Bournemouth, UK; Ms Michelle Bennett, Melbourne , Australia; Nicolai Hjordt Hansen, Denmark; Mr Stephen Scott, Blackpool, UK; Mr T Eyre, Enfield. UK; Miss K Wood, Ealing, UK; Mr G de Mondt, Essen, Belgium; Ms Kirstie McDonald, Queenstown, NZ; Miss C Green, France; Miss Maartje Bakers, Tilburg, Netherlands; Mr Nir Levi, Israel; Mr J Weeden, Sydney, Australia; Mr G Bowler, Sydney, Australia.

Anne McLachlan

Anne McLachlan has a deep regard for Egypt within its North African and Middle Eastern contexts. She enjoys travelling there every year, building up her experiences as a life-long explorer and resident of the region. Her passion for Egypt makes her an ideal and practical guide to this entrancing country. As a prelude to the present volume, her field work has taken her by jeep, train, river boat and aircraft to Upper Egypt to give enhanced coverage of the monuments and facilities at Luxor and the West Bank tomb areas, where the Egyptian authorities are doing so much now to improve both the quality of the monuments and access to them. This volume also benefits from intensive studies on site of the Aswan region, where the author finds some of her favourite places in a most tranquil atmosphere.

Keith McLachlan

Keith McLachlan first made the trans-Saharan trek in 1958 and has kept in close touch with Egypt and wider events in North Africa, the Middle Eastern world and Libya since that time, recently through regular annual travel as an advisor to governments and companies involved in regional affairs. In writing the current *Egypt Handbook*, he journeyed frequently to Cairo and the Nile Delta, Sinai and the Mediterranean coast, the Red Sea diving resorts, Sharm el-Sheikh, Luxor West Bank and Aswan.

Keith McLachlan is emeritus professor at the School of Oriental & African Studies and a well-known scholar on regional economy and society as well as a consultant on Middle Eastern affairs. He has a long-acquaintance with the quirks of travel in Egypt and its neighbours as researcher, explorer and guide. He has recently published books on Islamic material culture and economy of the Middle East.